Lecture Notes in Computer Science   14561

Founding Editors

Gerhard Goos
Juris Hartmanis

Editorial Board Members

The series Lecture Notes in Computer Science (LNCS), including its subseries Lecture Notes in Artificial Intelligence (LNAI) and Lecture Notes in Bioinformatics (LNBI), has established itself as a medium for the publication of new developments in computer science and information technology research, teaching, and education.

LNCS enjoys close cooperation with the computer science R & D community, the series counts many renowned academics among its volume editors and paper authors, and collaborates with prestigious societies. Its mission is to serve this international community by providing an invaluable service, mainly focused on the publication of conference and workshop proceedings and postproceedings. LNCS commenced publication in 1973.

Hwajeong Seo · Suhri Kim
Editors

Information Security and Cryptology – ICISC 2023

26th International Conference
on Information Security and Cryptology, ICISC 2023
Seoul, South Korea, November 29 – December 1, 2023
Revised Selected Papers, Part I

 Springer

Editors
Hwajeong Seo 🆔
Hansung University
Seoul, Korea (Republic of)

Suhri Kim 🆔
Sungshin Women's University
Seoul, Korea (Republic of)

ISSN 0302-9743   ISSN 1611-3349 (electronic)
Lecture Notes in Computer Science
ISBN 978-981-97-1234-2   ISBN 978-981-97-1235-9 (eBook)
https://doi.org/10.1007/978-981-97-1235-9

This Springer imprint is published by the registered company Springer Nature Singapore Pte Ltd.
The registered company address is: 152 Beach Road, #21-01/04 Gateway East, Singapore 189721, Singapore

Paper in this product is recyclable.

Preface

The 26th International Conference on Information Security and Cryptology (ICISC 2023) was held from November 29 – December 1, 2023. This year's conference was hosted by the KIISC (Korea Institute of Information Security and Cryptology).

The aim of this conference is to provide an international forum for the latest results of research, development, and applications within the field of information security and cryptology. This year, we received 78 submissions and were able to accept 31 papers at the conference. The challenging review and selection processes were successfully conducted by program committee (PC) members and external reviewers via the EasyChair review system. For transparency, it is worth noting that each paper underwent a double-blind review by at least three PC members. For the LNCS post-proceeding, the authors of selected papers had a few weeks to prepare their final versions, based on the comments received from the reviewers.

The conference featured three invited talks, given by Rei Ueno, Tung Chou, and Anubhab Baksi. We thank the invited speakers for their kind acceptances and stimulating presentations. We would like to thank all authors who have submitted their papers to ICISC 2023, as well as all PC members. It is a truly wonderful experience to work with such talented and hardworking researchers. We also appreciate the external reviewers for assisting the PC members. Finally, we would like to thank all attendees for their active participation and the organizing members who successfully managed this conference. We look forward to seeing you again at next year's ICISC.

November 2023

Hwajeong Seo
Suhri Kim

Organization

General Chair

Yoojae Won   Chungnam National University, South Korea

Organizing Chairs

Young-Ho Park   Sejong Cyber University, South Korea
Junbeom Hur   Korea University, South Korea

Organizing Committee

Daewan Han   National Security Research Institute, South Korea
Hyun-O Kwon   Korea Internet & Security Agency, South Korea
Jeong Nyeo Kim   Electronics and Telecommunications Research
                                Institute, South Korea
Jungsuk Song   Korea Institute of Science and Technology
                                Information, South Korea
Kihyo Nam   UMLogics, South Korea
Jonghwan Park   Sangmyung University, South Korea
Jongsung Kim   Kookmin University, South Korea
Youngjoo Shin   Korea University, South Korea
Dongyoung Koo   Hansung University, South Korea
Changhee Hahn   Seoul National University of Science and
                                Technology, South Korea
Hyunsoo Kwon   Inha University, South Korea

Program Chairs

HwaJeong Seo   Hansung University, South Korea
Suhri Kim   Sungshin Women's University, South Korea

Program Committee

Wenling Wu	Institute of Software Chinese Academy of Sciences, China
Zhenfu Cao	East China Normal University, China
Swee-Huay Heng	Multimedia University, Malaysia
Taehwan Park	National Security Research Institute, South Korea
Toshihiro Yamauchi	Okayama University, Japan
Jiqiang Lu	Beihang University, China
Joonsang Baek	University of Wollongong, Australia
Katsuyuki Okeya	Hitachi High-Tech Corporation, Japan
Keita Emura	Kanazawa University, Japan
Bimal Roy	Indian Statistical Institute, India
Dongseong Kim	University of Queensland, Australia
Donghoon Chang	IIIT-Delhi, India
Hung-Min Sun	National Tsing Hua University, Taiwan
Iraklis Leontiadis	Inpher, USA
Baodong Qin	Xi'an University of Posts and Telecommunications, China
Xinyi Huang	Fujian Normal University, China
Sherman S. M. Chow	Chinese University of Hong Kong, China
Daniel Slamanig	Universität der Bundeswehr München, Germany
Reza Azarderakhsh	Florida Atlantic University, USA
Ben Lee Wai Kong	Gachon University, South Korea
Anubhab Baksi	Nanyang Technological University, Singapore
Olivier Sanders	Orange Labs, France
Kwangsu Lee	Sejong University, South Korea
Munkyu Lee	Inha University, South Korea
Jooyoung Lee	KAIST, South Korea
SeogChung Seo	Kookmin University, South Korea
Jaehong Seo	Hanyang University, South Korea
Jihye Kim	Kookmin University, South Korea
Jongsung Kim	Kookmin University, South Korea
Aaram Yun	Ewha Woman's University, South Korea
Taekyoung Youn	Dankook University, South Korea
Jungyeon Hwang	Sungshin Women's University, South Korea
Minhye Seo	Duksung Women's University, South Korea
Dohyun Kim	Catholic University of Pusan, South Korea
Seongmin Kim	Sungshin Women's University, South Korea
Haehyun Cho	Soongsil University, South Korea
Myungseo Park	Kangnam University, South Korea
Dongyoung Koo	Hansung University, South Korea

Hyojin Jo	Soongsil University, South Korea
Wonsuk Choi	Korea University, South Korea
Daehee Jang	Kyunghee University, South Korea
Yeonjoon Lee	Hanyang University, South Korea
Jonghwan Park	Sangmyung University, South Korea
Seungkwang Lee	Dankook University, South Korea
Yongwoo Lee	Inha University, South Korea
Konwoo Kwon	Hongik University, South Korea
Youngjoo Shin	Korea University, South Korea
Ilgu Lee	Sungshin Women's University, South Korea
Joohee Lee	Sungshin Women's University, South Korea
Joonwoo Lee	Chungang University, South Korea
Dongyoung Roh	National Security Research Institute, South Korea
Changmin Lee	Korea Institute for Advanced Study, South Korea
Heeseok Kim	Korea University, South Korea
Seunghyun Park	Hansung University, South Korea
Kiwoong Park	Sejong University, South Korea
Sokjoon Lee	Gachon University, South Korea
Byoungjin Seok	Seoul National University of Science and Technology, South Korea
Taejin Lee	Hoseo University, South Korea
Donghyun Kwon	Pusan National University, South Korea
Kyunbaek Kim	Chonnam National University, South Korea
Dooho Choi	Korea University, South Korea
Seongkwang Kim	Samsung SDS, South Korea
Jihoon Kwon	Samsung SDS, South Korea
Seunghyun Seo	Hanyang University, South Korea
Namsu Chang	Sejong Cyber University, South Korea

Contents – Part I

Signature Schemes

Contents – Part II

Korean Post Quantum Cryptography

Cryptanalysis and Quantum Cryptanalysis

Enhancing the Related-Key Security of **PIPO** Through New Key Schedules

Seungjun Baek[1], Giyoon Kim[1], Yongjin Jeon[1], and Jongsung Kim[1,2($\boxtimes$)]

[1] Department of Financial Information Security, Kookmin University,
Seoul, Republic of Korea
{hellosj3,gi0412,idealtop18,jskim}@kookmin.ac.kr
[2] Department of Information Security, Cryptology, and Mathematics,
Kookmin University, Seoul, Republic of Korea

Abstract. In this paper, we present new key schedules for the PIPO block cipher that enhance its security in the related-key setting. While PIPO has demonstrated noteworthy resistance against attacks in the single-key setting, its security in the related-key setting is very vulnerable owing to its simple key schedule. Given the lightweight property of PIPO, we tweak the key schedule algorithm of PIPO by applying computation only within a single register or from one register to another in key states. By adopting our new key schedules, the tweaked version of PIPO achieves better resistance to related-key attacks and demonstrates competitive implementation results in an 8-bit AVR environment. We expect that this paper will contribute to a better understanding of the PIPO block cipher.

Keywords: symmetric-key cryptography · PIPO · block cipher · related-key attacks · key schedule

1 Introduction

Plug-In Plug-Out (PIPO) [11], proposed at ICISC 2020, is a lightweight block cipher with a substitution permutation network (SPN) structure that supports 64-bit block size and 128- and 256-bit keys. PIPO was designed to be suitable for the AVR embedded processor, which is a typical 8-bit microcontroller. PIPO-128 achieved the highest speed in an 8-bit AVR environment among lightweight block ciphers such as SIMON [3], CRAFT [5], PRIDE [1], and RECTANGLE [19]. PIPO is also a block cipher standard that was approved by the Telecommunications Technology Association (TTA) of Korea in 2022 [16]. Since PIPO was developed, its security has been scrutinized by several cryptographers, and its full-round security has not yet been broken in the single-key setting.

This work was supported by Institute for Information & communications Technology Promotion (IITP) grant funded by the Korea government (MSIT) (No. 2017-0-00520, Development of SCR-Friendly Symmetric Key Cryptosystem and Its Application Modes).

In designing a lightweight block cipher, related-key attacks are often dismissed because, from a practical perspective, they are unlikely to occur. Nevertheless, a block cipher vulnerable to a related-key attack presents some security concerns. It may not be suitable for other cryptographic primitives that use block ciphers as building blocks, e.g., block cipher-based hash functions. A concrete real-world example is the use of a hash function based on the block cipher TEA [10]. Microsoft's Xbox architecture employed a Davies–Meyer hash function instantiated with TEA, and a security vulnerability related to related-key characteristics of TEA was exploited in a hacking [18]. Another security concern arises when secret keys are frequently updated in protocols or when differences can be incorporated through fault attacks.

Recently, several analyses [14, 17] of related-key characteristics for PIPO have been proposed. In these analyses, researchers have reported PIPO's full-round characteristics based on iterative characteristics with a high probability. This weakness is attributed to PIPO's simple key schedule. Given that cryptographers repeatedly analyze the related-key security of PIPO, enhancing its resistance against related-key attacks might give them confusions. Furthermore, considering that PIPO is designed for embedded processors, it could also be employed to construct a hash function, which motivates us to scrutinize its security in the context of related-key setting.

Our Contributions. In this paper, we propose tweaks to the key schedule algorithm of PIPO-128. We take into account two conditions for tweaking PIPO-128's key schedule. First, our proposed tweaks must ensure better related-key security than the original PIPO-128. This is achieved by rotating the registers of key states in the key schedule algorithm to break the 2-round iterative related-key differential characteristics that occur. We also add additional bit-rotation within a register to further improve security. Second, we strive to ensure that the tweaked PIPO algorithm has minimal overhead in an 8-bit AVR environment. To inherit the lightweight nature of PIPO-128 while keeping implementation cost low, we completely exclude nonlinear operators, such as AND or OR gates, in the proposed tweaks. Instead, we mainly apply computation within a single register or from one register to another.

We evaluate the related-key security of our tweaks in terms of the number of active S-boxes in a characteristic. We first construct a Mixed Integer Linear Programming (MILP) model for PIPO-128 and evaluate the number of active S-boxes. Comparing our tweak to the original PIPO-128, we achieve more than twice the number of active S-boxes in characteristics with large rounds. For example, the 10-round characteristic of the original PIPO-128 had five active S-boxes, while ours has 11. While this measurement may not yield the characteristic with the lowest probability, it is sufficient to demonstrate the related-key security of PIPO-128. We also examine the implementation efficiency of our tweaks in an 8-bit AVR environment. Even though our tweaks involve slightly more computation compared to the original PIPO-128, their overhead is minimal. Thus, we preserve the lightweight property of PIPO-128. Furthermore, we confirm that our tweaks are useful for PIPO-256 as well.

Paper Organization. Section 2 describes the specifications of PIPO and related-key differential attacks. Section 3 describes our new tweaks for PIPO's key schedule. Section 4 describes security analysis for the tweaked PIPO in the related-key setting. Section 5 describes our implementation results for the tweaked PIPO in an 8-bit AVR environment. Section 6 presents our conclusion.

2 Preliminaries

2.1 Description of PIPO

Figure 1 depicts the process of PIPO [11,12]. The internal state of PIPO is represented by an 8×8 bit matrix. In the bit matrix, the least significant bit (LSB) is located at the top right and is filled from right to left. When one row is filled, the next row is filled again from the right.

The plaintext is XORed with the whitening key and then undergoes a sequence of r rounds. For PIPO-128, r is 13, while for PIPO-256, r is 17. Each round consists of three layers: S-layer, R-layer, and round key and constant XOR additions.

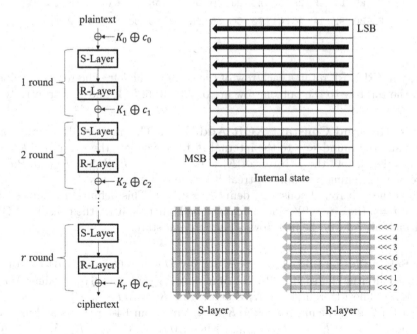

Fig. 1. Description of PIPO

S-Layer (SL). PIPO uses the defined 8-bit S-box as shown in Table 1. Each column in the state is independently substituted using eight S-boxes. The top bit of the state becomes the LSB of the S-box input value.

Table 1. PIPO S-box

	_0	_1	_2	_3	_4	_5	_6	_7	_8	_9	_A	_B	_C	_D	_E	_F
0_	5E	F9	FC	00	3F	85	BA	5B	18	37	B2	C6	71	C3	74	9D
1_	A7	94	0D	E1	CA	68	53	2E	49	62	EB	97	A4	0E	2D	D0
2_	16	25	AC	48	63	D1	EA	8F	F7	40	45	B1	9E	34	1B	F2
3_	B9	86	03	7F	D8	7A	DD	3C	E0	CB	52	26	15	AF	8C	69
4_	C2	75	70	1C	33	99	B6	C7	04	3B	BE	5A	FD	5F	F8	81
5_	93	A0	29	4D	66	D4	EF	0A	E5	CE	57	A3	90	2A	09	6C
6_	22	11	88	E4	CF	6D	56	AB	7B	DC	D9	BD	82	38	07	7E
7_	B5	9A	1F	F3	44	F6	41	30	4C	67	EE	12	21	8B	A8	D5
8_	55	6E	E7	0B	28	92	A1	CC	2B	08	91	ED	D6	64	4F	A2
9_	BC	83	06	FA	5D	FF	58	39	72	C5	C0	B4	9B	31	1E	77
A_	01	3E	BB	DF	78	DA	7D	84	50	6B	E2	8E	AD	17	24	C9
B_	AE	8D	14	E8	D3	61	4A	27	47	F0	F5	19	36	9C	B3	42
C_	1D	32	B7	43	F4	46	F1	98	EC	D7	4E	AA	89	23	10	65
D_	8A	A9	20	54	6F	CD	E6	13	DB	7C	79	05	3A	80	BF	DE
E_	E9	D2	4B	2F	0C	A6	95	60	0F	2C	A5	51	6A	C8	E3	96
F_	B0	9F	1A	76	C1	73	C4	35	FE	59	5C	B8	87	3D	02	FB

R-Layer (RL). RL rotates each row of the state to the left. The rotation values from the top row to the bottom row are 0, 7, 4, 3, 6, 5, 1, and 2, respectively.

Round Key and Constant XOR Additions. This layer XORs round constants and the round keys to the internal state. We denote the i-th round key as K_i. We also denote the j-th row of K_i is k_j^i, i.e., $K_i = k_7^i||k_6^i|| \cdots ||k_0^i$. In PIPO, there is a whitening key, and we treat it as the 0-th round key K_0.

c_i is the i-th round constant, defined as $c_i = i$. This definition includes the case of $i = 0$ (i.e., $c_0 = 0$). Since c_i cannot be higher than 19, the constant XOR addition only affects the 0-th row of the internal state.

Key Schedule. For PIPO-128, the master key MK is split into two 64-bit states and used alternately (see Fig. 2). Let $MK = MK_1||MK_0$ for 64-bit values MK_0 and MK_1. The i-th round key K_i is defined by $K_i = MK_{i \pmod 2}$.

For PIPO-256, the master key MK is split into four 64-bit states and used in sequence. That is, $K_i = MK_{i \pmod 4}$ where $MK = MK_3||MK_2||MK_1||MK_0$ for 64-bit values MK_0, MK_1, MK_2, and MK_3.

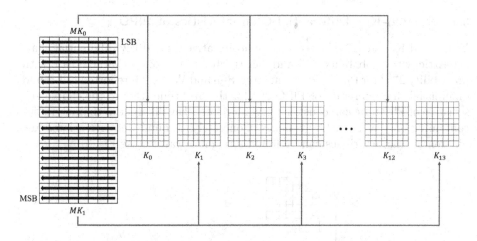

Fig. 2. Key schedule of PIPO-128

2.2   Related-Key Differential Attack

Related-key attack, independently introduced by Biham [6] and Knudsen [13], is a powerful cryptanalytic tool for the analysis of block ciphers. In this attack, the adversary can obtain the encryption of plaintexts under several related keys, where the relationship between the keys is known to (or can be chosen by) the adversary. Kelsey et al. [9] introduced the related-key differential attack. The adversary can ask for the encryption of plaintext pairs with a chosen difference of α, using unknown keys that have a difference of ΔK in a manner that is known or chosen by the adversary. To attack an n-bit cipher, the adversary exploits a related-key differential characteristic $\alpha \to \beta$ for target (sub-)cipher E with a probability p larger than 2^{-n}, i.e.,

$$Pr_{(P,K)}[E_K(P) \oplus E_{K \oplus \Delta K}(P \oplus \alpha) = \beta] = p > 2^{-n},$$

where P represents a plaintext. Here, the adversary's task is to find a related-key characteristic with as high a probability as possible. This attack is based on the key schedule and on the encryption/decryption algorithms, so a cipher with a weak key schedule may be vulnerable to this kind of attack.

3   New Key Schedules of PIPO

In this section, we propose new key schedules of PIPO to enhance the security in the related-key setting. We first observe the existing iterative related-key differential characteristics for PIPO-128 and PIPO-256. Here, we omit the constant addition, as it is not relevant to our analysis.

3.1   Related-Key Differential Characteristics of PIPO

Yadav and Kumar [17] showed a 2-round iterative related-key differential characteristic with probability 2^{-4} and constructed a full-round characteristic with probability 2^{-24} for PIPO-128. Soon after, Sun and Wang [14] reported full-round differential characteristics of PIPO-256 for the first time. Due to the simple key schedule of PIPO, we can construct several related-key differential characteristics containing only a few active S-boxes. Concretely, 2-round iterative related-key differential characteristics can be found straightforwardly (see Fig. 3).

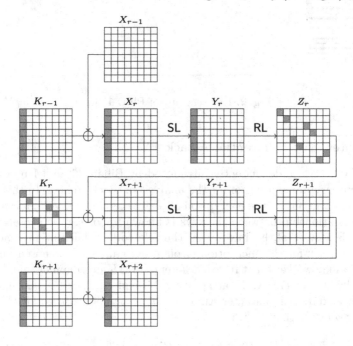

Fig. 3. 2-round iterative related-key differential characteristics of PIPO-128

In the transition $X_r \xrightarrow{\text{SL}} Y_r \xrightarrow{\text{RL}} Z_r$, the 2-round characteristic is constructed by setting ΔX_r and ΔZ_r as iterative keys. Considering the differential distribution table (DDT) of PIPO, there are 224 entries with probability 2^{-4} (see Table 2). Since the difference of X_r can also be placed in the remaining seven columns, there are a total of $224 \times 8 = 1792$ characteristics.

Table 2. Distribution of non-trivial probabilities in DDT of PIPO's S-box

DDT value	2	4	6	8	10	12	16
# of entries	12552	6226	651	951	9	7	224
probability	2^{-7}	2^{-6}	$2^{-5.415}$	2^{-5}	$2^{-4.678}$	$2^{-4.415}$	2^{-4}

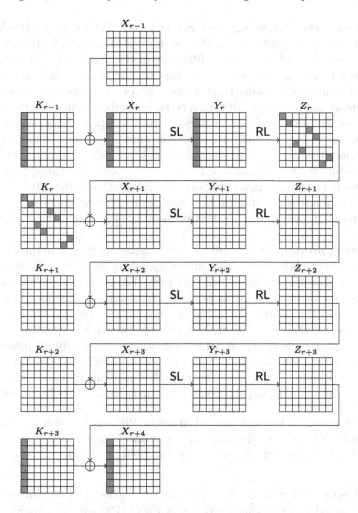

Fig. 4. 4-round iterative related-key differential characteristics of PIPO-256

Similarly, there exists a full-round differential characteristic with probability 2^{-16} for PIPO-256 based on the 4-round iterative differential characteristic (see Fig. 4).

3.2 Introducing New Key Schedules: KS1 and KS2

We propose new key schedules for PIPO-128. There are two factors to consider in order to simultaneously satisfy the related-key security and implementation efficiency of our key schedules. Note that we are not considering changing the entire algorithm of PIPO-128; we are only changing the key schedule. Our considerations for these tweaks are as follows:

1. **Increasing resistance against related-key differential attacks** - In PIPO-128's key schedule, the master key is divided into two 64-bit key states, and the attacker determines the difference of the two states by selecting the difference of the master key. Given this simple key schedule, the initially selected difference remains fixed within the two key states and is XORed throughout the entire algorithm every two rounds. Ultimately, there are 2-round iterative differential characteristics resulting from this property, so our main goal is to prevent such characteristics from occurring. To increase resistance against related-key differential attacks, we induce diffusion within the key schedule in the column-wise as well as row-wise directions. Specifically, we measure the minimum number of active S-boxes using the MILP tool. This number enables us to establish the bounds on the probability of differential characteristics, considering the best probability of 2^{-4} from the PIPO S-box's DDT table.

2. **Achieving minimal overhead** - When considering tweaks to the key schedule, one might choose to apply various operators to induce diffusion of differences within key states. Recall that PIPO-128 is a block cipher optimized for 8-bit microcontrollers, so it primarily relies on computations in terms of register level throughout the encrypting/decrypting process. To inherit this advantage, we strictly limit our key schedule tweaks to computing within a single register or from one register to another. Specifically, to preserve the low implementation cost, we completely exclude nonlinear operators such as AND or OR gates. Finally, we tweak the key schedule in a way that ensures security while minimizing the overhead in an 8-bit AVR environment.

Now we introduce two new key schedules of PIPO-128, which we refer to as KS1 and KS2. We refer to the original key schedule of PIPO-128 as KS0. The evaluation of their related-key security is discussed in Sect. 4.

KS1. KS1 is our first proposal for PIPO-128's key schedule. Our aim is to eliminate the 2-round iterative characteristics of PIPO-128 (see Fig. 3) in KS1. To do this, we simply rotate each row register within each of the two key states by 1 in the upward direction. For the first two rounds, two key states are input as MK_0 and MK_1, but from then on, rotation is applied to each register every two rounds. If we apply this operation to the key schedule, a 2-round iterative pattern is easily broken due to the RL of PIPO-128. In Fig. 5, we describe one example demonstrating our claim. We distinguish the differences between two key states: one represented by the color orange and the other by the color blue. In addition, we use hatch patterns to denote all possible differences. Here, we can see that the difference cancellation does not occur in the transition $X_2 \xrightarrow{\text{SL}} Y_2 \xrightarrow{\text{RL}} Z_2 \rightarrow X_3$. This is because the possible differences caused by ΔX_2 are not canceled out, mainly due to the rotation of the key state. In this way, difference cancellation patterns are prevented by applying rotations of registers. Therefore, KS1 can amplify the diffusion of key differences more than the original one. KS1 is represented as follows:

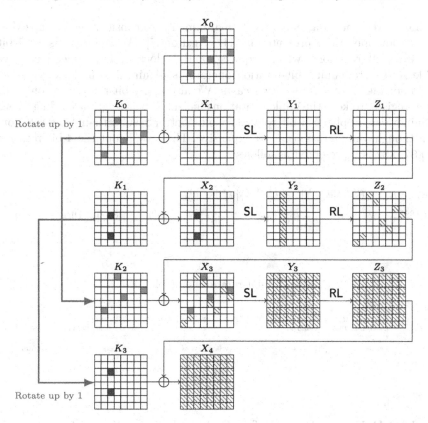

Fig. 5. Breaking the occurrence of the 2-round iterative characteristic of PIPO-128

$$(K_{r-1}, K_r) = (k_7^{r-1} || k_6^{r-1} || \cdots || k_0^{r-1}, k_7^r || k_6^r || \cdots || k_0^r)$$
$$\xrightarrow{2 \ rounds} (K_{r+1}, K_{r+2}) = (k_0^{r+1} || k_7^{r+1} || \cdots || k_1^{r+1}, k_0^{r+2} || k_7^{r+2} || \cdots || k_1^{r+2}).$$

In the rotation of two key states, one may consider rotating or changing only a few registers in each state. Let the attacker choose a key difference in the unchanged registers in one key state, typically one bit, and then set the difference determined by the RL operation in the unchanged registers in the other state. Since the differences in the unchanged registers are fixed, a 2-round characteristic occurs repeatedly. This is not a desirable property for us, so we do not adopt this method.

KS2. While KS1 offers better related-key security compared to KS0, there is still room for further improvement in security. The focus of KS2 is to improve the related-key security of KS1 by applying bit-rotation to one register in each key state. In KS1, there is no row-wise directional diffusion of the key difference, allowing us to consider bit-rotation within the registers. Since our goal is to minimize overhead in an 8-bit AVR environment, we consider the optimized 8-bit rotation operations presented in [11] based on [7]. We mainly consider 1-bit and 4-bit left rotations, which require 2 and 1 clock cycles, respectively (see Table 3). The remaining bit-rotation operations require 3 to 5 clock cycles, so we do not take into account other cases. We also apply bit-rotation to only one upper register to keep the implementation efficient. Surprisingly, according to our examinations, applying 4-bit rotation yields better results than 1-bit rotation, even though 4-bit rotation is less expensive. Thus, we adopt the 4-bit rotation for KS2. KS2 is represented as follows:

$$(K_{r-1}, K_r) = (k_7^{r-1}||k_6^{r-1}||\cdots||k_0^{r-1}, k_7^r||k_6^r||\cdots||k_0^r)$$
$$\xrightarrow{2\ rounds} (K_{r+1}, K_{r+2}) = (k_0^{r+1}||k_7^{r+1}||\cdots||(k_1^{r+1} \lll 4), k_0^{r+2}||k_7^{r+2}||\cdots||(k_1^{r+2} \lll 4)).$$

Table 3. 8-bit rotations on 8-bit AVR

⋘ 1	⋘ 2	⋘ 3	⋘ 4	⋘ 5	⋘ 6	⋘ 7
LSL X1 ADC X1, ZERO	LSL X1 ADC X1, ZERO LSL X1 ADC X1, ZERO	SWAP X1 BST X1, 0 LSR X1 BLD X1, 7	SWAP X1	SWAP X1 LSL X1 ADC X1, ZERO	SWAP X1 LSL X1 ADC X1, ZERO LSL X1 ADC X1, ZERO	BST X1, 0 LSR X1 BLD X1, 7
2 cycles	4 cycles	4 cycles	1 cycle	3 cycles	5 cycles	3 cycles

4 MILP-Based Search for Related-Key Characteristics for PIPO with New Key Schedules

Now, we present a security analysis for new key schedules for PIPO-128. We adopt the MILP framework for bit-oriented ciphers proposed by Sun et al. [15] and describe the MILP model for PIPO-128. To optimize the model, we use the Gurobi MILP solver. We utilized the MILES tool [17] for generating linear inequalities of the PIPO-128 S-box. Finally, we apply our MILP model to search for related-key characteristics for PIPO-128 with new key schedules and present the results. We also present some results for PIPO-256.

4.1 MILP Model for PIPO

Generating Linear Inequalities of S-Box. Yadav and Kumar [17] proposed the MILES tool to minimize the number of linear inequalities for large S-boxes. Minimizing the number of inequalities directly affects the efficiency of MILP model. Thus, we utilize the MILES tool to generate linear inequalities of the PIPO S-box. As described in [17], we obtain 4474 linear inequalities for the S-box, and 35792 inequalities are needed for the SL of one round of PIPO.

Variables and Constraints. We represent the difference of all cells in each round as a set of binary variables x_i. Each variable x_i can take on values 0 or 1, signifying inactive and active bits, respectively. The binary variables $x_0, x_1, \cdots, x_{63}$ represent a 64-bit plaintext difference, and the difference for the next round state is updated as $x_{64}, x_{65}, \cdots, x_{127}$, and so on. To reduce the number of variables in the MILP model, the output bits of SL in the first round are set to the variables in the next round with RL^{-1} applied, and the process is repeated for each subsequent round. This process in the first round is represented as follows:

$$
\begin{bmatrix}
x_7 & x_6 & x_5 & x_4 & x_3 & x_2 & x_1 & x_0 \\
x_{15} & x_{14} & x_{13} & x_{12} & x_{11} & x_{10} & x_9 & x_8 \\
x_{23} & x_{22} & x_{21} & x_{20} & x_{19} & x_{18} & x_{17} & x_{16} \\
x_{31} & x_{30} & x_{29} & x_{28} & x_{27} & x_{26} & x_{25} & x_{24} \\
x_{39} & x_{38} & x_{37} & x_{36} & x_{35} & x_{34} & x_{33} & x_{32} \\
x_{47} & x_{46} & x_{45} & x_{44} & x_{43} & x_{42} & x_{41} & x_{40} \\
x_{55} & x_{54} & x_{53} & x_{52} & x_{51} & x_{50} & x_{49} & x_{48} \\
x_{63} & x_{62} & x_{61} & x_{60} & x_{59} & x_{58} & x_{57} & x_{56}
\end{bmatrix}
\xrightarrow[\text{1-round}]{\text{SL}}
\begin{bmatrix}
x_{71} & x_{70} & x_{69} & x_{68} & x_{67} & x_{66} & x_{65} & x_{64} \\
x_{78} & x_{77} & x_{76} & x_{75} & x_{74} & x_{73} & x_{72} & x_{79} \\
x_{83} & x_{82} & x_{81} & x_{80} & x_{87} & x_{86} & x_{85} & x_{84} \\
x_{90} & x_{89} & x_{88} & x_{95} & x_{94} & x_{93} & x_{92} & x_{91} \\
x_{101} & x_{100} & x_{99} & x_{98} & x_{97} & x_{96} & x_{103} & x_{102} \\
x_{108} & x_{107} & x_{106} & x_{105} & x_{104} & x_{111} & x_{110} & x_{109} \\
x_{112} & x_{119} & x_{118} & x_{117} & x_{116} & x_{115} & x_{114} & x_{113} \\
x_{121} & x_{120} & x_{127} & x_{126} & x_{125} & x_{124} & x_{123} & x_{122}
\end{bmatrix}
$$

Here, we construct linear inequalities based on the input and output variables of SL. Since SL is applied column-wise, the linear inequalities are also constructed in such a manner.

To search a related-key differential characteristics, we represent the difference of the master key as a set of binary variables k_i. For PIPO-128, its 128-bit key is represented by $k_0, k_1, \cdots, k_{127}$ and for PIPO-256, the 256-bit key is represented by $k_0, k_1, \cdots, k_{255}$.

In our model, the XOR operation of the difference is used for XORing the internal state and the key to generate a new internal state. x_{in} and k_{in} are the state bit and corresponding key bit, respectively, and x_{out} is the corresponding output bit. The following inequalities are used to describe the XOR operation:

$$
\begin{cases}
x_{in} + k_{in} - x_{out} \geq 0, \\
x_{in} - k_{in} + x_{out} \geq 0, \\
-x_{in} + k_{in} + x_{out} \geq 0, \\
x_{in} + k_{in} + x_{out} \leq 2.
\end{cases}
$$

In addition, we use the following set of the inequalities to check the number of active S-boxes of a characteristic:

$$
\begin{cases}
x_{64\cdot(r-1)+i} + x_{64\cdot(r-1)+i+8} + x_{64\cdot(r-1)+i+16} + x_{64\cdot(r-1)+i+24} \\
\quad + x_{64\cdot(r-1)+i+32} + x_{64\cdot(r-1)+i+40} + x_{64\cdot(r-1)+i+48} + x_{64\cdot(r-1)+i+56} - a_{(r,i)} \geq 0, \\
a_{(r,i)} - x_{64\cdot(r-1)+i} \geq 0, \\
a_{(r,i)} - x_{64\cdot(r-1)+i+8} \geq 0, \\
a_{(r,i)} - x_{64\cdot(r-1)+i+16} \geq 0, \\
a_{(r,i)} - x_{64\cdot(r-1)+i+24} \geq 0, \\
a_{(r,i)} - x_{64\cdot(r-1)+i+32} \geq 0, \\
a_{(r,i)} - x_{64\cdot(r-1)+i+40} \geq 0, \\
a_{(r,i)} - x_{64\cdot(r-1)+i+48} \geq 0, \\
a_{(r,i)} - x_{64\cdot(r-1)+i+56} \geq 0,
\end{cases}
$$

where $a_{(r,i)}$ denotes whether the i-th column from the right is active.

Objective Function. Our goal is to minimize the number of active S-boxes of a characteristic. Thus, when finding a r-round characteristic, our objective function is

$$
\text{Minimize} \underbrace{\sum a_{(1,i)}}_{\text{Round 1}} + \underbrace{\sum a_{(2,i)}}_{\text{Round 2}} + \cdots + \underbrace{\sum a_{(r,i)}}_{\text{Round } r}.
$$

4.2 Results

We apply our MILP model to PIPO-128 with KS0, KS1, and KS2. Due to the large search space, we only compare these results up to 10 rounds of PIPO-128. In the case of KS2 in round 10, we were unable to prove that this is the best result since the MILP solver did not terminate within a reasonable amount of time. We imposed a one-month time constraint for this case and ran the solver. Our results are summarized in Table 4.

We can observe that in rounds 1 to 2, the results for three key schedules are identical since the first two key states are the same as K_0 and K_1. The change occurs starting from round 5, which is due to the differential diffusion resulting from additional operations on key states. In particular, in KS0, there are rounds where active S-boxes do not exist every two rounds, whereas, in KS1 and KS2, after round 3, there is at least one active S-box in each round. In comparing KS0 and KS1, the difference in the number of active S-boxes begins to appear from round 9, and considering the results up to round 10, this difference is expected to increase as the number of rounds increases. This difference is more pronounced when comparing KS0 and KS2. Furthermore, even if the number of active S-boxes in round 10 of KS2 may not be optimal, we need to consider at least three additional active S-boxes to reach a full-round PIPO. Thus, by adopting KS2 as the key schedule for the tweaked version of PIPO, we expect that there will be no related-key differential characteristics with a probability higher than 2^{-64}.

Table 4. Comparison of related-key differential characteristics for PIPO-128 according to KS0, KS1, and KS2

Round	KS0		KS1		KS2	
	#(Active S-box)	$-\log_2 p$	#(Active S-box)	$-\log_2 p$	#(Active S-box)	$-\log_2 p$
1	0	0	0	0	0	0
2	0	0	0	0	0	0
3	1	4	1	4	1	4
4	2	8	2	8	2	8
5	2	8	3	13	3	13
6	3	12	4	22.415	4	23
7	3	12	5	29	5	30
8	4	16	6	33.415	6	36.415
9	4	16	7	38.415	8	46.415
10	5	20	8	47.415	11*	60.830

KS0 represents the original key schedule of PIPO-128.
*Number of active S-boxes are not confirmed to be optimal.

On the Results for PIPO-256. We try to apply the approach of the key schedule KS1 to PIPO-256, and we refer to it as KS1*. That is, we simply rotate each row register within each of the four key states by 1 in the upward direction. In the same way as with PIPO-128, four key states are input as MK_0, MK_1, MK_2, and MK_3 in the first four rounds. As a result, we see that even when KS1* is adopted for PIPO-256, we can achieve better related-key security than the original key schedule (see Table 5).

We also attempted to apply the approach of KS2 to PIPO-256. However, due to the larger search space, the MILP solver did not terminate after 14 rounds. Furthermore, the results are either the same as or inferior to those obtained using KS1. Thus, we only present the results adopting KS1*.

5   Implementations

In this section, we compare our implementation results with the original PIPO-128 and other lightweight block ciphers. We used Atmel Studio 6.2 and compiled all implementations with optimization level 3. Our target processor was an ATmega128 running at 8 MHz, as in [11]. Since we could not find a reference assembly code for PIPO-128, we developed the code and analyzed it for a fair comparison. We also adopted a metric to measure overall performance on low-end devices, RANK, which is calculated as

$$RANK = (10^6/CPB)/(ROM + 2 \times RAM),$$

where the code size represents ROM. Table 6 compares results for PIPO-128 on 8-bit AVR environment according to key schedules. Results for other block ciphers can be found in [11].

Table 5. Comparison of related-key differential characteristics for PIPO-256 according to KS0*, KS1*

Round	KS0*		KS1*	
	#(Active S-box)	$-\log_2 p$	#(Active S-box)	$-\log_2 p$
1	0	0	0	0
2	0	0	0	0
3	0	0	0	0
4	0	0	0	0
5	1	4	1	4
6	1	4	1	4
7	1	4	1	4
8	2	8	2	8
9	2	8	3	13
10	2	8	4	20.415
11	2	8	4	22
12	3	12	6	31.415
13	3	12	8	39
14	3	12	10	51.245
15	3	12	11	60.660
16	4	16	12	67

We refer to the original key schedule of PIPO-256 as KS0.

Table 6. Comparison of PIPO-128 on 8-bit AVR according to key schedules with other lightweight block ciphers

Block cipher	Code size (bytes)	RAM (bytes)	Execution time (cycles per byte)	RANK
PIPO-64/128(KS0)	354	31	197	12.09
SIMON-64/128 [3]	290	24	253	11.69
PIPO-64/128(KS1)	354	31	249	8.85
PIPO-64/128(KS2)	354	31	251	8.78
RoadRunneR-64/128 [2]	196	24	477	8.59
RECTANGLE-64/128 [19]	466	204	403	2.84
PRIDE-64/128 [1]	650	47	969	1.39
SKINNY-64/128 [4]	502	187	877	1.30
PRESENT-64/128 [8]	660	280	1,349	0.61
CRAFT-64/128 [5]	894	243	1,504	0.48

We also implemented PIPO-256 with KS0* and KS1* in the same environment. Both cases require the same code size and RAM: 354 bytes of code and 47 bytes of RAM. With regard to the execution time, PIPO-256 with KS0* requires 253 CPB, whereas with KS1*, it requires 321 CPB. Therefore, the RANK metrics for them are 8.82 and 6.95, respectively.

6   Conclusion

In this paper, we presented two new key schedules, KS1 and KS2, for the PIPO block cipher, aiming to enhance PIPO's related-key security. By applying KS1 and KS2 to PIPO-128, we achieved better related-key security compared to original PIPO-128. We also applied KS1 to PIPO-256 and obtained interesting results regarding security. We obtained comparative implementation results in an 8-bit AVR environment by completely excluding nonlinear operators and only applying computation within a single register or from one register to another. The significance of this study lies in enhancing related-key security of PIPO without significantly increasing the implementation cost.

References

1. Albrecht, M.R., Driessen, B., Kavun, E.B., Leander, G., Paar, C., Yalçın, T.: Block ciphers – focus on the linear layer (feat. PRIDE). In: Garay, J.A., Gennaro, R. (eds.) CRYPTO 2014. LNCS, vol. 8616, pp. 57–76. Springer, Heidelberg (2014). https://doi.org/10.1007/978-3-662-44371-2_4
2. Baysal, A., Şahin, S.: RoadRunneR: a small and fast bitslice block cipher for low cost 8-bit processors. In: Güneysu, T., Leander, G., Moradi, A. (eds.) LightSec 2015. LNCS, vol. 9542, pp. 58–76. Springer, Cham (2016). https://doi.org/10.1007/978-3-319-29078-2_4
3. Beaulieu, R., Shors, D., Smith, J., Treatman-Clark, S., Weeks, B., Wingers, L.: The SIMON and SPECK block ciphers on AVR 8-bit microcontrollers. In: Eisenbarth, T., Öztürk, E. (eds.) LightSec 2014. LNCS, vol. 8898, pp. 3–20. Springer, Cham (2015). https://doi.org/10.1007/978-3-319-16363-5_1
4. Beierle, C., et al.: The SKINNY family of block ciphers and its low-latency variant MANTIS. In: Robshaw, M., Katz, J. (eds.) CRYPTO 2016. LNCS, vol. 9815, pp. 123–153. Springer, Heidelberg (2016). https://doi.org/10.1007/978-3-662-53008-5_5
5. Beierle, C., Leander, G., Moradi, A., Rasoolzadeh, S.: CRAFT: lightweight tweakable block cipher with efficient protection against DFA attacks. IACR Trans. Symmetric Cryptol. 2019(1), 5–45 (2019). https://doi.org/10.13154/tosc.v2019.i1.5-45 https://doi.org/10.13154/tosc.v2019.i1.5-45
6. Biham, E.: New types of cryptanalytic attacks using related keys. J. Cryptol. 7(4), 229–246 (1994). https://doi.org/10.1007/BF00203965
7. Corporation, A.: ATmega128(L) datasheet. https://www.microchip.com/wwwproducts/en/ATmega128. Accessed 4 Oct 2023
8. Engels, S., Kavun, E.B., Paar, C., Yalçın, T., Mihajloska, H.: A non-linear/linear instruction set extension for lightweight ciphers. In: 21st IEEE Symposium on Computer Arithmetic, ARITH 2013, Austin, TX, USA, 7–10 April 2013, pp. 67–75. IEEE Computer Society (2013). https://doi.org/10.1109/ARITH.2013.36
9. Kelsey, J., Schneier, B., Wagner, D.: Key-schedule cryptanalysis of IDEA, G-DES, GOST, SAFER, and triple-DES. In: Koblitz, N. (ed.) CRYPTO 1996. LNCS, vol. 1109, pp. 237–251. Springer, Heidelberg (1996). https://doi.org/10.1007/3-540-68697-5_19
10. Kelsey, J., Schneier, B., Wagner, D.: Related-key cryptanalysis of 3-WAY, Biham-DES,CAST, DES-X, NewDES, RC2, and TEA. In: Han, Y., Okamoto, T., Qing,

S. (eds.) ICICS 1997. LNCS, vol. 1334, pp. 233–246. Springer, Heidelberg (1997). https://doi.org/10.1007/BFb0028479

11. Kim, H., et al.: PIPO: a lightweight block cipher with efficient higher-order masking software implementations. In: Hong, D. (ed.) ICISC 2020. LNCS, vol. 12593, pp. 99–122. Springer, Cham (2021). https://doi.org/10.1007/978-3-030-68890-5_6

12. Kim, H., et al.: A new method for designing lightweight S-boxes with high differential and linear branch numbers, and its application. IEEE Access 9, 150592–150607 (2021). https://doi.org/10.1109/ACCESS.2021.3126008

13. Knudsen, L.R.: Cryptanalysis of LOKI 91. In: Seberry, J., Zheng, Y. (eds.) AUSCRYPT 1992. LNCS, vol. 718, pp. 196–208. Springer, Heidelberg (1993). https://doi.org/10.1007/3-540-57220-1_62

14. Sun, L., Wang, M.: SoK: modeling for large s-boxes oriented to differential probabilities and linear correlations. IACR Trans. Symmetric Cryptol. 2023(1), 111–151 (2023). https://tosc.iacr.org/index.php/ToSC/article/view/10310

15. Sun, S., Hu, L., Wang, P., Qiao, K., Ma, X., Song, L.: Automatic security evaluation and (related-key) differential characteristic search: application to SIMON, PRESENT, LBlock, DES(L) and other bit-oriented block ciphers. In: Sarkar, P., Iwata, T. (eds.) ASIACRYPT 2014. LNCS, vol. 8873, pp. 158–178. Springer, Heidelberg (2014). https://doi.org/10.1007/978-3-662-45611-8_9

16. TTAK.KO-12.0382: 64-bit Block Cipher PIPO. Telecommunications Technology Association of Korea (2022). https://www.tta.or.kr/tta/ttaSearchView.do?key=77&rep=1&searchStandardNo=TTAK.KO-12.0382&searchCate=TTAS

17. Yadav, T., Kumar, M.: Modeling large s-box in MILP and a (related-key) differential attack on full round PIPO-64/128. In: Batina, L., Picek, S., Mondal, M. (eds.) SPACE 2022. LNCS, vol. 13783, pp. 3–27. Springer, Cham (2022). https://doi.org/10.1007/978-3-031-22829-2_1

18. ZDNet: New xbox security cracked by Linux fans. https://www.zdnet.com/article/new-xbox-security-cracked-by-linux-fans/. Accessed 4 Oct 2023

19. Zhang, W., Bao, Z., Lin, D., Rijmen, V., Yang, B., Verbauwhede, I.: RECTANGLE: a bit-slice lightweight block cipher suitable for multiple platforms. Sci. China Inf. Sci. 58(12), 1–15 (2015). https://doi.org/10.1007/s11432-015-5459-7

Distinguisher and Related-Key Attack on HALFLOOP-96

Jinpeng Liu[1,2] and Ling Sun[1,2,3(✉)]

[1] Key Laboratory of Cryptologic Technology and Information Security,
Ministry of Education, Shandong University, Jinan, China
[2] School of Cyber Science and Technology, Shandong University, Qingdao, China
`lingsun@sdu.edu.cn`
[3] Quan Cheng Shandong Laboratory, Jinan, China

Abstract. HALFLOOP-96 is a 96-bit tweakable block cipher used in high frequency radio to secure automatic link establishment messages. In this paper, we concentrate on its differential properties in the contexts of conventional, related-tweak, and related-key differential attacks. Using automatic techniques, we determine the minimum number of active S-boxes and the maximum differential probability in each of the three configurations. The resistance of HALFLOOP-96 to differential attacks in the conventional and related-tweak configurations is good, and the longest distinguishers in both configurations consist of five rounds. In contrast, the security of the cipher against differential attacks in the related-key configuration is inadequate. The most effective related-key distinguisher we can find spans eight rounds. The 8-round related-key differential distinguisher is then utilised to initiate a 9-round weak-key attack. With $2^{92.96}$ chosen-plaintexts, 38.77-bit equivalent information about the keys can be recovered. Even though the attack does not pose a significant security threat to HALFLOOP-96, its security margin in the related-key configuration is exceedingly narrow. Therefore, improper use must be avoided in the application.

Keywords: Differential cryptanalysis · Related-tweak · Related-key · HALFLOOP-96

1 Introduction

HALFLOOP is a family of tweakable block ciphers. It was created to encrypt protocol data units before transmission during automatic link establishment (ALE). HALFLOOP has been standardised in the most recent revision of MIL-STD-188-141D [1], the interoperability and performance standards for medium and high frequency radio systems issued by the United States Department of Defence.

The three versions of HALFLOOP, namely HALFLOOP-24, HALFLOOP-48, and HALFLOOP-96, possess the same key size of 128 bits while exhibiting differing state sizes of 24 bits, 48 bits, and 96 bits, correspondingly. The three variants of HALFLOOP are used in various generations of ALE systems:

H. Seo and S. Kim (Eds.): ICISC 2023, LNCS 14561, pp. 19–40, 2024.
https://doi.org/10.1007/978-981-97-1235-9_2

HALFLOOP-24 in the second generation (2G) system, HALFLOOP-48 in the third generation (3G) system, and HALFLOOP-96 in the fourth generation (4G) system.

The announcement of HALFLOOP is not accompanied by a public cryptanalysis. Dansarie *et al.* [12] presented the first public cryptanalytic result on HALFLOOP-24 and proposed a number of differential attacks [5] for ciphertext-only, known-plaintext, chosen-plaintext, and chosen-ciphertext scenarios. Despite having a 128-bit key size, the results of the attack indicate that HALFLOOP-24 is incapable of providing 128-bit security. Note that [12] only assesses the security of HALFLOOP-24 and does not examine the security of the other two variants.

Despite the fact that many HALFLOOP operations are derived from AES [2], HALFLOOP-96 is the most similar to AES of the three HALFLOOP variants. It is common knowledge that AES is susceptible to relate-key differential attacks, and full-round attacks on AES-192 and AES-256 are proposed in [6,7]. Consequently, the similarity between AES and HALFLOOP-96 drives us to investigate the security of HALFLOOP-96 in the context of related-key differential attacks.

1.1   Our Results

Motivated by recognising the resistance of HALFLOOP-96 to differential attack in the relate-key setting, we examine its differential property in the contexts of conventional, related-tweak, and related-key differential attacks. Automatic methods based on the Boolean satisfiability problem (SAT) are employed to find the lower bound on the number of active S-boxes and the upper bound on the differential probability for each of the three configurations.

❖ The resistance of HALFLOOP-96 to standard differential attacks is acceptable. The longest distinguisher with a probability above 2^{-95} covers five rounds. The probability of the optimal 5-round differential characteristic is 2^{-92}, whereas the accumulated probability of the best 5-round differential we can discover is $2^{-89.18}$. Due to the limited accumulated effect of differential characteristics, there is no effective 6-round distinguisher.

❖ Comparing the security of HALFLOOP-96 in the related-tweak setting to the security of the cipher in the conventional differential setting, there is no significant decline. The bounds on the active S-boxes and differential probability in the related-tweak setting are identical to those in the conventional setting, commencing from the sixth round. For more than five rounds, the differential characteristics returned by the SAT solver are the same as those with zero tweak differences. Therefore, starting with the sixth round, the performance of related-tweak differential characteristics is not superior to that of traditional differential characteristics.

❖ In the related-key setting, HALFLOOP-96 has a low resistance to differential attack. The maximum number of rounds covered by a related-key differential characteristic is eight. The probability of the unique 8-round related-key differential characteristic is 2^{-124}, whereas the probability of the key schedule is

2^{-34} and the probability of the round function is 2^{-90}. The security margin in this case is limited, considering the ten rounds of HALFLOOP-96.

Using the newly discovered 8-round related-key differential distinguisher, we launch a 9-round related-key differential attack to recover partial information about the key pair. It takes $2^{92.96}$ chosen-plaintexts and $2^{92.96}$ 9-round encryptions to retrieve 38.77 bits of equivalent key information. The attack has a 90% success probability and is effective against 2^{94} key pairs with a specified difference. Although the attack does not pose an actual security threat to HALFLOOP-96, the security margin of the cipher in the setting for related-key attack is reduced to only one round. Hence, it is crucial to take measures to avoid the improper use of the application.

Outline. Section 2 goes over the target cipher HALFLOOP-96 as well as differential cryptanalysis. Section 3 describes the procedure for developing SAT models to seek for differential distinguishers of HALFLOOP-96. Section 4 provides the differential properties of the cipher in the conventional, related-tweak, and related-key configurations. The 9-round related-key differential on HALFLOOP-96 is detailed in Sect. 5. Section 6 serves as the conclusion of the paper.

2   Preliminaries

In this section, the cipher examined in the paper is initially reviewed. Next, the primary concept of differential cryptanalysis is presented.

2.1   Description of HALFLOOP-96

HALFLOOP [1] is a tweakable block cipher family with three distinct variants. HALFLOOP-96 employs 96-bit blocks and has 128-bit key K and 64-bit tweak T. Many operations in HALFLOOP-96 are derived from AES [2].

Initialisation After receiving the plaintext $m = m_0 \| m_1 \| \cdots \| m_{11}$, where $m_i \in \mathbb{F}_2^8$, $0 \leqslant i \leqslant 11$, the internal state IS is created by setting IS as

$$\text{IS} = \begin{bmatrix} m_0 & m_4 & m_8 \\ m_1 & m_5 & m_9 \\ m_2 & m_6 & m_{10} \\ m_3 & m_7 & m_{11} \end{bmatrix}.$$

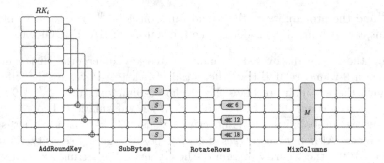

Fig. 1. Round function of HALFLOOP-96.

A single encryption round consists of the four operations depicted in Fig. 1: AddRoundKey (ARK), SubBytes (SB), RotateRows (RR), and MixColumns (MC). The encryption process consists of $r = 10$ rounds, with the last round replacing the MixColumns operation with AddRoundKey. The definitions of the four operations are as follows.

AddRoundKey (ARK) The round key RK_i is bitwise added to the state in the i-th round.

SubBytes (SB) An 8-bit S-box S is applied to each byte of the state, which is identical to the S-box used by AES (cf. [2]).

RotateRows (RR) As shown in Fig. 1, this operation rotates the rows of the state to the left by a variable number of bit positions.

MixColumns (MC) This operation is the same as the MixColumn transformation used in AES. The columns of the state are regarded as polynomials over the finite field $\mathbb{F}_{2^8}$, with the irreducible binary polynomial denoted as $m(x) = x^8 + x^4 + x^3 + x + 1$. Each column is multiplied modulo $x^4 + 1$ by a fixed polynomial $c(x)$ given by $c(x) = 3 \cdot x^3 + x^2 + x + 2$. The aforementioned process can instead be represented as a matrix multiplication utilising the matrix M over $\mathbb{F}_{2^8}$. In this case, the matrix M is defined as

$$M = \begin{bmatrix} 2 & 3 & 1 & 1 \\ 1 & 2 & 3 & 1 \\ 1 & 1 & 2 & 3 \\ 3 & 1 & 1 & 2 \end{bmatrix}. \tag{1}$$

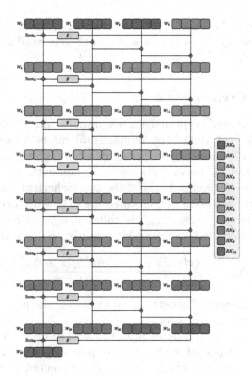

Fig. 2. Key schedule of HALFLOOP-96.

Key Schedule The key schedule resembles that of AES-128 closely. Denote K and T as $K_0\|K_1\|K_2\|K_3$ and $T_0\|T_1$, respectively, where K_i ($0 \leqslant i \leqslant 3$) and T_j ($j = 0, 1$) are 32-bit words. K and T are utilised to generate a linear array of 4-byte words $W_0, W_1, \ldots, W_{32}$, which are then employed to create the round keys. The first four words are initialised with

$$W_0 = K_0 \oplus T_0, W_1 = K_1 \oplus T_1, W_2 = K_2, W_3 = K_3.$$

The remaining words are derived using the subsequent two functions.

RotWord The function accepts the input word $a_0\|a_1\|a_2\|a_3$, performs a cyclic permutation, and returns the output word $a_1\|a_2\|a_3\|a_0$.

SubWord The function takes a 4-byte input word and applies the S-box S to each of the four bytes to generate a 4-byte output word.

Each subsequent word W_i ($4 \leqslant i \leqslant 32$ and $i \bmod 4 \neq 0$) is the XOR of the two preceding words W_{i-1} and W_{i-4}. For words in positions i that are a multiple of four, $g = $ SubWord $\circ$ RotWord is applied to W_{i-1} prior to the XOR, and a round constant $\text{Rcon}_{i/4}$ is XORed with the result. Eight round constants are involved in the key schedule of HALFLOOP-96, which are

$$\text{Rcon}_1 = \text{0x01000000}, \text{Rcon}_2 = \text{0x02000000}, \text{Rcon}_3 = \text{0x04000000},$$
$$\text{Rcon}_4 = \text{0x08000000}, \text{Rcon}_5 = \text{0x10000000}, \text{Rcon}_6 = \text{0x20000000},$$
$$\text{Rcon}_7 = \text{0x40000000}, \text{Rcon}_8 = \text{0x80000000}.$$

To obtain the round keys RK_0, RK_1, ..., and RK_{10} for HALFLOOP-96, it is necessary to repackage the 4-byte words into 12-byte words. The key schedule is illustrated in Fig. 2.

2.2   Differential Cryptanalysis

The concept of differential cryptanalysis was initially introduced by Biham and Shamir [5] at CRYPTO 1990. The fundamental methodology involves using plaintext pairs (P, P') linked by a constant *input difference* Δ_{in}, commonly described as the XOR operation between two plaintexts. The attacker subsequently calculates the difference between the two ciphertexts (C, C') to identify a non-random occurrence of an *output difference* Δ_{out} with a certain likelihood.

The pair of differences $(\Delta_{in}, \Delta_{out})$ is called a *differential*. The differential probability of the differential over an n-bit primitive E_K is computed as

$$\text{Pr}_{E_K}(\Delta_{in}, \Delta_{out}) = \frac{\{x \in \mathbb{F}_2^n \mid E_K(x) \oplus E_K(x \oplus \Delta_{in}) = \Delta_{out}\}}{2^n}.$$

The *weight* of the differential is determined by taking the negative logarithm of its probability, using a base of two.

The task of evaluating the differential probability of a differential in order to discover a valid differential for a cryptographic algorithm with several iterations is known to be quite challenging. The differential is usually localised by constructing *differential characteristics*, which enable the tracking of differences occurring after each round. Let $(\Delta_0 = \Delta_{in}, \Delta_1, \ldots, \Delta_r = \Delta_{out})$ be an r-round differential characteristic of the given differential $(\Delta_{in}, \Delta_{out})$. Suppose the r-round encryption E_K can be represented as the composition of r round functions denoted by $f_{k_{r-1}} \circ f_{k_{r-2}} \circ \cdots \circ f_{k_0}$. Given the premise that the round keys k_0, k_1, ..., and k_{r-1} are independent and uniformly random, the differential probability of the differential characteristic can be calculated as

$$\text{Pr}_{E_K}(\Delta_0, \Delta_1, \ldots, \Delta_r) = \prod_{i=0}^{r-1} \text{Pr}_{f_{k_i}}(\Delta_i, \Delta_{i+1}).$$

As discussed in [14], a fixed differential might encompass several differential characteristics, and the probability of the differential is determined by aggregating the probabilities associated with each differential characteristic. This probability may be computed as

$$\text{Pr}_{E_K}(\Delta_{in}, \Delta_{out}) = \sum_{\Delta_1, \Delta_2, \ldots, \Delta_{r-1} \in \mathbb{F}_2^n} \text{Pr}_{E_K}(\Delta_{in}, \Delta_1, \ldots, \Delta_{r-1}, \Delta_{out}).$$

In practical applications, the comprehensive search for all characteristics inside a differential and the precise calculation of their probabilities are unattainable due to the constraints imposed by limited computational resources. A common way of handling this is to find the differential characteristics with a higher probability in the differential, and the summation of probabilities of these characteristics approximates the probability of the differential.

After finding an r-round differential $(\Delta_{\mathsf{in}}, \Delta_{\mathsf{out}})$ with probability p_0 ($p_0 > 2^{1-n}$), we can launch an attack against the $(r+1)$-round encryption $\widehat{E}_K = f_{k_r} \circ E_K$. The following is a summary of the attack procedure.

① Select N pairs of plaintexts (P, P') whose difference $P \oplus P'$ equals Δ_{in}. Query the encryption oracle to obtain pairs of corresponding ciphertexts (C, C').

② Create a counter $\mathsf{Ctr}[k_r^{(i)}]$ for each possible value $k_r^{(i)}$ of the subkey k_r, $0 \leqslant i \leqslant 2^n - 1$. For each pair (C, C'), determine the value of $f_{k_r^{(i)}}^{-1}(C) \oplus f_{k_r^{(i)}}^{-1}(C')$ for each $k_r^{(i)}$. If the equation $f_{k_r^{(i)}}^{-1}(C) \oplus f_{k_r^{(i)}}^{-1}(C') = \Delta_{\mathsf{out}}$ is valid, increment the counter $\mathsf{Ctr}[k_r^{(i)}]$ by one.

③ If the threshold is set to τ, the key guess $k_r^{(i)}$ is sorted into a candidate list only if the counter value $\mathsf{Ctr}[k_r^{(i)}]$ is at least τ.

The counter that keeps track of the number of pairs confirming the differential conforms to the binomial distribution $\mathcal{B}(N, p_0)$ when the correct key guess is made, as the attack procedure specifies. The counter under the wrong key guess follows a binomial distribution $\mathcal{B}(N, p)$, where p is the probability of a pair matching the differential given a wrong key guess, which is equal to $p = 2^{1-n}$.

As a statistical cryptanalysis, differential cryptanalysis is inevitably confronted with two errors. The symbol ε_0 denotes the likelihood that the candidate list does not include the right key. The likelihood of a key guess that is not correct remaining in the candidate list is represented by the symbol ε_1. Hence, the probability of success (P_S) in the attack, denoting the likelihood of the right key being included in the candidate list, may be expressed as $1 - \varepsilon_0$. When the value of N is sufficiently large, the approximations for ε_0 and ε_1 may be derived using the methodology presented in [8] as

$$
\varepsilon_0 \approx \frac{p_0 \cdot \sqrt{1 - (\tau - 1)/N}}{(p_0 - (\tau - 1)/N) \cdot \sqrt{2 \cdot \pi \cdot (\tau - 1)}} \cdot \exp\left[-N \cdot D\left(\frac{\tau - 1}{N} \middle\| p_0\right)\right],
$$
$$
\varepsilon_1 \approx \frac{(1 - p) \cdot \sqrt{\tau/N}}{(\tau/N - p) \cdot \sqrt{2 \cdot \pi \cdot N \cdot (1 - \tau/N)}} \cdot \exp\left[-N \cdot D\left(\frac{\tau}{N} \middle\| p\right)\right],
$$
(2)

where $D(p\|q) \triangleq p \cdot \ln\left(\frac{p}{q}\right) + (1 - p) \cdot \ln\left(\frac{1-p}{1-q}\right)$ represents the Kullback-Leibler divergence between two Bernoulli distributions with parameters p and q.

2.3   Related-Key and Related-Tweak Differential Cryptanalysis

One notable distinction between differential cryptanalysis and related-key differential cryptanalysis is the utilisation of differential propagations. In related-key differential cryptanalysis, the focus is on exploiting the differential propagation while encrypting plaintexts P and P' with distinct keys, even if these plaintexts happen to be identical. The formal representation of an r-round *related-key differential* is denoted by the triple $(\Delta_{in}, \Delta_{out}, \Delta_{key})$, where Δ_{key} signifies the difference between the keys. The probability is calculated as

$$\Pr\nolimits_{E_K}(\Delta_{in}, \Delta_{out}, \Delta_{key}) = \frac{\{x \in \mathbb{F}_2^n \mid E_K(x) \oplus E_{K \oplus \Delta_{key}}(x \oplus \Delta_{in}) = \Delta_{out}\}}{2^n}.$$

AES is widely acknowledged as vulnerable to related-key differential attacks, as evidenced by the suggested full-round attacks on AES-192 and AES-256 in [6,7]. Given that HALFLOOP-96 has the highest degree of similarity to AES among the three HALFLOOP variations, our focus lies on examining its differential property in the context of a related-key attack.

It is also feasible to initialise related-tweak differential cryptanalysis for tweakable block ciphers. Differential propagation is utilised when P and P', which might potentially be identical, are encrypted using the same key and distinct tweaks. The *related-tweak differential* is denoted by $(\Delta_{in}, \Delta_{out}, \Delta_{tweak})$, where Δ_{tweak} signifies the difference between the tweaks. In contrast to related-key differential cryptanalysis, related-tweak differential cryptanalysis is considered a more feasible approach because the adversary knows the value of the tweak.

3   Automatic Search of Differential Distinguishers

Identifying a differential with a non-negligible probability is a pivotal and arduous stage in a differential attack. At the EUROCRYPT 1994, Matsui [18] introduced a pioneering approach called the branch and bound algorithm, which offered a systematic methodology for investigating the best differential characteristic. When considering tailored optimisations for certain ciphers, it is indisputable that branch and bound algorithms exhibit high efficiency [13]. However, the ability to prevent memory overflow through the precise selection of search nodes is a challenge requiring proficiency in cryptanalysis and programming.

The introduction of automatic search techniques [19] has dramatically simplified the process of identifying differential characteristics. The main aim is to transform the task of finding differential characteristics into some well-studied mathematical problems. With some publicly accessible solvers for these mathematical problems, the optimal differential characteristics can be identified. Due to its relatively straightforward implementation, automatic approaches have been widely employed in the search for distinguishers in various attacks.

The mathematical problems that are commonly encountered include mixed integer linear programming (MILP), Boolean satisfiability problem (SAT), satisfiability modulus theories (SMT), and constraint satisfaction problem (CSP). The classification of automatic search methods is based on the mathematical issues they address. The search for differential characteristics in ciphers with 8-bit S-boxes may be conducted using MILP method as described in [3,9,15], SAT method as described in [4,23], and SMT method as described in [16]. In this study, the SAT method proposed in [23] is chosen for efficiently generating SAT models for S-boxes.

This section provides a comprehensive description of the SAT models necessary for searching for differential characteristics of HALFLOOP-96.

3.1 Boolean Satisfiability Problem

A *Boolean formula* is comprised of Boolean variables, the operations AND (conjunction, $\wedge$), OR (disjunction, $\vee$), and NOT (negation, $\bar{\cdot}$), and brackets. The *Boolean satisfiability problem* (SAT) pertains to ascertaining the existence of a valid assignment for all Boolean variables such that the given Boolean formula holds. If this condition is met, the formula is known as *satisfiable*. In the absence of such a designated task, the formula in question is considered *unsatisfiable*. SAT is the first problem proven to be NP-complete [11]. However, significant advancements have been made in developing efficient solvers capable of handling a substantial volume of real-world SAT problems.

This work employs the solver CryptoMiniSat [21] for distinguisher search. CryptoMiniSat necessitates that Boolean formulae be expressed in *conjunctive normal form* (CNF), whereby many *clauses* are made in conjunction with each other, and each clause consists of a disjunction of variables, which may be negated. CryptoMiniSat additionally provides support for *XOR clauses* that are formed of XOR operations on variables. This feature greatly simplifies the process of constructing models for HALFLOOP-96. Converting distinguisher searching problems into Boolean formulae is critical in developing automatic models.

3.2 SAT Models for Linear Operations of HALFLOOP-96

For the m-bit vector Δ, the i-th bit ($0 \leqslant i \leqslant m - 1$) is denoted by $\Delta[i]$, while $\Delta[0]$ represents the most significant bit.

Model 1 (XOR, [17]). *For the m-bit XOR operation, the input differences are represented by Δ_0 and Δ_1, and the output difference is denoted by Δ_2. Differential propagation is valid if and only if the values of Δ_0, Δ_1 and Δ_2 validate all of the following XOR clauses.*

$$\Delta_0[i] \oplus \Delta_1[i] \oplus \Delta_2[i] = 0, 0 \leqslant i \leqslant m - 1.$$

To build the model for the MC operation, we employ the procedure described in [24]. First, the *primitive representation* [22] M of the matrix M (cf. Eq. (1)) is created.

$$
\mathbb{M} =
\begin{bmatrix}
0\,1\,0\,0\,0\,0\,0\,0 & 1\,1\,0\,0\,0\,0\,0\,0 & 1\,0\,0\,0\,0\,0\,0\,0 & 1\,0\,0\,0\,0\,0\,0\,0 \\
0\,0\,1\,0\,0\,0\,0\,0 & 0\,1\,1\,0\,0\,0\,0\,0 & 0\,1\,0\,0\,0\,0\,0\,0 & 0\,1\,0\,0\,0\,0\,0\,0 \\
0\,0\,0\,1\,0\,0\,0\,0 & 0\,0\,1\,1\,0\,0\,0\,0 & 0\,0\,1\,0\,0\,0\,0\,0 & 0\,0\,1\,0\,0\,0\,0\,0 \\
1\,0\,0\,0\,1\,0\,0\,0 & 1\,0\,0\,1\,1\,0\,0\,0 & 0\,0\,0\,1\,0\,0\,0\,0 & 0\,0\,0\,1\,0\,0\,0\,0 \\
1\,0\,0\,0\,0\,1\,0\,0 & 1\,0\,0\,0\,1\,1\,0\,0 & 0\,0\,0\,0\,1\,0\,0\,0 & 0\,0\,0\,0\,1\,0\,0\,0 \\
0\,0\,0\,0\,0\,0\,1\,0 & 0\,0\,0\,0\,0\,1\,1\,0 & 0\,0\,0\,0\,0\,1\,0\,0 & 0\,0\,0\,0\,0\,1\,0\,0 \\
1\,0\,0\,0\,0\,0\,0\,1 & 1\,0\,0\,0\,0\,0\,1\,1 & 0\,0\,0\,0\,0\,0\,1\,0 & 0\,0\,0\,0\,0\,0\,1\,0 \\
1\,0\,0\,0\,0\,0\,0\,0 & 1\,0\,0\,0\,0\,0\,0\,1 & 0\,0\,0\,0\,0\,0\,0\,1 & 0\,0\,0\,0\,0\,0\,0\,1 \\
1\,0\,0\,0\,0\,0\,0\,0 & 0\,1\,0\,0\,0\,0\,0\,0 & 1\,1\,0\,0\,0\,0\,0\,0 & 1\,0\,0\,0\,0\,0\,0\,0 \\
0\,1\,0\,0\,0\,0\,0\,0 & 0\,0\,1\,0\,0\,0\,0\,0 & 0\,1\,1\,0\,0\,0\,0\,0 & 0\,1\,0\,0\,0\,0\,0\,0 \\
0\,0\,1\,0\,0\,0\,0\,0 & 0\,0\,0\,1\,0\,0\,0\,0 & 0\,0\,1\,1\,0\,0\,0\,0 & 0\,0\,1\,0\,0\,0\,0\,0 \\
0\,0\,0\,1\,0\,0\,0\,0 & 1\,0\,0\,0\,1\,0\,0\,0 & 1\,0\,0\,1\,1\,0\,0\,0 & 0\,0\,0\,1\,0\,0\,0\,0 \\
0\,0\,0\,0\,1\,0\,0\,0 & 1\,0\,0\,0\,0\,1\,0\,0 & 1\,0\,0\,0\,1\,1\,0\,0 & 0\,0\,0\,0\,1\,0\,0\,0 \\
0\,0\,0\,0\,0\,1\,0\,0 & 0\,0\,0\,0\,0\,0\,1\,0 & 0\,0\,0\,0\,0\,1\,1\,0 & 0\,0\,0\,0\,0\,1\,0\,0 \\
0\,0\,0\,0\,0\,0\,1\,0 & 1\,0\,0\,0\,0\,0\,0\,1 & 1\,0\,0\,0\,0\,0\,1\,1 & 0\,0\,0\,0\,0\,0\,1\,0 \\
0\,0\,0\,0\,0\,0\,0\,1 & 1\,0\,0\,0\,0\,0\,0\,0 & 1\,0\,0\,0\,0\,0\,0\,1 & 0\,0\,0\,0\,0\,0\,0\,1 \\
1\,0\,0\,0\,0\,0\,0\,0 & 1\,0\,0\,0\,0\,0\,0\,0 & 0\,1\,0\,0\,0\,0\,0\,0 & 1\,1\,0\,0\,0\,0\,0\,0 \\
0\,1\,0\,0\,0\,0\,0\,0 & 0\,1\,0\,0\,0\,0\,0\,0 & 0\,0\,1\,0\,0\,0\,0\,0 & 0\,1\,1\,0\,0\,0\,0\,0 \\
0\,0\,1\,0\,0\,0\,0\,0 & 0\,0\,1\,0\,0\,0\,0\,0 & 0\,0\,0\,1\,0\,0\,0\,0 & 0\,0\,1\,1\,0\,0\,0\,0 \\
0\,0\,0\,1\,0\,0\,0\,0 & 0\,0\,0\,1\,0\,0\,0\,0 & 1\,0\,0\,0\,1\,0\,0\,0 & 1\,0\,0\,1\,1\,0\,0\,0 \\
0\,0\,0\,0\,1\,0\,0\,0 & 0\,0\,0\,0\,1\,0\,0\,0 & 1\,0\,0\,0\,0\,1\,0\,0 & 1\,0\,0\,0\,1\,1\,0\,0 \\
0\,0\,0\,0\,0\,1\,0\,0 & 0\,0\,0\,0\,0\,1\,0\,0 & 0\,0\,0\,0\,0\,0\,1\,0 & 0\,0\,0\,0\,0\,1\,1\,0 \\
0\,0\,0\,0\,0\,0\,1\,0 & 0\,0\,0\,0\,0\,0\,1\,0 & 1\,0\,0\,0\,0\,0\,0\,1 & 1\,0\,0\,0\,0\,0\,1\,1 \\
0\,0\,0\,0\,0\,0\,0\,1 & 0\,0\,0\,0\,0\,0\,0\,1 & 1\,0\,0\,0\,0\,0\,0\,0 & 1\,0\,0\,0\,0\,0\,0\,1 \\
1\,1\,0\,0\,0\,0\,0\,0 & 1\,0\,0\,0\,0\,0\,0\,0 & 1\,0\,0\,0\,0\,0\,0\,0 & 0\,1\,0\,0\,0\,0\,0\,0 \\
0\,1\,1\,0\,0\,0\,0\,0 & 0\,1\,0\,0\,0\,0\,0\,0 & 0\,1\,0\,0\,0\,0\,0\,0 & 0\,0\,1\,0\,0\,0\,0\,0 \\
0\,0\,1\,1\,0\,0\,0\,0 & 0\,0\,1\,0\,0\,0\,0\,0 & 0\,0\,1\,0\,0\,0\,0\,0 & 0\,0\,0\,1\,0\,0\,0\,0 \\
1\,0\,0\,1\,1\,0\,0\,0 & 0\,0\,0\,1\,0\,0\,0\,0 & 0\,0\,0\,1\,0\,0\,0\,0 & 1\,0\,0\,0\,1\,0\,0\,0 \\
1\,0\,0\,0\,1\,1\,0\,0 & 0\,0\,0\,0\,1\,0\,0\,0 & 0\,0\,0\,0\,1\,0\,0\,0 & 1\,0\,0\,0\,0\,1\,0\,0 \\
0\,0\,0\,0\,0\,1\,1\,0 & 0\,0\,0\,0\,0\,1\,0\,0 & 0\,0\,0\,0\,0\,1\,0\,0 & 0\,0\,0\,0\,0\,0\,1\,0 \\
1\,0\,0\,0\,0\,0\,1\,1 & 0\,0\,0\,0\,0\,0\,1\,0 & 0\,0\,0\,0\,0\,0\,1\,0 & 1\,0\,0\,0\,0\,0\,0\,1 \\
1\,0\,0\,0\,0\,0\,0\,1 & 0\,0\,0\,0\,0\,0\,0\,1 & 0\,0\,0\,0\,0\,0\,0\,1 & 1\,0\,0\,0\,0\,0\,0\,0
\end{bmatrix}
$$

is the matrix representation of M over $\mathbb{F}_2$. The notation $\mathbb{M}_{i,j}$ represents the element located in the i-th row and j-th column of the matrix $\mathbb{M}$. The SAT model can then be constructed using XOR clauses.

Model 2 (Matrix Multiplication). *For matrix multiplication with the 32×32 matrix $\mathbb{M}$, the input and output differences are represented by Δ_0 and Δ_1 respectively. Differential propagation is valid if and only if the values of Δ_0 and Δ_1 satisfy all the XOR clauses in the subsequent.*

$$
\bigoplus_{\{j \,\mid\, 0 \leqslant j \leqslant 31 \text{ s.t. } \mathbb{M}_{i,j}=1\}} \Delta_0[j] \oplus \Delta_1[i] = 0, 0 \leqslant i \leqslant 31.
$$

3.3   SAT Model for the S-Box of HALFLOOP-48

The method in [23] is utilised to construct the SAT model for the S-box. We commence our analysis with the SAT model that is focused on active S-boxes. In addition to using 16 Boolean variables $\Delta_0 = (\Delta_0[0], \Delta_0[1], \ldots, \Delta_0[7])$ and $\Delta_1 = (\Delta_1[0], \Delta_1[1], \ldots, \Delta_1[7])$ to represent the input and output differences of the S-box, it is necessary to incorporate an auxiliary Boolean variable denoted as w. The value assigned to w is one for active S-boxes and zero for inactive S-boxes, assuming the propagation $\Delta_0 \to \Delta_1$ is possible. Based on the given criteria, the set

$$\mathcal{V}_1 = \left\{ \Delta_0 \| \Delta_1 \| w \; \middle| \; \begin{array}{l} \Delta_0, \Delta_1 \in \mathbb{F}_2^8, w \in \mathbb{F}_2 \\ w = \begin{cases} 1, & \text{if } \mathrm{Pr}_S(\Delta_0, \Delta_1) < 1 \\ 0, & \text{if } \mathrm{Pr}_S(\Delta_0, \Delta_1) = 1 \end{cases} \end{array} \right\}$$

encompasses potential values for $\Delta_0 \| \Delta_1 \| w$. In order to maintain the constraint that $\Delta_0 \| \Delta_1 \| w$ remains within the bounds of the set $\mathcal{V}_1$, a clause is generated for each 17-bit vector $v \notin \mathcal{V}_1$,

$$\bigvee_{i=0}^{7} (\Delta_0[i] \oplus v[i]) \vee \bigvee_{i=0}^{7} (\Delta_1[i] \oplus v[i+8]) \vee (w \oplus v[16]) = 1,$$

which may serve as a candidate for the SAT model of the S-box. These clauses comprise an initial version of the SAT model for the search oriented to active S-boxes. The use of the initial version of the SAT model without modification would impede the search process of the automatic method due to the large size of the set $\mathbb{F}_2^{17} \backslash \mathcal{V}_1$, which is $2^{17} - 32386 = 98686$. To reduce the size of the S-box model, we employ the Espresso algorithm [10] to simplify the model[1]. The final SAT model oriented to active S-boxes is composed of 7967 clauses.

The SAT model oriented to differential probability can be created similarly. The probabilities of possible differential propagations $\Delta_0 \to \Delta_1$ for the 8-bit S-box S can take values from the set $\{2^{-7}, 2^{-6}, 1\}$. Motivated by the two-step encoding method described in [23], we introduce two Boolean variables u_0 and u_1 for each S-box to encode the differential probability of possible propagations.

$$\mathcal{V}_2 = \left\{ \Delta_0 \| \Delta_1 \| u_0 \| u_1 \; \middle| \; \begin{array}{l} \Delta_0, \Delta_1 \in \mathbb{F}_2^8, u_0, u_1 \in \mathbb{F}_2 \\ u_0 \| u_1 = \begin{cases} 1\|1, & \text{if } \mathrm{Pr}_S(\Delta_0, \Delta_1) = 2^{-7} \\ 0\|1, & \text{if } \mathrm{Pr}_S(\Delta_0, \Delta_1) = 2^{-6} \\ 0\|0, & \text{if } \mathrm{Pr}_S(\Delta_0, \Delta_1) = 1 \end{cases} \end{array} \right\}$$

is an optional set of values that may be assigned to the vector $\Delta_0 \| \Delta_1 \| u_0 \| u_1$. Thus, the weight of a potential propagation can be determined by $u_0 + 6 \cdot u_1$. To ensure that $\Delta_0 \| \Delta_1 \| u_0 \| u_1$ never takes values outside of the set $\mathcal{V}_2$, we should generate a clause for each 18-bit $\nu \notin \mathcal{V}_2$,

$$\bigvee_{i=0}^{7} (\Delta_0[i] \oplus \nu[i]) \vee \bigvee_{i=0}^{7} (\Delta_1[i] \oplus \nu[i+8]) \vee (u_0 \oplus \nu[16]) \vee (u_1 \oplus \nu[17]) = 1.$$

---

[1] A modern, compilable re-host of the Espresso heuristic logic minimizer can be found at https://github.com/classabbyamp/espresso-logic.

These clauses constitute an initial version of the SAT model oriented to differential probability. ESPRESSO algorithm is once again employed to reduce the size of the model. The final S-box model oriented to differential probability is composed of 8728 clauses.

3.4   SAT Model for the Objective Function

We aim to identify differential characteristics that exhibit fewer active S-boxes and high probability. The objective function can be mathematically expressed as $\sum_{i=0}^{\ell} u_i \leqslant \vartheta$, where u_i $(0 \leqslant i \leqslant \ell)$ are Boolean variables that indicate the activation status of the S-boxes or encode the differential probability of possible propagations for the S-boxes. Let ϑ denote a predetermined upper limit for either the number of active S-boxes or the weight of the differential characteristics. The sequential encoding method [20] is utilised to transform this inequality into clauses.

Model 3 (Objective Function, [20]). *The following clauses provide validity assurance for the objective function* $\sum_{i=0}^{\ell} u_i \leqslant 0$.

$$\overline{u_i} = 1, 0 \leqslant i \leqslant \ell.$$

For the objective function $\sum_{i=0}^{\ell} u_i \leqslant \vartheta$ *with* $\vartheta > 0$, *it is necessary to incorporate auxiliary Boolean variables* $a_{i,j}$ $(0 \leqslant i \leqslant \ell - 1, 0 \leqslant j \leqslant \vartheta - 1)$. *The objective function is valid if and only if the following clauses hold.*

$$\overline{u_0} \vee a_{0,0} = 1$$
$$\overline{a_{0,j}} = 1, \ 1 \leqslant j \leqslant \vartheta - 1$$
$$\left. \begin{array}{l} \overline{u_i} \vee a_{i,0} = 1 \\ \overline{a_{i-1,0}} \vee a_{i,0} = 1 \\ \left. \begin{array}{l} \overline{u_i} \vee \overline{a_{i-1,j-1}} \vee a_{i,j} = 1 \\ \overline{a_{i-1,j}} \vee a_{i,j} = 1 \end{array} \right\} 1 \leqslant j \leqslant \vartheta - 1 \\ \overline{u_i} \vee \overline{a_{i-1,\vartheta-1}} = 1 \end{array} \right\} 1 \leqslant i \leqslant \ell - 2$$
$$\overline{u_\ell} \vee \overline{a_{\ell-1,\vartheta-1}} = 1$$

3.5   Finding More Differential Characteristics

Using the models presented in Sects. 3.2, 3.3 and 3.4, we can identify differential characteristics with fewer active S-boxes and high probabilities. To improve the probability evaluation of the differential, we should fix the input and output differences in the automatic model and find as many other differential characteristics as feasible. To prevent the solver from returning the same solution after obtaining a single differential characteristic, we should add a clause to the SAT problem. Assume that $v \in \mathbb{F}_2^\omega$ is a solution for the ω Boolean variables x_0, x_1, ..., $x_{\omega-1}$ returned by the SAT solver. Two index sets

$$v|_0 = \{i | 0 \leqslant i \leqslant \omega - 1 \text{ s.t. } v[i] = 0\}, \text{ and } v|_1 = \{i | 0 \leqslant i \leqslant \omega - 1 \text{ s.t. } v[i] = 1\}.$$

are generated based on the value of v. Adding the clause

$$\bigvee_{i \in v|_0} x_i \vee \bigvee_{i \in v|_1} \overline{x_i} = 1$$

to the SAT problem guarantees that the solver will not find v again.

4 Differential Distinguishers of HALFLOOP-96

This section presents an analysis of the differential characteristics of HALFLOOP-96 in three attack settings: conventional, related-tweak, and related-key. These characteristics are determined using the methodology in Sect. 3.

Table 1. Differential properties of HALFLOOP-96.

Round	1	2	3	4	5	6	7	8	9	10
#S	1	5	8	11	14	17	20	23	26	29
#S$_T$	0	1	3	8	14	17	20	23	26	29
#S$_K$	0	0	1	5	11	14	16	19	24	29
P	2^{-6}	2^{-30}	2^{-48}	2^{-70}	2^{-92}	2^{-113}	2^{-134}	2^{-155}	2^{-176}	2^{-197}
P$_T$	1	2^{-6}	2^{-18}	2^{-53}	2^{-91}	2^{-113}	2^{-134}	2^{-155}	2^{-176}	2^{-197}
P$_K$	1	1	2^{-6}	2^{-31}	2^{-66}	2^{-87}	2^{-106}	2^{-124}	2^{-154}	2^{-197}

#S, #S$_T$, and #S$_K$: The number of active S-boxes in conventional, related-tweak, and related-key settings.

P, P$_T$, and P$_K$: Differential probabilities in conventional, related-tweak, and related-key settings.

4.1 Conventional Differential Distinguishers of HALFLOOP-96

The lower bound on the number of active S-boxes and the upper bound on the differential probability are calculated in the standard differential attack scenario. The outcomes of 1 to 10 rounds of HALFLOOP-96 are displayed in Table 1.

The longest differential characteristic with a probability greater than 2^{-95} spans five rounds, and the SAT solver indicates that there are 3207 5-round

Table 2. Information about three 5-round differentials with probability $2^{-89.18}$.

Index	Input difference	Output difference
1	0x00000058060000000660000	0x101030205f6a3535e8c09d2e
2	0x0600000000066000000000058	0x5f6a3535e8c09d2e10103020
3	0x00660000000005806000000	0xe8c09d2e101030205f6a3535

differential characteristics with probability 2^{-92}. A thorough analysis reveals that the 3207 characteristics stem from 2214 distinct differentials. We search for all differential characteristics in the 2214 differentials with probabilities more significant than 2^{-110} by fixing the input and output differences in the automatic search. The largest accumulated probability of the differential is $2^{-89.18}$, and there are three differentials with the highest probability, whose input and output differences are shown in Table 2. Six 5-round characteristics exist in the first differential with the highest probability of 2^{-92}, as depicted in Fig. 3.

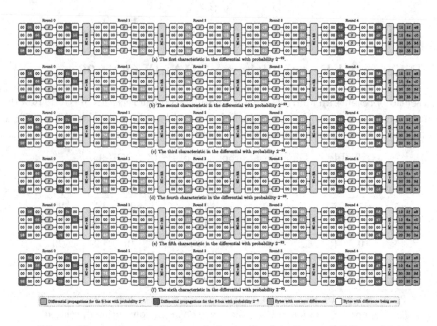

Fig. 3. Six dominated characteristics in the first 5-round differential.

Even though the probability of the optimal 6-round differential characteristic of HALFLOOP-96 is less than 2^{-95}, we question the existence of 6-round differentials with accumulated probabilities greater than 2^{-95}. To find the answer, we first search for all 6-round differential characteristics with a probability of 2^{-113} and determine that 1272 characteristics meet the condition. Note that the 1272 characteristics come from 1017 different differentials. Then, we fix the input and output differences in the automatic search and discover all differential characteristics with probabilities greater than 2^{-135} for each of the 1017 differentials. The maximal accumulated probability of 6-round differentials reaches $2^{-110.87}$, indicating that these differentials cannot support a valid differential attack. The longest differential distinguisher for HALFLOOP-96 comprises five rounds.

4.2 Related-Tweak Differential Distinguishers of HALFLOOP-96

The evaluation of active S-boxes and differential probabilities should include the key schedule in the context of a related-tweak attack. Table 1 displays the minimum number of active S-boxes and maximum differential probabilities for one to ten rounds of HALFLOOP-96 in the related-tweak attack configuration.

From the sixth round, the bounds on the active S-boxes and probabilities in the related-tweak setting are identical to those in the conventional setting, as shown in Table 1. The differential characteristics returned by the SAT solver for more than five rounds do not have non-zero tweak differences. Accordingly, beginning with the sixth round, related-tweak differential characteristics do not perform better than conventional ones. Given that the optimal differential in the conventional differential attack setting has already reached five rounds, the advantage of the adversary in the related-tweak setting is insignificant.

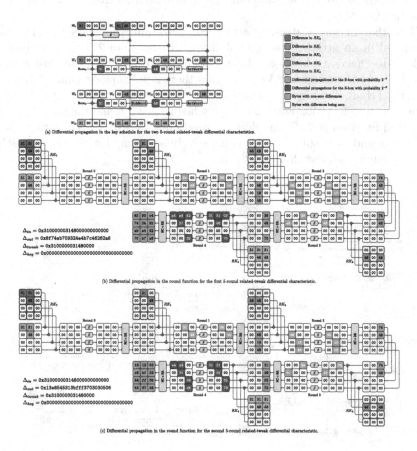

Fig. 4. Two 5-round related-tweak differential characteristics with probability 2^{-91}.

The minor advantage resides in the existence of 5-round related-tweak differential characteristics with a probability of 2^{-91}, whereas the probability of the optimal 5-round characteristic in the conventional setting is 2^{-92}. We find two 5-round related-tweak differential characteristics with a probability of 2^{-91} using the SAT solver. The probability in the key schedule is 2^{-12} and the probability in the round function is 2^{-79} for both characteristics. In addition, after searching exhaustively with the automatic procedure for all characteristics with probabilities greater than 2^{-120}, we are unable to identify a clustering effect for the two characteristics. Figure 4 exhibits the two characteristics.

4.3 Related-Key Differential Distinguishers of HALFLOOP-96

In the context of a related-key attack, the calculation of active S-boxes and differential probabilities must consider the key schedule. Table 1 displays the bounds on the active S-boxes and differential probabilities from one to ten cycles of HALFLOOP-96.

Note that in the related-key attack configuration, the characteristics may be utilised in an attack if the probability is greater than 2^{-127}. According to Table 1, the effective related-key differential characteristic with the most rounds is eight. We verify using the SAT solver that there is only one 8-round related-key differential characteristic with probability 2^{-124}. Figure 5 illustrates the 8-round characteristic. The probability in the key schedule is 2^{-34}, and the probability in the round function is 2^{-90}. In addition, we do not identify the clustering effect for the 8-round distinguisher after exhaustively searching for all characteristics with probability no less than 2^{-150}.

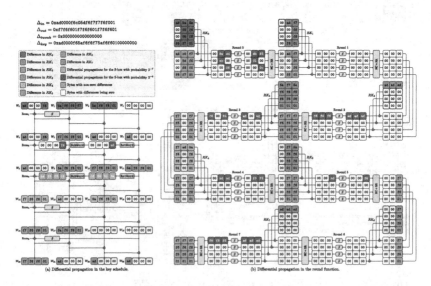

Fig. 5. 8-round related-key differential characteristics with probability 2^{-124}.

5   Related-Key Differential Attack on HALFLOOP-96

In this section, we employ the 8-round related-key differential distinguisher in Sect. 4.3 to launch a 9-round related-key differential attack on HALFLOOP-96. Note that the attack is a weak-key attack, as the probability of the key schedule shown in Fig. 5 is 2^{-34}. In other words, only one pair of keys out of 2^{34} pairs of keys with a difference of $\Delta_{key} = $ 0xad0000f65af6f6f75af6f60100000000 is susceptible to the following attack. In this circumstance, a valid attack must ensure the time complexity is less than 2^{94}.

In the attack, one round is appended after the distinguisher, and the key-recovery procedure is depicted in Fig. 6. $\mathcal{S}$ structures are prepared for the attack. Each structure contains 2^{80} plaintexts, where ten bytes $P[0, 3\text{-}11]$ of the plaintext P traverse all possible values while the remaining two are fixed to random constants. Then, a single structure can be used to create 2^{79} pairs with a difference of $\Delta P = $ 0xad0000f6c05df6f7f7f6f001, bringing the total number of pairs to $N = \mathcal{S} \cdot 2^{79}$. Therefore, the data complexity of the attack is $\mathcal{S} \cdot 2^{80}$ chosen-plaintexts.

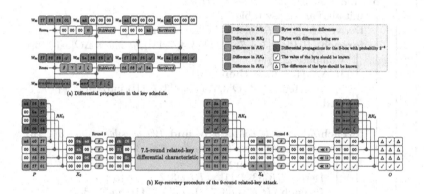

(a) Differential propagation in the key schedule.

(b) Key-recovery procedure of the 9-round related-key attack.

Fig. 6. 9-round related-key differential attack on HALFLOOP-96.

In the attack, an empty hash table $\mathbb{H}$ is created. For each output pair (O, O') returned by the encryption oracle, if the conditions

$$\Delta O[0\text{-}2] = \text{0x5af6f6}, \quad \Delta O[5] \oplus \Delta O[9] = \Delta O[6] \oplus \Delta O[10] = \text{0xf6}.$$

are fulfilled, the quadruple $(P, P', O[3,4,7,11], O'[3,4,7,11])$ will be inserted into $\mathbb{H}$ at index $\Delta O[8\text{-}10]$. Consequently, $\mathbb{H}$ contains approximately $N \cdot 2^{-40}$ quadruples, and each index $\Delta O[8\text{-}10]$ corresponds to approximately $N \cdot 2^{-64}$ quadruples. The index $\Delta O[8\text{-}10]$ that renders differential propagation of either 0xf6 $\to \Delta O[8] \oplus$ ad or 0xf6 $\to \Delta O[9]$ impossible for the S-box is then eliminated from $\mathbb{H}$. After this stage, there are approximately $2^{24} \cdot (127/256)^2 = 2^{21.98}$ indexes remaining in $\mathbb{H}$. The time complexity of this phase is dominated by the time to query the encryption oracle, which corresponds to line 3 of Algorithm 1 and is equivalent to $\mathsf{T}_{\mathsf{L}3} = \mathcal{S} \cdot 2^{79} \cdot 2 = \mathcal{S} \cdot 2^{80}$ 9-round encryptions.

For each index $\Delta O[8\text{-}10]$ in $\mathbb{H}$, we guess the value of $RK_9[4]$ and initialise an empty table $\mathbb{T}_1$. After deriving the value of $RK_9'[4] = RK_9[4] \oplus \Delta O[8] \oplus 5\mathsf{a}$, the value of $\Delta X_8[4]$ for each quadruple at index $\Delta O[8\text{-}10]$ can be computed.

Algorithm 1: 9-round related-key differential attack

1 Create $\mathcal{S} \cdot 2^{79}$ pairs (P, P') from $\mathcal{S}$ structures
2 Initialise an empty hash table $\mathbb{H}$
3 Obtain the value of (O, O') for each (P, P') by querying the encryption oracle
4 **if** $\Delta O[0\text{-}2] = \mathsf{0x5af6f6}$ **and** $\Delta O[5] \oplus \Delta O[9] = \Delta O[6] \oplus \Delta O[10] = \mathsf{0xf6}$ **then**
5 $\quad \mid$ $(P, P', O[3, 4, 7, 11], O'[3, 4, 7, 11])$ is inserted into $\mathbb{H}$ at index $\Delta O[8\text{-}10]$
6 **end**
7 **foreach** *index* $\Delta O[8\text{-}10]$ *of* $\mathbb{H}$ **do**
8 $\quad \mid$ **if** $\mathsf{0xf6} \to \Delta O[8] \oplus \mathsf{ad}$ **or** $\mathsf{0xf6} \to \Delta O[9]$ *are impossible propagations* **then**
9 $\quad \quad \mid$ Remove the index $\Delta O[8\text{-}10]$ from $\mathbb{H}$
10 $\quad \mid$ **else**
11 $\quad \quad \mid$ **foreach** *8-bit possible values of* $RK_9[4]$ **do**
12 $\quad \quad \quad \mid$ Initialise an empty table $\mathbb{T}_1$
13 $\quad \quad \quad \mid$ Derive $RK_9'[4] = RK_9[4] \oplus \Delta O[8] \oplus \mathsf{0x5a}$
14 $\quad \quad \quad \mid$ **foreach** $(P, P', O[3, 4, 7, 11], O'[3, 4, 7, 11])$ *at index* $\Delta O[8\text{-}10]$ **do**
15 $\quad \quad \quad \quad \mid$ Compute $\Delta X_8[4]$
16 $\quad \quad \quad \quad \mid$ **if** $\Delta X_8[4] = \mathsf{0xad}$ **then**
17 $\quad \quad \quad \quad \quad \mid$ Inserted $(P, P', O[3, 7, 11], O'[3, 7, 11])$ into table $\mathbb{T}_1$
18 $\quad \quad \quad \quad \mid$ **end**
19 $\quad \quad \quad \mid$ **end**
20 $\quad \quad \quad \mid$ **foreach** *63 possible values of* α' **and** *127 possible values of* ζ **do**
21 $\quad \quad \quad \quad \mid$ **foreach** *24-bit possible values of* $RK_9[3, 7, 11]$ **do**
22 $\quad \quad \quad \quad \quad \mid$ Initialise an empty table $\mathbb{T}_2$
23 $\quad \quad \quad \quad \quad \mid$ Derive $RK_9'[3, 7, 11] = RK_9[3, 7, 11] \oplus (\alpha' \| (\alpha' \oplus \zeta) \| \zeta)$
24 $\quad \quad \quad \quad \quad \mid$ **foreach** $(P, P', O[3, 7, 11], O'[3, 7, 11])$ *in* $\mathbb{T}_1$ **do**
25 $\quad \quad \quad \quad \quad \quad \mid$ Compute $\Delta X_8[3, 7, 11]$
26 $\quad \quad \quad \quad \quad \quad \mid$ **if** $\Delta X_8[3] = \Delta X_8[7] = \Delta X_8[11] = \alpha' \oplus \mathsf{0x01}$ **then**
27 $\quad \quad \quad \quad \quad \quad \quad \mid$ Inserted (P, P') into table $\mathbb{T}_2$
28 $\quad \quad \quad \quad \quad \quad \mid$ **end**
29 $\quad \quad \quad \quad \quad \mid$ **end**
30 $\quad \quad \quad \quad \quad \mid$ Count the number of pairs Ctr in $\mathbb{T}_2$
31 $\quad \quad \quad \quad \quad \mid$ **if** $\mathsf{Ctr} \geqslant \tau$ **then**
32 $\quad \quad \quad \quad \quad \quad \mid$ Derive candidates for $RK_0[4, 5, 8, 10]$ with (P, P') in $\mathbb{T}_2$
33 $\quad \quad \quad \quad \quad \quad \mid$ Output $RK_0[4, 5, 8, 10] \| RK_9[3, 4, 7, 11] \| \alpha' \| \zeta \| \Delta[8\text{-}10]$
34 $\quad \quad \quad \quad \quad \mid$ **end**
35 $\quad \quad \quad \quad \mid$ **end**
36 $\quad \quad \quad \mid$ **end**
37 $\quad \quad \mid$ **end**
38 $\quad \mid$ **end**
39 **end**

If $\Delta X_8[4] = \texttt{0xad}$, the quadruple $(P, P', O[3,7,11], O'[3,7,11])$ is inserted into table $\mathbb{T}_1$. The approximate number of quadruples in $\mathbb{T}_1$ is $N \cdot 2^{-64} \cdot 2^{-8} = N \cdot 2^{-72}$. This phase, which corresponds to line 14 of Algorithm 1, has a time complexity of $\mathsf{T}_{\mathsf{L}14} = 2^{21.98} \cdot 2^8 \cdot N \cdot 2^{-64} \cdot 2/12 = \mathcal{S} \cdot 2^{42.40}$ one-round encryptions.

Since the difference $\Delta RK_9[3,7,11]$ is related to undetermined values α' and ζ, the following attack should enumerate the values of α' and ζ. Noting that $\texttt{5a} \to \zeta$ is a possible propagation for the S-box, ζ can take on one of 127 possible values. Since $\texttt{ad} \to \alpha' \oplus \texttt{0x01}$ and $\alpha' \to \Delta O[10]$ must be possible propagations for the S-box, the probability that a random 8-bit vector validates the two constraints for the case of α' is $(127/256)^2 = 2^{-2.02}$. Therefore, α' has an average of 63 possible values. Then, for all 63 possible values of α' and 127 possible values of ζ, we estimate the value of $RK_9[3,7,11]$ and create an empty table $\mathbb{T}_2$. After deriving the values of $RK_9'[3] = RK_9[3] \oplus \alpha'$, $RK_9'[7] = RK_9[7] \oplus \alpha' \oplus \zeta$, and $RK_9'[11] = RK_9[11] \oplus \zeta$, it is possible to calculate the value of $\Delta X_8[3,7,11]$. If $\Delta X_8[3] = \Delta X_8[7] = \Delta X_8[11] = \alpha' \oplus \texttt{0x01}$, the quadruple in $\mathbb{T}_1$ will be inserted into $\mathbb{T}_2$. Consequently, $\mathbb{T}_2$ contains approximately $N \cdot 2^{-72} \cdot 2^{-24} = N \cdot 2^{-96}$ quadruples. This step, which corresponds to line 24 of Algorithm 1, has a time complexity of $\mathsf{T}_{\mathsf{L}24} = 2^{21.98} \cdot 2^8 \cdot 63 \cdot 127 \cdot 2^{24} \cdot N \cdot 2^{-72} \cdot 3 \cdot 2/12 = \mathcal{S} \cdot 2^{72.95}$ one-round encryptions.

We set a counter Cnt in order to remember the number of quadruples in $\mathbb{T}_2$. Based on the analysis presented above, the value of Cnt follows a binomial distribution with parameters $\mathcal{B}(N, p_0 = 2^{-90})$ for a correct key guess and $\mathcal{B}(N, p = 2^{-96})$ otherwise. The threshold τ is set to two correct pairs, and the success probability P_S is set to 90.00%. Using Eq. (2), we determine $\mathcal{S} = 2^{12.96}$ and $\varepsilon_1 = 2^{-14.77}$. Therefore, there are $\varepsilon_1 \cdot 2^{21.98} \cdot 2^{32} \cdot 63 \cdot 127 = \varepsilon_1 \cdot 2^{66.95}$ candidates for $RK_9[3,4,7,11] \| \alpha' \| \zeta \| \Delta[8\text{-}10]$ that satisfy the condition at line 30 of Algorithm 1. Utilising the property of the four active S-boxes in the first round, as depicted in Fig. 6(b), and relying on right pairs, additional information about the key can be recovered. Take the S-box at $X_0[4]$ as an illustration. Since the input difference $\texttt{0x9a}$ must be propagated to the output difference $\texttt{0xdb}$, there are only four possible values for $X_0[4]$ and $X_0'[4]$, which are $\texttt{0x00}$, $\texttt{0x72}$, $\texttt{0x9a}$, and $\texttt{0xe8}$. This restriction allows us to screen out candidates for $RK_0[4]$ with a probability of 2^{-6}. Likewise, the constraints on $X_0[5]$, $X_0[8]$ and $X_0[10]$ yield a sieving probability of 2^{-18}. There are a total of $\varepsilon_1 \cdot 2^{66.95} \cdot 4^4 = \varepsilon_1 \cdot 2^{74.95}$ candidates for $RK_0[4,5,8,10] \| RK_9[3,4,7,11] \| \alpha' \| \zeta \| \Delta[8\text{-}10]$. This phase, corresponding to line 31 of Algorithm 1, has a maximal time complexity of $\mathsf{T}_{\mathsf{L}31} = \varepsilon_1 \cdot 2^{66.95}$ one-round encryptions. We recover equivalently $1/\varepsilon_1 + 6 \cdot 4 = 38.77$ bits of information about the key pair. As a result, the total time complexity of the attack is $\mathsf{T}_{\mathsf{L}3} + (\mathsf{T}_{\mathsf{L}14} + \mathsf{T}_{\mathsf{L}24} + \mathsf{T}_{\mathsf{L}31})/9 = 2^{92.96}$ 9-round encryptions. Given that the hash table $\mathbb{H}$ dominates memory consumption, the memory complexity of the attack is $2^{56.96}$ bytes.

Remark 1. We attempt to recover the remaining key bits as well. However, the time required to seek the remaining key bits exhaustively exceeds 2^{94}. The recovery of complete information about the key is an intriguing future endeavour.

6   Conclusion

This paper focuses on the differential distinguishers and related-key differential attacks on HALFLOOP-96. SAT problems are utilised to model the search for differential distinguishers. We use the SAT solver to determine the minimum number of active S-boxes and the maximum differential probability for the conventional, related-tweak, and related-key differential attack configurations. By applying the newly discovered 8-round related-key differential distinguisher, we launch a 9-round related-key differential attack against the cipher. The attack is weak-key and effective against 2^{94} key pairs with a specified difference. Although the attack does not pose a real security threat to HALFLOOP-96, the security margin of the cipher in the setting for related-key attacks is minimal. Consequently, care must be taken to avoid misuse.

Acknowledgements. The research leading to these results has received funding from the National Natural Science Foundation of China (Grant No. 62272273, Grant No. 62002201, Grant No. 62032014), the National Key Research and Development Program of China (Grant No. 2018YFA0704702), and the Major Basic Research Project of Natural Science Foundation of Shandong Province, China (Grant No. ZR202010220025). Ling Sun gratefully acknowledges the support by the Program of TaiShan Scholars Special Fund for young scholars (Grant No. tsqn202306043).

References

1. Interoperability and performance standards for medium and high frequency radio systems. United States Department of Defense Interface Standard MIL-STD-188-141D
2. Specification for the advanced encryption standard (AES). Federal Information Processing Standards Publication 197 (2001). http://csrc.nist.gov/publications/fips/fips197/fips-197.pdf
3. Abdelkhalek, A., Sasaki, Y., Todo, Y., Tolba, M., Youssef, A.M.: MILP modeling for (large) S-boxes to optimize probability of differential characteristics. IACR Trans. Symmetric Cryptol. **2017**(4), 99–129 (2017). https://doi.org/10.13154/tosc.v2017.i4.99-129
4. Ankele, R., Kölbl, S.: Mind the gap - A closer look at the security of block ciphers against differential cryptanalysis. In: Cid, C., Jacobson Jr., M. (eds.) SAC 2018. LNCS, vol. 11349, pp. 163–190. Springer, Cham (2018). https://doi.org/10.1007/978-3-030-10970-7_8
5. Biham, E., Shamir, A.: Differential cryptanalysis of DES-like cryptosystems. In: Menezes, A.J., Vanstone, S.A. (eds.) CRYPTO 1990. LNCS, vol. 537, pp. 2–21. Springer, Heidelberg (1991). https://doi.org/10.1007/3-540-38424-3_1
6. Biryukov, A., Khovratovich, D.: Related-key cryptanalysis of the full AES-192 and AES-256. In: Matsui, M. (ed.) ASIACRYPT 2009. LNCS, vol. 5912, pp. 1–18. Springer, Heidelberg (2009). https://doi.org/10.1007/978-3-642-10366-7_1
7. Biryukov, A., Khovratovich, D., Nikolić, I.: Distinguisher and related-key attack on the full AES-256. In: Halevi, S. (ed.) CRYPTO 2009. LNCS, vol. 5677, pp. 231–249. Springer, Heidelberg (2009). https://doi.org/10.1007/978-3-642-03356-8_14

8. Blondeau, C., Gérard, B., Tillich, J.: Accurate estimates of the data complexity and success probability for various cryptanalyses. Des. Codes Cryptogr. **59**(1–3), 3–34 (2011). https://doi.org/10.1007/s10623-010-9452-2

9. Boura, C., Coggia, D.: Efficient MILP modelings for Sboxes and linear layers of SPN ciphers. IACR Trans. Symmetric Cryptol. **2020**(3), 327–361 (2020). https://doi.org/10.13154/tosc.v2020.i3.327-361

10. Brayton, R.K., Hachtel, G.D., McMullen, C.T., Sangiovanni-Vincentelli, A.L.: Logic Minimization Algorithms for VLSI Synthesis. The Kluwer International Series in Engineering and Computer Science, vol. 2. Springer, Heidelberg (1984). https://doi.org/10.1007/978-1-4613-2821-6

11. Cook, S.A.: The complexity of theorem-proving procedures. In: Harrison, M.A., Banerji, R.B., Ullman, J.D. (eds.) Proceedings of the 3rd Annual ACM Symposium on Theory of Computing, 3–5 May 1971, Shaker Heights, Ohio, USA, pp. 151–158. ACM (1971). https://doi.org/10.1145/800157.805047

12. Dansarie, M., Derbez, P., Leander, G., Stennes, L.: Breaking HALFLOOP-24. IACR Trans. Symmetric Cryptol. **2022**(3), 217–238 (2022). https://doi.org/10.46586/tosc.v2022.i3.217-238

13. Kim, S., Hong, D., Sung, J., Hong, S.: Accelerating the best trail search on AES-like ciphers. IACR Trans. Symmetric Cryptol. **2022**(2), 201–252 (2022). https://doi.org/10.46586/tosc.v2022.i2.201-252

14. Lai, X., Massey, J.L., Murphy, S.: Markov ciphers and differential cryptanalysis. In: Davies, D.W. (ed.) EUROCRYPT 1991. LNCS, vol. 547, pp. 17–38. Springer, Heidelberg (1991). https://doi.org/10.1007/3-540-46416-6_2

15. Li, T., Sun, Y.: Superball: a new approach for MILP modelings of Boolean functions. IACR Trans. Symmetric Cryptol. **2022**(3), 341–367 (2022). https://doi.org/10.46586/tosc.v2022.i3.341-367

16. Liu, Y., et al.: STP models of optimal differential and linear trail for S-box based ciphers. Sci. China Inf. Sci. **64**(5) (2021). https://doi.org/10.1007/s11432-018-9772-0

17. Liu, Y., Wang, Q., Rijmen, V.: Automatic search of linear trails in ARX with applications to SPECK and Chaskey. In: Manulis, M., Sadeghi, A.-R., Schneider, S. (eds.) ACNS 2016. LNCS, vol. 9696, pp. 485–499. Springer, Cham (2016). https://doi.org/10.1007/978-3-319-39555-5_26

18. Matsui, M.: On correlation between the order of S-boxes and the strength of DES. In: De Santis, A. (ed.) EUROCRYPT 1994. LNCS, vol. 950, pp. 366–375. Springer, Heidelberg (1995). https://doi.org/10.1007/BFb0053451

19. Mouha, N., Wang, Q., Gu, D., Preneel, B.: Differential and linear cryptanalysis using mixed-integer linear programming. In: Wu, C.-K., Yung, M., Lin, D. (eds.) Inscrypt 2011. LNCS, vol. 7537, pp. 57–76. Springer, Heidelberg (2012). https://doi.org/10.1007/978-3-642-34704-7_5

20. Sinz, C.: Towards an optimal CNF encoding of Boolean cardinality constraints. In: van Beek, P. (ed.) CP 2005. LNCS, vol. 3709, pp. 827–831. Springer, Heidelberg (2005). https://doi.org/10.1007/11564751_73

21. Soos, M., Nohl, K., Castelluccia, C.: Extending SAT solvers to cryptographic problems. In: Kullmann, O. (ed.) SAT 2009. LNCS, vol. 5584, pp. 244–257. Springer, Heidelberg (2009). https://doi.org/10.1007/978-3-642-02777-2_24

22. Sun, B., et al.: Links among impossible differential, integral and zero correlation linear cryptanalysis. In: Gennaro, R., Robshaw, M. (eds.) CRYPTO 2015, Part I. LNCS, vol. 9215, pp. 95–115. Springer, Heidelberg (2015). https://doi.org/10.1007/978-3-662-47989-6_5

23. Sun, L., Wang, M.: SoK: modeling for large s-boxes oriented to differential proba-
    bilities and linear correlations. IACR Trans. Symmetric Cryptol. **2023**(1), 111–151
    (2023). https://doi.org/10.46586/tosc.v2023.i1.111-151
24. Sun, L., Wang, W., Wang, M.: More accurate differential properties of LED64 and
    midori64. IACR Trans. Symmetric Cryptol. **2018**(3), 93–123 (2018). https://doi.
    org/10.13154/tosc.v2018.i3.93-123

Revisiting Key Switching Techniques with Applications to Light-Key FHE

Ruida Wang[1,2], Zhihao Li[1,2], Benqiang Wei[1,2], Chunling Chen[1,2], Xianhui Lu[1,2(✉)], and Kunpeng Wang[1,2(✉)]

[1] State Key Laboratory of Information Security,
Institute of Information Engineering, Chinese Academy of Sciences, Beijing, China
{luxianhui,wangkunpeng}@iie.ac.cn
[2] School of Cyber Security, University of Chinese Academy of Sciences,
Beijing, China

Abstract. Fully Homomorphic Encryption (FHE) allows for data processing while it remains encrypted, enabling privacy-preserving outsourced computation. However, FHE faces challenges in real-world applications, such as communication overhead and storage limitations, due to the large size of its evaluation key.

This paper revisits existing *key switching* algorithms widely used in FHE, which may account for over 90% of the total evaluation key size. Although these algorithms work towards the same goal, they differ significantly in functionality, computational complexity, noise management and key size. We close their functional gap and reanalyze them under a common standard, proposing theorems and comparative results to provide a flexible time-space trade-off when designing FHE applications.

To validate the efficacy of our theoretical results, we propose a light-key bootstrapping method using a lower-sized key switching variant. This approach reduces the key size of the well-known GINX bootstrapping by a factor of 88.8%. It also outperforms the state-of-the-art light-key FHE by reducing 48.4% bootstrapping key size and 8% transfer key size.

Keywords: FHE · Key Switching · Light-Key Bootstrapping

1 Introduction

Fully Homomorphic Encryption (FHE) allows data to be processed while encrypted, enabling users to delegate computation to an untrusted party without the risk of data leakage. This opens up the potential for privacy-preserving outsourced computation in various applications, such as cloud computing [1,19], the internet of things (IoT) [26,29] and machine learning [10,20]. The process involves the client (data owner) encrypting their sensitive data, generating the necessary evaluation keys for homomorphic operations, and transmitting them to the server (computing party). The server performs homomorphic evaluations on the ciphertext and returns the encrypted results, as shown in Fig. 1.

H. Seo and S. Kim (Eds.): ICISC 2023, LNCS 14561, pp. 41–64, 2024.
https://doi.org/10.1007/978-981-97-1235-9_3

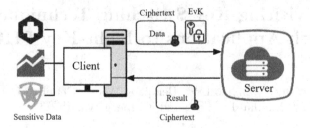

Fig. 1. Client-server model of FHE applications. Evk denotes the evaluation keys.

One issue faced by Fully Homomorphic Encryption (FHE) is the storage and the communication cost. FHE is based on lattice encryption schemes, resulting in large ciphertext and key sizes. In word-wise encryption schemes, the evaluation keys often have sizes of gigabytes [4,14,16,17]. While FHEW-like bit-wise encryption schemes reduce the evaluation key size by one order of magnitude, they still face limitations in real-world applications due to their key size of about 200 MB. More precisely, there is a strong preference for clients to generate and transmit keys with the smallest possible size. This is due to the fact that clients typically operate on devices with constrained computing power and limited storage space, sometimes even on mobile devices [13,28].

From the server's perspective, research has demonstrated that hardware acceleration can yield over a ten times boost in the efficiency of homomorphic encryption operations [15,25,30]. However, these solutions are memory-constrained due to their limited on-chip storage. These challenges promote us to explore techniques to reduce the size of evaluation keys.

This paper concentrates on the key switching algorithm, whose key size may account for over 90% of the total evaluation key in FHEW-like schemes, as shown in Table 1.

Table 1. The proportion of key switching key size in the total evaluation key size of different bootstrapping methods. The parameters resources is within brackets. In the transfer model [18], the transfer key is a seed of the evaluation key. Section 6.4 provides a detailed description of the transfer model.

Methods	Evaluation key size	Key switching key size	Transfer key size
GINX [21]	250 MB	229.1 MB (91.6%)	16.48 MB
LFHE [18]	175 MB	84.6 MB (48.3%)	881 KB
GINX$_{our}$	27.91 MB	27.2 KB (0.1%)	13.96 MB
LFHE$_{our}$	90.38 MB	54.2 KB (0.06%)	810.1 KB

Key switching is an essential operation in FHEW-like cryptosystems that enables changing the encryption key without revealing the plaintext. Various types of key switching have been described in this literature, including LWE-to-(R)LWE key switching, and RLWE-to-RLWE key switching. Chillotti et al.

shows that the former scheme can evaluate a linear Lipschitz morphism on ciphertext almost for free during switching keys [7]. Depending on the confidentiality of the morphism, it can be further divided into public functional key switching and private functional key switching. Even for the same switching type, there are different computation methods, these algorithms differ in functionality, key size, computational complexity, and noise management. A unified comparison is currently lacking, and there is no theoretical basis for selecting proper key switching algorithms when designing FHE applications. This motivates us to comprehensively revisit known key switching algorithms.

Functional Key Switching Algorithms. Our first contribution is to fill the functional gap in key switching algorithms. TFHE's key switching can compute a linear Lipschitz morphism while switching keys [7]. This property is not presented in the LWE-to-LWE key switching proposed by Chen et al. [3], or the commonly used RLWE-to-RLWE key switching algorithm. We fill this gap by decomposing all key switching algorithms into *gadget products*[1], and embedding the linear Lipschitz morphism in it. The linear property ensures that the morphism can be correctly calculated by scalar multiplication, while the Lipschitz property helps manage noise growth. As a result, we provide functional variants of all known key switching algorithms, which may have independent interests beyond this paper. For instance, we demonstrate that the scheme switching algorithm [9] (or the same EvalSquareMult algorithm [18]) can be regarded as a specific case of our proposed RLWE-to-RLWE private functional key switching algorithm for the morphism $f(x) = \mathbf{sk} \cdot x$, where $\mathbf{sk}$ is the secret key.

Comparison Between Key Switching Algorithms. Comparing key switching algorithms can be challenging since they are proposed and analyzed using different baselines, such as algebraic structures, the key distributions, and the gadget decomposition methods[2]. In this work, we present a comprehensive reanalysis of the existing key switching algorithms and our proposed functional variants under a common standard. We use the power of two cyclotomic ring, which is commonly used in FHE schemes, binary key distribution, and the canonical approximate gadget decomposition [7]. We propose noise growth formulas and provide performance data in terms of key sizes and computational complexity. Our work serves as a theoretical basis for the practical selection of key switching algorithms when designing FHE applications.

Light-Key Bootstrapping Algorithm. To validate the efficacy of our theoretical results, we propose the light-key bootstrapping variants using a lower-sized key switching algorithm. For the well-known GINX bootstrapping, this approach reduces the bootstrapping key size by 88.8% and the transfer key size by 15.3%. For the state-of-the-art light-key bootstrapping, this approach outperforms Kim

---

[1] The gadget product is the computational units for scalar multiplication in FHEW-like cryptosystems.

[2] The gadget decomposition is a technique used to decompose large numbers into smaller digits. This helps control error growth in FHE algorithms.

et al.'s LFHE method [18] by reducing 48.4% bootstrapping key size and 8% transfer key size.

Related Work. Figure 1 illustrates that the client must generate and transmit two components: the ciphertext and the evaluation keys. This paper focuses on reducing the size of the evaluation key. However, the ciphertext size is also significantly larger than plaintext due to the lattice-based encryption. Currently, Naehrig et al. have introduced techniques named hybrid homomorphic encryption (HHE or transciphering) [2,8,11,24]. This technique allows the client to encrypt messages with a symmetric cipher. The server then evaluates the decryption circuit homomorphically to obtain the ciphertext under HE form for further processing. Our future work involves integrating HHE with our research, to develop fully homomorphic encryption applications with minimal transmission size.

Organization. The rest of the paper is organized as follows: Sect. 2 reviews the notations and crypto primitives; Sect. 3 revisits the gadget product as the basic computational unit of key switching algorithms; Sect. 4 and Sect. 5 analyzes the LWE-to-LWE key switching algorithms and RLWE-to-RLWE key switching algorithms, respectively; Sect. 6 constructs the light-key bootstrapping algorithm based on the analysis results; Sect. 7 concludes the paper.

2 Preliminaries

2.1 Notations

Let $\mathbb{A}$ be a set. Define $\mathbb{A}^n$ as the set of vectors with n elements in $\mathbb{A}$, $\mathbb{A}_q$ as the set $\mathbb{A}$ module q, where the elements' scope is $[-q/2, q/2) \cap \mathbb{A}$. Use $\mathbb{Z}$ to denote the set of integers, $\mathbb{R}$ to denote the set of real numbers, and $\mathbb{B} = \mathbb{Z}_2$ represents the set of binary numbers. Denote $\mathcal{R}$ as the set of integer coefficient polynomials modulo $X^N + 1$, where N is a power of 2 Then $\mathcal{R}$ is the $2N$-th cyclotomic ring.

Use regular letters to represent (modular) integers like $a \in \mathbb{Z}_q$, while bold letters to represent polynomials $\mathbf{a} \in \mathcal{R}$ or vectors $\mathbf{a} \in \mathbb{Z}^n$. The notation a_i refers to the i-th coefficient/term of $\mathbf{a}$. The floor, ceiling, and rounding functions are written as $\lfloor \cdot \rfloor$, $\lceil \cdot \rceil$ $\lfloor \cdot \rceil$, respectively. A function f is R-Lipschitz means that it satisfies $\|f(x) - f(y)\|_\infty \leq R\|x - y\|_\infty$, where $\| \cdot \|_\infty$ is the infinity norm.

2.2 Gadget Decomposition

Given a gadget vector $\mathbf{v} = (v_0, v_1, ..., v_{l-1})$, the gadget decomposition of a ring element $\mathbf{t} \in R$ is to find $(\mathbf{t}_0, ..., \mathbf{t}_{l-1})$ to minimize the decomposition error $\varepsilon_{\text{gadget}}(\mathbf{t}) = \sum_i v_i \mathbf{t}_i - \mathbf{t}$. ϵ denotes its infinite norm, that is, $\|\sum_i v_i \mathbf{t}_i - \mathbf{t}\|_\infty \leq \epsilon$. In this paper, we use the canonical approximate gadget decomposition, where $\mathbf{v} = (\lceil \frac{q}{B^l} \rceil, \lceil \frac{q}{B^l} \rceil B, ..., \lceil \frac{q}{B^l} \rceil B^{l-1})$, thus $\epsilon \leq \frac{1}{2} \lceil \frac{q}{B^l} \rceil$. We say B is the gadget base and l is the gadget length.

2.3   Learning with Errors

The security of FHEW-like cryptosystem is based on the (ring) learning with errors problem [22,27]. We summarize the three kinds of ciphertexts as follow:

- **LWE:** Giving positive integers n and q, the LWE encryption of the message $m \in \mathbb{Z}$ is a vector $(\mathbf{a}, b) \in \mathbb{Z}_q^{n+1}$, where $b = -\mathbf{a} \cdot \mathbf{sk} + m + e$. The vector $\mathbf{a}$ is uniformly sampled from $\mathbb{Z}_q^n$, the secret key $\mathbf{sk}$ is sampled from a key distribution χ, the error e is sampled from an error distribution χ'.
- **RLWE:** RLWE is a ring version of LWE on $\mathcal{R}_q$. The RLWE encryption of the message $\mathbf{m} \in \mathcal{R}_q$ is a pair $(\mathbf{a}, \mathbf{b}) \in \mathcal{R}_q^{n+1}$, where $\mathbf{b} = -\mathbf{a} \cdot \mathbf{sk} + \mathbf{m} + \mathbf{e}$. The vector $\mathbf{a}$ is uniformly sampled from $\mathcal{R}_q$, the secret key $\mathbf{sk}$ is sampled from a key distribution χ, and each coefficient of the error e_i is sampled from χ'.
- **RGSW:** The RGSW encryption of the message $\mathbf{m} \in \mathcal{R}_q$ can be expressed as: $\mathrm{RGSW}_{\mathbf{sk}}(\mathbf{m}) = (\mathrm{RLWE}'_{\mathbf{sk}}(\mathbf{sk} \cdot \mathbf{m}), \mathrm{RLWE}'_{\mathbf{sk}}(\mathbf{m}))$, where RLWE' is the gadget RLWE ciphertext defined as follows:

  Given a gadget vector $\mathbf{v} = (v_0, v_1, ..., v_{l-1})$, the notion (R)LWE' refers to the gadget (R)LWE ciphertext is defined as:
  $\mathrm{LWE}'_{\mathbf{sk}}(m) = (\mathrm{LWE}_{\mathbf{sk}}(v_0 \cdot m), \mathrm{LWE}_{\mathbf{sk}}(v_1 \cdot m), ..., \mathrm{LWE}_{\mathbf{sk}}(v_{l-1} \cdot m))$,
  $\mathrm{RLWE}'_{\mathbf{sk}}(\mathbf{m}) = (\mathrm{RLWE}_{\mathbf{sk}}(v_0 \cdot \mathbf{m}), \mathrm{RLWE}_{\mathbf{sk}}(v_1 \cdot \mathbf{m}), ..., \mathrm{RLWE}_{\mathbf{sk}}(v_{l-1} \cdot \mathbf{m}))$.

Remark 1. These definitions (following Micciancio and Polyakov [23]) use different notions compared to the original TFHE papers [5–7]. Specifically, TFHE uses real torus $\mathbb{T} = \mathbb{R}/\mathbb{Z}$ and $\mathbb{T}_N[X] = \mathcal{R}/\mathbb{Z}$ to describe the message and ciphertext spaces, but implements $\mathbb{T}$ by $\mathbb{Z}_q$ with $q = 2^{32}$ or $q = 2^{64}$. Thus we straightforwardly use $\mathbb{Z}_q$ instead of $\mathbb{T}$.

Remark 2. In FHEW-like cryptosystem, the gadget (R)LWE is mainly used as the evaluation key and appears as an auxiliary input in algorithms such as key switching. To simplify the presentation and facilitate the understanding of the key switching algorithm, which is the main focus of this paper, we provide a formal definition and notation of gadget (R)LWE.

2.4   Bootstrapping

The error rate of the LWE/RLWE ciphertext will significantly affect the decryption failure probability, which can be calculated by $1 - \mathrm{erf}\left(\frac{q}{8\sqrt{2}\sigma}\right)$, where σ is the standard deviation of the error. We then introduce the bootstrapping algorithm to reduce the error rate. FHEW-like bootstrapping can evaluate a 1-in/1-out LUT function while refreshing ciphertext noise. It typically contains the following operations: blind rotation (BR), sample extraction (SE), key switching, and modulus switching (MS).

As the goal of bootstrapping is to refresh the noise in the ciphertext, it is necessary to pay extra attention and precisely control the noise generated in each step of the bootstrapping algorithm itself. The basic strategy is to execute the BR step, which mainly generates the new noise, under a large modulus. Then recovering the LWE ciphertext form through SE, reducing the modulus while eliminating the blind rotation noise size through MS, and recovering the original key through key switching algorithm. We introduce two typical bootstrapping work flows as follows:

GINX Bootstrapping [5–7]. $\text{LWE}_{571,2^{11}} \xrightarrow{\text{BR}} \text{RLWE}_{1024,2^{25}} \xrightarrow{\text{SE}} \text{LWE}_{1024,2^{25}}$
$\xrightarrow{\text{MS}} \text{LWE}_{1024,2^{14}} \xrightarrow{\text{LtL}} \text{LWE}_{571,2^{14}} \xrightarrow{\text{MS}} \text{LWE}_{571,2^{11}}$.

Remark 3. The above parameters are taken from Lee's recent article [21], with a security level of 128-bit. Due to the update of attack methods, the security level of the parameters in TFHE articles [5–7] has been reduced to 115-bit.

LFHE Bootstrapping [18]. $\text{LWE}_{571,2^{11}} \xrightarrow{\text{BR}} \text{RLWE}_{2048,2^{54}} \xrightarrow{\text{MS}} \text{RLWE}_{2048,2^{27}}$
$\xrightarrow{\text{RtR}} \text{RLWE}_{1024,2^{27}} \xrightarrow{\text{SE}} \text{LWE}_{1024,2^{27}} \xrightarrow{\text{MS}} \text{LWE}_{1024,2^{14}} \xrightarrow{\text{LtL}} \text{LWE}_{571,2^{14}} \xrightarrow{\text{MS}}$
$\text{LWE}_{571,2^{11}}$.

To display the switching of the keys and modulus, we use the form $(\text{R})\text{LWE}_{n,q}$ to represent ciphertexts, where n is the dimension of the secret key vector (or polynomial) and q represents the modulus of the ciphertext. LtL stands for LWE to LWE key switching, and both of the above bootstrapping algorithms use its storage version (for a summary and comparison between different versions, see Sect. 4). RtR stands for RLWE to RLWE key switching.

3   Gadget Products

The gadget product is used to calculate the scalar multiplication in FHEW-like cryptosystem. It works by gadget decomposing the plaintext scalar and then multiplying the corresponding gadget (R)LWE ciphertexts. This algorithm can reduce the noise growth of scalar multiplication and is widely used in core algorithms such as external product [7] and key switching. This section summarizes three types of gadget products, and analyze their differences in terms of noise growth, auxiliary input size and computational complexity. The first one is the canonical gadget product primarily used for external product. It was first abstracted as a separate algorithm by Micheli et al. in 2023 [9].

Gadget Product: The canonical gadget product $\odot : \mathbb{Z} \times (\text{R})\text{LWE}' \to (\text{R})\text{LWE}$ is defined as:

$$t \odot (\text{R})\text{LWE}'_{\mathbf{sk}}(\mathbf{m}) := \sum_{i=0}^{l-1} t_i \cdot (\text{R})\text{LWE}_{\mathbf{sk}}(v_i \cdot \mathbf{m})$$

$$= (\text{R})\text{LWE}_{\mathbf{sk}}\left(\sum_{i=0}^{l-1} v_i \cdot t_i \cdot \mathbf{m}\right)$$

$$= (\text{R})\text{LWE}_{\mathbf{sk}}(t \cdot \mathbf{m} + \varepsilon_{\mathsf{gadget}}(t) \cdot \mathbf{m}),$$

Lemma 1. *[18] Let B and l denote the base and the length of the gadget decomposition, respectively, then the error variance of the result of the gadget product is bounded by*

$$\sigma^2_{\odot,\mathsf{input}} \le \frac{1}{12} l B^2 \sigma^2_{\mathsf{input}} + \frac{1}{3}\mathsf{Var}(\mathbf{m})\epsilon^2$$

where $\sigma^2_{\mathsf{input}}$ is the error variance of the input LWE' ciphertext, and $\mathsf{Var}(\mathbf{m})$ is the variance of the message $\mathbf{m}$.

Lemma 1 is derived from [18] proposition.1 with the fact $\epsilon \le \frac{1}{2}\lceil \frac{q}{B^l} \rceil$. This method use the modular multiplication to compute the gadget product. However, for a fixed input $(\text{R})\text{LWE}'_{\mathbf{sk}}(\mathbf{m})$, there is an time-space trade-off that reduces the computational complexity by using additional storage. Specifically, since the range of t_i is bounded by the gadget base B, one can pre-compute and store all possible values of $(\text{R})\text{LWE}'_{\mathbf{sk}}(v_i \cdot t_i \cdot \mathbf{m})$, then use modular addition instead of modular multiplication. This method was first used in the FHEW bootstrapping algorithm proposed by Ducas et al. in 2015 [12], which inspired us to summarize a store version of the gadget product. We denote this method using operator $\oplus$:

Gadget Product (Store Version): The store version $\oplus : \mathbb{Z} \times (\text{R})\text{LWE}' \to (\text{R})\text{LWE}$ is defined as:

$$t \oplus (\text{R})\text{LWE}'_{\mathbf{sk}}(\mathbf{m}) := \sum_{i=0}^{l-1} (\text{R})\text{LWE}'_{\mathbf{sk}}(v_i \cdot t_i \cdot \mathbf{m})$$

$$= (\text{R})\text{LWE}_{\mathbf{sk}}\left(\sum_{i=0}^{l-1} v_i \cdot t_i \cdot \mathbf{m}\right)$$

$$= (\text{R})\text{LWE}_{\mathbf{sk}}(t \cdot \mathbf{m} + \varepsilon_{\mathsf{gadget}}(t) \cdot \mathbf{m}),$$

Corollary 1. *Let B and l denote the base and the length of the gadget decomposition, respectively, then the error variance of the result of the gadget product (store version) is bounded by*

$$\sigma^2_{\oplus,\mathsf{input}} \le l\sigma^2_{\mathsf{input}} + \frac{1}{3}\mathsf{Var}(\mathbf{m})\epsilon^2$$

where $\sigma^2_{\mathsf{input}}$ is the error variance of the input LWE' ciphertext, and $\mathsf{Var}(\mathbf{m})$ is the variance of the message $\mathbf{m}$.

The store version of gadget product use l times modular addition instead of modular multiplication. Thus Corollary 1 can be directly derived from Lemma 1 by replacing multiplication error growth with addition error growth.

Lastly, we introduce the ring version of the gadget product, denoted by $\odot_R$:

Gadget Product (Ring Version): The Ring gadget product $\odot_R : \mathcal{R} \times$ RLWE$' \to$ RLWE is defined as:

$$\mathbf{t} \odot_R \text{RLWE}'_{\mathbf{sk}}(\mathbf{m}) := \sum_{i=0}^{l-1} \mathbf{t}_i \cdot \text{RLWE}_{\mathbf{sk}}(v_i \cdot \mathbf{m})$$

$$= \text{RLWE}_{\mathbf{sk}} \left(\sum_{i=0}^{l-1} v_i \cdot \mathbf{t}_i \cdot \mathbf{m} \right)$$

$$= \text{RLWE}_{\mathbf{sk}} \left(\mathbf{t} \cdot \mathbf{m} + \varepsilon_{\text{gadget}}(\mathbf{t}) \cdot \mathbf{m} \right),$$

Corollary 2. *Let n denote the dimension of the ring polynomial of RLWE ciphertexts, B and l denote the base and the length of the gadget decomposition, respectively, then the error variance of the result of the gadget product is bounded by*

$$\sigma^2_{\odot_R,\text{input}} \le \frac{1}{12} n l B^2 \sigma^2_{\text{input}} + \frac{1}{3} n \text{Var}(\mathbf{m}) \epsilon^2$$

where σ^2_{input} is the error variance of the input RLWE$'$ ciphertext, and $\text{Var}(\mathbf{m})$ is the variance of $\mathbf{m}$.

This algorithm is a ring version of the gadget product. Notice that since polynomial dimension n causes an exponential increase in polynomial gadget decomposition results, it is impractical to accelerate computation by pre-storing all possible RLWE$'_{\mathbf{sk}}(v_i \cdot \mathbf{t}_i \cdot \mathbf{m})$. In other words, the store version of the ring gadget product is not practical and we do not consider it. The error growth of the ring gadget product needs to take into account the expansion factor of the ring. In this paper, we use a power-of-two cyclotomic ring, with an expansion factor of $\sqrt{n}$ for the two-norm, resulting in a factor of n when evaluating the noise variance. Then Corollary 2 can be derived from Lemma 1.

Comparison. The computational complexity and auxiliary input size of the three gadget products are listed in Table 2. From Lemma 1 and the corollaries in this section, we can conclude that in terms of error growth, $\odot_R = \odot > \oplus$. From Table 2, it is evident that in terms of computational complexity, $\odot_R > \odot > \oplus$, in terms of the size of auxiliary inputs, $\oplus > \odot_R = \odot$.

As the key switching algorithm is always a combination of scalar multiplication and addition, these algorithms can be re-written using the three types of gadget products. This novel perspective makes it easier to examine key switching algorithms, provides insights into their comparison in terms of correctness, error growth, computational complexity, and key size. Our analysis can serve as a guideline for time-space trade-offs in the implementation of the key switching. We then revisit LWE-to-LWE key switching algorithms in Sect. 4, and RLWE-to-RLWE key switching algorithms in Sect. 5.

Table 2. Comparison between different version of the gadget product, where l and B are the gadget length and base, MA and MM denote the modular addition and modular multiplication operations. NTT is the number theoretic transform algorithm (with $O(ln \log n)$ MM computational complexity) used in polynomial multiplication.

Calculation	Computation Complexity	Auxiliary Input (in (R)LWE$'$)
$\odot$	ln MM	1
$\oplus$	l MA	B
$\odot_R$	l NTT$+ln$ MM	1

4   LWE-to-LWE Key Switching

Chillotti et al. proposed in the TFHE series [5–7] that their key switching algorithm can calculate a R-Lipschitz linear morphism while switching keys. This section generalizes all existing LWE-to-LWE key switching algorithms into functional versions, and classifies key switching algorithms into public functional key switching and private functional key switching (following Chilloti et al. [7]) based on whether the Lipschitz morphism needs to be kept confidential (Fig. 2).

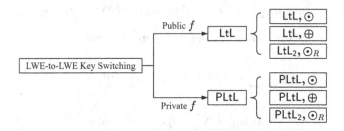

Fig. 2. Six LWE-to-LWE key switching algorithms revisited in this section.

4.1   Public Functional Key Switching

LWE-to-LWE Using Canonical Gadget Product

- Input: $\mathrm{LWE}_{\mathbf{sk}}(m) = (\mathbf{a}, b)$, and a public R-Lipschitz linear morphism $f : \mathbb{Z} \to \mathbb{Z}$
- Switching key: $\mathsf{LtLK} = \mathrm{LWE}'_{\mathbf{sk}'}(sk_i)_{i \in [1,n]}$
- Output: $\mathrm{LWE}_{\mathbf{sk}'}(f(m))$
- Algorithm:

$$\mathsf{LtL}^f_{\mathbf{sk} \to \mathbf{sk}'}(\mathrm{LWE}_{\mathbf{sk}}(m)) := \sum_{i=1}^{n} f(a_i) \odot \mathrm{LWE}'_{\mathbf{sk}'}(sk_i) + (0, f(b)).$$

This algorithm was first proposed by Chillotti et al. [7], and we formalize it using gadget product. We then re-analyze the error growth of this algorithm, and update the theorem 4.1 in [7] for two reasons.

Firstly, TFHE used binary gadget decomposition for scalars in the key switching algorithm. But currently FHEW-like cryptosystems generally use the standard approximate gadget decomposition (power-of-B), as what we considered. Secondly, TFHE utilized the torus algebraic structure in its theoretical analysis, rather than the power of 2 cyclotomic ring used in the implementation. Thus it did not consider the coefficient $1/12$ when calculating the variance of the uniform distribution, resulting in a less compact error bound in theorem 4.1 [7].

Correctness and Error Analysis

Theorem 1. *Let n denote the dimension of the LWE ciphertexts, B and l denote the base and the length of the gadget decomposition, respectively, then the error variance of the result of the LWE to LWE public functional key switching algorithm is bounded by:*

$$\sigma_{\mathsf{LtL}}^2 \le \frac{1}{12}nlB^2\sigma_{\mathsf{LtLK}}^2 + \frac{1}{6}n\epsilon^2 + R^2\sigma_{\mathsf{input}}^2,$$

where ϵ is the gadget decomposition error, $\sigma_{\mathsf{input}}^2$ is the error variance of the input LWE ciphertext, and σ_{LtLK}^2 is the error variance of the switching key.

Proof. Basing the correctness of the gadget product, we have,

$$\sum_{i=1}^{n} f(a_i) \odot \mathrm{LWE}'_{\mathbf{sk}'}(sk_i) + (0, f(b))$$

$$= \mathrm{LWE}_{\mathbf{sk}'}\left(\sum_{i=1}^{n} f(a_i \cdot sk_i) + f(b)\right)$$

$$= \mathrm{LWE}_{\mathbf{sk}'}\left(f(m) + f(e)\right),$$

then we measure the error variance based on Lemma 1:

$$\sigma_{\mathsf{LtL}}^2 = n\sigma_{\odot,\mathsf{LtLK}}^2 + \mathrm{Var}(f(e)) \le \frac{1}{12}nlB^2\sigma_{\mathsf{LtLK}}^2 + \frac{1}{6}n\epsilon^2 + R^2\sigma_{\mathsf{input}}^2.$$

Store Version. As we analyzed in Sect. 3, the LtL algorithm, which uses the canonical gadget product, also has a corresponding store version. It only requires modifications to the auxiliary input and calculation method:

- Switching key:$\mathsf{LtLK} = \mathrm{LWE}'_{\mathbf{sk}'}(j \cdot sk_i)_{i \in [1,n], j \in [0, B-1]}$
- Algorithm:

$$\mathsf{LtL}^f_{\mathbf{sk} \to \mathbf{sk}'}(\mathrm{LWE}_{\mathbf{sk}}(m)) := \sum_{i=1}^{n} f(a_i) \oplus \mathrm{LWE}'_{\mathbf{sk}'}(sk_i) + (0, f(b)).$$

It can be derived from Table 2 that, the store version is faster and has smaller noise growth compared to the canonical LtL algorithm. However, the trade-off is an increase in key size by a factor of B, where B is the base for gadget decomposition.

LWE-to-LWE Using Ring Gadget Product

- Input: $\mathrm{LWE}_{\vec{sk}}(m) = (\vec{a}, b)$, and a public R-Lipschitz linear morphism $f : \mathbb{Z} \to \mathbb{Z}$
- Switching key: $\mathsf{LtL_2K} = \mathrm{RLWE}'_{\mathbf{sk}'}(\mathbf{sk})$, where $\mathbf{sk} = \sum_{i=0}^{l-1} sk_i X^{-i}$, $\mathbf{sk}' = \sum_{i=0}^{l-1} sk'_i X^{-i}$
- Output: $\mathrm{LWE}_{\vec{sk}'}(f(m)) = (\vec{a}', b')$
- Algorithm:

$$(\mathbf{a}', \mathbf{b}') := \sum_{i=1}^{n} f(a_i) X^i \odot_R \mathrm{RLWE}'_{\mathbf{sk}'}(\mathbf{sk}) + (0, f(b)),$$

$$\mathsf{LtL2}^f_{\vec{sk} \to \vec{sk}'}(\mathrm{LWE}_{\vec{sk}}(m)) := (a'_0, a'_1, ..., a'_{n-1}, b'_0).$$

Remark 4. This algorithm involves the conversion between vectors and polynomials. Thus to avoid confusion, we use $\vec{a}$ to represent vectors in this algorithm, while $\mathbf{a}$ to represent polynomials. The notation a_i is the i-th term of the vector $\vec{a}$, and $[\mathbf{a}]_i$ is the i-th coefficient of the polynomial $\mathbf{a}$.

This switching method was proposed by Chen et al. [3]. We formalize it using ring gadget product, and first extend it to the functional version. Therefore, the error growth of this algorithm must take into account the Lipschitz morphism. In addition, Chen et al. only considered the exact gadget decomposition, which is a special case ($q \leq B^l$) of the canonical approximate gadget decomposition we use. This also prompts us to re-analyze the error.

Correctness and Error Analysis

Theorem 2. *Let n denote the dimension of the LWE ciphertexts, B and l denote the base and the length of the gadget decomposition, respectively, then the error variance of the result of the LWE to LWE using RtR algorithm is bounded by:*

$$\sigma^2_{\mathsf{LtL2}} \leq \frac{1}{12} nl B^2 \sigma^2_{\mathsf{LtL2K}} + \frac{1}{6} n\epsilon^2 + R^2 \sigma^2_{\mathsf{input}},$$

where $\sigma^2_{\mathsf{input}}$ is the error variance of the input LWE ciphertext, and $\sigma^2_{\mathsf{LtL2K}}$ is the error variance of the switching key.

Table 3. Comparison between different version of the public LWE-to-LWE key switching, where q is the ciphertext modulus, l and B are the gadget length and base, MA and MM denote the modular addition and modular multiplication operations.

Method	Computation complexity	Key size (in bits)
LtL, $\odot$	$O(ln^2)$ MM	$ln(n+1)\log q$
LtL, $\oplus$	$(ln+n+1)$ MA	$Bln(n+1)\log q$
LtL$_2$, $\odot_R$	$O(ln\log n)$ MM	$2ln\log q$

Proof. Basing the correctness of the ring gadget product, we have,

$$b_0' + \sum_{i=1}^{n} a_i' sk_i' = [\mathbf{b}' + \mathbf{a}' \cdot \mathbf{sk}']_0$$

$$= \sum_{i=1}^{n} f(a_i \cdot sk_i) + f(b)$$

$$= f(m) + f(e),$$

thus $(a_0', a_1', ..., a_{n-1}', b_0')$ is the LWE ciphertext of $f(m)$ under secret key $\vec{sk}'$, then we measure the error variance based on Corollary 2:

$$\sigma_{\mathsf{LtL}_2}^2 = \sigma_{\odot_R, \mathsf{LtL}_2\mathsf{K}}^2 + \mathsf{Var}(f(e)) \ \leq \ \frac{1}{12} nlB^2 \sigma_{\mathsf{LtLK}}^2 + \frac{1}{6} n\epsilon^2 + R^2 \sigma_{\mathsf{input}}^2$$

Comparison. The computational complexity and key size of LWE-to-LWE public functional key switching algorithms are listed in Table 3. From the theorems in this section, we can conclude that in terms of error growth, we have $(\mathsf{LtL}, \odot) = (\mathsf{LtL}_2, \odot_R) > (\mathsf{LtL}, \oplus)$. From Table 2, it is evident that $(\mathsf{LtL}, \odot) > (\mathsf{LtL}_2, \odot_R) > (\mathsf{LtL}, \oplus)$ in computational complexity. In terms of the key size, we have $(\mathsf{LtL}, \oplus) > (\mathsf{LtL}, \odot) > (\mathsf{LtL}_2, \odot_R)$.

Comparison results indicate that $(\mathsf{LtL}, \odot)$ is inferior to $(\mathsf{LtL}_2, \odot_R)$ in all aspects. Thus when we care more about the computational efficiency and error control of the algorithm, $(\mathsf{LtL}, \oplus)$ is the best choice. On the other hand, if key size (which affects transfer size and storage space) is of greater concern, we should use $(\mathsf{LtL}_2, \odot_R)$ as the substitute.

4.2   Private Functional Key Switching

In the public functional key switching algorithm, the Lipschitz morphism f is used as a public input. However, f should be kept confidential in some cases. For example, it is related to the secret key or derived from a protected model. Chillotti et al. proposed private functional key switching algorithm for this situation [7], where the morphism f is secretly encoded within the algorithm's switching key. In this section, we first revisit this canonical algorithm. Then we introduce two novel algorithms. The first is the store version of private functional key switching, which we extended based on the method of Ducas et al. [12]. The second is the ring version, extended based on Chen et al.'s methods [3].

Private LWE-to-LWE Using Canonical Gadget Product

- Input: $\mathrm{LWE}_{\mathbf{sk}}(m) = (\mathbf{a}, b)$
- Switching key: $\mathsf{PLtLK} = (\mathrm{LWE}'_{\mathbf{sk}'}(f(sk_i))_{i \in [1,n]}, \mathrm{LWE}'_{\mathbf{sk}'}(f(1)))$, where $f : \mathbb{Z} \to \mathbb{Z}$ is a private R-Lipschitz linear morphism
- Output: $\mathrm{LWE}_{\mathbf{sk}'}(f(m)) = (\mathbf{a}', b')$
- Algorithm:

$$\mathsf{PLtL}^f_{\mathbf{sk} \to \mathbf{sk}'}(\mathrm{LWE}_{\mathbf{sk}}(m)) := \sum_{i=1}^{n} a_i \odot \mathrm{LWE}'_{\mathbf{sk}'}(f(sk_i)) + b \odot \mathrm{LWE}'_{\mathbf{sk}'}(f(1)).$$

Store Version. This version only requires modifications to the switching key and calculation method:

- Switching key:$\mathsf{PLtLK} = (\mathrm{LWE}'_{\mathbf{sk}'}(j \cdot f(sk_i)), \mathrm{LWE}'_{\mathbf{sk}'}(j \cdot f(1)))$, where $i \in [1, n]$, $j \in [0, B-1]$, $f : \mathbb{Z} \to \mathbb{Z}$ is a private R-Lipschitz linear morphism
- Algorithm:

$$\mathsf{PLtL}^f_{\mathbf{sk} \to \mathbf{sk}'}(\mathrm{LWE}_{\mathbf{sk}}(m)) := \sum_{i=1}^{n} a_i \oplus \mathrm{LWE}'_{\mathbf{sk}'}(f(sk_i)) + b \oplus \mathrm{LWE}'_{\mathbf{sk}'}(f(1)).$$

Private LWE-to-LWE Using Ring Gadget Product

- Input: $\mathrm{LWE}_{\vec{sk}}(m) = (\vec{a}, b)$
- Switching key: $\mathsf{LtL_2K} = (\mathrm{RLWE}'_{\mathbf{sk}'}(\mathbf{sk}), \mathrm{RLWE}'_{\mathbf{sk}'}(f(1)))$, where $\mathbf{sk} = \sum_{i=0}^{l-1} f(sk_i)X^{-i}$, $\mathbf{sk}' = \sum_{i=0}^{l-1} sk_i'X^{-i}$, $f : \mathbb{Z} \to \mathbb{Z}$ is a private R-Lipschitz linear morphism
- Output: $\mathrm{LWE}_{\vec{sk}'}(f(m)) = (\vec{a}', b')$
- Algorithm:

$$(\mathbf{a}', \mathbf{b}') := \sum_{i=1}^{n} a_i X^i \odot_R \mathrm{RLWE}'_{\mathbf{sk}'}(\mathbf{sk}) + b \odot_R \mathrm{RLWE}'_{\mathbf{sk}'}(f(1)),$$

$$\mathsf{LtL2}^f_{\vec{sk} \to \vec{sk}'}(\mathrm{LWE}_{\vec{sk}}(m)) := (a_0', a_1', ..., a_{n-1}', b_0').$$

Table 4. Comparison between different versions of the private LWE-to-LWE key switching, where q is the ciphertext modulus, l and B are the gadget length and base, MA and MM denote the modular addition and modular multiplication operations.

Method	Computation complexity	Key size (in bits)
PLtL, $\odot$	$O(ln^2)$ MM	$l(n+1)^2 \log q$
PLtL, $\oplus$	$(ln+n+l+1)$ MA	$Bl(n+1)^2 \log q$
PLtL$_2$, $\odot_R$	$O(ln \log n)$ MM	$2l(n+1) \log q$

Correctness, Error Growth and Comparison. The correctness and error analysis of these algorithms are similar to those in Sect. 4.1. For self completeness, we include them in Appendix A.1. The computational complexity and key size of LWE-to-LWE private functional key switching algorithms are listed in Table 4.

A comparison of Table 3 and Table 4 reveals that the computational complexity and key size of private algorithms are both larger than the corresponding public algorithms. The comparison results between these three methods are similar to those in Sect. 4.1: (PLtL, $\oplus$) is more suitable for computation-priority scenarios, while (PLtL$_2$, $\odot_R$) is more suitable for storage-priority scenarios.

5   RLWE-to-RLWE Key Switching

Besides LWE-to-LWE key switching, LWE-to-RLWE and RLWE-to-RLWE key switching are also largely described in the literature. However, LWE-to-RLWE algorithms are highly similar to LWE-to-LWE algorithms. Therefore, we put the whole section in the Appendix A.3 for readers to refer to the algorithms and theorems. RLWE-to-RLWE key switching is different. To the best of our knowledge, it can only be calculated through ring gadget product.

In this section, we extend this method into functional versions, which support calculation of both public and private Lipschitz functions. We also prove that the widely-used scheme switching algorithm [9] (or EvalSquareMult algorithm [18]) is a special case of our extended private functional key switching algorithm.

5.1   Public Functional Key Switching

RLWE-to-RLWE Using Ring Gadget Product

- Input: $\text{RLWE}_{\mathbf{sk}}(\mathbf{m}) = (\mathbf{a}, \mathbf{b})$, and a public R-Lipschitz linear morphism f : $\mathcal{R} \to \mathcal{R}$
- Switching key: $\text{RtRK} = \text{RLWE}'_{\mathbf{sk}'}(\mathbf{sk})$
- Output: $\text{RLWE}_{\mathbf{sk}'}(f(\mathbf{m})) = (\mathbf{a}', \mathbf{b}')$
- Algorithm:

$$\text{RtR}_{\mathbf{sk} \to \mathbf{sk}'}(\text{RLWE}_{\mathbf{sk}}(\mathbf{m})) := f(\mathbf{a}) \odot_R \text{RLWE}'_{\mathbf{sk}'}(\mathbf{sk}) + (0, f(\mathbf{b})).$$

Correctness and Error Analysis

Theorem 3. *Let n denote the dimension of the ring polynomial of RLWE ciphertexts, B and l denote the base and the length of the gadget decomposition, respectively, then the error variance of the result of the LWE to LWE public functional key switching algorithm is bounded by:*

$$\sigma_{\mathsf{RtR}}^2 \leq \frac{1}{12} n l B^2 \sigma_{\mathsf{RtRK}}^2 + \frac{1}{6} n \epsilon^2 + \sigma_{\mathsf{input}}^2,$$

where $\sigma_{\mathsf{input}}^2$ is the error variance of the input RLWE ciphertext, and σ_{RtLR}^2 is the error variance of the switching key.

Proof. Basing the correctness of the Ring gadget product, we have,

$$f(\mathbf{a}) \odot_R \mathrm{RLWE}'_{\mathbf{sk'}}(\mathbf{sk}) + (0, f(\mathbf{b}))$$
$$= \mathrm{RLWE}_{\mathbf{sk'}}(f(\mathbf{a} \cdot \mathbf{sk}) + f(\mathbf{b}))$$
$$= \mathrm{RLWE}_{\mathbf{sk'}}(f(\mathbf{m}) + f(\mathbf{e})).$$

then we measure the error variance based on Lemma 2:

$$\sigma_{\mathsf{RtR}}^2 = \sigma_{\odot_R, \mathsf{RtRK}}^2 + \mathsf{Var}(\mathbf{e}) \leq \frac{1}{12} n l B^2 \sigma_{\mathsf{RtRK}}^2 + \frac{1}{6} n \epsilon^2 + R^2 \sigma_{\mathsf{input}}^2.$$

5.2 Private Functional Key Switching

Private RLWE-to-RLWE Using Ring Gadget Product

- Input: $\mathrm{RLWE}_{\mathbf{sk}}(\mathbf{m}) = (\mathbf{a}, \mathbf{b})$
- Switching key: $\mathsf{RtRK} = (\mathrm{RLWE}'_{\mathbf{sk'}}(f(\mathbf{sk})), \mathrm{RLWE}'_{\mathbf{sk'}}(f(1)))$, where $f : \mathcal{R} \to \mathcal{R}$ is a private R-Lipschitz linear morphism
- Output: $\mathrm{RLWE}_{\mathbf{sk'}}(f(\mathbf{m})) = (\mathbf{a'}, \mathbf{b'})$
- Algorithm:

$$\mathsf{RtR}_{\mathbf{sk} \to \mathbf{sk'}}(\mathrm{RLWE}_{\mathbf{sk}}(\mathbf{m})) := \mathbf{a} \odot_R \mathrm{RLWE}'_{\mathbf{sk'}}(f(\mathbf{sk})) + \mathbf{b} \odot_R \mathrm{RLWE}'_{\mathbf{sk'}}(f(1)).$$

The correctness and error analysis of this algorithm is similar to Theorem 3. We put it in Appendix A.2 for self completeness. When the private Lipschitz morphism is $f(x) = \mathbf{sk} \cdot x$, our algorithm becomes: $\mathbf{a} \odot_R \mathrm{RLWE}'_{\mathbf{sk'}}(\mathbf{sk}^2)) + \mathbf{b} \odot_R \mathrm{RLWE}'_{\mathbf{sk'}}(\mathbf{sk}) = \mathbf{a} \odot_R \mathrm{RLWE}'_{\mathbf{sk'}}(\mathbf{sk}^2)) + (\mathbf{b}, 0)$, where the right side is the well-known scheme switching algorithm [9] (or EvalSquareMult algorithm [18]).

6   Light-Key Bootstrapping

To illustrate the effectiveness of our result, we apply the above analysis to construct light-key bootstrapping algorithms. First, we modify the classical GINX bootstrapping [7], for which our method provides a time-space trade-off. We then improve the LFHE (light-key FHE) bootstrapping proposed by Kim et al. [18], which is specifically designed to reduce the key size. We optimize their result and yield the bootstrapping algorithm with the smallest key (Table 5).

Table 5. Security and Parameters.

Parameters	Q	Q_{RtR}	Q_{LtL}	q	N	N_{RtR}	n	l_{br}	l_{ak}	l_{sqk}	l_{RtR}	l_{LtL}
GINX [21]	25	–	14	11	1024	–	571	4	–	–	–	2
GINX_our	25	–	15	11	1024	–	571	4	–	–	–	13
LFHE [18]	54	27	14	11	2048	1024	571	3	5	2	2	3
LFHE_our	54	27	15	11	2048	1024	571	3	5	2	2	13

6.1　Security and Parameters

GINX bootstrapping algorithm use $(\mathsf{LtL}, \oplus)$ for key switching due to its higher efficiency and lower noise growth. However, the large key size of $(\mathsf{LtL}, \oplus)$ results in the key switching key occupying 91.6% of the GINX bootstrapping key (see Table 1). LFHE replace part of the key switching from $(\mathsf{LtL}, \oplus)$ to $(\mathsf{RtR}, \odot_R)$, which has a smaller key size. However, it still retains an $(\mathsf{LtL}, \oplus)$ step, so that the key switching key still occupies 48.3% of the LFHE bootstrapping key.

In order to construct light-key bootstrapping algorithms, our idea is to use $(\mathsf{LtL_2}, \odot_R)$ to replace $(\mathsf{LtL}, \oplus)$ in GINX and LFHE bootstrapping. However, a direct adoption would not work since the noise growth of $(\mathsf{LtL_2}, \odot_R)$ is much higher than that of $(\mathsf{LtL}, \oplus)$ under the same parameters. Therefore, to ensure algorithm security and control noise introduced by bootstrapping itself, we made necessary adjustments to the bootstrapping parameters, see tab.6.1. This set of parameters ensures that the security level of algorithms exceeds 128-bit[3], and the decryption failure rate due to noise accumulation is less than 2^{-324}.

q and n denotes the modulus and dimension of the ciphertext before bootstrapping. Q, N, l_{br}, l_{ak}, and l_{sqk} are the parameters used for blind rotation, representing the modulus and ring dimension of the blind rotation key, and the gadget length in blind rotation, automorphism, and SquareKeyMult (the latter two are used in LFHE), respectively. Q_{RtR}, N_{RtR}, and l_{RtR} denote the modulus, ring dimension, and gadget decomposition length of the RtR key switching key. Q_{LtL} and l_{LtL} represent the modulus and gadget decomposition length of the $\mathsf{LtL_2}$ key switching key.

6.2　Work Flow

The improved GINX and LFHE bootstrapping are shown as follows (all abbreviations are defined in previous section, or check Sect. 2.4 for explanations):

$\mathbf{GINX_{our}}$: $\mathrm{LWE}_{571,2^{11}} \xrightarrow{\mathsf{BR}} \mathrm{RLWE}_{1024,2^{25}} \xrightarrow{\mathsf{SE}} \mathrm{LWE}_{1024,2^{25}} \xrightarrow{\mathsf{MS}} \mathrm{LWE}_{1024,2^{15}}$ $\xrightarrow{\mathsf{LtL_2}} \mathrm{LWE}_{571,2^{15}} \xrightarrow{\mathsf{MS}} \mathrm{LWE}_{571,2^{11}}$

$\mathbf{LFHE_{our}}$: $\mathrm{LWE}_{571,2^{11}} \xrightarrow{\mathsf{BR}} \mathrm{RLWE}_{2048,2^{54}} \xrightarrow{\mathsf{MS}} \mathrm{RLWE}_{2048,2^{27}} \xrightarrow{\mathsf{RtR}} \mathrm{RLWE}_{1024,2^{27}}$ $\xrightarrow{\mathsf{SE}} \mathrm{LWE}_{1024,2^{27}} \xrightarrow{\mathsf{MS}} \mathrm{LWE}_{1024,2^{15}} \xrightarrow{\mathsf{LtL_2}} \mathrm{LWE}_{571,2^{15}} \xrightarrow{\mathsf{MS}} \mathrm{LWE}_{571,2^{11}}$

---

[3] Test by LWE estimator, https://bitbucket.org/malb/lwe-estimator/src/master/.

[4] calculate by $1 - \mathrm{erf}\left(\frac{q}{8\sqrt{2}\sigma}\right)$, where erf represents the Gaussian error function.

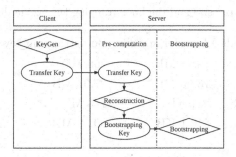

Fig. 3. The transfer model of TFHE bootstrapping.

6.3 Key Size

This section analyze the bootstrapping key size. Since the modulus switching and sample extraction algorithms do not require evaluation keys, the bootstrapping key includes two parts: the blind rotation key and the key switching key.

GINX$_{\text{our}}$: The blind rotation key contains n RGSW ciphertexts, with each having $4l_{\text{br}}N \log Q$ bits. This results in a blind rotation key size of 27.88 MB. We use LtL$_2$ instead of LtL$_1$, the key contains 1 RLWE$'$ ciphertext with a size of $2nl_{\text{LtL}} \log Q_{\text{LtL}}$ bits. Thus the key switching key size is 27.2 KB. The total key size is 27.91 MB.

LFHE$_{\text{our}}$: The blind rotation key also contains n RGSW ciphertexts, resulting in a blind rotation key size of 90.33 MB. The RtR key switching key contains 1 RLWE$'$ ciphertext with a size of $2Nl_{\text{RtR}} \log Q_{\text{RtR}}$ bits, resulting in a key size of 27 KB. The LtL$_2$ key switching key size is 27.2 KB. The total is 90.38 MB.

6.4 Transfer Model and Transfer Key Size

LFHE [18] proposed a transfer model, see Fig. 3. The client transmits a transfer key (a seed) to the server. Then the server runs the reconstruction algorithm to obtain the complete bootstrapping key, and performs the bootstrapping algorithm. In this model, client and server utilize a common reference string (CRS) to generate the **a**-components of each transferred LWE and RLWE ciphertext. Thus only the b(or **b** for RLWE)-components of the ciphertext needs to be transmitted. LFHE's blind rotation algorithm is specifically designed for the transfer model and uses a pached blind rotation key to reduce the bootstrapping transfer key size to within 1 MB. We also calculate the transfer key size of our improved algorithms under the transfer model.

GINX$_{\text{our}}$: The blind rotation key contains n RGSW ciphertexts, with each needing to transfer $2l_{\text{br}}N \log Q$ bits. This results in a blind rotation transfer key size of 13.94 MB. We use LtL$_2$ instead of LtL$_1$, the key contains 1 RLWE$'$ ciphertext, with a transfer key size of $nl_{\text{LtL}} \log Q_{\text{LtL}}$ bits. This results in a key switching transfer key size of 13.6 KB. The total is 13.96 MB (Table 6).

Table 6. Transfer key size and the bootstrapping key size in different methods.

Methods	Transfer key size	Bootstrapping key size
GINX	16.48 MB	250 MB
GINX_{our}	13.96 MB	27.91 MB
LFHE	881 KB	175 MB
LFHE_{our}	810.1 KB	90.38 MB

LFHE$_{\text{our}}$: The packed blind rotation key contains 1 RLWE ciphertext and $(\log N + 1)$ RLWE$'$ ciphertexts. Each RLWE ciphertext needs to transfer $N \log Q$ bits, each RLWE$'$ ciphertext needs to transfer $N l_{\text{ak}}(l_{\text{sqk}}) \log Q$ bits. This results in a blind rotation transfer key size of 783 KB. The RtR key switching key contains 1 RLWE$'$ ciphertext and has a transfer size of $N l_{\text{RtR}} \log Q_{\text{RtR}}$ bits, resulting in a transfer key size of 13.5 KB. The LtL_2 transfer key size is 13.6 KB. The total key size is 810.1 KB.

For GINX bootstrapping, our method reduces the bootstrapping key size by 88.8% and the transfer key size by 15.3%. We do not want to oversell this result, but take it as a trade-off method towards practical TFHE applications. For LFHE bootstrapping, our method outperforms Kim's method [18] by reducing 48.4% bootstrapping key size and 8% transfer key size.

7 Conclusion

The key switching algorithm is crucial in real-world fully homomorphic encryption (FHE) applications due to its significant impact on the key size and efficiency of the FHE system. This paper revisits currently known key switching algorithms, expands their functionality, carefully recalculates the error growth, and provide a comparison of different algorithms under the same benchmark. Our analysis is applied to the bootstrapping algorithm, resulting in optimal light-key FHE. This paper can be served as an reference for the time-space trade-off of key switching algorithms and assists to build FHE applications with different computational and storage requirements.

Acknowledgments. We are grateful for the helpful comments from the anonymous reviewers of ICISC 2023. This work was supported by CAS Project for Young Scientists in Basic Research (Grant No. YSBR-035).

A   Appendix

A.1   LWE-to-LWE Key Switching

Private LWE-to-LWE Using Canonical Gadget Product

Theorem 4. *Let n denote the dimension of the LWE ciphertexts, B and l denote the base and the length of the gadget decomposition, respectively, then the error variance of the result of the LWE to LWE public functional key switching algorithm is bounded by:*

$$\sigma^2_{\mathsf{PLtL}} \leq \frac{1}{12}(n+1)lB^2\sigma^2_{\mathsf{LtLK}} + \frac{1}{6}R^2n\epsilon^2 + +\frac{1}{3}n\mathsf{Var}(f(1))\epsilon^2 + R^2\sigma^2_{\mathsf{input}},$$

where $\sigma^2_{\mathsf{input}}$ is the error variance of the input LWE ciphertext, and σ^2_{LtLK} is the error variance of the switching key.

Proof. Basing the correctness of the gadget product, we have,

$$\sum_{i=1}^{n} a_i \odot \mathsf{LWE}'_{\mathbf{sk}'}(f(sk_i)) + b \odot \mathsf{LWE}'_{\mathbf{sk}'}(f(1))$$

$$= \mathsf{LWE}_{\mathbf{sk}'}\left(\sum_{i=1}^{n} f(a_i \cdot sk_i) + f(b)\right)$$

$$= \mathsf{LWE}_{\mathbf{sk}'}\left(f(m) + f(e)\right),$$

then we measure the error variance based on Lemma 1:

$$\sigma^2_{\mathsf{PLtL}} = \sum_{i=1}^{n} \sigma^2_{\odot,\mathsf{LWE}'_{\mathbf{sk}'}(f(sk_i))} + \sigma^2_{\odot,\mathsf{LWE}'_{\mathbf{sk}'}(f(1))} + \mathsf{Var}(f(e))$$

$$\leq \frac{1}{12}(n+1)lB^2\sigma^2_{\mathsf{LtLK}} + \frac{1}{3}n\mathsf{Var}(f(sk_i)\epsilon^2 + \frac{1}{3}n\mathsf{Var}(f(1))\epsilon^2 + R^2\sigma^2_{\mathsf{input}}.$$

$$\leq \frac{1}{12}(n+1)lB^2\sigma^2_{\mathsf{LtLK}} + \frac{1}{6}R^2n\epsilon^2 + +\frac{1}{3}n\mathsf{Var}(f(1))\epsilon^2 + R^2\sigma^2_{\mathsf{input}}.$$

Private LWE-to-LWE Using Ring Gadget Product

Theorem 5. *Let n denote the dimension of the LWE ciphertexts, B and l denote the base and the length of the gadget decomposition, respectively, then the error variance of the result of the LWE to LWE using RtR algorithm is bounded by:*

$$\sigma^2_{\mathsf{PLtL_2}} \leq \frac{1}{6}NlB^2\sigma^2_{\mathsf{LtL_2K}} + \frac{1}{6}R^2n\epsilon^2 + \frac{1}{3}n\mathsf{Var}(f(1))\epsilon^2 + R^2\sigma^2_{\mathsf{input}},$$

where $\sigma^2_{\mathsf{input}}$ is the error variance of the input LWE ciphertext, and $\sigma^2_{\mathsf{PLtL_2K}}$ is the error variance of the switching key.

Proof. Basing the correctness of the ring gadget product, we have,

$$b_0' + \sum_{i=1}^{n} a_i' sk_i' = [\mathbf{b}' + \mathbf{a}' \cdot \mathbf{sk}']_0 \;=\; \sum_{i=1}^{n} f(a_i \cdot sk_i) + f(b) = f(m) + f(e),$$

thus $(a_0', a_1', ..., a_{n-1}', b_0')$ is the LWE ciphertext of $f(m)$ under secret key $\vec{sk}'$, then we measure the error variance based on Corollary 2:

$$\sigma_{\mathsf{LtL}_2}^2 = \sigma_{\odot R, \mathrm{RLWE}_{\mathbf{sk}'}'(\mathbf{sk})}^2 + \sigma_{\odot R, \mathrm{RLWE}_{\mathbf{sk}'}'(f(1))}^2 + \mathsf{Var}(f(\mathbf{e}))$$

$$\leq \frac{1}{6} NlB^2 \sigma_{\mathsf{LtL}_2\mathsf{K}}^2 + \frac{1}{3} n \mathsf{Var}(f(sk_i))\epsilon^2 + \frac{1}{3} n \mathsf{Var}(f(1))\epsilon^2 + R^2 \sigma_{\mathrm{input}}^2$$

$$\leq \frac{1}{6} NlB^2 \sigma_{\mathsf{LtL}_2\mathsf{K}}^2 + \frac{1}{6} R^2 n\epsilon^2 + \frac{1}{3} n \mathsf{Var}(f(1))\epsilon^2 + R^2 \sigma_{\mathrm{input}}^2.$$

A.2   RLWE-to-RLWE Key Switching

Private RLWE-to-RLWE

Theorem 6. *Let n denote the dimension of the ring polynomial of RLWE ciphertexts, B and l denote the base and the length of the gadget decomposition, respectively, then the error variance of the result of the LWE to LWE public functional key switching algorithm is bounded by:*

$$\sigma_{\mathsf{RtR}}^2 \leq \frac{1}{12} nlB^2 \sigma_{\mathsf{RtRK}}^2 + \frac{1}{6} n\epsilon^2 + \sigma_{\mathrm{input}}^2,$$

where $\sigma_{\mathrm{input}}^2$ is the error variance of the input RLWE ciphertext, and σ_{RtLR}^2 is the error variance of the switching key.

Proof. Basing the correctness of the Ring gadget product, we have,

$$\mathbf{a} \odot_R \mathrm{RLWE}_{\mathbf{sk}'}' (f(\mathbf{sk})) + \mathbf{b} \odot_R \mathrm{RLWE}_{\mathbf{sk}'}' (f(1))$$
$$= \mathrm{RLWE}_{\mathbf{sk}'} (f(\mathbf{a} \cdot \mathbf{sk}) + f(\mathbf{b}))$$
$$= \mathrm{RLWE}_{\mathbf{sk}'} (f(\mathbf{m}) + f(\mathbf{e})).$$

then we measure the error variance based on Lemma 2:

$$\sigma_{\mathsf{RtR}}^2 = \sigma_{\odot R, \mathrm{RLWE}_{\mathbf{sk}'}'(f(\mathbf{sk}))}^2 + \sigma_{\odot R, \mathrm{RLWE}_{\mathbf{sk}'}'(f(1))}^2 + \mathsf{Var}(f(\mathbf{e}))$$

$$\leq \frac{1}{6} nlB^2 \sigma_{\mathsf{RtRK}}^2 + \frac{1}{3} n \mathsf{Var}(f(\mathbf{sk}))\epsilon^2 + \frac{1}{3} n \mathsf{Var}(f(1))\epsilon^2 + R^2 \sigma_{\mathrm{input}}^2$$

$$\leq \frac{1}{6} nlB^2 \sigma_{\mathsf{RtRK}}^2 + \frac{1}{6} R^2 n\epsilon^2 + \frac{1}{3} n \mathsf{Var}(f(1))\epsilon^2 + R^2 \sigma_{\mathrm{input}}^2$$

A.3   LWE-to-RLWE Key Switching

Public LWE-to-RLWE Functional Key Switching
Input: $\mathrm{LWE}_{\mathbf{sk}}(m) = (\mathbf{a}, b)$, and a public R-Lipschitz morphism $f : \mathbb{Z} \to \mathbb{Z}$

Switching key: $\mathsf{LtRK} = \mathrm{RLWE}'_{\mathbf{sk}'}(sk_i)_{i \in [1,n]}$
Output: $\mathrm{RLWE}_{\mathbf{sk}'}(f(m)) = (\mathbf{a}', \mathbf{b}')$
Algorithm:

$$\mathsf{LtR}^f_{\mathbf{sk} \to \mathbf{sk}'}(\mathrm{LWE}_{\mathbf{sk}}(m)) := \sum_{i=1}^n f(a_i) \odot \mathrm{RLWE}'_{\mathbf{sk}'}(sk_i) + (0, f(b)).$$

Correctness and Error Analysis

Theorem 7. *Let n denote the dimension of the LWE ciphertexts, B and l denote the base and the length of the gadget decomposition, respectively, then the error variance of the result of the LWE to LWE public functional key switching algorithm is bounded by:*

$$\sigma^2_{\mathsf{LtR}} \leq \frac{1}{12} n l B^2 \sigma^2_{\mathsf{LtRK}} + \frac{1}{6} n \epsilon^2 + R^2 \sigma^2_{\mathsf{input}},$$

where $\sigma^2_{\mathsf{input}}$ is the error variance of the input LWE ciphertext, and σ^2_{LtLK} is the error variance of the switching key.

Proof. Basing the correctness of the gadget product, we have,

$$\sum_{i=1}^n f(a_i) \odot \mathrm{RLWE}'_{\mathbf{sk}'}(sk_i) + (0, f(b))$$

$$= \mathrm{RLWE}_{\mathbf{sk}'} \left(\sum_{i=1}^n f(a_i \cdot sk_i) + f(b) \right)$$

$$= \mathrm{RLWE}_{\mathbf{sk}'} (f(m) + f(e)),$$

then we measure the error variance based on Lemma 1:

$$\sigma^2_{\mathsf{LtR}} = n\sigma^2_{\odot,\mathsf{LtRK}} + \mathsf{Var}(f(e)) \leq \frac{1}{12} n l B^2 \sigma^2_{\mathsf{LtLK}} + \frac{1}{6} n \epsilon^2 + R^2 \sigma^2_{\mathsf{input}}$$

Private LWE-to-RLWE Functional Key Switching
Input: $\mathrm{LWE}_{\mathbf{sk}}(m) = (\mathbf{a}, b)$
Switching key: $\mathsf{PLtRK} = (\mathrm{RLWE}'_{\mathbf{sk}'}(f(sk_i))_{i \in [1,n]}, \mathrm{RLWE}'_{\mathbf{sk}'}(f(1)))$, where $f : \mathbb{Z} \to \mathbb{Z}$ is a private R-Lipschitz linear morphism
Output: $\mathrm{RLWE}_{\mathbf{sk}'}(f(m)) = (\mathbf{a}', \mathbf{b}')$
Algorithm:

$$\mathsf{PLtR}^f_{\mathbf{sk} \to \mathbf{sk}'}(\mathrm{LWE}_{\mathbf{sk}}(m)) := \sum_{i=1}^n a_i \odot \mathrm{RLWE}'_{\mathbf{sk}'}(f(sk_i)) + b \odot \mathrm{RLWE}'_{\mathbf{sk}'}(f(1)).$$

Correctness and Error Analysis

Theorem 8. *Let n denote the dimension of the LWE ciphertexts, B and l denote the base and the length of the gadget decomposition, respectively, then the error variance of the result of the LWE to LWE public functional key switching algorithm is bounded by:*

$$\sigma^2_{\mathsf{PLtR}} \leq \frac{1}{12}(n+1)lB^2\sigma^2_{\mathsf{LtLK}} + \frac{1}{6}R^2(n+1)\epsilon^2 + R^2\sigma^2_{\mathsf{input}},$$

where $\sigma^2_{\mathsf{input}}$ is the error variance of the input LWE ciphertext, and σ^2_{LtLK} is the error variance of the switching key.

Proof. Basing the correctness of the gadget product, we have,

$$\sum_{i=1}^{n} a_i \odot \mathrm{RLWE}'_{\mathbf{sk}'}(f(sk_i)) + b \odot \mathrm{RLWE}'_{\mathbf{sk}'}(f(1))$$

$$= \mathrm{RLWE}_{\mathbf{sk}'}\left(\sum_{i=1}^{n} f(a_i \cdot sk_i) + f(b)\right)$$

$$= \mathrm{RLWE}_{\mathbf{sk}'}\left(f(m) + f(e)\right),$$

then we measure the error variance based on Lemma 1:

$$\sigma^2_{\mathsf{PLtR}} = (n+1)\sigma^2_{\odot,\mathsf{PLtRK}} + \mathsf{Var}(f(e))$$

$$\leq \frac{1}{12}(n+1)lB^2\sigma^2_{\mathsf{LtLK}} + \frac{1}{6}R^2(n+1)\epsilon^2 + R^2\sigma^2_{\mathsf{input}}.$$

References

1. Amuthan, A., Sendhil, R.: Hybrid GSW and DM based fully homomorphic encryption scheme for handling false data injection attacks under privacy preserving data aggregation in fog computing. J. Ambient. Intell. Humaniz. Comput. **11**, 5217–5231 (2020)
2. Canteaut, A., et al.: Stream ciphers: a practical solution for efficient homomorphic-ciphertext compression. J. Cryptol. **31**(3), 885–916 (2018)
3. Chen, H., Dai, W., Kim, M., Song, Y.: Efficient homomorphic conversion between (ring) LWE ciphertexts. In: Sako, K., Tippenhauer, N.O. (eds.) ACNS 2021. LNCS, vol. 12726, pp. 460–479. Springer, Cham (2021). https://doi.org/10.1007/978-3-030-78372-3_18
4. Cheon, J.H., Han, K., Kim, A., Kim, M., Song, Y.: Bootstrapping for approximate homomorphic encryption. In: Nielsen, J.B., Rijmen, V. (eds.) EUROCRYPT 2018. LNCS, vol. 10820, pp. 360–384. Springer, Cham (2018). https://doi.org/10.1007/978-3-319-78381-9_14
5. Chillotti, I., Gama, N., Georgieva, M., Izabachène, M.: Faster fully homomorphic encryption: bootstrapping in less than 0.1 seconds. In: Cheon, J.H., Takagi, T. (eds.) ASIACRYPT 2016. LNCS, vol. 10031, pp. 3–33. Springer, Heidelberg (2016). https://doi.org/10.1007/978-3-662-53887-6_1

6. Chillotti, I., Gama, N., Georgieva, M., Izabachène, M.: Faster packed homomorphic operations and efficient circuit bootstrapping for TFHE. In: Takagi, T., Peyrin, T. (eds.) ASIACRYPT 2017. LNCS, vol. 10624, pp. 377–408. Springer, Cham (2017). https://doi.org/10.1007/978-3-319-70694-8_14
7. Chillotti, I., Gama, N., Georgieva, M., Izabachène, M.: TFHE: fast fully homomorphic encryption over the torus. J. Cryptol. **33**(1), 34–91 (2020)
8. Cosseron, O., Hoffmann, C., Méaux, P., Standaert, F.X.: Towards case-optimized hybrid homomorphic encryption. In: Agrawal, S., Lin, D. (eds.) ASIACRYPT 2022. LNCS, vol. 13793, pp. 32–67. Springer, Cham (2022). https://doi.org/10.1007/978-3-031-22969-5_2
9. De Micheli, G., Kim, D., Micciancio, D., Suhl, A.: Faster amortized FHEW bootstrapping using ring automorphisms. Cryptology ePrint Archive (2023)
10. Deviani, R.: The application of fully homomorphic encryption on XGBoost based multiclass classification. JIEET (J. Inf. Eng. Educ. Technol.) **7**(1), 49–58 (2023)
11. Dobraunig, C., et al.: Rasta: a cipher with low ANDdepth and few ANDs per bit. In: Shacham, H., Boldyreva, A. (eds.) CRYPTO 2018. LNCS, vol. 10991, pp. 662–692. Springer, Cham (2018). https://doi.org/10.1007/978-3-319-96884-1_22
12. Ducas, L., Micciancio, D.: FHEW: bootstrapping homomorphic encryption in less than a second. In: Oswald, E., Fischlin, M. (eds.) EUROCRYPT 2015. LNCS, vol. 9056, pp. 617–640. Springer, Heidelberg (2015). https://doi.org/10.1007/978-3-662-46800-5_24
13. Gomes, F.A., de Matos, F., Rego, P., Trinta, F.: Analysis of the impact of homomorphic algorithm on offloading of mobile application tasks. In: 2023 IEEE 20th Consumer Communications & Networking Conference (CCNC), pp. 961–962. IEEE (2023)
14. Halevi, S., Shoup, V.: Bootstrapping for HElib. J. Cryptol. **34**(1), 7 (2021)
15. Jiang, L., Lou, Q., Joshi, N.: Matcha: a fast and energy-efficient accelerator for fully homomorphic encryption over the torus. In: Proceedings of the 59th ACM/IEEE Design Automation Conference, pp. 235–240 (2022)
16. Jutla, C.S., Manohar, N.: Modular Lagrange interpolation of the mod function for bootstrapping of approximate HE. Cryptology ePrint Archive (2020)
17. Jutla, C.S., Manohar, N.: Sine Series Approximation of the Mod Function for Bootstrapping of Approximate HE. Springer, Cham (2022)
18. Kim, A., Lee, Y., Deryabin, M., Eom, J., Choi, R.: LFHE: fully homomorphic encryption with bootstrapping key size less than a megabyte. Cryptology ePrint Archive (2023)
19. Kocabas, O., Soyata, T.: Towards privacy-preserving medical cloud computing using homomorphic encryption. In: Virtual and Mobile Healthcare: Breakthroughs in Research and Practice, pp. 93–125. IGI Global (2020)
20. Lee, J.W., et al.: Privacy-preserving machine learning with fully homomorphic encryption for deep neural network. IEEE Access **10**, 30039–30054 (2022)
21. Lee, Y., et al.: Efficient FHEW bootstrapping with small evaluation keys, and applications to threshold homomorphic encryption. In: Hazay, C., Stam, M. (eds.) EUROCRYPT 2023. LNCS, vol. 14006, pp. 227–256. Springer, Cham (2023). https://doi.org/10.1007/978-3-031-30620-4_8
22. Lyubashevsky, V., Peikert, C., Regev, O.: On ideal lattices and learning with errors over rings. In: Gilbert, H. (ed.) EUROCRYPT 2010. LNCS, vol. 6110, pp. 1–23. Springer, Heidelberg (2010). https://doi.org/10.1007/978-3-642-13190-5_1
23. Micciancio, D., Polyakov, Y.: Bootstrapping in FHEW-like cryptosystems. In: Proceedings of the 9th on Workshop on Encrypted Computing & Applied Homomorphic Cryptography, pp. 17–28 (2021)

24. Naehrig, M., Lauter, K., Vaikuntanathan, V.: Can homomorphic encryption be practical? In: Proceedings of the 3rd ACM Workshop on Cloud Computing Security Workshop, pp. 113–124 (2011)
25. Nam, K., Oh, H., Moon, H., Paek, Y.: Accelerating n-bit operations over TFHE on commodity CPU-FPGA. In: Proceedings of the 41st IEEE/ACM International Conference on Computer-Aided Design, pp. 1–9 (2022)
26. Peralta, G., Cid-Fuentes, R.G., Bilbao, J., Crespo, P.M.: Homomorphic encryption and network coding in IoT architectures: advantages and future challenges. Electronics 8(8), 827 (2019)
27. Regev, O.: On lattices, learning with errors, random linear codes, and cryptography. J. ACM 56(6), 34:1–34:40 (2009)
28. Ren, W., et al.: Privacy-preserving using homomorphic encryption in mobile IoT systems. Comput. Commun. 165, 105–111 (2021)
29. Shrestha, R., Kim, S.: Integration of IoT with blockchain and homomorphic encryption: challenging issues and opportunities. In: Advances in Computers, vol. 115, pp. 293–331. Elsevier (2019)
30. Ye, T., Kannan, R., Prasanna, V.K.: FPGA acceleration of fully homomorphic encryption over the torus. In: 2022 IEEE High Performance Extreme Computing Conference (HPEC), pp. 1–7. IEEE (2022)

Optimized Quantum Implementation of SEED

Yujin Oh, Kyungbae Jang, Yujin Yang, and Hwajeong Seo[✉]

Division of IT Convergence Engineering, Hansung University, Seoul, South Korea
hwajeong84@gmail.com

Abstract. With the advancement of quantum computers, it has been demonstrated that Grover's algorithm enables a potential reduction in the complexity of symmetric key cryptographic attacks to the square root. This raises increasing challenges in considering symmetric key cryptography as secure. In order to establish secure post-quantum cryptographic systems, there is a need for quantum post-quantum security evaluations of cryptographic algorithms. Consequently, NIST is estimating the strength of post-quantum security, driving active research in quantum cryptographic analysis for the establishment of secure post-quantum cryptographic systems.

In this regard, this paper presents a depth-optimized quantum circuit implementation for SEED, a symmetric key encryption algorithm included in the Korean Cryptographic Module Validation Program (KCMVP). Building upon our implementation, we conduct a thorough assessment of the post-quantum security for SEED. Our implementation for SEED represents the first quantum circuit implementation for this cipher.

Keywords: Quantum Circuit · SEED · Korean Block Cipher · Grover Algorithm

1 Introduction

Quantum computers are the new and upcoming computing paradigm which are based on quantum mechanical principles (such as superposition and entanglement), and will be able to solve certain classes of problems significantly faster than the classical computers. Quantum computers are being developed by many top-tier companies and research institutions.

The introduction of the Shor algorithm [1], which is known for its ability to solve the integer factorization problem and the discrete logarithm problem in polynomial time, poses significant risks to public-key cryptography designed based on these problems. Similarly, the Grover search algorithm [2], known for its ability to reduce the complexity of data search by a square root factor, can have a significant impact on the security of symmetric key cryptography.

NIST has proposed criteria for estimating the quantum attack complexity on the AES family and a parameter called MAXDEPTH, which represents the maximum circuit depth that a quantum computer can execute, in its evaluation criteria document for post-quantum cryptography standardization [3,4]. Both of these aspects need to be considered to evaluate the quantum security strength of a cipher. Detailed explanations on these topics will be provided in Sect. 2.4, 5.

Based on these NIST criteria, continuous efforts have been made to estimate the complexity of Grover's key search for symmetric-key ciphers and evaluate post-quantum security [5–7]. In addition to AES, research has also been conducted on estimating quantum resources for well-known lightweight block ciphers such as SPECK, GIFT, and PRESENT [8–10], as well as lightweight block ciphers selected as finalists in the Lightweight Cryptography (LWC) competition, including SPARKLE [11,12] and ASCON [13,14].

In this paper, we propose an optimized quantum circuits for SEED, which is a symmetric key encryption algorithms included as validation subjects in the Korean Cryptographic Module Validation Program (KCMVP). Since these cryptographic algorithms are widely used in cryptographic modules in Korea, it is of great importance to estimate quantum resources and measure the quantum security strength of these ciphers. Using the proposed quantum circuit as a basis, we assess the post-quantum security strength of SEED in accordance with NIST criteria.

1.1 Our Contribution

The contribution in this paper is manifold and can be summarized as follows:

1. **Quantum Circuit Implementation of SEED.** We demonstrate the first implementation of a quantum circuit for SEED, which is the one of Korean cipher.
2. **Low-Depth Implementation of SEED.** In our quantum circuit implementation of SEED, we focus to optimize a low Toffoli depth and full depth. We implement the Itoh-Tsujii algorithm for S-box optimization. For the implementation, we utilize the WISA'22 quantum multiplication, and a squaring based on PLU factorization. Further, we enhance the efficiency of depth optimization by using an optimal quantum adder(which is called CDKM adder) and implementing parallelization for applicable components.
3. **Post-quantum Security Assessment of SEED.** We estimate the cost of Grover's key search using an our implemented quantum circuit for SEED in order to assess the quantum security of SEED. During this assessment, we compare the estimated cost of Grover's key search for SEED with the security levels defined by NIST.

2 Preliminaries

2.1 SEED Block Cipher

SEED is a block cipher of Feistel structure operates on 128-bit block and 128-bit key. It consists of 16 rounds and each round has a round function F.

A 128-bit block is divided into 64-bit blocks, and the right 64-bit block (R_0) serves as the input to the F function with 64-bit round key. The output of F function is XORed to the left 64-bit block (L_0). The overall structure of SEED cipher is shown in Fig. 1.

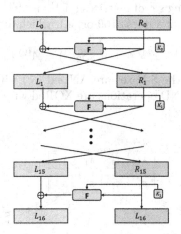

Fig. 1. Overall structure of SEED cipher.

F Function. The input of F function (Fig. 2) is 64-bit block and 64-bit round key $RK_i = (K_{i,0}, K_{i,1})$. The 64-bit block is divided into two 32-bit blocks (C, D) and each block is XORed with the round key. The F function consists of XOR operations ($\oplus$), modular additions ($\boxplus$), and G functions.

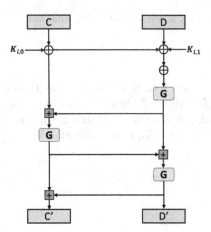

Fig. 2. Process of the F function.

G Function. The 32-bit input block of the G function (Fig. 3) is divided into 8-bit blocks (X_{0-3}) and each block becomes input for the S-boxes.

To compute the output of an S-box, it involves exponentiation of $x \in \mathbb{F}_{2^8}/(x^8 + x^6 + x^5 + x + 1)$, matrix-vector multiplication, and XORing a single constant. Specifically, two distinct S-boxes (S_1 and S_2) are employed, each using its own corresponding set of matrices ($A^{(1)}$ or $A^{(2)}$), exponentiation values (x^{247} or x^{251}), and constant values (169 or 56), which are as follows:

$$S_1(x) = A^{(1)} \cdot x^{247} \oplus 169, \quad S_2(x) = A^{(2)} \cdot x^{251} \oplus 56 \qquad (1)$$

The output values of the S-boxes are ANDed (&) with the constants m_{0-3}, and the results of these AND operations are XORed with each other to compute the final output (i.e., Z_{0-3}).

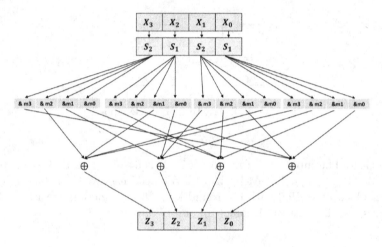

Fig. 3. Process of the G function.

Key Schedule. In the key schedule (Fig. 4), the 128-bit key is divided into four blocks ($A\|B\|C\|D$, where $\|$ denotes concatenation), and key constant values(KC_i) are utilized. Additionally, operations such as shift ($\gg$, $\ll$), modular addition, modular subtraction ($\boxminus$), and G function are applied.

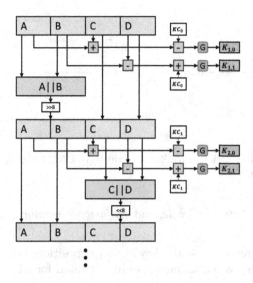

Fig. 4. Process of the key schedule

2.2 Quantum Gates

This section describes commonly used quantum gates (Fig. 5) for implementing quantum circuits of block ciphers (note that this is not an exhaustive list of all possible gates that can be used).

The X gate acts like a NOT operation on a classical computer, reversing the state of the qubit that goes through it. The Swap gate exchanges the states of two qubits. The CNOT gate behaves like an XOR operation on a classical computer. In CNOT(a, b), the input qubit a is the control qubit, and b is the target qubit. When the control qubit a is in the state 1, the target qubit b is flipped. As a result, the value of $a \oplus b$ is stored in the qubit b (i.e., $b = a \oplus b$), while the state of qubit a remains unchanged. The Toffoli gate, represented as Toffoli(a, b, c), acts like an AND operation on a classical computer. It requires three input qubits, with the first two qubits (a and b) serving as control qubits. Only when both control qubits are in the state 1, the target qubit c is flipped. The result of the operation a & b is XORed with the qubit c (i.e., $c = c \oplus (a$ & $b)$), while the states of qubits a and b are preserved.

2.3 Grover's Key Search

Grover's algorithm searches for a specific data from an unsorted set of N with a search complexity of $O(\sqrt{N})$. In cryptography, for an encryption scheme that uses a k-bit key, a classical computer requires a search of $O(2^k)$ complexity for exhaustive key search. However, using Grover's algorithm, a quantum computer can perform this search with a complexity of only $O(\sqrt{2^k})$, which is reduced by a square root. In this section, we divide the progress of Grover's key search into

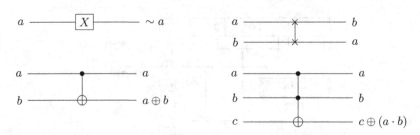

Fig. 5. Quantum gates: X (left top), Swap (right top), CNOT (left bottom) and Toffoli (right bottom) gates.

three stages: *Input Setting*, *Oracle*, and *Diffusion Operator*, and describe them as follows.

1. *Input Setting*: Prepare a k-qubit key in a superposition state using Hadamard gates. In this case, equal amplitudes are generated for all 2^k possible states.

$$H^{\otimes k}|0\rangle^{\otimes k} = |\psi\rangle = \left(\frac{|0\rangle + |1\rangle}{\sqrt{2}}\right) = \frac{1}{2^{k/2}}\sum_{x=0}^{2^k-1}|x\rangle \qquad (2)$$

2. In the *oracle*, the target encryption algorithm(Enc) is implemented through a quantum circuit. This circuit encrypts a known plaintext(p) in a superposition state using a pre-prepared key (as set in the input setting), producing ciphertexts for every possible key value. Subsequently, these generated ciphertexts are compared with the known ciphertexts (performed in $f(x)$). Upon discovering a match (i.e., when $f(x) = 1$ in Eq. (3)), the sign of the desired key state to be recovered is negated (i.e., $(-1)^{f(x)}$ in Eq. (4)). Finally, the implemented quantum circuit reverses the generated ciphertexts back to the known plaintext for the next iteration.

$$f(x) = \begin{cases} 1 \text{ if } Enc_{key}(p) = c \\ 0 \text{ if } Enc_{key}(p) \neq c \end{cases} \qquad (3)$$

$$U_f(|\psi\rangle|-\rangle) = \frac{1}{2^{k/2}}\sum_{x=0}^{2^k-1}(-1)^{f(x)}|x\rangle|-\rangle \qquad (4)$$

3. The *Diffusion Operator* serves to amplify the amplitude of the target key state indicated by the oracle, identifying it by flipping the sign of said amplitude to negative. The quantum circuit for the diffusion operator is typically straightforward and does not require any special techniques to implement. Additionally, the overhead of the diffusion operator is usually negligible compared to the oracle, and therefore it is generally ignored when estimating the cost of Grover's algorithm [5–7]. Lastly, the Grover's algorithm provides a high probability of measuring the solution key by performing a sufficient number of iterations of the oracle and the diffusion operator to amplify the amplitude of the target key state.

2.4   NIST Security Criteria

NIST establishes security levels and estimates the required resources for block cipher and hash function attack costs for post-quantum security [3]. The estimates provided by NIST for the security levels defined and the number of classical and quantum gates for the attacks are as follows:

- **Level 1:** Any attempt to breach the defined security standards should necessitate computational capabilities equal to or greater than those required to perform a key search on a 128-bit key block cipher, such as AES128. ($2^{170} \rightarrow 2^{157}$).
- **Level 3:** Any attempt to breach the defined security standards should necessitate computational capabilities equal to or greater than those required to perform a key search on a 192-bit key block cipher, such as AES192. ($2^{233} \rightarrow 2^{221}$).
- **Level 5:** Any attempt to breach the defined security standards should necessitate computational capabilities equal to or greater than those required to perform a key search on a 256-bit key block cipher, such as AES256. ($2^{298} \rightarrow 2^{285}$).

Level 1, 3, and 5 are based on the Grover's key search cost for AES, while Level 2 and 4 rely on the collision attack cost for SHA3. Additionally, for Levels 2 and 4, estimates are provided only for classical gates, not quantum attacks. In our implementation of SEED, which is a symmetric key cipher, we primarily focus on Levels 1, 3, and 5.

NIST sets the Grover's key search cost for AES-128, 192, and 256 based on the quantum circuits implemented by Grassl et al. [5], resulting in Levels 1, 3, and 5. During the execution of the Grover's key search, the number of gates and depth continue to increase, while the number of qubits remains constant. Therefore, the estimates provided by NIST are derived from the product of the total gates and total depth of the quantum circuit, excluding the number of qubits(AES-128, 192, and 256 as 2^{170}, 2^{233}, 2^{298}, respectively).

The estimates for Grover's key search on the quantum circuit from [5], which NIST used as a basis for setting security levels, are notably high. Subsequent efforts to optimize AES quantum circuits have led to a reduction in the cost of quantum attacks. In 2019, Jaques et al. presented optimized quantum circuits for AES at Eurocrypt '20 [15]. Based on this, NIST redefines the quantum attack costs for AES-128, 192, and 256 as 2^{157}, 2^{221}, 2^{285}, respectively [4].

Moreover, NIST proposes a restriction on circuit depth known as MAXDEPTH. This restriction stems from the challenge of executing highly prolonged sequential computations. In other words, it arises from the challenge of prolonged calculations due to sequential repetitions of quantum circuits in Grover's key search (especially in the Grover oracle). The MAXDEPTH specified by NIST is as follows. ($2^{40} < 2^{64} < 2^{96}$)

3   Proposed Quantum Implementation of SEED

In this section, we present our optimized quantum circuit implementation of SEED. Our optimization goal in implementation is to minimize the depth while allowing a reasonable number of qubits.

3.1   Implementation of S-Box

In quantum computers, the utilization of look-up table-based methods for implementing S-boxes is not appropriate. Thus, we employ quantum gates to implement the S-boxes based on *Boolean* expression of Eq. 1. We use x^{247} or x^{251} in the S-box implementation, and these values can be expressed using primitive polynomials in $\mathbb{F}_{2^8}/(x^8 + x^6 + x^5 + x + 1)$ as follows: The S-boxes are in $\mathrm{GF}(2^8)$, so they can be modified with inversion as follows:

$$(x^{-1})^8 \equiv x^{247} \mod p(x)$$

$$(x^{-1})^4 \equiv x^{251} \mod p(x) \tag{5}$$

$$p(x) = x^8 + x^6 + x^5 + x + 1$$

We can obtain the value by multiplying the inverse by the square. And then, following the Itoh Tsujii inversion algorithm [16], the x^{-1} can be computed:

$$x^{-1} = x^{254} = ((x \cdot x^2) \cdot (x \cdot x^2)^4 \cdot (x \cdot x^2)^{16} \cdot x^{64})^2 \tag{6}$$

To compute the inversion of x, squaring and multiplication are used (as shown in Eq. 6). In squaring, modular reduction can be employed PLU factorization because it is a linear operation. By using PLU factorization, it can be implemented without allocating additional ancilla qubits (i.e., in-place), using only the CNOT gates. Upon applying the PLU factorization, we obtain the following:

$$
\begin{pmatrix}
0&0&0&0&1&1&1&0\\
0&0&0&0&1&1&0&0\\
0&1&0&0&0&1&0&1\\
0&0&0&0&0&1&1&0\\
0&0&1&0&0&0&1&0\\
0&0&0&0&1&1&0&1\\
0&0&0&1&1&1&0&1\\
0&0&0&0&0&1&0&0
\end{pmatrix}
=
\begin{pmatrix}
1&0&0&0&0&0&0&0\\
0&0&0&0&1&0&0&0\\
0&1&0&0&0&0&0&0\\
0&0&0&0&0&1&0&0\\
0&0&1&0&0&0&0&0\\
0&0&0&0&0&0&0&1\\
0&0&0&1&0&0&0&0\\
0&0&0&0&0&0&1&0
\end{pmatrix}
\cdot
\begin{pmatrix}
1&0&0&0&0&0&0&0\\
0&1&0&0&0&0&0&0\\
0&0&1&0&0&0&0&0\\
0&0&0&1&0&0&0&0\\
0&0&0&0&1&0&0&0\\
0&0&0&0&0&1&0&0\\
0&0&0&0&0&1&1&0\\
0&0&0&0&1&0&0&1
\end{pmatrix}
\cdot
\begin{pmatrix}
1&0&0&0&1&1&1&0\\
0&1&0&0&0&1&0&1\\
0&0&1&0&0&0&1&0\\
0&0&0&1&1&1&0&1\\
0&0&0&0&1&1&0&0\\
0&0&0&0&0&1&1&0\\
0&0&0&0&0&0&1&0\\
0&0&0&0&0&0&0&1
\end{pmatrix}
\tag{7}
$$

These three matrices consist of a permutation matrix, a lower triangular matrix, and an upper triangular matrix, respectively. Figure 6 demonstrates the implementation of quantum circuit of squaring using only CNOT gates, utilizing these three matrices.

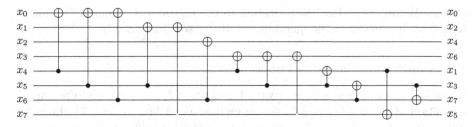

Fig. 6. Squaring in $\mathbb{F}_{2^8}/(x^8 + x^6 + x^5 + x + 1)$

For implementing multiplication in quantum, we adopt the method proposed in [17], which employs the Karatsuba multiplication instead of schoolbook multiplication [18]. The Karatsuba algorithm, when applied in the context of quantum computers, can lead to a reduction in the number of Toffoli gates (as it decrease the number of AND operations). This efficiency makes it a valuable technique for quantum computing.

In [17], a special Karatsuba algorithm is used, which enables the quantum multiplication with a Toffoli depth of one. By applying the Karatsuba algorithm recursively, all the AND operations for multiplication become independent. Additionally, by allocating more ancilla qubits, it becomes possible to operate all Toffoli gates in parallel, leading to a Toffoli depth of one.

Actually, allocating additional ancilla qubits is a known overhead in their method [17]. However, it is important to note that their method is more effective when used in conjunction with other operations rather than as a stand-alone multiplication. The authors of [17] mention that the ancilla qubits allocated for multiplication can be initialized (i.e., clean state) using reverse operations. This means that if it is not a stand-alone multiplication, the ancilla qubits can be reused in ongoing operations.

In Eq. 6, multiple multiplications are performed to compute the inverse of the input x. Indeed, the method proposed in [17] is well-suited for implementing quantum circuits for inversion. Concretely, in our implementation, ancilla qubits are allocated only once for the initial multiplication $(x \cdot x^2)$, and for subsequent multiplications, the initialized ancilla qubits are reused without incurring any additional cost.

As a result, we successfully optimize the number of qubits and the Toffoli-related metrics such as, the number of Toffoli gates, Toffoli depth, and full depth[1].

Using these methods of squaring and multiplication, we can obtain the exponentiation values $(x^{247}$ and $x^{251})$. And then, we compute the multiplication of the exponentiation values $(x^{247}$ and $x^{251})$ and the matrices $(A^{(1)}$ and $A^{(2)})$. Since the matrices $A^{(1)}$ and $A^{(2)}$ are constant, the matrix-vector multiplication (classical-quantum) can be implemented in-place without requiring additional

---

[1] The full depth is naturally reduced thanks to the reduction in the Toffoli depth.

qubits. We apply the PLU factorization to the matrices $A^{(1)}$ and $A^{(2)}$, similar to how we implemented the quantum circuit for squaring (Eq. 7).

3.2 Implementation of G Function

In the G function, four S-boxes (two $S1$ and two $S2$) are used, and the implementation of these S-boxes follows the method described in Sect. 3.1. Each S-box requires 38 ancilla qubits, which can be initialized using reverse operations, enabling their reuse. Therefore, if the four S-boxes are implemented sequentially, the number of ancilla qubits can be saved by using only 38 of them. However, in this case, the depth of the circuit increases due to the sequential operations. Thus, considering the trade-off, we implement the four S-boxes in parallel to reduce the circuit depth. This is achieved by allocating a total of 152 (38×4) ancilla qubits at first. Additionally, these ancilla qubits are initialized (i.e., returning to 0), allowing the 4 sets of ancilla qubits to be reused in the G function of the next round.

3.3 Implementation of Key Schedule

Algorithm 1 describes the proposed quantum circuit implementation of the key schedule. In the key schedule, two 32-qubit subkeys ($K_{i,0}$ and $K_{i,1}$) are generated. To reduce the circuit depth, the implementation is parallelized by operating two processes simultaneously. For this, we allocate two sets of 152 ancilla qubits to implement two G functions in parallel. Also, for parallel processing, the operations with KeyConstant values of quantum state also need to be implemented in parallel. To enable parallel processing, two pairs of qubits (32×2) are allocated to store the KeyConstant values (using on $K_{i,0}, K_{i,1}$ respectively) in our implementation.

Due to the different KeyConstant values used in each round, it is necessary to allocate and store new qubits every time. Instead of allocating new qubits in each round, we utilize reverse operations to initialize and reuse the qubits. The reverse operation for the KeyConstant of quantum state involves only X gates, which have a trivial overhead on the circuit depth. Thanks to this approach, we can effectively parallelize the quantum circuit for the key schedule, resulting in a reduced circuit depth while using a reasonable number of qubits.

For implementing addition in quantum, we utilize the CDKM adder [19], an enhanced version of the quantum ripple-carry adder, which is implemented using X, CNOT, and Toffoli gates. The CDKM adder proves to be effective for n-qubit addition when $n \geq 4$, making it a suitable choice for SEED, where $n = 8$. This adder requires only one ancilla qubit and optimizes the circuit depth. Specifically, it utilizes one ancilla qubit, $(2n-3)$ Toffoli gates, $(5n-7)$ CNOT gates, $(2n-6)$ X gates, and achieves a circuit depth of $(2n+3)$.

In Shift operation, it can be implemented using swap gates, but in our approach, we utilize logical swaps that change the index of qubits, avoiding the use of quantum gates.

Algorithm 1. Quantum circuit implementation of SEED Key Schedule.

Input: A, B, C, D, c_0, c_1 $ancilla_0$, $ancilla_1$
Output: key_0, key_1, C, D
//Each operation in parallel.
1: **for** $0 \leq i \leq 16$ **do**
2:    $KC\_Q_0 \leftarrow$ Constant_XOR($KC[i]$, KC_Q_0)
3:    $KC\_Q_1 \leftarrow$ Constant_XOR($KC[i]$, KC_Q_1)

4:    $C_2 \leftarrow$ allocate new 32 qubits
5:    $D_2 \leftarrow$ allocate new 32 qubits

6:    $C_2 \leftarrow$ Copy32(C, C_2)
7:    $D_2 \leftarrow$ Copy32(D, D_2)

8:    $C_2 \leftarrow$ CDKM(A, C_2,c_0)
9:    $D_2 \leftarrow$ CDKM_minus(B, D_2, c_1)

10:   $C_2 \leftarrow$ CDKM_minus(KC_Q_0, C_2, c_0)
11:   $D_2 \leftarrow$ CDKM(KC_Q_1, D_2, c_1)

12:   $key_0 \leftarrow$ G function(C_2, $ancilla_0$)
13:   $key_1 \leftarrow$ G function(D_2, $ancilla_1$)

14:   //Initialize qubitsthrough reverse to reuse.
15:   $KC\_Q_0 \leftarrow$ Constant_XOR($KC[i]$, KC_Q_0)
16:   $KC\_Q_1 \leftarrow$ Constant_XOR($KC[i]$, KC_Q_1)

17:   **if** i % 2 == 0 **then**
18:      RightShift(A, B)   ▷ logical Swap
19:   **else**
20:      LeftShift(C, D)   ▷ logical Swap
21: return key_0, key_1, C, D

4 Performance of the Proposed Quantum Circuits

In this part, we present the performance of our SEED quantum circuit implementation. Our proposed quantum circuits of cryptographys are implemented using the ProjectQ tool provided by IBM. ProjectQ provides ClassicalSimulator, which can simulate simple quantum gates mentioned in Sect. 2.2, and Resource-Counter, which can measure circuit resources, as internal libraries. Classical-Simulator has the advantage of providing enough quantum resources to run our proposed quantum circuit. Real quantum computers still provide limited quantum resources that are not sufficient to run cryptography. Therefore, the circuits are run through the simulator provided by ProjectQ and the quantum resources are measured.

Table 1 and 2 show the quantum resources required to implement our SEED quantum circuits. Table 1 provides a comprehensive analysis of quan-

Table 1. Required quantum resources for SEED quantum circuit implementation

Cipher	#X	#CNOT	#Toffoli	Toffoli depth	#Qubit	Depth	TD-M cost
SEED	8116	409,520	41,392	321	41,496	11,837	13,320,216

Table 2. Required decomposed quantum resources for SEED quantum circuit implementation

Cipher	#Clifford	#T	T-depth	#Qubit	Full depth	FD-M cost
SEED	748,740	289,680	1,284	41,496	34,566	1,434,350,736

tum resources at the NCT (NOT, CNOT, Toffoli) level. The Toffoli gate can be decomposed into 8 Clifford gates and 7T gates and Table 2 presents the decomposed quantum resource costs for the quantum circuit implementation of SEED. Additionally, our implementation focuses on optimizing the circuit depth while considering the trade-off for using qubit, and we also perform metrics to evaluate these trade-offs such as Toffoli depth × qubit count ($TD \times M$) and full depth × qubit count ($FD \times M$).

5   Evaluation of Grover's Search Complexity

We adopt the methodology detailed in Sect. 2.3 to estimate the cost of Grover's key search for SEED. Grover's search can be estimated based on our implemented SEED quantum circuit. Since the overhead of the diffusion operator can be considered insignificant compared to the oracle when most of the quantum resources are used for implementing the target cipher in the quantum circuit, it can be disregarded.

Additionally, the Grover oracle is comprised of two consecutive executions of the SEED quantum circuit. The first one constitutes the encryption circuit, while the second one is the reverse operation of encryption circuit to return back to the state prior to encryption. Therefore, the oracle requires twice the cost of implementing a quantum circuit, not including of qubits. The number of iterations of Grover key search for k-bit key length is about $\sqrt{2^k}$. In [20], Grover's key search algorithm was analyzed in detail and the optimal number of iterations was suggested to be $\lfloor \frac{\pi}{4}\sqrt{2^k} \rfloor$. In conclusion, including Grover iterations, the Grover's key search cost for SEED is approximately Table 2 $\times 2 \times \lfloor \frac{\pi}{4}\sqrt{2^k} \rfloor$, as shown in Table 3.

Table 3. Cost of the Grover's key search for SEED

Cipher	Total gates	Total depth	Cost (complexity)	#Qubit	TD-M cost	FD-M cost
SEED	$1.559 \cdot 2^{84}$	$1.657 \cdot 2^{79}$	$1.291 \cdot 2^{164}$	41,497	$1.246 \cdot 2^{88}$	$1.049 \cdot 2^{95}$

6 Conclusion

We can assess the post-quantum security of SEED based on the cost of Grover's key search obtained earlier (in Sect. 5). In 2016, NIST defined post-quantum security levels by considering the estimated costs of Grover's key search attacks on AES-128, 192, and 256. Nevertheless, with the declining costs of AES attacks, NIST revised the cost assessments to align with the respective security levels in 2019.

According to Table 3, the Grover's key search attack cost for SEED is calculated to be $1.291 \cdot 2^{164}$. This leads to the assessment that SEED attains post-quantum security Level 1.

In summary, this paper presents the first implementation of a quantum circuit for SEED. We focus on optimizing Toffoli and full depths utilizing parallelization and optimized multiplication, squaring and an adder. By analyzing the cost of Grover's key search attack, we confirm that SEED achieves post-quantum security Level 1. Furthermore, we provide $TD \times M$ and $FD \times M$ costs to consider the trade-off between depth and qubits.

Acknowledgment. This work was supported by the National Research Foundation of Korea (NRF) grant funded by the Korea government (MSIT). (No. RS-2023-00277994, Quantum Circuit Depth Optimization for ARIA, SEED, LEA, HIGHT, and LSH of KCMVP Domestic Cryptographic Algorithms, 80%) and this work was supported by Institute of Information & communications Technology Planning & Evaluation (IITP) grant funded by the Korea government (MSIT) (No.2022-0-00627, Development of Lightweight BIoT technology for Highly Constrained Devices, 20%).

References

1. Shor, P.: Algorithms for quantum computation: discrete logarithms and factoring. In: Proceedings 35th Annual Symposium on Foundations of Computer Science, pp. 124–134 (1994)
2. Grover, L.K.: A fast quantum mechanical algorithm for database search. In: Miller, G.L. (ed.) Proceedings of the Twenty-Eighth Annual ACM Symposium on the Theory of Computing, Philadelphia, Pennsylvania, USA, 22–24 May 1996, pp. 212–219. ACM (1996)
3. NIST. Submission requirements and evaluation criteria for the post-quantum cryptography standardization process (2016). https://csrc.nist.gov/CSRC/media/Projects/Post-Quantum-Cryptography/documents/call-for-proposals-final-dec-2016.pdf

4. NIST. Call for additional digital signature schemes for the post-quantum cryptography standardization process (2022). https://csrc.nist.gov/csrc/media/Projects/pqc-dig-sig/documents/call-for-proposals-dig-sig-sept-2022.pdf

5. Grassl, M., Langenberg, B., Roetteler, M., Steinwandt, R.: Applying Grover's algorithm to AES: quantum resource estimates (2015)

6. Jaques, S., Naehrig, M., Roetteler, M., Virdia, F.: Implementing Grover oracles for quantum key search on AES and LowMC. Cryptology ePrint Archive, Report 2019/1146 (2019). https://eprint.iacr.org/2019/1146

7. Jang, K., Baksi, A., Song, G., Kim, H., Seo, H., Chattopadhyay, A.: Quantum analysis of AES. Cryptology ePrint Archive (2022)

8. Jang, K., Song, G., Kim, H., Kwon, H., Kim, H., Seo, H.: Efficient implementation of present and gift on quantum computers. Appl. Sci. **11**(11), 4776 (2021)

9. Jang, K., Baksi, A., Kim, H., Seo, H., Chattopadhyay, A.: Improved quantum analysis of speck and LowMC (full version). Cryptology ePrint Archive (2022)

10. Anand, R., Maitra, A., Mukhopadhyay, S.: Evaluation of quantum cryptanalysis on SPECK. In: Bhargavan, K., Oswald, E., Prabhakaran, M. (eds.) INDOCRYPT 2020. LNCS, vol. 12578, pp. 395–413. Springer, Cham (2020). https://doi.org/10.1007/978-3-030-65277-7_18

11. Yang, Y., Jang, K., Kim, H., Song, G., Seo, H.: Grover on SPARKLE. In: You, I., Youn, T.Y. (eds.) WISA 2022. LNCS, vol. 13720, pp. 44–59. Springer, Cham (2023). https://doi.org/10.1007/978-3-031-25659-2_4

12. Jagielski, A., Kanciak, K.: Quantum resource estimation for a NIST LWC call finalist. Quantum Inf. Comput. **22**(13&14), 1132–1143 (2022)

13. Roy, S., Baksi, A., Chattopadhyay, A.: Quantum implementation of ASCON linear layer. Cryptology ePrint Archive (2023)

14. Oh, Y., Jang, K., Baksi, A., Seo, H.: Depth-optimized implementation of ASCON quantum circuit. Cryptology ePrint Archive (2023)

15. Jaques, S., Naehrig, M., Roetteler, M., Virdia, F.: Implementing Grover oracles for quantum key search on AES and LowMC. In: Canteaut, A., Ishai, Y. (eds.) EUROCRYPT 2020. LNCS, vol. 12106, pp. 280–310. Springer, Cham (2020). https://doi.org/10.1007/978-3-030-45724-2_10

16. Itoh, T., Tsujii, S.: A fast algorithm for computing multiplicative inverses in GF (2m) using normal bases. Inf. Comput. **78**(3), 171–177 (1988)

17. Jang, K., Kim, W., Lim, S., Kang, Y., Yang, Y., Seo, H.: Optimized implementation of quantum binary field multiplication with Toffoli depth one. In: You, I., Youn, T.Y. (eds.) WISA 2022. LNCS, vol. 13720, pp. 251–264. Springer, Cham (2023). https://doi.org/10.1007/978-3-031-25659-2_18

18. Cheung, D., Maslov, D., Mathew, J., Pradhan, D.K.: On the design and optimization of a quantum polynomial-time attack on elliptic curve cryptography. In: Kawano, Y., Mosca, M. (eds.) TQC 2008. LNCS, vol. 5106, pp. 96–104. Springer, Heidelberg (2008). https://doi.org/10.1007/978-3-540-89304-2_9

19. Cuccaro, S.A., Draper, T.G., Kutin, S.A., Moulton, D.P.: A new quantum ripple-carry addition circuit. arXiv preprint quant-ph/0410184 (2004)

20. Boyer, M., Brassard, G., Høyer, P., Tapp, A.: Tight bounds on quantum searching. Fortschr. Phys. **46**, 493–505 (1998)

Depth-Optimized Quantum Implementation of ARIA

Yujin Yang[1] , Kyungbae Jang[2] , Yujin Oh[3] , and Hwajeong Seo[3(✉)]

[1] Department of IT Convergence Engineering, Hansung University,
Seoul 02876, South Korea
[2] Department of Information Computer Engineering, Hansung University,
Seoul 02876, South Korea
[3] Department of Convergence Security, Hansung University,
Seoul 02876, South Korea
hwajeong84@gmail.com

Abstract. The advancement of large-scale quantum computers poses a threat to the security of current encryption systems. In particular, symmetric-key cryptography significantly is impacted by general attacks using the Grover's search algorithm. In recent years, studies have been presented to estimate the complexity of Grover's key search for symmetric-key ciphers and assess post-quantum security. In this paper, we propose a depth-optimized quantum circuit implementation for ARIA, which is a symmetric key cipher included as a validation target the Korean Cryptographic Module Validation Program (KCMVP). Our quantum circuit implementation for ARIA improves the full-depth by more than 88.8% and Toffoli-depth by more than 98.7% compared to the implementation presented in Chauhan et al.'s SPACE'20 paper. Finally, we present the cost of Grover's key search for our circuit and evaluate the post-quantum security strength of ARIA according to relevant evaluation criteria provided NIST.

Keywords: Depth-Optimized Quantum Circuit · Korean Block Ciphers · ARIA · Grover's Search Algorithm

1 Introduction

Quantum computers, built upon principles of quantum mechanics like quantum superposition and entanglement, have the capability to solve specific problems at a faster rate compared to classical computers. As a result, many companies and research institutions are concentrating on quantum computer development. However, it is known that the advancement of large-scale quantum computers has the potential to pose a threat to the security of current cryptographic systems. In particular, symmetric-key cryptography can be significantly compromised by general attacks using the Grover's search algorithm, which can reduce the data search complexity. As a result, in recent years, studies have

© The Author(s), under exclusive license to Springer Nature Singapore Pte Ltd. 2024
H. Seo and S. Kim (Eds.): ICISC 2023, LNCS 14561, pp. 79–96, 2024.
https://doi.org/10.1007/978-981-97-1235-9_5

been presented to estimate the complexity of recovering secret keys in existing symmetric-key ciphers using the Grover's search algorithm and evaluate post-quantum security based on these findings [8, 10, 11, 14, 15, 22, 25].

ARIA is a symmetric-key cryptography algorithm optimized for ultra-light environments and hardware implementation, and is included as a validation target in the Korean Cryptographic Module Validation Program (KCMVP). This means that ARIA is widely used in verified cryptographic modules, so it is very important to measure ARIA's quantum security strength for future preparedness against emerging threats. Fortunately, there is already a study that measured the quantum security strength of ARIA in 2020 [2]. However, since [2] primarily focuses on qubit optimization, there is also a need for research that addresses the recent emphasis on optimizing depth.

In a document guiding evaluation criteria for post-quantum cryptography standardization, NIST provided a criteria for estimating quantum attack complexity and proposed a parameter called MAXDEPTH, which refers to the maximum circuit depth that a quantum computer can execute. In order to evaluate the strength of quantum security, not only the quantum attack complexity but also the MAXDEPTH related to execution must be considered. Further elaboration on this topic can be found in Sects. 2.4 and 4.

The paper is structured as follows. Section 2 offers the background for this paper. Section 2.1 provides an introduction to ARIA. In Sect. 2.2, the quantum gates utilized to implement quantum circuits are covered. In Sect. 2.3 Grover's key search is examined because it relates to measuring quantum resources, and in Sect. 2.4, NIST post-quantum security and MAXDEPTH are covered because they are crucial for estimating security strength. Following this, in Sects. 3, the design of quantum circuits for ARIA is suggested, drawing upon the information presented in Sect. 2. Section 4.2 presents the cost of Grover's key search for our circuit and evaluates ARIA's post-quantum security strength based on the estimates. Lastly, Sect. 5 delves into the summarizing conclusions and outlines potential directions for future research.

1.1   Our Contribution

This paper makes the following contributions:

1. **Low depth quantum implementation of ARIA**. In our implementation of the ARIA quantum circuit, our main focus is minimizing the Toffoli depth and ensuring full depth. We achieve a reduction in Toffoli depth and full depth through various techniques for optimization.
2. **Various techniques for optimization**. We utilize various techniques for optimization to reduce the depth. For optimizing binary field operations, we choose a multiplication optimizer that implements the Karatsuba algorithm in parallel and a squaring method using linear layer optimization method. Furthermore, we enhance implementing parallel processing for applicable components.

3. **Evaluation of post-quantum security**. We estimate the resources required for implementing quantum circuits for ARIA. The resource estimation for the ARIA quantum circuit also includes the comparison with previous research. Furthermore, we evaluate the quantum security of ARIA by estimating the cost of Grover's key search based on the implemented quantum circuit and comparing them with the security levels provided by NIST.

2 Background

2.1 ARIA Block Cipher

ARIA [17], which stands for Academy, Research Institute, and Agency, is a Korean symmetric key block cipher jointly developed by the three organizations mentioned above. Since the adoption of ARIA as a national standard encryption algorithm in 2004, it has been widely used for secure communication and data protection. Especially, ARIA holds significance as symmetric key ciphers included in the validation subjects of the KCMVP. ARIA has an interface similar to AES, a symmetric key block cipher standard, because its designers considered the design principles of AES during its development. It has an Involutional Substitution-Permutation Network (ISPN) structure optimized for lightweight hardware implementation. The input/output size of ARIA is fixed at 128-bit, and only the key size is different as 128, 192, and 256-bit.

Round Function The round function is made of three main operations: *AddRoundKey*, *Substitution layer*, and *Diffusion layer*.

In the *AddRoundKey*, the round key suitable for each round is XORed to intermediate state.

In the *Substitution layer*, the input 128-bit state is divided into 8-bit units, and substitutions are performed using the S-boxes. ARIA employs a total of four S-boxes $(S_1, S_1^{-1}, S_2, S_2^{-1})$, which include the inverse S-boxes. The S_1, S_1^{-1} are identical to the ones used in AES, and the S_2, S_2^{-1} are newly designed S-boxes specifically for ARIA. These S-boxes used in ARIA are generated by applying an affine transformation to the functions x^{-1} and x^{247} over $GF(2^8)$. The S-boxes $S_1(x), S_2(x)$ are obtained by performing multiplication between 8×8 non-singular matrix (**A** or **B**) and the function (x^{-1} or x^{247}), followed by XOR with 8×1 vector. This can be expressed as follows:

$$S_1(x) = \mathbf{A} \cdot x^{-1} \oplus [1,1,0,0,0,1,1,0]^{\mathrm{T}},$$
$$S_2(x) = \mathbf{B} \cdot x^{247} \oplus [0,1,0,0,0,1,1,1]^{\mathrm{T}}$$

$$\text{where} \quad \mathbf{A} = \begin{pmatrix} 1\,0\,0\,0\,1\,1\,1\,1 \\ 1\,1\,0\,0\,0\,1\,1\,1 \\ 1\,1\,1\,0\,0\,0\,1\,1 \\ 1\,1\,1\,1\,0\,0\,0\,1 \\ 1\,1\,1\,1\,1\,0\,0\,0 \\ 0\,1\,1\,1\,1\,1\,0\,0 \\ 0\,0\,1\,1\,1\,1\,1\,0 \\ 0\,0\,0\,1\,1\,1\,1\,1 \end{pmatrix} \quad \text{and} \quad \mathbf{B} = \begin{pmatrix} 0\,1\,0\,1\,1\,1\,1\,0 \\ 0\,0\,1\,1\,1\,1\,0\,1 \\ 1\,1\,0\,1\,0\,1\,1\,1 \\ 1\,0\,0\,1\,1\,1\,0\,1 \\ 0\,0\,1\,0\,1\,1\,0\,0 \\ 1\,0\,0\,0\,0\,0\,0\,1 \\ 0\,1\,0\,1\,1\,1\,0\,1 \\ 1\,1\,0\,1\,0\,0\,1\,1 \end{pmatrix} \quad (1)$$

ARIA features two types of S-box layers consisting of four S-boxes. *Type 1* comprises four 32-bit sets consisting of S_1, S_2, S_1^{-1}, and S_2^{-1} in this order. Since the two types are the inverse relationship to each other, *Type 2* is the inverse of *Type 1* (i.e., Type1^{-1} = Type2). *Type 1* is used for odd rounds and *Type 2* for even rounds in the round function. The two types of S-box layers in ARIA are shown in Fig. 1.

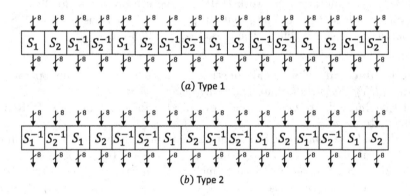

(a) Type 1

(b) Type 2

Fig. 1. Two types of S-box layers in ARIA

The Diffusion layer performs byte-wise matrix multiplication by multiplying the given 16 × 16 involution binary matrix with the output of the substitution layer. The involution binary matrix does not require a separate implementation of the inverse matrix during the decryption process, as its inverse matrix is the same as itself.

The detailed composition of the round function differs depending on whether the round is odd, even, or final. The main difference between odd and even rounds lies in the type of the S-box layer used: odd rounds use a *Type 1*, whereas even rounds use a *Type 2*. In the final round, the diffusion step is omitted and the AddRoundKey is performed once more. A brief outline of the round function of ARIA is shown in Fig. 2.

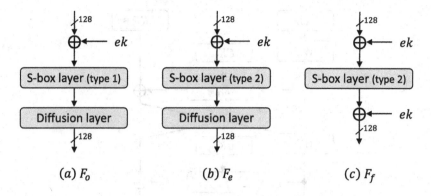

Fig. 2. Brief outline of round function of ARIA.

Key Schedule. In the *key initialization step* (Fig. 3), 128-bit initial constants W_0, W_1, W_2, and W_3 are generated as essential components for generating a round key. During this step, the round functions F_o and F_e are utilized.

$$KL||KR = MK||0\cdots0. \tag{2}$$

Equation 2 represents the formula used to generate the input values KL and KR in the key initialization step. This equation is derived from the master key MK. Since the concatenated result of KL and KR, which are each 128-bit, is fixed to 256-bit (i.e., $KL||KR$), if MK is smaller than 256, padding is performed to match the size by filling the insufficient bits with 0s. The 128-bit initial round constant keys $CK_{1,2,3}$ are the 128-bit constant values of the rational part of π^{-1}. The order of using the 128-bit initial round constant keys $CK_{1,2,3}$ depends on the length of MK. Figure 3 shows the key initialization step.

In the *key generation phase*, a round key is generated and used as the key for each round. The round keys $ek_{1\sim17}$ are obtained by applying rotations ($\lll, \ggg$) and XOR operations to the initial constants $W_{0\sim3}$ generated during the key initialization step.

The round key in all ARIA instances has a size of 128 bits. The number of rounds for ARIA-128, 192, and 256 are 12, 14, and 16, respectively. Additionally, an extra round key is used in the AddRoundKey operation for the final round, resulting in a total of 13, 15, and 17 round keys for ARIA-128, 192, and 256, respectively. The round keys ek_i are generated as follows:

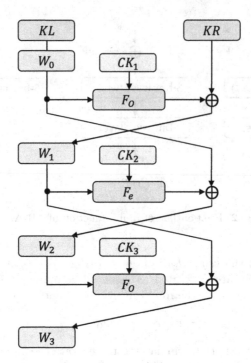

Fig. 3. Key Initialization of ARIA

$$
\begin{aligned}
ek_1 &= (W_0) \oplus (W_1 \ggg 19), & ek_2 &= (W_1) \oplus (W_2 \ggg 19) \\
ek_3 &= (W_2) \oplus (W_3 \ggg 19), & ek_4 &= (W_0 \ggg 19) \oplus (W_3) \\
ek_5 &= (W_0) \oplus (W_1 \ggg 31), & ek_6 &= (W_1) \oplus (W_2 \ggg 31) \\
ek_7 &= (W_2) \oplus (W_3 \ggg 31), & ek_8 &= (W_0 \ggg 31) \oplus (W_3) \\
ek_9 &= (W_0) \oplus (W_1 \lll 61), & ek_{10} &= (W_1) \oplus (W_2 \lll 61) \\
ek_{11} &= (W_2) \oplus (W_3 \lll 61), & ek_{12} &= (W_0 \lll 61) \oplus (W_3) \\
ek_{13} &= (W_0) \oplus (W_1 \lll 31), & ek_{14} &= (W_1) \oplus (W_2 \lll 31) \\
ek_{15} &= (W_2) \oplus (W_3 \lll 31), & ek_{16} &= (W_0 \lll 31) \oplus (W_3) \\
ek_{17} &= (W_0) \oplus (W_1 \lll 19)
\end{aligned}
\tag{3}
$$

2.2   Quantum Gates

Since in the quantum computer environment they do not provide logic gates such as AND, OR, and XOR, quantum gates are used as replacements for logic gates. This section describes commonly used quantum gates (Fig. 4) for implementing quantum circuits of block ciphers (note that this is not an exhaustive list of all possible gates that can be used).

The X gate acts like a NOT operation on a classical computer, reversing the state of the qubit that goes through it. The Swap gate exchanges the states of two qubits. The CNOT gate behaves like an XOR operation on a classical computer. In CNOT(a, b), the input qubit a is the control qubit, and b is the target qubit. When the control qubit a is in the state 1, the target qubit b is flipped. As a result, the value of $a \oplus b$ is stored in the qubit b (i.e., $b = a \oplus b$), while the state of qubit a remains unchanged. The Toffoli gate, represented as Toffoli(a, b, c), acts like an AND operation on a classical computer. It requires three input qubits, with the first two qubits (a and b) serving as control qubits. Only when both control qubits are in the state 1, the target qubit c is flipped. The result of the operation a & b is XORed with the qubit c (i.e., $c = c \oplus (a$ & $b)$), while the states of qubits a and b are preserved. The Toffoli gate consists of 8 Clifford gates and 7 T gates. The T-count of the standard Toffoli gate [18] is 7 and the T-depth is 6. Many studies are reporting the implementation of Toffoli gate circuits with minimized depth and T-depth [1,7,16,21,23]. Among these, we utilized Amy et al.'s Toffoli gate implementation [1], which has a T-depth of 4 and a full-depth of 8.

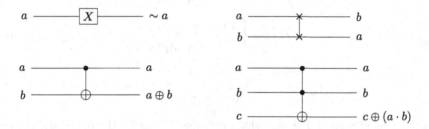

Fig. 4. Quantum gates: X (left top), Swap (right top), CNOT (left bottom) and Toffoli (right bottom) gates.

2.3   Grover's Key Search

Grover's search algorithm is a quantum algorithm that enables rapid searching for specific data within an unstructured database set N, reducing the search complexity from $O(N)$ to $O(\sqrt{N})$. When applied to an n-bit secret key search in symmetric key encryption, it reduces the search complexity from $O(2^n)$ resulting from a brute-force attack to $O(2^{n/2})$, halving the security level in theory. Grover's key search algorithm operates in three sequential steps as follows:

1. *Initialization*: Input the n-qubit key into the Hadamard gate to create a superposition of states $|\psi\rangle$ in which all 2^n computational basis states have equal amplitudes.

$$H|0\rangle = \left(\frac{|0\rangle + |1\rangle}{\sqrt{2}}\right) \tag{4}$$

$$|\psi\rangle = (H|0\rangle)^{\otimes n} = \left(\frac{|0\rangle + |1\rangle}{\sqrt{2}}\right)^{\otimes n} = \frac{1}{\sqrt{2^n}} \sum_{x=0}^{2^n-1} |x\rangle \tag{5}$$

2. *Oracle Operator*: The quantum circuit for the target cipher encrypts the known plaintext using keys (prepared keys) generated through a superposition of states in the Oracle and produces ciphertext for all key values. Within the Oracle operator (U_f), the function $f(x)$ in Eq. 6 compares the ciphertext generated by the circuit to the known ciphertext. The function $f(x)$ returns 0 if the generated ciphertext and the known ciphertext do not match and 1 if they do. When a match is identified, the state of the corresponding key in Eq. 7, i.e., its amplitude, becomes negative because $f(x)$ is equal to 1. If no match is found, $(-1)^0$ equals 1, so the amplitude remains positive.

$$f(x) = \begin{cases} 1 \text{ if } Enc_{key}(p) = c \\ 0 \text{ if } Enc_{key}(p) \neq c \end{cases} \tag{6}$$

$$U_f(|\psi\rangle|-\rangle) = \frac{1}{\sqrt{2^n}} \sum_{x=0}^{2^n-1} (-1)^{f(x)} |x\rangle |-\rangle \tag{7}$$

3. *Diffusion Operator*: The diffusion operator (D) serves the purpose of transforming a key state (target key state) with a negative amplitude into a symmetric state. This transformation involves computing the average value of all key states and then subtracting this average value from each key state element (I_n). During the second step, if the amplitude of the key state is initially negative, subtracting a negative number results in a positive value, thereby amplifying only the amplitude of that value.

$$D = 2|s\rangle \langle s| - I_n \tag{8}$$

In order to increase the probability of measuring the solution key, steps 2 and 3 must be repeated sufficiently. In general, when the number of repetitions is $\frac{\pi}{4}\sqrt{2^n}$, it has the highest measurement probability.

2.4   NIST Post-quantum Security and MAXDEPTH

In order to analyze the algorithms submitted during the post-quantum cryptography standardization, NIST provided security standards based on the security strength range specified in the existing NIST standard for symmetric cryptography in a related document [19, 20]. This post-quantum security baseline is based on the complexity of quantum attacks against AES and SHA-2/3 variants. The following is a summary of the criteria for estimating the complexity of quantum attacks provided in NIST's document [20]:

- **Level 1**: Any attempt to compromise the applicable security definition should demand computational resources that are equal to or exceed the resources needed to conduct a key search on a 128-bit key block cipher, such as AES-128.
- **Level 3**: Any attempt to compromise the applicable security definition should demand computational resources that are equal to or exceed the resources needed to conduct a key search on a 192-bit key block cipher, such as AES-192.
- **Level 5**: Any attempt to compromise the applicable security definition should demand computational resources that are equal to or exceed the resources needed to conduct a key search on a 256-bit key block cipher, such as AES-256.

Grover's search algorithm is recognized as one of the most efficient quantum attacks for targeting symmetric key ciphers, and NIST also acknowledges this fact. The difficulty presented by attacks at Levels 1, 3, and 5 is assessed according to the cost needed for Grover's key search on AES-128, 192, and 256, respectively. This cost is determined by multiplying the total gate count by the depth of Grover's key search circuit. Through studies published over the past few years that optimized AES quantum circuits to reduce Grover's key search costs, NIST has defined the costs for Levels 1, 3, and 5 as 2^{157}, 2^{221}, and 2^{285}, respectively in their recent document [20] by citing the costs of depth-optimized quantum circuit implementations for AES [15] presented by Jaques et al. at Eurocrypt'20.

It should be mentioned that the quantum circuit implementation by Jaques et al. [15] has a few programming-related problems. Nevertheless, Jang et al. addressed and examined these issues in their research [11], showing that the cost values mentioned in [15] can be roughly achieved using their optimized AES quantum circuits. As far as our current understanding goes, the most notable outcomes are detailed in [11] (Level 1, 3, and 5 cost $2^{157}, 2^{192}, 2^{274}$).

Additionally, we must also consider an approach called MAXDEPTH. NIST introduced a parameter called MAXDEPTH, which signifies the maximum circuit depth the quantum computer is able to execute, as an excessively large depth can lead to execution challenges in terms of time. The depth limits (i.e. MAXDEPTH) for quantum attacks provided by NIST range as follows: (no more than 2^{40}, 2^{64}, 2^{96}).

3   Proposed Quantum Implementation of ARIA

This section describes our optimized quantum circuit implementation of ARIA. We compare the results of the previous work [2], which implemented ARIA as a quantum circuit, and examine the optimized components.

3.1   Implementation of S-Box

In classical computers, the S-box of most block ciphers, including AES, employs a predefined look-up table. However, in a quantum computing environment, it is more efficient to implement the S-box using multiplicative inversion and affine transformation, primarily because of the limited number of qubits [5].

While the tool LIGHTER-R [6] efficiently constructs quantum circuits based on existing S-boxes, it has a limitation in its applicability, as it can only be used with 4-bit S-boxes, making it unsuitable for ARIA's S-box. The recent studies [4,26] aim to enhance LIGHTER-R tools to build quantum circuits for S-boxes that are previously beyond its reach. However, since these tools also concentrate on 4-bit S-boxes, they cannot be employed to implement quantum circuits for ARIA's S-box. Therefore, it is necessary to obtain the multiplicative inverse and perform the affine transformation to implement the quantum circuit of ARIA's S-box.

In order to find ARIA's S-box S_1 and S_2, The inverse of x (i.e., x^{-1}) and the exponentiation value x^{247} of Eq. 1 in Sect. 2.1 must be obtained. x^{247} in S_2 can be expressed as follows using the primitive polynomial $m(x)$ in the environment of $GF(2^8)$:

$$x^{247} \equiv (x^{-1})^8 \equiv (((x^{-1})^2)^2)^2 \mod m(x)$$
$$m(x) = x^8 + x^4 + x^3 + x + 1 \tag{9}$$

Likewise, the multiplicative inverse of x in the environment of $GF(2^8)$ is equal to x^{254}. The multiplicative inverse can be efficiently obtained using the Itoh-Tsujii algorithm [9]. Therefore, by applying the Itoh-Tsuji algorithm, it can be expressed as an expression consisting of square and multiplication as follows:

$$x^{-1} = x^{254} = ((x \cdot x^2) \cdot (x \cdot x^2)^4 \cdot (x \cdot x^2)^{16} \cdot x^{64})^2 \tag{10}$$

In order to increase the operation speed, the squaring operation is generally performed by converting the irreducible polynomial having linearity through modular reduction into a matrix form. Since this corresponds to a linear operation, it can be implemented as an in-place structure using only the XOR operation by using the XZLBZ [24], a heuristic search algorithm based on factorization in binary matrices.

The squaring operation in ARIA is implemented using CNOT gates and SWAP gates through modular reduction and XZLBZ [24]. This implementation utilizes 10 CNOT gates and has a circuit depth of 7. Figure 5 depicts the quantum circuit for the squaring operation in ARIA.

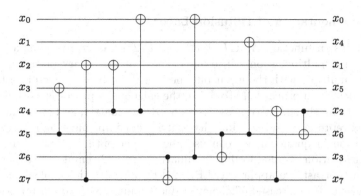

Fig. 5. Quantum circuit implementation for Squaring in $\mathbb{F}_{2^8}/(x^8 + x^4 + x^3 + x + 1)$

For multiplication, Jang et al.'s Toffoli-depth optimized Karatsuba quantum multiplication [13], first announced at WISA'22, is used. By employing the Karatsuba algorithm, which is known for reducing the number of multiplications, the number of Toffoli gates required for a multiplication can be reduced. Jang et al.'s multiplication applies the Karatsuba algorithm recursively to perform all multiplications, i.e., AND operations, independently. In order to achieve a Toffoli depth of 1, more ancilla qubits are allocated to execute Toffoli gates in parallel. This method is only used for multiplications between quantum-quantum values.

In [2], the authors employed the schoolbook multiplication method [3]. In contrast, in our work, by adopting the Toffoli-depth optimized Karatsuba multiplication [13], we achieve a significant reduction in quantum resources. Table 1 compares the quantum resources required for multiplication by adopting different methods [3,13]. In Table 1, we can see that overall quantum resources have been reduced, and, in particular, Toffoli-depth have been optimized.

Table 1. Quantum resources required for multiplication.

Source	#Clifford	#T	Toffoli depth	Full depth
CMMP [3]	435	448	28	195
J++ [13]	390	189	1	28

✳: The multiplication size n is 8.

After obtaining the exponentiation values, matrix-vector multiplication between the exponentiation and the matrix is computed by applying the XZLBZ methods because it involves the product of classical and quantum values. Multiplying vector would have originally required applying 8 CNOT gates, but by taking advantage of the fact that the given vector is a constant, resources are saved by applying X gates only to the positions where inversion is necessary.

3.2 Implementation of Diffusion Layer

ARIA's diffusion function $A : GF(2^8)^{16} \to GF(2^8)^{16}$ is expressed as a 16×16 binary matrix multiplication. Since one element of the binary matrix is a byte, in order to multiply with the input bit, the byte must be converted to a bit unit and the calculation proceeded. To do so, the calculation proceeds assuming that the element 0 in the matrix represents an 8×8 zero matrix, and the element 1 in the matrix represents an 8×8 identity matrix. For implementing matrix-vector multiplication in quantum, we can use linear layer optimization methods (i.e. PLU Factorization, Gauss-Jordan elimination etc.) [2] employed PLU factorization. In contrast, we applied XZLBZ [24] to optimize the implementation of the linear layer for increased efficiency. Table 2 compares the quantum resources used in the implementation of the Diffusion layer between [2] and our approach. In the case of [2], since 96 CNOT operations are required per byte, a total of 768 ($= 96 \times 8$) CNOT gates are used. In contrast, for XZLBZ, since 47 CNOT operations are required per byte, 376 ($= 47 \times 8$) CNOT gates are used in total. Consequently, Table 2 demonstrates a reduction of 51.04% and 45.16% in CNOT gates and depths, respectively, while maintaining the same number of qubits.

Table 2. Quantum resources required for Diffusion layer.

Source	#CNOT	qubit	Depth
PLU factorization	768	128	31
XZLBZ [24]	376	128	17

3.3 Implementation of Key Schedule

In the key initialization phase, the 128-qubit W_1, W_2, and W_3 are generated using round functions. Since K_L is used only for the generation of W_0, instead of allocating new qubits for W_0, K_L is utilized as a substitute, resulting in a reduction of 128 qubits. In addition, when performing the XOR operation of K_R and $W_{1 \sim 3}$, since K_R is a constant, the X gate are applied to W1 only when the bit of K_R is 1. By replacing the CNOT gates with cheaper X gates, the number of gates and gate cost are reduced. In contrast, our implementation in the key initialization stage employs 192 X gates and 87544 CNOT gates, leading to a reduction of approximately 49% in X gates and about 45% in CNOT gates compared to [2].

In the key generation stage, a round key ek used as an encryption key for each round is generated using $W_{0 \sim 3}$. If W_0 is used in the generation of ek, we reduce the gate cost by applying the X gates instead of the CNOT gates as in the generation of W_0.

Since the value of ek is different for each round, new qubits must be allocated and stored each time. However, instead of allocating new qubits for ek every round, we initialize and reuse the qubits by performing a reverse operation on the round key generation at the end of every round. Since the reverse operation on key generation, which is related to CNOT gates and X gates, has little effect on the depth, it is more efficient to perform the reverse operation than to allocate 128 ancilla qubits every round.

Algorithm 1. Quantum circuit implementation of key schedule for ARIA.

Input: master key MK, key length l, vector a, b, ancilla qubit anc, round number r
Output: round key ek

$\qquad\qquad\qquad\qquad\qquad\qquad\qquad\qquad\qquad\qquad\qquad\qquad$ ▷ Key Initialization
1: $W_1 \leftarrow F_o(MK[: 128], a, b, anc)$ $\qquad\qquad\qquad\qquad\qquad$ ▷ $MK[: 128]$ is K_L
2: Constant_XOR($W_1[l - 128 : 128], MK[l - 128 : l]$) $\qquad$ ▷ $MK[l - 128 : l]$ is K_R

3: $W_2 \leftarrow F_e(W_1, a, b, anc)$
4: $W_2 \leftarrow \text{CNOT128}(MK[: 128], W_2)$

5: $W_3 \leftarrow F_o(W_2, a, b, anc)$
6: $W_3 \leftarrow \text{CNOT128}(W_1, W_3)$

7: $num = [19, 31, 67, 97, 109]$ $\qquad\qquad\qquad\qquad\qquad\qquad\qquad$ ▷ Key Generation
8: **for** $i \leftarrow 0$ to r **do**
9: $\qquad$ **if** $i = 0 \pmod 4$ **then**
10: $\qquad\qquad$ Constant_XOR($ek, MK[: 128]$)
11: $\qquad$ **else**
12: $\qquad\qquad$ $ek \leftarrow \text{CNOT128}(W_{(i\%4)}, ek)$
13: $\qquad$ $ek \leftarrow \text{CNOT128}(W_{(i+1)\%4} \ggg num[i\%4], ek)$
14: **return** ek

---

4   Evaluation

In this section, we estimate and analyze the quantum circuit resources for ARIA. The proposed quantum circuits cannot yet be implemented in large-scale quantum computers. Therefore, we use ProjectQ, a quantum programming tool, on a classical computer instead of real quantum computer to implement and simulate quantum circuits. A large number of qubits can be simulated using ProjectQ's own library, `ClassicalSimulator`, which is restricted to simple quantum gates (such as X, SWAP, CNOT, and Toffoli). With the aid of this functionality, the `ClassicalSimulator` is able to test the implementation of a quantum circuit by classically computing the output for a particular input. For the estimation of quantum resources, another internal library called `ResourceCounter` is needed. `ResourceCounter` solely counts quantum gates and circuit depth, doesn't run quantum circuits, in contrast to `ClassicalSimulator`.

4.1 Performance of the Proposed Quantum Circuit

Table 3 and 4 represent the quantum resources required to implement our proposed quantum circuits for ARIA. These tables compare the quantum resources between the quantum circuit proposed by Chauhan et al. [2] and our proposed quantum circuit. Table 3 shows quantum resources for ARIA at the NCT (NOT, CNOT, Toffoli) gate level, while Table 4 presents quantum resources for ARIA at the Clifford+T level, achieved by decomposing the Toffoli gate. In [2], the decomposed quantum resources were not explicitly provided, so the quantum resources in Table 4 are extrapolated based on the information provided in the paper [2]. Furthermore, our implementation places a primary emphasis on circuit depth optimization while carefully considering the balance with qubit utilization. We conduct assessments that encompass circuit complexity metrics, such as $TD\text{-}M$ cost and $FD\text{-}M$ cost, where $TD\text{-}M$ cost represents the multiplication of Toffoli depth (TD) and the number of qubits (M), while $FD\text{-}M$ cost signifies the multiplication of Full depth (FD) and the number of qubits (M).

Table 3. Required quantum resources for ARIA quantum circuit implementation

Cipher	Source	#X	#CNOT	#Toffoli	Toffoli depth	#Qubit	Depth	$TD\text{-}M$ cost
ARIA-128	CS [2]	1,595	231,124	157,696	4,312	1,560	9,260	6,726,720
	This work	1,408	272,392	25,920	60	29,216	3,091	1,752,960
ARIA-192	CS [2]	1,851	273,264	183,368	5,096	1,560	10,948	7,949,760
	This work	1,624	315,144	29,376	68	32,928	3,776	2,239,104
ARIA-256	CS [2]	2,171	325,352	222,208	6,076	1,688	13,054	10,256,288
	This work	1,856	352,408	32,832	76	36,640	4,229	2,784,640

Table 4. Required decomposed quantum resources for ARIA quantum circuit implementation

Cipher	Source	#Clifford	#T	T-depth	#Qubit	Full depth
ARIA-128	CS [2]$^\lozenge$	1,494,287	1,103,872	17,248	1,560	37,882
	This work	481,160	181,440	240	29,216	4,241
ARIA-192	CS [2]$^\lozenge$	1,742,059	1,283,576	20,376	1,560	44,774
	This work	551,776	205,632	272	32,928	5,083
ARIA-256	CS [2]$^\lozenge$	2,105,187	1,555,456	24,304	1,688	51,666
	This work	616,920	229,824	304	36,640	5,693

$\lozenge$ Extrapolated result

4.2 Evaluation of Grover's Search Complexity

In this section, we evaluate the quantum security of ARIA by estimating the cost of Grover's key search for this algorithm. As described in Sect. 2.3, the overhead of the diffusion operator can be considered insignificant compared to the overhead of the oracle, so it is disregarded when estimating the cost of the Grover's key search. Therefore, the optimal number of iterations for Grover's key search for a cipher using a k-bit key is approximately $\lfloor \frac{\pi}{4}\sqrt{2^k} \rfloor$.

According to [15], finding a unique key requires r plaintext-ciphertext pairs, where r needs to be at least $\lceil$key size/block size$\rceil$. To calculate the quantum resources required for Grover's key search in the block cipher, the decomposed quantum resources need to be multiplied by 2, r, and $\lfloor \frac{\pi}{4}\sqrt{2^k} \rfloor$.

In the case of ARIA with the key size of 192 or 256 bits, the value of r is 2, indicating that the multiplication by r cannot be omitted. Therefore, the Grover's key search cost for ARIA is approximately Table 4 $\times r \times 2 \times \lfloor \frac{\pi}{4}\sqrt{2^k} \rfloor$ (see Table 5).

Table 5. Cost of the Grover's key search for ARIA

Cipher	Source	Total gates (G)	Full depth (FD)	Cost (complexity)	#Qubit (M)	TD-M	FD²-M	FD²-G
ARIA-128	CS [2]	$1.946 \cdot 2^{85}$	$1.816 \cdot 2^{79}$	$1.767 \cdot 2^{165}$	1,561	$1.26 \cdot 2^{86}$	$1.257 \cdot 2^{170}$	$1.604 \cdot 2^{245}$
	This work	$1.985 \cdot 2^{83}$	$1.626 \cdot 2^{76}$	$1.614 \cdot 2^{160}$	29,217	$1.313 \cdot 2^{84}$	$1.179 \cdot 2^{168}$	$1.312 \cdot 2^{237}$
ARIA-192	CS [2]	$1.133 \cdot 2^{119}$	$1.073 \cdot 2^{113}$	$1.216 \cdot 2^{232}$	3,121	$1.489 \cdot 2^{118}$	$1.754 \cdot 2^{237}$	$1.304 \cdot 2^{345}$
	This work	$1.135 \cdot 2^{117}$	$1.949 \cdot 2^{109}$	$1.106 \cdot 2^{227}$	65,857	$1.677 \cdot 2^{116}$	$1.908 \cdot 2^{236}$	$1.078 \cdot 2^{337}$
ARIA-256	CS [2]	$1.627 \cdot 2^{150}$	$1.238 \cdot 2^{145}$	$1.007 \cdot 2^{296}$	3,377	$1.921 \cdot 2^{150}$	$1.264 \cdot 2^{302}$	$1.247 \cdot 2^{441}$
	This work	$1.268 \cdot 2^{149}$	$1.092 \cdot 2^{142}$	$1.385 \cdot 2^{291}$	73,281	$1.043 \cdot 2^{149}$	$1.409 \cdot 2^{300}$	$1.511 \cdot 2^{433}$

Cost is an indicator that can be compared with the security criteria provided by NIST. After comparing with the quantum attack cost ($\mathbf{2^{157}}$, $\mathbf{2^{221}}$, and $\mathbf{2^{285}}$) described in Sect. 2.4, it can be confirmed that all instances of ARIA attain the suitable level of security for their respective key sizes. We conduct evaluations, including metrics such as $TD\text{-}M$ cost, where $TD\text{-}M$ cost represents the multiplication of Toffoli depth(TD) and qubit count(M), to assess these trade-offs.

To take NIST's MAXDEPTH (mentioned in Sect. 2.4) into account, one cannot disregard parallelization. When comparing Full depth(FD) and NIST MAXDEPTH in Table 5, only ARIA-128 meets the MAXDEPTH requirement (ARIA-128 $< 2^{96}$). If the full depth (FD) exceeds MAXDEPTH, as in the case of ARIA-192 and ARIA-256, reducing FD by FD/MAXDEPTH requires Grover instances to operate in parallel by a factor of FD^2/MAXDEPTH^2. In this scenario, while MAXDEPTH can be decreased, M increases by a factor of FD^2/MAXDEPTH^2, resulting in a final value of $(FD^2/\text{MAXDEPTH}^2) \times M$. Ultimately, $FD^2 - M$ represents the cost of $FD - M$, considering parallelization for Grover search. Similar to $TD^2 - M$, $FD^2 - M$ also denotes the cost of $TD - M$, considering parallelization for Grover search. Additionally, $FD^2\text{-}G$ represents the cost of $FD\text{-}G$ considering Grover search parallelization, where $FD^2\text{-}G$ is obtained by multiplying FD^2 by the number of total gates (G). However, according to [12,15], parallelization of Grover's key search is highly inefficient; therefore, instead of directly imposing a MAXDEPTH limit on the cost, the focus should be on minimizing the costs of relevant metrics (e.g., $FD^2 - M, FD^2 - G$, $TD^2 - M$). The results for the relevant metrics ($FD^2 - M, FD^2 - G$) can be found in Table 5.

Without considering MAXDEPTH, it may appear that optimization has not been achieved, as the increase in qubits(M) is perceived to be more significant compared to the increase in full depth(FD). However, when observing the metric $FD^2 - M$, which accounts for MAXDEPTH, it is evident that optimization has indeed progressed compared to the previous results. In other words, when considering MAXDEPTH, our circuit showcases depth optimization while maintaining an appropriate trade-off with qubits.

5 Conclusion

In this paper, we propose optimized quantum circuit for ARIA, focusing on circuit depth optimization. We utilize various techniques such as optimized multiplication and squaring methods in binary fields, along with parallelization, to reduce both Toffoli and full depths while ensuring a reasonable number of qubits. As a result, our quantum circuit implementation for ARIA achieves the depth improvement of over 88.8% and Toffoli depth by more than 98.7% compared to the implementation proposed in Chauhan et al.'s SPACE'20 paper [2]. Based on our quantum circuits, we estimate the quantum resources and the cost of Grover's attacks for the proposed circuit. We then evaluate the security strength based on the criteria provided by NIST. We demonstrate that ARIA achieves post-quantum security levels 1, 3, and 5, respectively, for all key sizes: 128, 192, and 256 bits (according to the recent standards [20]). Additionally, we have shown that only ARIA-128 satisfies the MAXDEPTH limit. We discuss the metrics considering MAXDEPTH, and all of them have been identified as optimized compared to the compared paper's results.

Our future plan involves optimizing ARIA's quantum circuits further, with greater consideration for the MAXDEPTH limit.

Acknowledgment. This work was supported by the National Research Foundation of Korea (NRF) grant funded by the Korea government (MSIT). (No. RS-2023-00277994, Quantum Circuit Depth Optimization for ARIA, SEED, LEA, HIGHT, and LSH of KCMVP Domestic Cryptographic Algorithms, 80%) and this work was supported by Institute of Information & communications Technology Planning & Evaluation (IITP) grant funded by the Korea government(MSIT) (No. 2022-0-00627, Development of Lightweight BIoT technology for Highly Constrained Devices, 20%).

References

1. Amy, M., Maslov, D., Mosca, M., Roetteler, M., Roetteler, M.: A meet-in-the-middle algorithm for fast synthesis of depth-optimal quantum circuits. IEEE Trans. Comput. Aided Des. Integr. Circuits Syst. **32**(6), 818–830 (2013)

2. Chauhan, A.K., Sanadhya, S.K.: Quantum resource estimates of Grover's key search on ARIA. In: Batina, L., Picek, S., Mondal, M. (eds.) Security, Privacy, and Applied Cryptography Engineering. SPACE 2020. LNCS, vol. 12586, pp. 238–258. Springer, Cham (2020). https://doi.org/10.1007/978-3-030-66626-2_13

3. Cheung, D., Maslov, D., Mathew, J., Pradhan, D.K.: On the design and optimization of a quantum polynomial-time attack on elliptic curve cryptography. In: Kawano, Y., Mosca, M. (eds.) Theory of Quantum Computation, Communication, and Cryptography. TQC 2008. LNCS, vol. 5106, pp. 96–104. Springer, Berlin, Heidelberg (2008). https://doi.org/10.1007/978-3-540-89304-2_9

4. Chun, M., Baksi, A., Chattopadhyay, A.: Dorcis: depth optimized quantum implementation of substitution boxes. Cryptology ePrint Archive (2023)

5. Chung, D., Lee, S., Choi, D., Lee, J.: Alternative tower field construction for quantum implementation of the AES S-box. IEEE Trans. Comput. **71**(10), 2553–2564 (2021)

6. Dasu, V.A., Baksi, A., Sarkar, S., Chattopadhyay, A.: LIGHTER-R: optimized reversible circuit implementation for SBoxes. In: 32nd IEEE International System-on-Chip Conference (SOCC) 2019, pp. 260–265. IEEE (2019)

7. Fedorov, A., Steffen, L., Baur, M., da Silva, M.P., Wallraff, A.: Implementation of a Toffoli gate with superconducting circuits. Nature **481**(7380), 170–172 (2012)

8. Grassl, M., Langenberg, B., Roetteler, M., Steinwandt, R.: Applying Grover's algorithm to AES: quantum resource estimates (2015)

9. Itoh, T., Tsujii, S.: A fast algorithm for computing multiplicative inverses in GF (2m) using normal bases. Inf. Comput. **78**(3), 171–177 (1988)

10. Jang, K., Baksi, A., Kim, H., Seo, H., Chattopadhyay, A.: Improved quantum analysis of speck and LowMC (full version). Cryptology ePrint Archive (2022)

11. Jang, K., Baksi, A., Song, G., Kim, H., Seo, H., Chattopadhyay, A.: Quantum analysis of AES. Cryptology ePrint Archive (2022)

12. Jang, K., et al.: Quantum implementation of aim: aiming for low-depth. Cryptology ePrint Archive (2023)

13. Jang, K., Kim, W., Lim, S., Kang, Y., Yang, Y., Seo, H.: Optimized implementation of quantum binary field multiplication with toffoli depth one. In: You, I., Youn, T.Y. (eds.) Information Security Applications. WISA 2022. LNCS, vol. 13720, pp. 251–264. Springer, Cham (2023). https://doi.org/10.1007/978-3-031-25659-2_18

14. Jang, K., Song, G., Kim, H., Kwon, H., Kim, H., Seo, H.: Efficient implementation of present and gift on quantum computers. Appl. Sci. **11**(11), 4776 (2021)

15. Jaques, S., Naehrig, M., Roetteler, M., Virdia, F.: Implementing grover oracles for quantum key search on AES and LowMC. In: Canteaut, A., Ishai, Y. (eds.) Advances in Cryptology – EUROCRYPT 2020. EUROCRYPT 2020. LNCS, vol. 12106, pp. 280–310. Springer, Cham (2020). https://doi.org/10.1007/978-3-030-45724-2_10

16. Jones, C.: Low-overhead constructions for the fault-tolerant toffoli gate. Phys. Rev. A **87**(2), 022328 (2013)

17. Kwon, D., et al.: New block cipher: aria. In: Lim, J.I., Lee, D.H. (eds.) Information Security and Cryptology – ICISC 2003. ICISC 2003. LNCS, vol. 2971, pp. 432–445. Springer, Berlin, Heidelberg (2004). https://doi.org/10.1007/978-3-540-24691-6_32

18. Nielsen, M.A., Chuang, I.: Quantum computation and quantum information (2002)

19. NIST.: Submission requirements and evaluation criteria for the post-quantum cryptography standardization process (2016). https://csrc.nist.gov/CSRC/media/Projects/Post-Quantum-Cryptography/documents/call-for-proposals-final-dec-2016.pdf

20. NIST.: Call for additional digital signature schemes for the post-quantum cryptography standardization process (2022). https://csrc.nist.gov/csrc/media/Projects/pqc-dig-sig/documents/call-for-proposals-dig-sig-sept-2022.pdf
21. Ralph, T., Resch, K., Gilchrist, A.: Efficient Toffoli gates using qudits. Phys. Rev. A **75**(2), 022313 (2007)
22. Roy, S., Baksi, A., Chattopadhyay, A.: Quantum implementation of ASCON linear layer. Cryptology ePrint Archive (2023)
23. Selinger, P.: Quantum circuits of t-depth one. Phys. Rev. A **87**(4), 042302 (2013)
24. Xiang, Z., Zeng, X., Lin, D., Bao, Z., Zhang, S.: Optimizing implementations of linear layers. IACR Trans. Symmetric Cryptol. 120–145 (2020)
25. Yang, Y., Jang, K., Kim, H., Song, G., Seo, H.: Grover on SPARKLE. In: You, I., Youn, T.Y. (eds.) Information Security Applications. WISA 2022. LNCS, vol. 13720, pp. 44–59. Springer, Cham (2023). https://doi.org/10.1007/978-3-031-25659-2_4
26. Yongjin, J., Baek, S., Kim, J.: A novel framework to construct quantum circuits of s-boxes: applications to 4-bit S-Boxes (2023)

Finding Shortest Vector Using Quantum NV Sieve on Grover

Hyunji Kim[1], Kyoungbae Jang[1], Yujin Oh[1], Woojin Seok[2], Wonhuck Lee[2], Kwangil Bae[2], Ilkwon Sohn[2], and Hwajeong Seo[1(✉)]

[1] IT Department, Hansung University, Seoul, South Korea
`hwajeong84@gmail.com`
[2] Korea Institute of Science and Technology Information (KISTI), Seoul, South Korea
{`wjseok,livezone,kibae,d2estiny`}`@kisti.re.kr`

Abstract. Quantum computers, especially those with over 10,000 qubits, pose a potential threat to current public key cryptography systems like RSA and ECC due to Shor's algorithms. Grover's search algorithm is another quantum algorithm that could significantly impact current cryptography, offering a quantum advantage in searching unsorted data. Therefore, with the advancement of quantum computers, it is crucial to analyze potential quantum threats.

While many works focus on Grover's attacks in symmetric key cryptography, there has been no research on the practical implementation of the quantum approach for lattice-based cryptography. Currently, only theoretical analyses involve the application of Grover's search to various Sieve algorithms.

In this work, for the first time, we present a quantum NV Sieve implementation to solve SVP, posing a threat to lattice-based cryptography. Additionally, we implement the extended version of the quantum NV Sieve (i.e., the dimension and rank of the lattice vector). Our extended implementation could be instrumental in extending the upper limit of SVP (currently, determining the upper limit of SVP is a vital factor). Lastly, we estimate the quantum resources required for each specific implementation and the application of Grover's search.

In conclusion, our research lays the groundwork for the quantum NV Sieve to challenge lattice-based cryptography. In the future, we aim to conduct various experiments concerning the extended implementation and Grover's search.

Keywords: Shortest Vector Problem · Lattice based cryptography · Quantum NV Sieve · Quantum attack · Grover's search

1 Introduction

As outlined in IBM's roadmap[1], if a stable quantum computer with more than 10,000 qubits is developed, public key algorithms (such as Rivest, Shamir, Adle-

---

[1] https://www.ibm.com/quantum/roadmap.

© The Author(s), under exclusive license to Springer Nature Singapore Pte Ltd. 2024
H. Seo and S. Kim (Eds.): ICISC 2023, LNCS 14561, pp. 97–118, 2024.
https://doi.org/10.1007/978-981-97-1235-9_6

man (RSA) and Elliptic curve cryptography (ECC)) may be decrypted within polynomial time through Shor algorithm [1].

Additionally, If a search count of $O(2^k)$ on a classical computer is required, Grover's algorithm can find results with a maximum of $O(\sqrt{2^n})$ searches.

As quantum computers developed, the current cryptography system is under threat. Therefore, migration to a secure cryptography system and analysis of potential quantum attacks are very important issues.

Among the categories of post-quantum cryptography, there are lattice-based ciphers (e.g. LWE (Learning with Error)). Currently, much research has been conducted on estimating the cost of Grover attacks on symmetric key cryptography [2–6].

However, research on practical quantum attacks on lattice-based cryptography is lacking. As mentioned earlier, to establish a secure post-quantum security system, it is crucial to analyze potential quantum attacks on various cryptographic methods. Therefore, in this paper, we propose a quantum implementation for NV Sieve that can solve SVP (Shortest Vector Problem) for lattice-based cryptography. In addition, we present an implementation considering the dimension and rank expansion of the lattice and estimate the quantum cost for an attack through quantum NV Sieve.

1.1 Our Contributions

1. **For the first time in our knowledge, Quantum NV Sieve implementation to solve SVP**
   There is theoretical research that applies Grover's search to Sieve algorithms to solve SVP [7]. However, as far as we know, there is no implementation for these yet. In this work, we implement NV Sieve, an attack that can threaten lattice-based cryptosystems by solving SVP, as a quantum circuit. Through this, an oracle that can be applied to Grover's search is created.
2. **Extension implementation considering multiple conditions (dimension, rank) of lattice-based cryptography**
   In addition to the basic NV Sieve implementation, we present an extended implementation that takes into account the dimension and rank of the lattice. Our extended implementation can help raise the SVP upper limit that NV Sieve can solve.
3. **Resource estimation for Quantum NV Sieve logic and Grover's search**
   Grover's search algorithm has an advantage that can compute all possibilities at once. By applying Grover's search to NV Sieve, a solution that satisfies the condition can be found with quantum advantage. This approach requires an oracle, and our implementation can be used as an oracle for Grover's search. In this work, we estimate the quantum cost for each case-specific implementation.
   Based on our quantum circuits, we estimate the required quantum resources for Grover's search (on NV Sieve). This is affected by quantum resources and

the number of iterations. We get the appropriate iteration of Grover's search and also get the quantum cost of Grover's search attack.[2]

1.2 Organization of the Paper

The remainder of this paper is organized as follows. In Sect. 2, classical NV Sieve, SVP (Shortest Vector Problem), and background for quantum implementation are described. In Sect. 3, the implementation of the quantum NV Sieve is proposed. Section 4 demonstrates the results of the experiment and further discussion about that. Finally, Sect. 5 concludes the paper.

2 Prerequisites

2.1 Lattice

Lattice. Lattice (L) is a set of points made up of a linear combination of basis vectors (B). Since it is made up of points, there can be more than one shortest vector (e.g. $x, -x \in L$). Equation 1 represent a lattice, and x is an integer in Eq. 1, and $(b_1, ..., b_n)$ means the basis vector.

$$L(b_1, ..., b_n) = \Sigma_{i=1}^{n}(x_i \cdot b_i, x_i \in Z) \tag{1}$$

Basis. As noted earlier, the lattice is based on basis vectors. A basis vector (B) is a set of vectors that can constitute all lattice points. The vector (arrow sign) in Fig. 1 represents the basis in the lattice. Each vector (b_i) constituting the basis vector has a length of m and consists of a total of n components. Here, the length of each vector and the number of vectors constituting the basis vector, respectively, are called Dimension (m) and Rank (n). Generally, a full-rank lattice is used $(m = n)$.

Here, the basis vector consisting of one lattice is not unique. As shown in Fig. 1, the basis vectors on a lattice with the same lattice points are different. If a lattice is created with a vector created by multiplying one basis vector by another, the two basis vectors create the same lattice.

However, these basis vectors have a good basis and a bad basis. A good basis is generally composed of a short vector, and a bad basis is created by multiplying the good basis by a matrix such as an unimodular matrix[3] several times. Therefore, finding a bad basis from a good basis is easy because only matrix multiplication several times is required. However, in the opposite case, finding a good basis from a bad basis becomes a very difficult task. This can be seen as similar to generating a public key from a private key in public key cryptography. (i.e. obtaining a private key by factorizing a very large public key

---

[2] Detailed estimation of Grover's search while varying the parameters of the NV sieve remains for our future work.

[3] https://en.wikipedia.org/wiki/Unimodular_matrix.

Fig. 1. Two different basis vectors generating the same lattice.

into prime factors.) Similarly, in lattice-based cryptography, a bad basis is used as the public key, and a good basis is used as the private key. Here, the good basis and the bad basis are basis vectors that generate the same lattice. Constructing the public and private keys in this way makes it difficult to decrypt messages in lattice-based encryption.

2.2   Shortest Vector Problem (SVP)

SVP, known as the basic problem of lattice-based cryptography, is the problem of finding the shortest vector on a lattice that is not a zero vector. Miklo's Ajtai [8] revealed that SVP is an NP-hard problem. In addition, it was later revealed that it had almost the same level of difficulty as the Closest Vector Problem (CVP), which is another lattice-based problem. SVP is a problem of finding the shortest vector by using the basis of the lattice as input. However, the solution is not always unique because one vector can have an opposite vector with the same size.

When a bad basis vector is used as input, the difficulty of solving the SVP increases. If a good basis is used as an input, there is a high possibility that the shortest vector will be included in the already input good basis. If a bad basis is used, the opposite scenario occurs. Additionally, as the rank of the lattice (the number of vectors constituting the lattice) increases, it becomes more difficult to solve.

The lattice-based cryptography is generally used when the rank is 500 or higher. Therefore, solving lattice-based cryptography is a very challenging work. Furthermore, as mentioned earlier, one can easily derive a bad basis (public key) from a good basis (private key). However, it is difficult to find a good basis (private key) from a bad basis (public key) due to information asymmetry. Thus, solving lattice-based cryptography is challenging due to its reliance on one-wayness (the computation in one direction is straightforward but difficult in the reverse direction).

In this way, lattice-based cryptography is based on lattice problems (SVP, CVP, etc.), and the security level of lattice-based cryptography is based on the difficulty of solving the lattice problem. For example, RSA's security strength is based on the difficulty of prime factorization. In other words, lattice-based cryptography is designed by utilizing one-wayness such as information asymmetry.

To solve such lattice-based cryptography, the lattice problem must be solved. Solving SVP, a representative lattice problem, lattice-based cryptosystems such as LWE can be threatened.

Algorithms to Solve SVP. Several algorithms, such as AKS and Sieve, have been proposed to solve the lattice problem, which underpins lattice-based cryptography. However, these algorithms generally target low-dimensional lattices with a rank of about 50~60. There are also algorithms that target high-dimensional lattices, but finding the shortest vector in a high-dimensional lattice is a very difficult problem. Therefore, there's a need for an approximate algorithm that can reduce the problem from a high-dimensional lattice to a low-dimensional one. As a result, to solve SVP, an exact algorithm that accurately finds the shortest vector in the low-dimensional lattice is needed and important.

Approximate algorithms that reduce high-dimensional to low-dimensional lattice (e.g., Lenstra, Lenstra, and Lovász (LLL) [9], block Korkine-Zolotarev (BKZ) [10]) have also been widely studied. Also, it is efficient in high-dimension lattices. However, as shown in Fig. 2, the method for finding exactly short vectors belongs to the exact algorithm, and the best practical and theoretical SVP solution should be accurate and efficient in low dimensions. Therefore, for now, it is important to take an approach that accurately solves SVP in low dimensions. It is then important to determine the upper limit (highest dimension of lattice) that can be solved.

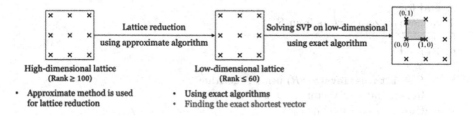

Fig. 2. Flow chart of approximate and exact algorithms for solving SVP.

2.3 Survey on the Exact Algorithms for SVP

Well-known exact algorithms include AKS [11] and NV Sieve [12]. AKS is the most famous early exact algorithm, but it has the disadvantage of using many parameters and having high time and space complexity. Moreover, due to the absence of optimal parameters, actual implementation, or analysis, it is deemed an impractical algorithm. Subsequently, NV Sieve, an exact algorithm, was introduced to address these limitations of AKS. It offers benefits such as reduced time and space complexity, practicality, and the possibility for actual implementation and evaluation. Additionally, building upon the NV Sieve algorithm, several

Sieve algorithms, including the List Sieve and Gaussian Sieve, have been presented [13–17].

However, only the theoretical complexity of the Sieve algorithm on quantum computers (using Grover's search) has been calculated [7]. There is no practical implementation or analysis for this.

2.4   NV Sieve Algorithm

Reasons and Overview for Selecting the NV Sieve Algorithm. NV Sieve is more practical and efficient than AKS and serves as the foundation for numerous Sieve algorithms. So, in our work, NV Sieve is selected as an exact algorithm for solving the SVP problem. Although there are algorithms with lower time and space complexity than NV Sieve, quantum computing can incur significant costs when implementing algorithms that require additional procedures. Of course, a simple algorithm is not necessarily efficient when executed on a quantum computer.

Algorithm 1. NV Sieve algorithm for finding short lattice vectors

---

Input: An reduced basis (B) in lattice (L) using the LLL algorithm, a sieve factor γ ($\frac{2}{3} < \gamma < 1$), S is an empty set, and a number N
Output: A non-zero short vector of L
1: **for** $i = 1$ to N **do**
2:      $S \leftarrow$ Sampling B using sampling algorithm
3: **end for**
4: Remove all zero vectors from S.
5: $S_0 \leftarrow S$
6: **Repeat**
7:      $S_0 \leftarrow S$
8:      $S \leftarrow$ latticesieve$(S, \gamma R)$ using Algorithm 2.
9:      Remove all zero vectors from S.
10: **until** S becomes an empty set.
11: **Return** $v_0 \in S_0$ such that $||v_0|| = \min||v||, v \in S_0$

Details of NV Sieve Algorithm. Algorithm 1 briefly shows the main process of NV Sieve. The goal of NV Sieve is to find the shortest vector excluding zero vectors while losing as few vectors as possible. The input is the basis vector of the lattice reduced through the approximate algorithm (i.e., LLL), and the output is the shortest vector, not the zero vector. As mentioned earlier, the shortest vector may not be one. In addition, γR, the sieve factor, is a geometric element in the range of $\frac{2}{3} < \gamma R < 1$, and the closer it is to 1, the better. The reduction range of the lattice, which will be explained later, is determined by the corresponding sieve factor.

The overall structure is as follows. First, a set S is generated by randomly sampling from the basis received as input. Next, the zero vector is removed from S to generate S_0, and then the `latticesieve` is repeatedly performed with S and γ as input. After this, the output vectors with zero vectors removed are stored in S_0, and the process is repeated until S becomes an empty set. Finally, it is completed by returning the shortest vector among the vectors belonging to S_0.

Algorithm 2. The `latticesieve` algorithm in NV Sieve

Input: A subset S in L and sieve factor γ ($0.666 < \gamma < 1$)
Output: S' (Short enough vector, not zero vector)
1: Initialize C, S' to empty set.
2: $R \leftarrow max_{v \in S}\|v\|$
3: **for** $v \in S$ **do**
4:     **if** $\|v\| \leq \gamma R$ **then**
5:         $S' \leftarrow S' \cup \{v\}$
6:     **else**
7:         **if** $\exists c \in C \|v - c\| \leq \gamma R$ **then**
8:             $S' \leftarrow S' \cup \{v - c\}$
9:         **else**
10:             $C \leftarrow C \cup \{v\}$
11:         **end if**
12:     **end if**
13: **end for**
14: **return** S'

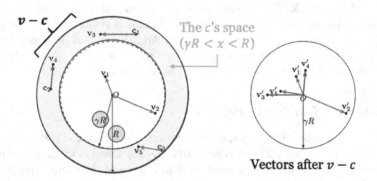

Fig. 3. The core logic in NV Sieve (See line 7 in Algorithm 2).

Algorithm 2 shows the lattice sieve algorithm in NV Sieve and shows the detailed process. This sieve algorithm is the core logic of NV Sieve, and its purpose is as follows.

- In order to minimize the loss for short vectors, a point on the lattice called c is randomly selected. c is a sufficient number of points on the lattice belonging to $\gamma R < x < R$ and belongs to the yellow area in Fig. 3.
- The search range (γR) is reduced by the sieve factor γ to obtain a vector shorter. Here, R means the maximum length among the vectors belonging to the vector set received as input.

The core logic of the NV sieve mentioned earlier in more detail is as follows.

1. First, initialize C and S'. Afterward, vectors with a length shorter than γR are stored in S'. (S' is used to store vectors within the γR range.)
2. However, there will be vectors longer than γR. For this, the process as in line 7 is performed to minimize loss for short vectors on the lattice, which is the goal of NV Sieve.
   A vector longer than γR is subtracted from a point on the lattice called c. If the result is shorter than γR, then it is stored in S'. If the length is longer than γR, it is stored in C. In other words, when the vector after subtraction starts from O (origin point), if it is within the range of γR, it is stored in S'.
3. Finally, by returning S', vectors with a length shorter than γR are selected. By performing this process repeatedly, sufficiently short vectors are obtained, and the shortest vector among them is found.

Important Factors Related to the Complexity. The parts that affect the complexity of NV Sieve's algorithm are as follows. The first part is measuring the number of points in c. There are a sufficiently large number of points on the lattice, and we need to find a point c that can be used to create a vector with a length shorter than γR. Therefore, it is important to find the number of c. Next, as the size of the initially given vector set S increases, complexity increases. As the rank of S increases, the number of c also increases because c is also a vector on the lattice and a subset of S. This is related to the complexity related to the number of c mentioned above. Additionally, as mentioned earlier, lattice problems with large ranks are difficult to solve, so the size of the target basis vector set affects the complexity of the algorithm.

2.5   Grover's Search Algorithm

Grover's search algorithm is a quantum search algorithm for tasks with n-bit complexity and has $O(\sqrt{2^n})$ of complexity ($O(2^n)$ for classical). The data (n-bit) for the target of the search must exist in a state of quantum superposition, so given by:

$$H^{\otimes n}|0\rangle^{\otimes n}(|\psi\rangle) = \left(\frac{|0\rangle + |1\rangle}{\sqrt{2}}\right) = \frac{1}{2^{n/2}} \sum_{x=0}^{2^n-1} |x\rangle \qquad (2)$$

Thanks to quantum advantage, all search targets are computed simultaneously as a probability.

Grover's algorithm consists of two modules: Oracle and Diffusion operator. Oracle is a quantum circuit that implements logic that can return a solution to the problem to be solved. Then it returns a solution by inverting the decision qubit at the end of the circuit as follows.

$$f(x) = \begin{cases} 1 \text{ if } Oracle_{\psi(n)} = Solution \\ 0 \text{ if } Oracle_{\psi(n)} \neq Solution \end{cases} \tag{3}$$

Afterwards, the probability of the returned solution is amplified through the diffusion operator. By repeating this process, the probability of observing the correct solution is increased. The number of such repetitions is expressed as Grover iteration. The most important thing in Grover's search is the optimal implementation of the quantum circuit that designs the oracle.

The diffusion operator has a fixed implementation method and is often excluded from resource estimation [5,18] because the overhead is so small that it is negligible. Therefore, the final efficiency is determined depending on the quantum circuit in the oracle.

2.6 Quantum Circuit

Qubits. A qubit (quantum bit) is the basic unit of computation in a quantum computer and can have probabilities of 0 and 1 at the same time (superposition). So, 2^n states can be expressed with n qubits. Additionally, qubits exist in a superposition state and are calculated, but are determined as a single classical value the moment they are measured. In quantum computing, classical bits are used to store the results of measuring the state of the qubit.

Quantum Gates. Quantum gates operate as logical gates in quantum circuits. By applying a quantum gate to a qubit, the state of the qubit can be controlled. There are several quantum gates (see Fig. 4). Each gate can be used to configure superposition, entanglement, invert, and copy, and can be utilized to perform various operations such as addition and multiplication.

3 Quantum NV Sieve for Solving SVP

3.1 System Overview

According to the results of theoretical calculations, Quantum NV Sieve with Grover's search is expected to have less time complexity than classical NV Sieve $(log_2^{0.415}$ to $log_2^{0.312})$ [7]. However, no implementation is presented. To the best of our knowledge, our work presents the first implementation of various cases of the NV Sieve algorithm for solving SVP using quantum circuits. However, given the current state of quantum computers in the Noisy Intermediate-Scale Quantum

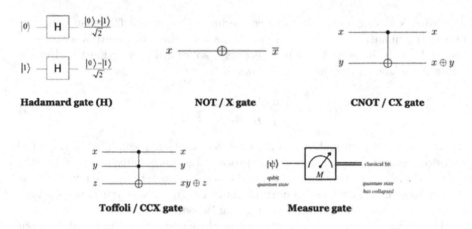

Fig. 4. Quantum gates.

(NISQ) era and the challenges encountered during implementation, achieving results akin to the theoretical complexity remains challenging. Starting with our work, we plan to further improve our approach, which we remain for our future work.

As noted earlier, solving SVP, the fundamental problem of lattice-based encryption, can threaten grid-based encryption systems (e.g., LWE). Furthermore, among several algorithms, the Exact algorithm, that accurately finds short vectors, is an important part of the process of solving lattice problems.

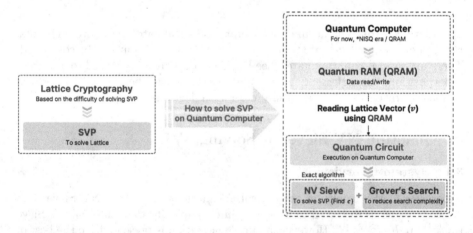

Fig. 5. Overview of Quantum NV Sieve.

We implemented the NV Sieve algorithm, which solves the SVP problem among several lattice problems (e.g., SVP, CVP, etc.), on a quantum computer.

Figure 5 shows the overview of the quantum NV Sieve algorithm. In other words, this is the overall relationship between the quantum NV Sieve we present and the configuration diagram for solving SVP on a quantum computer.

First, since Grover's search must be applied, the logic of the NV Sieve (oracle) must be implemented using the quantum circuit. In other words, since the purpose of NV Sieve is to find the short vector c that satisfies the condition ($\|v - c\| \leq \gamma R$), the NV Sieve logic for searching c must be implemented as an oracle. Then, Grover's search algorithm should be performed on the implemented oracle. The factors that determine the performance of NV Sieve in classical are finding the number of large numbers of c and the corresponding computational and memory complexity. However, when using quantum NV Sieve, it is possible to calculate numerous cases for c at once. Therefore, there are advantages in terms of computational and memory complexity.

Meanwhile, v, which is not the search target but is a vector on the lattice, needs to be loaded from quantum memory. However, it is difficult to access actual QRAM (Quantum RAM). In addition, many studies, such as [19], are conducted on the premise that queries can be made to QRAM. Therefore, in this implementation, QRAM is implemented as a very simple quantum circuit (Explicit QRAM: data is written directly to the quantum circuit, and the value is loaded from the corresponding memory qubit).

3.2 Implementation of NV Sieve on Quantum Circuit

We implement/design the quantum circuit for line 7 in Algorithm 2. It operates classically except where quantum NV sieve algorithms are used. In other words, quantum is applied to operations on a sufficiently large number of c. In a classical computer, we need to know how many c there are and perform a size comparison on all c. However, in the implementation of the quantum NV sieve, a size comparison is performed on all cases of c at once. Details are described in Algorithm 3.

The overall steps in Algorithm 3 are as follows:

1. **Data load from explicit QRAM (line 3):** It is difficult to actually access QRAM. Therefore, we implement a simple explicit QRAM on a quantum circuit. This is actually close to QROM (Quantum Read-only Memory) because it can only read data to be used.
2. **Prepare c in superposition state (line 4~5):** Apply the Hadamard gate to c, Grover's search target, and prepare it in a superposition state. Since v is not a search target, it doesn't make it a superposition state.
3. **Prepare $(sqr\_rR)^2$ (line 6): Prepare the squared γR.**
4. **Overflow handling (line 8~15):** To handle overflow that occurs during the calculation process, the highest bit of the data qubit is copied to the highest qubit. Through this, data expressed in 2-qubits is made to have the same value even when converted to 3-qubits.
5. **Complement function for signed vector (line 17~18):** For data involving signed vectors, the complement operation is utilized to repurpose

---

Algorithm 3. The quantum NV Sieve on the quantum circuit.

Input: Quantum circuit (QNV), A subset S in L and sieve factor γ ($\frac{2}{3} < \gamma < 1$)
Output: c_0, c_1

1: Initiate quantum registers and classical registers. $\triangleright$ *carry, qflag, sqr_result*, etc.
2: // Input setting (Each vector is allocated 3 qubits to address the overflow)
3: $v_0, v_1 \leftarrow$ Data load from memory qubits
4: $QNV.Hadamard(c_0)$
5: $QNV.Hadamard(c_1)$
6: $QNV.x(sqr\_rR[i])$ $\triangleright 0 \leq i < 6$

7: // To address the overflow of target qubits
8: $vflag[0] \leftarrow QNV.cx(v_0[1], vflag[0])$
9: $v_0[2] \leftarrow QNV.cx(vflag[0], v_0[2])$

10: $cflag[0] \leftarrow QNV.cx(c_0[1], cflag[0])$
11: $c_0[2] \leftarrow QNV.cx(cflag[0], c_0[2])$

12: $vflag[1] \leftarrow QNV.cx(v_1[1], vflag[1])$
13: $v_1[2] \leftarrow QNV.cx(vflag[1], v_1[2])$

14: $cflag[1] \leftarrow QNV.cx(c_1[1], cflag[1])$
15: $c_1[2] \leftarrow QNV.cx(cflag[1], c_1[2])$

16: // Two's complement for subtraction using adder
17: $c_0 \leftarrow$ Two's complement$(QNV, c_0, qflag0, zero)$
18: $c_1 \leftarrow$ Two's complement$(QNV, c_1, qflag1, zero)$

19: // $v + \bar{c}$
20: $c_0 \leftarrow$ Addition$(QNV, v_0, c_0, carry)$
21: $c_1 \leftarrow$ Addition$(QNV, v_1, c_1, carry)$

22: // Two's complement for correct squaring
23: $c_0 \leftarrow$ Two's complement_negative$(QNV, c_0, qflag2, carry, zero)$
24: $c_1 \leftarrow$ Two's complement_negative$(QNV, c_1, qflag3, carry, zero)$

25: // Duplicating qubit for squaring
26: $dup\_c_0 \leftarrow QNV.cx(c_0, dup\_c_0)$
27: $dup\_c_1 \leftarrow QNV.cx(c_1, dup\_c_1)$

28: // Squaring elements of vectors
29: $sqr\_result[2] \leftarrow$ Squaring$(QNV, c_0, dup\_c_0, sqr\_result[0], sqr\_result[1], sqr\_result[2], carry, 6)$
30: $sqr\_result[5] \leftarrow$ Squaring$(QNV, c_1, dup\_c_1, sqr\_result[3], sqr\_result[4], sqr\_result[5], carry, 6)$

31: // Addition for squared results to calculate the size of the vector
32: $sqr\_result[5] \leftarrow$ Addition$(QNV, sqr\_result[2], sqr\_result[5], carry, 6)$

33: // Two's complement for subtraction using adder
34: $sqr\_result[5] \leftarrow$ Two's complement_6bit$(QNV, sqr\_result[5], qflag4, carry, zero, zero1, zero2)$

35: // Size comparison between $(rR)^2$ and $(||v - c||)^2$ $\triangleright ((rR)^2 - (||v - c||)^2)$
36: $sqr\_result[5] \leftarrow$ Addition$(QNV, sqr\_rR, sqr\_result[5], carry, 6)$ $\triangleright$ No square root
37: **return** c_0, c_1

---

the adder as a subtractor. When comparing vector magnitudes at the conclusion of the quantum circuit, the complement operation is currently applied solely to positive vectors.

6. **Three-qubit addition (line 20~21):** For vector elements $(v+\bar{c})$, a 3-qubit ripple carry adder is applied between v and the complements of c.

7. **Apply complement function for 3-qubits to ensure correct square value (line 23~24):** In the complement system, 11_2 is -1, but if the complement operation for negative numbers is not performed before the square operation, 11_2 is recognized as 3. Then, the result is 9. Therefore the complement operation must be applied for the correct result of squaring.

8. **Duplicate the target qubits for squaring (line 26~27):** In a quantum circuit, performing calculations on identical qubits is not feasible; therefore, the value must be copied to a different qubit.

9. **Squaring each element to calculate the size of the vector (line 29~30):** The size of a vector is the root of the sum of the squares of each element. However, in our oracle only size comparison between γR and $||v-c||$ is required. Therefore, the root operation is removed in our approach. So we only need the squaring operation of the vector at this stage.

10. **6-qubit addition of each element of the vector after squaring (line 32):** To calculate the size of a vector, a square operation is required for each element.

11. **6-qubit complement for positive values (line 34):** The value after squaring is naturally a positive value. However, as in the previous part of the quantum circuit, we perform a complement operation to use the adder as a subtractor. Here, since it is the value after squaring a 3-qubit vector, a complement operation on 6-qubits must be performed.

12. **Size comparison through 6-qubit addition for $(\gamma R)^2$ and $(\overline{||v-c||^2})$ (line 36):** As mentioned earlier, the size of the vector can be obtained by performing the root operation. However, in our method, since the only purpose is size comparison, the root operation is not performed.

13. **Check the MSB (Most Significant Bit):** We have to check the MSB of the result value performed in step 13. If MSB is 0, $(\gamma R)^2$ is larger than $\overline{||v-c||^2}$. Therefore, MSB of 0 means that $||v-c||^2$ is a short vector that falls within the range of the condition. Therefore, we can add vector $v-c$ to the list that stores short vectors (Classical).

Conversely, if MSB is 1, it means that it is a negative sign, which means that it is a vector that does not satisfy the condition. Therefore, it is not added to the short vector list.

Implementation Details for Core Functions in Quantum NV Sieve

– **Data load and input Setting $(v, c, (\gamma R)^2)$:** In our implementation, we use a simple QRAM structure. After allocating a memory qubit for value storage, the values are stored in the corresponding memory qubit. Afterward, the cx gate is used to read the values stored in the memory qubit, and the values are loaded into the input vector v. In other words, it is copying values from quantum memory to input qubits for the oracle. Additionally, Grover's search is repeated for each v, and v is not a search target, so it is not prepared in a superposition state.

Fig. 6 shows the input setting process for c, the search target. What must be found through Grover's search algorithm is the c value that satisfies the condition, and the $v - c$ vector at that time must be returned. Therefore, the Hadamard gate is applied to all qubits for c, generating a superposition state with the same probability of 0 and 1.

Next, a process is needed to set $(\gamma R)^2$ required for the conditional expression. This applies the x gate to the qubit to express 1 (the same as setting the v value). However, the γR is determined in each iteration. So, in our implementation, its squaring value is calculated in a classical method and then set as input. Therefore, since it is a square value for 2 qubit data, 4 qubits are allocated.

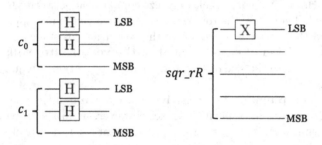

Fig. 6. Preparation c (c_0 and c_1) and $(\gamma R)^2$ (sqr_rR).

- **Overflow handling:** In this work, we will cover cases where overflow may occur during the NV Sieve calculation process. When the dimension is 2, there are cases where 2-qubits are exceeded during the calculation. Therefore, the calculation of NV Sieve is performed by upscaling to 3-qubit. Figure 7 shows the quantum circuit for the overflow handling process. For example, if the dimension is 2, data can be represented by two qubits. Therefore, the value of the second qubit (with an index of qubit is 1) is copied to the $qflag$. Afterward, upscaling is completed by copying the $qflag$ to the highest qubit that is set to 0. Through this process, the value expressed through 3 qubits can be expressed equally with 2 qubits.
- **Two's Complement (2-qubit, 4-qubit, positive and negative cases):** Fig. 8 shows the quantum circuit for 2's complement for positive values. As mentioned earlier, an additional qubit (ancilla qubit, $qflag$) is needed as a control qubit. When the target qubit to which the complement will be applied is c, the MSB is $c[1]$ (lowest qubit). Therefore, the value of the lower qubit is copied to the control qubit through the cx gate. Here, bit inversion and addition of LSB and 1 must be performed only when the value is positive. However, if MSB is zero, the value of the control qubit is 0, so the value of the

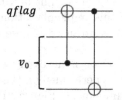

Fig. 7. Upscaling quantum circuit to handle the overflow.

control qubit must be inverted. But, after applying the x gate to $qflag$, the value of the control qubit is 1, so complement logic is performed. After bit inversion, to add the value of 1 to the LSB, create a new qubit array, input $qflag$ as the lowest bit first, and then append the value of 0. Afterwards, addition is performed through a 2 qubit adder between the 1's complement (2 qubits) and the new qubit array (2 qubits).

The quantum circuit for 2's complement for the negative values is performed to calculate the correct squaring on the signed data. This uses control qubits like two's complement when positive. However, for negative numbers, the MSB itself is 1, so there is no need to apply the x gate to $qflag$ (omit the x gate for $qflag$). Therefore, the bit is inverted through the cx gate without additional work. Afterward, the process for adding 1 to LSB is also performed in the same way.

The 2's complement quantum circuit for 4 qubits is similar to the 2-qubit complement quantum circuit, which is performed only when the number is positive. However, since it is 4 qubits, the MSB is $c[3]$ (Only the index of MSB is different). Therefore, after copying the value to $qflag$, apply the x gate to invert all bits. Afterwards, a new qubit with the state of $[0,0,0,1]$ is assigned and a 4-qubit addition is performed. Through this, 2's complement operations on 4 qubits can be performed.

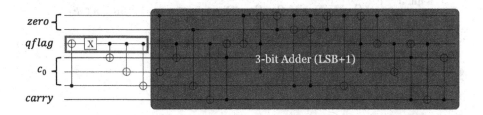

Fig. 8. Two's complement quantum circuit for a positive value (3-qubit).

– **Addition:** Addition is a very important and basic operation among quantum circuit operations. In this implementation, Ripple-Carry Adders such as 3-qubit and 4-qubit adders are used. These are the method proposed in Cuccaro's paper [20].

– **Squaring:** The square operation is necessary to find the size of the vector. An integer square operation is performed on the value converted to a positive number through the 2's complement. Figure 9 depicts the square operation. The squaring is equivalent to multiplying the same value, so a and b are the same value. However, operations using the same qubit repeatedly are impossible in quantum circuits. In other words, as shown in Fig. 9, the value a must be copied to another qubit (b) through the cx gate. Additionally, performing a multiplication on 3 qubits affects up to 6 qubits, so two 6-qubit arrays (ab and ba) are created to store the result.

The process is as follows. First, multiply a and b, which represent the same value, like integer multiplication. However, all elements are qubits and therefore have a value of 0 or 1. If even one element is 0, the result value is 0, and only if both elements are 1, the result value is 1. These operations correspond to the ccx (Toffoli) gate. Therefore, the ccx gate is applied to all elements of a and b. Afterward, the results are saved in an appropriate location. Here, the location where the calculation results are saved gray circle in each array. In addition, the results of 6-qubit addition are stored in *Second* and *Third* array in Fig. 9. However, since *First*, *Second* and *Third* are 6-qubit arrays, the top three qubits of *First* are set to 0, and the remainders of *Second* are set to 0. Finally, the square operation is completed by applying a 6-qubit adder to *First*, *Second* and *Third*. The adder used is CDKM adder, an in-place ripple carry adder, so the final result value is stored in *Third*.

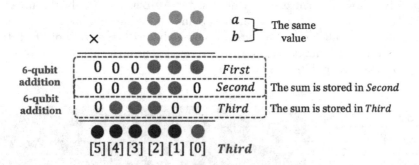

Fig. 9. The integer squaring for 3-qubits.

3.3   Implementation for Dimension Expansion

Increasing dimension means that the range of bits that can be expressed by each element of the vector increases. In other words, operations on 2 qubits must be changed to operations on n ($n < 2$) qubits. In our work, we implement the case where the dimension is increased to 4. This indicates that our implementation is scalable in terms of dimensionality. In this case, the 3-qubit adder must become a 5-qubit adder, and the 3-qubit two's complement must become a 5-qubit two's complement. Therefore, in accordance with this increased data range, the range of functions for calculations must also be expanded.

3.4 Implementation for Rank Expansion

Even if the rank of the input vector increases, the formula for calculating the size of the vector remains the same. Therefore, it is implemented by allocating additional qubits as needed depending on the number of extended rank. Neither the type nor the scope of the operation used changes. The same operation is performed on the elements of the new vector. In the case of the addition, it can be implemented by adding another vector to the result of adding two vectors. Hence, our implementation offers scalability as the rank of the input lattice vector increases.

4   Evaluation

4.1   Experiment Environment

Our implementation utilized Qiskit[4], a quantum computing platform. The cloud platform provides IBM's real hardware and simulators. Additionally, programming can be possible using Python and Qiskit's grammar, allowing access to the quantum computing environment. We use the 'matrix_product_state' simulator, which can provide relatively large-scale qubits.

4.2   Result of Quantum NV Sieve

Table 1 shows the results of each step of our implementation for quantum NV Sieve. The complement expression of x is $\bar{x}$, and the abbreviation of the previous step is sometimes used in the next step to prevent the output term from becoming long. On the other hand, we present results for Default, Ex_DIM, and Ex_RANK. The extension to dimension (Ex_DIM) increases the length of the vector ($v_0 = \{0,1\}$ to $v_0 = \{0,0,0,1\}$). The extension to rank (Ex_RANK) increases the number of elements ($V = \{v_0, v_1\}$ to $V = \{v_0, \ldots, v_n\}$).

Through the result of quantum NV Sieve logic, we present a scalable implementation that takes into account various situations on the lattice. Correct values are output at all steps. This allows us to verify the suitability of our quantum NV Sieve for practical implementation. Furthermore, this extended implementation can help raise the SVP upper limit that NV Sieve can solve. In our work, we confirmed that the NV Sieve algorithm operates accurately on a quantum circuit. Based on our work, we can expect that the possibility of solving the larger problem will increase as the scale of quantum computers expands.

---

[4] https://qiskit.org/.

Table 1. Results from each step of quantum NV Sieve to check whether it has been implemented correctly. (`Default`: 2-dimension and 2-rank, `Ex_DIM`: 4-dimension and 2-rank, `Ex_RANK`: 2-dimension and 3-rank)

Output	Default	Ex_DIM	Ex_RANK
v_0	000	00111	000
v_1	001	00011	001
v_2	None	None	001
c_0	001	11001	001
c_1	000	00101	001
c_2	None	None	111
$(\gamma R)^2$	000001	0000000001	000001
$\overline{c_0}$ (when positive)	111	11001	111
$\overline{c_1}$ (when positive)	000	11011	111
$\overline{c_2}$ (when positive)	None	None	111
$v_0 + \overline{c_0}: (vc_0)$	111	00000	111
$v_1 + \overline{c_1}: (vc_1)$	001	11110	000
$v_2 + \overline{c_2}: (vc_2)$	None	None	000
$(vc_0)^2$	001	0000000000	001
$(vc_1)^2$	001	0000000100	000
$(vc_2)^2$	None	None	000
$(vc_0)^2 + (vc_1)^2 + (vc_2)^2: (Sum_v c)$	000010	0000000100	000001
$\overline{Sum_v c}$	111110	1111111100	111111
$\gamma R + \overline{Sum_v c}$	111111	1111111101	000000
MSB	1	1	0
Shots	100		

4.3   Resource Estimation of Quantum NV Sieve

Table 2 shows the resource estimation of quantum NV Sieve. Since this is a resource estimate for Oracle, the result also includes resources for reverse operation. Contrary to the traditional Grover's search that identifies a single solution, the NV Sieve yields multiple outcomes. That is, it may produce multiple short vectors meeting the condition, with probabilities varying based on the number of shots. Therefore, determining the correct Grover's iteration is a very important issue.

The required quantum resources increase as the rank and dimension of the target vector increase. Even if the dimension is doubled, the total quantum cost increases by about 8.38 times, and even if the rank increases by just one, the total cost increases by about 1.98 times. However, a real lattice will have larger dimensions and ranks. Therefore, if the dimension and rank increase simultaneously, the quantum cost of the quantum NV Sieve is expected to increase enormously.

$$2 \cdot \#gates \cdot FD \cdot iter \tag{4}$$

Additionally, when applying Grover, the total number of gates ($\#gates$) mentioned in Table 2 must be multiplied by full depth (FD). Then, we need to multiply by 2 (reverse operation) and multiply by the number of Grover's iterations ($iter$). In other words, the formula for calculating Grover's attack cost is as shown in Eq. 4. That is, in addition to quantum resources (i.e. the number of gates and circuit depth), Grover's iteration affects the attack cost. Table 3 is calculated from Table 2 and Eq. 4. Table 3 shows the required quantum resources for Grover's search on NV Sieve. The number of qubits in every case increases by 1 because of the decision qubit. And, we get the appropriate iteration for these cases. Therefore, we calculate Grover's search cost on NV Sieve (Default, Ex_RANK and Ex_DIM).

Table 2. Resource Estimation of Quantum NV Sieve oracle.

Case	#CNOT	#1qCliff	#T	T-depth	full depth	#Qubit
Default	291	69	124	396	1126	74
Ex_RANK	420	90	181	576	1631	105
Ex_DIM	685	224	296	878	2342	179

Table 3. Required quantum resources for Grover's search on NV Sieve.

Case	Total gates	Full depth	T-depth	Quantum cost	#Qubit
Default	972	2259	792	2195748	75
Ex_RANK	1403	3271	1152	4589213	106
Ex_DIM	2436	4714	1756	11483304	180

※: The appropriate iteration is 1.

4.4 Further Discussion

According to our implementation mentioned above, it is expected that quantum gain can be obtained through Grover's search. Of course, there will certainly be implementation challenges as follows. Also, in the current quantum computing environment, it is believed that there will be many difficulties from an implementation perspective to derive results similar to the theoretically proposed complexity of the quantum NV Sieve.

- **Grover's iteration:** Since iteration affects the cost, finding an iteration for a problem that has multiple solutions is the most important challenge in the practical implementation of Quantum NV Sieve. In this work, we get the proper iteration that ensures that only the correct answer is derived. We are conducting experiments on other cases (other extended implementations), and the results will be published in future research.

- **Increase the upper limit:** The important thing to solve the current SVP is to accurately find short vectors and increase the upper limit of the dimension that can be solved. In other words, the Sieve algorithm belongs to the exact algorithm, and it is important to solve it accurately starting from low dimensions. Therefore, we should start experimenting with low dimensions and ranks, as we do now, and then work our way up to higher limits.

- **Optimizing the oracle circuit:** In order to improve the efficiency of the quantum NV Sieve and maximize the benefits that arise from applying quantum, it is thought that optimal implementation of the oracle will be important. In other words, it appears that the optimal implementation of the oracle (NV Sieve quantum circuit), which determines the efficiency of quantum costs in Grover's search, must be progressed to solve SVP on a higher-dimensional and rank lattice and obtain greater quantum advantages.

- **NISQ era:** As the resource estimation results indicate, quite a bit of attack cost is required despite the small dimensions and rank. Therefore, it is believed that there will be limitations in allowing general users to treat lattice vectors with higher rank and dimension. In other words, it is thought that solving SVP for high dimensions ($50 \sim 60$ dimensions) such as classical is difficult for now.

5   Conclusion

In conclusion, there are quantum threats to traditional cryptographic systems, especially as quantum computing technology advances. While the most of research has focused on the potential impact of Grover's algorithm on symmetric key cryptography, the field of quantum attacks on lattice-based cryptography on Grover's search remains underexplored.

To address this gap and solve SVP on quantum computers, our work introduces a practical implementation of Quantum NV Sieve, designed to solve the SVP for hacking lattice-based cryptography. This implementation is an oracle that is a vital component of Grover's search algorithm. Furthermore, our work extends the Quantum NV Sieve implementation to handle various conditions (i.e., expansion of dimensions and rank of the lattice) thereby increasing its applicability and impact.

We estimate the quantum resources required for each case-specific implementation (oracle) and predict the cost of Grover's attacks when applied in conjunction with their Quantum NV Sieve. Like this, in a rapidly evolving quantum field, our research addresses the new potential quantum threats practically.

In our future work, we plan to find the correct Grover's iteration on other extended cases in the condition that there are multiple solutions, and successfully sieve the short vectors.

References

1. Shor, P.W.: Algorithms for quantum computation: discrete logarithms and factoring. In: Proceedings 35th Annual Symposium on Foundations of Computer Science, pp. 124–134. IEEE (1994)
2. Jang, K., Choi, S., Kwon, H., Kim, H., Park, J., Seo, H.: Grover on Korean block ciphers. Appl. Sci. **10**(18), 6407 (2020)
3. Jang, K., Choi, S., Kwon, H., Seo, H.: Grover on speck: quantum resource estimates, Cryptology ePrint Archive (2020)
4. Jang, K., Song, G., Kim, H., Kwon, H., Kim, H., Seo, H.: Efficient implementation of present and gift on quantum computers. Appl. Sci. **11**(11), 4776 (2021)
5. Jang, K., Baksi, A., Kim, H., Song, G., Seo, H., Chattopadhyay, A.: Quantum analysis of AES. Cryptology ePrint Archive (2022)
6. Rahman, M., Paul, G.: Grover on katan: quantum resource estimation. IEEE Trans. Quantum Eng. **3**, 1–9 (2022)
7. Laarhoven, T., Mosca, M., Van De Pol, J.: Finding shortest lattice vectors faster using quantum search. Des. Codes Crypt. **77**, 375–400 (2015)
8. Ajtai, M.: The shortest vector problem in L2 is NP-hard for randomized reductions. In: Proceedings of the Thirtieth Annual ACM Symposium on Theory of Computing, pp. 10–19 (1998)
9. Nguyen, P.Q., Vallée, B.: The LLL Algorithm. Springer, Heidelberg (2010). https://doi.org/10.1007/978-3-642-02295-1
10. Schnorr, C.-P., Euchner, M.: Lattice basis reduction: improved practical algorithms and solving subset sum problems. Math. Program. **66**, 181–199 (1994)
11. Ajtai, M., Kumar, R., Sivakumar, D.: A sieve algorithm for the shortest lattice vector problem. In: Proceedings of the Thirty-Third Annual ACM Symposium on Theory of Computing, pp. 601–610 (2001)
12. Nguyen, P.Q., Vidick, T.: Sieve algorithms for the shortest vector problem are practical. J. Math. Cryptol. **2**(2), 181–207 (2008)
13. Wang, X., Liu, M., Tian, C., Bi, J.: Improved Nguyen-Vidick heuristic sieve algorithm for shortest vector problem. In: Proceedings of the 6th ACM Symposium on Information, Computer and Communications Security, pp. 1–9 (2011)
14. Zhang, F., Pan, Y., Hu, G.: A three-level sieve algorithm for the shortest vector problem. In: Lange, T., Lauter, K., Lisonek, P. (eds.) Selected Areas in Cryptography – SAC 2013. SAC 2013. LNCS, vol. 8282, pp. 29–47. Springer, Berlin, Heidelberg (2014). https://doi.org/10.1007/978-3-662-43414-7_2
15. Laarhoven, T.: Sieving for shortest vectors in lattices using angular locality-sensitive hashing. In: Gennaro, R., Robshaw, M. (eds.) Advances in Cryptology – CRYPTO 2015. CRYPTO 2015. LNCS, vol. 9215, pp. 3–22. Springer, Berlin, Heidelberg (2015). https://doi.org/10.1007/978-3-662-47989-6_1
16. Becker, A., Gama, N., Joux, A.: Speeding-up lattice sieving without increasing the memory, using sub-quadratic nearest neighbor search. Cryptology ePrint Archive (2015)
17. Micciancio, D., Voulgaris, P.: Faster exponential time algorithms for the shortest vector problem. In: Proceedings of the Twenty-First Annual ACM-SIAM Symposium on Discrete Algorithms, pp. 1468–1480. SIAM (2010)
18. Jaques, S., Naehrig, M., Roetteler, M., Virdia, F.: Implementing Grover oracles for quantum key search on AES and LowMC. In: Canteaut, A., Ishai, Y. (eds.) Advances in Cryptology – EUROCRYPT 2020. EUROCRYPT 2020. LNCS, vol. 12106, pp. 280–310. Springer, Cham (2020). https://doi.org/10.1007/978-3-030-45724-2_10

19. Kaplan, M., Leurent, G., Leverrier, A., Naya-Plasencia, M.: Quantum differential and linear cryptanalysis, arXiv preprint arXiv:1510.05836 (2015)
20. Cuccaro, S.A., Draper, T.G., Kutin, S.A., Moulton, D.P.: A new quantum ripple-carry addition circuit, arXiv preprint quant-ph/0410184 (2004)

Experiments and Resource Analysis of Shor's Factorization Using a Quantum Simulator

Junpei Yamaguchi[1]([✉]), Masafumi Yamazaki[1], Akihiro Tabuchi[1],
Takumi Honda[1], Tetsuya Izu[1], and Noboru Kunihiro[2]

[1] Fujitsu Limited, Kanagawa, Japan
{j-yamaguchi,izu}@fujitsu.com
[2] University of Tsukuba, Tsukuba, Japan

Abstract. Shor's algorithm on actual quantum computers has succeeded only in factoring small composite numbers such as 15 and 21,
and simplified quantum circuits to factor the specific integers are used
in these experiments. In this paper, we factor 96 RSA-type composite
numbers up to 9-bit using a quantum computer simulator. The largest
composite number $N = 511$ was factored in approximately 2 h on the
simulator. In our experiments, we implement Shor's algorithm with basic
circuit construction, which does not require complex tricks to reduce the
number of qubits, and we give some improvements to reduce the number of gates, including MIX-ADD method. This is a flexible method
for selecting the optimal ADD circuit which minimizes the number of
gates from the existing ADD circuits for each of the many ADD circuits
required in Shor's algorithm. Based on our experiments, we estimate
the resources required to factor 2048-bit integers. We estimate that the
Shor's basic circuit requires 2.19×10^{12} gates and 1.76×10^{12} depth when
10241 qubits are available, and 2.37×10^{14} gates and 2.00×10^{14} depth
when 8194 qubits are available.

Keywords: Shor's algorithm · integer factorization · quantum
computer · quantum computer simulator

1 Introduction

The security of RSA, one of the standardized public key cryptosystems, is based
on the difficulty of the integer factorization problem of large composite numbers.
The current factorization record by a classical computer is the factorization of an
829-bit integer [6], so that RSA with larger than 2048-bit integer is considered
to be secure for the time being. On the other hand, it is known that the integer
factorization problem can be solved in polynomial time by Shor's algorithm
by using an ideal quantum computer [18]. Some factorization experiments on
quantum computers by using Shor's algorithm have been reported only for $N =$
15 and 21 [1,13–17] because of the difficulty of realizing ideal quantum computers

© The Author(s), under exclusive license to Springer Nature Singapore Pte Ltd. 2024
H. Seo and S. Kim (Eds.): ICISC 2023, LNCS 14561, pp. 119–139, 2024.
https://doi.org/10.1007/978-981-97-1235-9_7

– quantum computers free from the limitation of the number of quantum bits (qubits) and the noise on the qubits[1]. To make matters worse, these experiments used the simplified Shor's circuits in which qubits and gates are reduced as much as possible by using the properties of the integers to be factored and their factors to be found. Since such experiments do not lead to accurate quantum resource estimation, the implementation of Shor's algorithm which can factor general composite numbers and its resource evaluation based on factoring experiments are required.

Various quantum circuits of Shor's algorithm for general composite numbers have been proposed. Kunihiro summarized basic circuits [12], which use $2n$ controlling qubits as a 1st qubit sequence for an n-bit composite number. On the other hand, advanced circuits have also been proposed [4,8]. These circuits use a technique to reduce the qubits of the 1st sequence from $2n$ to 1, which requires a complex quantum operation, repeatedly performing observations and quantum gate operations depending on the observation results.

Despite some efforts to estimate circuit resources for factoring 2048-bit integers with noisy qubits [8,9], it is too difficult to give exact estimates for factoring such large integers.

There are two major problems to break the situation. The first problem is the lack of computational resources, specifically, the number of qubits available on quantum computers. Although IBM has recently developed a 433-qubit processor [10], because of the effects of the noise, it is still difficult to process Shor's algorithm even on such computers. The second problem to be solved is the lack of experimental results for Shor's algorithm. To estimate the circuit resources for factoring 2048-bit integers, more experimental results on the same computing environments are needed.

Contribution of this Paper

This paper has three contributions. First, we implemented the basic circuits of Shor's algorithm applicable to general composite numbers, and succeeded in factoring 96 RSA-type composite numbers up to 9-bit on a quantum computer simulator running on a supercomputer. The largest composite number $N = 511$ was factorized in 2 h on the simulator. We used the simulator *mpiQulacs* developed by Fujitsu [11], a State Vector (SV) type simulator that records all qubit states in memory with no noise and allows to simulate an ideal quantum computation [11]. This paper focuses on the basic circuits because the current large scale quantum simulator cannot handle the advanced circuit due to its complexity. Our implementations are based on the well-known techniques [4,12], but we provide some bug-fixes, improvements (including the second contribution) and comparisons of required resource.

---

[1] Very recently, Yan et al. proposed a new quantum factoring algorithm which requires a fewer number of qubits [21] and gave a new estimation for factoring 2048-bit integers. However, the validity of the algorithm and the correctness of the estimation are under the analysis.

Second, we propose a flexible ADD method, MIX-ADD, to reduce the elementary gates and the depth of the basic circuit. The dominant circuit in Shor is Mod-EXP which computes a modular exponentiation $f_{a,N}(x) = a^x \bmod N$. Mod-EXP can be constructed from ADD circuits, and there are three well-known ADD circuits: R-ADD, GT-ADD, and Q-ADD [12]. The basic circuit requires $5n + 1$ qubits for R-ADD, and $4n + 2$ qubits for GT/Q/MIX-ADD for n-bit composite numbers to be factored. MIX-ADD reduces the gates and the depth by selecting the optimal ADD circuit which minimizes the number of gates from R/GT/Q-ADD for each ADD circuit called multiple times in Mod-EXP. Our analysis shows that R/MIX/Q/GT-ADD require more gates in this order for larger n. MIX-ADD can factor larger composite numbers more efficiently in an environment where the number of available qubits is limited like the present.

Finally, we gave estimations of the number of gates and the depth for the Shor's basic circuits. We generated some quantum circuits for $n = 8, \ldots, 24$, and evaluated the resources of the circuit. Based on these data, we estimated the circuit resources required to factor 2048-bit integers. In our estimation, the basic circuit requires 10241 qubits, 2.19×10^{12} gates and 1.76×10^{12} depth for R-ADD, and 8194 qubits, 2.37×10^{14} gates and 2.00×10^{14} depth for MIX-ADD.

The rest of the paper is organized as follows: Sect. 2 describes the construction of Shor's quantum circuit, in particular the modular exponentiation circuit Mod-EXP using ADD circuits. Then, in Sect. 3, concrete constructions of Mod-EXP from R-ADD, GT-ADD, Q-ADD and MIX-ADD are explained. Section 4 summarizes factoring experiments by Shor's quantum circuit using the quantum computer simulator including the estimation for 2048-bit integers.

2   Quantum Circuit of Shor's Algorithm

This section describes quantum circuits of Shor's algorithm for general composite numbers based on known techniques [4,12]. In this paper, we consider the following quantum gates as the elementary gates for evaluating the number of gates and the depth: 1-qubit gates including the Hadamard gate, NOT gate, the rotation gate and the phase-shift gate, Controlled NOT (C-NOT) gate, and Toffoli (C^2-NOT) gate.

2.1   Shor's Algorithm and Factorization

Suppose we want to factor an n-bit composite number N. For an integer a coprime to N, the order of a with regard to N is defined as the smallest positive integer r such that $a^r \equiv 1 \bmod N$. In 1994, Shor proposed a quantum algorithm to compute the order r of a with regard to N in polynomial time [18]. The integer N can be factored by using Shor's algorithm in the following way:

i) Choose an integer a from $\{2, \ldots, N - 1\}$. If $\gcd(a, N) \neq 1$ then output $\gcd(a, N)$ and terminate (since a factor of N larger than 1 is found).
ii) Compute the order r from a and N by quantum order finding algorithm.

iii) If r is even, $a^{r/2}+1 \not\equiv 0 \bmod N$ and $\gcd(a^{r/2}\pm 1, N) \neq 1$, output $\gcd(a^{r/2}\pm 1, N)$ and terminates. Otherwise, return step i).

Note that step i) and iii) can be proceeded by classical computers. On the other hand, step ii) can be computed by the quantum order finding algorithm on a quantum computer in the following way:

1. Generate an initial state $|\phi_0\rangle = |0\ldots0\rangle|0\ldots01\rangle$, where the 1st qubit sequence has m qubits, while the 2nd qubit sequence has n qubits.
2. Apply the Hadamard operation H_m to the 1st sequence:

$$|\phi_1\rangle = H_m(|\phi_0\rangle) = \frac{1}{\sqrt{2^m}} \sum_{x=0}^{2^m-1} |x\rangle|0\ldots01\rangle.$$

3. Apply the operation $U_{f_{a,N}}$ which corresponds to a modular exponentiation $f_{a,N}(x) = a^x \bmod N$, to the 2nd sequence:

$$|\phi_2\rangle = U_{f_{a,N}}(|\phi_1\rangle) = \frac{1}{\sqrt{2^m}} \sum_{x=0}^{2^m-1} |x\rangle|f_{a,N}(x)\rangle.$$

4. Apply the Inverse Quantum Fourier Transform to the 1st sequence.
5. Observe the 1st sequence, an approximation of a multiple of $2^m/r$ is obtained.
6. Repeat Step 1–5 until r can be estimated.

The parameter m is determined from the approximation precision in Step 5, $m = 2n$ is used usually and in this paper.

2.2   Construction of Mod-EXP from ADD

Above steps except Step 3 can be easily realized by elementary gates. On the other hand, Step 3 requires complex circuits called Mod-EXP [12]. This subsection describes how to realize Mod-EXP from elementary gates. In fact, Mod-EXP can be constructed from ADD circuits, by transforming Mod-EXP to the following circuits step-by-step:

- Mod-EXP(a) : $|x\rangle|1\rangle \rightarrow |x\rangle|a^x \bmod N\rangle$
- Mod-MUL(d) : $|y\rangle \rightarrow |dy \bmod N\rangle$
- Mod-PS(d) : $|y\rangle|t\rangle \rightarrow |y\rangle|t + dy \bmod N\rangle$
- Mod-ADD(d) : $|y\rangle \rightarrow |y + d \bmod N\rangle$
- ADD(d) : $|y\rangle \rightarrow |y + d\rangle$

Construction of Mod-EXP from Mod-MUL. For an exponent x represented in binary, namely, $x = \sum_{i=0}^{m-1} 2^i x_i$, a modular exponentiation Mod-EXP(a) is computed by a repetition of multiplying $d_i = a^{2^i} \bmod N$ and taking modulus by N, since $a^x \bmod N = a^{\sum_{i=0}^{m-1} 2^i x_i} \bmod N = \prod_{i=0}^{m-1} a^{2^i x_i} \bmod N$. In other words, Mod-EXP(a) can be computed by a repetition of the modular multiplication Mod-MUL(d_i) controlled by $|x_i\rangle$, so that Mod-EXP(a) requires m controlled-Mod-MULs, which is denoted by $C(x_i)$-Mod-MUL.

Construction of Mod-MUL from Mod-PS. The modular multiplication Mod-MUL(d) for an integer $0 \le d < N$ and an n-bit integer y can be computed by using modular product-sums Mod-PSs in the following way:

$$|y\rangle \underbrace{|0\ldots0\rangle}_{n} \xrightarrow{\text{Mod-PS}(d)} |y\rangle |0 + dy \bmod N\rangle \xrightarrow{\text{SWAP}} |dy \bmod N\rangle |y\rangle$$

$$\xrightarrow{\text{Mod-PS}(-d^{-1})} |dy \bmod N\rangle |y + (-d^{-1})(dy \bmod N) \bmod N\rangle$$

$$= |dy \bmod N\rangle |0\rangle.$$

Since $d_i = a^{2^i} \bmod N$ and $\gcd(a, N) = 1$, there always exists the inverse $d^{-1} \bmod N$. Thus, Mod-MUL can be computed by two Mod-PSs and one n-qubit SWAP with n auxiliary qubits $|R_2\rangle = |0\ldots0\rangle$. Especially, $C(x_i)$-Mod-MUL requires two $C(x_i)$-Mod-PSs and one n-qubit C-SWAP. Moreover, an n-qubit C-SWAP can be realized by n 1-qubit C-SWAPs, and one 1-qubit C-SWAP can be realized by two C-NOTs and one Toffoli gate.

Construction of Mod-PS from Mod-ADD. When the 2nd sequence is represented as $|y\rangle = |y_{n-1}\ldots y_0\rangle$, for an integer $0 \le d < N$, we have $dy = \sum_{j=0}^{n-1} d2^j y_j$. Thus, a modular product-sum Mod-PS(d) on a bit sequence $|R_2\rangle$ can be computed by a repetition $R_2 \leftarrow R_2 + d2^j \bmod N$ if $y_j = 1$ for $j = 0, 1, \ldots, n-1$, which is equivalent to $C(y_j)$-Mod-ADD($d2^j \bmod N$). That is, Mod-PS can be realized by n 1-controlled Mod-ADDs, and $C(x_i)$-Mod-PS can be realized by n 2-controlled Mod-ADDs, namely, $C(x_i, y_j)$-Mod-ADDs.

Construction of Mod-ADD from ADD. There are two constructions, Type 1 and Type 2 for realizing $C(x_i, y_j)$-Mod-ADD [12]. From the efficiency point of view, Type 2 is optimal for R-ADD and Q-ADD, while Type 1 for GT-ADD. Due to space limitation, we omit describing the details.

2.3 Construction of ADD

This subsection describes how to construct ADD circuits from the elementary gates in three ways: R-ADD, GT-ADD, and Q-ADD. Here, we consider the circuit to add an n-bit integer $p = p_{n-1}\ldots p_0$ to an n-qubit register $|R_2\rangle = |R_{2,n-1}\ldots R_{2,0}\rangle$. Considering the carry-over, the result is represented by $|R_1 R_2\rangle$ with 1-qubit register $|R_1\rangle$. All ADD circuits use another 1-qubit register $|R_3\rangle$, and R-ADD uses further $(n-1)$-qubit sequence $|c\rangle$. In total, GT-ADD and Q-ADD require $m + n + 1 + n + 1 = m + 2n + 2 = 4n + 2$ qubits, while R-ADD requires $m + 2n + 2 + (n-1) = m + 3n + 1 = 5n + 1$ qubits. On the other hand, the number of elementary gates is estimated by $270n^3$ for R-ADD, $16/3n^5$ for GT-ADD, and $97n^4$ for Q-ADD [12].

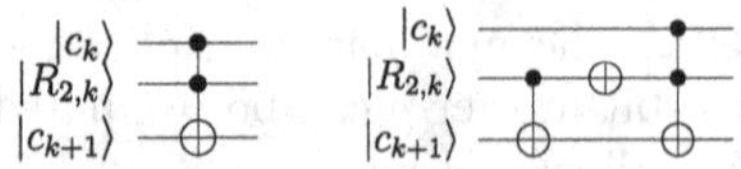

(a) $p_k = 0$ (b) $p_k = 1$ (a) $p_k = 0$ (b) $p_k = 1$

Fig. 1. CARRY Circuit   **Fig. 2.** SUM Circuit

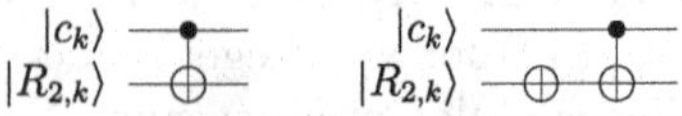

Construction of R-ADD. R-ADD is a ripple carry adder [5,20], which computes $R_2 + p$ by using the following addition table:

$$
\begin{array}{c}
 \quad c_{n-1} \quad c_{n-2} \quad \cdots \quad c_1 \\
 \quad R_{2,n-1} \; R_{2,n-2} \cdots R_{2,1} \; R_{2,0} \\
+) \quad \quad p_{n-1} \quad p_{n-2} \quad \cdots \quad p_1 \quad p_0 \\
\hline
R_1 \; R_{2,n-1} \; R_{2,n-2} \cdots R_{2,1} \; R_{2,0}
\end{array}
$$

Here, $c = c_{n-1} \ldots c_1$ is an auxiliary $(n-1)$-bit register with initial value 0, which is used for storing carry-overs. R-ADD consists of three circuits, CARRY (for computing carry bits), SUM (for computing additions), and CARRY^{-1} (for resetting carry bits). As in Figure 2 of Vedral, Barenco and Ekert's paper [20], R-ADD firstly computes all carry-overs by using CARRY circuit described in Fig. 1 for $k = 0, 1, \ldots, n-1$ (set $c_n = R_1$ when $k = n-1$). When $p_{n-1} = 1$, apply the NOT gate to $R_{2,n-1}$. Finally, for $k = n-1, \ldots, 0$, update $R_{2,k}$ by using SUM circuit described in Fig. 2 and reset c_k by using CARRY^{-1} circuit, which is reverse circuit of CARRY. When $k = 0$, CARRY^{-1} is omitted. Thus, R-ADD can be constructed from Toffoli gates, C-NOT gates, and NOT gates.

Type 2 Mod-ADD requires 1-controlled R-ADD and 2-controlled R-ADD, which require not only C-NOT gate and Toffoli gate, but 3-controlled NOT and 4-controlled NOT gates. Barenco et al. showed two conversions from a C^k-NOT gate to Toffoli gates [3]. The first conversion converts a C^k-NOT gate to $2k-3$ Toffoli gates by using $k-2$ clean auxiliary qubits (qubits with their state known to be $|0\rangle$). The second converts a C^k-NOT gate to $4k-8$ Toffoli gates by using $k-2$ dirty (unclean) auxiliary qubits. Both auxiliary qubits return to their initial state after the usage. According to Kunihiro's paper [12], the first conversion is used for all C^k-NOT gates.

Construction of GT-ADD. For $k = 0, 1, \ldots, n-1$, GT-ADD adds p by repeatedly computing $R_2 \leftarrow R_2 + 2^k$ when $p_k = 1$. An addition by 2^k can be realized by C^ℓ-NOT gates ($1 \leq \ell \leq n-k$) and one NOT gate as in Fig. 3. Type 1 Mod-ADD requires, in addition to GT-ADD, 1/2/3-controlled GT-ADD, which consists of NOT gates, C-NOT gates, Toffoli gates, and C^ℓ-NOT gates ($3 \leq \ell \leq n+3$). Both conversions described in Sect. 2.3 can be used in GT-ADD, however, since it is difficult to allocate clean qubits, Kunihiro used the second conversion for all C^ℓ-NOT gates [12].

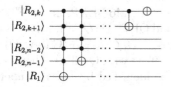
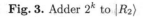

Fig. 3. Adder 2^k to $|R_2\rangle$

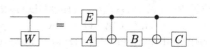

Fig. 4. Conversion of 1-controlled R_k

Construction of Q-ADD. Q-ADD is an adder using the Quantum Fourier Transform (QFT) [4,7]. For simplicity, we set $|R_{2,n}\rangle := |R_1\rangle$ and assume that $|R_2\rangle$ has $n+1$ qubits in this subsection. Also set $p_n = 0$. Unlike R/GT-ADD, Q-ADD computes $|R_2\rangle \leftarrow |R_2 + p \bmod 2^{n+1}\rangle$. Denote the state after applying QFT to the register $|R_2\rangle$ (Figure 9 in [4]) as $\phi(|R_2\rangle)$. Then, Q-ADD computes in the following way: for $j = n, n-1, \ldots, 0$, and for $k = 1, 2, \ldots, j+1$, apply the Z-rotation gate $R_k = (1, 0; 0, e^{2\pi i/2^k})$ to $\phi(|R_{2,j}\rangle)$ when $p_{j-k+1} = 1$. Inverse QFT (QFT^{-1}) is required to obtain the result of the addition. Thus, Q-ADD can be realized by rotation gates except QFT/QFT^{-1}.

Type 2 Mod-Add requires 1/2-controlled Q-ADDs, that is, 1/2-controlled R_k gates are required. Here, 1-controlled R_k gate can be realized by 2 C-NOTs and 4 1-qubit gates, and 2-controlled R_k gate can be realized by 6 C-NOTs and 8 1-qubit gates [3].

Construction of 1/2-controlled R_k is as follows. Arbitrary unitary matrix W can be represented by

$$W = \Phi(\delta)Rz(\alpha)Ry(\theta)Rz(\beta) \tag{1}$$

for parameters $\alpha, \beta, \theta, \delta \in [0, 2\pi]$, where

$$\Phi(x) = \begin{pmatrix} e^{ix} & 0 \\ 0 & e^{ix} \end{pmatrix}, \; Ry(x) = \begin{pmatrix} \cos x/2 & \sin x/2 \\ -\sin x/2 & \cos x/2 \end{pmatrix}, \; Rz(x) = \begin{pmatrix} e^{ix/2} & 0 \\ 0 & e^{-ix/2} \end{pmatrix}.$$

Then 1-controlled W gate can be represented as in Fig. 4, where

$$A = Rz(\alpha)Ry(\theta/2), B = Ry(-\theta/2)Rz(-(\alpha+\beta)/2),$$
$$C = Rz((\beta-\alpha)/2), E = Rz(-\delta)\Phi(\delta/2).$$

Thus, 1-controlled R_k can be realized by 2 C-NOTs and 4 1-qubit gates as in Fig. 4 by determining parameters $\alpha, \beta, \theta, \delta$. Similarly, 2-controlled R_k gate can be realized by 6 C-NOTs and 8 1-qubit gates from Lemma 6.1 in [3].

2.4 Required Resources

This section summarizes the resources required in Shor's circuit to factor an n-bit integer.

Shor's circuit has three main circuits, Hadamard, Mod-EXP, and QFT^{-1}. Required number of gates for each of Hadamard and QFT^{-1} is $O(n^2)$, while Mod-EXP requires $G_{\text{ModEXP}}(\text{R-ADD}) = 270n^3$ with R-ADD, $G_{\text{ModEXP}}(\text{GT-ADD}) = 16/3n^5$ with GT-ADD, and $G_{\text{ModEXP}}(\text{Q-ADD}) = 97n^4$ with Q-ADD. Therefore, required number of gates for Shor's circuit can be identified by these numbers: $G_{\text{Shor}}(\text{R-ADD}) = 270n^3$, $G_{\text{Shor}}(\text{GT-ADD}) = 16/3n^5$, and $G_{\text{Shor}}(\text{Q-ADD}) = 97n^4$. Unfortunately, no estimation for the depth is known. Required numbers of qubits are $Q_{\text{Shor}}(\text{R-ADD}) = 5n + 1$ with R-ADD, and $Q_{\text{Shor}}(\text{GT-ADD}) = Q_{\text{Shor}}(\text{Q-ADD}) = 4n + 2$ with GT-ADD and Q-ADD.

3   Implementation of Shor's Quantum Circuit

This section describes how to implement Mod-EXP with each of R-ADD, GT-ADD, and Q-ADD, respectively, based on Kunihiro's paper [12]. We also show bug-fixes and improvements from them. Moreover, we propose Mod-EXP with MIX-ADD method. This requires $4n+2$ qubits same as the case of GT/Q-ADD, but consists of fewer gates compared with GT/Q-ADD.

3.1   Mod-EXP with R-ADD

We use Type 2 Mod-ADD in order to minimize the number of gates. We also apply the following bug-fixes and improvements.

Bug-Fix on Converting C^3-NOT, C^4-NOT to Toffoli Gate. The first conversion described in Sect. 2.3 is used in [12] for all C^k-NOT ($k = 3, 4$) gates in 1/2-controlled R-ADD, however, $k - 2$ clean qubits are not available in some cases. In such cases we propose to take the following procedures. When $k = 3$ and no clean qubit is available, then use the second conversion described in Sect. 2.3. When $k = 4$, use the second conversion if no qubit is available, and use the conversion described in Fig. 6 if 1-qubit is available, which is given by greedy method described later. Compared to the first conversion, 1 Toffoli gate is increased when $k = 3$, and 3/1 Toffoli gates are increased when $k = 4$ with 0/1 clean qubit. Though this increases the number of gates in Mod-EXP, it does not affect the order since it is at most $O(n)$ (explained later).

Greedy Method. Suppose $1 \leq c \leq k - 3$ clean qubits and sufficient dirty qubits are available. Our greedy method converts a C^k-NOT to Toffoli gates as follows.

1. Generate a null circuit circ.
2. Let X be a set of indices of k control qubits.
3. Select two indices from X, and delete these indices from X.
4. Select one clean qubit with changing its status as 'dirty' in clean qubit management, and add its index to X.
5. Generate a Toffoli gate, controlled by selected indexed-qubits and targeted to the selected clean qubit.

6. Add the generated Toffoli gate to `circ`.
7. Repeat Step 2–6 c times.
8. Generate a C^{k-c}-NOT gate controlled by $(k-c)$ indices in X, and targeted to the same qubit as the original C^k-NOT gate, and convert to $4(k-c)-8$ Toffoli gates by using the 2nd conversion, and add to `circ`.
9. Add all Toffoli gates generated in Step 2–7 in the reversed order to `circ`.
10. Output `circ`.

The number of Toffoli gates generated by the greedy method is $c+4(k-c)-8+c = 4k-8-2c$. See Appendix 1 and 2 for examples of our greedy method.

Clean Qubits Management. It is difficult to figure out which qubit is clean or not manually when C^k-NOT conversion is required. So we implemented the management function to automatically list the status of auxiliary qubits.

- When a quantum gate is added to the circuit, set the status of the target qubit of the gate as 'dirty' (not clean). If the gate makes the status clean (such as CARRY^{-1}), set 'clean'.
- Use 'clean' qubits in C^k-NOT conversion.

This management minimizes the number of gates of Mod-EXP.

The Number of Gates After Bug-Fix. In Step 2 of Shor's algorithm, we apply the Hadamard gate to the m-qubit sequence. By changing this operation to applying the Hadamard gate to x_i just before each $C(x_i)$-Mod-MUL, $x_{i+1}, \ldots, x_{m-1}$ can be used as clean qubits in $C(x_i)$-Mod-MUL. Thus, for $i = 0, \ldots, m-3$, x_{i+1}, x_{i+2} can be used as clean qubits and there is no increase on the number of gates because the first conversion can be applied same as in the Kunihiro's paper [12]. On the other hand, when $i = m-2, m-1$, available clean qubits are less than 2, and additional circuits are required.

The number of gates for Bug-fix Mod-EXP with R-ADD is given as follows. $C(x_i, y_j)$-Mod-ADD in Mod-EXP consists of 3 C^2-R-ADDs, 1 C-R-ADD, 1 C^2-NOT, 2 C-NOTs and 3 NOTs. In the case for $i = 0, \ldots, m-3$, C^4/C^3-NOT is converted to 5/3 Toffoli gates because two clean qubits are available. Hence, $C(x_i, y_j)$-Mod-ADD consists of $135/2n - 155/2$ elementary gates. For $i = m-2, m-1$, we count the number of gates to be added from this number. For $i = m-2$, there is no additional gates in the first and last C^2-R-ADD(d) in Type 1 $C(x_i, y_j)$-Mod-ADD, because two clean qubits (x_{m-1} and R_3) are available. On the other hand, additional gates are required in C^2-R-ADD$(2^n - d)$ due to lack of clean qubits. Specifically, two clean qubits x_{m-1} and c_{n-1} are available in C^2-CARRY for c_j and C^2-CARRY^{-1} for c_j for $j = 1, \ldots, n-2$, but just one in C^2-CARRY for c_{n-1}, c_n and C^2-CARRY^{-1} for c_{n-1}. Each C^4-NOT gate in these three CARRYs is converted to 6 Toffoli gates by the greedy method for $k = 4, c = 1$. This leads to the addition of 3 elementary gates compared to the case for $i = 0, \ldots, m-3$. Hence, $C(x_i, y_j)$-Mod-ADD consists of $135/2n - 149/2$ elementary gates. For $i = m-1$, additional gates are required as shown in Table 1,

Table 1. The number of required clean qubits, available clean qubits and the number of additional gates in each controlled ADD in Mod-ADD Type-2 [12] with R-ADD for $i = m - 1$

	C^2-ADD(d) at Step 1-1 and 7			C-ADD at Step 3			C^2-ADD($2^n - d$) at Step 5		
	required	available	#gates	required	available	#gates	required	available	#gates
CARRY c_{n-2}	2	R_3, c_{n-1}	+0	1	c_{n-1}	+0	2	c_{n-1}	+1
CARRY c_{n-1}	2	R_3	+1	1	–	+1	2	–	+7/2
CARRY R_1	2	R_3	+1	1	–	+1	2	–	+7/2
SUM $R_{2,n-1}$	2	R_3	+0	0	–	+0	1	–	+1
CARRY^{-1} c_{n-1}	2	R_3	+1	1	–	+1	2	–	+7/2
CARRY^{-1} c_{n-2}	2	R_3, c_{n-1}	+0	1	c_{n-1}	+0	2	c_{n-1}	+1

then $C(x_i, y_j)$-Mod-ADD consists of $135/2n - 55$ elementary gates. Therefore, Bug-fix Mod-EXP with R-ADD consists of

$$\begin{aligned}
G_{\text{ModEXP}}(\text{R-ADD}) &= 2n(m-2)(135/2n - 155/2) + 2n(135/2n - 149/2) \\
&\quad + 2n(135/2n - 55) + 3mn \\
&= 270n^3 - 304n^2 + 51n
\end{aligned}$$

elementary gates, where $3mn$ is the number of elementary gates for C-SWAPs in Mod-MUL. The gates increased by the lack of clean qubits is at most $O(n)$.

3.2   Mod-EXP with GT-ADD

For implementing Mod-EXP with GT-ADD, Type 1 Mod-ADD is used to minimize the number of gates. Kunihiro used the second conversion described in Sect. 2.3 for converting C^k-NOT gates (for $3 \le k \le n+3$) to Toffoli gates. This paper proposes to use clean qubits as much as possible by the greedy method to decrease the number of gates.

Greedy Method in Mod-EXP. For all conversions from C^k-NOT gates ($3 \le k \le n+3$) to Toffoli gates appeared in Mod-EXP with GT-ADD, we use the 1st conversion described in Sect. 2.3 when more than or equal to $k - 2$ clean qubits are available, the greedy method when 1 to $k - 3$ clean qubits are available, and the 2nd conversion when no clean qubit is available. We also use the clean qubit management in the greedy method.

The Number of Gates with Greedy Method. The number of gates for Mod-EXP with GT-ADD with the greedy method is given as follows. Type 1 $C(x_i, y_j)$-Mod-ADD consists of the following four gates. Each gate can be converted to elementary gates as shown in Case 1–4.

1. C^3-GT-ADD with $m - i - 1$ cleans,
2. 2 C^3-GT-ADDs with $m - i$ cleans,

3. C^2-GT-ADD with $m - i - 1$ cleans,
4. 2 C^3-NOTs and 4 C^2-NOTs.

Case 1. C^3-GT-ADD consists of $(n-k+4)/2$ C^k-NOTs $(4 \leq k \leq n+3)$ and $n/2$ C^3-NOTs on average. In the case for $0 \leq i \leq n-2$, all C^k-NOTs can be converted to Toffoli gates by the 1st conversion because $n + 1$ clean qubits are available. Hence, the number of gates is given as $n_1(i) = 1/2 \sum_{k=4}^{n+3}(n-k+4)(2k-3)+3/2n$. For $n-1 \leq i \leq m-2$, we convert C^k-NOT to Toffoli gates by the 1st conversion for $3 \leq k \leq m - i + 1$ and the greedy method for $m - i + 2 \leq k \leq n + 3$. Hence, the number of gates is $n_1(i) = 1/2 \sum_{k=m-i+2}^{n+3}(n-k+4)(4k-8-2(m-i-1)) + 1/2 \sum_{k=4}^{m-i+1}(n-k+4)(2k-3)+3/2n$. For $i = m - 1$, we use the 2nd conversion, then the number of gates is $n_1(i) = 1/2 \sum_{k=4}^{n+3}(n - k + 4)(4k - 8) + 3/2n$.

Case 2. In the same way as Case 1, the number of gates is $n_2(i) = 1/2 \sum_{k=3}^{n+2}(n-k+3)(2k-3) + n/2$ for $0 \leq i \leq n$, $n_2(i) = 1/2 \sum_{k=m-i+3}^{n+2}(n-k+3)(4k-8-2(m-i)) + 1/2 \sum_{k=3}^{m-i+2}(n-k+3)(2k-3) + n/2$ for $n + 1 \leq i \leq m - 1$.

Case 3. In the same way as Case 1, the number of gates is $n_3(i) = 1/2 \sum_{k=3}^{n+2}(n-k+3)(2k-3) + n/2$ for $0 \leq i \leq n-1$, $n_3(i) = 1/2 \sum_{k=m-i+2}^{n+2}(n-k+3)(4k-8-2(m-i-1)) + 1/2 \sum_{k=3}^{m-i+1}(n-k+3)(2k-3) + n/2$ for $n \leq i \leq m - 2$, and $n_3(i) = 1/2 \sum_{k=3}^{n+2}(n-k+3)(4k-8) + n/2$ for $i = m - 1$.

Case 4. Each C^3-NOT can be converted to 3 Toffoli gates for $0 \leq i \leq m - 2$, and 4 for $i = m - 1$.

Mod-EXP with GT-ADD with the greedy method consists of

$$G_{\text{ModEXP}}(\text{GT-ADD}) = 2n\left\{ \sum_{i=0}^{m-1}(n_1(i)+n_2(i)+n_3(i)+4)+6(2n-1)+8 \right\} + 3mn$$

$$= 3n^5 + 15n^4 + \frac{51}{2}n^3 + \frac{103}{2}n^2 + 8n$$

elementary gates. The greedy method reduces the fifth-order coefficient from 16/3 to 3.

3.3   Mod-EXP with Q-ADD

This subsection describes how to implement Mod-EXP with Q-ADD.

Bug-Fix in Q-ADD. Since Q-ADD requires to apply QFT to the registers $|R_1 R_2\rangle$, QFT just before $C(x_0)$-Mod-MUL in Q-ADD (Figure 2 in [4]), and QFT^{-1} just before C-SWAP and QFT just before C-SWAP in $C(x_i)$-Mod-MUL should be added. Thus the number of gates are increased to $4n + 2$ QFTs for Mod-EXP from the original [12]. Furthermore, the original number of gates did not consider C-SWAP, so that mn Toffoli gates and $2mn$ C-NOTs should be added. However, since these increase is at most $O(n^3)$, it does not effect on the total number of Mod-EXP at all.

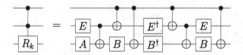

Fig. 5. Conversion of 2-controlled Rotation Gate

Change of Mod-ADD. When Type 2 Mod-ADD is used for Q-ADD, 4 QFTs and 4 QFT^{-1}s are required, and the number of gates of Mod-EXP will be increased (the order is same, but the coefficient becomes larger). So, we propose to use Beauregard's Mod-ADD which requires 2 QFTs and 2 QFT^{-1}s [4].

Gate Reduction of Controlled Rotation Gate Conversion. When 1/2-controlled R_k gates are converted to elementary gates, one 1-qubit gate can be reduced by setting parameters properly. In fact, set $\alpha = \beta = -\pi/2^k$, $\theta = 0$, $\delta = \pi/2^k$ in (1) for $W = R_k$, then C becomes an identity matrix and can be omitted. Similarly, setting $\alpha = \beta = -\pi/2^{k-1}$, $\theta = 0$, $\delta = \pi/2^{k-1}$ for 2-controlled R_k gates reduces one 1-qubit gate as in Fig. 5, where † denotes an inversion.

The Number of Gates After Bug-Fix. Mod-EXP consists of $2mn$ Beauregard's Mod-ADDs, $2m + 2$ QFTs (or QFT^{-1}) and mn C-SWAPs. Mod-ADD also consists of as follows.

- 3 C^2-Q-ADDs, each of which consists of $(n+2-k)/2$ C^2-R_k for $1 \leq k \leq n+1$,
- C-Q-ADD, which consists of $(n+2-k)/2$ of C-R_k for $1 \leq k \leq n+1$,
- Q-ADD, which consists of $(n+2-k)/2$ of R_k for $1 \leq k \leq k$,
- 4 QFTs, each QFT consists of $n+1$ H gates and $n+2-k$ C-R_k for $2 \leq k \leq n+1$,
- 2 C-NOTs and 2 NOTs.

Hence, Mod-ADD consists of $G_{\text{ModADD}}(\text{Q-ADD}) = 21n^2/4 + 47n/4 + 21/2$ elementary gates because C^2/C-R_k can be converted to 13/5 elementary gates. And QFT consists of $G_{\text{QFT}}(n + 1) = 5/2n^2 + 7n/2 + 1$ elementary gates. Therefore, Mod-EXP with Q-ADD consists of

$$G_{\text{ModEXP}}(\text{Q-ADD}) = 2mn \times G_{\text{ModADD}}(\text{Q-ADD}) + (2m+2) \times G_{\text{QFT}}(n+1) + 3mn$$
$$= 85n^4 + 201n^3 + 147n^2 + 11n + 2$$

elementary gates. The fourth-order coefficient is reduced from 97 to 85 by the gate reduction.

3.4   Mod-EXP with MIX-ADD

This subsection proposes a MIX-ADD method, which uses different ADD methods in Mod-EXP depending on the number of available clean qubits to minimize the number of elementary gates.

Definition of MIX-ADD. The original Mod-EXP uses just one ADD circuit such as R/GT/Q-ADD, but in the case of $4n + 2$ qubits circuit, the number of gates for Mod-EXP can be reduced by selecting the optimal ADD for each ADD in Mod-EXP. We call this construction Mod-EXP with MIX-ADD. Considering the order of the number of gates for each ADD, R-ADD is top priority, next Q-ADD, then GT-ADD. However, R-ADD is available only if $n - 1$ clean auxiliary qubits are available as carry qubits. In $C(x_i)$-Mod-MUL in Mod-EXP, we can use R-ADD for $0 \leq i \leq n$ because $m - i + 1$ clean qubits $(x_{i+1}, \ldots, x_{m-1})$ are available. On the other hand, we use Q-ADD for $n + 1 \leq i \leq m - 1$ to minimize the number of gates. In applying Q-ADD from the middle of Mod-EXP, QFT is added in the following three points. The first is after $C(x_{n-2})$-Mod-MUL, the second is QFT^{-1} before C-SWAP and QFT after C-SWAP in Mod-MUL for $n + 1 \leq i \leq m - 1$, and the third is after $C(x_{m-1})$-Mod-MUL.

The Number of Gates. The number of gates for Mod-EXP with MIX-ADD is computed in the same way as in Sect. 3.1 and Sect. 3.3. Therefore, we have

$$G_{\text{ModEXP}}(\text{MIX-ADD}) = 2n(n - 1)(135/2n - 155/2) + 2n(135/2n - 149/2)$$
$$+ 2n(135/2n - 55) + 2n(n - 1) \times G_{\text{ModADD}}(\text{Q-ADD})$$
$$+ 2n \times G_{\text{QFT}}(n + 1) + 3mn$$
$$= \frac{85}{2}n^4 + 193n^3 - \frac{83}{2}n^2 - 163n,$$

which is about half the number of gates for Mod-EXP with Q-ADD.

4   Experimental Results

This section reports our factorization results based on our implementation described in Sect. 3 by using the quantum computer simulator *mpiQulacs* [11], a distributed version of the quantum simulator *Qulacs* [19]. We used an A64FX-based cluster system similar to *Todoroki* [11] with 512 nodes, which enables 39-qubit operations. A64FX is an ARM-based CPU that is also equipped in the world's top Fugaku supercomputer.

The experiments were conducted by the following steps:

1. For an n-bit RSA-type composite number (a product of two different odd primes) N, choose a which induces the factorization (for efficiency reason).
2. Generate the quantum circuit for factoring N by Shor's algorithm. Here we have four choices for ADD circuit.
3. Input the quantum circuit to the simulator.
4. Observe the 1st bit sequence 10,000 times to estimate the order r.
5. Output $\gcd(a^{r/2} \pm 1, N)$.

Note that, since the observation in Step 4 does not destroy the quantum state, it is sufficient to run each quantum circuit once in the experiments.

Table 2. Factorization of N up to 7-bit (with 1-node).

N	n	a	R-ADD				GT-ADD				Q-ADD				MIX-ADD			
			Q	G	D	T	Q	G	D	T	Q	G	D	T	Q	G	D	T
15	4	2	21	12937	10507	2.4	18	12595	9838	0.91	18	38967	20208	3.5	18	22815	14273	1.6
21	5	2	26	26155	20779	89.9	22	25325	18824	5.2	22	78334	40409	18	22	47273	28866	10.4
33	6	5	31	46935	36870	–	26	44461	31436	92	26	145620	76578	404	26	87251	53343	228
35	6	2	31	47662	37775	–	26	55387	38869	115	26	155329	79693	426	26	93174	55541	241
39	6	2	31	47843	38214	–	26	61941	43483	129	26	160315	81152	441	26	95233	56408	246
51	6	2	31	46991	37413	–	26	55755	39348	116	26	152468	78285	421	26	90995	54677	237
55	6	2	31	47845	38513	–	26	61899	43507	129	26	160613	80877	441	26	95368	56384	246
57	6	5	31	47555	38028	–	26	51360	36346	107	26	154085	78686	431	26	91616	55062	238
65	7	3	36	76341	59902	–	30	82676	56199	2430	30	251424	132329	10545	30	150521	90940	5915
69	7	2	36	78035	61939	–	30	98774	66690	2866	30	271832	138888	11329	30	162705	95730	6362
77	7	2	36	77066	61391	–	30	104285	70616	3033	30	267042	135177	11125	30	159450	93522	6275
85	7	2	36	75704	60041	–	30	99407	67570	2906	30	256625	132179	10719	30	153316	91241	6011
87	7	2	36	78196	62751	–	30	120027	80999	3485	30	284083	142164	11792	30	167554	97300	6524
91	7	2	36	77819	62369	–	30	116234	78729	3369	30	279204	141000	11594	30	165151	96642	6435
93	7	2	36	77659	62319	–	30	108070	73227	3150	30	276912	140313	11516	30	163710	96243	6380
95	7	2	36	78550	63480	–	30	125960	85061	3664	30	289797	144364	12098	30	169991	98446	6610
111	7	2	36	78692	63633	–	30	124959	84533	3646	30	289793	144261	12020	30	170163	98552	6648
115	7	2	36	78591	63151	–	30	109922	74503	3188	30	282238	141557	11809	30	168210	97753	6568
119	7	2	36	78563	63477	–	30	122960	83264	3577	30	287020	142555	11978	30	170386	98332	6620
123	7	2	36	78691	63672	–	30	118337	80519	3452	30	286730	143475	11899	30	170798	99083	6643

4.1   Naive Circuit

Firstly, we factored small RSA-type composite numbers up to 7-bit with 1-node by using Shor's quantum circuits generated by our implementation. Table 2 shows the required resources and timings for factorization, where Q, G, D, T denote the number of required qubits, the number of elementary gates, the depth of Shor's circuit, and the timing data in seconds. Since we used 1-node only, 30 qubits are available for factorization. Thus, circuits with R-ADD for 6-bit and 7-bit integers cannot be proceeded (denoted by '–' in the table).

As in the table, required resources depend on the parameters N and n, but on n mainly. The ratio D/G seems to be a constant depending on the features of R-ADD, GT-ADD, Q-ADD, and MIX-ADD. Since Q-ADD has many 1-qubit operations and is easy to parallelize, so that the ratio D/G is smaller (0.50–0.53 for Q-ADD and 0.57–0.63 for MIX-ADD) compared to other ADDs (0.79 to 0.81 for R-ADD, 0.68–0.79 for GT-ADD). Though G and D are expected in the following order, $O(n^3)$ for R-ADD, $O(n^4)$ for Q-ADD and MIX-ADD, and $O(n^5)$ for GT-ADD, the results differ from expected ones. The reason is that the composite numbers are so small that other terms rather than the dominant term affect. The difference may be smaller for larger parameters.

4.2   Optimized Circuit

Then, we factor 8-bit and 9-bit integers with 512-nodes. GT-ADD is used for the experiment because it requires less number of qubits and gates compared to other ADDs in the case of these small integers. In order to decrease the number

Table 3. Factorization of N up to 9-bit with GT-ADD (with 512-nodes).

N	n	a	Q	G	D	T	N	n	a	Q	G	D	T	N	n	a	Q	G	D	T
129	8	7	34	152780	100141	256	259	9	2	38	288684	183065	6143	395	9	2	38	319088	203494	7307
133	8	2	34	169108	111205	247	265	9	6	38	272685	173346	5620	403	9	2	38	307506	195485	6271
141	8	2	34	183453	120170	287	267	9	2	38	309270	196137	6572	407	9	2	38	338095	214301	7907
143	8	2	34	207514	135907	311	287	9	2	38	359003	228259	7511	411	9	2	38	335319	214006	7404
145	8	6	34	158918	105271	262	291	9	2	38	308155	195603	6542	413	9	2	38	327370	208569	6648
155	8	2	34	198473	130150	311	295	9	2	38	334848	212590	6370	415	9	2	38	359587	228199	7723
159	8	2	34	217743	142924	335	299	9	2	38	321523	204402	7094	417	9	5	38	267426	171328	5940
161	8	3	34	155238	103030	238	301	9	2	38	317493	202575	6461	427	9	2	38	324243	207582	6862
177	8	5	34	168876	111997	259	303	9	2	38	353151	224856	7559	437	9	2	38	314856	200771	5925
183	8	2	34	207468	136410	297	305	9	3	38	285798	182560	6350	445	9	2	38	339458	216426	6572
185	8	3	34	180752	119593	282	309	9	2	38	309354	196737	6358	447	9	2	38	373035	237421	7448
187	8	2	34	208281	137192	328	319	9	2	38	367923	233944	7419	451	9	2	38	306484	195876	5999
201	8	7	34	170050	112064	244	321	9	7	38	260877	166496	5899	453	9	2	38	286538	183164	6146
203	8	2	34	193163	126762	285	323	9	2	38	304490	193554	5956	469	9	2	38	303229	193946	6246
205	8	3	34	178117	117326	276	327	9	2	38	322336	204745	6115	471	9	2	38	343707	219148	7473
209	8	3	34	165014	109327	243	329	9	3	38	285506	182113	6099	473	9	3	38	303975	194528	6933
213	8	2	34	184210	121450	272	335	9	2	38	349246	222013	8104	481	9	3	38	281077	180267	6815
215	8	2	34	204621	134697	327	339	9	2	38	317273	201779	7109	485	9	2	38	305606	195586	6502
217	8	5	34	178741	118044	255	341	9	2	38	291468	186213	6363	489	9	7	38	302012	193333	7218
219	8	2	34	204160	134522	299	355	9	2	38	310783	197410	7491	493	9	2	38	329162	210756	6188
221	8	2	34	200121	131790	283	365	9	2	38	322926	206125	6346	497	9	3	38	296472	189877	5750
235	8	2	34	198443	130597	285	371	9	2	38	324641	206674	6287	501	9	2	38	322414	207063	6335
237	8	2	34	193348	127347	286	377	9	3	38	316691	202612	6676	505	9	6	38	313370	200596	6811
247	8	2	34	208086	136900	289	381	9	2	38	321134	204686	5860	511	9	3	38	395310	252188	8226
249	8	11	34	186487	123502	292	391	9	2	38	326281	207709	6697							
253	8	2	34	202159	133987	306	393	9	5	38	281956	179878	6014							

of gates and the depth as much as possible, we used `optimize_light` option of *Qulacs* which unifies successive 1-qubit gates to one gate. However, the effect was very limited: it reduce the number of gates by only 1%.

Since factorization of 9-bit integers require 38-qubits, and 256-nodes are sufficient for the computation, other 256-nodes can be used for the speed-up. To do so, we used the `fused_swap_option` option of *mpiQulacs* which enables to distribute tasks to identified nodes for efficient computation.

Table 3 summarizes the factorization results. As in the table, we have succeeded factoring all RSA-type integers up to 9-bit. The largest integer we factored here was $N = 511$, which requires 8226 s (2.3 h). On the other hand, `optimize_light` option works very well for Q-ADD, since Q-ADD uses a lot of successive 1-qubit gates. In fact, the optimized quantum circuit for factoring $N = 511$ with Q-ADD requires 225523 gates and 187618 depth, and it factors $N = 511$ in 7050 s (1.96 h) in the experiment.

4.3 Resource Estimation of Basic Circuit

Finally, we estimated the quantum circuit resources for factoring 1024-bit and 2048-bit integers. For each $8 \leq n \leq 24$, we generated 10 composite numbers N

Table 4. Circuit estimation for factoring 1024/2048-bit integers

	$n = 1024$			$n = 2048$		
	qubits	gates	depth	qubits	gates	depth
Kunihiro [12]	3074	2.90×10^{11}	–	6146	2.32×10^{12}	–
R-ADD	5121	2.74×10^{11}	2.20×10^{11}	10241	2.19×10^{12}	1.76×10^{12}
GT-ADD	4098	3.33×10^{15}	1.02×10^{15}	8194	1.07×10^{17}	3.23×10^{16}
Q-ADD	4098	2.87×10^{13}	2.43×10^{13}	8194	4.58×10^{14}	3.88×10^{14}
MIX-ADD	4098	1.49×10^{13}	1.26×10^{13}	8194	2.37×10^{14}	2.00×10^{14}

randomly (170 composite numbers in total). Then, we generated the quantum circuit for each N with the `optimize_light` option, and evaluated the number of elementary gates and the depth. Here, we used R-ADD since resources become smaller than others for larger N's. Next, we computed the average of resources for each n. See Appendix 3 for the detailed values from this experiment.

From average values for $8 \leq n \leq 24$, we obtain approximation polynomials

$$G_{\text{R-ADD}}(n) = 254.84981n^3 - 338.63513n^2 - 177.31878n + 3112.36316,$$
$$D_{\text{R-ADD}}(n) = 204.72160n^3 - 265.74807n^2 - 515.61678n + 5232.47162,$$

using least squares method with assuming that $G(n) = O(n^3)$ and $D(n) = O(n^3)$. Then, by substituting $n = 1024$ and $n = 2048$ to these polynomials, we obtain approximations as in Table 4. Compared to the estimation by Kunihiro, our estimation decreases by about 5.6% for the number of gates. We do not discuss the feasibility of such a huge quantum computer, however, if the quantum circuit for factoring a 2048-bit integer is proceeded by an ideal quantum computer which can proceed the operation in the same speed as Google's Sycamore [2], that took 200 s to sample 10^6 times with a circuit with depth 40, factoring requires about 101.70 days, which seems infeasible by the current quantum technology.

As in the R-ADD case, we obtain the approximation polynomials for GT-ADD, Q-ADD and MIX-ADD

$$G_{\text{GT-ADD}}(n) = 2.931n^5 + 20.169n^4, \qquad D_{\text{GT-ADD}}(n) = 0.883n^5 + 21.875n^4,$$
$$G_{\text{Q-ADD}}(n) = 25.983n^4 + 59.060n^3, \qquad D_{\text{Q-ADD}}(n) = 21.993n^4 + 44.503n^3,$$
$$G_{\text{MIX-ADD}}(n) = 13.378n^4 + 136.287n^3, \quad D_{\text{MIX-ADD}}(n) = 11.309n^4 + 107.630n^3,$$

with assuming that $G(n) = O(n^k)$ and $D(n) = O(n^k)$ for $k = 5, 4, 4$, respectively. Since k is large, we compute the approximation polynomials only in the upper two degrees. We obtain approximations for $n = 1024$ and 2048 as in Table 4. Factoring a 2048-bit composite number requires about 5107, 61.4 and 31.7 years (GT, Q and MIX-ADD, respectively). MIX-ADD requires less time than GT/Q-ADD, but more time than R-ADD. However, MIX-ADD is useful in environments where the number of available qubits is limited since MIX-ADD requires fewer qubits than R-ADD.

5   Concluding Remarks

In this paper, we have proposed the MIX-ADD method that can flexibly select the optimal ADD circuit for each of the ADD circuits in the Mod-EXP.

This method reduces the number of elementary gates and the depth in Shor's quantum circuit while maintaining a lower qubit requirement compared to R-ADD. Next, we have implemented Shor's algorithm for factoring general composite numbers using 4 different ADD (R-ADD, GT-ADD, Q-ADD and MIX-ADD), and successfully factored 96 RSA-type composite numbers up to 9-bit using the quantum computer simulator developed by Fujitsu. Finally, we have estimated the number of gates and depth required of Shor's quantum circuit for larger composite numbers by actually generating quantum circuits, and gave the estimation for 1024 and 2048-bit integers.

A new finding obtained from our experiments is that the required resources related to Shor's algorithm can be evaluated based on actual implementation rather than theoretical analysis, at least for small parameters, by using the quantum simulator. The effectiveness of improvements can be assessed through actual implementation and experiments on quantum simulators.

Our implementations are based on the basic construction of Shor's quantum circuit. Future work will involve experiments and resource estimation using advanced circuits that apply complex techniques to reduce the number of qubits, as well as under noisy conditions.

Acknowledgments. We would like to thank Shintaro Sato, Hirotaka Oshima, Kazunori Maruyama, Masayoshi Hashima and Kohta Nakashima from Fujitsu for their efforts in using the quantum computer simulator. The sixth author conducted the research supported by JST CREST JPMJCR2113 and JPSP KAKENHI Grant Number JP21H03440.

Appendix 1. Examples of Greedy Method

Figure 6 shows an example of our greedy method for $k = 4, c = 1$, and Fig. 7 for $k = 5, c = 1, 2$. The number of Toffoli gates is 6 for $k = 4, c = 1$, 8 for $k = 5, c = 2$, and 10 for $k = 5, c = 1$, which matches $4k - 8 - 2c$.

Appendix 2. Effectiveness of Greedy Method

In order to show the superiority of our greedy method, we factored RSA-type composite numbers up to 7-bit with 1-node, without and with the greedy method for GT-ADD. Results are summarized in Table 5, where results in the 'Greedy' column coincide with the results shown at 'GT-ADD' column in Table 2. As shown in the table, the greedy method reduces the number of gates to about 66–71%, and the depth to about 45–56%. Since the generated Toffoli gates by the greedy method can be parallelized easily, the effect on the depth is much larger than that on the number of gates. Our analysis in Sect. 3.2 shows that the greedy method reduces the number of gates to about 56.25% (calculated as $3/(16/3) \times 100$) when n is sufficiently large.

Appendix 3. Data for Circuit Estimation in Sect. 4.3

Figure 8 shows the average values and the approximation polynomials described in Sect. 4.3. Table 6 summarizes the average values, lowest values, and highest values for the R-ADD case. There is virtually no difference between them.

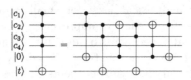

Fig. 6. Conversion from a C^4-NOT to C^2-NOTs with 1 clean qubit

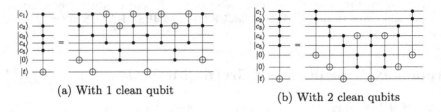

(a) With 1 clean qubit

(b) With 2 clean qubits

Fig. 7. Conversion from a C^5-NOT to C^2-NOTs

Table 5. Factorization of N with GT-ADD without and with the greedy method

GT-ADD				No Greedy			Greedy			Ratio		
N	n	a	Q	G_0	D_0	T_0	G_1	D_1	T_1	G_1/G_0	D_1/D_0	T_1/T_0
15	4	2	18	17881	17763	1.5	12595	9838	0.91	0.71	0.56	0.61
21	5	2	22	37044	36867	10.1	25325	18824	5.2	0.69	0.52	0.52
33	6	5	26	66679	66433	227	44461	31436	92	0.67	0.48	0.41
35	6	2	26	83216	82966	282	55387	38869	115	0.67	0.47	0.41
39	6	2	26	93136	92886	315	61941	43483	129	0.67	0.47	0.41
51	6	2	26	83790	83541	285	55755	39348	116	0.67	0.48	0.41
55	6	2	26	93156	92906	315	61899	43507	129	0.67	0.47	0.41
57	6	5	26	77400	77151	262	51360	36346	107	0.67	0.48	0.41
65	7	3	30	126462	126133	6814	82676	56199	2430	0.66	0.45	0.36
69	7	2	30	151490	151157	8121	98774	66690	2866	0.66	0.45	0.36
77	7	2	30	159842	159509	8546	104285	70616	3033	0.66	0.45	0.36
85	7	2	30	152208	151875	8165	99407	67570	2906	0.66	0.45	0.36
87	7	2	30	183909	183575	9864	120027	80999	3485	0.66	0.45	0.36
91	7	2	30	178045	177711	9537	116234	78729	3369	0.66	0.45	0.36
93	7	2	30	165750	165417	8857	108070	73227	3150	0.66	0.45	0.36
95	7	2	30	193219	192885	10358	125960	85061	3664	0.66	0.45	0.36
111	7	2	30	191313	190979	10257	124959	84533	3646	0.66	0.45	0.36
115	7	2	30	168479	168145	9048	109922	74503	3188	0.66	0.45	0.36
119	7	2	30	188369	188035	10112	122960	83264	3577	0.66	0.45	0.36
123	7	2	30	181029	180695	9692	118337	80519	3452	0.66	0.45	0.36

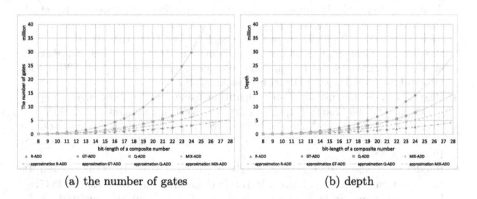

(a) the number of gates   (b) depth

Fig. 8. Average values of the number of gates and the depth of Shor's circuit for n-bit integers. The dashed lines represent approximation polynomials.

Table 6. Resources of optimized Shor's circuit with R-ADD

n	Average		Lowest		Highest	
	gates	depth	gates	depth	gates	depth
8	109654	87762.8	107372	85241	111100	89648
9	159835.8	128291.1	158641	126288	162018	130662
10	223161.5	179300.9	218662	173506	225187	182354
11	299715.2	240530.5	297074	238494	302068	243438
12	393551.7	315677.3	387423	309689	397390	320203
13	503860	403660.2	497511	396630	508398	409619
14	633082.9	507259.3	627831	500757	641738	517706
15	783469.7	627229.6	779900	622474	788900	634906
16	958542.6	769055.5	953155	761892	967134	781641
17	1152195	922632.6	1146738	915406	1157066	929076
18	1373845.4	1100267	1366213	1087255	1384917	1115100
19	1628078.6	1307037.4	1618600	1293395	1644736	1331018
20	1901953.5	1525742.6	1886368	1503536	1909138	1535936
21	2213048.9	1776710.5	2203974	1764214	2222441	1789865
22	2549491.8	2045255.8	2532631	2023007	2562329	2062360
23	2919664.5	2342540.3	2907098	2320299	2936593	2366786
24	3326305.5	2669232.6	3295857	2629337	3349921	2701801

References

1. Amico, M., Saleem, Z.H., Kumph, M.: Experimental study of Shor's factoring algorithm using the IBM Q Experience. Phys. Rev. A **100**(1), 012305 (2019). https://doi.org/10.1103/PhysRevA.100.012305
2. Arute, F., Arya, K., Babbush, R., Bacon, D., Bardin, J.C., Barends, R., et al.: Quantum supremacy using a programmable superconducting processor. Nature **574**(7779), 505–510 (2019). https://doi.org/10.1038/s41586-019-1666-5
3. Barenco, A., Bennett, C.H., Cleve, R., DiVincenzo, D.P., Margolus, N., Shor, P., et al.: Elementary gates for quantum computation. Phys. Rev. A **52**(5), 3457 (1995). https://doi.org/10.1103/PhysRevA.52.3457
4. Beauregard, S.: Circuit for Shor's algorithm using 2n+3 qubits. arXiv preprint quant-ph/0205095 (2002). https://doi.org/10.48550/arXiv.quant-ph/0205095
5. Beckman, D., Chari, A.N., Devabhaktuni, S., Preskill, J.: Efficient networks for quantum factoring. Phys. Rev. A **54**(2), 1034 (1996). https://doi.org/10.1103/PhysRevA.54.1034
6. Boudot, F., Gaudry, P., Guillevic, A., Heninger, N., Thomé, E., Zimmermann, P.: Factorization of RSA-250 (2020). https://web.archive.org/web/20200228234716/. https://lists.gforge.inria.fr/pipermail/cado-nfs-discuss/2020-February/001166.html
7. Draper, T.G.: Addition on a quantum computer. arXiv preprint quant-ph/0008033 (2000). https://doi.org/10.48550/arXiv.quant-ph/0008033

8. Gidney, C., Ekerå, M.: How to factor 2048 bit RSA integers in 8 hours using 20 million noisy qubits. Quantum **5**, 433 (2021). https://doi.org/10.22331/q-2021-04-15-433

9. Gouzien, E., Sangouard, N.: Factoring 2048-bit RSA integers in 177 days with 13 436 qubits and a multimode memory. Phys. Rev. Lett. **127**(14), 140503 (2021). https://doi.org/10.1103/PhysRevLett.127.140503

10. IBM: 433-qubits quantum processor, Osprey. https://research.ibm.com/blog/next-wave-quantum-centric-supercomputing

11. Imamura, S., Yamazaki, M., Honda, T., Kasagi, A., Tabuchi, A., Nakao, H., et al.: mpiqulacs: a distributed quantum computer simulator for A64FX-based cluster systems. arXiv preprint arXiv:2203.16044 (2022). https://doi.org/10.48550/arXiv.2203.16044

12. Kunihiro, N.: Exact analyses of computational time for factoring in quantum computers. IEICE Trans. Fundam. Electron. Commun. Comput. Sci. **88**(1), 105–111 (2005). https://doi.org/10.1093/ietfec/e88-a.1.105

13. Lanyon, B.P., Weinhold, T.J., Langford, N.K., Barbieri, M., James, D.F., Gilchrist, A., et al.: Experimental demonstration of a compiled version of Shor's algorithm with quantum entanglement. Phys. Rev. Lett. **99**(25), 250505 (2007). https://doi.org/10.1103/PhysRevLett.99.250505

14. Lu, C.Y., Browne, D.E., Yang, T., Pan, J.W.: Demonstration of a compiled version of Shor's quantum factoring algorithm using photonic qubits. Phys. Rev. Lett. **99**(25), 250504 (2007). https://doi.org/10.1103/PhysRevLett.99.250504

15. Lucero, E., Barends, R., Chen, Y., Kelly, J., Mariantoni, M., Megrant, A., et al.: Computing prime factors with a Josephson phase qubit quantum processor. Nat. Phys. **8**(10), 719–723 (2012). https://doi.org/10.1038/nphys2385

16. Martin-Lopez, E., Laing, A., Lawson, T., Alvarez, R., Zhou, X.Q., O'brien, J.L.: Experimental realization of Shor's quantum factoring algorithm using qubit recycling. Nat. Photonics **6**(11), 773–776 (2012). https://doi.org/10.1038/nphoton.2012.259

17. Politi, A., Matthews, J.C., O'brien, J.L.: Shor's quantum factoring algorithm on a photonic chip. Science **325**(5945), 1221–1221 (2009). https://doi.org/10.1126/science.1173731

18. Shor, P.W.: Algorithms for quantum computation: discrete logarithms and factoring. In: 35th FOCS, pp. 124–134. IEEE Computer Society Press (1994). https://doi.org/10.1109/SFCS.1994.365700

19. Suzuki, Y., Kawase, Y., Masumura, Y., Hiraga, Y., Nakadai, M., Chen, J., et al.: Qulacs: a fast and versatile quantum circuit simulator for research purpose. Quantum **5**, 559 (2021). https://doi.org/10.22331/q-2021-10-06-559

20. Vedral, V., Barenco, A., Ekert, A.: Quantum networks for elementary arithmetic operations. Phys. Rev. A **54**(1), 147 (1996). https://doi.org/10.1103/PhysRevA.54.147

21. Yan, B., Tan, Z., Wei, S., Jiang, H., Wang, W., Wang, H., et al.: Factoring integers with sublinear resources on a superconducting quantum processor. arXiv preprint arXiv:2212.12372 (2022). https://doi.org/10.48550/arXiv.2212.12372

Quantum Circuits for High-Degree and Half-Multiplication for Post-quantum Analysis

Rini Wisnu Wardhani[1] , Dedy Septono Catur Putranto[2,3] ,
and Howon Kim[1(✉)]

[1] School of Computer Science and Engineering, Pusan National University,
Busan 609735, South Korea
{rini.wisnu,howonkim}@pusan.ac.kr
[2] IoT Research Center, Pusan National University, Busan 609735, South Korea
dedy.septono@pusan.ac.kr
[3] Blockchain Platform Research Center, Pusan National University,
Busan 609735, South Korea

Abstract. Along with the possibility of accelerated polynomial multiplication, the Toom-Cook k–way multiplication technique has drawn significant interest in the field of post-quantum cryptography due to its ability to serve as a part of the lattice-based algorithm. In contrast, the growing likelihood of attacks based on multiplication, specifically correlation power analysis attacks, has heightened vulnerability and emphasized the need to examine the feasibility of employing the polynomial multiplication method as a potential alternative in the era of post-quantum. This study examines thoroughly an elaborate mathematical procedure designated as high-degree and half-multiplication, focusing on the design of an efficient multiplication technique. The proposed polynomial multiplication is intended to be enhanced in terms of asymptotic performance analysis and quantum resource utilization. Through the utilization of the Toom-Cook 8.5-way method, we reach the lowest asymptotic performance and quantum resources usage for multiplication operation in comparison to the existing Toom-Cook-based multiplication designs with $186n^{\log_9 17} - 202n$ Toffoli count and $n(\frac{17}{9})^{1-\frac{\log 17}{(2\log 17 - \log 9)}} \log_9 n \approx n^{1.053}$ Toffoli depth. The designed multiplication yields a qubit count of $n(\frac{17}{9})^{\frac{\log 17}{(2\log 17 - \log 9)}} \log_9 n$, or approximately $n^{1.236}$. We further compare its asymptotic performance and quantum resource efficiency to other Toom-Cook-based multiplications to determine its efficacy.

R.W. Wardhani—This research was supported by the MSIT (Ministry of Science and ICT), Korea, under the Convergence Security Core Talent Training Business (Pusan National University), support program (IITP-2023-2022-0-01201) supervised by the IITP (Institute for Information & Communications Technology Planning & Evaluation, 50%) and by the Institute for Information & Communications Technology Planning & Evaluation (IITP) grant funded by the Korea government (MSIT) (No. 2019-0-00033, Study on Quantum Security Evaluation of Cryptography based on Computational Quantum Complexity, 50%).

Keywords: High-degree and half-multiplication · Toom-Cook · Post-Quantum Cryptography · Correlation Power Analysis · Quantum

1   Introduction

The Toom-Cook, a method based on [11, 33], is widely acknowledged as an effective approach for solving large number multiplication algorithms. The approach being referred to is a mathematical method employed for the efficient multiplication of polynomials. This method involves breaking down the multiplication process into smaller multiplications (sub-multiplications) and additions, thereby minimizing the overall computing complexity. The use of this technique is prevalent throughout diverse domains, including computer algebra systems, cryptography, and signal processing, with the aim of enhancing the efficiency of polynomial multiplication processes.

Besides the number theoretic transform (NTT)-based polynomial multiplication, the Toom-Cook-based or Karatsuba-based polynomial multiplication algorithms have experienced a resurgence in popularity after the commencement of the National Institute of Standards and Technology's (NIST) post-quantum standardization program [22, 25]. Several studies (i.e., [14, 22], and [25]) have put forth a new approach to Toom-Cook multiplication, taking into account the NIST adoption of the module learning with errors (MLWE) algorithm, which forms the basis of many lattice-based cryptography schemes, as the forthcoming standard.

In terms of Toom-Cook multiplication implementation, to optimize performance and reduce implementation costs, Putranto et al. [31] propose employing a Toom-Cook-based multiplier based on several Toom-Cook calculation strategies, including [7, 13, 21, 34]. The analysis of the asymptotic performance of multiplication algorithms and the corresponding costs associated with their quantum implementation offers effectiveness in multiplication operations and valuable perspectives on the importance of multiplication algorithms within the realm of post-quantum cryptography (PQC) and mitigating the risk of side-channel attacks (SCA). Meanwhile, Mera et al. [25], provide a proposition consisting of two innovative strategies aimed at enhancing the efficiency of polynomial multiplications based on the Toom-Cook algorithm. These techniques are then implemented within the Saber post-quantum key encapsulation mechanism.

Recently, the present study [22] investigates the vulnerabilities of the Toom-Cook algorithm in the reference implementation of the Saber cryptographic scheme. It introduces a novel approach by conducting a single-trace attack on Toom-Cook, utilizing the soft-analytical side-channel attack technique. In accordance with this, Mujdei et al. [27] undertook a comparative examination of the complexity associated with attacking various multiplication schemes, multiplication algorithms, and parameter selections. This study utilized the correlation power analysis (CPA) technique, which was first introduced by Brier et al. in their influential paper released in 2004 [10], to prove the existing Toom-Cook vulnerability, particularly the Toom-Cook 4-way PQC algorithm, against the attacks.

The examination of the feasibility of polynomial multiplication as a prospective alternative within the context of PQC holds significant importance. Lattice-based cryptographic systems commonly employ either the NTT with time complexity of $(\mathcal{O}(n \log n))$ [29] or the Toom-Cook/Karatsuba algorithm with time complexity of $(\mathcal{O}(n^{1+\epsilon})$, where $0 < \epsilon < 1)$, [11,17,33], to achieve efficient polynomial multiplication involving n coefficients [27]. In this paper, we will explore the utilization of a new and advantageous multiplication operation derived from Toom's approach, considering that Toom-Cook-based multiplication, especially degrees up to 4, is part of the lattice-based post-quantum algorithm approach, which is also associated with attacks. Further, the proposed multiplication is intended to be integrated into a quantum cryptanalysis circuit with the aim of facilitating an evaluation of post-quantum security.

In this study, we refer to Bodrato's research on high-degree Toom'n'half balanced and unbalanced multiplication [8] to elucidate the functioning of Toom's method for polynomials. To the best of our knowledge, this study is the first to utilize high-degree and half-multiplication compounds in quantum circuits, specifically Toom-Cook-based multiplication exceeding 8°. The primary objective in the design of high-degree and half-multiplication quantum circuits is to reach lower asymptotic performance analyses and minimize the utilization of quantum resources during the execution of multiplication operations. The contributions of this paper can be succinctly summarized as follows:

1. We elaborate a comprehensive analysis of multiplication strategies (i.e., [21,34], and [31]), with a specific emphasis on the high-degree and half-multiplication technique, the Toom-Cook 8.5-way method. Referring to [8], we conduct computation steps like splitting, evaluation, recursive multiplication, interpolation, and recomposition in a certain order, to reach the goal of yielding the best asymptotic performance analysis and the lowest amount of quantum resource use.

2. We design the Toom-Cook 8.5-way multiplier in a quantum environment, yielding the lowest asymptotic performance analysis for the multiplier and the minimum quantum resource utilization with qubit count $n(\frac{17}{9})^{\frac{\log 17}{(2 \log 17 - \log 9)}} \log_9 n \approx n^{1.236}$, $186 n^{\log_9 17} - 202n$ Toffoli count, and $n(\frac{17}{9})^{1 - \frac{\log 17}{(2 \log 17 - \log 9)}} \log_9 n \approx n^{1.053}$ Toffoli depth.

3. We then investigate the asymptotic performance and quantum resource use of various multiplication algorithms, namely the naïve schoolbook method, the Karatsuba algorithm, and existing Toom-Cook-based multiplication up to 8.5°. Additionally, we provide a thorough analysis and evaluation of various factors, including qubit count, Toffoli count, and Toffoli depth, for the purpose of assessing the space-time complexity and drawing up a comprehensive comparison metric to the multiplication operation.

The organization of the paper is as follows: Sect. 1 provides an overview of the background insights relevant to our work. Section 2 provides a brief overview of high-degree and half-multiplication, particularly in the context of Toom-Cook-based multiplication. Section 3 outlines a detailed procedure for designing the proposed high-degree and half-multiplication, the Toom-Cook 8.5-way. In Sect. 4, we provide a concise insight into the utilization and underlying principles of multiplication-based attacks with CPA and address multiplication usage in cryptanalysis circuits that led to a post-quantum security evaluation. In Sect. 5, we analyze and compare the computational complexity in terms of space and time for designs involving proposed multiplication. Future work discussion and conclusions are formulated in Sect. 6 and Sect. 7.

2   High-Degree and Half-Multiplication

The Schoolbook Multiplication algorithm, which has a time complexity of $\mathcal{O}(n^2)$, is considered the most basic and straightforward approach for multiplying polynomials of degree n, which is equivalent to a variant of the Toom-Cook 1-way algorithm. Meanwhile, the Karatsuba algorithm can be considered a variant of the Toom-Cook 2-way algorithm, in which the original number is divided into two smaller sub-numbers. The reduction of four multiplications to three results in the Karatsuba method yield efficiency compared to naive with a complexity value of $(n^{log(3)/log(2)}) \equiv \mathcal{O}(n^{1.58})$.

The Toom-Cook algorithm, specifically the Toom-Cook k-way algorithm for multiplication, is a divide-and-conquer approach that bears resemblance to Karatsuba multiplication. However, unlike Karatsuba multiplication which divides each polynomial into two equal parts during each recursive step, the Toom-Cook k-way multiplication divides two large integers f and g into k smaller parts, each with a length of l. In general, the time complexity of the Toom-Cook k–way algorithm can be expressed as $\mathcal{O}(c(k)n^e)$, where e is calculated as the logarithm of $(2k - 1)$ divided by the logarithm of k. The term n^e represents the time spent on sub-multiplications, while c denotes the time spent on additions and multiplication by small constants.

The computational procedures encompass many steps such as splitting, evaluation, recursive multiplication, interpolation, and recomposition, which have already received extensive study in other works [8,13,21,31,34]. This study concentrates its attention on effective multiplication, specifically exploring its complexity before delving into the realm of quantum circuits for high-degree and half-multiplication in quantum architecture.

In the first step in Toom's splitting step, in order to divide a given quantity into k segments using Toom's k–way algorithm, it is necessary to choose a base $B = b^i$ that satisfies the condition where the number of integer digits both m and n when expressed in base B does not exceed k. A commonly selected option for the variable i is provided by Eq. 1, then, the variables m and n are partitioned into their respective base B digits, denoted as m_i and n_i.

$$i = max\left\{ \left\lfloor \frac{\lceil \log_b m \rceil}{k_m} \right\rfloor, \left\lfloor \frac{\lceil \log_b n \rceil}{k_n} \right\rfloor \right\} + 1 \tag{1}$$

Subsequently, the aforementioned digits are employed as coefficients in polynomials p and q of degree $(k - 1)$, satisfying the condition that $p(B)$ equals m

and $q(B)$ equals n. The rationale for the defining of these polynomials lies in the fact that by calculating their product, denoted as $r(x) = p(x)q(x)$, the resulting value $r(B)$ will correspond to the multiplication of $m \times n$.

In the case where the multiplicands have different magnitudes, it is advantageous to employ different values of k for m and n, denoted as k_m and k_n. An instance in this condition is the high-degree and half-multiplication Toom-Cook k-way; for example (using terminology, high-degree and half-multiplication), Toom-Cook 8.5-way corresponds to the Toom-Cook algorithm with the specific values of $k_m = 9$ and $k_n = 8$. In this particular scenario, the selection of the variable i in the equation $B = b^i$ is commonly determined by Eq. 1.

3   Quantum Toom-Cook 8.5-Way Multiplier Design

Zanoni et al. [34] introduce a conventional computational implementation of a balanced Toom-Cook 8-way algorithm for the purpose of integer multiplication and squaring. The authors successfully achieved a degree of 7 in their Toom-Cook-based multiplication version. In their comprehensive study, Dutta et al. [13] provide an in-depth elucidation of the Toom-Cook 2.5-way technique employed in the realm of quantum computing. The authors primarily concentrate on the identification of the maximum count of Toffoli gates and qubits attainable by means of a rigorous examination of the recursive tree inherent to the algorithm.

The research undertaken by Larasati et al. [21] shows findings that demonstrate the possibility of the k–way Toom-Cook method, which employs higher-order polynomial interpolation, to exhibit lower asymptotic complexity in comparison to alternative approaches such as Toom-Cook 2.5-way. In their study, Larasati et al. [21] expound upon the Toom-Cook 3-way algorithm by incorporating the division gate. They augment their analysis by drawing upon the research conducted by Bodrato et al. [7], resulting in a singular instance of accurate division by three circuits in every iteration. Moreover, the cost related to the remaining division was reduced by the usage of the circuit's unique properties. The aforementioned accomplishment was attained through the use of a circuit that employs a constant multiplication by reciprocal technique, complemented with the requisite swap operations [21].

Referring to [31], the following part provides a detailed description of the sequential procedure for implementing our quantum Toom-Cook 8.5-way Multiplication algorithm, while also highlighting the distinctions between this approach and the Toom-Cook 8-way multiplication method for the purpose of clarification. The comparison between the recursion tree structures of Toom-Cook 8-way and Toom-Cook 8.5-way is depicted in Fig. 1. In the present context, Fig. 2 draws a comparative analysis of quantum circuits pertaining to the multiplications of Toom-Cook 8-way and Toom-Cook 8.5-way.

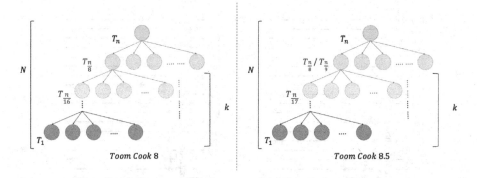

Fig. 1. The Toom–Cook 8-way and 8.5-way Multiplication Recursion Tree Structure, where T represents the Toom–Cook k–way Multiplication and n and N represent the bit length for each level and the overall depth of the tree, respectively.

3.1 Computation Steps

Focusing on the Toom–Cook 8.5-way strategy design, this work explains and undertakes a thorough investigation of high-degree and half-multiplication methods based on the Toom–Cook algorithm within the context of polynomial multiplication. We incorporate several prior research findings, including [31], and [8]. The processes of computation include splitting, evaluation, recursive multiplication, interpolation, and recomposition, as discussed in previous studies [8,21,31,34]. To offer a succinct explanation of the approach, the quantities to be multiplied, referred to as the input operands, are represented by the variables x and y. The variable x is used to represent the complete numerical input. The subscripts $x_0, x_1, x_{-1}, x_{-2}, \ldots$ are used to signify the individual components of the input. On the other hand, the notations $x(0), x(1), x(-1), x(-2), \ldots$ are employed to indicate the results obtained by evaluating the variable x at certain places.

Splitting. As shown by Eqs. 2 and 3, the specified inputs, denoted as x and y, are divided into eight smaller pieces of length $\frac{n}{8}$. The radix j in the equations can be determined in advance through the calculation of Eq. 4.

$$x = x_7 s^{7j} + x_6 s^{6j} + x_5 s^{5j} + x_4 s^{4j} + x_3 s^{3j} + x_2 s^{2j} + x_1 s^j + x_0 \qquad (2)$$

$$y = y_8 s^{8j} + y_7 s^{7j} + y_6 s^{6j} + y_5 s^{5j} + y_4 s^{4j} + y_3 s^{3j} + y_2 s^{2j} + y_1 s^j + y_0 \qquad (3)$$

$$j = max\left\{ \left\lfloor \frac{\lceil \log_2 x \rceil}{9} \right\rfloor, \left\lfloor \frac{\lceil \log_2 y \rceil}{8} \right\rfloor \right\} + 1 \qquad (4)$$

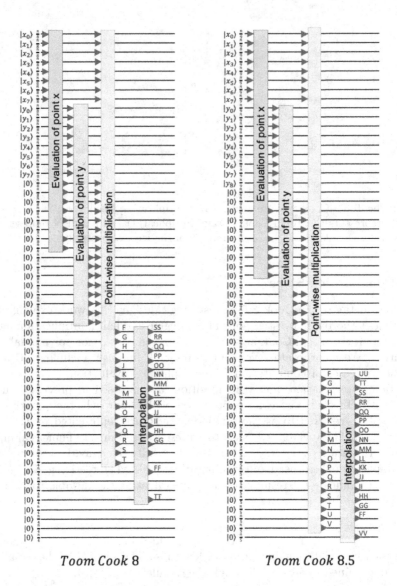

Fig. 2. Quantum Circuits Comparison for the Toom-Cook 8-way and Toom-Cook 8.5-way Multiplication Algorithms. The function block boxes serve as representations of the individual steps involved in constructing the Toom-Cook quantum circuit. The quantum circuit utilized in the multiplication algorithm uses red triangles to denote the input and output of each respective operation within the function blocks. A notation symbol is employed to denote the quantum state of the input, with each line representing a required register in the quantum circuit. The presence of triangles positioned on the left side of a block serves to highlight the location of its input entry point. The output location on the right side is symbolized by triangles. To maintain simplicity, the ancilla registers are omitted from the display. (Color figure online)

$F = x_0 y_0$

$G = (x_7 + x_6 + x_5 + x_4 + x_3 + x_2 + x_1 + x_0)(y_8 + y_7 + y_6 + y_5 + y_4 + y_3 + y_2 + y_1 + y_0)$

$H = (-x_7 + x_6 - x_5 + x_4 - x_3 + x_2 - x_1 + x_0)(y_8 + -y_7 + y_6 - y_5 + y_4 - y_3 + y_2 - y_1 + y_0)$

$I = (128x_7 + 64x_6 + 32x_5 + 16x_4 + 8x_3 + 4x_2 + 2x_1 + x_0)(256y_8 + 128y_7 + 64y_6 + 32y_5$
$\quad + 16y_4 + 8y_3 + 4y_2 + 2y_1 + y_0)$

$J = (-128x_7 + 64x_6 - 32x_5 + 16x_4 - 8x_3 + 4x_2 - 2x_1 + x_0)(256y_8 + -128y_7 + 64y_6 - 32y_5$
$\quad + 16y_4 - 8y_3 + 4y_2 - 2y_1 + y_0)$

$K = (16384x_7 + 4096x_6 + 1024x_5 + 256x_4 + 64x_3 + 16x_2 + 4x_1 + x_0)$
$(65536y_8 + 16384y_7 + 4096y_6 + 1024y_5 + 256y_4 + 64y_3 + 16y_2 + 4y_1 + x_0)$

$L = (-16384x_7 + 4096x_6 - 1024x_5 + 256x_4 - 64x_3 + 16x_2 - 4x_1 + x_0)$
$(65536y_8 - 16384y_7 + 4096y_6 - 1024y_5 + 256y_4 - 64y_3 + 16y_2 - 4y_1 + y_0)$

$M = (2097152x_7 + 262144x_6 + 32768x_5 + 4096x_4 + 512x_3 + 64x_2 + 8x_1 + x_0)$
$(16777216y_8 + 2097152y_7 + 262144y_6 + 32768y_5 + 4096y_4 + 512y_3 + 64y_2 + 8y_1 + y_0)$

$N = (-2097152x_7 + 262144x_6 - 32768x_5 + 4096x_4 - 512x_3 + 64x_2 - 8x_1 + x_0)$
$(16777216y_8 + -2097152y_7 + 262144y_6 - 32768y_5 + 4096y_4 - 512y_3 + 64y_2 - 8y_1 + y_0)$

$O = (268435456x_7 + 16777216x_6 + 1048576x_5 + 65536x_4 + 4096x_3 + 256x_2 + 16x_1 + x_0)$
$(4294967296y_8 + 268435456y_7 + 16777216y_6 + 1048576y_5 + 65536y_4 + 4096y_3 + 256y_2 + 16y_1 + y_0)$

$P = (-268435456x_7 + 16777216x_6 - 1048576x_5 + 65536x_4 - 4096x_3 + 256x_2 - 16x_1 + x_0)$
$(4294967296y_8 - 268435456y_7 + 16777216y_6 - 1048576y_5 + 65536y_4 - 4096y_3 + 256y_2 - 16y_1 + y_0)$

$Q = (0.0078125x_7 + 0.015625x_6 + 0.03125x_5 + 0.0625x_4 + 0.125x_3 + 0.25x_2 + 0.5x_1 + x_0)$
$(0.00390625y_8 + 0.0078125y_7 + 0.015625y_6 + 0.03125y_5 + 0.0625y_4 + 0.125y_3 + 0.25y_2 + 0.5y_1 + y_0)$

$R = (-0.0078125x_7 + 0.015625x_6 - 0.03125x_5 + 0.0625x_4 - 0.125x_3 + 0.25x_2 - 0.5x_1 + x_0)$
$(0.00390625y_8 - 0.0078125y_7 + 0.015625y_6 - 0.03125y_5 + 0.0625y_4 - 0.125y_3 + 0.25y_2 - 0.5y_1 + y_0)$

$S = (0.00006103515625x_7 + 0.000244140625x_6 + 0.0009765625x_5 + 0.00390625x_4 + 0.015625x_3$
$\quad + 0.0625x_2 + 0.25x_1 + x_0)(0.0000152587890625y_8 + 0.00006103515625y_7 + 0.000244140625y_6$
$\quad + 0.0009765625y_5 + 0.00390625y_4 + 0.015625y_3 + 0.0625y_2 + 0.25y_1 + y_0)$

$T = (-0.00006103515625x_7 + 0.000244140625x_6 - 0.0009765625x_5 + 0.00390625x_4 - 0.015625x_3$
$\quad + 0.0625x_2 - 0.25x_1 + x_0)(0.0000152587890625y_8 - 0.00006103515625y_7 + 0.000244140625y_6$
$\quad - 0.0009765625y_5 + 0.00390625y_4 - 0.015625y_3 + 0.0625y_2 - 0.25y_1 + y_0)$

$U = (0.000000476837158203125x_7 + 0.000003814697265625x_6 + 0.000030517578125x_5 + 0.000244140625x_4$
$\quad + 0.001953125x_3 + 0.015625x_2 + 0.125x_1 + x_0)(0.00000000596046447753906y_8$
$\quad + 0.000000476837158203125y_7 + 0.000003814697265625y_6 + 0.000030517578125y_5 + 0.000244140625y_4$
$\quad + 0.001953125y_3 + 0.015625y_2 + 0.125y_1 + y_0)$

$V = (-0.000000476837158203125x_7 + 0.000003814697265625x_6 - 0.000030517578125x_5$
$\quad + 0.000244140625x_4 - 0.001953125x_3 + 0.015625x_2 - 0.125x_1 + x_0)(0.00000000596046447753906y_8$
$\quad - 0.000000476837158203125y_7 + 0.000003814697265625y6 - 0.000030517578125y_5 + 0.000244140625y_4$
$\quad - 0.001953125y_3 + 0.015625y_2 - 0.125y_1 + y_0)$

$$(5)$$

Evaluation. We employ $x_1 = 0$, $x_2 = 1$, $x_3 = -1$, $x_4 = 2$, $x_5 = -2$, $x_6 = 4$, $x_7 = -4$, $x_8 = 8$, $x_9 = -8$, $x_{10} = 16$, $x_{11} = -16$, $x_{12} = 0.5$, $x_{13} = -0.5$, $x_{14} = 0.25$, $x_{15} = -0.25$, $x_{16} = -0.125$, and $x_{17} = -0.125$ to obtain $x(0)$, $x(1)$, $x(-1)$, $x(2)$, $x(-2)$, $x(4)$, $x(-4)$, $x(8)$, $x(-8)$, $x(16)$, $x(-16)$, $x(0.5)$, $x(-0.5)$, $x(0.25)$, $x(-0.25)$, $x(0.125)$ and $x(-0.125)$ for the evaluating points x and y, each of the 17 predefined evaluation points. Figure 3 and Fig. 4 illustrate the evaluation points x and y for the evaluation stage in the Toom-Cook 8.5-way multiplications design. The exact equation for the evaluation points $x(0)$, $x(1)$,

$x(-1)$, $x(2)$, $x(-2)$, $x(4)$, $x(-4)$, $x(8)$, $x(-8)$, $x(16)$, $x(-16)$, $x(0.5)$, $x(-0.5)$, $x(0.25)$, $x(-0.25)$, $x(0.125)$ and $x(-0.125)$ is not included in this work. However, it can be inferred from the evaluation multiplication equation, Eq. 5.

Recursive Multiplication. A single iteration of non-recursive point-wise multiplication for Toom-Cook 8.5-way multiplication utilizes a total of 17 multiplications, each with smaller bit lengths. To multiply each component of $x(0)$, $x(1)$, $x(-1)$, $x(2)$, $x(-2)$, $x(4)$, $x(-4)$, $x(8)$, $x(-8)$, $x(16)$, $x(-16)$, $x(0.5)$, $x(-0.5)$, $x(0.25)$, $x(-0.25)$, $x(0.125)$ and $x(-0.125)$, the result is expressed in Eq. 5, denoted as $F, G, H, I, J, K, L, M, N, O, P, Q, R, S, T, U$, and V, respectively.

Interpolation. The process of interpolation can be represented mathematically using a matrix, which is the opposite process of multiplying a point, as demonstrated in Eq. 6. It needs to be noticed that, in the aforementioned procedure, an inverse matrix derived from the sub-multiplication of coefficients $(k_0 \ldots k_{16})$ in Eq. 5 is employed. To facilitate comprehension, the inverse matrix is represented as described in Eq. 6.

Recomposition. The recomposition from the interpolation result is indicated as $VV, UU, TT, SS, RR, QQ, PP, OO, NN, MM, LL, KK, JJ, II, HH, GG$, and FF in Eq. 7 below. The final product of Toom-Cook 8.5-way multiplication is the xy Equation.

$$
\begin{pmatrix} VV \\ TT \\ SS \\ RR \\ QQ \\ PP \\ OO \\ NN \\ MM \\ LL \\ KK \\ JJ \\ II \\ HH \\ GG \\ FF \end{pmatrix}
=
\begin{pmatrix} 1 & 0 & \cdots & 0 & 0 \\ \vdots & & \cdots & & \vdots \\ & & & & \\ & & & & \\ & & & & \\ & & & & \\ & & & & \\ & & & & \\ & & & & \\ & & & & \\ & & & & \\ & & & & \\ & & & & \\ \vdots & & \cdots & & \vdots \\ 0 & 0 & \cdots & 0 & 1 \end{pmatrix}^{-1}
\begin{pmatrix} F \\ G \\ H \\ I \\ J \\ K \\ L \\ M \\ N \\ O \\ P \\ Q \\ R \\ S \\ T \\ U \end{pmatrix}
\tag{6}
$$

$$
\begin{aligned}
xy = {} & FF2^{16j} + GG2^{15j} + HH2^{14j} + II2^{13j} + JJ2^{12j} + KK2^{11j} + LL2^{10j} + MM2^{9j} \\
& + NN2^{8j} + OO2^{7j} + PP2^{6j} + QQ2^{5j} + RR2^{4j} + SS2^{3j} + TT2^{2j} + UU2^{j} + VV
\end{aligned}
\tag{7}
$$

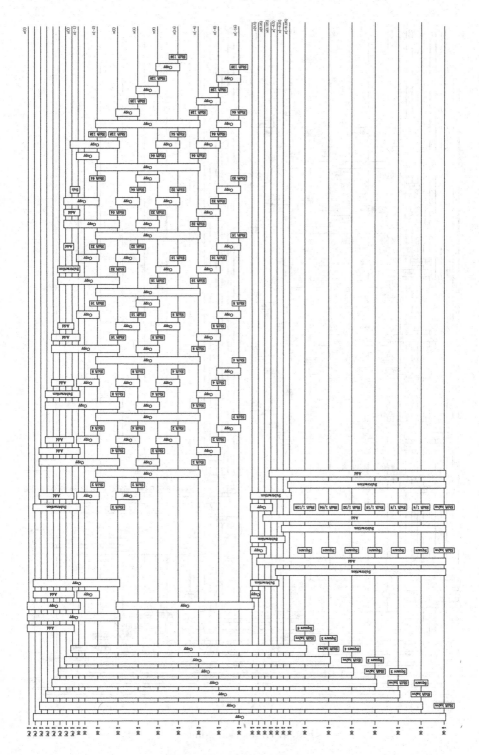

Fig. 3. Evaluation point x

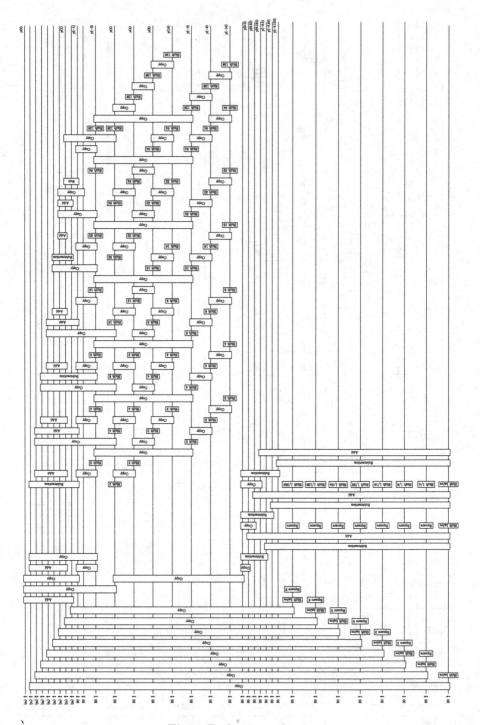

Fig. 4. Evaluation point y

4 Toom-Cook-Based Polynomial Multiplication in the Post-quantum

Numerous investigations have been conducted pertaining to the enhancement of public-key cryptosystems, aiming to protect against potential attacks deriving from both classical and quantum computing paradigms. The period character-ized by the need for quantum-resistant encryption is commonly denoted as the PQC era, as elucidated in [1]. According to the NIST PQC standardization pro-cess, the two main algorithms that are suggested for a range of applications, including digital signatures, are Crystals-Kyber [9] for public-key setup and Crystals-Dilithium [24] Lattice-based encryption is expected to exhibit optimal efficiency and resilience against quantum attacks, rendering it a feasible solution within the domain of PQC and appears to be the most rapid implementation as in [5,6,23,26]. Dilithium, Falcon, FrodoKEM, Kyber, NTRU, NTRU Prime, and Saber are seven of the fifteen candidates in the NIST third round that use lattice-based cryptography [1]. In this subsection, we present a brief example of the usage and implementation of Toom-Cook-based multiplication in the Saber and Kyber PQC algorithm, as well as the potential vulnerability that arises from the utilization of lower-degree multiplication.

The primary focus of public key cryptography (PKC) implementation is on compactness, power efficiency, and energy consumption, with a secondary con-sideration given to throughput or delay [14]. This is due to its main purpose of generating shared secret keys. While the majority of other research concentrates on optimizing NTT-based multiplications, [14] research optimizes a Toom-Cook-based multiplier to an exceptional degree. A memory-efficient striding Toom-Cook with delayed interpolation yields a highly compact, low-power implemen-tation that allows for a very regular memory access scheme. They demonstrate the multiplier's effectiveness and integrate it into one of the four NIST finalists, the Saber post-quantum accelerator. The results of the runtime analysis for a post-quantum lattice-based cryptographic algorithm, specifically a key encapsu-lation mechanism, are displayed in Fig. 5. In this figure, our focus is solely on the Kyber algorithm. The analysis is conducted by comparing the algorithm's run-time behavior and memory consumption statistics, as documented in the work by Mujdei et al. [27].

Polynomial multiplications, such as Toom-Cook and NTT, play a crucial role in lattice-based post-quantum encryption by serving as the essential constituents. Lattice-based cryptographic systems commonly employ either the NTT with time complexity of $(\mathcal{O}(n \log n))$ [29] or the Toom-Cook/Karatsuba algorithm with time complexity of $(\mathcal{O}(n^{1+\epsilon})$, where $0 < \epsilon < 1)$, [11,17,33], to achieve efficient polynomial multiplication involving n coefficients [27]. These multipli-cations facilitate the division of the resultant sub-polynomial, as highlighted in [27]. The Saber algorithm employs an additional division of the resultant sub-polynomials into two Karatsuba layers, followed by the execution of a 16-coefficient schoolbook operation [27]. Figure 6 displays an image that portrays an occurrence of Toom-Cook-based multiplication executed within the Saber structures. We redraw from the work of Mera et al. [25] to demonstrate the

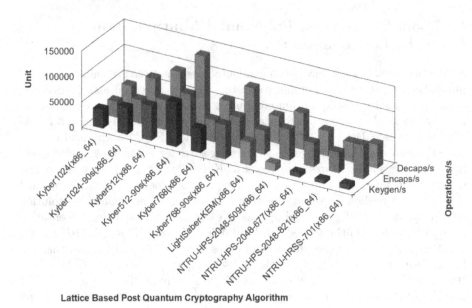

Lattice Based Post Quantum Cryptography Algorithm

Fig. 5. Runtime analysis of Open Quantum Safe Lattice-based Cryptographic algorithms (Key Encapsulation Mechanisms)

application of the Toom-Cook 4-way method in the implementation of the Saber post-quantum cryptography algorithm.

The exploitation of side-channel information, such as power consumption, electromagnetic radiation, and execution time, has been shown to be a method for gaining unauthorized access to sensitive data [19]. CPA is widely recognized as a very effective technique that leverages the correlation between a device's power consumption and the data it is processing. This approach exploits power fluctuations that are caused by mathematical processes such as multiplication. Hence, the evaluation of potential risks associated with multiplication exploitation in side-channel analysis attacks, particularly when utilizing the CPA approach, is crucial during the construction of cryptographic algorithms. This concern arises due to the frequent use of arithmetic multiplication as a sub-operation multiplier in real implementations.

The architectural design of all NTRU versions exhibits a common structure, characterized by the presence of four Karatsuba layers, with the exception of *ntruhps*2048509, which features three layers [27]. Further, variations in the schoolbook thresholds are observed [27]. Mujdei et al. conducted an experimental analysis to investigate the potential occurrence of CPA peaks when employing the schoolbook sub-operation in the processing of 3-way and 4-way Toom-Cook within the lattice-based PQC algorithm. The post-quantum algorithm *ntruhps*4096821 elaborated in [27], can be subjected to a multiplication-based attack utilizing side-channel measurements. Mujdei et al. study encompasses an examination of the variance plot of 500 instances of schoolbook multiplication,

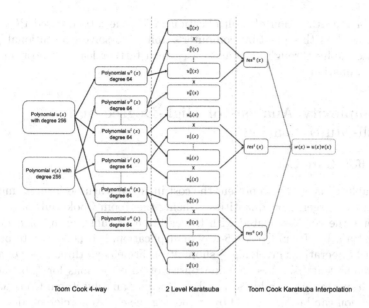

Fig. 6. The Toom-Cook 4-way and Karatsuba Multiplication Utilization in the Saber Post-Quantum Cryptography Algorithm

wherein a comprehensive analysis reveals the identification of a total of 72 apparent peaks. These peaks are specifically associated with the targeted algorithm as described in the work by [27].

PQC refers to a collection of cryptographic methods, specifically algorithms developed for the purpose of public key encapsulation, that are widely acknowledged for their ability to withstand possible attacks from quantum computers. The main goal of PQC is to strengthen and optimize mathematical methods and standards in anticipation of the emergence of quantum computing. Proficiency in mathematical approaches is essential for the development of PQC algorithms that can effectively withstand SCA. Furthermore, the utilization of effective mathematical techniques is imperative in the construction of quantum circuits, which can be employed for the creation of cryptanalysis circuits. The primary function of these cryptanalysis circuits is to evaluate the resilience of a method.

Efficient arithmetic operations, particularly multiplication, play a vital role in conducting comprehensive investigations within the domain of quantum-based cryptanalysis. According to Roche [32], Parent et al. [28], Gidney [15], Banegas et al. [3], and Putranto et al. [30,31], the development of a fundamental arithmetic constructor that demonstrates efficiency in terms of space use and time consumption is crucial for expediting the cryptanalysis process. The primary objective of these investigations is to reduce the complexity that is typically encountered during the execution of quantum cryptanalysis. The efficacy of basic mathematical operations, particularly multiplication, can significantly impact the predictive analysis of the utilization of multiplication inside the lattice-based PQC algorithm, as well as the quantum computer's ability to solve conventional public key cryptography through cryptanalysis, which further leads to post-quantum security evaluation.

5   Complexity Analysis of High-Degree and Half-Multiplication

5.1   Toffoli Gate Count

The variable T_n is used to represent the cost incurred when performing multiplication on two larger n-bit quantities utilizing the Toom-Cook multiplier. Thus, A_n denotes the cost associated with the addition or substracting of n bits. To implement a n-bit Toom-Cook 8.5-way multiplication, it is necessary to perform a total of 17 operations involving $\frac{n}{9}$ submultiplications and three types of adders with different lengths. These adders consist of 46 operations for $\frac{n}{9}$-bit adders, 272 operations for $\frac{2n}{9}$-bit adders. The Toffoli cost of an n-bit Toom-Cook 8.5-way multiplication can be determined by employing the equation referenced as Eq. 8. Furthermore, the cost increases to 9 for recursive implementations, and Eq. 10 becomes equivalent when the Toffoli cost of $A_n = 2n$ is substituted.

$$T_n = 17T_{\frac{n}{9}} + 46A_{\frac{n}{9}} + 272A_{\frac{2n}{9}} \tag{8}$$

$$\begin{aligned} T_n &= 17^{\log_9 n}T_1 + 46(A\frac{n}{9} + 23A\frac{n}{81} + \cdots + 23^{\log_9(n)-1}A_1) \\ &+ 272(A\frac{2n}{9} + 136A\frac{2n}{81} + \cdots + 95^{\log_9(n)-1}A_2) \end{aligned} \tag{9}$$

$$T_n = 17^{\log_9 n} + \sum_{i=0}^{\log_9(n)-1}\left[92n(\frac{17}{9})^i\right] \tag{10}$$

By utilizing the geometric series calculation $\sum_{i=0}^{m-1} r^i = \frac{1-r^m}{1-r}$, it is possible to determine the Toffoli cost of a recursive implementation, as denoted by Eq. 11. The result obtained from Eq. 11 does not consider the typical uncomputation procedure carried out in a quantum environment. The strategy mentioned in this study is also discussed in previous research conducted by [13,21,28], and Putranto et al. [31]. Equation 12 in this study incorporates the concept of uncomputed process to prevent a significant increase in the previously determined cost. It is important to acknowledge that the definition of "clean cost" used in the subsequent equation aligns with Larasati et al.'s [21] and Putranto et al.'s [31] definitions.

$$T_n = 17^{\log_9 n} + 92n\left(\frac{1 - \left(\frac{17}{9}\right)^{\log_9 n}}{1 - \left(\frac{17}{9}\right)}\right)$$

$$= n^{\log_9 17} + 92n\left(\frac{1 - n^{\log_9\left(\frac{17}{9}\right)}}{1 - \left(\frac{17}{9}\right)}\right) \tag{11}$$

$$= 93n^{\log_9 17} - 101n$$

$$T_{n(clean)} = 186n^{\log_9 17} - 202n \tag{12}$$

5.2 Space-Time Complexity Analysis

Bennett in [4] introduced the technique for measuring asymptotic performance improvements in the context of space consumption in the context of space-time complexity analysis. This technique is utilized extensively in reversible computing, which makes time and space complexity analysis possible and enables time-efficient finite-space computing [20]. This method will allow us to evaluate the difference in the cost of the successfully optimized multiplication and compare it to the results of previous studies. We determined the optimal cost of multiplication by following the procedures outlined in [13,21,28], and [31].

In the Toom-Cook 8.5-way algorithm, 17 simultaneous multiplications were done in a recursive way to make a quinary eight structure. There are 17^l nodes of size $9^{-l}n$ for an input of size n at level l, and this input has a total circuit cost of $n(\frac{15}{9})^l$. Equations 13–15 depict the total price of the quinary tree. For determining the optimal tree height k for optimal performance, use Eq. 15.

$$n\sum_{i=0}^{N}\left(\frac{17}{9}\right)^i, \quad N = \log_9 n \tag{13}$$

$$n\sum_{i=0}^{N-k-1}\left(\frac{17}{9}\right)^i = \frac{1}{9^{N-k}}\sum_{i=0}^{k-1}\left(\frac{17}{9}\right)^i \tag{14}$$

In a pattern similar to Eq. 12, the identity of the geometric series enables us to locate the boundaries indicated by Eq. 15. Thus, the space can be reduced, as shown in qubit count Eq. 16. The obtained result from Eq. 16, approximately equal to $\mathcal{O}(n^{1.245})$, is lower than the initially required space assessed with Eq. 17, which is confined to the value $\mathcal{O}(n^{\log_9 15}) \approx \mathcal{O}(n^{n^{1.30229}})$.

$$k \leq \frac{N}{2 - \frac{\log 9}{\log 17}} \approx 0.8167N \tag{15}$$

$$QC = \mathcal{O}\left(n\left(\frac{17}{9}^{\left(\frac{\log 17}{2\log 17 - 2\log 9}\right)\log_9 n}\right)\right) \approx \mathcal{O}(n^{1.236}) \tag{16}$$

$$n \sum_{k=0}^{\log_9 n - 1} \left(\frac{17}{9}\right)^k = n \left(\frac{1 - \left(\frac{17}{9}\right)^{\log_9 n}}{1 - \frac{17}{9}}\right) \tag{17}$$

The Toffoli depth of a circuit is a prevalent way to describe its time complexity [2,13]. It can be calculated by multiplying the number of subtrees S_k at the $k - th$ level by the corresponding depth D_k. Consequently, we can express the Toffoli depth T_d as in Eq. 18.

$$S_k = 17^{\left(1 - \frac{\log 17}{2 \log 17 - \log 9}\right) \log_9 n}$$

$$D_k = \frac{n}{9^{\left(1 - \frac{\log 17}{2 \log 17 - \log 9}\right) \log_9 n}} \tag{18}$$

$$T_d = S_k D_k = n \left(\frac{17}{9}\right)^{\left(1 - \frac{\log 17}{2 \log 15 - \log 9}\right) \log_9 n} \approx n^{1.0530}$$

5.3 Complexity Analysis Comparison

The naïve multiplication, which is equivalent to the Toom-Cook 1-way, exhibits a time complexity of $\mathcal{O}(n^2)$, where n represents the size of the input. The Toffoli depth of Naive is also of the order $\mathcal{O}(n \log n)$, according to a more in-depth study done in [12]. In the context of asymptotic performance analysis in quantum implementation, it is observed that the schoolbook technique necessitates a qubit count of $\mathcal{O}(n)$, as well as a Toffoli count and depth values of $\mathcal{O}(n^2)$. The costs associated with quantum multiplication are characterized by a qubit count of $(4n + 1)$, a Toffoli depth of $(4n^2 - 4n + 1)$, and a Toffoli count of $(4n^2 - 3n)$ [13,21].

Karatsuba multiplication, a multiplication equivalency with the Toom-Cook 2-way approach, resulted in a qubit count of $\mathcal{O}(n^{\log_2(3)})$ for both the qubit count and Toffoli count. The improvement study reveals asymptotic values for qubit count ($\mathcal{O}(n^{1.427})$), Toffoli count ($\mathcal{O}(n^{\log_2(3)})$), and Toffoli depth ($\mathcal{O}(n^{1.158})$) [13,21,28]. Parent et al. [28] determined the values of the qubit count, denoted as $n^{1.427}$, the Toffoli count, denoted as $\mathcal{O}(n^{\log_2 3})$, and the Toffoli depth, denoted as $n^{1.158}$ for Karatsuba. Recently, the Karatsuba variant proposed by Putranto et al. [30] demonstrates a reduction in CNOT usage, changing the $\mathcal{O}(n^2)$ CNOT in the prior work to $\mathcal{O}(n^{\log_2(3)})$.

According to Dutta et al. [13], the Toom-Cook 2.5-way algorithm offers a potential approach for reducing the cost of developing quantum systems by achieving the qubit count ($n^{1.404}$), Toffoli count ($49n^{\log_6 16}$), and Toffoli depth ($n^{1.143}$). Later, Larasati et al. [21] present a comprehensive examination of the asymptotic performance metrics for qubit count, Toffoli count, and Toffoli depth. They report an estimated value of $n^{1.353}$ for the qubit count, $\mathcal{O}(n^2)$ for the Toffoli count, and $n^{1.112}$ for the Toffoli depth.

Table 1. Asymptotic Performance and Quantum Implementation Cost Multipliers Comparison. In order to provide a comprehensive analysis of the advancements in complexity multiplication research, specifically focusing on the Karatsuba and Toom-Cook-based approaches, we provide our results pertaining to cost evaluation. This evaluation is conducted utilizing the Toffoli count, qubit count, and Toffoli depth as metrics to assess the space-time complexity.

No	Reference	Multiplication Algorithm	Asymptotic Performance Analysis			Cost of Quantum Implementation of Multiplication			
			Qubit Count	Toffoli Count	Toffoli Depth	Qubit Count	Toffoli Count	Toffoli Depth	CNOT
1	Kepley and Steinwandt (2015,[18])	Karatsuba	$O(n^{\log_2 3})$	$O(n^{\log_2 6})$	-	-	-	-	$O(n^{\log_2 3})$
2	Parent et al. (2017, [28])	Karatsuba	$O(n^{1.427})$	$O(n^{\log_2 3})$	$O(n^{1.158})$	$n(\frac{3}{2})^{\frac{\log 15}{(2\log 15-\log 8)}\log_2 n} \approx n^{1.427}$	$42n^{\log_2 3}$	$n(\frac{3}{2})^{1-\frac{\log 15}{(2\log 15-\log 8)}\log_2 n} \approx n^{1.158}$	-
3	Dutta et al. (2018, [13])	Toom-Cook 2.5-way	$O(n^{1.404})$	$O(n^{\log_2 5})$	$O(n^{1.143})$	$n(\frac{3}{2})^{\frac{\log 15}{(2\log 15-\log 8)}\log_2 n} \approx n^{1.404}$	$49n^{\log_2 16}$	$n(\frac{3}{2})^{1-\frac{\log 15}{(2\log 15-\log 8)}\log_2 n} \approx n^{1.143}$	-
4	Larasati et al.(2021,[21])	Toom-Cook 3-way	$O(n^{1.35})$	$O(n^{2})$	$O(n^{1.112})$	$n(\frac{3}{2})^{\frac{\log 15}{(2\log 15-\log 8)}\log_2 n} \approx n^{1.35}$	$8n^2 + 66n^{\log_2 5} - 72$	$n(\frac{3}{2})^{1-\frac{\log 15}{(2\log 15-\log 8)}\log_2 n} \approx n^{1.113}$	-
5	Van Hoof (2020, [16])	Karatsuba	$3n$	$O(n^{\log_2 3})$	-	-	-	-	$O(n^2)$
6	Putranto et al. (2023, [30])	Karatsuba	$3n$	$O(n^{\log_2 3})$	-	-	-	-	$O(n^{\log 3})$
7	Putranto et al. (2023, [31])	Toom Cook 2-way	$O(n^{1.588})$	$O(n^{\log_2 3})$	$O(n^{1.217})$	$n(\frac{3}{2})^{\frac{\log 15}{(2\log 15-\log 8)}\log_2 n} \approx n^{1.588}$	$34n^{\log_2 3} - 32n$	$n(\frac{3}{2})^{1-\frac{\log 15}{(2\log 15-\log 8)}\log_2 n} \approx n^{1.217}$	-
8	Putranto et al. (2023, [31])	Toom Cook 4-way	$O(n^{1.513})$	$O(n^{\log_4 7})$	$O(n^{1.09})$	$n(\frac{3}{2})^{\frac{\log 15}{(2\log 15-\log 8)}\log_2 n} \approx n^{1.513}$	$122n^{\log_4 7} - 160n$	$n(\frac{3}{2})^{1-\frac{\log 15}{(2\log 15-\log 8)}\log_2 n} \approx n^{1.09}$	-
9	Putranto et al. (2023, [31])	Toom Cook 8-way	$O(n^{1.245})$	$O(n^{\log_8 15})$	$O(n^{1.0569})$	$n(\frac{15}{8})^{\frac{\log 15}{(2\log 15-\log 8)}\log_8 n} \approx n^{1.245}$	$112n^{\log_8 15} - 128n$	$n(\frac{15}{8})^{1-\frac{\log 15}{(2\log 15-\log 8)}\log_8 n} \approx n^{1.0569}$	-
10	our	Toom-Cook 8.5-way	$O(n^{1.236})$	$O(n^{\log_9 17})$	$O(n^{1.053})$	$n(\frac{17}{9})^{\frac{\log 17}{(2\log 17-\log 9)}\log_9 n} \approx n^{1.236}$	$186n^{\log_9 17} - 202n$	$n(\frac{17}{9})^{1-\frac{\log 17}{(2\log 17-\log 9)}\log_9 n} \approx n^{1.053}$	-

Recently, from Putranto et al. [31] elaboration, they exhibit a better asymptotic performance analysis in terms of qubit count for the Toom-Cook 8-way approach. Specifically, it is approximated by qubit count with $n(\frac{15}{8})^{\frac{\log 15}{(2\log 15 - \log 8)}} \log_8 n$, which is of the order $O(n^{1.245})$. In the context of Toffoli depth, which is relevant to efficient computation, the Toom-Cook 8-way design results in a lower bound on logical depth of $O(n^{1.0569})$ and a Toffoli count of $O(n^{\log_8 15})$.

In the present study, as presented in Table 1, a comparative analysis of various multiplication methods reveals that the Toom-Cook high-degree and half-multiplier, established in this research, demonstrates the lowest desired asymptotic performance in terms of qubit count, Toffoli count, and Toffoli depth when compared to other approaches. In terms of cost, the proposed multiplication in quantum implementation demonstrates lower quantum resources when compared to the alternative Toom-Cook strategy. The high-degree and half-multiplication, specifically the Toom-Cook 8.5-way approach, involves a qubit count of $O(n^{1.236})$, a logical Toffoli depth of $n(\frac{17}{9})^{1-\frac{\log 17}{(2\log 17 - \log 9)}} \log_9 n \approx n^{1.053}$, and a Toffoli count of $186n^{\log_9 17} - 202n$.

6 Discussion

Empirical research has provided evidence indicating that while higher-order procedures may exhibit superior efficiency, the incorporation of the division operation, a crucial component of the k–way Toom-Cook method, can provide difficulties in terms of identifying an effective strategy. In the current research, as shown in Table 1, using the Toom-Cook-8.5 approach and yielding complexity analysis ($O(n^{1.236})$ qubit Count, $O(n^{\log_9 17})$ Toffoli Count, and Toffoli Depth of $O(n^{1.053})$), we established the optimal utilization of resources for multiplication operations. Nevertheless, the design multiplication was not incorporated into the

PQC algorithm, and the notable cryptanalysis using the Shor algorithm technique was also not performed. In later stages, it is imperative to also enhance the implementation of a higher degree in the PQC algorithm and provide a more comprehensive examination of multiplication-based attacks employing SCA, or correlation power analysis, methodologies.

Further, it should be noted that the efficiency of the recently developed Toom-Cook method exceeds that of the currently employed Toom-Cook-based multiplication techniques, Karatsuba, and naive schoolbooks. This demonstrates a higher level of efficiency in comparison to existing multipliers based on the Toom-Cook method currently utilized as part of the lattice-based algorithm, the Toom-Cook 4-way approach. In this work, the multiplication is also designed in a quantum environment, facilitating its integration into quantum circuits for cryptanalysis (e.g., [3, 30]). This integration will thereafter enable the evaluation of security in the post-quantum era.

7   Conclusions

The present study undertook a thorough examination of high-degree and half-multiplication, focusing particularly on the Toom-Cook 8.5-way algorithm. The study demonstrated the achievement of the lowest or most optimal multiplication, which is distinguished by its lower asymptotic performance and fewer demands on quantum resources compared to other multiplications. The proposed multiplication was subjected to asymptotic performance analysis, resulting in a qubit count of $n(\frac{17}{9})^{\frac{\log 17}{(2\log 17 - \log 9)}} \log_9 n \approx n^{1.236}$, approximately $\mathcal{O}(n^{1.236})$. Additionally, the Toom-Cook 8.5-way has a Toffoli count of $186n^{\log_9 17} - 202n$ and a Toffoli depth of $n(\frac{17}{9})^{1-\frac{\log 17}{(2\log 17 - \log 9)}} \log_9 n \approx n^{1.053}$ for multiplication.

The alternative methods that have been proposed have the potential to reduce the computational resources needed and can result in efficient multiplication with high degrees of multiplication. As part of planned future research, the suggested multiplication operation could be used as an alternative to constructing lattice-based post-quantum algorithms while lowering the risks of attacks that use multiplication. Furthermore, the multiplication technique is intended to be incorporated into a quantum cryptanalysis circuit in order to enhance the efficiency of evaluating post-quantum security.

References

1. Alagic, G., et al.: Status report on the third round of the NIST post-quantum cryptography standardization process. US Department of Commerce, NIST (2022)
2. Amy, M.: Algorithms for the optimization of quantum circuits. Master's thesis, University of Waterloo (2013)
3. Banegas, G., Bernstein, D.J., van Hoof, I., Lange, T.: Concrete quantum cryptanalysis of binary elliptic curves. IACR Trans. Cryptogr. Hardw. Embed. Syst. **2021**(1), 451–472 (2021)

4. Bennett, C.H.: Time/space trade-offs for reversible computation. SIAM J. Comput. **18**(4), 766–776 (1989)

5. Bisheh-Niasar, M., Azarderakhsh, R., Mozaffari-Kermani, M.: High-speed NTT-based polynomial multiplication accelerator for post-quantum cryptography. In: 2021 IEEE 28th Symposium on Computer Arithmetic (ARITH), pp. 94–101. IEEE (2021)

6. Bisheh-Niasar, M., Azarderakhsh, R., Mozaffari-Kermani, M.: Instruction-set accelerated implementation of CRYSTALS-Kyber. IEEE Trans. Circ. Syst. I Regul. Pap. **68**(11), 4648–4659 (2021)

7. Bodrato, M.: Towards optimal Toom-Cook multiplication for univariate and multivariate polynomials in characteristic 2 and 0. In: Carlet, C., Sunar, B. (eds.) WAIFI 2007. LNCS, vol. 4547, pp. 116–133. Springer, Cham (2007). https://doi.org/10.1007/978-3-540-73074-3_10

8. Bodrato, M.: High degree Toom'n'half for balanced and unbalanced multiplication. In: 2011 IEEE 20th Symposium on Computer Arithmetic, pp. 15–22. IEEE (2011)

9. Bos, J., et al.: CRYSTALS-Kyber: a CCA-secure module-lattice-based KEM. In: 2018 IEEE European Symposium on Security and Privacy (EuroS&P), pp. 353–367. IEEE (2018)

10. Brier, E., Clavier, C., Olivier, F.: Correlation power analysis with a leakage model. In: Joye, M., Quisquater, J.J. (eds.) CHES 2004. LNCS, vol. 3156, pp. 16–29. Springer, Heidelberg (2004). https://doi.org/10.1007/978-3-540-28632-5_2

11. Cook, S.A., Aanderaa, S.O.: On the minimum computation time of functions. Trans. Am. Math. Soc. **142**, 291–314 (1969)

12. Draper, T.G., Kutin, S.A., Rains, E.M., Svore, K.M.: A logarithmic-depth quantum carry-lookahead adder. Quantum Inf. Comput. **6**(4), 351–369 (2006)

13. Dutta, S., Bhattacharjee, D., Chattopadhyay, A.: Quantum circuits for Toom-Cook multiplication. Phys. Rev. A **98**(1), 012311 (2018)

14. Ghosh, A., et al.: A 334 microwatt 0.158 mm^2 ASIC for post-quantum key-encapsulation mechanism saber with low-latency striding Toom-Cook multiplication authors version. arXiv preprint arXiv:2305.10368 (2023)

15. Gidney, C.: Asymptotically efficient quantum Karatsuba multiplication. arXiv preprint arXiv:1904.07356 (2019)

16. van Hoof, I.: Space-efficient quantum multiplication polynomials for binary finite fields with sub–quadratic Toffoli gate count. Quantum Inf. Comput. **20**(9&10), 721–735 (2020). https://doi.org/10.26421/QIC20.9-10-1

17. Karatsuba, A.A., Ofman, Y.P.: Multiplication of many-digital numbers by automatic computers. In: Doklady Akademii Nauk, vol. 145, pp. 293–294. Russian Academy of Sciences (1962)

18. Kepley, S., Steinwandt, R.: Quantum circuits for $\mathbb{F}_{2^n}$-multiplication with sub-quadratic gate count. Quantum Inf. Process. **14**(7), 2373–2386 (2015). https://doi.org/10.1007/s11128-015-0993-1

19. Kocher, P., Jaffe, J., Jun, B.: Differential power analysis. In: Wiener, M. (ed.) CRYPTO 1999. LNCS, vol. 1666, pp. 388–397. Springer, Heidelberg (1999). https://doi.org/10.1007/3-540-48405-1_25

20. Král'ovič, R.: Time and space complexity of reversible pebbling. In: Pacholski, L., Ružička, P. (eds.) SOFSEM 2001. LNCS, vol. 2234, pp. 292–303. Springer, Heidelberg (2001). https://doi.org/10.1007/3-540-45627-9_26

21. Larasati, H.T., Awaludin, A.M., Ji, J., Kim, H.: Quantum circuit design of toom 3-way multiplication. Appl. Sci. **11**(9), 3752 (2021)

22. Li, Y., Zhu, J., Huang, Y., Liu, Z., Tang, M.: Single-trace side-channel attacks on the Toom-Cook: the case study of saber. IACR Trans. Cryptogr. Hardw. Embed. Syst. **2022**(4), 285–310 (2022)
23. Liu, Z., Choo, K.K.R., Grossschadl, J.: Securing edge devices in the post-quantum internet of things using lattice-based cryptography. IEEE Commun. Mag. **56**(2), 158–162 (2018)
24. Lyubashevsky, V.: Fiat-Shamir with aborts: applications to lattice and factoring-based signatures. In: Matsui, M. (ed.) ASIACRYPT 2009. LNCS, vol. 5912, pp. 598–616. Springer, Heidelberg (2009). https://doi.org/10.1007/978-3-642-10366-7_35
25. Mera, J.M.B., Karmakar, A., Verbauwhede, I.: Time-memory trade-off in Toom-Cook multiplication: an application to module-lattice based cryptography. Cryptology ePrint Archive (2020)
26. Micciancio, D., Regev, O.: Post-quantum cryptography, chapter lattice-based cryptography. Computing **85**(1–2), 105–125 (2008)
27. Mujdei, C., Wouters, L., Karmakar, A., Beckers, A., Mera, J.M.B., Verbauwhede, I.: Side-channel analysis of lattice-based post-quantum cryptography: exploiting polynomial multiplication. ACM Trans. Embed. Comput. Syst. (2022)
28. Parent, A., Roetteler, M., Mosca, M.: Improved reversible and quantum circuits for Karatsuba-based integer multiplication. In: 12th Conference on the Theory of Quantum Computation, Communication, and Cryptography (TQC 2017), pp. 7:1–7:15. Springer (2017)
29. Pollard, J.M.: The fast Fourier transform in a finite field. Math. Comput. **25**(114), 365–374 (1971)
30. Putranto, D.S.C., Wardhani, R.W., Larasati, H.T., Ji, J., Kim, H.: Depth-optimization of quantum cryptanalysis on binary elliptic curves. IEEE Access **11**, 45083–45097 (2023)
31. Putranto, D.S.C., Wardhani, R.W., Larasati, H.T., Kim, H.: Space and time-efficient quantum multiplier in post quantum cryptography era. IEEE Access **11**, 21848–21862 (2023)
32. Roche, D.S.: Space-and time-efficient polynomial multiplication. In: Proceedings of the 2009 International Symposium on Symbolic and Algebraic Computation, pp. 295–302 (2009)
33. Toom, A.L.: The complexity of a scheme of functional elements realizing the multiplication of integers. In: Soviet Mathematics Doklady, vol. 3, pp. 714–716 (1963)
34. Zanoni, A.: Toom-cook 8-way for long integers multiplication. In: 2009 11th International Symposium on Symbolic and Numeric Algorithms for Scientific Computing, pp. 54–57. IEEE (2009)

Side Channel Attack

Extended Attacks on ECDSA with Noisy Multiple Bit Nonce Leakages

Shunsuke Osaki[✉] and Noboru Kunihiro

University of Tsukuba, Ibaraki, Japan
s2220571@u.tsukuba.ac.jp, kunihiro@cs.tsukuba.ac.jp

Abstract. It is well known that in ECDSA signatures, the secret key can be recovered if more than a certain number of tuples of random nonce partial information, corresponding message hash values, and signatures are leaked. There exist two established methods for recovering a secret key, namely lattice-based attack and Fourier analysis-based attack. When using the Fourier analysis-based attack, the number of signatures required for the attack can be evaluated through a precise calculation of the modular bias even if the leaked nonce contains errors. Previous works have focused on two cases: error-free cases and the case for the first MSB has errors among all of the nonce leakage. In this study, we extend the technique to the noisy multiple bits case to calculate the precise value of the modular bias for the case that multiple bits (say, l bits from MSB) have errors. Aranha et al. (ACM CCS 2020) introduced a linear programming problem with parameters to evaluate the number of signatures, time, and memory required for a Fourier analysis-based attack. They also employed a SageMath module to optimize the number of signatures and time required for the attack. Furthermore, we show by experiments that 131-bit ECDSA is vulnerable when the first MSB of the nonce is leaked without error and when 2 MSBs are leaked with an error rate 0.1 each, which implies that total error rate is about 0.19. We then show that the latter case requires less signatures to recover the secret key.

Keywords: ECDSA · Fourier analysis-based attack · Side-channel attack

1 Introduction

The Elliptic Curve Digital Signature Algorithm (ECDSA) is a digital signature algorithm that utilizes elliptic curves. It is widely used in various systems such as SSH, SSL/TLS, Bitcoin, and others. Therefore, evaluating the potential for leakage of secret information and the effect it may have on the overall security of a system is critical.

A nonce (Number used only ONCE) is secret information that is randomly generated during the signing process. However, it is possible to leak nonces through side-channel attacks. An attack is reduced to the Hidden Number Problem (HNP) if a certain number of pairs of nonce partial bits, corresponding

© The Author(s), under exclusive license to Springer Nature Singapore Pte Ltd. 2024
H. Seo and S. Kim (Eds.): ICISC 2023, LNCS 14561, pp. 163–184, 2024.
https://doi.org/10.1007/978-981-97-1235-9_9

message hash values, and signatures are available [5]. Lattice-based and Fourier-analysis-based attacks are known as methods that solve HNPs.

A lattice-based attack can find a secret key with a relatively small number of signatures if the MSBs of the nonce are known without errors. If the secret key is 160-bit and the 2 bits in a nonce is leaked [1,7,9]; if the secret key is 256-bit and the 3 bits in a nonce is leaked [1,9]; or if the secret key is 384-bit and the 4 bits in a nonce is leaked [1,9], then several dozens to several thousands of signatures can be used to recover the secret key in a few minutes to hours. Lattice-based attacks require more than 2 bits of nonce information without errors but do not require many signatures.

In a Fourier analysis-based attack, recovering the secret key is possible when the MSBs of the nonce are known without errors. If the key length is 192-bit [3] or 256-bit [11], the signatures can be solved with a 1 or 2 bits leak with small errors, respectively. It was reported that several hundreds of millions of signatures and several days were required to solve the problem using workstations and clusters in those cases. In addition, the attack can also be successful if more MSBs are obtained with errors, but it requires many signatures, computational cost and time.

Aranha et al. [3] found vulnerabilities in OpenSSL 1.0.2 and 1.1.0, etc., against side-channel attacks that leak the MSB of ECDSA nonce, and used these vulnerabilities in their attacks. They estimated the number of signatures and costs of time, and memory of an attack when the 1 bit nonce is leaked with errors by estimating the modular bias. The number of signatures, cost of time, and memory required for the attack are also obtained by using the 4-list sum algorithm for linear combination, which is critical in Fourier analysis-based attacks. They then reduced the problem of optimizing the number of signatures to a linear programming problem and solved it using the Mixed Integer Linear Program module of SageMath to optimize the number of signatures, costs of memory, and time required for the attack [10].

1.1 Our Contributions

In this paper, we estimate the number of signatures, costs of time, and memory required for an attack in the case of multiple bits by estimating the modular bias when multiple MSBs with errors are obtained. In previous studies, modular bias has only been formulated for MSB leakage with errors or multiple bit leakage without errors. We have successfully generalized the formulation of the module bias. This allows us to estimate the modular bias in any case and to obtain an estimate of the number of signatures needed to recover a secret key.

We also focus on changes to the number of signatures when the error rate changes. Then, the optimal parameters are selected based on the evaluation of the number of obtained signatures. We extend their optimization program with a generalized modular bias to find the number of signatures required to recover the secret key. We also perform an actual attack against 131-bit ECDSA and confirm that it is possible to recover the secret key. Furthermore, we show from both theoretical analysis for modular bias and experiment that the secret key is successfully recovered with fewer signatures when each of the 2 bits is leaked with an error rate of 0.1 than when the nonce is leaked with 1 bit without error.

2   Preliminaries

2.1   ECDSA Signature Generation Algorithm

The set of solutions $(x, y) \in \mathbb{F} \times \mathbb{F}$ of an elliptic curve E defined over a field F with an infinity point O is a commutative group derived from the chord-and-tangent rule.

The signature generation algorithm of the ECDSA is shown in Algorithm 1. The secret key sk is λ-bit. The secret information (i.e., nonce k) is randomly generated in the first line of Algorithm 1. In this study, we consider the case in which the MSBs of k are leaked.

Algorithm 1. ECDSA signature generation

Input: prime number q, secret key sk $\in \mathbb{Z}_q$, message msg $\in \{0,1\}^*$, base point on elliptic curve G, and cryptographic hash function $H : \{0,1\}^* \to \mathbb{Z}_q$
Output: valid signatures (r, s)
1: k is chosen at random from $\mathbb{Z}_q$
2: $R = (r_x, r_y) \leftarrow kG; r \leftarrow r_x \bmod q$
3: $s \equiv (H(\mathsf{msg}) + r \cdot \mathsf{sk}) / k \bmod q$
4: **return** (r, s)

2.2   Hidden Number Problem with Errors

The function $\mathrm{MSB}_n(x)$ returns the top n bits of x for a positive integer x. Let b be a positive integer, $\{0,1\}^b$ be a fixed distribution on χ_b, and the error bit sequence e be sampled from χ_b. The probabilistic algorithm $\mathrm{EMSB}_{\chi_b}(x)$ takes x, b as input and returns $\mathrm{MSB}_b(x) \oplus e$. For each $i = 1, \ldots, M$, let z_i be $z_i \equiv k_i - h_i \cdot \mathsf{sk} \bmod q$ and h_i, k_i be uniform random values on $\mathbb{Z}_q$. The HNP is the problem of finding sk that satisfies the aforementioned equations given the $h_i, z_i, \mathrm{EMSB}_{\chi_b}(k_i)$ obtained for each $i = 1, \ldots, M$.

The ECDSA signature (r, s) is generated according to Algorithm 1, nonce $k \in \mathbb{Z}_q$ is chosen uniformly at random, and $s \equiv (H(\mathsf{msg}) + r \cdot \mathsf{sk}) / k \pmod{q}$ is satisfied. This yields the following equation.

$$H(\mathsf{msg}) / s \equiv k - (r/s) \cdot \mathsf{sk} \bmod q$$

If the MSBs of k are obtained, we obtain an instance of HNP as $z \equiv H(\mathsf{msg}) / s \pmod{q}$ and $h \equiv r/s \pmod{q}$,

2.3   Bias Function and Sample Bias

We follow the idea of [3] and first show definitions of bias function and sample bias.

Definition 1. *Let K be a random variable over $\mathbb{Z}_q$. The modulus bias $B_q(K)$ is defined as*

$$B_q(K) = E\left[\exp\left((2\pi K/q)\,i\right)\right]$$

Let $E(K)$ denote the expected value of random variable K and let i be an imaginary unit. In the same way, the sample bias of the set of points $K = \{k_i\}_{i=1}^{M}$ in $\mathbb{Z}_q$ is defined as

$$B_q(K) = \frac{1}{M}\sum_{i=1}^{M}\exp\left((2\pi k_i/q)\,i\right) \tag{1}$$

By fast Fourier transform (FFT), the computational complexity is $O(M\log M)$. For some positive integer l, let the higher l bits of K be fixed to a certain constant, and the remaining $(\lambda - l)$ bits be random. The following equation is given in [11].

$$\lim_{q\to\infty}|B_q(K)| = \frac{2^l}{\pi}\cdot\sin\left(\frac{\pi}{2^l}\right) \tag{2}$$

If no bits are fixed, its absolute value of sample bias is estimated as $1/\sqrt{M}$. In addition, we can easily see that $\lim_{l\to\infty}\lim_{q\to\infty}|B_q(K)| = 1$ from Eq. (2).

The following lemma is given in [3].

Lemma 1. *Suppose that the random variable K follows the following distribution on $\mathbb{Z}_q$ for $b \in \{0,1\}$, all $\varepsilon \in [0, 1/2]$ and even $q > 0$.*

$$\begin{cases} \Pr[K = k_i] = (1-b)\cdot\frac{1-\varepsilon}{q/2} + b\cdot\frac{\varepsilon}{q/2} & \text{if } 0 \le k_i < q/2 \\ \Pr[K = k_i] = b\cdot\frac{1-\varepsilon}{q/2} + (1-b)\cdot\frac{\varepsilon}{q/2} & \text{if } q/2 \le k_i < q \end{cases}$$

Letting K_b be a uniform distribution over $[bq/2, (b+1)\,q/2)$, the modular bias of K is given by

$$B_q(K) = (1-2\varepsilon)\,B_q(K_b). \tag{3}$$

It can be easily verified that $|B_q(K_0)| = |B_q(K_1)|$. Note that Eq. (3) considers only 1 bit leakage. The absolute value of $B_q(K)$ is given by

$$|B_q(K)| = (1-2\varepsilon)\cdot\frac{2}{\pi}\sin\frac{\pi}{2}. \tag{4}$$

2.4   Fourier Analysis-Based Attack

Bleichenbacher introduced Fourier analysis based attack in [4]. First, we consider a naive search method to obtain the secret key sk using the bias function, which is shown in Algorithm 2. Let M be the number of signatures obtained. In the case in which the input sample $\{(z_i, h_i)\}_{i=1}^{M}$ is biased K_i, we randomly select a candidate secret key $w \in \mathbb{Z}_q$ and then calculate $K_w = \{z_i + h_i w \bmod q\}_{i=1}^{M}$. Next, we compute $|B_q(K_w)|$ under Eq. (1). If $w = \mathrm{sk}$, then K_w is biased and $|B_q(K_w)|$ has the peak. Then finding the correct key sk is possible. However, this method is inefficient because it must search w in all $\mathbb{Z}_q$.

Algorithm 2. Naive search

Input: $(h_i, z_i)_{i=1}^{M}$: HNP samples over $\mathbb{Z}_q$
Output: Correct secret key sk
1: // *Select a candidate w for the secret key.*
2: **for** $w = 1$ to $q - 1$ **do**
3:     Calculate $K_w = \{z_i + h_i w \bmod q\}_{i=1}^{M}$.
4:     Calculate $|B_q(K_w)|$.
5: **end for**
6: **return** w which maximizes $|B_q(K_w)|$.

De Mulder et al. [8] and Aranha et al. [2] proposed a method to efficiently search for a secret key without performing an exhaustive search. Their methods perform a linear combination of input samples to satisfy $h'_j < L_{\mathrm{FFT}}$ until M' samples are obtained. Consequently, a new linear combined sample $\left\{(h'_j, z'_j)\right\}_{j=1}^{M'}$ is generated. The width of the peak w is extended from 1 to approximately q/L_{FFT}, showing that recovering the higher $\log L_{\mathrm{FFT}}$ bits of the secret key is possible. In a Fourier analysis-based attack, the entire secret key is recovered by repeating this process.

Let λ' be the number of already recovered bits in sk. At the first step of Fourier analysis-based attack, $\lambda' = \log L_{\mathrm{FFT}}$. Letting the higher λ' bits of sk be $\mathrm{sk_{hi}}$ and the unknown lower $(\lambda - \lambda')$ bits be $\mathrm{sk_{lo}}$, sk can be expressed as $\mathrm{sk} = 2^{\lambda - \lambda'} \mathrm{sk_{hi}} + \mathrm{sk_{lo}}$. Thus, the new HNP formula for the case in which the higher λ' bits of sk has already been recovered can be rewritten as

$$k \equiv z + h \cdot \left(2^{\lambda - \lambda'} \mathrm{sk_{hi}} + \mathrm{sk_{lo}}\right) \bmod q$$

$$k \equiv z + h \cdot 2^{\lambda - \lambda'} \mathrm{sk_{hi}} + h \cdot \mathrm{sk_{lo}} \bmod q$$

$$k \equiv \hat{z} + h \cdot \mathrm{sk_{lo}} \bmod q,$$

where $\hat{z} = z + h \cdot 2^{\lambda - \lambda'} \mathrm{sk_{hi}}$. Thus, we obtain the new HNP samples $\{(\hat{z}_i, h_i)\}_{i=1}^{M}$. When the Fourier analysis-based attack is repeated, λ' increases. The $\hat{z}$ is updated in each repetition and, finally, the whole of sk can be recovered.

Algorithm 3 shows Bleichenbacher's attack framework for a Fourier analysis-based attack. The range reduction phase of the algorithm considers two constraints on linear combinations for efficient key searches, namely, small and sparse linear combinations.

In the small linear combination constraint, it should be satisfied that $\omega_{i,j} \in \{-1, 0, 1\}$ and $h'_j = \sum_{i=1}^{M} \omega_{i,j} h_i < L_{\mathrm{FFT}}$. This constraint is used to reduce the

---

Algorithm 3. Bleichenbacher's attack framework

Input: $\{(h_i, z_i)\}_{i=1}^{M}$: Sample of HNP over $\mathbb{Z}_q$. M': Number of linear combinations to find. L_{FFT}: FFT table size.

Output: $\text{MSB}(\text{sk})_{\log L_{\text{FFT}}}$.

1: **Range reduction**
2: For all $j \in [1, M']$, the coefficients are $\omega_{i,j} \in \{-1, 0, 1\}$, and the linear combination pairs are denoted as $(h'_j, z'_j) = (\sum_i \omega_{i,j} h_i, \sum_i \omega_{i,j} z_i)$. In this case, we generate M' sample $\{(h'_j, z'_j)\}_{j=1}^{M'}$ that satisfies the following two conditions.

    (1) Small : $0 \le h'_j < L_{\text{FFT}}$.
    (2) Sparse : $|B_q(K)|^{\Omega_j} \gg 1/\sqrt{M'}$, where $\Omega_j := \sum_i |\omega_{i,j}|$ for all $j \in [1, M']$.

3: **Bias computation**
4: $Z := (Z_0, \ldots Z_{L_{\text{FFT}}-1}) \leftarrow (0, \ldots, 0)$
5: **for** $j = 1$ to M' **do**
6:    $Z_{h'_j} \leftarrow Z_{h'_j} + \exp\left((2\pi z'_j/q)\,\mathrm{i}\right)$
7: **end for**
8: Let $w_i = iq/L_{\text{FFT}}$, $\{B_q(K_{w_i})\}_{i=0}^{L_{\text{FFT}}-1} \leftarrow \text{FFT}(Z)$
   $= \left(B_q(K_{w_0}), B_q(K_{w_1}), \ldots, B_q\left(K_{w_{L_{\text{FFT}}-1}}\right)\right)$.
9: Find i that maximizes $|B_q(K_{w_i})|$.
10: **return** $\text{MSB}(w_i)_{\log L_{\text{FFT}}}$.

---

search range by linear combinations. To enable h'_j to be smaller, we can take linear combinations with a greater number of h_i (i.e., a fewer number of $\omega_{i,j} = 0$). The fewer the number of linear combinations, the smaller L_{FFT} becomes, and thus the width of the peak, q/L_{FFT} increase. However, if too many linear combinations are taken, the peak value decreases exponentially. Although the original peak value is $|B_q(K)|$, the peak bias after linear combinations is $|B_q(K)|^{\Omega_j}$, due to constraint, which exponentially decreases if we take Ω_j linear combinations. If the peak value is sufficiently larger than the average of the noise $1/\sqrt{M'}$, it can be distinguished. Therefore, constraints are imposed as sparse linear combinations to distinguish them from noise values.

The constraints of sparse linear combinations limit the number of linear combinations that can be taken such that the peak value is prevented from becoming too small. Now, estimating the number of samples M' after the linear combination (assuming that Ω_j is constant) depends only on $|B_q(K)|$, and finding the modular bias in a rigorous manner is critical. In a Fourier analysis-based attack, bias computation is performed using FFT, which has a computational complexity of $O(L_{\text{FFT}} \log L_{\text{FFT}})$ and can thus be calculated efficiently. However, range reduction is not known to be inefficient and requires considerable computational time. Table 3 in [3] shows that the bias computation (FFT) consumes 1 hour, but range reduction (collision) consumes 42 hours when the key length is 162-bit, and the nonce is 1 bit leak with $\varepsilon = 0.027$.

2.5 $\mathcal{K}$-List Sum Problem

Let the birthday problem be the problem of choosing $x_1 \in \mathcal{L}_1$ and $x_2 \in \mathcal{L}_2$ from 2 lists $\mathcal{L}_1$ and $\mathcal{L}_2$ with random n bits elements that satisfy $x_1 \oplus x_2 = 0$. In addition, given a list of $\mathcal{K}$ with n bits values, the problem of selecting 1 of elements from each list and finding a pair of values for which the XOR of those $\mathcal{K}$ values is 0 is known as the Generalized Birthday Problem (GBP). In [12], Bleichenbacher observed similarities between GBP and the Fourier analysis-based attack [4]. The $\mathcal{K}$-list sum algorithm solves $\mathcal{K}$-list sum problem [6] which is the GBP subproblem.

Aranha et al. [3] used the $\mathcal{K}$-list sum algorithm to increase the number of samples while increasing the widths of peaks through linear combination. Algorithm 4 shows a 1-fold 4-list sum algorithm. Algorithm 4 first finds the pairs from two of the given four lists such that the higher a bits of the sum is a certain value, and it stores the sum in sorted lists $\mathcal{L}'_1$ and $\mathcal{L}'_2$. Next, from $\mathcal{L}'_1$ and $\mathcal{L}'_2$, select a pair (x'_1, x'_2) whose higher n bits are equal and calculate the absolute difference $|x'_1 - x'_2|$, where the higher n bits are 0. We then obtain sorted lists with $(\lambda - n)$ bits elements. Because the higher a bits are first chosen to be equal, we only need to check whether $(a - n)$ bits are equal. The algorithm increases the $M = 2^m = 2^{a+2}$ sequences of length λ received as input to 2^{3a+v-n} sequences of length $(\lambda - n)$ by linear combination.

Algorithm 4. Parameterized 4-list sum algorithm based on Howgrave–Graham–Joux

---

Input: $\{\mathcal{L}_i\}_{i=1}^{4}$: Sorted list of uniform random samples of λ bits uniform random samples of length 2^a. n: Number of higher bits to be discarded in each round. $v \in [0, a]$: Parameter

Output: $\mathcal{L}'$: List of $(\lambda - n)$-bit samples

1: For each $c \in [0, 2^v)$:

  (a) Search for a pair $(x_1, x_2) \in \mathcal{L}_1 \times \mathcal{L}_2$ satisfying $\mathrm{MSB}_a (x_1 + x_2) = c$. Output a new sorted list $\mathcal{L}'_1$ with $x_1 + x_2$ as $2^a \cdot 2^a \cdot 2^{-a} = 2^a$ elements. Similarly, for $\mathcal{L}_3, \mathcal{L}_4$, the sorted list $\mathcal{L}'_2$ is obtained.

  (b) Search for a pair $(x'_1, x'_2) \in \mathcal{L}'_1 \times \mathcal{L}'_2$ satisfying $\mathrm{MSB}_n (|x'_1 - x'_2|) = 0$. Output a new sorted list $\mathcal{L}'$ with $|x'_1 - x'_2|$ as $2^a \cdot 2^a \cdot 2^{-(n-a)} = 2^{3a-n}$ elements.

2: **return** $\mathcal{L}'$

Algorithm 5 is an iterative 4-list sum algorithm that calls Algorithm 4 as a subroutine. If 2^a is the length of each sublist, it can be expressed as $M = 2^m = 4 \cdot 2^a = 2^{a+2}$. Let n be the number of higher bits to be nullified, and let $N = 2^n$. $M' = 2^{m'} < 2^{2a}$ is the number of samples output with the higher n bits as 0. In addition, v is the number of iterations in range reduction with $v \in [0, a]$, and $T = 2^t = 2^{a+v}$ and T is the time complexity. From [6], it holds that $TM^2 = N$. Now, the N is $2^4 M' N$ and therefore the following holds.

$$2^4 M' N = TM^2 \tag{5}$$

From Eq. (5), we obtain

$$m' = 3a + v - n \qquad (6)$$

Let r be the number of times the attacker repeats the 4-list sum algorithm. By iterating, find a small linear combination of 4^r integers that satisfies the budget parameter of the FFT table so that it is less than $L_{FFT} = 2^{\ell_{FFT}}$ and so that the FFT computation is tractable. In this case, the trade-off equation for each round $i = 0, \ldots, r - 1$ can be rewritten as

$$m'_i = 3a_i + v_i - n_i, \qquad (7)$$

where $m_{i+1} = m'_i$. The output of the i-th round is used for the input of the $i + 1$-th round.

Table 1 lists the constraints of a linear programming problem when Algorithm 5 is optimized in terms of time, memory, and the number of signatures. Consider the optimization case in which m_{in} is minimized. Let t_{max} be the maximum time spent in each round, m_{max} be the maximum memory, and $\ell_{FFT} = \log L_{FFT}$ be the memory size for the FFT. These are quantities determined by the amount that can be spent (i.e., cost). The α is a slack parameter that enables the peak to be more observable and depends on the maximum possible noise value. This value can be estimated by examining the distribution of $\{h'_j\}_{j=1}^{M'}$ and is given by approximately $\sqrt{2 \ln (2L_{FFT}/\varepsilon)}$ [3].

Letting $m_r := \log M'$, $m_r = 2 (\log \alpha - 4^r \log |B_q (K)|)$ is derived from the constraint sparse linear combinations. Estimating $|B_q (K)|$ is sufficient to estimate the number of samples M' required after linear combination. In addition, $|B_q (K)|$ is the only value related to the number of bits l in the leaked nonce. Depending on the length λ of the secret key, each n_i is differently chosen and the choice of n_is affects other parameters.

Algorithm 5. Iterative HGJ 4-list sum algorithm

Input: $\mathcal{L}$: List of $M = 4 \times 2^a$ uniforml random λ-bit samples. $\{n_i\}_{i=0}^{r-1}$: The number of higher bits to be discarded in each round. $\{v_i\}_{i=0}^{r-1}$: Parameters where $v_i \in [0, a_i]$.
Output: $\mathcal{L}'$: List of $(\lambda - \sum_{i=0}^{r-1} n_i)$-bit samples with length 2^{m_r}.
1: Let $a_0 = a$.
2: For each $i = 0, \ldots, r - 1$:

    (a) Divide $\mathcal{L}$ into four lists $\mathcal{L}_1, \mathcal{L}_2, \mathcal{L}_3, \mathcal{L}_4$ of length 2^{a_i} and sort each list.
    (b) Give parameters n_i and v_i and $\{\mathcal{L}_i\}_{i=1}^{4}$ to Algorithm 4. Obtain a single list $\mathcal{L}'$ of length $2^{m_{i+1}} = 2^{3a_i + v_i - n_i}$. Let $\mathcal{L} := \mathcal{L}'$ and $a_{i+1} = m_{i+1}/4$.

3: **return** $\mathcal{L}'$

Table 1. Linear programming problem based on iterative HGJ 4-list sum algorithm (Algorithm 5). Each column is a constraint to optimize time and space and data [3].

	Time	Space	Data
minimize	$t_0 = \ldots = t_{r-1}$	$m_0 = \ldots = m_{r-1}$	m_{in}
subject to	—	$t_i \leq t_{\max}$	$t_i \leq t_{\max}$
subject to	$m_i \leq m_{\max}$	—	$m_i \leq m_{\max}$
subject to	$m_{i+1} = 3a_i + v_i - n_i$		$i \in [0, r-1]$
	$t_i = a_i + v_i$		$i \in [0, r-1]$
	$v_i \leq a_i$		$i \in [0, r-1]$
	$m_i = a_i + 2$		$i \in [0, r-1]$
	$m_{i+1} \leq 2a_i$		$i \in [0, r-1]$
	$m_{\text{in}} = m_0 + f$		
	$\lambda \leq \ell_{\text{FFT}} + f + \sum_{i=0}^{r-1} n_i$		
	$m_r = 2\left(\log \alpha - 4^r \log\left(|B_q\left(\boldsymbol{K}\right)|\right)\right)$		

3 Modular Bias for Multiple Bit Leakage

Aranha et al. [3] discussed the security of ECDSA only for 1 bit noisy leakage. Considering practical circumstances, more bit leakage can be obtained. This section will analyze the security for the case where more noisy bits are obtained.

3.1 Modular Bias for 2 Bits Leakage

We extend the evaluation of the modular bias for a single noisy bit case presented in Eq. (3) to one when the nonce leaks multiple bits with errors. We begin with the most simple case: modular bias for $l = 2$ and extend the result for general l. The modular bias is also given for the case in which each bit has a different error rate. The nonce obtained by a side-channel attack is not necessarily completely error-free. Thus far, evaluation of the case of nonce leakage with errors has been limited to the case of 1 bit leakage as done by Aranha et al. [3]. This work allows us to evaluate and discuss the security of the ECDSA in more detail by estimating the modular bias in the case of multiple bit leakage.

Lemma 2 (Modular bias for $l = 2$). *Suppose that the random variable $\boldsymbol{K}$ follows the following distribution over $\mathbb{Z}_q$ for $b \in \{0, 1, 2, 3\}$, $\varepsilon_1, \varepsilon_2 \in [0, 1/2]$ and even $q > 0$.*

$$\begin{cases} \Pr\left[K = k_i\right] = \frac{(1-b)(2-b)(3-b)}{6} \cdot \frac{(1-\varepsilon_1)(1-\varepsilon_2)}{q/4} + \frac{b(2-b)(3-b)}{2} \cdot \frac{\varepsilon_1\varepsilon_2}{q/4} \\ \qquad -b\left(1-b\right)\left(3-b\right) \cdot \frac{\varepsilon_1(1-\varepsilon_2)}{q/4} + \frac{b(1-b)(2-b)}{6} \cdot \frac{(1-\varepsilon_1)\varepsilon_2}{q/4} \quad \text{if } 0 \le k_i < q/4 \\ \Pr\left[K = k_i\right] = \frac{(1-b)(2-b)(3-b)}{6} \cdot \frac{(1-\varepsilon_1)\varepsilon_2}{q/4} + \frac{b(2-b)(3-b)}{2} \cdot \frac{(1-\varepsilon_1)(1-\varepsilon_2)}{q/4} \\ \qquad -b\left(1-b\right)\left(3-b\right) \cdot \frac{\varepsilon_1\varepsilon_2}{q/4} + \frac{b(1-b)(2-b)}{6} \cdot \frac{\varepsilon_1(1-\varepsilon_2)}{q/4} \quad \text{if } q/4 \le k_i < q/2 \\ \Pr\left[K = k_i\right] = \frac{(1-b)(2-b)(3-b)}{6} \cdot \frac{\varepsilon_1(1-\varepsilon_2)}{q/4} + \frac{b(2-b)(3-b)}{2} \cdot \frac{(1-\varepsilon_1)\varepsilon_2}{q/4} \\ \qquad -b\left(1-b\right)\left(3-b\right) \cdot \frac{(1-\varepsilon_1)(1-\varepsilon_2)}{q/4} + \frac{b(1-b)(2-b)}{6} \cdot \frac{\varepsilon_1\varepsilon_2}{q/4} \quad \text{if } q/2 \le k_i < 3q/4 \\ \Pr\left[K = k_i\right] = \frac{(1-b)(2-b)(3-b)}{6} \cdot \frac{\varepsilon_1\varepsilon_2}{q/4} + \frac{b(2-b)(3-b)}{2} \cdot \frac{\varepsilon_1(1-\varepsilon_2)}{q/4} \\ \qquad -b\left(1-b\right)\left(3-b\right) \cdot \frac{(1-\varepsilon_1)\varepsilon_2}{q/4} + \frac{b(1-b)(2-b)}{6} \cdot \frac{(1-\varepsilon_1)(1-\varepsilon_2)}{q/4} \quad \text{if } 3q/4 \le k_i < q \end{cases}$$

Let K_b be a uniform distribution over $[bq/4, (b+1)\,q/4)$. The modular bias of K is then given by

$$B_q\left(K\right) = \{(1 - 2\varepsilon_1)\left(1 - \varepsilon_2\right) + \mathrm{i}\left(1 - 2\varepsilon_1\right)\varepsilon_2\} B_q\left(K_b\right).$$

Proof. See Appendix A.

Remark 1. We now consider the case in which $\varepsilon_2 = 0.5$, (i.e., the same case in which no bias exists in the second bit, which is completely random). In this case, the absolute value of the bias is given by

$$|B_q\left(K\right)| = |(1 - 2\varepsilon_1) \times 0.5 + \mathrm{i}\left(1 - 2\varepsilon_1\right) \times 0.5| \cdot \frac{2^2}{\pi} \sin\frac{\pi}{2^2} = (1 - 2\varepsilon_1) \cdot \frac{2^1}{\pi} \sin\frac{\pi}{2^1}. \quad \cdot$$

We can easily verify that the value is equal to Eq. (4), which is the expression for $l = 1$. In addition, it is better to point out that the bias is 0 regardless of the value of ε_2 in the case of $\varepsilon_1 = 0.5$.

3.2 Generalization to Modular Bias for Multiple Bit Leakage

We next generalize the modular bias to the case in which the higher l bits of the nonce leaks with errors. To simplify the discussion, consider the case where each bit contains an error with probability ε. Given l, let K_b be a uniform distribution over $\left[bq/2^l, (b+1)\,q/2^l\right)$. $b \in \{0, 1, \ldots, 2^l - 1\}$. We can easily verify that all of $|B_q\left(K_b\right)|$ are equal regardless of the value of b. Therefore, it is enough to obtain $B_q\left(K_0\right)$. Let $\mathcal{H}\left(j\right)$ be the Hamming weight when j is expressed in binary. If the higher l bits of the nonce are all 0 and no errors occur, K_0 corresponding to $b = 0$ is uniformly distributed over $\left[0, q/2^l\right)$. When an error is contained in each bit with probability ε, each bit is 1 with probability ε. Thus, the number of bits containing errors is the same as the number of 1 bits and can be expressed in terms of Hamming weights. In addition, the number of error-free bits is $l - \mathcal{H}\left(j\right)$. From this, for the higher l bits, if an error occurs in each bit with an error rate of ε, the modular bias is expressed as

$$\left\{ \sum_{j=0}^{2^l-1} \exp\left(\frac{2j\pi}{2^l}\mathrm{i}\right) \varepsilon^{\mathcal{H}(j)} \left(1 - \varepsilon\right)^{l-\mathcal{H}(j)} \right\} B_q\left(K_0\right). \qquad (8)$$

We next simplify the term $\sum_{j=0}^{2^l-1} \exp\left(2j\pi\mathrm{i}/2^l\right) \varepsilon^{\mathcal{H}(j)} (1-\varepsilon)^{l-\mathcal{H}(j)}$ appeared in Eq. (8).

$$
\sum_{j=0}^{2^l-1} \exp\left(\frac{2j}{2^l}\pi\mathrm{i}\right) \varepsilon^{\mathcal{H}(j)} (1-\varepsilon)^{l-\mathcal{H}(j)}
$$

$$
= \sum_{j=0}^{2^{l-1}-1} \exp\left(\frac{4j}{2^l}\pi\mathrm{i}\right) \varepsilon^{\mathcal{H}(2j)} (1-\varepsilon)^{l-\mathcal{H}(2j)} + \sum_{j=0}^{2^{l-1}-1} \exp\left(\frac{4j+2}{2^l}\pi\mathrm{i}\right) \varepsilon^{\mathcal{H}(2j+1)} (1-\varepsilon)^{l-\mathcal{H}(2j+1)}
$$

$$
= \sum_{j=0}^{2^{l-1}-1} \exp\left(\frac{2j}{2^{l-1}}\pi\mathrm{i}\right) \varepsilon^{\mathcal{H}(2j)} (1-\varepsilon)^{l-1+1-\mathcal{H}(2j)}
$$

$$
+ \sum_{j=0}^{2^{l-1}-1} \exp\left(\frac{2j}{2^{l-1}}\pi\mathrm{i} + \frac{2}{2^l}\pi\mathrm{i}\right) \varepsilon^{\mathcal{H}(2j)+1} (1-\varepsilon)^{l-(\mathcal{H}(2j)+1)}
$$

$$
= \sum_{j=0}^{2^{l-1}-1} \exp\left(\frac{2j}{2^{l-1}}\pi\mathrm{i}\right) \varepsilon^{\mathcal{H}(j)} (1-\varepsilon)^{l-1-\mathcal{H}(j)} \times \left\{ (1-\varepsilon) + \varepsilon \exp\left(\frac{2}{2^l}\pi\mathrm{i}\right) \right\}
$$

$$
= \prod_{j=1}^{l} \left((1-\varepsilon) + \varepsilon \exp\left(\frac{2\pi\mathrm{i}}{2^j}\right) \right)
$$

During the equation transformation, we use the equation $\mathcal{H}(2j+1) = \mathcal{H}(j)+1$ for a non-negative integer j. Note that in the case of $b=0$, we just consider the Hamming distance to the binary representation $00\cdots0$ of the l-bit. In the general b case, we slightly modify to consider the Hamming distance to the binary representation of b. From this, the bias with error is expressed by the following theorem.

Theorem 1. *The modular bias for the l-bit nonce leakage with error rate ε is given by*

$$
\prod_{j=1}^{l} \left((1-\varepsilon) + \varepsilon \exp\left(\frac{2\pi\mathrm{i}}{2^j}\right) \right) B_q\left(\boldsymbol{K}_b\right). \tag{9}
$$

For the absolute value of the modular bias, the following holds and can be expressed without using complex numbers.

Corollary 1. *The absolute value of the modular bias for the l-bit nonce leakage with error rate ε is given by*

$$
\left| \prod_{j=1}^{l} \left((1-\varepsilon) + \varepsilon \exp\left(\frac{2\pi\mathrm{i}}{2^j}\right) \right) \right| \left| B_q\left(\boldsymbol{K}_b\right) \right|
$$

$$
= \sqrt{\prod_{j=1}^{l} \left(1 - 4\varepsilon(1-\varepsilon)\sin^2\frac{\pi}{2^j} \right)} \left| B_q\left(\boldsymbol{K}_b\right) \right|. \tag{10}
$$

Here, a simple calculation confirms that the absolute value of the modular bias is 0 in Eq. (8)–(10) if $\varepsilon = 0.5$.

Corollary 1 can be used to find the absolute value of the modular bias for a given number of bits and the leakage error rate. The concrete values are shown in Table 2. Each column is the number of bits leaked by the nonce, and each row is the value of the nonce's error rate.

Only the values for $\varepsilon = 0$ are shown in Table 1 of [8]. Only the values for $l = 1$ are shown in Lemma 4.2 of [3]. With the help of Corollary 1, we can calculate the precise absolute value of the modilar bias for arbitrary ε and l (as shown in yellow in the table).

These values are extended to Fig. 1 shows the modular bias plotted for each error rate. We can find that the value increases as l increases and depends on the error rate. It converges to some value that depends on the error rate ε at approximately $l = 6$. Moreover, we can see that the graph for $\varepsilon = 0.01$ has almost the same shape as that for $\varepsilon = 0$. In [3], they attacked in $\varepsilon = 0.01$ and $\varepsilon = 0.027$ cases and succeeded in recovering the secret keys.

The modular bias for $\varepsilon = 0.1$ and $l \geq 2$ is larger than that for $\varepsilon = 0$ and $l = 1$. This means that the number of signatures for a 2 bits leak with an error rate of 0.1 is less than that for a 1-bit leak with no errors. Thus, fewer signatures are required for a successful attack. We give experimental reults comaring two cases in Sect. 4.2.

Table 2. Absolute values of modular bias

l	1	2	3	4	5	6
$\varepsilon = 0$	0.6366	0.9003	0.9749	0.9935	0.9983	0.9999
$\varepsilon = 0.01$	0.6238	0.8735	0.9427	0.9605	0.9649	0.9660
$\varepsilon = 0.1$	0.5092	0.6522	0.6870	0.6957	0.6978	0.6984
$\varepsilon = 0.3$	0.2546	0.2742	0.2780	0.2788	0.2790	0.2791
$\varepsilon = 0.4$	0.1273	0.1298	0.1302	0.1303	0.1304	0.1304

3.3   Case for Different Error Rate of Each Bit

Equation (10), as presented in Sect. 3.2, shows the absolute value of the modular bias for which the error rates of each bit are equal (say, ε). We next show the modular bias for the different error rates of each bit.

Again, we consider $\boldsymbol{K_0}$ and we attempt to update the value corresponding to $\prod_{j=1}^{l} \left((1 - \varepsilon) + \varepsilon \exp\left(2\pi i/2^j\right) \right)$ in Eq. (9). The values up to $j = 1$ and $j = 2$ are $(1 - \varepsilon) - \varepsilon$ and $((1 - \varepsilon) - \varepsilon)((1 - \varepsilon) + \varepsilon i)$, respectively. Thus, we are considering cases when the MSBs do not contain errors and when MSBs contain errors. Multiplying by $1 - \varepsilon$ and εi enables us to consider those cases in

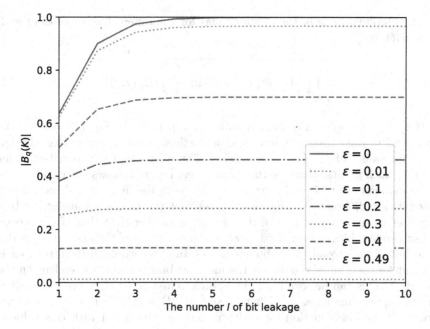

Fig. 1. Modular bias under multiple bit leakage with errors.

which the second MSB error is not included and when it is included, respectively. In general j, $1 - \varepsilon$ and $\varepsilon \exp\left(2\pi i/2^j\right)$ can be considered as the error-free bits and error-containing bits, respectively. In other words, at the j-th factor, $((1-\varepsilon)-\varepsilon)\cdots((1-\varepsilon)+\varepsilon \exp\left(2\pi i/2^j\right))$ is considered as each 2^{j-1} combination of the $(j-1)$ bits from the MSB to the $(j-1)$-th bit, with and without errors. Therefore, to establish the case in which the j-th bit does not include an error, we multiply by $1-\varepsilon$. To create the case where the j-th bit contains an error, we multiply by $\varepsilon \exp\left(2\pi i/2^j\right)$. From this, we can say that the j-th ε represents the error rate of the j-th bit from the MSB. If the error rate of each leaked bit in the nonce is different, we denote ε_j as the error rate of the j-th MSB. The modular bias in the case in which the error rate is different for each bit of Theorem 1 is as in the following theorem.

Theorem 2. *The modular bias when the nonce leaks l-bit with an error rate ε_j is given by*

$$\prod_{j=1}^{l} \left((1-\varepsilon_j) + \varepsilon_j \exp\left(\frac{2\pi i}{2^j}\right)\right) B_q\left(\boldsymbol{K}_b\right). \tag{11}$$

In the case of $l = 2$, it matches Lemma 2.

The absolute value of the modular bias for the different error rates of each bit is given by

$$\sqrt{\prod_{j=1}^{l} \left(1 - 4\varepsilon_j \left(1 - \varepsilon_j\right) \sin^2 \frac{\pi}{2^j}\right)} \left|B_q\left(\boldsymbol{K}\right)\right|. \tag{12}$$

If $\varepsilon_j = \varepsilon$ for all j, Eq. (12) is equal to Eq. (10). As Eq. (12) shows, the error rates of the higher bits have a greater effect on the modular bias. Table 3 shows the values of $\sin^2\left(\pi/2^j\right)$ for each j. This shows that the contribution for $j = 1$ is much greater than for the other cases. Figure 2 shows the exact values of the modular bias when the error rates between the first bit and second and after bits are different. The figure indicates that the absolute value of the bias is greater when the error rate of the first bit is smaller than that of the second and subsequent bits as compared to when the error rate of the first bit is greater than that of the second and subsequent bits. In other words, if the error rate is different for each bit of the nonce, the modular bias is highly dependent on the first MSB. This can be seen from the approximated equation, since for small x, $\sin^2 x$ is approximated as x^2. That is, $\sin^2\left(\pi/2^j\right) \approx \pi^2/2^{2j}$ if $j \geq 5$. A visual explain of the bias function for multi-bit leakage associated with this value is shown in Appendix B.

Table 3. Values of $\sin^2 \dfrac{\pi}{2^j}$ at each j.

j	1	2	3	4	5	6	$\cdots$	10
$\sin^2(\pi/2^j)$	1	0.5	0.146	0.038	0.009	0.002	$\cdots$	0.000009

The term $\sqrt{1 - 4\varepsilon_j\left(1 - \varepsilon_j\right)\sin^2\left(\pi/2^j\right)}$ in Eq. (12) can be expressed as

$$\sqrt{1 - 4\varepsilon_j\left(1 - \varepsilon_j\right)\left(\pi^2/2^{2j}\right)} \tag{13}$$

from the above approximation. We can see that this term rapidly converges to 1 as $l \to \infty$, regardless of the value of ε_j.

Intuitively, the proof of Lemma 2 shows that $\Pr\left[\boldsymbol{K} = k_i\right]$ is designed so that one term of each $\Pr\left[\boldsymbol{K} = k_i\right]$ remains depending on the value of b. Related figures are shown in Figs. 3 and 4. Figure 3 shows the modular bias for the 2 bits case, and Fig. 4 shows the modular bias for the 3 bits case. The sum of the absolute values of the four or eight vectors is 1, respectively. The absolute value of the sum of these vectors is the absolute value of the modular bias. An interesting fact is that a vector with 2 or 3 bits wrong has a smaller effect on the absolute value of the modular bias than a vector with only 1 bits wrong. In addition, Figs. 3 and 4 show the sum of the vectors is 0 if $\varepsilon_1 = 0.5$, which is mentioned at the end of Remark 1.

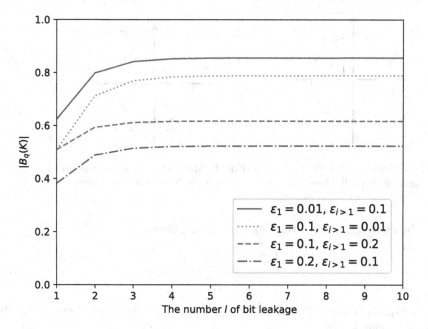

Fig. 2. Modular bias for different error rate for each bit of nonce

3.4 The Number of Signatures Required for Key-Recovery and Error Rates

The constraint of sparse linear combinations is given by $|B_q(K)|^{\Omega_j} \gg \alpha/\sqrt{M'}$. Suppose that $|B_q(K)|$ α are given for this inequality. We can satisfy the inequality by choosing smaller Ω_j, which is the number of linear combinations, or larger M', which is the number of samples after linear combination. The number of samples after linear combination required for r rounds is given by the following equation based on the error rate and bias.

$$M' \gg \alpha / \left(\sqrt{\prod_{j=1}^{l} \left(1 - 4\varepsilon_j (1 - \varepsilon_j) \sin^2 \frac{\pi}{2^j}\right)} |B_q(K_b)| \right)^{2 \times 4^r} \tag{14}$$

From the fact that $v_i \leq a_i$ in the input of Algorithm 5 and Eq. (7), we obtain $m_{i+1} \leq 4m_i - n_i - 8$. We then have the following.

$$m' = m_r \leq 4^r m_0 - \sum_{i=0}^{r-1} 4^{r-i-1} n_i - \frac{8}{3} (4^r - 1) \tag{15}$$

In the 4-list sum algorithm, it holds that $t_i = a_i + v_i$, $m_i = a_i + 2$, and $v_i \leq a_i$ in the input of Algorithm 5. Accordingly, the inequations $t_i \leq 2m_i - 4$ are obtained.

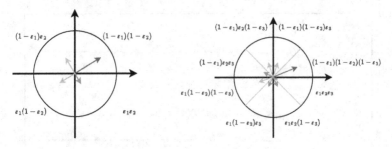

Fig. 3. Modular bias illustrated on the unit circle with 2 bits leakage.   **Fig. 4.** Modular bias illustrated on the unit circle with 3 bits leakage.

We then have the sum of time complexity as follows.

$$\sum_{i=0}^{r-1} t_i \leq 2 \sum_{i=0}^{r-1} m_i - 4r \tag{16}$$

From Eqs. (14) and (15), the estimated number of signatures required for the attack is bounded by

$$M \geq \frac{1}{\prod_{j=1}^{l} \left(1 - 4\varepsilon_j \left(1 - \varepsilon_j\right) \sin^2\left(\pi/2^j\right)\right)} \times \frac{1}{\{(2^l/\pi) \cdot \sin\left(\pi/2^l\right)\}^2} \times 2^{\mathcal{A}}, \tag{17}$$

where

$$\mathcal{A} = \sum_{i=0}^{r-1} 4^{-i-1} n_i + \frac{8}{3}\left(1 - 4^{-r}\right). \tag{18}$$

From Eq. (17), we can see that a higher error rate increases the number of signatures required and that an increase in the length of the known nonce reduces the number of signatures required. For example, from Table 2, a comparison of $\varepsilon = 0.01$ and $\varepsilon = 0.1$ when $l = 2$ reveals that $0.8725^2/0.6522^2 \approx 1.79$ times increase. In addition, comparing $l = 3$ and $l = 1$ for $\varepsilon = 0.01$, we see that $0.9427^2/0.6238^2 \approx 2.284$ times increase in the number of signatures. Furthermore, we find that the error rate and size of the bias do not affect the number of signatures required, whereas the number of rounds is varied. Note that the values for $l = 1$ are completely consistent with the evaluation of Aranha et al.

To understand Eq. (17), we can break it down into three separate parts and analyze each one individually.

Third term, represented by $2^{\mathcal{A}}$, remains constant regardless of any changes to l or ε. By utilizing Eqs. (17) and (18), we can determine that the number of required signatures for an attack is solely dependent on r and n_is, provided that l and ε remain unchanged. These values are utilized in the calculation of $\mathcal{A}$. Moreover, if r is fixed, it depends only on n_is. Therefore, the number of signatures required for the attack depends on the value of n_i. Here, n_i is represented by constraints such as $m_{i+1} = 3a_i + v_i - n_i$ and $\lambda - \ell_{\text{FFT}} - f \leq \sum_{r=0}^{r-1} n_i$ as given in Table 1. M is minimized if the equality holds. It is also multiplied by the square of the inverse of the modular bias. Considering each value in Table 2, we find that the number of signatures required increases significantly for high error rates.

The initial component of Eq. (17) is referred to as the *penalty* term, which is always greater than 1, except when all ε_j values are zero. Moreover, as the value of ε_j increases, this term also increases, ultimately leading to an increase in M. This aligns with our natural intuitions.

The value of the second term is determined solely by the parameter l. As l increases, this term gradually decreases and approaches 1, but it always remains greater than 1. As l increases, the required signatures decrease, which intuitively makes sense. The penalty term prevents the second term from reducing M, and its significance increases with an increase in ε_j. However, it does not completely eliminate the possibility of the second term reducing M.

Combing Eq. (17) with Eq. (13), we can estiamte the contribution j-th MSB leakage. We can see that as l becomes larger, M will decrease, but its rate of decrease will be negligibly small.

4 Experimental Results

4.1 Extension to Multiple Bit Leakage with Errors

Aranha et al. [3] have posted a script on GitHub [10] for solving linear programming problems based on Table 1. In this script, ε is freely changeable. On the other hand, the number l of nonce bits to leak is fixed to $l = 1$. In a Fourier analysis-based attack, the leakage bit length and error rate affect only $|B_q(\boldsymbol{K})|$ in the constraints of Table 1. Therefore, we can easily obtain the script for multiple bits leakage by replacing the $|B_q(\boldsymbol{K})|$ evaluation equation for the [10] script with Eq. (10).

We first naively optimize the number of signatures for multiple bit leakage with errors using a script with only $|B_q(\boldsymbol{K})|$ modifications. Figure 5 shows the optimal number of signatures for each ε and l. Here, $\lambda = 162$, $m_{\text{max}} = 40$, $\ell_{\text{FFT}} = 40$, $t_{\text{max}} = 80$, $r = 2$. In addition, α depends only on the value of ε because L_{FFT} is fixed.

4.2 Attack Experiment

For 131-bit ECDSA, we recover the secret key when nonces have 1 bit leakage without error and when 2 bits leakage, each with an error rate of 0.1. The computer used in the experiments has Intel Xeon Silver 4214R CPU $\times 2$ and 256 GB of DDR4 RAM. The parameters for the $l = 1, \varepsilon = 0$ and $l = 2, \varepsilon = 0.1$

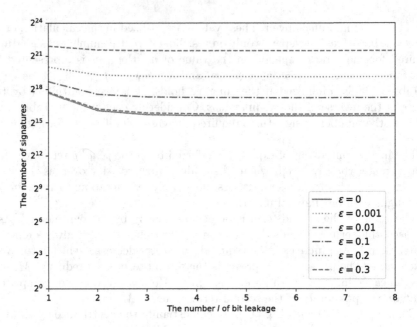

Fig. 5. The number of signatures required for the extended [3] script.

cases are shown in Table 4. Table 5 shows the obtained $M' = 2^{m'} = 2^{m_2}$, mean value of bias and peak bias as a result of range reduction. In both cases, the top 29 bits were successfully recovered. The experimental results show that $l = 2, \varepsilon = 0.1$ successfully recovers the secret key with a smaller bias value. Note that the error rate of 2 bits is 0.19, since the error rate of each bit is 0.1.

Table 4. Paramenters of attack experiment.

	a_0	a_1	v_0	v_1	n_0	n_1
$(l, \varepsilon) = (1, 0)$	22	24	18	18	48	55
$(l, \varepsilon) = (2, 0.1)$	22	24	18	16	48	55

From the experimental results, when $l = 2, \varepsilon = 0.1$, the secret key was successfully recovered with about $1/16$ of the number of samples after linear combination than when $l = 1, \varepsilon = 0$. Furthermore, the time required for range reduction is about 0.26 times smaller. Although the value of M' is changed by the parameter v in this case, the number of signatures required can be changed by changing other parameters, and it can be inferred that the 2 bits leakage requires a smaller number of signatures.

Next, the parameters in Table 4 were changed to $a_0 = 20, a_1 = 23$, and $v_1 = 18$ to confirm the experiment in the case with errors. As a result, $M' = 2^{23.0}$,

Table 5. Experiment result.

	M'	Average noise	Peak bias	Range reduction time (sec)
$(l, \varepsilon) = (1, 0)$	$2^{28.1}$	1.5×10^{-5}	1.5×10^{-4}	5957
$(l, \varepsilon) = (2, 0.1)$	$2^{22.1}$	2.0×10^{-6}	1.7×10^{-5}	1555

the time was 1984 seconds, and the secret key is successfully recovered. This shows that $l = 2, \varepsilon = 0.1$ can be recovered with fewer signatures and in less time than without errors.

5   Conclusion

We first evaluated the number of signatures by finding the formula of the modular bias for multiple bit leakage in the nonce. The modular bias as indicated by De Mulder et al. [8] and Aranha et al. [3] was extended to the case in which the MSBs of the nonce were leaked with multiple errors. We then proved Theorem 1. As the modular bias can now be calculated for any l, ε, we can now estimate the required number of signatures using a linear combination algorithm. In addition, the absolute value of the modular bias was given by Corollary 1. This corollary indicates that the error rate of the first MSB of the nonce has a greater effect on the modular bias than the error rates of the other bits. We then provided an estimate of the number of signatures required for various error rates.

We evaluated the number of signatures and computation time by obtaining the parameters of the 4-list sum algorithm. Then, we performed an attack on 131-bit ECDSA with $l = 2, \varepsilon = 0.1$, and succeeded in recovering the secret key with fewer signatures with $l = 1, \varepsilon = 0$.

Acknowledgements. This work was supported by JST CREST Grant Number JPMJCR2113 and JSPS KAKENHI Grant Number 21H03440.

A   Proof of Lemma 2

The proof for $b = 0$ is as follows. Note that for simplicity, we denote $\exp\left(2\pi i k_i / q\right)$ by $\mathcal{E}_q\left(k_i\right)$.

$$B_q\left(\boldsymbol{K}\right) = \boldsymbol{E}\left[\exp\left(2\pi i \boldsymbol{K}/q\right)\right] = \sum_{k_i \in \mathbb{Z}_q} \mathcal{E}_q\left(k_i\right) \cdot \Pr\left[\boldsymbol{K} = k_i\right]$$

$$= \frac{\left(1 - \varepsilon_1\right)\left(1 - \varepsilon_2\right)}{q/4} \sum_{k_i \in [0, q/4)} \mathcal{E}_q\left(k_i\right) + \frac{\left(1 - \varepsilon_1\right)\varepsilon_2}{q/4} \sum_{k_i \in [q/4, q/2)} \mathcal{E}_q\left(k_i\right)$$

$$+ \frac{\varepsilon_1\left(1 - \varepsilon_2\right)}{q/4} \sum_{k_i \in [q/2, 3q/4)} \mathcal{E}_q\left(k_i\right) + \frac{\varepsilon_1\varepsilon_2}{q/4} \sum_{k_i \in [3q/4, q)} \mathcal{E}_q\left(k_i\right)$$

$$= \frac{(1-\varepsilon_1)(1-\varepsilon_2)}{q/4} \sum_{k_i \in [0,q/4)} \mathcal{E}_q(k_i) + \frac{(1-\varepsilon_1)\varepsilon_2}{q/4} \sum_{k_i^{(1)} \in [0,q/4)} \mathcal{E}_q\left(k_i^{(1)} + q/4\right)$$

$$+ \frac{\varepsilon_1(1-\varepsilon_2)}{q/4} \sum_{k_i^{(2)} \in [0,q/4)} \mathcal{E}_q\left(k_i^{(2)} + q/2\right) + \frac{\varepsilon_1\varepsilon_2}{q/4} \sum_{k_i^{(3)} \in [0,q/4)} \mathcal{E}_q\left(k_i^{(3)} + 3q/4\right)$$

$$= \frac{(1-\varepsilon_1)(1-\varepsilon_2)}{q/4} \sum_{k_i \in [0,q/4)} \mathcal{E}_q(k_i) + i\frac{(1-\varepsilon_1)\varepsilon_2}{q/4} \sum_{k_i^{(1)} \in [0,q/4)} \mathcal{E}_q\left(k_i^{(1)}\right)$$

$$- \frac{\varepsilon_1(1-\varepsilon_2)}{q/4} \sum_{k_i^{(2)} \in [0,q/4)} \mathcal{E}_q\left(k_i^{(2)}\right) - i\frac{\varepsilon_1\varepsilon_2}{q/4} \sum_{k_i^{(3)} \in [0,q/4)} \mathcal{E}_q\left(k_i^{(3)}\right)$$

$$= \frac{(1-2\varepsilon_1)(1-\varepsilon_2)}{q/4} \sum_{k_i \in [0,q/4)} \mathcal{E}_q(k_i) + i\frac{(1-2\varepsilon_1)\varepsilon_2}{q/4} \sum_{k_i \in [0,q/4)} \mathcal{E}_q(k_i)$$

$$= \{(1-2\varepsilon_1)(1-\varepsilon_2) + i(1-2\varepsilon_1)\varepsilon_2\} B_q(K_b)$$

B Visual Explanation of the Bias Function for Multi-bit Leakage

In this appendix, Eq. (9) is represented graphically. In Eq. (9), at each j, $(1-\varepsilon)+$ $\exp(2\pi i/2^j)$ can be understood as a point in the complex plane with 1 and $\exp(2\pi i/2^j)$ endowed by $1-\varepsilon : \varepsilon$. The endpoints in the complex plane at $j = 1, 2$ and $j = 3, 4$ in Figs. 6 and 7, respectively, are indicated by red dots. ε and $1-\varepsilon$ in the figures represent ratios. When $j = 1$, the two points 1 and -1 are endowed by $1-\varepsilon : \varepsilon$, and the red point is in the complex plane at coordinates $1 - 2\varepsilon$. When $j = 2$, we endow 1 and i, and when $j = 3$, we endow 1 and $\exp(\pi i/4)$ with $1-\varepsilon : \varepsilon$.

As j increases, $\exp(2\pi i/2^j)$ approximates 1. Therefore, $\exp(2\pi i/2^j)$ and the interior point of 1 also approximates 1. Figures 6 and 7 also show that the interior point approximates 1 in the complex plane. The absolute value also approximates 1.

Table 2 shows that as l increases, the value does not readily increase. As explained in Sect. 3.3, this is because $\sin^2(\pi/2^j)$ is closer to 0. This can also be observed in Figs. 6 and 7.

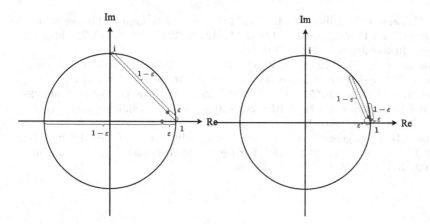

Fig. 6. When the first and second bits leak.

Fig. 7. When the third and fourth bits leak.

References

1. Albrecht, M.R., Heninger, N.: On bounded distance decoding with predicate: breaking the "lattice barrier" for the hidden number problem. In: Canteaut, A., Standaert, F.X. (eds.) EUROCRYPT 2021. LNCS, vol. 12696, pp. 528–558. Springer, Cham (2021). https://doi.org/10.1007/978-3-030-77870-5_19

2. Aranha, D.F., Fouque, P., Gérard, B., Kammerer, J., Tibouchi, M., Zapalowicz, J.: GLV/GLS decomposition, power analysis, and attacks on ECDSA signatures with single-bit nonce bias. In: Sarkar, P., Iwata, T. (eds.) ASIACRYPT 2014. LNCS, vol. 8873, pp. 262–281. Springer, Heidelberg (2014). https://doi.org/10.1007/978-3-662-45611-8_14

3. Aranha, D.F., Novaes, F.R., Takahashi, A., Tibouchi, M., Yarom, Y.: Ladderleak: breaking ECDSA with less than one bit of nonce leakage. In: ACM CCS 2020, pp. 225–242 (2020). https://doi.org/10.1145/3372297.3417268

4. Bleichenbacher, D.: On the generation of one-time keys in DL signature schemes. In: Presentation at IEEE P1363 Working Group Meeting, p. 81 (2000)

5. Boneh, D., Venkatesan, R.: Hardness of computing the most significant bits of secret keys in Diffie-Hellman and related schemes. In: Koblitz, N. (eds.) CRYPTO 1996. LNCS, vol. 1109, pp. 129–142. Springer, Heidelberg (1996). https://doi.org/10.1007/3-540-68697-5_11

6. Dinur, I.: An algorithmic framework for the generalized birthday problem. Des. Codes Cryptogr. **87**(8), 1897–1926 (2019). https://doi.org/10.1007/s10623-018-00594-6

7. Liu, M., Nguyen, P.Q.: Solving BDD by enumeration: an update. In: Dawson, E. (eds.) CT-RSA 2013. LNCS, vol. 7779, pp. 293–309. Springer, Heidelberg (2013). https://doi.org/10.1007/978-3-642-36095-4_19

8. Mulder, E.D., Hutter, M., Marson, M.E., Pearson, P.: Using bleichenbacher's solution to the hidden number problem to attack nonce leaks in 384-bit ECDSA. In: Bertoni, G., Coron, JS. (eds.) CHES 2013. LNCS, vol. 8086, pp. 435–452. Springer, Heidelberg (2013). https://doi.org/10.1007/978-3-642-40349-1_25

9. Sun, C., Espitau, T., Tibouchi, M., Abe, M.: Guessing bits: improved lattice attacks on (EC)DSA with nonce leakage. IACR TCHES **2022**(1), 391–413 (2022). https://doi.org/10.46586/tches.v2022.i1.391-413

10. Takahashi, A.: LadderLeak attack ECDSA (2020). https://github.com/akiratk0355/ladderleak-attack-ecdsa/blob/master/tradeoffs-submit.ipynb

11. Takahashi, A., Tibouchi, M., Abe, M.: New bleichenbacher records: fault attacks on QDSA signatures. IACR TCHES **2018**(3), 331–371 (2018). https://doi.org/10.13154/tches.v2018.i3.331-371

12. Wagner, D.A.: A generalized birthday problem. In: Yung, M. (eds.) CRYPTO 2002. LNCS, vol. 2442, pp. 288–303. Springer, Heidelberg (2002). https://doi.org/10.1007/3-540-45708-9_19

Single Trace Analysis of Comparison Operation Based Constant-Time CDT Sampling and Its Countermeasure

Keon-Hee Choi[1], Ju-Hwan Kim[1], Jaeseung Han[1], Jae-Won Huh[1], and Dong-Guk Han[1,2(✉)]

[1] Department of Financial Information Security, Kookmin University, Seoul, Republic of Korea
{dy1637,zzzz2605,gjwodnjs987,jae1115,christa}@kookmin.ac.kr
[2] Department of Information Security, Cryptology, and Mathematics, Kookmin University, Seoul, Republic of Korea

Abstract. Cumulative Distribution Table (CDT) sampling is a Gaussian sampling technique commonly used for extracting secret coefficients or core matrix values in lattice-based Post-Quantum Cryptography (PQC) algorithms like FrodoKEM and FALCON. This paper introduces a novel approach: a single trace analysis (STA) method for comparison operation based constant-time CDT sampling, as employed in SOLMAE—a candidate for Korean Post-Quantum Cryptography (KPQC) first-round digital signature Algorithm. The experiment is measuring power consumption during the execution of SOLMAE's sampling operation on an 8-bit AVR compiler microcontrollers unit (MCU) using ChipWhisperer-Lite. By utilizing STA, this paper recovered output of comparison operation based constant-time CDT sampling. The source of CDT sampling leakage is investigated through an in-depth analysis of the assembly code. The 8-bit AVR MCU conducts comparison operations on values exceeding 8 bits by dividing them into 8-bit blocks. Consequently, the execution time of a CDT sampling operation is influenced by the outcome of each block's comparison operation due to conditional branching. To address these concerns, this paper begins by summarizing trends in CDT sampling related research to design robust countermeasures against single trace analysis. Furthermore, a novel implementation method for comparison operation based constant-time CDT sampling against STA is proposed. This assembly-level implementation removes branching statements and performs comparative operations on all data words. Through experimental validation, this paper demonstrates the safety of the proposed countermeasure algorithm against STA.

Keywords: Side Channel Analysis · Single Trace Analysis · PQC · Gaussian sampling · CDT sampling · KPQC · SOLMAE · AVR

© The Author(s), under exclusive license to Springer Nature Singapore Pte Ltd. 2024
H. Seo and S. Kim (Eds.): ICISC 2023, LNCS 14561, pp. 185–201, 2024.
https://doi.org/10.1007/978-981-97-1235-9_10

1   Introduction

The usage of public key cryptographic algorithms, such as Public-key Encryption (PKE)/Key Encapsulation Mechanism (KEM) and Digital Signature Algorithm (DSA), is widespread across various fields. However, it has been demonstrated that these algorithms will become vulnerable in the future due to the emergence of quantum computers and Shor's algorithm. [1,2] To address these security concerns, the National Institute of Standards and Technology (NIST) initiated the PQC standardization competition in 2016. The objective of this competition is to develop public-key cryptographic algorithms that can resist attacks from quantum computers. Currently, a subround is in progress following the final round of the competition. Additionally, as part of the competition, new algorithms are being proposed that build upon the shortlisted and selected algorithms. The competition was divided into two main areas for public-key cryptography, namely PKE/KEM and Digital Signature. Importantly, numerous lattice-based algorithms have been proposed in both areas. In these lattice-based cryptographic algorithms, important values are extracted from the Gaussian distribution, and the method employed to extract them using a table is known as CDT sampling. In other words, CDT sampling is a crucial role in lattice-based algorithms.

There are many ways to implement CDT sampling. The first proposed CDT sampling has been analyzed using the technique proposed by [3], resulting in the proposal of constant-time CDT sampling. This constant-time CDT sampling was implemented using subtraction in FrodoKEM and Lizard. Additionally, [4,5] proposed STA for CDT sampling then secret value of FrodoKEM was leaked. Repeatedly, CDT sampling is very important. In this paper, we study in detail the security of side channel analysis for comparison operation based CDT sampling in MITAKA [6] and SOLMAE [7], which are a similar structure of the Falcon. Importantly, the security of side channel analysis for these comparison operation based CDT sampling techniques has not been studied before this work. This paper recovery the sampling value of CDT sampling through STA for vulnerability that is variable the operating time of CDT sampling depending on the results of comparative operations in 8-bit AVR MCU. To validate this vulnerability, the paper employs ChipWhisperer-Lite to measure power consumption during CDT sampling on the Atmel XMEGA-128, using the AVR compiler for the 8-bit processor. Additionally, using assembly code root cause analysis, the paper proposes a secure constant-time CDT sampling method using comparison operations to counter STA.

1.1   Contribution

This paper addresses the safety of comparison operation based constant-time CDT sampling from a side-channel analysis perspective, which has not been previously studied. In addition, by analyzing the power consumption traces used in SOLMAE, we identified the *basesampler* in the overall cryptographic operation algorithm. This increases the feasibility of the STA in this paper. So, this paper describes the reason for vulnerability in comparison operation-based

CDT sampling in great detail. Experiments have confirmed that CDT sampling in 8-bitAVR MCU varies in operating time depending on comparison operation results. The cause analysis was performed using an assembly code. In the 8-bit AVR MCU, during CDT sampling operations, when comparing values larger than 8 bits, the process is divided into 8-bit units. The analysis reveals that the operation concludes the moment the result is determined, resulting in a change in execution time. In essence, not all blocks undergo comparison operations, and this behavior is closely associated with the presence of branch statements.

A novel STA is propose for comparison operation based CDT sampling. Additionally, a new CDT sampling implementation method is propose to resist side-channel analysis, contributing to the development of secure algorithms for CDT sampling. The practical implementation removes the branch statements from the assembly code and presents a structure where all blocks can be compared. Experimental verification demonstrates the resistance to STA through power consumption trace analysis.

1.2   Organization

The remainder of this paper introduces STA for CDT sampling through a total of five sections. In Sect. 2, it provides detailed explanation of lattice, LWE, and NTRU, emphasizing the significance of Gaussian sampling. This highlights the importance of CDT sampling, the two implementation methods, and the imperative need to investigate the security of comparison based CDT sampling, which has not been previously explored. Moving on to Sect. 3, it presents the experimental setup and target implementation. Section 4 delves into a side channel analysis of CDT sampling based on comparison operations. Here, it detailed describe the application method of STA and the cause of the vulnerability. In Sect. 5, we present the implementation of CDT sampling in which vulnerabilities are mitigated through an analysis of the underlying causes. To demonstrate their resistance against the attack technique proposed in this paper, it collect actual a power consumption trace. Finally, Sect. 6 addresses conclusions and future research directions.

2   Backgrounds

In this section, we provide an introductory overview of lattice-based cryptography [8], LWE, and NTRU encryption schemes. Following that, we delve into the Gaussian distribution and proceed to describe CDT sampling, which is of paramount importance as a module. We then elaborate on timing side-channel analysis conducted on the original CDT sampling, followed by an in-depth description of a STA of the subtraction operation based constant-time CDT sampling.

2.1 Lattice

Definition 1. Lattice: Given n linearly independent vectors $\mathbf{b_1}, \mathbf{b_2}, ..., \mathbf{b_n} \in \mathbb{R}^m$, the lattice $\mathcal{L}(\mathbf{b_1}, \mathbf{b_2}, ..., \mathbf{b_n})$ is defined as the set of all linear combinations of $\mathbf{b_1}, \mathbf{b_2}, ..., \mathbf{b_n}$ with integer coefficients, i.e.,

$$\mathcal{L}(\mathbf{b_1}, \mathbf{b_2}, ..., \mathbf{b_n}) = \left\{ \sum_{i=1}^{n} x_i \mathbf{b_i} \mid x_i \in \mathbb{Z} \right\}.$$

We refer to $\mathbf{b_1}, \mathbf{b_2}, ..., \mathbf{b_n}$ as a basis of the lattice.

Equivalently, if we define $\mathbf{B}$ as the $m \times n$ matrix whose columns are $\mathbf{b_1}, \mathbf{b_2}, ..., \mathbf{b_n}$, then the lattice generated by $\mathbf{B}$ is

$$\mathcal{L}(\mathbf{B}) = \{\mathbf{Bx} \mid \mathbf{x} \in \mathbb{Z}^n\}.$$

2.2 NTRU and LWE

The first public key cipher based on Lattice was proposed by A.M. in 1997, and since then, various studies have been conducted to create efficient encryption algorithms [9]. In Lattice-based encryption, efficiency primarily refers to speed and key size. NTRU, proposed by Hoffstein et al. in 1996 [10], is known for its fast encryption process. Falcon, MITAKA, and SOLMAE are examples of NTRU-based encryption algorithms [6,7,11].

Definition 2. NTRU: Let q be a positive integer, and $z(x) \in \mathbb{Z}$ be a monic polynomial. Then, a set of NTRU secrets consists of four polynomials $f, g, F, G \in R_q$ which satisfy the NTRU equation:

$$fG - gF \equiv q \mod z(x).$$

And define h as $h \leftarrow g \cdot f^{-1} \mod q$. Then, given h, find f and g.

LWE was proposed by Regev in 2005 [12]. LWE is known to be NP-hard, even when adding small values of noise. CRYSTAL-KYBER and CRYSTAL-Dilithium are examples of LWE-based cryptographic algorithms [13,14].

Definition 3. LWE: Let n and q be positive integers, and let χ be a distribution over $\mathbb{Z}$. For a vector $s \in \mathbb{Z}_q^n$, the LWE distribution $\mathcal{A}_{s,\chi}$ over $\mathbb{Z}_q^n \times \mathbb{Z}_q$ obtained by choosing $a \in \mathbb{Z}_q^n$ and an integer error e from χ. The distribution returns the pair $(a, \langle a, s \rangle + e \mod q)$.

There are two important concepts of LWE.

- **Search-LWE problem:** Given m independent samples $(a_i, b_i) \in \mathbb{Z}_q^n \times \mathbb{Z}_q$ drawn from $\mathcal{A}_{s,\chi}$, find s.
- **Decision-LWE problem:** Given m independent samples $(a_i, b_i) \in \mathbb{Z}_q^n \times \mathbb{Z}_q$, distinguish whether each sample is drawn from the uniform distribution or from $\mathcal{A}_{s,\chi}$.

2.3   Discrete Gaussian Distribution

In this paper, CDT sampling is the method to extract random values from Gaussian distribution. Prior to CDT sampling, the definition of the discrete Gaussian distribution on the lattice is given as follows.

Definition 4. Discrete Gaussian Distribution over Lattice: Let $\forall c \in \mathbb{R}^n$, $\sigma \in \mathbb{R}^+$,

$$\forall x \in \mathbb{R}^n, \rho_{\sigma,c}(x) = exp(\frac{-\pi \| x - c \|^2}{\sigma^2}).$$

Then, for $\forall c \in \mathbb{R}^n$, $\sigma \in \mathbb{R}^+$, n-dimensional lattice $\mathcal{L}$, define the Discrete Gaussian Distribution over $\mathcal{L}$ as:

$$\forall x \in \mathcal{L}, \mathcal{D}_{L,\sigma,c}(x) = \frac{\rho_{\sigma,c}(x)}{\rho_{\sigma,c}(\mathcal{L})}.$$

2.4   CDT Sampling

Some lattice-based schemes based on LWE extract the error from a Gaussian distribution. Similarly, certain lattice-based schemes based on NTRU create essential values from a Gaussian distribution. CDT sampling is an efficient method for extracting values from these Gaussian distributions, and ensuring the security of such CDT sampling is of utmost importance. The CDT table stores specific probability values of the Gaussian distribution. CDT sampling is an algorithm that randomly generates probability values and determines the range within which the generated values fall among those stored in the table. The value to be sampled at this point corresponds to the determined index. There are several ways to implement CDT sampling, and this paper deals with the safety study of implementing CDT sampling based on comparison operations.

Algorithm 1. The CDT sampling vulnerable to timing attack

    Input : CDT table Ψ, σ, τ
  Output : Sampled value S
1: $rnd \leftarrow [0, \tau\sigma] \cap \mathbb{Z}$ uniformly at random
2: sign $\leftarrow [0, 1] \cap \mathbb{Z}$ uniformly at random
3: $i \leftarrow 0$
4: **while** $(rnd > \Psi[i])$ **do**
5:    $i + +$
6: **end while**
7: $S \leftarrow ((-\text{sign}) \wedge i) + \text{sign}$
8: **return** S

The initially proposed CDT sampling Algorithm 1 was found to be vulnerable to the timing attack proposed by [3]. This vulnerability arises due to the different timing of the *while* loop termination. As a remedy, constant-time CDT sampling utilizes *for* statements. There are two ways to implement this: CDT sampling based on comparison operations and CDT sampling based on subtraction operations.

Algorithm 2. The subtraction operation based CDT sampling

    Input : CDT table Ψ of length ℓ, σ, τ
    Output : Sampled value S
1: $rnd \leftarrow [0, \tau\sigma)$ uniformly at random
2: sign $\leftarrow [0, 1] \cap \mathbb{Z}$ uniformly at random
3: $S \leftarrow 0$
4: **for** $i = 0$ to $\ell - 1$ **do**
5:    $S \mathrel{+}= (\Psi[i] - rnd) \gg 63$
6: **end for**
7: $S \leftarrow ((-\text{sign}) \wedge S) + \text{sign}$
8: **return** S

Both methods are available for schemes that use CDT sampling. However, only subtraction based CDT sampling has been suggested to be vulnerable. Algorithm 2 is an example of subtraction operation based CDT sampling. LWE-based lattice-based schemes commonly employ this algorithm [15,16]. Additionally, it has been proposed to perform STA by the power differences between negative and positive numbers [4,5]. Moreover, an attack to find the secret key of a cryptographic algorithm has been proposed using this method.

Algorithm 3. The comparison operation based CDT sampling: half-Gaussian table access CDT

    Input : CDT table Ψ of length ℓ, σ, τ
    Output : Sampled value S
1: $rnd \leftarrow [0, \tau\sigma)$ uniformly at random
2: sign $\leftarrow [0, 1] \cap \mathbb{Z}$ uniformly at random
3: $S \leftarrow 0$
4: **for** $i = 0$ to $\ell - 1$ **do**
5:    $S \mathrel{+}= (rnd \geq \Psi[i])$
6: **end for**
7: $S \leftarrow ((-\text{sign}) \wedge S) + \text{sign}$
8: **return** S

On the other hand, NTRU-based lattice-based schemes often utilize CDT sampling based on comparison operations, especially in [6,7,17] which employs hybrid sampling. Algorithm 3 is the comparison based CDT sampling. Unlike conventional methods, it performs sampling from Gaussian distribution using comparison operations.

3   Experiment Setup

In this section, the experimental environment and the CDT sampling code employed in the STA experiments are described. The C code of SOLMAE, a candidate from the KPQC Round 1 digital signature category, was implemented in the AtmelXMEGA128 environment. Power consumption traces were collected during the operation for analysis.

3.1   Implimentation of Comparison Operation Based CDT Sampling

The *BaseSampler* function implemented in SOLMAE and MITAKA employs a comparison operation based CDT sampling approach. Thus, this paper utilizes the reference code of SOLMAE, which was proposed as a candidate for KPQC Round 1 digital signature. Specifically, our focus is on the *BaseSampler* function within the code. The sampling technique in SOLMAE follows the sampling outlined in [17] and employs a table to generate values from a half-Gaussian distribution. The *BaseSampler* function is illustrated in Listing 1.1. The CDT table contains 13 values arranged in ascending order, which are sequentially compared against the randomly selected value "r" from the reference code.

```
int base_sampler()
{
  uint64_t r = get64(); //get randomly 64 bits from RNG.
  int res = 0;
  for (int i = 0; i < TABLE_SIZE; i++)
    res += (r >= CDT[i]);
  return res;
}
```

Listing 1.1. *BaseSampler* function C code

3.2   Target Device of Experiment

The board utilized in this paper consists of an AtmelXMEGA128 (8-bit processor) and Chipwhisperer-Lite. The AtmelXMEGA128 is an 8-bit AVR MCU. The *BaseSampler* function implemented in *SOLMAE* operates on the AtmelXMEGA128 board, while Chipwhisperer-Lite is employed to collect the power consumption data during the *BaseSampler* function operation Fig. 1.

The experimental steps conducted in this paper are as follows:

- Collection of power consumption data during the comparison operation-based CDT sampling.
- Analysis of the assembly language, considering different compiler optimization levels, to identify vulnerabilities in the comparison operations.
- Investigation of comparison operation vulnerabilities using real-world traces.

Fig. 1. AtmelXMEGA128(8-bit AVR MCU) and Chipwhisperer-Lite

– Acquisition of output values for the newly proposed CDT sampling algorithm through STA.

This paper demonstrates that vulnerable implementations of comparison operations, which could be realistic in a commercialized environment, can expose the actual values of CDT sampling. Furthermore, a CDT sampling algorithm resistant to side-channel attacks is proposed.

4   Side Channel Analysis of Comparison Operation Based Constant-Time CDT Sampling

4.1   Description of the Cause of Vulnerability

The security of comparison operations heavily depends on the specific implementation technique and enviroment like compiler. Let us consider the comparison of two multi-word numbers, denoted as A and B in Fig. 2.

Various methods can be employed to compare these numbers. One common approach is to initiate the comparison with the most significant words. Compare A and B as follows:

1. Check if A_0 is greater than B_0. If so, $A > B$.
2. Check if A_0 is less than B_0. If true, $A < B$.
3. Check if A_0 and B_0 are equal. If true, continue to compare the next word until the comparison ends.

This implementation is vulnerable to side channel analysis. For instance, let's consider two scenarios: (1) $A_0 > B_0$ and (2) $A_0 = B_0, A_1 < B_1$. In these situations, the execution time of the comparison operations may differ. As a result, timing vulnerabilities arise, which can be exploited through STA to distinguish

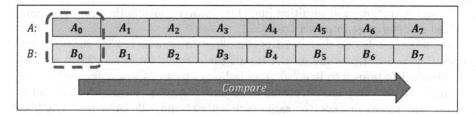

Fig. 2. The comparison of two multi-word numbers, denoted as A and B. A and B are each 8 blocks.

between the two scenarios. Therefore, a comparison algorithm resistant to STA is required.

```
<base_sampler>:
    ...
    24c:                    ldi  r22, 0x00
    24e:                    ldi  r23, 0x00
    250:                    ldd  r24, Z+7
    252:                    cp   r25, r24
    254:                    brcs .+74          ; 0x2a0 <base_sampler+0x92>
    256:                    cp   r24, r25
    258:                    brne .+66          ; 0x29c <base_sampler+0x8e>
    25a:                    ldd  r24, Z+6
    25c:                    cp   r20, r24
    25e:                    brcs .+64          ; 0x2a0 <base_sampler+0x92>
    260:                    cp   r24, r20
    262:                    brne .+56          ; 0x29c <base_sampler+0x8e>
    ...
    29c:                    ldi  r22, 0x01     ; 1
    29e:                    ldi  r23, 0x00     ; 0
    2a0:                    add  r18, r22
    2a2:                    adc  r19, r23
    ...
```

Listing 1.2. Base Sampler() assembly code

In this section, the vulnerabilities associated with various implementations of weak comparison operations are explored. The assembly code of the *BaseSampler* function used in *SOLMAE* is examined for various optimization levels (Level: 0, 1, 2, 3, s) provided by the AtmelXMEGA128. The assembly code depicted in Listing 1.2 illustrates the part of *BaseSampler* function for the optimized s-level. It is evident that the comparisons are performed sequentially, word by word. Notably, vulnerabilities in the word based comparison method are evident. The process of performing comparison operations for each optimization level follows a similar pattern as shown in Listing 1.2. Subsequent instructions are dependent on the results of the word comparisons, leading to variations in executed operations and resulting in distinct power consumption patterns manifested as differences in power traces.

In more detail, the first word is compared in lines 252, 254, and the next operation varies depending on the result. First, calculate $r25 - r24$. If a carry occurred, then branch to line 2a0. This indicates that $r24$ was a greater number than $r25$. If no carry has occurred, go to lines 256, 258. Then, calculate $r24 - r25$. If the values are not the same between $r24$ and $r25$, branch to line 29c. This means that $r25$ was a greater number than $r24$. If the values were the same, compare the next two words by executing the following lines. Repeat this process until the comparison operation is finally completed. In other words, the vulnerability appears in the fact that the processing method in the branch statement varies depending on the result of the comparison operation. This is an important point to understand for design of countermeasure.

4.2   Single Trace Analysis on the Comparison Operation Based Constant-Time CDT Sampling

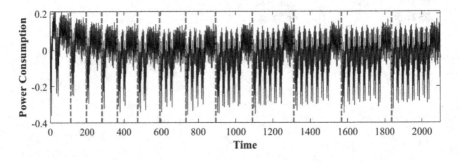

Fig. 3. The power consumption trace of maximum r on $uint64\_t$

The *BaseSampler* function utilized in SOLMAE implements CDT sampling through comparison operations, as depicted in Listing 1.1. The comparison operations are performed between two operands of the $uint64\_t$ data type: a random variable r and each the 13 values stored in the CDT table. On an 8-bit processor, these comparison operations are performed by dividing them into 8 words. The aforementioned comparison operations have two vulnerabilities. First, the number of comparisons depends on the values being compared. Second, the value being added depends on the result of each comparison operation, i.e., an additional operation is required to add 1. Therefore, it is risky to work with data types larger than *word*.

Figure 3 shows the power consumption trace of the *CDTsampling* when r is set to the maximum value of the $uint64\_t$ data type (i.e., $2^{64} - 1$). From the power consumption trace, it is evident that the number of comparisons with

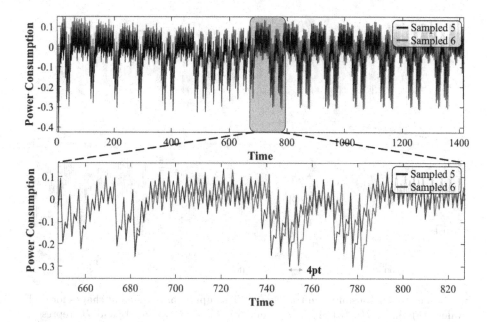

Fig. 4. Two power consumption traces differ by only one in sampling values. They differ by only one in r values

each CDT table differs, indicating variations in computation time based on the compared values.

Figure 4 shows two power consumption traces with only a difference of 1 in the values of 'r.' More precisely, the return values, sampled by the difference in 'r' values, also differ by one. The noted discrepancy is a result of the optional addition operation, leading to evident distinctions between the two traces. This is also related to the data type of the resulting value returned. Since the returned data type is a unit larger than the *word*, a difference also occurs in the addition operation. These discrepancies in power consumption traces enable the visual detection of any divergence in assembly instructions.

An increment of 1 of the sampling result occurs when r is greater than or equal to value of table in the comparison between r and the value of table. Furthermore, the values in the CDT table are arranged in ascending order. Consequently, once r becomes smaller than a particular value in the CDT table, the resulting value remains unchanged. This implies that if a comparison operation with a CDT table value greater than r is identified, the output of CDT sampling can be obtained. The power consumption traces of the first word in the comparison operation, as depicted in Fig. 5, exhibit distinct shapes for the scenarios where r is greater than, equal to, and less than the value in the CDT table, respectively. The visual distinctiveness of these power traces facilitates the acquisition of the CDT sampling value. This vulnerability arises from the inherent characteristics of the weak comparison operation, as discussed earlier.

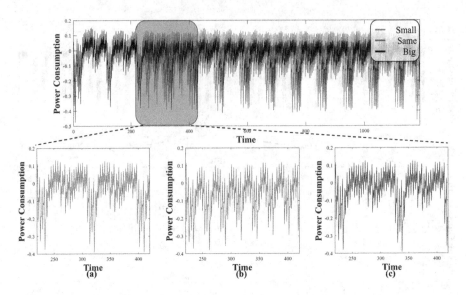

Fig. 5. The power consumption traces of CDT sampling have different shapes for each r value: (a) $A_0 < B_0$, (b) $A_0 = B_0$, and (c) $A_0 > B_0$ where A_i and B_i represent individual words.

5   Countermeasure

In the previous section, we highlighted the vulnerability of comparison operations when processing data larger than the word size of the processor. To address this issue and ensure the safety of comparison operation based constant-time CDT sampling, we propose a novel implementation method with countermeasure.

Before introducing the proposed countermeasure, we first provide an overview of trends in countermeasures related to CDT sampling. First, in [4] the CDT sampling method using Table was proposed. But it requires a large storage space. In addition, there is also the protection of sampling through the masking method proposed by [18] and the random shuffling method proposed by [19,20]. However, But these have memory overheads and time overheads. And analysis techniques related to these are being proposed. [21]. However, since there have not been many studies related to sampling using comparison operation, a new concept of implementing CDT sampling using comparison operation has been attempted.

In previous sections, the cause of vulnerability mentioned in this paper were attributed to the varying number of clock cycles depending on the branch statement in the 8-bit AVR MCU environment. Hence, the countermeasure proposed an implementation method that eliminates the discrepancy in the number of clock cycles. The proposed secure CDT sampling algorithm in this paper is denoted as Algorithm 4. The algorithm processes the r and the CDT table in word-sized blocks, corresponding to the processing units of the processor. The values in r, CDT table that exceed the word size are divided into n word blocks. Comparison operations are performed identically each block. However, if the outcome of a comparison operation is determined in the previous block, subsequent operations are only performed, i.e., it does not affect the result. Due to the inherent nature of comparison operations, methods employing them may result in branching. Branching commands such as 'brne' and 'brcc' are commonly used. In AVR instruction sets, 'brne' and 'brcc' differ by only 1 with respect to true and false conditions, allowing for an equal adjustment in the number of clock cycles for the operation. However, this implementation approach can be considered risky. Therefore, this paper introduces an assembly code that effectively eliminates the need for branch commands while implementing Algorithm 4.

Algorithm 4. STA-Resistant CDT sampling
___
   Input : -
   Output : Sampled value z
   1: $z \leftarrow 0$
   2: $r_i \xleftarrow{\$} [0, 2^{word\ size})$ uniformly random with $i = 0$ to n
   3: **for** $i = 0$ to $Table\_size - 1$ **do**
   4:    $gt \leftarrow 0, lt \leftarrow 0$
   5:    **for** $j = 0$ to $n - 1$ **do**
   6:       $gt\ |= (\neg(gt\ |\ lt))\&(r_j > CDT_{i,j})$
   7:       $lt\ |= (\neg(gt\ |\ lt))\&(r_j < CDT_{i,j})$
   8:    **end for**
   9:    $z\ += 1 \oplus lt$
   10: **end for**
   11: **return** z

```
<STA-Resistant CDT sampling>:
      . . .
      278:            ldi   r18, 0x00  ; 0
      27a:            cp    r22, r23
      27c:            adc   r18, r18
      27e:            and   r24, r18
      280:            or    r19, r24
      282:            mov   r24, r19
      284:            or    r24, r25
      286:            com   r24
      288:            ldi   r18, 0x00  ; 0
      28a:            cp    r23, r22
      28c:            adc   r18, r18
      . . .
```

Listing 1.3. The comparison operation of assembly implementation code of countermeasure

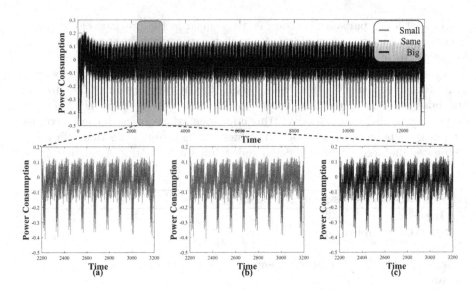

Fig. 6. The traces that overlap all three types of STA-Resident CDT sampling. And (a) $A_0 < B_0$, (b) $A_0 = B_0$, and (c) $A_0 > B_0$ where A_i and B_i represent individual words.

Listing 1.3 is a parts of the assembly code, representing the comparison operation in the proposed countermeasure. The blue and red lines in Listing 1.3 correspond to the comparison operations in Algorithm 4. Lines 278 and 288 initialize the value of register r18, where the result of the comparison operation will be stored, to zero. Lines 27a and 28a perform comparisons between registers r22 and r23 using 'cp' commands, respectively, and store the results in the carry flag. Lines 27c and 28c execute an addition operation on the initialized r18 using the 'adc' (add with carry) instruction. During this operation, the stored carry values are combined, resulting in the storage of the comparison operation's result within r18. This approach allowed me to eliminate the need for branching instructions, thus removing the vulnerabilities previously mentioned.

Figure 6 illustrates the power consumption traces of 3 different types of the Listing 1.3 operating in the 8-bit AVR MCU. The power consumption traces (a), (b), and (c), which are fully examined by overlapping with a, b, and c, represent the corresponding power consumption traces. Similar to Fig. 5, (a), (b), and (c) signify whether the most significant block of 'r' is greater than, equal to, or less than the value in the CDT table. The trace reveals that there are no discernible variations in the comparison time across different values. This serves as compelling evidence that CDT sampling demonstrates resistance against STA.

6   Conclusion and Futurework

This paper introduces a secure implementation of CDT sampling for Gaussian sampling techniques. CDT sampling is used by many algorithms to generate important values. And this paper presents an analysis of a previously unexplored vulnerability that STA in comparison operation-based CDT sampling. This paper identifies a vulnerability in which the operation time varies depending on the results of the comparison operation in 8-bit AVR MCU. The cause of the vulnerability was demonstrated through different of the number of instruction at the assembly stage. It was investigated that it was a vulnerability due to the difference in the number of clocks.

The feasibility of extracting CDT sampling outputs in real-world environments, such as AtmelXMEGA128, is demonstrated. AtmelXMEGA128 is an 8-bit AVR MCU and is used in various environments. We also employed different compiler options (0, 1, 2, 3, s) provided by Chipwhisperer in the AtmelXMEGA128 environment and verified the presence of the vulnerability across all of them. In this paper, we utilized the example of compiler option level 's,' which is set as the default among several available options. In this paper, we did not show power consumption traces for other options, as we observed that all options exhibited the same or even greater leakage. In addition, this paper deals with vulnerabilities that depend on the processor's word size and compiler. During our investigation, we observed that the number of clock cycles varied depending on the branch instruction employed. It also showed the impact of the attack by recovering the sampling value. This finding sheds light on the potential risks associated with future cryptographic algorithms that employ CDT sampling with vulnerable comparison operations, using SOLMAE as a case study. We conducted an analysis of power consumption traces to pinpoint the sections of the SOLMAE algorithm utilizing CDT sampling. This demonstrated the practical applicability of STA.

To address these concerns, a robust CDT sampling design is proposed, ensuring security against STA in real-world. To address these issues, our proposed countermeasure for CDT sampling in this paper aims to stabilize the number of clock cycles, irrespective of the branch statement used. So, First we delved into the countermeasure algorithms for CDT sampling that were previously explored. Our investigation revealed the existence of algorithms employing table-based comparison operations, masking methods, and shuffling techniques. And we present a method for implementing comparison operation based constant-time CDT sampling, designed to mitigate the security risks associated with the previously proposed STA. The algorithm is crafted to segment and store data in units processed by the processor, facilitating comparisons across all blocks. This design allows for sampling without reliance on the results of comparison operations.

In real-world implementations, caution is warranted branch statements. Branch statements, such as 'brne' and 'brcc' commands in 8-bit AVR MCU, introduce variability in clock cycles depending on the outcome of comparison operations. If the result of the branch leads to a distant address, the number of clock cycles will vary based on the outcome. In essence, it is the need for caution in employing branch statements. To address this variability, we propose a comparison operation based constant-time CDT sampling implementation method at the actual assembly code level. Instead of using branch statements, the results of comparison operations are stored in the result register using instructions that 'cp' and 'adc'. This approach ensures uniform operation time without relying on the specific outcome of the comparison operation. Additionally, this paper showed the power consumption traces using Chipwhisperer-Lite when operating proposed countermeasure algorithm in AtmelXMEGA128(8-bit AVR MCU) to demonstrate safety against STA.

The experimental environment of this paper is 8-bit AVR MCU. In the future, we plan to investigate the possibility of STA for comparison operation based constant-time CDT sampling in various environments.

References

1. Shor, P.W.: Polynomial-time algorithms for prime factorization and discrete logarithms on a quantum computer. SIAM Rev. **41**(2), 303–332 (1999)
2. Mosca, M.: Cybersecurity in an era with quantum computers: will we be ready? IEEE Secur. Priv. **16**(5), 38–41 (2018)
3. Kocher, P.C.: Timing attacks on implementations of Diffie-Hellman, RSA, DSS, and other systems. In: Koblitz, N. (ed.) CRYPTO 1996. LNCS, vol. 1109, pp. 104–113. Springer, Heidelberg (1996). https://doi.org/10.1007/3-540-68697-5_9
4. Kim, S., Hong, S.: Single trace analysis on constant time CDT sampler and its countermeasure. Appl. Sci. **8**(10), 1809 (2018)
5. Marzougui, S., Kabin, I., Krämer, J., Aulbach, T., Seifert, J.-P.: On the feasibility of single-trace attacks on the gaussian sampler using a CDT. In: Kavun, E.B., Pehl, M. (eds.) COSADE 2023. LNCS, vol. 13979, pp. 149–169. Springer, Cham (2023). https://doi.org/10.1007/978-3-031-29497-6_8
6. Espitau, T., et al.: Mitaka: a simpler, parallelizable, maskable variant of falcon. In: Dunkelman, O., Dziembowski, S. (eds.) EUROCRYPT 2022. LNCS, vol. 13277, pp. 222–253. Springer, Cham (2022). https://doi.org/10.1007/978-3-031-07082-2_9
7. Kim, K., et al.: Solmae algorithm specifications (2020). https://kpqc.or.kr/1
8. Regev, O.: Lecture notes of lattices in computer science, taught at the computer science Tel Aviv university (2009)
9. Ajtai, M., Dwork, C.: A public-key cryptosystem with worst-case/average-case equivalence. In: Proceedings of the Twenty-Ninth Annual ACM Symposium on Theory of Computing, pp. 284–293 (1997)
10. Hoffstein, J., Pipher, J., Silverman, J.H.: NTRU: a ring-based public key cryptosystem. In: Buhler, J.P. (ed.) ANTS 1998. LNCS, vol. 1423, pp. 267–288. Springer, Heidelberg (1998). https://doi.org/10.1007/BFb0054868
11. Fouque, P.-A., et al.: Falcon: fast-fourier lattice-based compact signatures over NTRU. Submission to the NIST's Post-quantum Cryptography Standardization Process, vol. 36, no. 5, pp. 1–75 (2018)
12. Regev, O.: On lattices, learning with errors, random linear codes, and cryptography. J. ACM (JACM) **56**(6), 1–40 (2009)
13. Bai, S., et al.: Crystals-dilithium: algorithm specifications and supporting documentation (2020)
14. Avanzi, R., et al.: Crystals-kyber algorithm specifications and supporting documentation. NIST PQC Round **2**(4), 1–43 (2019)

15. Bos, J., et al.: Frodo: take off the ring! practical, quantum-secure key exchange from LWE. In: Proceedings of the 2016 ACM SIGSAC Conference on Computer and Communications Security, pp. 1006–1018 (2016)
16. Cheon, J.H., Kim, D., Lee, J., Song, Y.: Lizard: cut off the tail! a practical post-quantum public-key encryption from LWE and LWR. In: Catalano, D., De Prisco, R. (eds.) SCN 2018. LNCS, vol. 11035, pp. 160–177. Springer, Cham (2018). https://doi.org/10.1007/978-3-319-98113-0_9
17. Howe, J., Prest, T., Ricosset, T., Rossi, M.: Isochronous gaussian sampling: from inception to implementation: With applications to the falcon signature scheme. In: Ding, J., Tillich, J.P. (eds.) PQCrypto 2020. LNCS, vol. 12100, pp. 53–71. Springer, Cham (2020). https://doi.org/10.1007/978-3-030-44223-1_4
18. Schneider, T., Paglialonga, C., Oder, T., Güneysu, T.: Efficiently masking binomial sampling at arbitrary orders for lattice-based crypto. In: Lin, D., Sako, K. (eds.) PKC 2019, Part II. LNCS, vol. 11443, pp. 534–564. Springer, Cham (2019). https://doi.org/10.1007/978-3-030-17259-6_18
19. Knuth, D.E.: Art of Computer Programming, Volume 2: Seminumerical Algorithms. Addison-Wesley Professional, Boston (2014)
20. Fisher, R.A., Yates, F.: Statistical tables for biological, agricultural and medical research. Hafner Publishing Company (1953)
21. Ngo, K., Dubrova, E., Guo, Q., Johansson, T.: A side-channel attack on a masked IND-CCA secure saber KEM implementation. IACR Trans. Cryptogr. Hardw. Embed. Syst. 676–707 (2021)

A Lattice Attack on CRYSTALS-Kyber with Correlation Power Analysis

Yen-Ting Kuo[(✉)] and Atsushi Takayasu

The University of Tokyo, Tokyo, Japan
{kuruwakuo,takayasu-a}@g.ecc.u-tokyo.ac.jp

Abstract. *CRYSTALS-Kyber* is a key-encapsulation mechanism, whose security is based on the hardness of solving the *learning-with-errors* (LWE) problem over module lattices. As in its specification, Kyber prescribes the usage of the *Number Theoretic Transform* (NTT) for efficient polynomial multiplication. Side-channel assisted attacks against *Post-Quantum Cryptography* (PQC) algorithms like Kyber remain a concern in the ongoing standardization process of quantum-computer-resistant cryptosystems. Among the attacks, *correlation power analysis* (CPA) is emerging as a popular option because it does not require detailed knowledge about the attacked device and can reveal the secret key even if the recorded power traces are extremely noisy. In this paper, we present a two-step attack to achieve a full-key recovery on lattice-based cryptosystems that utilize NTT for efficient polynomial multiplication. First, we use CPA to recover a portion of the secret key from the power consumption of these polynomial multiplications in the decryption process. Then, using the information, we are able to fully recover the secret key by constructing an LWE problem with a smaller lattice rank and solving it with lattice reduction algorithms. Our attack can be expanded to other cryptosystems using NTT-based polynomial multiplication, including Saber. It can be further parallelized and experiments on simulated traces show that the whole process can be done within 20 min on a 16-core machine with 200 traces. Compared to other CPA attacks targeting NTT in the cryptosystems, our attack achieves lower runtime in practice. Furthermore, we can theoretically decrease the number of traces needed by using lattice reduction if the same measurement is used. Our lattice attack also outperforms the state-of-the-art result on integrating side-channel hints into lattices, however, the improvement heavily depends on the implementation of the NTT chosen by the users.

Keywords: CRYSTALS-Kyber · lattice · side-channel attack · number theoretic transform

1 Introduction

1.1 Background

With the development of quantum computation, what is usually hard to solve on the traditional computer (factorization, DLP, etc.) will become efficiently

H. Seo and S. Kim (Eds.): ICISC 2023, LNCS 14561, pp. 202–220, 2024.
https://doi.org/10.1007/978-981-97-1235-9_11

solvable by applying Shor's algorithm [26], which will make the public-key cryptosystems most people use now unreliable. Thus, there is a significant interest in post-quantum cryptography (PQC) algorithms, which are based on mathematical problems presumed to resist quantum attacks. To standardize such algorithms, the National Institute of Standards and Technology (NIST) initiated a process to solicit and evaluate PQC candidates being submitted [22]. After three rounds of the process, they had identified four candidate algorithms for standardization and four more to be evaluated in round 4.

CRYSTALS-KYBER (Kyber) [2] is one out of the four candidates that are confirmed to be standardized in July, 2022, and it is the only public-key encryption and key-establishment algorithm. It belongs to the category of lattice-based cryptography, and in particular a module Learning With Errors (module-LWE) scheme. Kyber prescribes the usage of the Number Theoretic Transform (NTT) for efficient polynomial multiplication. Via point-wise multiplication of transformed polynomials, i.e., $ab = \text{NTT}^{-1}(\text{NTT}(a) \circ \text{NTT}(b))$, multiplication can be performed in time $O(n \log n)$, where n is the degree of polynomial a and b. Kyber has three parameter sets: Kyber512, Kyber768 and Kyber1024 with security level similar to that of AES128, AES192 and AES256.

Power analysis attacks, introduced by Kocher [15,16], exploit the fact that the instantaneous power consumption of a cryptographic device depends on the data it processes and on the operation it performs. There exist simple power analysis attacks on Kyber that can compromise a message or private key using only one or several traces. In particular, Primas et al. [24] and Pessl et al. [23] recover data passed through an NTT by templating the multiplications or other intermediate values within the NTT. Hamburg et al. [13] present a sparse-vector chosen ciphertext attack strategy, which leads to full long-term key recovery. These attacks are still limited in that they either require extensive profiling efforts or they are only applicable in specific scenarios like the encryption of ephemeral keys.

As opposed to above methods, Mujdei et al. [21] showed that leakage from the schoolbook polynomial multiplications after the incomplete NTT can be exploited through correlation power analysis (CPA) style attacks. CPA attacks exploit the dependency of power consumption on intermediate values, we provide an introduction of CPA attacks below and refer to work of Mangard et al. [18] for further details. The presented attack required 200 power traces to recover all the coefficients, which enables full key recovery. More precisely, they guess two coefficients at once within the range $\left(-\frac{q}{2}, \frac{q}{2}\right]$, implying a search over q^2 combinations.

In order to model the effect of these side-channel leakage, Dachman-Soled et al. [8] proposed a general lattice framework that quantifies the LWE security loss when revealing a so-called hint $(\mathbf{v}, \mathbf{w}, l) \in \mathbb{Z}_q^n \times \mathbb{Z}_q^m \times \mathbb{Z}$ satisfying

$$\langle (\mathbf{v}, \mathbf{w}), (\mathbf{s}, \mathbf{e}) \rangle = l.$$

The inner product of this equation is usually performed in $\mathbb{Z}_q$, which is referred to as *modular-hint*. They also dealt with leakage l before   mod q reduction, a so-called *perfect hint*. Their results was later improved by May and Nowakowski [19], where they only addressed hints for the secret **s** only, i.e., hints $(\mathbf{v}, l)$ with $\langle \mathbf{v}, \mathbf{s} \rangle = l$.

1.2 Our Contribution

In this paper, we propose a way that utilizes correlation power analysis to fully recover the secret key of Kyber. Our attack consists of two steps. First, by exploiting the correlation of Hamming weight of some intermediates and the power consumption of the decryption process in Kyber, precisely the part where we multiply the secret polynomial with ciphertext, we can recover some of the coefficients of the secret key in the NTT domain. Secondly, since there will be some ambiguity about whether the recovered coefficients are indeed correct, we sample part of the recovered coefficients and construct a lattice problem by Kannan's embedding proposed by [14]. Then one can recover the entire secret key by solving the lattice problem by using lattice reduction algorithms such as BKZ [5].

We also examined the attack on simulated traces of ARM cortex-M0 generated by a toolkit named ELMO [10]. Experiments show that we can indeed recover the secret key with 200 traces. With some fine-tuning on the acceptance threshold of power analysis, we can even have guaranteed success in sampling all correct coefficients with 600 traces and still have enough ones to construct a solvable lattice problem.

There are three parameter sets for Kyber, and our attack can be easily adapted to all parameter sets. The time it takes to recover the secret key is linear to the number of coefficients in the secret key. The power analysis part of our attack can be parallelized to further accelerate the process. Although the idea of our attack is similar to that of Mujdei *et al.* [21], we only require $O(q)$ search, which directly reflects on the runtime of the CPA. For reference, our attack is about 16 times faster than Mujdei *et al.* [21] without parallelization. Since our SCA and that of [21] use different methods of measurement, it is hard to compare the result. However, if we use the same measurement, by using the lattice reduction, we can theoretically decrease the number of required power traces. It may get some wrong coefficients by doing so, but we can fix that by sampling portion of recovered coefficients and using lattice reduction to find the rest of them.

For the lattice attack part of our attack, as opposed to the above methods, our approach uses divide-and-conquer methods in a way that we only consider a portion of the secret key at a time. That is, the hints $\langle \mathbf{v}, \mathbf{s} \rangle = l$ gathered from our method are inner products of vectors with smaller dimension. This can be done because in the computation of decryption of Kyber, the secret key is divided into blocks by the intrinsic property of module-LWE. Furthermore, the NTTs of each sub-key are usually incomplete since it can achieve fastest speed in that way [6]. Due to these properties of Kyber, The techniques of Dachman-Soled et al. [8] and May et al. [19] to solve the LWE instance are not suitable for our cases. Since we only consider a portion of the secret key at a time. The number of hints we need is extremely lower than their methods. However, we do need to perform multiple times of the lattice reduction to achieve a full key recovery.

Our lattice attack can be applied to other cryptosystems that utilizes NTT-based polynomial multiplications. For example, Saber [9] is a lattice-based KEM based on Module Learning With Rounding problem. Although it is not specifically designed to use NTT by choosing an *NTT-friendly* ring, it is still possible to achieve fast computation by NTT by enlarging the ring as shown in the work by Chung *et al.* [6]. However, the improvement from our attack depends on the implementation of the NTT, namely how many layers of NTT the implementation chooses to apply to it.

We use the official reference implementation of the Kyber key encapsulation mechanism provided by the authors [3] as the target. We also provide an efficient open-source Python implementation of our framework. The source code is available at https://github.com/kuruwa2/kyber-sca.

Organization. The rest of this paper is organized as follows. In Sect. 2, we introduce how Kyber is implemented with Number Theoretic Transform. In Sect. 3, we illustrate how to apply differential power analysis to the NTT part of Kyber. In Sect. 4, we construct a simpler lattice problem from the recovered coefficients and conduct an experiment by lattice reduction algorithm to determine the least number of coefficients we need to recover from differential power analysis. In Sect. 5, we analyze the success rate of our attack and conclude the paper.

2 Preliminaries

In this section, we explain the lattices and module-learning with errors problem, go into some details about Kyber, and review the Number Theoretic Transform.

2.1 Lattices

Let $\mathbf{B} = [\mathbf{b}_1, ..., \mathbf{b}_n] \in \mathbb{Z}^{m \times n}$ be an integer matrix. We denote by

$$\Lambda(\mathbf{B}) := \{\alpha_1 \mathbf{b}_1 + ... + \alpha_n \mathbf{b}_n \mid \alpha_i \in \mathbb{Z}\}$$

the lattice generated by $\mathbf{B}$. If the rows of $\mathbf{B}$ are linearly independent, $\mathbf{B}$ is a *basis matrix* of $\Lambda(\mathbf{B})$. The number of rows n in any basis matrix of some lattice Λ is called the *rank* of Λ. The *determinant* of a lattice Λ with basis matrix $\mathbf{B}$ is defined as

$$\det(\Lambda) := \sqrt{\det(\mathbf{B}\mathbf{B}^T)}$$

The determinant does not depend on the choice of basis. We also denote by $\lambda_i(\Lambda)$ the *i-th successive minimum* of Λ. A lattice vector $\mathbf{v} \in \Lambda$ such that $\|\mathbf{v}\| = \lambda_1(\Lambda)$ is called the *shortest vector* of Λ. $\lambda_1(\Lambda)$ can be estimated by the following heuristic.

Heuristic 1 *(Gaussian Heuristic) Let Λ be an n-dimensional lattice. Gaussian heuristic predicts that the norm of the shortest vector $\lambda_1(\Lambda)$ equals*

$$gh(\Lambda) := \sqrt{\frac{n}{2\pi e}} \det(\Lambda)^{1/n}.$$

2.2   Module-LWE

Learning with errors (LWE) problem [25] and its extension over rings [17] or modules are the basis of multiple NIST PQC candidates.

Let $\mathbb{Z}_q$ be the ring of integers modulo q and for given power-of-2 degree n, define $\mathcal{R}_q = \mathbb{Z}_q[x]/(x^n + 1)$ as the polynomial ring of polynomials modulo $x^n + 1$. For any ring $\mathcal{R}$, $\mathcal{R}^{\ell \times k}$ denotes the ring of $\ell \times k$-matrices over $\mathcal{R}$. We also simplify $\mathcal{R}^{\ell \times 1}$ to $\mathcal{R}^\ell$ if there is no ambiguity. Single polynomials are written without markup, vectors are bold lower case **a** and matrices are denoted with bold upper case **A**. β_η denotes the centered binomial distribution with parameter η and $\mho$ denote the uniform distribution. If χ is a probability distribution over a set S, then $x \leftarrow \chi$ denotes sampling $x \in S$ according to χ. If χ is only defined on $\mathbb{Z}_q$, $x \leftarrow \chi(\mathcal{R}_q)$ denotes sampling the polynomial $x \in \mathcal{R}_q$, where all coefficients of the coefficients in x are sampled from χ.

The learning with errors (LWE) problem was introduced by Regev [25] and its decision version states that it is hard to distinguish m uniform random samples $(\mathbf{a}_i, b_i) \leftarrow \mho(\mathbb{Z}_q^n \times \mathbb{Z}_q)$ from m LWE-samples of the form

$$\left(\mathbf{a}_i, b_i = \mathbf{a}_i^\top \mathbf{s} + e_i\right) \in \mathbb{Z}_q^n \times \mathbb{Z}_q,$$

where the secret vector $\mathbf{s} \leftarrow \beta_\eta(\mathbb{Z}_q^n)$ is fixed for all samples, $\mathbf{a}_i \leftarrow \mho(\mathbb{Z}_q^n)$ and $e_i \leftarrow \beta_\eta(\mathbb{Z}_q)$ is a small error. A module version of LWE, called Mod-LWE [4] essentially replaces the ring $\mathbb{Z}_q$ in the above samples by a quotient ring of the form $\mathcal{R}_q$ with corresponding error distribution $\beta_\eta(\mathcal{R}_q)$.

$$\left(\mathbf{a}_i, b_i = \mathbf{a}_i^\top \mathbf{s} + e_i\right) \in \mathcal{R}_q^{k \times 1} \times \mathcal{R}_q.$$

The rank of the module is k and the dimension of the ring $\mathcal{R}_q$ is n. The case $k = 1$ corresponds to the ring-LWE problem introduced in [17]. We also commonly integrate m number of samples by the matrix multiplication,

$$(\mathbf{A}, \mathbf{b} = \mathbf{A}\mathbf{s} + \mathbf{e}) \in \mathcal{R}_q^{m \times k} \times \mathcal{R}_q^m.$$

Let $\lambda_i(\Lambda)$ denote the i-th minimum of lattice Λ. The LWE problem can be considered as an average version of the *Bounded Distance Decoding* (BDD) problem: Given a vector such that its distance from the lattice is at most $\lambda_1(\Lambda)/2$, the goal is to find the closest lattice vector to it. A dual problem of BDD is the so-called *unique Shortest Vector Problem* (uSVP): Given $\gamma \geq 1$, and lattice Λ such that $\lambda_2(\Lambda) \geq \gamma \cdot \lambda_1(\Lambda)$, the goal is to find a non-zero vector $\mathbf{v} \in \Lambda$ of norm $\lambda_1(\Lambda)$. The reduction between LWE, BDD, and uSVP will be further discussed in Sect. 4.2.

2.3   CRYSTALS-Kyber

Kyber [2] is a Key Encapsulation Mechanism (KEM) submitted to the NIST standardization process, and it is among the four confirmed candidates to be standardized [22]. The security of Kyber is based on the module-LWE problem. For the three parameter sets in the proposal, Kyber512, Kyber768, and

Table 1. Parameter sets for Kyber [1].

name	n	k	q	η_1	η_2
Kyber512	256	2	3329	3	2
Kyber768	256	3	3329	2	2
Kyber1024	256	4	3329	2	2

Kyber1024, the parameters are all set to $n = 256$ and $q = 3329$. For most parameters $\eta = 2$ is used, except for Kyber512, where $\eta = 3$. The parameter sets differ in their module dimension $k = 2, 3$, and 4 respectively. The three parameter sets listed in Table 1.

Kyber consists of the CCA2-KEM Key Generation, PKE- and CCA2-KEM-Encryption, and CCA2-KEM-Decryption algorithms, which are summarized in Algorithms 1, 2, 3 and 4, respectively.

Algorithm 1. Kyber-CCA2-KEM Key Generation (simplified)

Output: Public key pk, secret key sk
1: Choose uniform seeds ρ, σ, z
2: $\mathcal{R}^{k \times k} \ni \hat{\mathbf{A}} \leftarrow \mathtt{Sample}_{\mathcal{U}}(\rho)$
3: $\mathcal{R}_q^k \ni \mathbf{s}, \mathbf{e} \leftarrow \mathtt{Sample}_{\beta_\eta}(\sigma)$
4: $\hat{\mathbf{s}} \leftarrow \mathrm{NTT}(\mathbf{s})$
5: $\hat{\mathbf{t}} \leftarrow \hat{\mathbf{A}} \circ \hat{\mathbf{s}} + \mathrm{NTT}(\mathbf{e})$
6: **return** $(pk := (\hat{\mathbf{t}}, \rho), sk := (\hat{\mathbf{s}}, pk, \mathrm{Hash}(pk), z))$

Algorithm 2. Kyber-PKE Encryption (simplified)

Input: Public key $pk = (\hat{\mathbf{t}}, \rho)$, message m, seed τ
Output: Ciphertext c
1: $\mathcal{R}^{k \times k} \ni \hat{\mathbf{A}} \leftarrow \mathtt{Sample}_{\mathcal{U}}(\rho)$
2: $\mathcal{R}_q^k \ni \mathbf{r}, \mathbf{e}_1, \mathcal{R}_q \ni e_2 \leftarrow \mathtt{Sample}_{\beta_\eta}(\tau)$
3: $\mathbf{u} \leftarrow \mathrm{NTT}^{-1}(\hat{\mathbf{A}}^\top \circ \mathrm{NTT}(\mathbf{r})) + \mathbf{e}_1$
4: $v \leftarrow \mathrm{NTT}^{-1}(\hat{\mathbf{t}}^\top \circ \mathrm{NTT}(\mathbf{r})) + e_2 + \mathtt{Encode}(m)$
5: **return** $c := (\mathbf{u}, v)$

In these algorithms, and in the rest of this paper, the notation $a \circ b$ means "pairwise" multiplication of polynomials, or vectors of polynomials, in the NTT domain. For example, if $a = (a_0, a_1)$ and $b = (b_0, b_1)$, $a \circ b = (a_0 b_0, a_1 b_1)$.

Kyber uses a variant of the Fujisaki-Okamoto transform [11] to build an IND-CCA2 secure KEM scheme. This transform applies an additional re-encryption of the decrypted message, using the same randomness as used for the encryption of the received ciphertext. The decryption is only valid if the re-computed ciphertext matches the received ciphertext.

Algorithm 3. Kyber-CCA2-KEM Encapsulation (simplified)

    Input: Public key $pk = (\hat{\mathbf{t}}, \rho)$
    Output: Ciphertext c, shared key K
1: Choose uniform m
2: $(\bar{K}, \tau) \leftarrow \mathtt{Hash}(m \parallel \mathtt{Hash}(pk))$
3: $c \leftarrow \mathtt{PKE.Enc}(pk, m, \tau)$
4: $K \leftarrow \mathtt{KDF}(\bar{K} \parallel \mathtt{Hash}(c))$
5: **return** (c, K)

Algorithm 4. Kyber-CCA2-KEM Decapsulation (simplified)

    Input: Secret key $sk = (\hat{\mathbf{s}}, pk, h, z)$, ciphertext $c = (\mathbf{u}, v)$
    Output: Shared key K
1: $m \leftarrow \mathtt{Decode}(v - \mathtt{NTT}^{-1}(\hat{\mathbf{s}}^\top \circ \mathtt{NTT}(\mathbf{u})))$
2: $(K, \tau) \leftarrow \mathtt{Hash}(m \parallel h)$
3: $c' \leftarrow \mathtt{PKE.Enc}(pk, m, \tau)$
4: **if** $c = c'$ **then**
5:     **return** $K := \mathtt{KDF}(K \parallel \mathtt{Hash}(c))$
6: **else**
7:     **return** $K := \mathtt{KDF}(z \parallel \mathtt{Hash}(c))$
8: **end if**

2.4 Number Theoretic Transform

For lattice-based schemes using polynomial rings, polynomial multiplications in en-/decryption are the most computationally expensive step. The Number Theoretic Transform (NTT) is a technique that can achieve efficient computation for those multiplications.

The NTT is similar to the Discrete Fourier Transform (DFT), but instead of over the field of complex numbers, it operates over a prime field $\mathbb{Z}_q$. It can be seen as a mapping between the coefficient representation of a polynomial from $\mathcal{R}_q$ (called the normal domain) to the evaluation of the polynomial at the n-th roots of unity (called the NTT domain). This bijective mapping is typically referred to as forward transformation. The mapping from the NTT domain to the normal domain is referred to as backward transformation or inverse NTT. In the NTT domain, the multiplication of polynomials can be achieved by pointwise multiplication, which is much cheaper than multiplication in the normal domain. Typically, one would perform the forward transformation, multiply the polynomials pointwisely in the NTT domain, and go back using the backward transformation. For $\mathcal{R}_q$ with a $2n$-th primitive root of unity ζ, the NTT transformation of an n-degree polynomial $f = \sum_{i=0}^{n-1} f_i x^i$ is defined as:

$$\hat{f} = \mathrm{NTT}(f) = \sum_{i=0}^{n-1} \hat{f}_i x^i, \quad \text{where} \quad \hat{f}_i = \sum_{j=0}^{n-1} f_j \zeta^{(2i+1)\cdot j}.$$

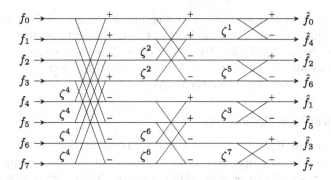

Fig. 1. 8-coefficient Cooley-Tukey decimation in time NTT

Similarly,

$$f = \text{NTT}^{-1}(\hat{f}) = \sum_{i=0}^{n-1} f_i x^i, \quad \text{where}$$

$$f_i = n^{-1} \sum_{j=0}^{n-1} \hat{f}_j \zeta^{-i\cdot(2j+1)}.$$

The NTT transform and its inverse can be applied efficiently by using a chaining of $\log_2 n$ butterflies. It is a divide and conquer technique that splits the input in half in each step and solves two problems of size $n/2$. The construction for an 8-coefficient NTT using the Cooley-Tukey butterfly [7] with decimation in time is depicted in Fig. 1, with the output being in bit-reversed order. Notice that both NTT and inverse NTT are a linear transform, thus they can be expressed by matrix multiplications, e.g. $[f_i]^\top = \mathbf{M}[\hat{f}_i]^\top$ for some $n \times n$ matrix $\mathbf{M}$.

Kyber uses an NTT-friendly ring. But in Kyber, only n-th primitive roots of unity exist, therefore the modulus polynomial x^n+1 only factors into polynomials of degree 2. Hence, the last layer between nearest neighbors of the NTT is skipped and in NTT domain multiplication is not purely point-wise, but multiplications of polynomials of degree 1. That is, the Kyber ring is effectively $\mathbb{F}_{q^2}[y]/(y^{128}+1)$, where $\mathbb{F}_{q^2}$ is the field $\mathbb{Z}_q[x]/(x^2-\zeta)$. Also note that in Kyber, polynomials in the NTT domain are always considered in bit-reversed order (cf. Fig. 1). Therefore, in the following bit-reversal is implicitly expected in the NTT domain and indices for NTT-coefficients are noted in regular order.

3 Correlation Power Analysis

In this section, we provide a comprehensive introduction to correlation power analysis (CPA) provided by Mangard et al. [18] in Sect. 3.1, and then we apply the idea to reveal the secret key of Kyber in Sect. 3.2.

The goal of CPA is to reveal secret keys of cryptographic devices based on a large number of power traces that have been recorded while the devices encrypt or decrypt different plaintexts. The probability of success for CPA depends on the quality and number of traces. Due to the fact that CPA does not require detailed knowledge about the attacked devices, it is the most popular type of power analysis attack. Furthermore, they can reveal the secret key even if the recorded power traces are extremely noisy.

3.1 General Description

We now discuss in detail how such an analysis reveals the secret keys of cryptographic devices in five steps. To reveal one coefficient we need to apply the five steps, however, step 2 can be applied only once and the power consumption can be used multiple time for each coefficient that needs to be recovered.

Step 1: Choosing an Intermediate Result of the Executed Algorithm. The first step of a CPA is to choose an intermediate result of the cryptographic algorithm that is executed by the device. This intermediate value needs to be a function $f(d, k)$, where d is a known non-constant data value and k is a small part of the key. In most attack scenarios, d is either the plaintext or the ciphertext.

Step2: Measuring the Power Consumption. The second step of a CPA is to measure the power consumption of the device while it encrypts or decrypts D different data blocks. For each of these encryption or decryption runs, the attacker needs to know the corresponding data value d that is involved in the calculation of the intermediate result chosen in Step 1. We denote these known data values by vector $\mathbf{d} = (d_1, ..., d_D)^\top$, where d_i denotes the data value in the i-th encryption or decryption process.

During each of these runs, the attacker records a power trace. We denote the power trace that corresponds to data block d_i by $\mathbf{t}_i^\top = (t_{i,1}, ..., t_{i,T})$, where T denotes the length of the trace. The attacker measures a trace for each of the D data blocks, and hence, the traces can be written as matrix $\mathbf{T}$ of size $D \times T$.

It is important that the measured traces are correctly aligned. This means that the power consumption values of each column t_j of the matrix $\mathbf{T}$ need to be caused by the same operation. In practice, attackers typically try to measure only the power consumption that is related to the targeted intermediate result. If the plaintext is known, the attacker sets the trigger of the oscilloscope to the sending of the plaintext from the PC to the cryptographic device and records the power consumption for a short period of time.

Step 3: Calculating Hypothetical Intermediate Values. The next step of the attack is to calculate a *hypothetical intermediate value* for every possible choice of k. We write these possible choices as vector $\mathbf{k} = (k_1, ..., k_K)$, where K denotes the total number of possible choices of k. In the context of CPA, we usually refer to the elements of this vector as key hypotheses. Given the data vector $\mathbf{d}$ and the key hypotheses $\mathbf{k}$, an attacker can easily calculate hypothetical intermediate values $f(d, k)$ for all D en-/decryption runs and for all K key hypotheses. This calculation results in a matrix $\mathbf{V}$ of size $D \times K$.

$$\mathbf{V} = [f(d_i, k_j)]_{D \times K}$$

A j-th column of $\mathbf{V}$ contains the intermediate results that have been calculated based on the key hypothesis k_j. It is clear that one column of $\mathbf{V}$ contains those intermediate values that have been calculated in the device during the D en-/decryption runs because $\mathbf{k}$ contains all possible choices for k. We refer to the index of this element as ck. Hence, k_{ck} refers to the key of the device. The goal of CPA is to find out which column of $\mathbf{V}$ has been processed during the D en-/decryption runs. We immediately know k_{ck} as soon as we know which column of $\mathbf{V}$ has been processed in the attacked device.

Step 4: Mapping Intermediate Values to Power Consumption Values. The next step of a CPA is to map the hypothetical intermediate values $\mathbf{V}$ to a matrix $\mathbf{H}$ of *hypothetical power consumption values*. For this purpose, the attacker typically uses models like *Hamming-weight model* or *Hamming-distance model* depending on the scenarios of attack. Using the techniques, the power consumption of the device for each hypothetical intermediate value $v_{i,j}$ is simulated in order to obtain a hypothetical intermediate value $h_{i,j}$.

The quality of the simulation strongly depends on the knowledge of the attacker about the analyzed device. The better the simulation of the attacker matches the actual power consumption characteristics of the device, the more effective the CPA is. The most commonly used power models to map $\mathbf{V}$ to $\mathbf{H}$ are the Hamming-distance and Hamming-weight models.

Step 5: Comparing the Hypothetical Power Consumption Values with the Power Traces. After having mapped $\mathbf{V}$ to $\mathbf{H}$, the final step of a CPA can be performed. In this step, each column $\mathbf{h}_i$ of the matrix $\mathbf{H}$ is compared with each column $\mathbf{t}_j$ of the matrix $\mathbf{T}$. This means that the attacker compares the hypothetical power consumption values of each key hypothesis with the recorded traces at every position. The result of this comparison is a matrix $\mathbf{R}$ of size $K \times T$, where each element $r_{i,j}$ contains the result of the comparison between the columns $\mathbf{h}_i$ and $\mathbf{t}_j$. The comparison is done based on the Pearson correlation coefficient,

$$r_{i,j} = \frac{\sum_{d=1}^{D}(h_{d,i} - \bar{h}_i) \cdot (t_{d,j} - \bar{t}_j)}{\sqrt{\sum_{d=1}^{D}(h_{d,i} - \bar{h}_i)^2 \cdot \sum_{d=1}^{D}(t_{d,j} - \bar{t}_j)^2}}$$

where $\bar{h}_i$ and $\bar{t}_j$ denote the mean values of the columns $\mathbf{h}_i$ and $\mathbf{t}_j$. It has the property that the value $r_{i,j}$ is the higher, the better columns $\mathbf{h}_i$ and $\mathbf{t}_j$ match. The key of the attacked device can hence be revealed based on the following observation.

The power traces correspond to the power consumption of the device while it executes a cryptographic algorithm using different data inputs. The intermediate result that has been chosen in step 1 is a part of this algorithm. Hence, the device needs to calculate the intermediate value $\mathbf{v}_{ck}$ during the different executions of the algorithm. Consequently, also the recorded traces depend on these intermediate values at some position. We refer to this position of the power traces as ct, i.e., the column $\mathbf{t}_{ct}$ contains the power consumption values that depend on the intermediate value $\mathbf{v}_{ck}$.

The hypothetical power consumption values $\mathbf{h}_{ck}$ have been simulated by the attacker based on the values $\mathbf{v}_{ck}$. Therefore, the columns $\mathbf{h}_{ck}$ and $\mathbf{t}_{ct}$ are strongly related. In fact, these two columns lead to the highest value in $\mathbf{R}$, i.e., the highest value of the matrix $\mathbf{R}$ is the value $r_{ck,ct}$. An attacker can hence reveal the index for the correct key ck and the moment of time ct by simply looking for the highest value in the matrix $\mathbf{R}$. The indices of this value are then the result of the CPA.

Sometimes, CPA produce high correlation coefficients for many key hypotheses at the time when targeted intermediate result is processed. The high correlation peaks for wrong keys are sometimes referred to as "ghost peaks". These peaks happen because the hypothetical intermediate values are correlated. The height of these correlations depends on the intermediate result that is attacked.

3.2   Application on CRYSTALS-Kyber

Our attack targets the decryption process of Kyber, i.e. line 1 of Algorithm 4, with the aim of recovering the victim's secret key $\hat{\mathbf{s}}$. To decrypt a message the recipient calculates $\mathrm{NTT}^{-1}(\hat{\mathbf{s}}^\top \circ \hat{\mathbf{u}})$, where $\hat{\mathbf{u}}$ is the decompressed ciphertext in the NTT domain and $\circ$ denotes the pairwise multiplication. The pairwise multiplication is done in the quotient ring $\mathbb{Z}_q[x]/(x^2 - \zeta_i)$ as we discussed in Sect. 2.4, where ζ_i are the primitive roots of unity of $\mathbb{Z}_q$. In such a ring, the product of two polynomials $a = a_0 + a_1 x$ and $b = b_0 + b_1 x$ can be easily computed as

$$ab = (a_0 b_0 + a_1 b_1 \zeta_i) + (a_0 b_1 + a_1 b_0)x \quad \mathrm{mod}\ q.$$

However, in most of the processors, modular multiplication is still expensive since it needs divisions by q. Fortunately, we can avoid the divisions by the Montgomery reduction algorithm summarized in Algorithm 5. By setting $R = 2^{16}$, division by R can be replaced by a simple bit shifting and $x \bmod R$ can be done by returning the lower 16 bits of x, which results in an integer between $-R/2$ and $R/2 - 1$. The algorithm works because first, t is chosen so that $a - tq$ is divisible by R. Second, t is in the range $[-R/2, R/2 - 1]$, thus $a - tq$ is in the range $[-qR + q, qR - 1]$, which guarantees that b is in the correct range.

Algorithm 5. Montgomery reduction

Input: Integers q, R with $\gcd(q, R) = 1$
    Integer $q^{-1} \in [-R/2, R/2 - 1]$ such that $qq^{-1} \equiv 1 \bmod R$
    Integer $a \in [-qR/2, qR/2 - 1]$
Output: Integer $b \in [-q+1, q-1]$ such that $b \equiv aR^{-1} \bmod q$
1: $t \leftarrow ((a \bmod R)q^{-1}) \bmod R$
2: $b \leftarrow (a - tq)/R$
3: **return** b

Let x_0 and y_0 be two integers in the range $[-q+1, q-1]$, we refer to the result of Montgomery reduction of $x_0 \times y_0$ by Algorithm 5 as $\mathtt{fqmul}(x_0, y_0)$. Then the product $r_0 + r_1 x = ab2^{-16}$ can be computed as follow:

$$r_0 \leftarrow \texttt{fqmul}(a_1, b_1)$$
$$r_0 \leftarrow \texttt{fqmul}(r_0, \zeta_i 2^{16})$$
$$r_0 \leftarrow \texttt{fqmul}(a_0, b_0) + r_0 \tag{1}$$
$$r_1 \leftarrow \texttt{fqmul}(a_1, b_0)$$
$$r_1 \leftarrow \texttt{fqmul}(a_0, b_1) + r_1.$$

The unwanted constant can be dealt within the inverse NTT together when we divide the coefficient by n, thus no extra multiplications is needed.

Now suppose we want to reveal the coefficients $(\hat{s}_{2i}, \hat{s}_{2i+1})$, notice that they are point-wisely multiplied by the ciphertext $(\hat{u}_{2i}, \hat{u}_{2i+1})$, then our first chosen intermediate value is $\texttt{fqmul}(\hat{s}_{2i+1}, \hat{u}_{2i+1})$, i.e. r_0 in the first line of Eq. (1). The intermediate value meets the requisite described in Sect. 3.1, and the total number of possible choices of $\hat{s}_{2i+1} \in [0, q-1]$ is q. Following the steps in Sect. 3.1, we can get a list of the most possible candidates of $\hat{s}_{2i+1}$. There can be some incorrect candidates with high score in this step, for example, $q - \hat{s}_{2i+1}$ can be such a candidate since the Hamming weight of $\texttt{fqmul}(q - \hat{s}_{2i+1}, \hat{u}_{2i+1})$ is strongly correlated with $\texttt{fqmul}(\hat{s}_{2i+1}, \hat{u}_{2i+1})$.

Now that we have some highly confident candidates for $\hat{s}_{2i+1}$, we can then use it and newly guessed $\hat{s}_{2i}$ to calculate the hypothetical value of r_1. And we can repeat the same process except that the intermediate values are now $\texttt{fqmul}(\hat{s}_{2i}, \hat{u}_{2i+1}) + \texttt{fqmul}(\hat{s}_{2i+1}, \hat{u}_{2i})$, i.e. r_1 in the last line of Eq. 1. Following the same steps, we can find the candidate with the highest correlation coefficient, and if it is higher than some threshold, we accept the guess. If not, we try the next candidate of $\hat{s}_{2i+1}$. If there is no candidate with high enough correlation coefficient, we just return failure. Then we guess the next one with same process targeting the next intermediate values.

The complexity can be easily calculated, if K is the number of possible keys, T is the scanned window size, D is the number of power traces, then we need TK computations of correlation coefficient of length D vectors to recover one coefficient of the secret key, which is linear to all the parameters. For Kyber512, we need to repeat the process above 256 times to recover the 512 coefficients in the NTT domain. The CPA process is identical across different parameter sets of Kyber, thus it is easy to adapt to Kyber768/1024 without any problem. It can also be parallelized as long as we know the starting point of each $\texttt{fqmul}$ in the power trace, since the length of all power traces is the same, we only need to evaluate the starting point once and store the result. For Kyber512 on a 16 core computer, our CPA can scan through all coefficients within 5 min.

However, we will run into some problems. If the correct coefficient $(\hat{s}_{2i}, \hat{s}_{2i+1})$ has high score, then it is likely that $(q - \hat{s}_{2i}, q - \hat{s}_{2i+1})$ has high score too, since the Hamming weight of them are highly correlated. So to prevent it from getting accepted, we can increase the threshold for acceptance, however, it may cause the correct ones to get rejected too. Furthermore, in some rare cases, $(q - \hat{s}_{2i}, q - \hat{s}_{2i+1})$ may have a higher score than the correct one and be accepted, we call such cases false positive. The way we deal with it is to sample the accepted guesses and hope the coefficients we sampled are all correct ones. The number of sampled coefficients will be further discussed in Sect. 4.

4   Lattice Attack

In this section, we describe how to construct a simpler LWE problem from the coefficients that have been recovered in the CPA attack, then we do a hardness analysis that determines the least number of coefficients needed to be recovered in the CPA.

4.1   Lattice Construction

Now we have some of the coefficients being recovered, the next step is to recover the unknown coefficients by the lattice attack. Because of the structure of incomplete NTT in Kyber, we know that coefficients are split into $2k$ groups of 128 ones. We will focus on one group and notice that the rest of the steps need to repeat $2k$ times to derive the full secret key.

Let $\mathbf{M} = [\mathbf{m}_0, \mathbf{m}_2, ..., \mathbf{m}_{254}]$ be the inverse NTT matrix as we mentioned in Sect. 2.4. Suppose we have recovered $128 - \ell$ coefficients in $\hat{\mathbf{s}}_i$, one of the groups in $\hat{\mathbf{s}}$, from the polynomial multiplication $\hat{\mathbf{s}} \circ \hat{\mathbf{u}}$, i.e., we need to recover the remaining ℓ coefficients. Let $A = \{a_0, a_1, ..., a_{127-\ell}\}$ be the indices that are successfully recovered in the CPA step, and $B = \{b_0, b_1, ..., b_{\ell-1}\}$ be the indices that are still unknown, then the inverse NTT $\mathrm{NTT}^{-1}(\hat{\mathbf{s}}_i) = \mathbf{M}\hat{\mathbf{s}}_i = \mathbf{s}_i \mod q$ can be split into two halves as followed:

$$\mathbf{M}_A \hat{\mathbf{s}}_{i,A} + \mathbf{M}_B \hat{\mathbf{s}}_{i,B} = \mathbf{s}_i \mod q,$$

where $\mathbf{M}_A := [\mathbf{m}_{a_0}, ..., \mathbf{m}_{a_{127-\ell}}]$ is a matrix whose columns are those of $\mathbf{M}$ whose indices are in A, $\hat{\mathbf{s}}_{i,A} = [\hat{s}_{a_0}, ..., \hat{s}_{a_{127-\ell}}]^\top$, and the similar definition for $\mathbf{M}_B$ and $\hat{\mathbf{s}}_{i,B}$.

Notice that $\mathbf{s}_i$ is an extremely short vector since it is the secret key sampled from β_η. By calling the known vector $\mathbf{t} = \mathbf{M}_A \hat{\mathbf{s}}_{i,A}$, the known basis $\mathbf{A} = -\mathbf{M}_B$, and an unknown vector $\mathbf{s}'_i = \hat{\mathbf{s}}_{i,B}$, we now have $\mathbf{t} = \mathbf{A}\mathbf{s}'_i + \mathbf{s}_i \mod q$, which is exactly the definition of an LWE problem. Compared to the original module-LWE problem in Kyber, this problem becomes simpler since the rank of $\mathbf{A}$ is less than the original one.

4.2 Hardness Analysis

We use the standard technique of Kannan's embedding to solve the LWE problem. First we treat the LWE problem as a BDD/uSVP problem and then apply a lattice reduction algorithm. For example, given the instance above $(\mathbf{A}, \mathbf{t} = \mathbf{As}'_i + \mathbf{s} \mod q)$, consider the lattice $\Lambda(\mathbf{B}_{BDD})$ generated by

$$\mathbf{B}_{BDD} = \begin{bmatrix} \mathbf{I}_\ell & \mathbf{A}' \\ \mathbf{0} & q\mathbf{I}_{n-\ell} \end{bmatrix},$$

where $[\mathbf{I}_\ell \mid \mathbf{A}']$ denotes the reduced row echelon matrix of $\mathbf{A}^\top$, which can be easily calculated by Gaussian elimination. We can then solve the BDD of $\Lambda(\mathbf{B}_{BDD})$ with respect to the target point $\mathbf{t}$ which reveals $\mathbf{s}'$ and $\mathbf{s}$.

Alternatively, we can reduce this BDD to uSVP by a technique called Kannan's embedding [14]. Given the BDD instance above, we consider the following basis matrix

$$\mathbf{B}_{Kan} = \begin{bmatrix} \mathbf{I}_l & \mathbf{A}' & \mathbf{0} \\ \mathbf{0} & q\mathbf{I}_{n-\ell} & \\ \hline \mathbf{t}^\top & & 1 \end{bmatrix}.$$

Recall that the lattice $\Lambda(\mathbf{B}_{Kan})$ contains all linear combinations of the vectors in $\mathbf{B}_{Kan}$. The equation $\mathbf{t} = \mathbf{As}'_i + \mathbf{s}_i \mod q$ can be written as $\mathbf{t} = \mathbf{As}'_i + \mathbf{s}_i + q\mathbf{k}$, where $\mathbf{k} \in \mathbb{Z}_q^n$, so there exists a row vector $[-\mathbf{s}''^\top \mid -\mathbf{k}'^\top \mid 1] \in \mathbb{Z}_q^{n+1}$ such that the shortest vector in $\Lambda(\mathbf{B}_{Kan})$ is $[-\mathbf{s}''^\top \mid -\mathbf{k}'^\top \mid 1] \cdot \mathbf{B}_{Kan} = [\mathbf{s}_i^\top \mid 1] \in \mathbb{Z}_q^{n+1}$.

The norm of vector $[\mathbf{s}_i^\top \mid 1]$ is $\sqrt{\|\mathbf{s}_i\|^2 + 1} \approx \sqrt{n}\sigma_s$. If this norm is smaller than the norm of the shortest vector estimated by the Gaussian Heuristic, this uSVP instance can be solved, and the more gap between the first and second successive minima, i.e., the bigger $\lambda_2(\Lambda(\mathbf{B}_{Kan}))/\lambda_1(\Lambda(\mathbf{B}_{Kan}))$ is, the easier the uSVP will be. Since the volume of the lattice $\Lambda(\mathbf{B}_{Kan})$ is $q^{n-\ell}$, $\lambda_2(\Lambda(\mathbf{B}_{Kan}))$ can be estimated by

$$\lambda_2(\Lambda(\mathbf{B}_{Kan})) \approx \sqrt{\frac{n+1}{2\pi e}} q^{(n-\ell)/(n+1)}.$$

To determine the least number of coefficients we must recover in the CPA step, we do an experiment on solving the SVP randomly generated by script. The result is shown in Fig. 2, where the blue line is the success rate of finding $[\mathbf{s}_i^\top \mid 1]$ by the BKZ algorithm[1] of block size 50 for 20 randomly generated $\mathbf{s}$, and the red line is the running time of the algorithm. From the result, the critical point of guaranteed success is on $\ell = 89$, $\ell = 90$ for Kyber512, Kyber768/1024, respectively. This means that in the CPA step, we need at least $128 - 89 = 39$ (or 38 for Kyber768/1024) recovered coefficients so that we can have a fully recovered secret key when using the BKZ algorithm of block size 50 to solve the reduced SVP problem. Notice that in order to do a full key recovery, the number of recovered coefficients need to be multiplied by $2k$, where k is the module dimension for each version of Kyber. The reason that Kyber768/1024 is easier to solve is because η of Kyber768/1024 is smaller than that of Kyber512.

---

[1] We ran the experiment using the BKZ implementation from `fpylll` in `Sage9.2`. See https://github.com/fplll/fpylll.

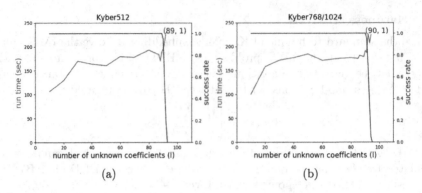

Fig. 2. Success rate and running time on randomly generated uSVP in the lattice $\mathbf{B}_{Kan}$ for (a) Kyber512 and (b) Kyber768/1024

5 Experiments

We experimented our attacks on simulated power traces of the ARM cortex-M0 processor, then estimate how many traces we need to conduct our attack.

5.1 ELMO

Our simulated traces were generated using the ELMO [10], which emulates the power consumption of an ARM Cortex M0 processor and produces noise-free traces. The tool reproduces the 3-stage pipeline of an M0 processor, which means that the algorithmic noise is taken into account. ELMO's quality has been established by comparing leakage detection results between simulated and real traces from a STM32F0 Discovery Board [20]. For reference, to conduct a successful key recovery power analysis on the lattice-based signature scheme FALCON, the required numbers of simulated power traces and real acquisitions are 2000 and 5000 [12].

5.2 Results

Table 2 gives the results of our experiment done on the simulated traces. The *threshold* is the minimum correlation coefficient of acceptance that we set as a parameter in Sect. 3.2. *Recovered rate* is the average number of successfully recovered coefficients, and *false positive* is the average number of coefficients that are accepted but turn out to be wrong. The *success rate* is the possibility of all 39/38 coefficients we randomly sample being the correct ones when we choose from all coefficients that are accepted by the CPA step, which can be directly calculated by $\binom{a-39}{b}/\binom{a}{b}$ if a is the *recovered rate* and b is the *false positive*. Therefore, it does not mean the overall success rate of our attack, the overall success rate will be arbitrarily closed to 1 if we keep sampling the coefficients as long as we have at least 39/38 correct ones.

Table 2. Experimental results on different acceptance threshold and trance number. Left hand side of success rate is for Kyber512 and right is for Kyber768/1024.

Threshold	Trace number	Recovered rate	False positive	Success rate
0.63	200	110.5/128	6/128	0.07(0.07)
	400	118.75/128	4.25/128	0.18(0.19)
	600	124.75/128	3/128	0.32(0.33)
	800	124.75/128	1.75/128	0.52(0.54)
0.65	200	98.75/128	4.5/128	0.10(0.11)
	400	109/128	4.25/128	0.15(0.16)
	600	112/128	2.25/128	0.39(0.40)
	800	116.25/128	1.5/128	0.55(0.56)
0.67	200	79.25/128	2.5/128	0.19(0.20)
	400	86/128	0.5/128	0.77(0.78)
	600	83.75/128	0.25/128	0.88(0.89)
	800	86.5/128	0/128	1(1)
0.69	200	58/128	1/128	0.33(0.34)
	400	53.25/128	0.25/128	0.82(0.82)
	600	49.75/128	0/128	1(1)
	800	49.5/128	0/128	1(1)

It can be seen that although adding trace numbers does not help much to increase the recovered coefficients, it does help to lower the false positive, which directly affects the success rate. Increasing the threshold of acceptance will also lower the false positive and recovered rate, but notice that if the recovered rate drops below 39, our attack may fail. Since the running time of the overall attack is dominated by CPA, we would argue that the fewer the number of power traces the better it is, as long as the success rate is higher than 0.05.

5.3 Application to Saber

Saber [9] is a lattice-based key encapsulation mechanism based on the Module Learning With Rounding problem. Saber is one of the round 3 candidates of the NIST post-quantum cryptography standardization competition. The polynomial ring used within Saber is $R_q = \mathbb{Z}_q[x]/(x^n+1)$ with $q = 2^{13}$ and $n = 256$ across all parameter sets. Saber also offers three security levels: Lightsaber with security level similar to AES-128, Saber with one similar to AES-192 and Firesaber with one similar to AES-256.

Because Saber was not specifically designed to benefit from NTT-based multiplication by using an *NTT-friendly* ring, it uses a combination of Toom-4 and Karatsuba to implement efficient polynomial arithmetic. However, as shown in the work by [6], NTTs can be used to obtain efficient polynomial arithmetic in finite fields modulo a power-of-two. They did this by choosing a prime $p > nq^2/2$

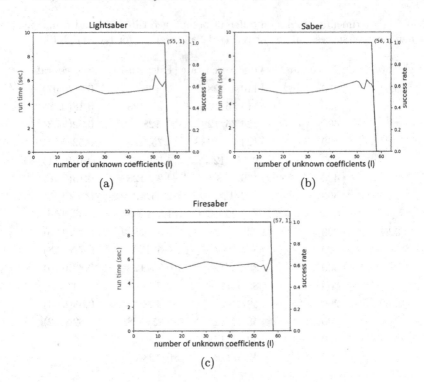

Fig. 3. Success rate and running time on randomly generated USVP for (a) Lightsaber, (b) Saber and (c) Firesaber

such that $n|(p-1)$, computing the multiplication by the NTT over $\mathbb{Z}_p[x]$, and then reducing the result back to $\mathbb{Z}_q[x]$. Since the modulus is much bigger in the NTT for Saber, the SCA for pointwise multiplication on Saber needs to target a smaller portion of the intermdeiate value, which results in smaller signal-to-noise ratio. In [21], a minimum of 10000 traces was required to mount a successful attack.

Figure 3 shows our lattice attack when applying to the SCA proposed by [21]. Since the implementation uses 6 layers of NTTs, we divide the coefficients into $512/2^6 = 8$ groups and find the minimum number of coefficients we needed to recover other one. We can see that it needs 9/8/7 coefficients out of 64 to guarantee a successful attack for each parameter sets of Saber, which means a total of 72/64/56 coefficients are needed. This saves about $86\% \sim 89\%$ of the running time for the SCA. Another way to see the improvement is the possibility to reduce the traces of SCA. Although by doing so, there may be incorrectly recovered coefficients, by our sampling approach as shown before, we only need portion of the coefficients correct to recover the whole secret key. We do want to point out that the improvement heavily depends on the implementation of the incomplete NTT of choice. That is, the less layers of incomplete NTTs an implementation chooses, the less coefficients we need to perform the lattice attack.

6   Conclusion

In this paper, we propose a combined CPA and lattice attack on Kyber. With 200 traces, our attack terminated within 20 min on a 16-core computer. Compared to other SCA targeting NTT in the cryptosystems, our attack achieves lower runtime in practice. Furthermore, there is potential for decreasing the number of traces by using lattice reduction if the same measurement is used.

Our future works are to migrate the attacks to real devices and other cryptosystems using the NTT transform multiplication like Saber or NTRU. We can also investigate the effect of popular countermeasures of CPA like masking and hiding on our attack.

Acknowledgement. This work was partially supported by JSPS KAKENHI Grant Number 19K20267, Japan, and JST CREST Grant Number JPMJCR2113, Japan.

References

1. Avanzi, R., et al.: CRYSTALS-Kyber (version 3.02) - submission to round 3 of the NIST post-quantum project. Specification document (2021)
2. Bos, J., et al.: CRYSTALS - Kyber: a CCA-secure module-lattice-based KEM. In: 2018 IEEE European Symposium on Security and Privacy (EuroS&P), pp. 353–367 (2018). https://doi.org/10.1109/EuroSP.2018.00032
3. Bos, J., et al.: Kyber (2023). https://github.com/pq-crystals/kyber
4. Brakerski, Z., Gentry, C., Vaikuntanathan, V.: (Leveled) fully homomorphic encryption without bootstrapping. In: Proceedings of the 3rd Innovations in Theoretical Computer Science Conference, ITCS 2012, pp. 309–325. Association for Computing Machinery (2012). https://doi.org/10.1145/2090236.2090262
5. Chen, Y., Nguyen, P.Q.: BKZ 2.0: better lattice security estimates. In: Lee, D.H., Wang, X. (eds.) Advances in Cryptology - ASIACRYPT 2011, pp. 1–20 (2011)
6. Chung, C.M.M., Hwang, V., Kannwischer, M.J., Seiler, G., Shih, C.J., Yang, B.Y.: NTT multiplication for NTT-unfriendly rings. Cryptology ePrint Archive, Paper 2020/1397 (2020). https://eprint.iacr.org/2020/1397
7. Cooley, J.W., Tukey, J.W.: An algorithm for the machine calculation of complex Fourier series. Math. Comput. **19**, 297–301 (1965)
8. Dachman-Soled, D., Ducas, L., Gong, H., Rossi, M.: LWE with side information: attacks and concrete security estimation. In: Micciancio, D., Ristenpart, T. (eds.) CRYPTO 2020, Part II. LNCS, vol. 12171, pp. 329–358. Springer, Cham (2020). https://doi.org/10.1007/978-3-030-56880-1_12
9. D'Anvers, J.P., Karmakar, A., Sinha Roy, S., Vercauteren, F.: Saber: module-LWR based key exchange, CPA-secure encryption and CCA-secure KEM. In: Joux, A., Nitaj, A., Rachidi, T. (eds.) Progress in Cryptology - AFRICACRYPT 2018, pp. 282–305 (2018)
10. ELMO: Evaluating leaks for the arm cortex-m0. https://github.com/sca-research/ELMO. Accessed 17 Oct 2022
11. Fujisaki, E., Okamoto, T.: Secure integration of asymmetric and symmetric encryption schemes. In: Wiener, M. (ed.) CRYPTO 1999. LNCS, vol. 1666, pp. 537–554. Springer, Heidelberg (1999). https://doi.org/10.1007/3-540-48405-1_34

12. Guerreau, M., Martinelli, A., Ricosset, T., Rossi, M.: The hidden parallelepiped is back again: power analysis attacks on Falcon. Cryptology ePrint Archive, Paper 2022/057 (2022). https://eprint.iacr.org/2022/057

13. Hamburg, M., et al.: Chosen ciphertext k-trace attacks on masked CCA2 secure Kyber. IACR Trans. Cryptogr. Hardw. Embed. Syst. **2021**(4), 88–113 (2021). https://doi.org/10.46586/tches.v2021.i4.88-113. https://tches.iacr.org/index.php/TCHES/article/view/9061

14. Kannan, R.: Minkowski's convex body theorem and integer programming. Math. Oper. Res. **12**(3), 415–440 (1987). http://www.jstor.org/stable/3689974

15. Kocher, P., Jaffe, J., Jun, B.: Differential power analysis. In: Wiener, M. (ed.) CRYPTO 1999. LNCS, vol. 1666, pp. 388–397. Springer, Heidelberg (1999). https://doi.org/10.1007/3-540-48405-1_25

16. Kocher, P.C.: Timing attacks on implementations of Diffie-Hellman, RSA, DSS, and other systems. In: Koblitz, N. (ed.) CRYPTO 1996. LNCS, vol. 1109, pp. 104–113. Springer, Heidelberg (1996). https://doi.org/10.1007/3-540-68697-5_9

17. Lyubashevsky, V., Peikert, C., Regev, O.: On ideal lattices and learning with errors over rings. J. ACM **60**(6) (2013). https://doi.org/10.1145/2535925

18. Mangard, S., Oswald, E., Popp, T.: Power Analysis Attacks: Revealing the Secrets of Smart Cards, 1st edn. Springer, New York (2010). https://doi.org/10.1007/978-0-387-38162-6

19. May, A., Nowakowski, J.: Too many hints - when LLL breaks LWE. Cryptology ePrint Archive, Paper 2023/777 (2023). https://eprint.iacr.org/2023/777

20. McCann, D., Oswald, E., Whitnall, C.: Towards practical tools for side channel aware software engineering: grey box' modelling for instruction leakages. In: Proceedings of the 26th USENIX Conference on Security Symposium, pp. 199–216 (2017)

21. Mujdei, C., Wouters, L., Karmakar, A., Beckers, A., Mera, J.M.B., Verbauwhede, I.: Side-channel analysis of lattice-based post-quantum cryptography: exploiting polynomial multiplication. ACM Trans. Embed. Comput. Syst. (2022). https://doi.org/10.1145/3569420

22. National Institute of Standards and Technology. Post-quantum cryptography standardization. https://csrc.nist.gov/projects/post-quantum-cryptography. Accessed 12 Oct 2022

23. Pessl, P., Primas, R.: More practical single-trace attacks on the number theoretic transform. Cryptology ePrint Archive, Paper 2019/795 (2019). https://eprint.iacr.org/2019/795

24. Primas, R., Pessl, P., Mangard, S.: Single-trace side-channel attacks on masked lattice-based encryption. Cryptology ePrint Archive, Paper 2017/594 (2017). https://eprint.iacr.org/2017/594

25. Regev, O.: On lattices, learning with errors, random linear codes, and cryptography. In: Proceedings of the 37th Annual ACM Symposium on Theory of Computing, vol. 56, pp. 84–93 (2005). https://doi.org/10.1145/1568318.1568324

26. Shor, P.: Algorithms for quantum computation: Discrete logarithms and factoring. In: Proceedings 35th Annual Symposium on Foundations of Computer Science, pp. 124–134 (1994). https://doi.org/10.1109/SFCS.1994.365700

Side-Channel Analysis on Lattice-Based KEM Using Multi-feature Recognition - The Case Study of Kyber

Yuan Ma[1,2], Xinyue Yang[1,2], An Wang[3], Congming Wei[3(✉)], Tianyu Chen[1], and Haotong Xu[3]

[1] SKLOIS, Institute of Information Engineering, CAS, Beijing, China
{mayuan,yangxinyue,chentianyu}@iie.ac.cn
[2] School of Cyber Security, University of Chinese Academy of Sciences, Beijing, China
[3] School of Cyberspace Science and Technology, Beijing Institute of Technology, Beijing, China
{wangan1,weicm,3120231257}@bit.edu.cn

Abstract. Kyber, selected as the next-generation standard for key encapsulation mechanism in the third round of the NIST post-quantum cryptography standardization process, has naturally raised concerns regarding its resilience against side-channel analysis and other physical attacks. In this paper, we propose a method for profiling the secret key using multiple features extracted based on a binary plaintext-checking oracle. In addition, we incorporate deep learning into the power analysis attack and propose a convolutional neural network suitable for multi-feature recognition. The experimental results demonstrate that our approach achieves an average key recovery success rate of 64.15% by establishing secret key templates. Compared to single-feature recovery, our approach bypasses the intermediate value recovery process and directly reconstructs the representation of the secret key. Our approach improves the correct key guess rate by 54% compared to single-feature recovery and is robust against invalid attacks caused by errors in single-feature recovery. Our approach was performed against the Kyber768 implementation from **pqm4** running on STM32F429 M4-cortex CPU.

Keywords: Lattice-Based cryptography · Side-channel analysis · Plaintext-checking oracle · Kyber · Convolutional neural network

1 Introduction

Classical public key cryptosystems rely on the intractability of certain mathematical problems. However, the rapid development of quantum algorithms and quantum computers poses a grave threat to these cryptographic schemes in use today. Integer factorization and discrete logarithm problems can be solved in polynomial time using Shor's algorithm [17]. Furthermore, a recent study estimated the possibility of factoring a 2048-bit RSA integer in 8 h using "20 million

H. Seo and S. Kim (Eds.): ICISC 2023, LNCS 14561, pp. 221–239, 2024.
https://doi.org/10.1007/978-981-97-1235-9_12

noisy qubits" [5]. Therefore, it is necessary to develop novel, post-quantum secure cryptographic primitives for long-term security.

In 2016, the National Institute of Standards and Technology (NIST) initiated a process [12] to select the best post-quantum cryptography (PQC) primitives for standardization. In July 2022, NIST announced the first group of winners from its six-year competition [2]. Lattice-based cryptography prevailed, with 3 out of 4 winners, demonstrating their foundational role in PQC standards. Among them, Kyber [16], the KEM part of the Cryptographic Suite for Algebraic Cipher Suite (CRYSTALS), was chosen by NIST as the only public key encryption or key encapsulation mechanism (KEM) algorithm for standardization [2]. Shortly after, the National Security Agency included Kyber in the suite of encryption algorithms recommended for national security systems [1]. Currently, the NIST PQC process has entered the fourth round.

In addition to other desired security properties, NIST has prioritized the resilience against side-channel attacks (SCAs), before deploying these PQC algorithms in real-world applications, particularly in scenarios where an attacker could physically access an embedded device.

SCAs were first introduced by Kocher in 1996 [9]. Research has shown that power consumption, electromagnetic emanations (EM), thermal signatures, or other physical phenomena are often correlated with encrypt and decrypt operations occurring on a device [10]. Thus enabling attackers to extract sensitive information such as the long-term secret key. Based on this approach, several SCAs against lattice-based KEMs in the NIST PQC standardization process have been proposed, such as [3,6,15,18–21]. Most of them are chosen-ciphertext attacks (CCAs) due to the fact that NIST PQC KEMs are always targeting CCA security.

The recovery goals of these CCAs can be categorized into two groups: one for decrypted messages recovery [18,20] and the other for key recovery [3,6,15, 19,21]. Since key recovery is more powerful than message recovery, we focus our study on key recovery SCAs. Guo et al. in [6] first proposed an oracle based on decryption-failure and instantiated the attack model to complete a timing attack on Frodo KEM. Xu et al. presented a full-decryption-based oracle in [21]. They proved that an attacker only needs 8 traces to recover a specific implementation of Kyber512 compiled at the optimization level -O0. D'Anvers et al. [3] exploited the variable runtime information of its non-constant-time decapsulation implementation on the LAC and successfully recovered its long-term secret key. This key recovery attack, named plaintext-checking (PC) oracle in [14] which was defined as a message-recovery-type attack, finds a link between the long-term secret key and specifically chosen messages and recovers the key by recovering the message. Ravi et al. [15] continue this attack conception by exploiting the leaked side information in Fujisaki-Okamoto (FO) transformation [4] or error correcting codes to propose a generic EM chosen-ciphertext SCA. Qin et al. [13] optimized the approach of [15] in terms of query efficiency. Ueno et al. in [19] further investigated the attack methods against adversaries. More appealing is that they implemented a deep-learning-based distinguisher to assist PC oracle attacks.

Our Contributions. In this paper, we proposed a novel multi-feature-based side-channel attack (Multi-feature-based SCA) by extracting profiling information from multi-features. Multi-feature-based SCA constructs templates of each secret key value based on a convolutional neural network (CNN) and successfully recovers the secret key of Kyber768. In addition to improving the success rate of recovering the secret key, our approach also eliminates the occurrence of invalid attacks. In summary, we make the following contributions:

- We propose a new profiling approach named Multi-feature-based SCA, which uses multiple features to build templates for the secret key. Our approach eliminates invalid attacks and can directly recover the secret key values, bypassing the intermediate step of recovering the decrypted message.
- We build a CNN to recognize secret keys. The experimental results prove the huge advantages of CNN in constructing templates, and its recognition accuracy reached around 90%.
- Furthermore, we instantiate the described attack framework on Kyber768 and show the details in each step of the new procedure. Compared to Ueno et al.'s [19] method, our approach demonstrates an average success rate enhancement of 27.45%. Additionally, when contrasted with Ravi et al.'s [15] method, our approach exhibits an average attack success rate improvement of 53.69%.

Outline. The remainder of this paper is organized as follows. In Sect. 2, we examine the details of Kyber and the conception of binary PC oracle. Then we enumerate some previous SCAs on it. Section 3 outlines the basic idea of our approach, Multi-feature-based SCA. In Sect. 4, we detail our experimental setup and illustrate our attack method and the CNN construction we used. We further demonstrate the effect of our approach on improving the probability of attack success. Lastly, Sect. 5 concludes our work.

2   Background

2.1   Kyber and the Binary PC Oracle

KEM is a public key cryptographic primitive that encapsulates a secret key. Kyber is a chosen-ciphertext secure (CCA-secure) KEM based on the Module-learning with error (M-LWE) problem. The M-LWE problem evolves from the Ring-LWE (R-LWE) problem, with their theoretical basis being to add noise to the $\mathbf{b} = \mathbf{A}\mathbf{s}$ problem, making it difficult to recover $\mathbf{b} = \mathbf{A}\mathbf{s} + \mathbf{e}$. However, in R-LWE problem, $\mathbf{s}$ and each column of $\mathbf{A}$ are chosen from a polynomial ring, while in M-LWE, $\mathbf{s}$ and each column of $\mathbf{A}$ are selected from a module. Therefore, the M-LWE problem offers more flexibility and computational efficiency.

In Kyber, define a polynomial ring $\mathcal{R}_q = \mathbb{Z}_q[x]/(x^n + 1)$, where modulus $q = 3329$ and $n = 256$. For every polynomial $f(x) = a_0 + a_1 x + a_2 x^2 + \cdots + a_{n-1}x^{n-1} \in \mathbb{R}_q$, each coefficient $a_i \in \mathbb{Z}_q$ $(0 \le i \le n-1)$, represents a ring with all elements are integers modulo q. Additions, subtractions, and multiplications of polynomials all require modulus $x^n + 1$. We use bolded uppercase letters for matrices and bolded lowercase letters for polynomial vectors. Matrix $\mathbf{A} \in \mathcal{R}_q^{k \times k}$, where its vector $(\mathbf{A}[0], \cdots, \mathbf{A}[k-1])$ represent a polynomial. $\mathbf{s}, \mathbf{e} \in \mathcal{B}_\eta^k$, where $\mathcal{B}_\eta$ represents the centered binomial distribution with parameter η, and can be generated by $\sum_{i=1}^{\eta}(a_i - b_i)$. In Kyber, a_i and b_i are uniformly random samples independently selected from $\{0, 1\}$.

Based on the above, Kyber provides three security levels with Kyber512 (NIST Security Level 1), Kyber768 (Level 3) and Kyber1024 (Level 5) with dimension $k = 2, 3$ and 4 respectively. In this paper, we focus on the implementation of Kyber768, but our approaches can also be applied to the other two sets. Parameters in Kyber768 are shown in Table 1. $k = 3$ means secret key $\mathbf{sk}$ has 3 polynomials. $(\eta_1, \eta_2) = (2, 2)$ means the coefficients in $\mathbf{sk}$ belong an integer between $[-2, 2]$. (d_u, d_v) were used in Compress and Decompress fuction.

Table 1. Parameters used in Kyber768

	Parameters				
	n	q	k	(η_1, η_2)	(d_u, d_v)
values	256	3329	3	$(2, 2)$	$(10, 4)$

Generally, a KEM consists of key generation, encapsulation, and decapsulation. But PC-based SCA is only against the decapsulation part. Thus, in Algorithm 1 and Algorithm 2, we only introduce the main parts of encapsulation and decapsulation of Kyber, ignoring details such as the Number Theoretic Transform (NTT).

Let $\lceil x \rfloor$ denotes the nearest integer to x. In the following, we first define two functions, $\text{Compress}_q(x, d)$ and $\text{Decompress}_q(x, d)$.

Definition 1. *The Compression function is defined as:* $\mathbb{Z}_q \to \mathbb{Z}_{2^d}$

$$\text{Compress}_q(x, d) = \left\lceil \frac{2^d}{q} \cdot x \right\rfloor \pmod{2^d}. \tag{1}$$

Definition 2. *The Decompression function is defined as:* $\mathbb{Z}_{2^d} \to \mathbb{Z}_q$

$$\text{Decompress}_q(x, d) = \left\lceil \frac{q}{2^d} \cdot x \right\rfloor. \tag{2}$$

We can get in [16], $\text{Compress}_q(x, d)$ and $\text{Decompress}_q(x, d)$ need polynomials for their inputs. The above operation is separately done on each coefficient in the input polynomial. Kyber uses a version of the FO transformation to achieve its stated security goals, i.e., for the chosen-plaintext secure (CPA-secure) to CCA-secure. In the following two algorithms, $\mathcal{G}$ represents a hash operation to get a 64-byte variant meanwhile, $\mathcal{H}$ represents a hash operation to get a 32-byte variant.

Algorithm 1. CCA-secure Kyber KEM based on FO transformation (Encaps)

Input: Public key **pk**
Output: Ciphertext $\mathbf{c} = (\mathbf{c_1}, \mathbf{c_2})$, session key k
1: $\mathbf{m} \leftarrow \{0,1\}^{256}$
2: $(\bar{K}, r) = \mathcal{G}(\mathbf{m} \| \mathcal{H}(\mathbf{pk}))$
3: $\triangleright c = \text{CPA.Encrypt}(\mathbf{pk}, \mathbf{m}, r)$
4:     $\mathbf{A} \leftarrow \mathcal{R}_q^{k \times k}$
5:     $\mathbf{r} \leftarrow \mathcal{B}_{\eta_1}^k$, $\mathbf{e_1}, \mathbf{e_2} \leftarrow \mathcal{B}_{\eta_2}^k$
6:     $\mathbf{u} = \mathbf{A}^T \mathbf{r} + \mathbf{e_1}$
7:     $\mathbf{v} = \mathbf{pk}^T \mathbf{r} + \mathbf{e_2} + \text{Decompress}_q(\mathbf{m}, 1)$
8:     $\mathbf{c_1} = \text{Compress}_q(\mathbf{u}, d_u)$
9:     $\mathbf{c_2} = \text{Compress}_q(\mathbf{v}, d_v)$
10: $k = \text{KDF}(\bar{K} \| \mathcal{H}(\mathbf{c}))$
11: **return** $\mathbf{c}, k$

During Algorithm 1, the message generates a 32-byte $\mathbf{m}$ from the 0,1 space. By $\mathbf{m}$ and $\mathcal{H}(\mathbf{pk})$, we can get the pre-shared secret $\bar{K}$ and a random coin r. In the encapsulation, a CPA-secure encryption operation is used to output $\mathbf{c_1}$ and $\mathbf{c_2}$. Then, the shared secret k is calculated from $\bar{K}$ and $\mathcal{H}(\mathbf{c})$ through the key-derivation function (KDF).

Algorithm 2. CCA-secure Kyber KEM based on FO transformation(Decaps)

Input: Ciphertext **c**, secret key **sk**
Output: Session key k
1: $\mathbf{pk}, \mathcal{H}(\mathbf{pk}), z \leftarrow \text{UnpackSK}(\mathbf{sk})$
2: $\triangleright \mathbf{m'} \leftarrow \text{CPA.Decrypt}(\mathbf{sk}, \mathbf{c})$
3:     $\mathbf{u'} = \text{Decompress}_q(\mathbf{c_1}, d_u)$
4:     $\mathbf{v'} = \text{Decompress}_q(\mathbf{c_2}, d_v)$
5:     $\mathbf{m'} = \text{Compress}_q(\mathbf{v'} - \mathbf{sk}^T \mathbf{u'}, 1)$
6: $(\bar{K'}, r') = \mathcal{G}(\mathbf{m'} \| \mathcal{H}(\mathbf{pk}))$ /* Attack loaction */
7: $\mathbf{c'} \leftarrow \text{CPA.Encrypt}(\mathbf{pk}, \mathbf{m'}, r')$
8: **if** $\mathbf{c} = \mathbf{c'}$ **then**
9:     **return** $k \leftarrow \text{KDF}(\bar{K'}, \mathbf{c})$
10: **else**
11:     **return** $k \leftarrow \text{KDF}(z, \mathbf{c})$
12: **end if**

CCA.Decaps first performs the CPA decryption. In CPA-secure decryption, from $\mathbf{c_1}$ and $\mathbf{c_2}$ using Compress, we obtained the plaintext $\mathbf{m'}$. Then, similar to CCA.Encaps, CCA.Decaps generates r' and $\bar{K'}$, and evaluates CPA.Encrypt $(\mathbf{pk}, \mathbf{m'}, r')$. This procedure is called re-encryption. At Algorithm 2 line 8, the algorithm executes equality checking, namely, examines whether the re-encryption result $\mathbf{c'}$ is equal to the ciphertext $\mathbf{c}$. If equals, the CCA.Decaps algorithm returns the shared secret k as the ciphertext is valid; otherwise, the algorithm returns a pseudorandom number of $KDF(z, c)$ (instead of $\perp$) as the ciphertext is invalid. Thus, the KEM scheme gives any active attacker no information about the PKE decryption result for invalid ciphertext.

The CPA-secure KEMs are vulnerable to chosen-ciphertext attacks when the secret key is reused. These attacks are generally operated in a key-mismatch or PC Oracle. The working principle of PC oracle is to recover one coefficient of the secret key polynomial at a time. Algorithm 3 depicts the PC oracle, in which the adversary sends ciphertext **c** and a reference message **m** to the oracle. The oracle tells whether **m** equals the CPA decryption result **m**' or not.

Algorithm 3. PC oracle

Input: Ciphertext **c**, message **m**
Output: 0 or 1
1: **m**' ← CPA.Decrypt(**sk**, **c**)
2: **if m = m**' **then**
3:    **return** 1
4: **else**
5:    **return** 0
6: **end if**

The key recovery process is based on the recovery of message **m**' in Algorithm 3. By constructing the selected ciphertext, we can combine every possible coefficient value in Kyber with a set of oracle response sequences. With multiple queries, we are able to recover this coefficient value. Using the rotation property of the polynomial ring, we are then able to recover the complete secret key polynomial of Kyber.

2.2 PC Oracle-Based SCA Attacks

The LWE-based KEM in the CPA model can be upgraded to a CCA-secure KEM through FO transformation. As we described in Sect. 2.1, using FO transformation, the attacker cannot obtain any prompt information about the decapsulation failure when decapsulating. This theoretically provides a strong security guarantee for CPA security KEM, which can prevent selected ciphertext attacks.

However, with the help of side information, such as analyzing the power or electromagnetic waveforms of certain operations during the decapsulation process, an attacker can directly discover the CPA-secure operations inside the CCA-secure model and launch the same attack.

At CHES 2020, Ravi et al. launched a PC oracle-based SCA attack against NIST KEM by utilizing side information leaked from the re-encryption process in the FO transform [15]. Taking the attack against Kyber as an example, the attacker only needs to control **m**' to be $O = (0, 0, 0, 0, \cdots)$ or $X = (1, 0, 0, 0, 0, \cdots)$. In this way, they build a PC Oracle with a side-channel waveform distinguisher. In [15], Ravi et al. used simple Euclidean distances to create a recognizer with profiled waveform templates. More specifically, they first collected two sets of re-encrypted waveforms with $\mathbf{m}' = \mathrm{O}$ and $\mathbf{m}' = \mathrm{X}$. Then, they performed a Test Vector Leakage Assessment (TVLA) between the two sets to select the Point of Interest (PoI). In the attack phase, they achieve binary classification by computing the Euclidean distance between the collected PoI waveforms and the two waveform templates. If each PC oracle query is correct, then Ravi et al. need 5 queries to recover a coefficient. In total, they need $256 \times 2 \times 5 = 2560$ queries to recover Kyber512.

After that, Qin et al. improved the query efficiency by using an optimal binary tree similar to Hoffman tree encoding to reduce the average number of queries to recover Kyber512 to 1312, which can be found in [13].

We call all the above recovery methods *single-feature recovery*, and if the value of the private key cannot be found based on the private key identifier obtained from a set of oracle queries, we call this case an invalid attack.

This type of key recovery approach designed by them cannot always tell the truth due to the influence of ambient noise and the accuracy of the side channel distinguisher itself. And since we cannot determine the location of the error, the complexity of brute force cracking is quite high. Therefore, additional techniques are needed to enhance the recovery procedure or tolerate the error. One commonly used technique is majority voting, which was also used in the Ravi et al. attack. With multiple votes, we can obtain a more accurate Oracle.

2.3 Convolutional Neural Network in SCAs

Convolutional neural networks are a powerful class of neural networks designed for processing image data. It has achieved widespread success across domains, including side-channel analysis. It is not surprising, as deep learning excels at identifying patterns and relationships, which aids in extracting information from power consumption time series. This is especially useful for template attacks.

In [11], Maghrebi et al. first applied deep learning in a side-channel context. They found that against unprotected cryptographic algorithm implementations, DL-based attacks are more effective than machine learning-based and traditional template attacks. Notably, their experimental results show that the feature extraction-based model performed very well on both datasets. This could be explained by the fact that CNN applies a nice features extraction technique based on filters allowing dealing with the most informative samples from the processed traces. The work of [8] also proves this.

At CHES 2022, Ueno et al. used CNN to design a side-channel distinguisher and achieve a similar binary classification [19]. With the CNN distinguisher, they can get higher accuracy of single-feature recognition.

2.4 Open Problem

We reproduce the method of Ravi and Ueno in [15] and [19] using energy analysis. As an example, 20 coefficient values are recovered, as shown in Fig. 1, the average success rate for recovering a single-feature (i.e., message $\mathbf{m}'$) using Ravi's method is 64.58%. However, for recovering the complete label, the entire attack fails even if one-bit feature is incorrectly recovered. Hence, the average success rate of secret key recovery using the method in [15] is only 10.46%.

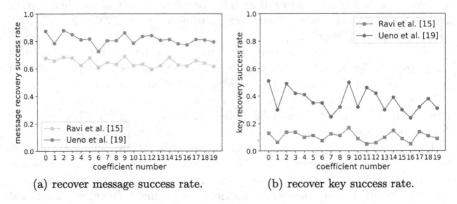

(a) recover message success rate.   (b) recover key success rate.

Fig. 1. The success rates of using Ravi [15] and Ueno [19] methods in recovering message bit and a certain secret key coefficient respectively.

As illustrated in Fig. 1, using Ueno's method in [19], the CNN model leads to significant performance gains, with the average success rate of recovering message $\mathbf{m}'$ directly improved from 64.58% to 81.4%. However, the success rate of secret key recovery using the method in [19] remains only 36.7%.

We also noticed that with both methods in [15] and [19], this attack approach of recovering the secret key value bit-by-bit according to the single-feature of $\mathbf{m}'$ has a very large invalid attack space. That is, the recovered binary label string may represent neither the correct secret key value nor the wrong secret key value, but rather a meaningless label string. Shockingly, the average occurrence probability of invalid attacks at 75.17% in [15], shown in Fig. 2. Although using CNN in [19] reduces the occurrence of this event, the proportion of invalid attacks still reaches over 50%.

So how to improve the success rate of attacks and avoid such invalid attacks?

3   Multi-feature-Based SCA on Kyber

In this section, we elucidate in detail the methodology for constructing multi-features of secret key and use it to recover Kyber768 using power analysis attacks. Using this approach, we eliminate the occurrence of invalid attacks.

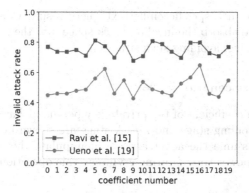

Fig. 2. Invalid attack rate in Ravi [15] and Ueno [19].

3.1 Construction of Multiple Features

In this part, we describe the full-key recovery framework of the new attack.

All previous attack methods take recovering m' as an intermediate step (including [15] and [19]), with the decrypted message value m' as the profiling target. In contrast, our approach bypasses this intermediate process and directly builds templates for the key. The comparison between the two approaches is illustrated in Fig. 3.

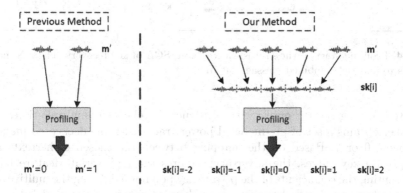

Fig. 3. Our profiling strategy.

In order to eliminate the invalid attack presented above, we propose a new profiling method that builds templates for secret keys from multi-features. We integrate the modeling and matching of m' and build a template for the secret key instead of the decrypted message m'. Instead of recovering the key's binary label bit by bit, the new key feature construction method stitches single-features

m' together based on a specific ciphertext query result. Compared to *single-feature recovery*, we absorb the invalid attack space into the guess space for the entire secret key value, avoiding such situation.

3.2 Our Attack Scenario

We denote the i-th coefficient of the private key polynomial as $\mathbf{sk}[i]$. The overall workflow of the profiling stage and attack stage are shown in Fig. 4 and Fig. 5, respectively. We assume the adversary can manipulate the target device and collect the leaked power traces during cryptographic operations.

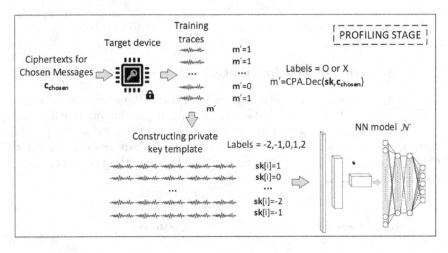

Fig. 4. Profiling stage of the Multi-feature-based SCA of key recovery. The NN model learns to find the combined message bit $\mathbf{m}'$.

By querying the PC oracle with constructed ciphertexts multiple times, the attacker obtains a set of pre-modeled power traces with the decrypted message m' being 0 or 1. Based on the mapping between the chosen ciphertexts and the private key values, the adversary acquires the multivariate feature labels representing the coefficients of the private key polynomial. Using the multivariate feature identifiers for each private key value, we construct the modeled power traces for $\mathbf{sk}[i]$ and label these traces based on the value of $\mathbf{sk}[i]$. Finally, they are fed into the network for training.

During the attack stage, as shown in Fig. 5, the attacker replaces the ciphertext with five preset chosen ciphertexts and polls the decrypted messages m' from the target device by decrypting these five chosen ciphertexts. After that, the five obtained traces are concatenated in order and preprocessed into the $\mathbf{sk}[i]$ template style during the modeling stage. Finally, the preprocessed power trace is fed into the trained network, which will directly output the value of this $\mathbf{sk}[j]$.

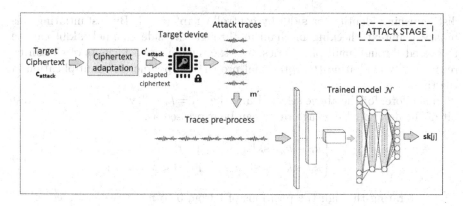

Fig. 5. Attack stage of the Multi-feature-based SCA of key recovery.

3.3 Generate Qualified Ciphertexts

The process of obtaining these five chosen ciphertexts is as follows:

In CCA.Decaps of Algorithm 2, an attacker can construct the ciphertext $\mathbf{c} = (\mathbf{u}, \mathbf{v})$. And set $\mathbf{u} = k_u \cdot x^0$ and $\mathbf{v} = k_v \cdot x^0$ where $(k_u, k_v) \in \mathbb{Z}_q$.

Let us take the example of recovering $\mathbf{sk}[0]$ (i.e., the lowest coefficient in the first polynomial of $\mathbf{sk}$). We take a long rectangle to represent a polynomial, and each small rectangle in it represents a coefficient. In Kyber768, the polynomial vector has three dimensions, so $\mathbf{sk}$ and $\mathbf{u}'$ each have three long rectangles. We omit certain modules, such as Compress operations. The connection between the decrypted $\mathbf{m}'$, the selected ciphertext $\mathbf{c}$ and the secret key is as shown in Fig. 6:

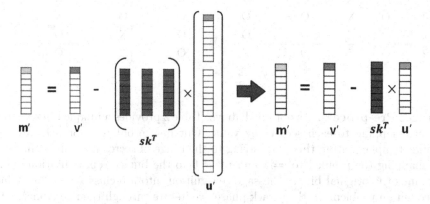

Fig. 6. The abstract compute relation for $\mathbf{m}'$ in line 5 in Algorithm 2. We fill the nonzero coefficients of each polynomial in $\mathbf{m}'$, $\mathbf{sk}$, $\mathbf{u}'$, and $\mathbf{v}'$ with a different color, with a white rectangle indicating that the coefficient is 0.

From Fig. 6, we can see that all coefficients in $\mathbf{m}'$ except for the lowest coefficient, the remaining are all zeros. This allows the attacker to establish a binary distinguishing identity for $\mathbf{sk}[0]$ by controlling $\mathbf{m}' = 0/1$. By instantiating this binary plaintext checking mechanism through the side channel, $\mathbf{sk}[0]$ can be recovered through multiple queries, and the remaining coefficients of $\mathbf{sk}$ can be recovered by exploiting the rotational property of polynomial multiplication in the ring.

Therefore, for the above selected $\mathbf{u}, \mathbf{v}$ (i.e., $\mathbf{u} = k_u \cdot x^0, \mathbf{v} = k_v \cdot x^0$), the lowest bit of the decrypted message $\mathbf{m}'[0]$ can be expressed as:

$$
\mathbf{m}'[0] = \begin{cases} k_v - k_u \cdot \mathbf{sk}[0] & \text{if} \quad t = 0 \\ k_v - k_u \cdot -\mathbf{sk}[n-t] & \text{if} \quad 0 < t \le n-1 \end{cases} \tag{3}
$$

By iterating through the positions of t from 0 to $n-1$, we can recover the coefficients of the first polynomial in secret key s in the order of $\mathbf{sk}[0], -\mathbf{sk}[n-1], -\mathbf{sk}[n-2], \ldots, -\mathbf{sk}[1]$.

Since the coefficient values of the secret key in Kyber768 are within $[-2, 2]$, we construct Table 2 to enumerate the mapping between the binary string representation of the decrypted message from a chosen ciphertext and the corresponding secret key value. Where X represents the decrypted $\mathbf{m}' = 1$, and O represents $\mathbf{m}' = 0$.

Table 2. Chosen ciphertext pairs

Coeff.	(k_u, k_v)						
	$(0,0)$	$(0, q/2)$	$(110, 657)$	$(240, 2933)$	$(110, 832)$	$(182, 2497)$	$(416, 1248)$
-2	O	X	X	O	X	O	X
-1	O	X	O	O	X	O	X
0	O	X	O	O	O	O	X
1	O	X	O	O	O	X	O
2	O	X	O	X	O	X	O

Traces Pre-process. As obtained above, Table 2 provides a unique binary label string mapping to each secret key value. Our new profiling approach directly builds templates from this label string to the range of secret key values, instead of mapping the profiled $\mathbf{m}' = 1$ and $\mathbf{m}' = 0$ to the binary representation. This expands the original binary message recognition into a 5-class secret key value recognition problem. In the attack phase, we iterate through the five ciphertexts constructed using Table 2 (last five columns), collecting the power traces over the last four rounds of the hash function during decapsulation for each ciphertext. These are concatenated to form the combined multivariate feature information.

4   Experiments

4.1   Equipment Setup

Our measurement setup is shown in Fig. 7. It consists of the Laptop, the versatile current amplifier, the STM32F429 target board, and the PicoScope 3403D Oscilloscope. We target the optimized unprotected implementation of Kyber768, taken from the public **pqm4** library [7], a benchmarking and testing framework for PQC schemes on the 32-bit ARM Cortex-M4 microcontroller. In our initialization, the implementation is compiled with **arm-none-eabi-gcc** using the optimization flag "-O1". We set the operating clock frequency of the target board to 16 MHz and utilized the power analysis side-channel for our experiments. For traces acquisition, we set the trigger at pin PC6, and the measurement results were collected on the oscilloscope with a sampling rate of 62.5 MSa/s.

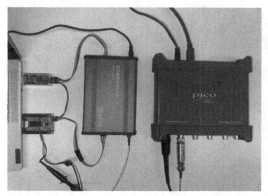 

Fig. 7. Equipment for trace acquisition and the board used in the experiment.

4.2   Target Operation

The ensuing problem is how to capture this leakage in the side channel. We assume that the attacker has the ability to completely manipulate the target device and is able to measure the power consumption during the execution of a cryptographic algorithm. Then during the inference phase, the adversary aims at recovering the unknown secret key, processed by the same device, by collecting a new set of power consumption traces. To guarantee a fair and realistic attack comparison, we stress the fact that the training and the attack data sets must be different.

Target Operation. Using the key recovery methods in Sect. 3, we find a chosen ciphertext correspondence that is sufficient to distinguish the values of the polynomial coefficients of the secret key. By means of the binary plaintext checking oracle described above, the attacker constructs a distinction of the decrypted message $\mathbf{m}'$. Exactly through the hash function execution process in the FO transformation, the attacker can amplify the difference of the decrypted message $\mathbf{m}'$ from 1 bit message bit to 256 bits.

The `KeccakF1600_StatePermute` function in $\mathcal{G}$ includes twelve for loops. Therefore, the target option we choose is the last four rounds of the hash operation, as shown in Fig. 8. That is, line 6 in Algorithm 2. The TVLA result of our target operation is as shown in Fig. 9:

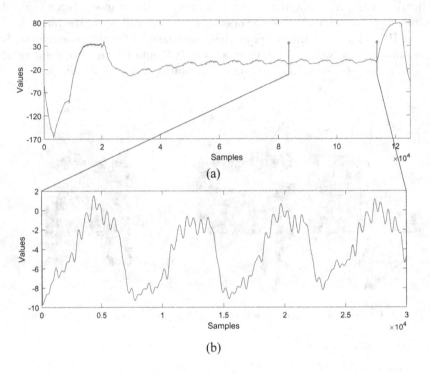

(a)

(b)

Fig. 8. Original power trace of Kyber768. (a) The whole hash operation $\mathcal{G}$ with twelve for loops in Kyber.KEM.Decaps() (i.e., line 6 in Algorithm 2); (b) The last four rounds of $\mathcal{G}$.

Traces Acquire. We set the STM32F429 microcontroller as a server and our laptop as a client. Every time we selected a random message $\mathbf{m}$ and encapsulated it with the public key into ciphertext $\mathbf{c}$ on the client, then we sent $\mathbf{c}$ to the server through a socket.

During the decapsulation of the profiling stage, we captured power traces and saved O or X (i.e., $\mathbf{m}' = 0$ or $\mathbf{m}' = 1$) as labels. For each type of template, we collected 9,000 traces, each with a length of 30,000. Then we combined the traces in order of the five chosen ciphertexts in Table 2. The templates we get

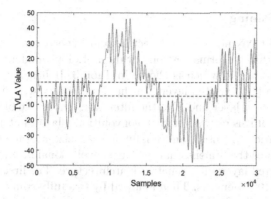

Fig. 9. TVLA results for the last four rounds between O and X.

are as shown in Fig. 10, and we only selected two localized positions for zoomed-in display (five values of **sk**[i] are represented by five lines with different colors respectively):

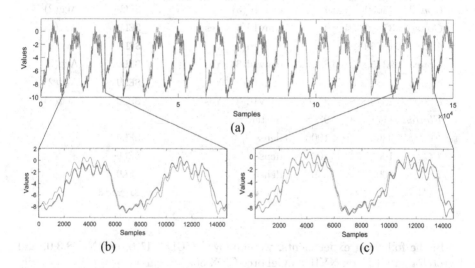

Fig. 10. Constructed template of **sk**[i]. (a) Complete template for **sk**[i] after trace pre-process; (b) and (c) The expansion of an interval somewhere in the template of **sk**[i].

In the attack stage, we only need to poll these five chosen ciphertexts in order and collect the same power traces as in the profiling stage for the same pre-processing.

4.3   Model Training

By adjusting the CNN network architecture and hyperparameters, we obtained the CNN model that performs best on our dataset. This model is inherited from [19]. The architecture of which is shown in Table 3. It has seven convolutional layers and four fully-connected layers. In the "Function" row, conv1d(F) denotes the operation at each layer and F is the filter size. The stride of the filter is two and the padding of it is one. After each convolutional layer, batch normalization and SeLU activation are used, and finally, a 2×2 size average pooling layer is connected to reduce the dimensionality. The convolutional layers are followed by four fully-connected layers in our network architecture. The first fully-connected layer consists of 1000 neurons. Then followed by two fully-connected layers with 200 neurons each. The final layer has 5 neurons and utilizes softmax activation for classification.

Table 3. NN architecture

	Input	Output	Function	Normalization	Activation	Pooling
$Conv1$	150000×1	4	conv1d(3)	Yes	SELU	Avg(2)
$Conv2$	75000×4	4	conv1d(3)	Yes	SELU	Avg(2)
$Conv3$	37500×4	4	conv1d(3)	Yes	SELU	Avg(2)
$Conv4$	18750×4	8	conv1d(3)	Yes	SELU	Avg(2)
$Conv5$	9375×8	8	conv1d(3)	Yes	SELU	Avg(2)
$Conv6$	4687×8	8	conv1d(3)	Yes	SELU	Avg(2)
$Conv7$	2343×8	8	conv1d(3)	Yes	SELU	Avg(2)
$Flatten$	1171×8	9368	flatten	–	–	–
$FC1$	9368	1000	dense	–	SELU	–
$FC2$	1000	200	dense	–	SELU	–
$FC3$	200	200	dense	–	SELU	–
$FC4$	200	5	dense	–	Sigmoid	–

In the following experiments, we employed CUDA 11.6, cuDNN 8.3.0, and Pytorch-gpu 1.13.1 on NVIDIA GeForce GTX 3050 to carry out the NN training. The Adam optimizer is utilized with a learning rate of 0.00005, the batch size was 128, and the number of epochs was 50. We used the cross-entropy loss function during training and validated it after each epoch.

4.4   Experimental Results and Comparison

The loss values of this model trained on our dataset for 50 epochs and the accuracy of the validation set are shown in Fig. 11. After 50 epochs of training, the model's loss stabilizes around 0.9 and the accuracy of the validation set improves to 88%.

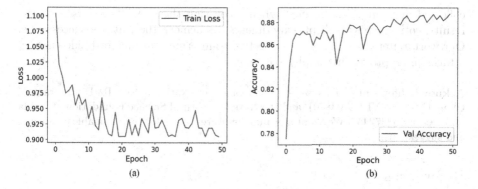

Fig. 11. Train loss (a) and validation accuracy (b) of our approach.

As shown in Fig. 12, our approach significantly improves the success probability of recovering secret key values. Compared to Ravi's method [15], the average attack success rate for a secret key value increases by 53.69%. It also outperforms distinguishing message **m′** using neural networks [19] by 27.45%. Our approach can also tolerate invalid attacks due to errors in *single-feature recovery*.

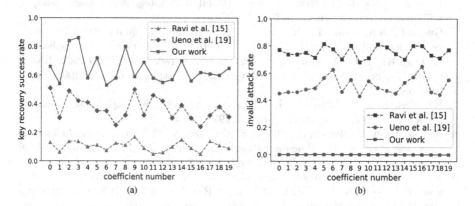

Fig. 12. Compare three methods of key recovery success rate (a) and invalid attack rate (b).

5 Conclusion

Our Multi-feature-based SCA is a novel attack technique that extracts secret key templates from multivariate features and employs the optimal CNN architecture. All attacks presented in this paper are performed directly on the target device. Our experimental results demonstrate that CNN can significantly improve profiling efficiency as an effective approach. Notably, our approach only uses the traces collected in a single experiment when recovering the secret key. Based on the results, voting across multiple experiments can achieve 100% attack success rate. Our work reiterates the need for effective countermeasures against side-channel attacks in cryptographic implementations.

Acknowledgements. This work is supported by National Key R&D Program of China (No. 2022YFB3103800), and the National Natural Science Foundation of China under Grant 62272457. We thank the anonymous reviewers for their valuable comments and suggestions.

References

1. Announcing the commercial national security algorithm suite 2.0. Technical report (2022)
2. Alagic, G., et al.: Status report on the third round of the nist post-quantum cryptography standardization process. US Department of Commerce, NIST (2022)
3. D'Anvers, J.P., Tiepelt, M., Vercauteren, F., Verbauwhede, I.: Timing attacks on error correcting codes in post-quantum schemes. In: Proceedings of ACM Workshop on Theory of Implementation Security Workshop, pp. 2–9 (2019)
4. Fujisaki, E., Okamoto, T.: Secure integration of asymmetric and symmetric encryption schemes. J. Cryptol. **26**, 80–101 (2013)
5. Gidney, C., Ekerå, M.: How to factor 2048 bit RSA integers in 8 hours using 20 million noisy qubits. Quantum **5**, 433 (2021)
6. Guo, Q., Johansson, T., Nilsson, A.: A key-recovery timing attack on post-quantum primitives using the Fujisaki-Okamoto transformation and its application on FrodoKEM. In: Micciancio, D., Ristenpart, T. (eds.) CRYPTO 2020. LNCS, vol. 12171, pp. 359–386. Springer, Cham (2020). https://doi.org/10.1007/978-3-030-56880-1_13
7. Kannwischer, M.J., Rijneveld, J., Schwabe, P., Stoffelen, K.: PQM4: post-quantum crypto library for the arm cortex-m4 (2019)
8. Kim, J., Picek, S., Heuser, A., Bhasin, S., Hanjalic, A.: Make some noise: unleashing the power of convolutional neural networks for profiled side-channel analysis. IACR Trans. Cryptogr. Hardware Embed. Syst. 148–179 (2019)
9. Kocher, P.C.: Timing attacks on implementations of Diffie-Hellman, RSA, DSS, and other systems. In: Koblitz, N. (ed.) CRYPTO 1996. LNCS, vol. 1109, pp. 104–113. Springer, Heidelberg (1996). https://doi.org/10.1007/3-540-68697-5_9
10. Koeune, F., Standaert, F.X.: A tutorial on physical security and side-channel attacks. In: International School on Foundations of Security Analysis and Design, pp. 78–108 (2004)
11. Maghrebi, H., Portigliatti, T., Prouff, E.: Breaking cryptographic implementations using deep learning techniques. In: Carlet, C., Hasan, M.A., Saraswat, V. (eds.) SPACE 2016. LNCS, vol. 10076, pp. 3–26. Springer, Cham (2016). https://doi.org/10.1007/978-3-319-49445-6_1
12. Moody, D.: Post-quantum cryptography standardization: announcement and outline of nist's call for submissions. In: International Conference on Post-Quantum Cryptography-PQCrypto (2016)
13. Qin, Y., Cheng, C., Zhang, X., Pan, Y., Hu, L., Ding, J.: A systematic approach and analysis of key mismatch attacks on lattice-based nist candidate kems. In: Advances in Cryptology-ASIACRYPT 2021: 27th International Conference on the

Theory and Application of Cryptology and Information Security, Singapore, 6–10 December 2021, Proceedings, Part IV, vol. 27, pp. 92–121. Springer, Heidelberg (2021). https://doi.org/10.1007/978-3-030-92068-5_4

14. Ravi, P., Roy, S.S.: Side-channel analysis of lattice-based PQC candidates. In: Round 3 Seminars, NIST Post Quantum Cryptography (2021)
15. Ravi, P., Roy, S.S., Chattopadhyay, A., Bhasin, S.: Generic side-channel attacks on cca-secure lattice-based pke and kems. IACR Trans. Cryptogr. Hardware Embed. Syst. 307–335 (2020)
16. Schwabe, P., et al.: Crystals-kyber: algorithm specifications and supporting documentation (version 3.0). In: NIST Post-Quantum Cryptography-Round 3 (2019)
17. Shor, P.W.: Algorithms for quantum computation: discrete logarithms and factoring. In: Proceedings 35th Annual Symposium on Foundations of Computer Science, pp. 124–134. IEEE (1994)
18. Sim, B.Y.: Single-trace attacks on message encoding in lattice-based KEMs. IEEE Access 8, 183175–183191 (2020)
19. Ueno, R., Xagawa, K., Tanaka, Y., Ito, A., Takahashi, J., Homma, N.: Curse of re-encryption: a generic power/em analysis on post-quantum kems. IACR Trans. Cryptogr. Hardware Embed. Syst. 296–322 (2022)
20. Wang, R., Ngo, K., Dubrova, E.: A message recovery attack on lwe/lwr-based pke/kems using amplitude-modulated em emanations. In: International Conference on Information Security and Cryptology, pp. 450–471. Springer, Heidelberg (2022). https://doi.org/10.1007/978-3-031-29371-9
21. Xu, Z., Pemberton, O., Roy, S.S., Oswald, D., Yao, W., Zheng, Z.: Magnifying side-channel leakage of lattice-based cryptosystems with chosen ciphertexts: the case study of kyber. IEEE Trans. Comput. 71(9), 2163–2176 (2021)

Not Optimal but Efficient:
A Distinguisher Based
on the Kruskal-Wallis Test

Yan Yan[1(✉)], Elisabeth Oswald[1], and Arnab Roy[1,2]

[1] University of Klagenfurt, Klagenfurt, Austria
yanyansmajesty@outlook.com
[2] University of Innsbruck, Innsbruck, Austria

Abstract. Research about the theoretical properties of side channel distinguishers revealed the rules by which to maximise the probability of first order success ("optimal distinguishers") under different assumptions about the leakage model and noise distribution. Simultaneously, research into bounding first order success (as a function of the number of observations) has revealed universal bounds, which suggest that (even optimal) distinguishers are not able to reach theoretically possible success rates. Is this gap a proof artefact (aka the bounds are not tight) or does a distinguisher exist that is more trace efficient than the "optimal" one? We show that in the context of an unknown (and not linear) leakage model there is indeed a distinguisher that outperforms the "optimal" distinguisher in terms of trace efficiency: it is based on the Kruskal-Wallis test.

Keywords: Distinguisher · Side Channel

1 Introduction

To exploit the information contained in side channels we use distinguishers: these are key-guess dependent functions, which are applied to the side channel observations and some auxiliary input (plaintext or ciphertext information), that attribute scores to key guesses. Optimal distinguishers [HRG14] are distinguishing rules derived by the process of maximising the likelihood of ranking the key guess that corresponds to the true secret value first (via their respective scores). The mathematical setup to derive optimal distinguishers is agnostic to estimation and trace efficiency, and thus an optimal distinguisher is not per construction the most trace efficient one. However, the optimal distinguishing rules that were derived in [HRG14] outperformed (experimentally) other distinguishers, or when not, [HRG14] showed mathematical equivalence between an optimal distinguishing rule and a classical rule. For instance, the correlation distinguisher turned out to be equivalent to the optimal rule in the situation where the leakage function is known and the noise is Gaussian.

H. Seo and S. Kim (Eds.): ICISC 2023, LNCS 14561, pp. 240–258, 2024.
https://doi.org/10.1007/978-981-97-1235-9_13

The situation in which an adversary is confronted with a new device that contains an unknown key is interesting because it corresponds to the "hardest challenge" for the adversary: they should recover the key with only information about the cryptographic implementation. Framing this in the context of side channel distinguishers, this leads to a type of distinguisher that neither requires assumptions about the noise distribution nor information about the device leakage distribution. Previous research has looked at distinguishers such as mutual information [GBTP08], Spearman's rank correlation [BGL08], and the Kolmogorov-Smirnov (KS) test [WOM11] in this context—these papers pre-date the seminal paper [HRG14] that establishes how to derive an optimal distinguishing rule.

Relatively recently only it was argued that the mutual information can be recovered as the optimal distinguishing rule [dCGHR18] if no assumptions about the device leakage distribution can be made. They also show experimentally that mutual information is the most trace efficient distinguisher in this setting. Next, better bounds for the estimation of the first order success rate (i.e. the probability to rank the key guess that corresponds to the true secret key first based on distinguishing scores) were derived in [dCGRP19]. The idea here was to derive these bounds independently of any specific distinguisher, purely based on the mutual information between the observed leakage and the key. The bounds were then compared to the respective optimal distinguishing rule. It turned out that there is a considerable gap between the optimal distinguisher and the bounds. This begs the question: could there indeed be a distinguisher that is more trace efficient than the one recovered as the optimal distinguishing rule?

1.1   Our Contributions

We find a more trace efficient distinguisher by switching to rank based statistics. Previous work has once touched on rank based statistics before (Spearman's rank correlation) but we seek out a method that works even if the relationship between the intermediate values and the device leakage is not monotonic: this leads us to explore the Kruskal-Wallis method. We show how to translate it to the side channel context **(the important trick here is to rank the traces itself prior to any partitioning)** and we demonstrate how to estimate the number of needed traces for statistical attack success. We extend the existing work here by **developing a lower bound for the number of needed traces**.

Following established practice we then provide experimental results that enable us to conclude also from a practical point of view that the anticipated theoretical advantages show in practice. We cover **a range of situations** where we explore different target functions and different device leakage functions. In terms of target functions, we use non-injective target functions (as required by the assumptions in [HRG14,dCGHR18]), and also injective target functions with the bit-dropping trick. For device leakage functions we cover functions that range from highly non-linear to linear. We investigate Gaussian and Laplacian noise. Our philosophy is to include settings from prevoius work and more. We also consider implementations based on shared out intermediate values. Experiments that vary all these factors are necessarily based on simulations. We also demonstrate that our observations translate to real device data by using traces from two AES implementations: one with and one without masking.

Our research exhibits, for the first time, in the setting where no information about the device leakage distribution is available, a distinguishing rule that is more trace efficient than the optimal distinguishing rule (MI). Our research also shows for the first time that a purely rank based distinguisher is effective in the context of masking.

We provide the necessary background about (rank based) distinguishers, and our notation in Sect. 2. Then we introduce the Kruskal-Wallis method and turn it into a distinguisher (alongside the analysis for the number of needed traces from a statistical point of view) in Sect. 3. In Sect. 4 we show and discuss the simulation results, and in Sect. 5 we show and discuss the results for the real traces. We conclude in Sect. 6.

2   Background

We try and use notation that is uncluttered whenever we refer to well established background, in particular, when it comes to known facts about distinguishers, and we "overload" variables so that they simultaneously refer to sets and random variables. For instance, we use L to refer to the set of observed traces, which we also know to have a distribution.

2.1   Side Channel Attacks and Notation

We assume that the side-channel leakage L can be expressed as a sum of a key dependent function M and some independent noise ε:

$$L = M(V_{k^*}) + \varepsilon.$$

The device leakage model M is not known in practice. It is a function of V, an intermediate value, which depends on some input word X and a fixed and unknown secret key word k^*. We assume that the noise follows a Gaussian distribution $\varepsilon \sim \mathcal{N}(0, \sigma)$.[1] The intermediate V is derived by the keyed cryptographic function f_{k^*}:

$$V_{k^*} = f_{k^*}(X).$$

In a side-channel attack, the adversary is given a set of leakages L and their corresponding inputs X.[2] To recover the correct (secret) key k^* embedded within the device, the adversary first computes the (predicted) intermediates V_k under all possible guesses of k, from the given input X. Then they compute the hypothetical leakage value $L_{\mathcal{H},k} = \mathcal{H}(V_k)$ by assuming a leakage function $\mathcal{H}$. In side-channel attacks that rely on a direct or proportional approximation of the device

---

[1] For readability we do not make input and key dependence explicit in the leakage L.
[2] Side-channel attacks are also possible by exploiting the output with $f_{k^*}^{-1}$.

leakage, the quality of $\mathcal{H}$ determines the success or efficiency of the corresponding attacks. When no model is known, then $\mathcal{H}$ is simply the identity function.

A distinguisher D is used to compute the distinguishing score d_k from the predicted intermediates V_k and the observed leakage L. In a successful side-channel attack, the correct key k^* is determined as the maximum distinguishing score(s):

$$k^* = \arg\max_k d_k = \arg\max_k D(L_{\mathcal{H},k}, L)$$

It is important to bear in mind that distinguishers are based on estimators of statistical quantities, thus in the formulas below we indicate this fact by placing a hat above the respective quantity. Distinguishers may or may not be based on some either assumed or known properties of the observed leakage L. In statistical jargon, statistics that require assumptions about the distribution are called "parametric" and statistics that do not require assumptions about the distribution are called "non-parametric". In this paper we work on the assumption that we are in a "first contact" scenario where the adversary utilises no information about L in their initial attack attempt: this hence requires them to use non-parametric statistics, thus a non-parametric distinguisher.

In all practical side-channel attacks, the targeted intermediate V_k is normally a part of operands being processed by the device during the cryptographic algorithms, and the key k is a chunk of the cryptographic key. The complete key recovery is done via performing multiple side-channel attacks on each of the key chunks (thus we use a divide and conquer strategy). Also observable leakage often is given as a real-valued vector: e.g. power traces consist of many measurement points. Distinguishers are either applied to individual trace points, or to specific subsets of trace points. Therefore, in our aim to keep the notation uncluttered, we do not include any variables for indices for trace points or the like. We implicitly understand that the distinguisher is applied to (many) trace points or sets of trace points individually.

2.2   Rank Transformations

Many statistical techniques that do not require assumptions about the underlying distributions have been developed by working on ranked data. Suppose that we have a set of leakages L: there are several ways in which ranks can be assigned to the leakages in the set. The two most natural types of assigning ranks are the following:

Type 1: The entire set is ranked from smallest to largest (or vice versa), and the smallest leakage having rank 1, the second smallest having rank 2, etc.

Type 2: The set L is partitioned according to some rule into subsets, then each subset is ranked independently of all other subset, by ordering the elements within a set (either from smallest to largest or vice versa).

Ties are resolved by assigning the average of the ranks that the ties would have received.

Any monotonic increasing function that is applied to the data does not change the ranking of the data. In our text we indicate that ranking takes place by applying the rank() function to the resp. variables. The type of ranking will be clear from the context.

2.3 Non-parametric Side-Channel Distinguishers

For the sake of completeness we provide a very brief description of the non-parametric side-channel distinguishers that we use as comparisons with are new distinguisher.

Difference of Means. The Difference of Means (DoM) [KJJ99] is often used as a baseline distinguisher, and it can be defined such that it makes minimal assumptions about the leakage distribution. For its' computation, the traces are divided into two groups $L_{V_k=0}$ and $L_{V_k=1}$ depending on whether a predicted single bit of a targeted intermediate is zero or one ($V_k = 0$ or $V_k = 1$). The distinguishing score is defined as the estimated difference of means (often one takes the absolute value)):

$$d_k = |\hat{\mathbb{E}}(L_{V_k=0}) - \hat{\mathbb{E}}(L_{V_k=1})|.$$

Spearman's Rank Correlation. This is a non-parametric alternative to Pearson's correlation, and it was investigated in [BGL08] against an AES implementation. It was shown to be significantly more efficient (in terms of success rate) compared to Pearson's correlation-based attack [BCO04] (a.k.a. CPA). In this attack, the adversary computes the hypothetical leakage from V_k by computing $L_{\mathcal{H},k}$ where $\mathcal{H}$ is guessed/assumed by the adversary. Then $L_{\mathcal{H},k}$ and L are ranked and the (absolute value of the) correlation coefficient is estimated as follows

$$d_k = \left| \frac{\hat{Cov}(\mathsf{rank}(L), \mathsf{rank}(L_{\mathcal{H},k}))}{\hat{\sigma}_{\mathsf{rank}(L)}\hat{\sigma}_{\mathsf{rank}(L_{\mathcal{H},k})}} \right|.$$

Notice that although the adversay must "guess" a hypothetical leakage model, there is no requirement for the device leakage to follow a Gaussian distribution.

Mutual Information. Mutual Information [GBTP08] analysis is a distinguishing method that can be used without the need for $\mathcal{H}$. The MI distinguishing score is computed by estimating the mutual information from a set of collected traces and the corresponding inputs or plaintexts:

$$d_k = \hat{I}(L, V_k) = \hat{H}(L) - \hat{H}(L|V_k)$$

where $\hat{H}$ and $\hat{I}$ denote the (estimated) Shannon's entropy and mutual information respectively. For estimating MI, different entropy estimation methods have been studied, but the most commonly applied and efficient method (over $\mathbb{R}$) is the so-called binning method that is used in the original proposal of MIA [GBTP08]. We also use this same estimation method in our experiments.

Note that MI requires that the target function f_k is not a bijection as discussed in [WOS14,dCGHR18]. When MIA is applied to cryptographic target that is a bijection, then the bit dropping technique [RGV14] that simply chops off a selected number bits from the output, is used. Although it is not necessary to supply MI with a hypothetical leakage model $\mathcal{H}$ this is frequently done in the literature, in particular by selecting the Hamming weight as $\mathcal{H}$.

Kolmogorov-Smirnov (KS). The KS test-based distinguisher [WOM11] is suggested as an alternative to using MI. The distinguishing score (of a key) is defined as the average of KS distances between the leakage distribution of L and leakage distributions of L_{V_k} for each predicted intermediate V_k i.e.

$$d_k = \hat{\mathbb{E}}_{V_k}\left(\sup_l |F_L(l) - F_{L_{V_k}}(l)|\right)$$

where $F_L(l)$ and $F_{L_{V_k}}(l)$ are the Cumulative Distribution Functions (CDFs) of L and L_{V_k} respectively. From a finite sample set A the empirical CDF is computed by $F_A(x) = \frac{1}{n}\sum_{a \in A} I_{a \leq x}$ where I is the indicator function and $|A| = n$.

3   The Kruskal-Wallis Test as Side-Channel Distinguisher

The Kruskal-Wallis test (KW) [KW52] is a non-parametric method for the *analysis of variance* (ANOVA): this means it does not require any distributional assumption about the leakage L. The KW test is based on the ranks of the observed data and it is often used to check whether (or not) multiple groups of samples are from the same distribution. In this section we explain how to construct a KW based distinguisher, and we discuss the salient properties of the resulting distinguisher.

3.1   The KW Statistic as a Distinguisher

In this section we describe how to compute the KW statistic in a side-channel setting, and we argue why it gives a sound side channel distinguisher. For a generic description of the KW statistic we refer the readers to Appendix A.

Informally, the KW test statistic is derived by first ranking the observed data, and second by grouping the data according to the resp. (key dependent) intermediate values. Then the tests checks if the groups can be distinguished from another or not, by comparing the variances between the groups and within the groups.

More formally, let us assume that we have N side channel leakages. We apply the type 1 rank transformation to the side channel leaks, and then work with the ranked data: rank(L). For each key guess k, the ranked data is grouped according to the respective intermediate V_k. Thus the set $R_k^i = \{\text{rank}(L) | V_k = i\}$ contains the ranks of leakages where the intermediate V_k equals i. Let $R_k^{i,j}$ refers to the j-th element in R_k^i. Suppose that we have t groups and the size of group R_k^i is n^i and so $N = \sum_{i=1}^{t} n^i$.

Let us assume that the group R_k^i has distribution F^i. The null hypothesis is that all the groups have the same distribution, and alternative hypotheses of KW test is that the groups can be distinguished:

$$H_0 : F^0 = F^1 = \ldots = F^{t-1} \tag{1}$$
$$H_a : F^i \neq F^j \quad \text{for some} \quad i, j \quad \text{s.t} \quad i \neq j.$$

The average of the ranks in R_i is given as:

$$\bar{R}_k^i = 1/n_i \sum_{j=1}^{n^i} R_k^{i,j}$$

and $\bar{R}_k = (N+1)/2$ the average of all $R_k^{i,j}$.
The KW test statistic is defined [KW52] as:

$$d_k = (N-1)\frac{\sum_{i=1}^{t} n_i (\bar{R}_k^i - \bar{R}_k)^2}{\sum_{i=1}^{t} \sum_{j=1}^{n_i} (R_k^{i,j} - \bar{R}_k)^2} \tag{2}$$

If the elements in R_k^i are all from the same distribution, then all $\bar{R}^i{}_k$ are expected to be close to $\bar{R}_k$ and thus the statistic d_k should be smaller, than when the elements in R_k^i are from different distributions. Thus large values of the test statistic imply that we reject the null hypothesis of the KW test (i.e. we have enough data to conclude that there are meaningful groups). We can use this test statistic readily as a side channel distinguisher: the groups are given by the key dependent intermediate values V_k. Thus, for $k = k^*$ we have a meaningful grouping of the ranked leakages, and thus the test statistic is large. If $k \neq k^*$, then the ranked side channel leaks are randomly assigned to different groups, which will lead to a small test statistic. Consequently the value of $d_{k^*} >= d_k$ for $\forall k$, which implies that it is a sound side channel distinguisher.

3.2   Properties of the KW Distinguisher

Side channel distinguisher are most useful if they can be applied in different settings, including higher order attacks. It is also beneficial to be able to derive sample size estimates. For some of the existing non-parametric, in particular in the case of MI, this is hard to achieved. We now explain what is possible for the KW distinguisher.

Application to Higher Order Attack Scenarios. In masked implementations, an intermediate value is represented as a tuple of shares. The leakage of a single share is uninformative, but a statistic that exploits the distribution of the entire tuple enables key recovery. The canonical way of applying distinguishers to masked implementations is via processing the observed leakage traces: a popular (processing) function is the multiplication of (mean-free) trace points [PRB09]. Such trace processing produces a new trace in which each point now is based on the joint leakage of multiple points (aka shares). Using the mean-free product to produce joint leakage is compatible with the Kruskal-Wallis distinguisher (if the mean-free product of two values is larger than the mean-free product of another two values then this property is preserved by ranking: it is a monotonically increasing function), and we show how well it performs in the experimental sections.

Computational Cost. The KW test is often compared to the Wilcoxon-Whitney-Mann test (MWW) [MW47] with respect to computation costs, which is another rank based non-parametric test. The major difference between the two is that MWW is applied to paired data against two values, whereas KW is applied to multiple groups. The latter thus naturally fits with the side channel setting where the intermediate values fall naturally in multiple (independent) groups. Applying MWW in the side channel setting increases the computational cost. For example, in case of t groups we need to apply MWW in the worst case $\binom{t}{2}$ times. Thus the KW test is a natural choice over the MWW test. We found that the computational cost of KW is of the same order as other generic distinguishers (MI, KS).

Number of Samples. For the KW statistic, the theoretical analysis [FZZ11, Theorem 1] shows how to estimate the sample size. The main result necessary for estimating the sample size in a KW test is that under the alternative hypothesis the KW statistic follow a non-central χ^2 distribution. Let $\lambda_i = n_i/N \geq \lambda_0$ for all i and a fixed $\lambda_0 > 0$. And let α be the confidence level and β be the power of the test. Then the estimated sample size is given as

$$\widetilde{N} = \frac{\tau_{\alpha,\beta}}{12 \sum_{i=1}^{t} \lambda_i \left(\sum_{s \neq i} \lambda_s (\hat{p}_{is} - 1/2) \right)^2}. \tag{3}$$

For each pair i, s s.t. $i \neq s$, the probability estimates $\hat{p}_{is}$ can be computed from the given data sample of size N as follows

$$\hat{p}_{is} = \frac{1}{N_i N_k} \sum_{j=1}^{N_i} \sum_{\ell=1}^{N_s} (\mathcal{I}(X_{s\ell} < X_{ij}) + \mathcal{I}(X_{s\ell} = X_{ij})/2)$$

where $\mathcal{I}$ is the indicator function, and $i, s \in \{1, 2, \ldots t\}$. Note that the second part of the above expression corresponds to the ties in ranking. In Eq. (3) $\tau_{\alpha,\beta}$ is solution to $\mathbb{P}(\chi_{t-1}^2(\tau) > \chi_{t-1,1-\alpha}^2) = 1 - \beta$ for some fixed α, β, and $\chi_{t-1,1-\alpha}^2$ is the $(1 - \alpha)$ quantile of central χ^2 distribution with $t - 1$ degrees of freedom.

The estimation of sample size following Eq. (3) is biased and needs to be adjusted. As explained in [FZZ11], an adjusted estimator $\widehat{N}$ is defined as follows

$$\widehat{N} = \widetilde{N} \cdot \frac{\mathsf{median}\{\chi^2_{t-1}(\hat{\tau})\}}{\hat{\tau}} \tag{4}$$

where $\hat{\tau} = N \cdot 12 \sum_{i=1}^{t} \lambda_i \left(\sum_{s \neq i} \lambda_s (\hat{p}_{is} - 1/2) \right)^2$.

Considering Correct and Incorrect Key Hypotheses. The application of sample size estimation technique requires care in the context of side-channel key recovery attack. Recall that in a statistical (hypothesis) testing there are two types of errors namely

1. **Type I error** α where the null hypothesis H_0 is rejected when the hypothesis H_0 is true, and
2. **Type II error** β where the null hypothesis H_0 is not rejected when the alternate hypothesis H_a is true.

In a successful attack the null hypothesis should not be rejected for any k where $k \neq k^*$ (thus we want α to be small). However, under the correct key guess $k = k^*$ the alternative hypothesis H_a is true and we should not fail to reject H_0. Hence, β should be small so that the power of the test $1 - \beta$ is large. In fact we wish to have a high power for both cases.

Thus we should perform the sample size estimation for both cases (correct and incorrect keys) and then take the maximum of these sample sizes as a conservative estimate. In statistical hypothesis testing typically it is ensured that the value of $\mathbb{P}(\text{Type I error}) \leq 0.1$ and $\mathbb{P}(\text{Type II error}) \leq 0.2$.

Example 1. In this example we show the sample size estimation for $N = 1000$ using simulated Hamming weight traces of AES Sbox where the Gaussian noise has $\sigma = 6$.

We choose $\alpha = 0.025$ (corresponding to the confidence level) and $\beta = 0.05$ (corresponding to the power of the test). First, using the technique as described above, we find the generic estimate of the sample size as per Eq. (3). For applying the leakage estimation (or KW attack) we extract the 4 Least Significant Bits (LSB) from the output of the Sbox.

For this experiment the degrees of freedom of the χ^2 distributions is $16 - 1 = 15$ (the number of different groups are 16 corresponding to the 4-bit output values obtained). Note that $\tau_{\alpha,\beta}$ depends only on the degrees of freedom, α and β. In this case $\tau_{\alpha,\beta} = 1.8506$. We compute $\widetilde{N}$ for different key choices. Here we only show the computation for one key that corresponds to the maximum $\widetilde{N}$. The estimation process is carried out in the same way for other keys.

Estimating λ_i and $\hat{p}_{is}$ from 1000 data points we obtain the $\widetilde{N} = \frac{1.8506}{.0041} \approx 451$. Since this is a biased estimate we obtain the adjusted estimate as

$$\widehat{N} = \widetilde{N} \cdot \frac{\mathsf{median}\{\chi^2_{t-1}(\hat{\tau})\}}{\hat{\tau}} = 451 \cdot \frac{\mathsf{median}\{\chi^2_{15}(4.1)\}}{4.1} \approx 2015. \tag{5}$$

Remark 1. For estimating the sample size in the context of side-channel attack, λ_i can be estimated from the target cryptographic function (instead of estimating it from the data). Suppose, the target function is 8-bit Sbox, and say 4 bits of the output is chosen for the attack. In this case, for all 2^8 input values, the number of elements n_i in each 2^4 groups can be computed.

Example 2. In this example we show the sample size estimation when traces are simulated from ARX function with a HW leakage model and Gaussian noise with $\sigma = 6$. We fix $N = 1000$ and follow the same process as in Example 1. Here we choose $\alpha = 0.001$ and $\beta = 0.1$.

We consider a key recovery attack (using KW statistic) which recovers 4-bit key chunk from each k_1 and k_2, in the usual divide and conquer process used for side-channel attack. The ARX function is defined as

$$A(x) = (x \oplus k_1) \boxplus (y \oplus k_2).$$

($\oplus$ denotes the bit-wise exclusive-or and $\boxplus$ the addition in $GF(2^{16})$). So, the degrees of freedom for the χ^2 distribution remains $16 - 1 = 15$. The biased sample size estimation gives $\widetilde{N} \approx 992$. After adjusting the bias as in Example 1 we get $\widehat{N} \approx 2212$.

Corollary 1. *The generic estimate $\widetilde{N}$ in Eq. (3) (and bias adjusted estimate $\widehat{N}$ in Eq. (4)) gives estimated lower bound on sample size.*

Proof. The sample estimate is derived from the fact that $\hat{\tau} \approx \tau_{\alpha,\beta}$. Recall that $\tau_{\alpha,\beta}$ is the solution to the equation

$$\mathbb{P}(\chi^2_{t-1}(\tau) > \chi^2_{t-1,1-\alpha}) = 1 - \beta.$$

for some fixed β. Now, if we obtain a $\hat{\tau}_1$ from the fixed sized data such that $\hat{\tau}_1 \geq \tau_{\alpha,\beta}$, then $\mathbb{P}(\chi^2_{t-1}(\tau_1) > \chi^2_{t-1,1-\alpha})$ will be more than $1 - \beta$. This is favourable since we want to maximise the power of the test. Thus we have

$$\hat{\tau} \geq \tau_{\alpha,\beta} \quad \Longrightarrow \quad \widetilde{N}^* \geq \frac{\tau_{\alpha,\beta}}{12 \sum_{i=1}^t \lambda_i \left(\sum_{s \neq i} \lambda_s (\hat{p}_{is} - 1/2) \right)^2} = \widetilde{N}$$

The lower bound on the bias adjusted estimate $\widehat{N}^*$ follows from this.

4   Experiments Based on Simulated Leakage

We now detail a range of experiments that are based on simulating side channel data. Experiments based on simulated data offer the advantage, over experiments based on data from devices, that we can efficiently vary implementation characteristics such as the leakage function, the cryptographic target function, and the signal to noise ratio. Therefore the inclusion of simulations is standard in research on distinguishers.

We display simulation outcomes in terms of the success rate as function of an increasing number of side channel observations. Our comparisons include the KW test, mutual information analysis (MI) with an identity leakage model, mutual information analysis with a Hamming weight leakage model (MI-HW), the Kolmogorov-Smirnov test and Spearman's test. We included MI-HW because of its wide use in the literature (and despite the obvious fact that it is no longer assumption free).

Before we discuss the outcomes, we provide an informal but detailed description of the choices for the cryptographic target functions V_k as well as the device leakage functions M.

4.1   Simulation Setup

Our choice of target functions V_k is informed by best-practice: it is well known that properties of the target function impact on distinguishability and therefore we aimed to select a function that is known to be "poor" target, to challenge all distinguishers. Our selection observed a further requirement imposed by the use of MI (as main comparison) that MI is only a sound distinguisher for non-injective target functions (if a target function is injective, then MI cannot distinguish any key candidates) [HRG14], and the bit-dropping trick must be used. Therefore, we selected as a poor non-injective target function V_{ni} the non-injective target function is the modular addition that is part of many ARX constructions, which is also the basis of modern permutation based ciphers such as SPARKLE:

$$V_{ni}(x_l, x_r, k_l, k_r) = (x_l \oplus k_l) \boxplus (x_r \oplus k_r)$$

where $x_l \| x_r \in \{0, 1\}^{32}$ is a state element, and $k_l \| k_r \in \{0, 1\}^{32}$ is the key, and $\boxplus$ is the addition modulo 2^{16}.

We also experimented with a function that is known to be an excellent target function, namely the AES SubBytes operation, which is injective, and thus the bit-dropping trick must be applied. To aid the flow of this submission, we include the results of this in the appendix (they are aligned with the results for the injective target function).

Our choice of leakage functions M is also informed by best-practice: leakage functions are also well known to impact on distinguisher performance. Linear leakage functions help distinguishers that are based on distributional assumptions or simple hypothetical leakage models. Highly non-linear leakage functions are representative of complex leakage originating in combinational logic ([LBS19] and [GMPO20]) are a motivating factor for studing "assumption free" distinguishers like MI, KS and KW.

In our experiments we thus use a range of device leakage functions, which are defined as follows. Let y_i be the ith bit of y. Then we consider two linear device leakage functions (Hamming weight and Randomly weighted bits), and two non-linear leakage functions (Strongly non-linear and Binary), as follows:

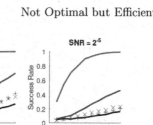

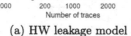

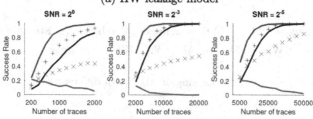

(a) HW leakage model

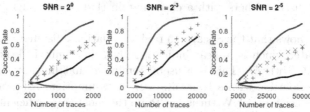

(b) Rrandomly weighted bits leakage model

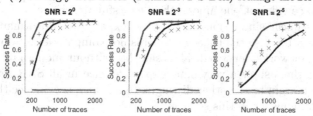

(c) Strongly non-linear (PRESENT S-Box) leakage model

(d) Binary leakage model

KW:—— MI:—— MI-HW:+ KS:× Spearman:——

Fig. 1. Simulations for Modular Addition as a Target

Hamming weight: $M(y) = \sum_{i=1}^{n} y_i$
Randomly weighted bits: $M(y) = \sum_{i=1}^{n} w_i y_i$ with $w \in [-1, 1]$
Strongly non-linear: $M(y) = S(y)$, with $S(y)$ defined to be the Present S-Box
Binary: $M(y) = \sum_i S(y)_i \pmod 2$, with $S(y)$ defined to be the Present S-Box

4.2   First Order Attack Simulations

Figure 1a shows that the Spearman rank correlation has indeed a significant advantage (because it uses the correct hypothetical leakage model), compared

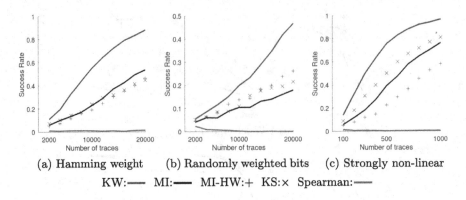

(a) Hamming weight   (b) Randomly weighted bits   (c) Strongly non-linear

KW:——   MI:——   MI-HW:+   KS:×   Spearman:——

Fig. 2. 2-share Boolean masking of ARX with different leakage models

to the other distinguishers. Note that the KW test-based attack outperforms the other generic distinguishers with a clear margin that is more significant in the lower SNRs.

Figure 1b shows that the Spearman rank correlation fails: more traces reduce the success rate, which is a clear indication that the "built in leakage model" is incompatible with M. This is a useful reminder that linear models are not necessarily compatible with a Hamming weight assumption. All model-free distinguishers succeed, and KW turns out to be the most trace efficient in all SNR settings. The MI and MI-HW distinguishers show similar performance while KS is the least trace efficient one among the successful attacks.

In the non-linear simulation (Fig. 1c) We expect that Spearmans rank correlation will fail because the leakage model is not compatible. However MI with the same model works very well, alongside MI without model and KS. These three distinguishers show a very similar performance in all SNR settings. KW shows a clear margin to the other distinguishers, which is evidence that it is the preferable distinguisher in this setting.

The last simulation (Fig. 1d) is a binary leakage model that represents an extreme case where the leakage is either 0 or 1 such that only a minimum resolution exists in the leakage values. In a high SNR setting, all assumption-free distinguishers recover the key. In low SNR seetings, the KW distinguisher show the quickest convergence to a high success rate, which is evidence that it is the preferable distinguisher in this setting.

4.3   Masked Implementation

We further extend our simulations to a masked implementation by simulating the leakages of a 2-shares Boolean masking scheme using the same leakage models as before. To perform an attack we use the a well understood, and frequently adopted approach of combining the leakages from all independent shares

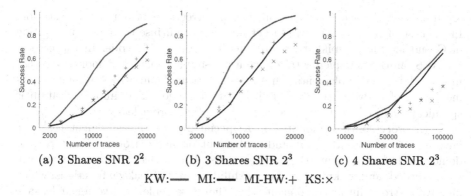

(a) 3 Shares SNR 2^2 (b) 3 Shares SNR 2^3 (c) 4 Shares SNR 2^3

KW:——   MI:——   MI-HW:+   KS:×

Fig. 3. Higher order Boolean masking of AES with Hamming weight leakage

via the centred product-combining function, [PRB09], which was also used in [BGP+11].[3]

The results of the simulations for the 2-share Boolean masking scheme are shown in Fig. 2a, 2b and 2c. For succinctness, we excluded the very low SNR settings of 2^{-3} and 2^{-5} (because the observations are the same as for the higher SNRs), and the results of binary leakage model (because all distinguishers failed in this setting). As is evident from the graphs, Spearman fails in all settings; among the successful attacks, KW turned out to be the most trace efficient distinguisher.

We then turn our attention to masking for the AES SubBytes operation, where Figs. 3a–3c show that KW provides a clear advantage for low order masking.

5   Experiments Based on Device Data

To complement our simulation results we also show experiments that were performed based on measurements from two processors. These processors are based on the ARM Cortex M0 and the ARM Cortex M3 architecture. We implemented the same target functions as before in the simulations.

To work with the masked implementation, we perform the same mean-free product combining pre-processing as in the simulations. Before showing the outcomes, we discuss the implementation characteristics in some more detail.

5.1   Implementation Characteristics and Experimental Setup

Our simulated experiments ranged from unprotected implementations to implementations based on sharing out intermediate values. For implementations that

---

[3] It is worth noting that there exists no known optimal multivariate implementation for the above mentioned side-channel distinguishers [BGP+11,WOM11], because the outcomes are highly sensitive to various factors, including leakage models, noise levels and methods for pre-processing, etc.

are unprotected we only ensure functional correctness of our implementation. In the case of the non-injective target function, we utilise the modular addition in C and let the compiler translate this into Assbembly code. In the case of the AES SubBytes implementation we use a simple table-based lookup. For the masked SubBytes implementation we use a custom Thumb-16 Assembly implementation of a two share ISW multiplication gadget. This implementation is specifically crafted to ensure that there are no first-order leaks.

Both processors are mounted in a special purpose measurement rig[4]. We have a state of the art scope and probe, but do not perform any filtering or de-noising before applying the distinguishers. The devices that we use are well characterised, and we know that they exhibit a range of leakage functions, which all have a strong linear component (thus they resemeble the two linear leakage functions that we considered in the simulations).

We apply the distinguishers to all trace points, and perform repeat experiments to determine the first order success rate. We then select the best point and plot the success rate graphs for this point only.

5.2   Experimental Results

Non-injective Target Function. Figure 4a shows the results of repeat attacks on the modular addition on the M0. In the corresponding simulated experiments, we supplied Spearman with the Hamming weight leakage model and as a result it outperformed the other distinguishers when the device leakage model was also the Hamming weight. To demonstrate that Spearmans succeess in the Hamming weight simulation really was because we supplied it with the Hamming weight model, we now supply it with only 4 bits of the intermediate values. We give the same 4 bit intermediate values also to MI, MI-HW, KS and KW.

Lacking the correct leakage model, Spearman now completely fails. All other side-channel distinguishers successfully recover the key. KW shows again a better success rate than the competitors.

Injective Target Function. Figure 4b shows the results of repeat attacks on the SubBytes operation on the M0. Now we supply Spearman once more with the Hamming weight leakage model, which gives it a significant advantage over the other distinguishers (because the device features signifant linear leakage in all trace points).

KW is the most trace efficient distinguisher among the other distinguishers. DoM is the least efficient one which might due to the fact that DoM can only exploit a single bit leakage whereas other distinguishers exploit all 4 bit leakages.

Masked Implementation. Figure 4c[5] shows a familiar picture: KW achieves a higher success rate by a clear margin over the other distinguishers. Spearman

---

[4] We refrain to include more details at this point in order to maintain the anonymity of the submission.

[5] Spearman and DoM are excluded from Fig. 4c as they failed against the masked implementation.

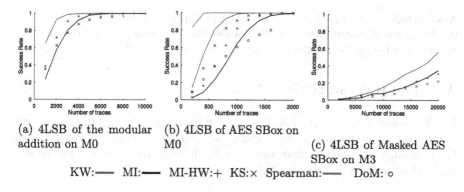

(a) 4LSB of the modular addition on M0

(b) 4LSB of AES SBox on M0

(c) 4LSB of Masked AES SBox on M3

KW:—— MI:—— MI-HW:+ KS:× Spearman:—— DoM: o

Fig. 4. Experiments based on real device data

failed, so we did not include it anymore. The picture also shows that MI-HW no longer shows any advantage over MI, which one should expect given that pre-processing is applied to the trace points as part of attacking the masking scheme.

6 Discussion and Conclusion

Of the distinguishers that we compared in this submission, Spearman and MI-HW are supplied with the Hamming weight leakage model. Theoretically, this gives them an advantage in situations where there is strong Hamming weight device leakage. We can see this advantage also experimentally: in all Hamming weight simulations, Spearman outperforms all other distinguishers, including MI-HW. This particular simulation showcases that iff the device leakage model is "simple" then there is no point in using MI, KS or KW.

In situations where the leakage model is unknown and HW based attack fail, they are the premise of our work, MI, KS, and KW are considerably better than Spearman (and MI-HW). When looking carefully at the experimental outcomes, then we can observe that the gap between the distinguishers decreases with lower SNR values. This behaviour is expected because of [MOS11], according to which they must, asymptotically speaking, get closer in terms of trace efficiency the lower the SNR.

All together our experiments provide strong evidence that MI is not the most trace efficient distinguisher setting where no leakage model is available, which is in contrast to [dCGHR18], who selected different distinguishers for comparison with MI.

Our results help clarify that "optimal distinguishers" are not necessarily the most trace efficient distinguishers, despite that in previous work they have always been identified as being more trace efficient (in their respective categories) than their "normal" counterparts.

Acknowledgment. Elisabeth Oswald and Yan Yan have been supported in part by the European Research Council (ERC) under the European Union's Horizon 2020 research and innovation programme (grant agreement No 725042).

A   The KW Statistic

Let X_{ij} where $i = 1,\dots,t$, $j = 1,\dots,n_i$ be independent random samples collected from a population having t groups and the sample size for group i is n_i. Let us assume that the random variables X_{ij} have distribution F_i. The generic null and alternative hypotheses of KW test are

$$H_0 : F_1 = F_2 = \dots = F_t \tag{6}$$
$$H_a : F_i \neq F_j \quad \text{for some} \quad i,j \quad \text{s.t} \quad i \neq j.$$

The observations are combined into one sample of size N where

$$N = \sum_{i=1}^{t} n_i$$

This combined sample is ranked. Suppose, $R_{i,j}$ is the ranking of the j-th sample from the group i, $\bar{R}_i$ the average rank of all samples from group i:

$$\bar{R}_i = n_i^{-1} \sum_{j=1}^{n_i} R_{i,j}$$

and $\bar{R} = (N+1)/2$ the average of all $R_{i,j}$.

The KW test statistic H_{KW} is defined [KW52] as:

$$H_{KW} = (N-1)\frac{\sum_{i=1}^{t} n_i(\bar{R}_i - \bar{R})^2}{\sum_{i=1}^{t}\sum_{j=1}^{n_i}(R_{i,j} - \bar{R})^2} \tag{7}$$

In Eq. (7) the denominator $\sum_{i=1}^{t} n_i(\bar{R}_i - \bar{R})^2$ describes the variation of ranks between groups, and the numerator $\sum_{i=1}^{t}\sum_{j=1}^{n_i}(R_{i,j} - \bar{R})^2$ describes the variation of ranks in the combined sample. Intuitively, if X_{ij} are all sampled from the same distribution, then all $\bar{R}_i$ are expected to be close to $\bar{R}$ and thus the statistics H_{KW} should be smaller, and vice versa. Large values of the test statistic results in rejecting the null hypothesis of the KW test.

B   Further Experimental Results

(Se Fig. 5).

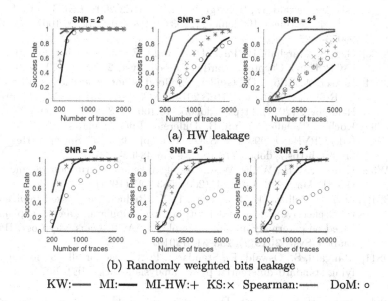

(a) HW leakage

(b) Randomly weighted bits leakage

KW:—— MI:—— MI-HW:+ KS:× Spearman:—— DoM: o

Fig. 5. Attacking the AES SubBytes target, dropping 4 most significant bits

References

[BCO04] Brier, E., Clavier, C., Olivier, F.: Correlation power analysis with a leakage model. In: Joye, M., Quisquater, J.-J. (eds.) CHES 2004. LNCS, vol. 3156, pp. 16–29. Springer, Heidelberg (2004). https://doi.org/10.1007/978-3-540-28632-5_2

[BGL08] Batina, L., Gierlichs, B., Lemke-Rust, K.: Comparative evaluation of rank correlation based DPA on an AES prototype chip. In: Wu, T.-C., Lei, C.-L., Rijmen, V., Lee, D.-T. (eds.) ISC 2008. LNCS, vol. 5222, pp. 341–354. Springer, Heidelberg (2008). https://doi.org/10.1007/978-3-540-85886-7_24

[BGP+11] Batina, L., Gierlichs, B., Prouff, E., Rivain, M., Standaert, F.-X., Veyrat-Charvillon, N.: Mutual information analysis: a comprehensive study. J. Cryptol. **24**(2), 269–291 (2011)

[dCGHR18] de Chérisey, E., Guilley, S., Heuser, A., Rioul, O.: On the optimality and practicability of mutual information analysis in some scenarios. Cryptogr. Commun. **10**(1), 101–121 (2018)

[dCGRP19] de Chérisey, E., Guilley, S., Rioul, O., Piantanida, P.: Best information is most successful mutual information and success rate in side-channel analysis. IACR Trans. Cryptogr. Hardw. Embed. Syst. **2019**(2), 49–79 (2019)

[FZZ11]   Fan, C., Zhang, D., Zhang, C.-H.: On sample size of the kruskal-wallis test with application to a mouse peritoneal cavity study. Biometrics **67**(1), 213–24 (2011)

[GBTP08] Gierlichs, B., Batina, L., Tuyls, P., Preneel, B.: Mutual information analysis. In: Oswald, E., Rohatgi, P. (eds.) CHES 2008. LNCS, vol. 5154, pp. 426–442. Springer, Heidelberg (2008). https://doi.org/10.1007/978-3-540-85053-3_27

[GMPO20] Gao, S., Marshall, B., Page, D., Oswald, E.: Share-slicing: Friend or foe? IACR Trans. Cryptogr. Hardw. Embed. Syst. **2020**(1), 152–174 (2020)

[HRG14]   Heuser, A., Rioul, O., Guilley, S.: Good is not good enough. In: Batina, L., Robshaw, M. (eds.) CHES 2014. LNCS, vol. 8731, pp. 55–74. Springer, Heidelberg (2014). https://doi.org/10.1007/978-3-662-44709-3_4

[KJJ99]   Kocher, P., Jaffe, J., Jun, B.: Differential power analysis. In: Wiener, M. (ed.) CRYPTO 1999. LNCS, vol. 1666, pp. 388–397. Springer, Heidelberg (1999). https://doi.org/10.1007/3-540-48405-1_25

[KW52]   Kruskal, W.H., Wallis, W.A.: Use of ranks in one-criterion variance analysis. J. Am. Stat. Assoc. **47**(260), 583–621 (1952)

[LBS19]   Levi, I., Bellizia, D., Standaert, F.-X.: Reducing a masked implementation's effective security order with setup manipulations and an explanation based on externally-amplified couplings. IACR Trans. Cryptogr. Hardw. Embed. Syst. **2019**(2), 293–317 (2019)

[MOS11]   Mangard, S., Oswald, E., Standaert, F.-X.: One for all - all for one: unifying standard differential power analysis attacks. IET Inf. Secur. **5**(2), 100–110 (2011)

[MW47]   Mann, H.B., Whitney, D.R.: On a test of whether one of two random variables is stochastically larger than the other. Ann. Math. Stat. **18**(1), 50–60 (1947)

[PRB09]   Prouff, E., Rivain, M., Bevan, R.: Statistical analysis of second order differential power analysis. IEEE Trans. Comput. **58**(6), 799–811 (2009)

[RGV14]   Reparaz, O., Gierlichs, B., Verbauwhede, I.: Generic DPA attacks: curse or blessing? In: Prouff, E. (ed.) COSADE 2014. LNCS, vol. 8622, pp. 98–111. Springer, Cham (2014). https://doi.org/10.1007/978-3-319-10175-0_8

[WOM11]   Whitnall, C., Oswald, E., Mather, L.: An exploration of the kolmogorov-smirnov test as a competitor to mutual information analysis. In: Prouff, E. (ed.) CARDIS 2011. LNCS, vol. 7079, pp. 234–251. Springer, Heidelberg (2011). https://doi.org/10.1007/978-3-642-27257-8_15

[WOS14]   Whitnall, C., Oswald, E., Standaert, F.-X.: The myth of generic DPA...and the magic of learning. In: Benaloh, J. (ed.) CT-RSA 2014. LNCS, vol. 8366, pp. 183–205. Springer, Cham (2014). https://doi.org/10.1007/978-3-319-04852-9_10

Signature Schemes

1-out-of-n Oblivious Signatures: Security Revisited and a Generic Construction with an Efficient Communication Cost

Masayuki Tezuka[(✉)] and Keisuke Tanaka

Tokyo Institute of Technology, Tokyo, Japan
`tezuka.m.ac@m.titech.ac.jp`

Abstract. 1-out-of-n oblivious signature by Chen (ESORIC 1994) is a protocol between the user and the signer. In this scheme, the user makes a list of n messages and chooses the message that the user wants to obtain a signature from the list. The user interacts with the signer by providing this message list and obtains the signature for only the chosen message without letting the signer identify which messages the user chooses. Tso et al. (ISPEC 2008) presented a formal treatment of 1-out-of-n oblivious signatures. They defined unforgeability and ambiguity for 1-out-of-n oblivious signatures as a security requirement.

In this work, first, we revisit the unforgeability security definition by Tso et al. and point out that their security definition has problems. We address these problems by modifying their security model and redefining unforgeable security. Second, we improve the generic construction of a 1-out-of-n oblivious signature scheme by Zhou et al. (IEICE Trans 2022). We reduce the communication cost by modifying their scheme with a Merkle tree. Then we prove the security of our modified scheme.

Keywords: 1-out-of-n oblivious signatures · Generic construction · Round-optimal · Merkle tree · Efficient communication cost

1 Introduction

1.1 Background

Oblivious Signatures. The notion of 1-out-of-n oblivious signatures by Chen [6] is an interactive protocol between a signer and a user. In an oblivious signature scheme, first, the user makes a list of n messages $M = (m_i)_{i \in \{1, \dots, n\}}$ and chooses one of message m_j in M that the user wants to obtain a signature. Then the user interacts with the signer by sending the list M with a first message μ at the beginning of the interaction. The signer can see the candidate messages M that the user wants to get signed, but cannot identify which one of

---

This work was supported by JST CREST Grant Number JPMJCR2113 and JSPS KAKENHI Grant Number JP23K16841.

H. Seo and S. Kim (Eds.): ICISC 2023, LNCS 14561, pp. 261–281, 2024.
https://doi.org/10.1007/978-981-97-1235-9_14

the messages in M is chosen by the user. After completing the interaction with the signer, the user can obtain a signature σ for only the chosen message m_j.

1-out-of-n oblivious signatures should satisfy ambiguity and unforgeability. Ambiguity prevents the signer from identifying which one of the messages the signer wants to obtain the signature in the interaction. Unforgeability requires that for each interaction, the user cannot obtain a signature of a message $m \notin M$ and can obtain a signature for only one message $m \in M$ where M is a list of message that the user sends to the signer at the beginning of the interaction.

Oblivious signatures can be used to protect the privacy of users. Chen [6] explained an application of oblivious signatures as follows. The user will buy software from the seller and the signature from the seller is needed to use the software. However, information about which software the user is interested in may be sensitive at some stage. In this situation, by using oblivious signatures, the user can make a list of n software and obtain a signature only for the one software that the user honestly wants to obtain without revealing it to the seller (signer). The oblivious signature can be used for e-voting systems [7,18].

Oblivious Signatures and Blind Signatures. Signatures with a similar flavor to oblivious signatures are blind signatures proposed by Chaum [5]. In a blind signature scheme, similar to an oblivious signature scheme, a user chooses a message and obtains a corresponding signature by interacting with the signer, but no message candidate list in the blind signature scheme. Typically, blind signatures satisfy blindness and one-more unforgeability (OMUF). Blindness guarantees that the signer has no idea what a message is being signed and prevents the signer from linking a message/signature pair to the run of the protocol where it was created. OMUF security prevents the user from forging a new signature.

From the point of view of hiding the contents of the message, it may seem that blind signatures are superior than oblivious signatures. But compared to blind signatures, oblivious signature has merits listed as follows.

- **Avoid Signing Disapprove Messages:** In blind signatures, since the signer has no information about the message that the user wants to obtain the signature, the signer cannot prevent users from obtaining a signature on the message that the signer does not want to approve.

  Partially blind signatures proposed by Abe and Fujisaki [1] mitigate this problem. This scheme allows the user and the signer to agree on a predetermined piece of common information `info` which must be included in the signed message. However, similar to blind signatures, the signer has no information for the blinded part of a message, partially blind signatures do not provide a full solution for the above problem.

  By contrast, oblivious signatures allow the signer to view a list of messages. If the message that the signer does not want to approve is included in the message list, the signer can refuse to sign. Thus, the ambiguity of oblivious signatures provides a better solution for the above problem.
- **Based on Weaker Assumptions:** Recent works on blind signatures are dedicated to constructing efficient round-optimal (i.e., 2-move signing interaction) blind signature schemes [2,4,8–16]. However, these schemes either

rely on at least one of strong primitives, models, or assumptions such as pairing groups [4,9–11,13,14], non-interactive zero-knowledge (NIZK) [2,8,15,16], the random oracle model (ROM) [8,14], the generic group model (GGM) [9], interactive assumptions [4,10,11,13], q-type assumptions [12], one-more assumptions [2], or knowledge assumptions [12].

By contrast, a generic construction of a round-optimal oblivious signature scheme without the ROM was proposed in the recent work by Zhou, Liu, and Han [21]. This construction uses a digital signature scheme and a commitment scheme. This leads to instantiations in various standard assumptions (e.g., DDH, DCR, Factoring, RSA, LWE) without the ROM. Thus, the round-optimal oblivious signature schemes can be constructed with weaker assumptions than round-optimal blind signature schemes.

Previous Works on Oblivious Signatures. The notion of oblivious signatures was introduced by Chen [6] and proposed 1-out-of-n oblivious signature schemes in the ROM. Following this seminal work, several 1-out-of-n oblivious signature schemes have been proposed.

Tso, Okamoto, and Okamoto [19] formalized the syntax and security definition of the 1-out-of-n oblivious signature scheme. They gave the efficient round-optimal (i.e., 2-move) 1-out-of-n oblivious signature scheme based on the Schnorr signature scheme. The security of this scheme can be proven under the DL assumption in the ROM.

Chiou and Chen [7] proposed a t-out-of-n oblivious signature scheme. This scheme needs 3 rounds for a signing interaction and the security of this scheme can be proven under the RSA assumption in the ROM.

You, Liu, Tso, Tseng, and Mambo [20] proposed the lattice-based 1-out-of-n oblivious signature scheme. This scheme is round-optimal and the security can be proven under the short integer solution (SIS) problem in the ROM.

In recent work by Zhou, Liu, and Han [21], a generic construction of a round-optimal 1-out-of-n oblivious signature scheme was proposed. Their scheme is constructed from a commitment scheme and a digital signature scheme without the ROM. By instantiating a signature scheme and commitment scheme from standard assumptions without the ROM, this generic construction leads 1-out-of-n oblivious signature schemes from standard assumptions without the ROM. As far as we know, their scheme is the first generic construction of a 1-out-of-n oblivious signature scheme without the ROM.

1.2 Motivation

The security model for a 1-out-of-n oblivious signature scheme is formalized by Tso [19]. Their security model is fundamental for subsequent works [20,21]. However, this security model has several problems. Here, we briefly review the unforgeability security model in [19] and explain the problems of their model. The formal description of this security game is given in Sect. 3.2

Definition of Unforgeability in [19]. Informally, the unforgeability for a 1-out-of-n oblivious signature scheme in [19] is defined by the following game.

Let A be an adversary that executes a user part and tries to forge a new signature. A engages in the signing interaction with the signer. A can make any message list M_i and any one message $m_{i,j_i} \in M_i$. Then, A engages the i-th signing interaction by sending M_i the signer at the beginning of the interaction. By interacting with the signer, A can obtain a signature σ_i on a message m_{i,j_i}. Let t be the number of signing interaction with the signer and A. Let $\mathbb{L}^{Sign} = \{m_{i,j_i}\}_{i \in \{1,...,t\}}$ be all messages that A has obtained signatures. A wins this game if A outputs a valid signature σ^* on a message $m^* \notin \mathbb{L}^{Sign}$. A 1-out-of-$n$ oblivious signature scheme satisfies unforgeability if for all PPT adversaries A cannot win the above game in non-negligible probability. However, the above security game has several problems listed below.

- **Problem 1: How to Store Messages in $\mathbb{L}^{Sign}$:** In the above security game, we need to store corresponding messages that A has obtained signatures. However, by ambiguity property, we cannot identify the message m_{i,j_i} that A selected to obtain a signature from a transcription of the i-th interaction with M_i. This problem can be addressed by forcing A to output (m_{i,j_i}, σ_i) at the end of each signing query. However, the next problem arises.
- **Problem 2: Trivial Attack:** One problem is the existence of a trivial attack on the security game. Let us consider the following adversary A that runs signing protocol execution twice. A chooses $M = (m_0, m_1)$ where m_0 and m_1 are distinct, and sets lists as $M_1 = M_2 = M$. In the 1st interaction, A chooses $m_0 \in M_1$, obtains a signature σ_0 on a message m_0, and outputs (m_0, σ_0) at the end of interaction. In the 2nd interaction, A chooses $m_1 \in M_2$, obtains a signature σ_1 on a message m_1, and outputs (m_0, σ_0) at the end of interaction. Then, A outputs a trivial forgery $(m^*, \sigma^*) = (m_1, \sigma_1)$. This problem occurs when A pretends to have obtained (m_0, σ_0) in the 2nd signing interaction. Since the security model lacks a countermeasure for this trivial attack, A succeeds in this trivial attack. The unforgeability security models in previous works [20,21] are based on the model by Tso et al. [19]. This trivial attack also works for these security models as well.

    Note that we only claim that the security model in [19] has problems. We do not intend to claim that existing constructions in [6,19–21] are insecure. Under an appropriate unforgeability security model, it may be possible to prove the security for these constructions. Some constructions seem to have structures that can address this trivial attack. Reassessing the unforgeability security of these constructions in an appropriate model is a future work.
- **Problem 3: Missing Adversary Strategy:** The security game does not capture an adversary with the following strategy. Let us consider an adversary A that executes the signing query only once. A interacts with the signer with a message list M and intends to obtain a signature σ^* on a message $m^* \notin M$, but give up outputting (m, σ) where $m \in M$ at the end of the signing query. The game only considers the adversary that outputting (m, σ) where $m \in M$ at the end of the signing query. At the heart of unforgeability security, we should guarantee that A cannot obtain a signature on a message which is not in the list M. Thus, we should consider this adversary strategy.

1.3   Our Contribution

The first contribution is providing a new security definition of the unforgeability security for a 1-out-of-n oblivious signature scheme. We address the problems described in the previous section. We refer the reader to Sect. 3.3 for more detail on our unforgeability security definition.

The second contribution is an improvement of a generic construction of 1-out-of-n oblivious signature schemes by [20]. This round-optimal construction is obtained by a simple combination of a digital signature scheme and a commitment scheme. However, a bottleneck of this scheme is the communication cost (See Fig. 1).

Scheme	$|\mathsf{vk}^{\mathsf{OS}}|$	$|\mu|$	$|\rho|$	$|\sigma^{\mathsf{OS}}|$
OS$_{\mathsf{ZLH}}$ [21]	$|\mathsf{vk}^{\mathsf{DS}}|$	$|c^{\mathsf{COM}}|$	$n|\sigma^{\mathsf{DS}}|$	$|\sigma^{\mathsf{DS}}| + |c^{\mathsf{COM}}| + |r^{\mathsf{COM}}|$
OS$_{\mathsf{Ours}}$ §4.2	$|\mathsf{vk}^{\mathsf{DS}}|$	$|c^{\mathsf{COM}}|$	$|\sigma^{\mathsf{DS}}|$	$|\sigma^{\mathsf{DS}}| + |c^{\mathsf{COM}}| + |r^{\mathsf{COM}}| + (\lceil \log_2 n \rceil + 1)\lambda + \lceil \log_2 n \rceil$

Fig. 1. Comparison with generic construction of 1-out-of-n oblivious signature schemes. $|\mathsf{vk}^{\mathsf{OS}}|$ represents the bit length of the verification key, $|\mu|$ represents the bit length of the first communication, $|\rho|$ represents the bit length of the second communication, and $|\sigma^{\mathsf{OS}}|$ represents the bit length of the 1-out-of-n oblivious signature scheme. In columns, λ denotes a security parameter. $|c^{\mathsf{COM}}|$ (resp. $|r^{\mathsf{COM}}|$) denotes the bit length of a commitment (resp. randomness) and $|\sigma^{\mathsf{DS}}|$ (resp. $|\mathsf{vk}^{\mathsf{DS}}|$) denotes the bit length of a digital signature (resp. verification key) used to instantiate the 1-out-of-n oblivious signature scheme.

Particular, if the user interacts with the signer with a message list $M = (m_i)_{i \in \{1,...,n\}}$ and the first communication message μ, then the signer sends n digital signatures $(\sigma_i^{\mathsf{DS}})_{i \in \{1,...,n\}}$ to the user as the second communication message where σ_i^{DS} is a signature on a message (m_i, μ). This means that the second communication message cost (size) is proportional to n.

We improve the second communication cost by using a Merkle tree. Concretely, instead of signing each (m_i, μ) where $m_i \in M$, we modify it to sign a message (root, μ) where root is a root of the Merkle tree computed from M. By this modification, we reduce the communication cost of the second round from n digital signatures to only one digital signature. As a side effect of our modification, the size of the obtained 1-out-of-n oblivious signature is increasing, but it is proportional to $\log n$. Our modification has the merit that the sum of a second communication message size and a signature size is improved from $O(n)$ to $O(\log n)$.

1.4   Road Map

In Sect. 2, we introduce notations and review commitments, digital signatures, and Merkle tree. In Sect. 3, we review 1-out-of-n oblivious signatures, revisit the definition of unforgeability by Tuo et al. [19], and redefine unforgeability. In Sect. 4, we give a generic construction of 1-out-of-n oblivious signature schemes with efficient communication cost by improving the construction by Zhou et al. [21] and prove security for our scheme. In Sect. 5, we conclude our result and discuss open problems.

2   Preliminaries

In this section, we introduce notations and review fundamental cryptographic primitives for constructing our 1-out-of-n oblivious signature scheme.

2.1   Notations

Let 1^λ be the security parameter. A function f is negligible in k if $f(k) \leq 2^{-\omega(\log k)}$. For a positive integer n, we define $[n] := \{1, \ldots, n\}$. For a finite set S, $s \xleftarrow{\$} S$ represents that an element s is chosen from S uniformly at random.

For an algorithm A, $y \leftarrow \mathsf{A}(x)$ denotes that the algorithm A outputs y on input x. When we explicitly show that A uses randomness r, we denote $y \leftarrow \mathsf{A}(x; r)$. We abbreviate probabilistic polynomial time as PPT.

We use a code-based security game [3]. The game Game is a probabilistic experiment in which adversary A interacts with an implied challenger C that answers oracle queries issued by A. The Game has an arbitrary amount of additional oracle procedures which describe how these oracle queries are answered. When the game Game between the challenger C and the adversary A outputs b, we write $\mathsf{Game}_\mathsf{A} \Rightarrow b$. We say that A wins the game Game if $\mathsf{Game}_\mathsf{A} \Rightarrow 1$. We implicitly assume that the randomness in the probability term $\Pr[\mathsf{Game}_\mathsf{A} \Rightarrow 1]$ is over all the random coins in the game.

2.2   Commitment Scheme

We review a commitment scheme and its security notion.

Definition 1 (Commitment Scheme). *A commitment scheme* COM *consists of a following tuple of algorithms* (KeyGen, Commit).

- KeyGen(1^λ) : *A key-generation algorithm takes as an input a security parameter* 1^λ. *It returns a commitment key* ck. *In this work, we assume that* ck *defines a message space, randomness space, and commitment space. We represent these space by* $\mathcal{M}_\mathsf{ck}$, Ω_ck, *and* $\mathcal{C}_\mathsf{ck}$, *respectively.*
- Commit(ck, $m; r$) : *A commit algorithm takes as an input a commitment key* ck, *a message* m, *and a randomness* r. *It returns a commitment* c. *In this work, we use the randomness* r *as the decommitment (i.e., opening) information for* c.

Definition 2 (Computational Hiding). *Let* $\mathsf{COM} = (\mathsf{KeyGen}, \mathsf{Commit})$ *a commitment scheme and* A *a PPT algorithm. We say that the* COM *satisfies computational hiding if for all* A, *the following advantage of the hiding game*

$$\mathsf{Adv}^{\mathsf{Hide}}_{\mathsf{COM}, \mathsf{A}}(1^\lambda) :=$$

$$\left| \Pr\left[b = b^* \middle| \begin{array}{l} \mathsf{ck} \leftarrow \mathsf{COM}.\mathsf{KeyGen}(1^\lambda), (m_0, m_1, \mathsf{st}) \leftarrow \mathsf{A}(\mathsf{ck}), \\ b \xleftarrow{\$} \{0, 1\}, c^* \leftarrow \mathsf{COM}.\mathsf{Commit}(\mathsf{ck}, m_b), b^* \leftarrow \mathsf{A}(c^*, \mathsf{st}) \end{array} \right] - \frac{1}{2} \right|$$

is negligible in λ.

Definition 3 (Strong Computational Binding). *Let* $\mathsf{COM} = (\mathsf{KeyGen}, \mathsf{Commit})$ *a commitment scheme and* A *a PPT algorithm. We say that the* COM *satisfies strong computational binding if the following advantage*

$$\mathsf{Adv}^{\mathsf{sBind}}_{\mathsf{COM}, \mathsf{A}}(1^\lambda) :=$$

$$\Pr\left[\begin{array}{l} \mathsf{Commit}(\mathsf{ck}, m; r) = \mathsf{Commit}(\mathsf{ck}, m'; r') \\ \wedge\, (m, r) \neq (m', r') \end{array} \middle| \begin{array}{l} \mathsf{ck} \leftarrow \mathsf{KeyGen}(1^\lambda), \\ ((m, r), (m', r')) \leftarrow \mathsf{A}(\mathsf{ck}) \end{array} \right]$$

is negligible in λ.

A commitment scheme with computational hiding and strong computational binding property can be constructed from a public key encryption (PKE) scheme with indistinguishable under chosen plaintext attack (IND-CPA) security. We refer the reader to [21] for a commitment scheme construction from a PKE scheme.

2.3 Digital Signature Scheme

We review a digital signature scheme and its security notion.

Definition 4 (Digital Signature Scheme). *A digital signature scheme* DS *consists of following four algorithms* $(\mathsf{Setup}, \mathsf{KeyGen}, \mathsf{Sign}, \mathsf{Verify})$.

- $\mathsf{Setup}(1^\lambda)$: *A setup algorithm takes as an input a security parameter* 1^λ. *It returns the public parameter* pp. *In this work, we assume that* pp *defines a message space and represents this space by* $\mathcal{M}_{\mathsf{pp}}$. *We omit a public parameter* pp *in the input of all algorithms except for* KeyGen.
- $\mathsf{KeyGen}(\mathsf{pp})$: *A key-generation algorithm takes as an input a public parameter* pp. *It returns a verification key* vk *and a signing key* sk.
- $\mathsf{Sign}(\mathsf{sk}, m)$: *A signing algorithm takes as an input a signing key* sk *and a message* m. *It returns a signature* σ.
- $\mathsf{Verify}(\mathsf{vk}, m, \sigma)$: *A verification algorithm takes as an input a verification key* vk, *a message* m, *and a signature* σ. *It returns a bit* $b \in \{0, 1\}$.

Correctness. DS *satisfies correctness if for all* $\lambda \in \mathbb{N}$, $\mathsf{pp} \leftarrow \mathsf{Setup}(1^\lambda)$ *for all* $m \in \mathcal{M}_{\mathsf{pp}}$, $(\mathsf{vk}, \mathsf{sk}) \leftarrow \mathsf{KeyGen}(\mathsf{pp})$, *and* $\sigma \leftarrow \mathsf{Sign}(\mathsf{sk}, m)$, $\mathsf{Verify}(\mathsf{vk}, m, \sigma) = 1$ *holds.*

We review a security notion called the strong existentially unforgeable under chosen message attacks (sEUF-CMA) security for digital signature.

Definition 5 (sEUF-CMA Security). *Let* DS = (Setup, KeyGen, Sign, Verify) *be a signature scheme and* A *a PPT algorithm. The strong existentially unforgeability under chosen message attacks (sEUF-CMA) security for* DS *is defined by the sEUF-CMA security game* $\mathsf{Game}_{\mathsf{DS},\mathsf{A}}^{\mathsf{sEUFCMA}}$ *between the challenger* C *and* A *in Fig. 2.*

GAME $\mathsf{Game}_{\mathsf{DS},\mathsf{A}}^{\mathsf{sEUFCMA}}(1^\lambda)$:

  $\mathbb{L}^{\mathsf{Sign}} \leftarrow \{\}$, $\mathsf{pp} \leftarrow \mathsf{Setup}(1^\lambda)$, $(\mathsf{vk},\mathsf{sk}) \leftarrow \mathsf{KeyGen}(\mathsf{pp})$, $(m^*,\sigma^*) \leftarrow \mathsf{A}^{\mathcal{O}^{\mathsf{Sign}}(\cdot)}(\mathsf{pp},\mathsf{vk})$
  If $\mathsf{Verify}(\mathsf{vk}, m^*, \sigma^*) = 1 \wedge (m^*,\sigma^*) \notin \mathbb{L}^{\mathsf{Sign}}$, return 1. Otherwise return 0.

Oracle $\mathcal{O}^{\mathsf{Sign}}(m)$:
  $\sigma \leftarrow \mathsf{Sign}(\mathsf{sk}, m)$, $\mathbb{L}^{\mathsf{Sign}} \leftarrow \mathbb{L}^{\mathsf{Sign}} \cup \{(m,\sigma)\}$, return σ.

Fig. 2. The sEUF-CMA security game $\mathsf{Game}_{\mathsf{DS},\mathsf{A}}^{\mathsf{sEUFCMA}}$.

The advantage of an adversary A *for the* sEUF-CMA *security game is defined by* $\mathsf{Adv}_{\mathsf{DS},\mathsf{A}}^{\mathsf{sEUFCMA}}(1^\lambda) := \Pr[\mathsf{Game}_{\mathsf{DS},\mathsf{A}}^{\mathsf{sEUFCMA}}(1^\lambda) \Rightarrow 1]$. DS *satisfies* sEUF-CMA *security if for all PPT adversaries* A, $\mathsf{Adv}_{\mathsf{DS},\mathsf{A}}^{\mathsf{sEUFCMA}}(1^\lambda)$ *is negligible in* λ.

2.4 Merkle Tree Technique

We review the collision resistance hash function family and the Merkle tree technique.

Definition 6 (Collision Resistance Hash Function Family). *Let* $\mathcal{H} = \{H_\lambda\}$ *be a family of hash functions where* $H_\lambda = \{H_{\lambda,i} : \{0,1\}^* \to \{0,1\}^\lambda\}_{i \in \mathcal{I}_\lambda}$. $\mathcal{H}$ *is a family of collision-resistant hash functions if for all PPT adversaries* A, *the following advantage*

$$\mathsf{Adv}_{\mathcal{H},\mathsf{A}}^{\mathsf{Coll}}(1^\lambda) := \Pr[H(x) = H(x')|H \xleftarrow{\$} H_\lambda, (x,x') \leftarrow \mathsf{A}(H)]$$

is negligible in λ.

Definition 7 (Merkle Tree Technique [17]). *The Merkle tree technique* MT *consists of following three algorithms* (MerkleTree, MerklePath, RootReconstruct) *with access to a common hash function* $H : \{0,1\}^* \to \{0,1\}^\lambda$.

- MerkleTree$^H(M = (m_0, \ldots, m_{2^k-1}))$: *A Merkle tree generation algorithm takes as an input a list of* 2^k *elements* $M = (m_0, \ldots, m_{2^k-1})$. *It constructs a complete binary tree whose height is* $k+1$ *(i.e., maximum level is* k*).*
  We represent a root node as w_ϵ *and a node in level* ℓ *as* $w_{b_1,\ldots,b_\ell}$ *where* $b_j \in \{0,1\}$ *for* $j \in [\ell]$. *The leaf node with an index* $i \in \{0,\ldots,2^k-1\}$

represents $w_{\mathsf{I2B}(i)}$ *where* I2B *is a conversion function from an integer* i *to the* k*-bit binary representation.*

Each leaf node with an index $i \in \{0, \dots, 2^k - 1\}$ *(i.e.,* $w_{\mathsf{I2B}(i)}$*) is assigned a value* $h_{\mathsf{I2B}(i)} = H(m_i)$*. Each level* j *internal (non-leaf) node* $w_{b_1, \dots b_j}$ *is assigned a value* $h_{b_1, \dots b_j} = H(h_{b_1, \dots b_j, 0} \| h_{b_1, \dots b_j, 1})$ *where* $h_{b_1, \dots b_j, 0}$ *and* $h_{b_1, \dots b_j, 1}$ *are values assigned to the left-children node* $w_{b_1, \dots b_j, 0}$ *and the right-children node* $w_{b_1, \dots b_j, 1}$*, respectively. The root node* w_ϵ *is assigned a hash value* $h_\epsilon = H(h_0 \| h_1)$ *and denote this value as* root*. This algorithm outputs a value* root *and the description* tree *which describes the entire tree.*

- MerklePath^H(tree, i) : *A Merkle path generation algorithm takes as an input a description of a tree* tree *and a leaf node index* $i \in \{0, \dots, 2^k - 1\}$*. Then, this algorithm computes* $(b_1, \dots b_k) = \mathsf{I2B}(i)$ *and outputs a list* path $= (h_{\overline{b_1}}, h_{b_1, \overline{b_2}}, \dots, h_{b_1, \dots, \overline{b_k}})$ *where* $\overline{b_j} = 1 - b_j$ *for* $j \in [k]$.

- RootReconstruct^H(path, m_i, i) : *A root reconstruction algorithm takes as an input a list* path $= (h_{\overline{b_1}}, h_{b_1, \overline{b_2}}, \dots, h_{b_1, \dots, \overline{b_k}})$*, an element* m_i*, and a leaf node index* $i \in \{0, \dots, 2^k - 1\}$*. This algorithm computes* $(b_1, \dots b_k) = \mathsf{I2B}(i)$ *and assigns* $h_{b_1, \dots b_k}$*. For* $i = k - 1$ *to* 1*, computes* $h_{b_1, \dots b_j} = H(h_{b_1, \dots b_j, 0} \| h_{b_1, \dots b_j, 1})$ *and outputs* root $= H(h_0 \| h_1)$.

Lemma 1 (Collision Extractor for Merkle Tree). *There exists the following efficient collision extractor algorithms* Ext$_1$ *and* Ext$_2$.

- Ext$_1$ *takes as an input a description of Merkle tree* tree *whose root node is assigned value* root *and* (m_i', path, i)*. If* tree *is constructed from a list* $M = (m_0, \dots, m_{2^k - 1})$*,* $m_i \neq m_i'$*, and* root $=$ RootReconstruct^H(path, m_i, i) *holds, it outputs a collision of the hash function* H.

- Ext$_2$ *takes as an input a tuple* $(m, j, \mathsf{path}, \mathsf{path}')$*. If* RootReconstruct^H(path, m, j) $=$ RootReconstruct^H(path', m, j) *and* path $\neq$ path' *hold, it outputs a collision of the hash function* H.

3   Security of Oblivious Signatures Revisited

In this section, first, we review a definition of a 1-out-of-n signature scheme and security notion called ambiguity. Next, we review the security definition of the unforgeability in [19] and discuss the problems of their security model. Then, we redefine the unforgeability security for a 1-out-of-n signature scheme.

3.1   (1, n)-Oblivious Signature Scheme

We review a syntax of a 1-out-of-n oblivious signature scheme and the security definition of ambiguity.

Definition 8 (Oblivious Signature Scheme). *a 1-out-of-n oblivious signature scheme* $(1, n)$-OS *consists of following algorithms* (Setup, KeyGen, U$_1$, S$_2$, U$_{\mathsf{Der}}$, Verify).

- Setup(1^λ) : *A setup algorithm takes as an input a security parameter 1^λ. It returns the public parameter* pp. *In this work, we assume that* pp *defines a message space and represents this space by* $\mathcal{M}_{pp}$. *We omit a public parameter* pp *in the input of all algorithms except for* KeyGen.
- KeyGen(pp) : *A key-generation algorithm takes as an input a public parameter* pp. *It returns a verification key* vk *and a signing key* sk.
- U$_1$(vk, $M = (m_0, \ldots, m_{n-1}), j$) : *This is a first message generation algorithm that is run by a user. It takes as input a verification key* vk, *a list of message* $M = (m_0, \ldots, m_{n-1})$, *and a message index* $j \in \{0, \ldots, n-1\}$. *It returns a pair of a first message and a state* (μ, st) *or* $\perp$.
- S$_2$(vk, sk, $M = (m_0, \ldots, m_{n-1}), \mu$) : *This is a second message generation algorithm that is run by a signer. It takes as input a verification key* vk, *a signing key* sk, *a list of message* $M = (m_0, \ldots, m_{n-1})$, *and a first message* μ. *It returns a second message* ρ *or* $\perp$.
- U$_{\mathsf{Der}}$(vk, st, ρ) : *This is a signature derivation algorithm that is run by a user. It takes as an input a verification key* vk, *a state* st, *and a second message* ρ. *It returns a pair of a message and its signature* (m, σ) *or* $\perp$.
- Verify(vk, m, σ) : *A verification algorithm takes as an input a verification key* vk, *a message* m, *and a signature* σ. *It returns a bit* $b \in \{0, 1\}$.

Correctness. $(1, n)$-OS *satisfies correctness if for all* $\lambda \in \mathbb{N}$, $n \leftarrow n(\lambda)$, pp $\leftarrow$ Setup(1^λ), *for all message set* $\mathcal{M} = (m_0, \ldots, m_{n-1})$ *such that* $m_i \in \mathcal{M}_{pp}$, (vk, sk) $\leftarrow$ KeyGen(pp), *for all* $j \in \{0, \ldots n-1\}$, $(\mu, \mathsf{st}) \leftarrow$ U$_1$(vk, M, j), $\rho \leftarrow$ S$_2$(vk, sk, M, μ), *and* $(m_j, \sigma) \leftarrow$ U$_{\mathsf{Der}}$(vk, st, ρ), Verify(vk, m_j, σ) = 1 *holds.*

Definition 9 (Ambiguity) *Let* $(1, n)$-OS $=$ (Setup, KeyGen, U$_1$, S$_2$, U$_{\mathsf{Der}}$, Verify) *be an oblivious signature scheme and* A *a PPT algorithm. The ambiguity for* $(1, n)$-OS *is defined by the ambiguity security game* Game$^{\mathsf{Amb}}_{(1,n)\text{-OS},A}$ *between the challenger* C *and* A *in Fig. 3.*

GAME Game$^{\mathsf{Amb}}_{(1,n)\text{-OS},A}(1^\lambda)$:
  pp $\leftarrow$ Setup(1^λ), (vk, sk) $\leftarrow$ KeyGen(pp),
  $(M = (m_0, \ldots, m_{n-1}), i_0, i_1, \mathsf{st}_A) \leftarrow$ A(pp, vk, sk)
  $b \xleftarrow{\$} \{0, 1\}$, $(\mu, \mathsf{st}_S) \leftarrow$ U$_1$(vk, M, i_b), $b^* \leftarrow$ A(μ, st_A).
  If $b^* = b$ return 1. Otherwise return 0.

Fig. 3. The ambiguity security game Game$^{\mathsf{Amb}}_{(1,n)\text{-OS},A}$.

The advantage of an adversary A *for the ambiguity security game is defined by* Adv$^{\mathsf{Amb}}_{(1,n)\text{-OS},A}(1^\lambda) := |\Pr[\text{Game}^{\mathsf{Amb}}_{(1,n)\text{-OS},A}(1^\lambda) \Rightarrow 1] - \frac{1}{2}|$. $(1, n)$-OS *satisfies ambiguity if for all PPT adversaries* A, Adv$^{\mathsf{Amb}}_{(1,n)\text{-OS},A}(1^\lambda)$ *is negligible in* λ.

3.2 Definition of Unforgeability Revisited

We review the security definition of unforgeability for $(1, n)$-OS in previous works in [19]. The unforgeability for a 1-out-of-n oblivious signature scheme in [19] is formalized by the following game between a challenger C and a PPT adversary A.

- C runs pp ← Setup(1^λ) and (vk, sk) ← KeyGen(pp), and gives (pp, vk) to A.
- A is allowed to engage polynomially many signing protocol executions.
  In an i-th $(1 \leq i \leq t)$ protocol execution,
  - A makes a list $M_i = (m_{i,0}, \ldots, m_{i,n-1})$ and chooses m_{i,j_i}.
  - A sends $(\mu_i, M_i = (m_{i,0}, \ldots, m_{i,n-1}))$ to C.
  - C runs $\rho_i \leftarrow S_2(\text{vk}, \text{sk}, M_i, \mu_i)$ and gives ρ_i to A.
- Let $\mathbb{L}^{\text{Sign}} = \{m_{1,j_1}, \ldots m_{t,j_t}\}$ be a list of messages that A has obtained signatures. A outputs a forgery (m^*, σ^*) which satisfies $m^* \notin \mathbb{L}^{\text{Sign}}$. A must complete all singing executions before it outputs a forgery.

If no PPT adversary A outputs a valid forgery in negligible probability in λ, $(1, n)$-OS satisfies the unforgeability security.

We point out three problems for the above security definition.

- **Problem 1: How to Store Messages in $\mathbb{L}^{\text{Sign}}$:** In the above security game, C needs to store corresponding messages that A has obtained signatures. However, by ambiguity property, C cannot identify the message m_{i,j_i} which is selected by the A from a transcription of the i-th interaction with M_i. This security model does not explain how to record an entry of $\mathbb{L}^{\text{Sign}}$.
- **Problem 2: Trivial Attack:** Let us consider the following adversary A that runs signing protocol execution twice. A chooses $M = (m_0, m_1)$ where m_0 and m_1 are distinct, and sets lists as $M_1 = M_2 = M$. In the 1st interaction, A chooses $m_0 \in M_1$, obtains a signature σ_0 on a message m_0, and outputs (m_0, σ_0) at the end of interaction. In the 2nd interaction, A chooses $m_1 \in M_2$, obtains a signature σ_1 on a message m_1, and outputs (m_0, σ_0) at the end of interaction. Then, A outputs a trivial forgery $(m^*, \sigma^*) = (m_1, \sigma_1)$. This attack is caused by the resubmitting of a signature (m_0, σ_0) at the end of the signing interaction. A pretends to have obtained (m_0, σ_0) in the 2nd signing interaction. However, there is no countermeasure in the security model.
- **Problem 3: Missing Adversary Strategy:** The security game does not capture an adversary with the following strategy. Let us consider an adversary A that executes the signing query only once. A interacts with the signer with a message list M and intends to forge a signature σ^* on a message $m^* \notin M$, but give up outputting (m, σ) where $m \in M$ at the end of signing query. Since the security game only considers the adversary that outputting (m, σ) where $m \in M$ at the end of the signing query, the security game cannot capture the this adversary A.

3.3 New Unforgeability Definition

We modify the unforgeability security model by Tso et al. [19] by addressing the problems in the previous sections in order and redefine the unforgeability security. Here, we briefly explain how to address these problems.

- **Countermeasure for Problem 1:** This problem is easy to fix by forcing A to output (m_{i,j_i}, σ_i) at the end of each signing interaction.
- **Countermeasure for Problem 2:** This attack is caused by the reuse of a signature at the end of signing interactions. That is A submits (m, σ) twice or more at the end of signing interactions.

  To address this problem, we introduce the signature resubmission check. This prevents resubmission of (m, σ) at the end of signing interactions. However, this is not enough to prevent the reuse of a signature. For example, if an oblivious signature has a re-randomizable property (i.e., The property that a signature is refreshed without the signing key), A can easily pass resubmission checks by randomizing a obtained signature σ to σ'.

  For this reason, normal unforgeability security is not enough. We address this issue by letting strong unforgeability security be a default for the security requirement.
- **Countermeasure for Problem 3:** This problem is addressed by adding another winning path for A. When A submits (m^*, σ^*) at the end of i-th signing interaction, if (m^*, σ^*) submitted by A at the end of signing query is valid and $m^* \notin M_i$, A wins the game where M_i is a list of messages send by A at the beginning of the i-th signing query.

By reflecting the above countermeasures to the unforgeability security model by Tso et al. [19], we redefine the unforgeability security model as the strong unforgeability under chosen message attacks under the sequential signing interaction (Seq-sEUF-CMA) security.

Definition 10 (Seq-sEUF-CMA Security). *Let* $(1, n)$-OS $=$ (Setup, KeyGen, $U_1, S_2, U_{\text{Der}},$ Verify) *be a 1-out-of-n oblivious signature scheme and* A *a PPT algorithm. The strong unforgeability under chosen message attacks under the sequential signing interaction (Seq-sEUF-CMA) security for* $(1, n)$-OS *is defined by the* Seq-sEUF-CMA *security game* $\text{Game}^{\text{Seq-sEUFCMA}}_{(1,n)\text{-OS},A}$ *between the challenger* C *and* A *in Fig. 4.*

The advantage of an adversary A *for the* Seq-sEUF-CMA *security game is defined by* $\text{Adv}^{\text{Seq-sEUFCMA}}_{(1,n)\text{-OS},A}(1^\lambda) := \Pr[\text{Game}^{\text{Seq-sEUFCMA}}_{(1,n)\text{-OS},A}(1^\lambda) \Rightarrow 1]$. $(1, n)$-OS *satisfies* Seq-sEUF-CMA *security if for all PPT adversaries* A, $\text{Adv}^{\text{Seq-sEUFCMA}}_{(1,n)\text{-OS},A}(1^\lambda)$ *is negligible in* λ.

Our security model is the sequential signing interaction model. One may think that it is natural to consider the concurrent signing interaction model. However, by extending our model to the concurrent signing setting there is a trivial attack. We discuss the security model that allows concurrent signing interaction in Sect. 5.

4   Our Construction

In this section, first, we review the generic construction by Zhou et al. [21]. Second, we propose our new generic construction based on their construction. Then, we prove the security of our proposed scheme.

GAME $\mathsf{Game}_{(1,n)\text{-OS},A}^{\mathsf{Seq\text{-}sEUFCMA}}(1^\lambda)$:

$\quad \mathbb{L}^{\mathsf{Sign}} \leftarrow \{\}, \mathbb{L}^{\mathsf{ListM}} \leftarrow \{\}, q^{\mathsf{Sign}} \leftarrow 0, q^{\mathsf{Fin}} \leftarrow 0$

$\quad \mathsf{pp} \leftarrow \mathsf{Setup}(1^\lambda), (\mathsf{vk}, \mathsf{sk}) \leftarrow \mathsf{KeyGen}(\mathsf{pp}), (m^*, \sigma^*) \leftarrow A^{\mathcal{O}^{\mathsf{Sign}}(\cdot, \cdot), \mathcal{O}^{\mathsf{Fin}}(\cdot, \cdot)}(\mathsf{pp}, \mathsf{vk})$

$\quad$ If $q^{\mathsf{Sign}} = q^{\mathsf{Fin}} \wedge \mathsf{Verify}(\mathsf{vk}, m^*, \sigma^*) = 1 \wedge (m^*, \sigma^*) \notin \mathbb{L}^{\mathsf{Sign}}$, return 1.

$\quad$ Otherwise return 0.

Oracle $\mathcal{O}^{\mathsf{Sign}}(M_{q^{\mathsf{Sign}}}, \mu)$:

$\quad$ If $q^{\mathsf{Sign}} \neq q^{\mathsf{Fin}}$, return $\perp$.

$\quad \rho \leftarrow \mathsf{S}_2(\mathsf{vk}, \mathsf{sk}, M, \mu)$, if $\rho = \perp$, return $\perp$.

$\quad$ If $\rho \neq \perp$, $q^{\mathsf{Sign}} \leftarrow q^{\mathsf{Sign}} + 1$, $\mathbb{L}^{\mathsf{ListM}} \leftarrow \mathbb{L}^{\mathsf{ListM}} \cup \{(q^{\mathsf{Sign}}, M_{q^{\mathsf{Sign}}})\}$, return ρ.

Oracle $\mathcal{O}^{\mathsf{Fin}}(m^*, \sigma^*)$:

$\quad$ If $q^{\mathsf{Sign}} \neq q^{\mathsf{Fin}} + 1$, return $\perp$.

$\quad$ If $\mathsf{Verify}(\mathsf{vk}, m^*, \sigma^*) = 0$, return the game output 0 and abort.

$\quad$ (//Oblivious signature resubmission check)

$\quad$ | If $(m^*, \sigma^*) \in \mathbb{L}^{\mathsf{Sign}}$, return the game output 0 and abort. |

$\quad$ Retrieve an entry $(q^{\mathsf{Sign}}, M_{q^{\mathsf{Sign}}}) \in \mathbb{L}^{\mathsf{ListM}}$.

$\quad$ If $m^* \in M_{q^{\mathsf{Sign}}}$, $\mathbb{L}^{\mathsf{Sign}} \leftarrow \mathbb{L}^{\mathsf{Sign}} \cup \{(m^*, \sigma^*)\}$, $q^{\mathsf{Fin}} \leftarrow q^{\mathsf{Fin}} + 1$, return "accept".

$\quad$ (//Capture adversaries that give up completing signing executions in the game.)

$\quad$ | If $m^* \notin M_{q^{\mathsf{Sign}}}$, return the game output 1 and abort. |

Fig. 4. The Seq-sEUF-CMA security game $\mathsf{Game}_{(1,n)\text{-OS},A}^{\mathsf{Seq\text{-}sEUFCMA}}$. The main modifications from previous works security game are highlighted in | white box |.

4.1 Generic Construction by Zhou et al. [21]

The generic construction of a 1-out-of-n signature scheme $(1, n)$-$\mathsf{OS}_{\mathsf{ZLH}}$ by Zhou et al. [21] is a combination of a commitment scheme COM and a digital signature scheme DS. Their construction $(1, n)$-$\mathsf{OS}_{\mathsf{ZLH}}[\mathsf{COM}, \mathsf{DS}] = (\mathsf{OS.Setup}, \mathsf{OS.KeyGen}, \mathsf{OS.U}_1, \mathsf{OS.S}_2, \mathsf{OS.U}_{\mathsf{Der}}, \mathsf{OS.Verify})$ is given in Fig. 5.

We briefly provide an overview of a signing interaction and an intuition for the security of their construction. In the signing interaction, the user chooses a message list $M = (m_i)_{i \in \{0, \ldots, n-1\}}$ and a specific message m_{j_i} that the user wants to obtain the corresponding signature. To hide this choice from the signer, the signer computes the commitment c on m_j with the randomness r. The user sends $(M, \mu = c)$ to the signer.

Here, we provide an intuition for the security of their construction. From the view of the signer, by the hiding property of the commitment scheme, the signer does not identify m_j from $(M, \mu = c)$. This guarantees the ambiguity of their construction. The signer computes a signature σ_i^{DS} on a tuple (m_i, c) for $i \in \{0, \ldots, n-1\}$ and sends $\rho = (\sigma_i^{\mathsf{DS}})_{i \in \{0, \ldots, n-1\}}$.

If the signer honestly computes c on $m_j \in M$, we can verify that m_{j_i} is committed into c by decommitting with r. An oblivious signature on m_j is obtained as $\sigma^{\mathsf{OS}} = (c, r, \sigma_j^{\mathsf{DS}})$. If a malicious user wants to obtain two signatures for two distinct messages $m, m' \in M$ or obtain a signature on $m^* \notin M$ from the signing protocol execution output $(M = (m_i)_{i \in \{0, \ldots, n-1\}}, \mu, \rho)$, the malicious user must

```
OS.Setup(1^λ) :
  ck ← COM.KeyGen(1^λ), pp^DS ← DS.Setup(1^λ), return pp^OS ← (ck, pp^DS).
OS.KeyGen(pp^OS = (ck, pp^DS)) :
  (vk^DS, sk^DS) ← DS.KeyGen(pp^DS), return (vk^OS, sk^OS) ← (vk^DS, sk^DS).
OS.U₁(vk^OS, M = (m₀,...,m_{n-1}), j ∈ {0,...,n-1}) :
  r ←$ Ω_ck, c ← COM.Commit(ck, m; r), μ ← c, st ← (M, c, r, j), return (μ, st).
OS.S₂(vk^OS, sk^OS = sk^DS, M = (m₀,...,m_{n-1}), μ = c) :
  For i = 0 to n-1, σ_i^DS ← DS.Sign(sk^DS, (m_i, c)).
  Return ρ ← (σ₀^DS,...,σ_{n-1}^DS).
OS.U_Der(vk^OS = vk^DS, st = (M = (m₀,...,m_{n-1}), c, r, j), ρ = (σ₀^DS,...,σ_{n-1}^DS)) :
  For i = 0 to n-1, if DS.Verify(vk^DS, (m_i, c), σ_i^DS) = 0, return ⊥.
  σ^OS ← (c, r, σ_j^DS), return (m_j, σ^OS).
OS.Verify(vk^OS = vk^DS, m, σ^OS = (c, r, σ^DS)) :
  If c ≠ COM.Commit(ck, m; r), return 0.
  If DS.Verify(vk^DS, (m, c), σ^DS) = 0, return 0.
  Otherwise return 1.
```

Fig. 5. The generic construction $(1,n)$-$\mathsf{OS}_{\mathsf{ZLH}}[\mathsf{COM}, \mathsf{DS}]$.

break either the sEUF-CMA security of DS or the strong binding property of COM. This guarantees the unforgeability security of their construction.

A drawback of their construction is the second communication cost. A second message ρ consists of n digital signatures. If n becomes large, it will cause heavy communication traffic. It is desirable to reduce the number of signatures in ρ.

4.2 Our Generic Construction

As explained in the previous section, the drawback of the construction by Zhou et al. [21] is the size of a second message ρ. To circumvent this bottleneck, we improve their scheme by using the Merkle tree technique. Concretely, instead of signing on (m_i, c) for each $m_i \in M$, we modify it to sign on (root, c) where root is a root of the Merkle tree computed from M. This modification allows us to reduce the number of digital signatures included in ρ from n to 1.

Now, we describe our construction. Let COM be a commitment scheme, DS a digital signature scheme, $\mathcal{H} = \{H_\lambda\}$ a hash function family, and MT = (MerkleTree, MerklePath, RootReconstruct) a Merkle tree technique in Sect. 2.4. To simplify the discussion, we assume that $n > 1$ is a power of 2.[1]

Our generic construction $(1,n)$-$\mathsf{OS}_{\mathsf{Ours}}[\mathcal{H}, \mathsf{COM}, \mathsf{DS}]$ = (OS.Setup, OS.KeyGen, OS.U₁, OS.S₂, OS.U_Der, OS.Verify) is given in Fig. 6.

---

[1] With the following modification, our scheme also supports the case where $n > 1$ is not a power of 2. Let k be an integer such that $2^{k-1} < n < 2^k$. We change a list of message $M = (m_0,...m_{n-1})$ which is given to OS.U₁ and OS.S₂ as a part of an input to an augmented message list $M' = (m'_0,...m'_{2^k-1})$ where $m'_i = m_i$ for $i \in \{0,...,n-1\}$, $m'_{n-1+i} = \phi || i$ for $i \in \{1,...2^k - n\}$, and ϕ is a special symbol representing that a message is empty.

```
OS.Setup(1^λ) :
   H ←$ H_λ, ck ← COM.KeyGen(1^λ), pp^DS ← DS.Setup(1^λ),
   Return pp^OS ← (H, ck, pp^DS).
OS.KeyGen(pp^OS = (ck, pp^DS)) :
   (vk^DS, sk^DS) ← DS.KeyGen(pp^DS), return (vk^OS, sk^OS) ← (vk^DS, sk^DS).
OS.U_1(vk^OS, M = (m_0, ..., m_{n-1}), j ∈ {0, ..., n-1}) :
   If there exists (t, t') ∈ {0, ..., n-1}^2 s.t. t ≠ t' ∧ m_t = m_{t'}, return ⊥.
   r ←$ Ω_ck, c ← COM.Commit(ck, m; r), μ ← c, st ← (M, c, r, j), return (μ, st).
OS.S_2(vk^OS, sk^OS = sk^DS, M = (m_0, ..., m_{n-1}), μ = c) :
   If there exists (t, t') ∈ {0, ..., n-1}^2 s.t. t ≠ t' ∧ m_t = m_{t'}, return ⊥.
   (root, tree) ← MerkleTree^H(M), σ^DS ← DS.Sign(sk^DS, (root, c)).
   Return ρ ← σ^DS.
OS.U_Der(vk^OS = vk^DS, st = (M = (m_0, ..., m_{n-1}), c, r, j), ρ = (σ_1^DS, ..., σ_n^DS)) :
   (root, tree) ← MerkleTree^H(M), path ← MerklePath^H(tree, j)
   If DS.Verify(vk^DS, (root, c), σ^DS) = 0, return ⊥.
   σ^OS ← (root, c, σ^DS, path, j, r), return (m_j, σ^OS).
OS.Verify(vk^OS = vk^DS, m, σ^OS = (root, c, σ^DS, path, j, r) :
   If root ≠ RootReconstruct^H(path, m, j), return 0.
   If c ≠ COM.Commit(ck, m; r), return 0.
   If DS.Verify(vk^DS, (root, c), σ^DS) = 0, return 0.
   Otherwise return 1.
```

Fig. 6. Our generic construction $(1, n)$-$\mathsf{OS_{Ours}}[\mathcal{H}, \mathsf{COM}, \mathsf{DS}]$.

4.3 Analysis

We analyze our scheme $(1, n)$-$\mathsf{OS_{Ours}}$. It is easy to see that our scheme satisfies the correctness. Now, we prove that our generic construction $(1, n)$-$\mathsf{OS_{Ours}}$ satisfies the ambiguity and the Seq-sEUF-CMA security.

Theorem 1. *If* COM *is computational hiding commitment,* $(1, n)$-$\mathsf{OS_{Ours}}[\mathcal{H},$ COM, DS] *satisfies the ambiguity.*

Proof. The ambiguity of our scheme can be proven in a similar way in [21]. Let A be an adversary for the ambiguity game of $(1, n)$-$\mathsf{OS_{Ours}}$. We give a reduction algorithm B that reduces the ambiguity security of our scheme to the computational hiding property of COM in Fig. 7.

Now, we confirm that B simulates the ambiguity game of $(1, n)$-$\mathsf{OS_{Ours}}$. In the case that $b = 0$, $c^* \leftarrow \mathsf{COM.Commit}(\mathsf{ck}, m_0^* = m_{i_0})$ holds. B simulates μ on the choice of m_{i_0} in this case. Similarly, in the case that $b = 1$, $c^* \leftarrow \mathsf{COM.Commit}(\mathsf{ck}, m_1^* = m_{i_1})$ holds. B simulates μ on the choice of m_{i_1} in this case. Since b is chosen uniformly at random from $\{0, 1\}$, B perfectly simulates the ambiguity game of $(1, n)$-$\mathsf{OS_{Ours}}$. We can see that $\mathsf{Adv}_{\mathsf{COM,B}}^{\mathsf{Hide}}(1^\lambda) = \mathsf{Adv}_{(1,n)\text{-}\mathsf{OS_{Ours}},A}^{\mathsf{Amb}}(1^\lambda)$ holds. Thus, we can conclude Theorem 1.   □

Theorem 2. *If* $\mathcal{H}$ *is a family of collision-resistant hash functions,* DS *satisfies the sEUF-CMA security, and* COM *is a strong computational binding commitment,* $(1, n)$-$\mathsf{OS_{Ours}}[\mathcal{H}, \mathsf{COM}, \mathsf{DS}]$ *satisfies the Seq-sEUF-CMA security.*

$B(1^\lambda, \mathsf{ck})$:

$H \xleftarrow{\$} H_\lambda$, $\mathsf{pp}^{\mathsf{DS}} \leftarrow \mathsf{DS.Setup}(1^\lambda)$, $\mathsf{pp}^{\mathsf{OS}} \leftarrow (H, \mathsf{ck}, \mathsf{pp}^{\mathsf{DS}})$,

$(\mathsf{vk}^{\mathsf{DS}}, \mathsf{sk}^{\mathsf{DS}}) \leftarrow \mathsf{DS.KeyGen}(\mathsf{pp}^{\mathsf{DS}})$, $(\mathsf{vk}^{\mathsf{OS}}, \mathsf{sk}^{\mathsf{OS}}) \leftarrow (\mathsf{vk}^{\mathsf{DS}}, \mathsf{sk}^{\mathsf{DS}})$,

$(M = (m_0, \ldots, m_{n-1}), i_0, i_1, \mathsf{st}_A) \leftarrow A(\mathsf{pp}^{\mathsf{OS}}, \mathsf{vk}^{\mathsf{OS}}, \mathsf{sk}^{\mathsf{OS}})$

$m_0^* \leftarrow m_{i_0}$, $m_1^* \leftarrow m_{i_1}$, send (m_0^*, m_1^*) to the challenger C and obtain

　a commitment c^* where $c^* \leftarrow \mathsf{COM.Commit}(\mathsf{ck}, m_b^*)$ and $b \xleftarrow{\$} \{0,1\}$ is chosen C.

$b' \leftarrow A(\mu = c^*, \mathsf{st}_A)$, return $b^* \leftarrow b'$.

Fig. 7. The reduction algorithm B.

Proof. Let A be a PPT adversary for the Seq-sEUF-CMA game of $(1,n)\text{-OS}_{\mathsf{Ours}}$. We introduce the base game $\mathsf{Game}^{\mathsf{Base}}_{(1,n)\text{-OS}_{\mathsf{Ours}},A}$ which simulates $\mathsf{Game}^{\mathsf{Seq\text{-}sEUFCMA}}_{(1,n)\text{-OS}_{\mathsf{Ours}},A}$. We provide $\mathsf{Game}^{\mathsf{Base}}_{(1,n)\text{-OS}_{\mathsf{Ours}},A}$ in Fig. 8.

$\mathsf{Game}^{\mathsf{Base}}_{(1,n)\text{-OS}_{\mathsf{Ours}},A}$ simulates the game $\mathsf{Game}^{\mathsf{Seq\text{-}sEUFCMA}}_{(1,n)\text{-OS}_{\mathsf{Ours}},A}$ by introducing flags (e.g., Final, $\mathsf{DS}_{\mathsf{reuse}}$) which are used for classifying forgery type and a table $\mathbb{T}$ which stores the computation of the signing oracle $\mathcal{O}^{\mathsf{Sign}}$. More precisely, the flag Final represents that a forgery $(m^*, \sigma^{*\mathsf{OS}} = (\mathsf{root}^*, c^*, \sigma^{*\mathsf{DS}}, \mathsf{path}^*, j^*, r^*))$ is submitted in the final output (Final = true) or $\mathcal{O}^{\mathsf{Fin}}$ (Final = false). The flag $\mathsf{DS}_{\mathsf{reuse}}$ represents that there is a pair $(\widetilde{m}, \widetilde{\sigma}^{\mathsf{OS}}) \neq (\widetilde{m}', \widetilde{\sigma}'^{\mathsf{OS}})$ in $\mathbb{L}^{\mathsf{Sign}}$ such that the first three elements of σ^{OS} are the same. i.e., $(\widetilde{\mathsf{root}}, \widetilde{c}, \widetilde{\sigma}^{\mathsf{DS}}) = (\widetilde{\mathsf{root}}', \widetilde{c}', \widetilde{\sigma}'^{\mathsf{DS}})$ holds. We represent that such a pair exists as $\mathsf{DS}_{\mathsf{reuse}} = $ true. The table $\mathbb{T}$ stores a tuple $(i, M, \mathsf{root}, c, \sigma^{\mathsf{DS}})$ where (M, c) is an input for an i-th $\mathcal{O}^{\mathsf{Sign}}$ query, $(\mathsf{root}, \mathsf{tree}) \leftarrow \mathsf{MerkleTree}^H(M)$, $\sigma^{\mathsf{DS}} \leftarrow \mathsf{DS.Sign}(\mathsf{sk}^{\mathsf{DS}}, (\mathsf{root}, c))$. The counter q^{Sign} represents the number of outputs that A received from the $\mathcal{O}^{\mathsf{Sign}}$ oracle and q^{Fin} represent the number of submitted signatures from A.

Now, we divide an adversary A into three types A_1, A_2, A_3 according to states of flags $\mathsf{DS}_{\mathsf{reuse}}$, $\mathsf{DS}_{\mathsf{forge}}$, and $\mathsf{COM}_{\mathsf{coll}}$ when A wins the game $\mathsf{Game}^{\mathsf{Base}}$.

- A_1 wins the game with $\mathsf{DS}_{\mathsf{forge}} = $ true.
- A_2 wins the game with $\mathsf{COM}_{\mathsf{coll}} = $ true.
- A_3 wins the game with $\mathsf{DS}_{\mathsf{forge}} = $ false $\wedge$ $\mathsf{COM}_{\mathsf{coll}} = $ false.

For adversaries A_1, A_2, and A_3, we can construct a reduction for the security of DS, COM, and H respectively. Now, we give reductions for these adversaries.

Reduction B^{DS}: A reduction B^{DS} to the sEUFCMA security game of DS is obtained by modifying $\mathsf{Game}^{\mathsf{Base}}_{(1,n)\text{-OS}_{\mathsf{Ours}},A}$ as follows. Instead of running $\mathsf{pp}^{\mathsf{DS}} \leftarrow \mathsf{DS.Setup}(1^\lambda)$ and $(\mathsf{vk}^{\mathsf{DS}}, \mathsf{sk}^{\mathsf{DS}}) \leftarrow \mathsf{DS.KeyGen}(\mathsf{pp}^{\mathsf{DS}})$, B^{DS} uses $(\mathsf{pp}^{\mathsf{DS}}, \mathsf{vk}^{\mathsf{DS}})$ given by the sEUFCMA security game of DS. For a signing query (M, c) from A, B^{DS} query (root, c) to the signing oracle of the sEUFCMA security game of DS, obtains $\sigma^{\mathsf{DS}} \leftarrow \mathsf{DS.Sign}(\mathsf{sk}^{\mathsf{DS}}, (\mathsf{root}, c))$, and returns σ^{DS}. To simplify the discussion, we assume that A makes distinct (M, c) to B^{DS}. (If A makes the same (M, c) more than once, B^{DS} simply outputs return $\sigma^{\mathsf{DS}} \leftarrow \mathsf{DS.Sign}(\mathsf{sk}^{\mathsf{DS}}, (\mathsf{root}, c))$ which was previously obtained by the signing oracle of the sEUFCMA security game where root is computed from M.)

$\text{Game}^{\text{Base}}_{(1,n)\text{-OS}_{\text{Ours}},\text{A}}(1^\lambda):$

  $\mathbb{L}^{\text{Sign}} \leftarrow \{\}, \mathbb{L}^{\text{ListM}} \leftarrow \{\}, \mathbb{T} \leftarrow \{\}, q^{\text{Sign}} \leftarrow 0, q^{\text{Fin}} \leftarrow 0, \text{Final} \leftarrow \text{false},$

  $\text{DS}_{\text{reuse}} \leftarrow \text{false}, \text{COM}_{\text{coll}} \leftarrow \text{false}, \text{DS}_{\text{forge}} \leftarrow \text{false}, \text{ck} \leftarrow \text{COM.KeyGen}(1^\lambda),$

  $\text{pp}^{\text{DS}} \leftarrow \text{DS.Setup}(1^\lambda), \text{pp}^{\text{OS}} \leftarrow (H, \text{ck}, \text{pp}^{\text{DS}}), (\text{vk}^{\text{DS}}, \text{sk}^{\text{DS}}) \leftarrow \text{DS.KeyGen}(\text{pp}^{\text{DS}}),$

  $(\text{vk}^{\text{OS}}, \text{sk}^{\text{OS}}) \leftarrow (\text{vk}^{\text{DS}}, \text{sk}^{\text{DS}}), (m^*, \sigma^{*\text{OS}}) \leftarrow \text{A}^{\mathcal{O}^{\text{Sign}}(\cdot,\cdot),\mathcal{O}^{\text{Fin}}(\cdot,\cdot)}(\text{pp}^{\text{OS}}, \text{vk}^{\text{OS}})$

  If $q^{\text{Sign}} \neq q^{\text{Fin}} \vee \text{OS.Verify}(\text{vk}^{\text{OS}}, m^*, \sigma^*) \neq 1 \vee (m^*, \sigma^{*\text{OS}}) \in \mathbb{L}^{\text{Sign}}$, return 0.

  $\text{Final} \leftarrow \text{true}, \mathbb{L}^{\text{Sign}} \leftarrow \mathbb{L}^{\text{Sign}} \cup \{(m^*, \sigma^{*\text{OS}})\}, q^{\text{Fin}} \leftarrow q^{\text{Fin}} + 1$

  Search a pair $(\widetilde{m}, \widetilde{\sigma}^{\text{OS}}) \neq (\widetilde{m}', \widetilde{\sigma}'^{\text{OS}})$ in $\mathbb{L}^{\text{Sign}}$ such that the first three

    elements of σ^{OS} are the same. i.e., $(\widetilde{\text{root}}, \widetilde{c}, \widetilde{\sigma}^{\text{DS}}) = (\widetilde{\text{root}}', \widetilde{c}', \widetilde{\sigma}'^{\text{DS}})$

  If there is no such a pair, $\text{DS}_{\text{forge}} \leftarrow \text{true}$, return 1.

    $(\text{Final} = \text{true} \wedge \text{DS}_{\text{reuse}} = \text{false} \wedge \text{DS}_{\text{forge}} = \text{true} \wedge \text{COM}_{\text{coll}} = \text{false})$

  $\text{DS}_{\text{reuse}} \leftarrow \text{true}.$

  Parse $\widetilde{\sigma}^{\text{OS}}$ as $(\text{root}^*, c^*, \sigma^{*\text{DS}}, \widetilde{\text{path}}, \widetilde{j}, \widetilde{r}), \widetilde{\sigma}'^{\text{OS}}$ as $(\text{root}^*, c^*, \sigma^{*\text{DS}}, \widetilde{\text{path}}', \widetilde{j}', \widetilde{r}').$

  If $(\widetilde{m}, \widetilde{r}) \neq (\widetilde{m}', \widetilde{r}'), \text{COM}_{\text{coll}} \leftarrow \text{true}$, return 1.

    $(\text{Final} = \text{true} \wedge \text{DS}_{\text{reuse}} = \text{true} \wedge \text{DS}_{\text{forge}} = \text{false} \wedge \text{COM}_{\text{coll}} = \text{true})$

  Otherwise, return 1.

    $(\text{Final} = \text{true} \wedge \text{DS}_{\text{reuse}} = \text{true} \wedge \text{DS}_{\text{forge}} = \text{false} \wedge \text{COM}_{\text{coll}} = \text{false})$

$\text{Oracle } \mathcal{O}^{\text{Sign}}(M = (m_0, \ldots, m_{n-1}), \mu = c):$

  If $q^{\text{Sign}} \neq q^{\text{Fin}}$, return $\bot$.

  If there exists a pair $(t \neq t' \in \{0, \ldots, n-1\})$ such that $m_t = m_{t'}$, return $\bot$.

  $(\text{root}, \text{tree}) \leftarrow \text{MerkleTree}^H(M), \sigma^{\text{DS}} \leftarrow \text{DS.Sign}(\text{sk}^{\text{DS}}, (\text{root}, c)),$

  $q^{\text{Sign}} \leftarrow q^{\text{Sign}} + 1, M_{q^{\text{Sign}}} \leftarrow M, \mathbb{L}^{\text{ListM}} \leftarrow \mathbb{L}^{\text{ListM}} \cup \{(q^{\text{Sign}}, M_{q^{\text{Sign}}})\},$

  $\mathbb{T} \leftarrow \mathbb{T} \cup \{(q^{\text{Sign}}, M_{q^{\text{Sign}}}, \text{root}, c, \sigma^{\text{DS}})\},$

  return $\rho \leftarrow \sigma^{\text{DS}}$ to A.

$\text{Oracle } \mathcal{O}^{\text{Fin}}(m^*, \sigma^{*\text{OS}}):$

  If $q^{\text{Sign}} \neq q^{\text{Fin}} + 1$, return $\bot$.

  If $\text{OS.Verify}(\text{vk}^{\text{OS}}, m^*, \sigma^{*\text{OS}}) \neq 1$, return the game output 0 and abort.

  If $(m^*, \sigma^{*\text{OS}}) \in \mathbb{L}^{\text{Sign}}$, return the game output 0 and abort.

  $\mathbb{L}^{\text{Sign}} \leftarrow \mathbb{L}^{\text{Sign}} \cup \{(m^*, \sigma^{*\text{OS}})\}, q^{\text{Fin}} \leftarrow q^{\text{Fin}} + 1$, retrieve $(q^{\text{Sign}}, M_{q^{\text{Sign}}}) \in \mathbb{L}^{\text{ListM}}.$

  If $m^* \in M_{q^{\text{Sign}}}$, return "accept" to A.

  Parse $\sigma^{*\text{OS}}$ as $(\text{root}^*, c^*, \sigma^{*\text{DS}}, \text{path}^*, j^*, r^*).$

  If $(q^{\text{Sign}}, *, \text{root}^*, c^*, \sigma^{*\text{DS}}) \in \mathbb{T}$ return the game output 1.

    $(\text{Final} = \text{false} \wedge \text{DS}_{\text{reuse}} = \text{false} \wedge \text{DS}_{\text{forge}} = \text{false} \wedge \text{COM}_{\text{coll}} = \text{false})$

  Search a pair $(\widetilde{m}, \widetilde{\sigma}^{\text{OS}}) \neq (\widetilde{m}', \widetilde{\sigma}'^{\text{OS}})$ in $\mathbb{L}^{\text{Sign}}$ such that the first three

    elements of σ^{OS} are the same. i.e., $(\widetilde{\text{root}}, \widetilde{c}, \widetilde{\sigma}^{\text{DS}}) = (\widetilde{\text{root}}', \widetilde{c}', \widetilde{\sigma}'^{\text{DS}})$

  If there is no such a pair, $\text{DS}_{\text{forge}} \leftarrow \text{true}$, return the game output 1.

    $(\text{Final} = \text{false} \wedge \text{DS}_{\text{reuse}} = \text{false} \wedge \text{DS}_{\text{forge}} = \text{true} \wedge \text{COM}_{\text{coll}} = \text{false})$

  $\text{DS}_{\text{reuse}} \leftarrow \text{true}.$

  Parse $\widetilde{\sigma}^{\text{OS}}$ as $(\text{root}^*, c^*, \sigma^{*\text{DS}}, \widetilde{\text{path}}, \widetilde{j}, \widetilde{r}), \widetilde{\sigma}'^{\text{OS}}$ as $(\text{root}^*, c^*, \sigma^{*\text{DS}}, \widetilde{\text{path}}', \widetilde{j}', \widetilde{r}').$

  If $(\widetilde{m}, \widetilde{r}) \neq (\widetilde{m}', \widetilde{r}'), \text{COM}_{\text{coll}} \leftarrow \text{true}$, return the game output 1.

    $(\text{Final} = \text{false} \wedge \text{DS}_{\text{reuse}} = \text{true} \wedge \text{DS}_{\text{forge}} = \text{false} \wedge \text{COM}_{\text{coll}} = \text{true})$

  Otherwise, return the game output 1.

    $(\text{Final} = \text{false} \wedge \text{DS}_{\text{reuse}} = \text{true} \wedge \text{DS}_{\text{forge}} = \text{false} \wedge \text{COM}_{\text{coll}} = \text{false})$

Fig. 8. The base game $\text{Game}^{\text{Base}}_{(1,n)\text{-OS}_{\text{Ours}},\text{A}}.$

If B^{DS} outputs 1 with the condition where $DS_{forge} = \text{true}$, there is the forgery $(\widetilde{root}, \widetilde{c}, \widetilde{\sigma}^{DS})$. Since $DS_{forge} = \text{true}$ holds, $DS_{reuse} = \text{false}$ holds. This fact implies that for $(m, \sigma^{OS}) \in \mathbb{L}^{Sign}$, the first three elements $(root, c, \sigma^{DS})$ of σ^{OS} are all distinct in $\mathbb{L}^{Sign}$ and valid signatures for DS (i.e., $DS.Verify(vk^{DS}, (root, c), \sigma^{DS}) = 1$). Moreover, B^{DS} makes q^{Sign} signing queries to signing oracle, $q^{Sign} < q^{Fin}$ holds where q^{Fin} is the number of entry in $\mathbb{L}^{Sign}$. Hence, there is a forgery $((\widetilde{root}, \widetilde{c}), \widetilde{\sigma}^{DS})$ of DS. By modifying $\text{Game}^{Base}_{(1,n)\text{-}OS_{Ours},A}$ to output this forgery $((\widetilde{root}, \widetilde{c}), \widetilde{\sigma}^{DS})$, we can obtain B^{DS}.

Reduction B^{COM}: A reduction B^{COM} to the strong computational binding property of COM is obtained by modifying $\text{Game}^{Base}_{(1,n)\text{-}OS_{Ours},A}$ as follows. B^{COM} uses ck given by the strong computational binding security game of COM.

If $\text{Game}_{OS_{Ours},A}$ outputs 1 with the condition where $COM_{coll} = \text{true}$, there is a collision $(\widetilde{m}, \widetilde{r}) \neq (\widetilde{m}', \widetilde{r}')$ such that $COM.Commit(ck, \widetilde{m}; \widetilde{r}) = COM.Commit(ck, \widetilde{m}'; \widetilde{r}')$ holds. Since if $COM_{coll} = \text{true}$ holds, $DS_{reuse} = \text{true}$ holds in $\text{Game}^{Base}_{OS_{Ours},A}$. This fact implies that there is a pair $(\widetilde{m}, \widetilde{\sigma}^{OS} = (root^*, c^*, \sigma^{*DS}, \widetilde{path}, \widetilde{j}, \widetilde{r})) \neq (\widetilde{m}', \widetilde{\sigma}'^{OS} = (root^*, c^*, \sigma^{*DS}, \widetilde{path}', \widetilde{j}', \widetilde{r}'))$. Since $(\widetilde{m}, \widetilde{\sigma}^{OS})$ and $(\widetilde{m}', \widetilde{\sigma}'^{OS})$ are valid signatures, $(\widetilde{m}, \widetilde{r}) \neq (\widetilde{m}', \widetilde{r}')$ and $COM.Commit(ck, \widetilde{m}; \widetilde{r}) = COM.Commit(ck, \widetilde{m}'; \widetilde{r}')$ hold. By modifying $\text{Game}^{Base}_{(1,n)\text{-}OS_{Ours},A}$ to output this collision $((\widetilde{m}, \widetilde{\sigma}^{OS}), (\widetilde{m}', \widetilde{\sigma}'^{OS}))$, we can obtain B^{COM}.

Reduction B^{Hash}: We explain how to obtain a reduction B^{Hash} to the collision resistance property from $\text{Game}^{Base}_{(1,n)\text{-}OS_{Ours},A}$. If $\text{Game}^{Base}_{(1,n)\text{-}OS_{Ours},A}$ outputs 1 with the condition where $\text{Final} = \text{false} \wedge DS_{reuse} = \text{false} \wedge DS_{forge} = \text{false}$, a collision a hash function can be found. Since $\text{Final} = \text{false} \wedge DS_{reuse} = \text{false} \wedge DS_{forge} = \text{false}$ holds, then $(q^{Sign}, *, root^*, c^*, \sigma^{*DS}) \in \mathbb{T}$ holds. Let $(M_{q^{Sign}}, c_{q^{Sign}})$ be an input for the q^{Sign}-th $\mathcal{O}^{Sign}$ query. Then, by the computation of $\mathcal{O}^{Sign}$ and table $\mathbb{T}$, $c^* = c_{q^{Sign}}$, $(root^*, tree^*) = \text{MerkleTree}^H(M_{q^{Sign}})$, and $DS.Verify(vk^{DS}, (root^*, c^*), \sigma^{*DS}) = 1$ holds. Since $m^* \notin M_{q^{Sign}}$, a collision of a hash function H can be computed by $(x, x') \leftarrow \text{Ext}_1(tree^*, (m^*, path^*, i^*))$. We modify $\text{Game}^{Base}_{(1,n)\text{-}OS_{Ours},A}$ to output this collision (x, x') in this case.

If $B^{Base}_{(1,n)\text{-}OS_{Ours},A}$ outputs 1 with the condition where $DS_{reuse} = \text{true} \wedge DS_{forge} = \text{false} \wedge COM_{coll} = \text{false}$ (regardless of the bool value Final), a collision of a hash function can be also found. Since $DS_{reuse} = \text{false} \wedge COM_{coll} = \text{false}$ holds, then there is a pair $(\widetilde{m}, \widetilde{\sigma}^{OS} = (root^*, c^*, \sigma^{*DS}, path, \widetilde{j}, \widetilde{r})) \neq (\widetilde{m}, \widetilde{\sigma}'^{OS} = (root^*, c^*, \sigma^{*DS}, \widetilde{path}', \widetilde{j}', \widetilde{r}))$ holds. From this fact, we can see that $(\widetilde{path}, \widetilde{j}) \neq (\widetilde{path}', \widetilde{j}')$ holds. If $j^* \neq \widetilde{j}$ holds, we can obtain a collision of a hash function H as $(x, x') \leftarrow \text{Ext}_1(tree^*, (m^*, path^*, i^*)$. If $j^* = \widetilde{j}$ holds, then $\widetilde{path} = \widetilde{path}'$ holds and thus we can compute a collision of a hash function as $(x, x') \leftarrow \text{Ext}_2(m, j^*, \widetilde{path}, \widetilde{path}')$. We modify $\text{Game}^{Base}_{(1,n)\text{-}OS_{Ours},A}$ to output this collision (x, x') in these case.

By reduction algorithms B^{DS}, B^{COM}, and B^{Hash} described above, we can bound the advantage $\text{Adv}^{Seq\text{-}sEUFCMA}_{(1,n)\text{-}OS,A}(1^\lambda)$ as

$$\mathsf{Adv}^{\text{Seq-sEUFCMA}}_{(1,n)\text{-OS},\mathsf{A}}(1^\lambda)$$

$$= \Pr[\mathsf{Game}^{\text{Seq-sEUFCMA}}_{(1,n)\text{-OS}_{\text{Ours}},\mathsf{A}}(1^\lambda) \Rightarrow 1]$$

$$= \Pr[\mathsf{Game}^{\text{Base}}_{(1,n)\text{-OS}_{\text{Ours}},\mathsf{A}}(1^\lambda) \Rightarrow 1]$$

$$= \Pr[\mathsf{Game}^{\text{Base}}_{(1,n)\text{-OS}_{\text{Ours}},\mathsf{A}}(1^\lambda) \Rightarrow 1 \wedge \mathsf{DS}_{\text{forge}} = \texttt{true}]$$

$$\quad + \Pr[\mathsf{Game}^{\text{Base}}_{(1,n)\text{-OS}_{\text{Ours}},\mathsf{A}}(1^\lambda) \Rightarrow 1 \wedge \mathsf{COM}_{\text{coll}} = \texttt{true}]$$

$$\quad + \Pr[\mathsf{Game}^{\text{Base}}_{(1,n)\text{-OS}_{\text{Ours}},\mathsf{A}}(1^\lambda) \Rightarrow 1 \wedge \mathsf{DS}_{\text{forge}} = \texttt{false} \wedge \mathsf{COM}_{\text{coll}} = \texttt{false}]$$

$$\leq \mathsf{Adv}^{\text{sEUFCMA}}_{\mathsf{DS},\mathsf{A}_1}(1^\lambda) + \mathsf{Adv}^{\text{sBind}}_{\mathsf{COM},\mathsf{A}_2}(1^\lambda) + \mathsf{Adv}^{\text{Coll}}_{\mathcal{H},\mathsf{A}_3}(1^\lambda).$$

By this fact, we can conclude Theorem 2. □

5 Conclusion

Summary of Our Results. In this paper, we revisit the unforgeability security for a 1-out-of-n oblivious signature scheme and point out problems. By reflecting on these problems, we define the Seq-sEUF-CMA security. We propose the improved generic construction of a 1-out-of-n oblivious signature scheme $(1,n)$-$\mathsf{OS}_{\text{Ours}}$. Compared to the construction by Zhou et al. [21], our construction offers a smaller second message size. The sum of a second message size and a signature size is improved from $O(n)$ to $O(\log n)$.

Discussion of Our Security Model. We introduce the Seq-sEUF-CMA security in Definition 10. It is natural to consider a model that allows concurrent signing interactions. However, if we straightforwardly extend our security model to a concurrent setting, there is a trivial attack.

Let us consider the following adversary A that runs signing protocol executions twice concurrently. A chooses two list $M_1 = (m_{1,0}, \ldots, m_{1,n-1})$ and $M_2 = (m_{2,0}, \ldots, m_{2,n-1})$ such that $M_1 \cap M_2 = \emptyset$ (i.e., there is no element m such that $m \in M_1 \wedge m \in M_2$). In the 1st interaction, A chooses $m_{1,0} \in M_1$, obtains a signature σ_1 on a message $m_{1,0}$. In the 2nd interaction A chooses $m_{2,0} \in M_2$, obtains a signature σ_2 on a message $m_{2,0}$. A finishes the 1st interaction by outputting $(m_{2,0}, \sigma_2)$. Since $m_{2,0} \notin M_1$, A trivially wins the unforgeability game. Due to this trivial attack, we cannot straightforwardly extend our security model to the concurrent signing interaction setting.

Our security model seems complex and redundant. Instead of the signature resubmission check, by introducing the algorithm Link which verifies a link between a signing interaction and a signature, it may be possible to define the unforgeability security more simply. We leave this formalization as a future work.

References

1. Abe, M., Fujisaki, E.: How to date blind signatures. In: Kim, K., Matsumoto, T. (eds.) ASIACRYPT 1996. LNCS, vol. 1163, pp. 244–251. Springer, Heidelberg (1996). https://doi.org/10.1007/BFb0034851

2. Agrawal, S., Kirshanova, E., Stehlé, D., Yadav, A.: Practical, round-optimal lattice-based blind signatures. In: Yin, H., Stavrou, A., Cremers, C., Shi, E. (eds.) Proceedings of the 2022 ACM SIGSAC Conference on Computer and Communications Security, CCS 2022, Los Angeles, CA, USA, 7–11 November 2022, pp. 39–53. ACM (2022)
3. Bellare, M., Rogaway, P.: The security of triple encryption and a framework for code-based game-playing proofs. In: Vaudenay, S. (ed.) EUROCRYPT 2006. LNCS, vol. 4004, pp. 409–426. Springer, Heidelberg (2006). https://doi.org/10.1007/11761679_25
4. Błaśkiewicz, P., et al.: Pseudonymous signature schemes. In: Li, K.-C., Chen, X., Susilo, W. (eds.) Advances in Cyber Security: Principles, Techniques, and Applications, pp. 185–255. Springer, Singapore (2019). https://doi.org/10.1007/978-981-13-1483-4_8
5. Chaum, D.: Blind signatures for untraceable payments. In: Chaum, D., Rivest, R.L., Sherman, A.T. (eds.) Advances in Cryptology: Proceedings of CRYPTO 1982, Santa Barbara, California, USA, 23–25 August 1982, pp. 199–203. Plenum Press, New York (1982)
6. Chen, L.: Oblivious signatures. In: Gollmann, D. (ed.) ESORICS 1994. LNCS, vol. 875, pp. 161–172. Springer, Heidelberg (1994). https://doi.org/10.1007/3-540-58618-0_62
7. Chiou, S., Chen, J.: Design and implementation of a multiple-choice e-voting scheme on mobile system using novel t-out-of-n oblivious signature. J. Inf. Sci. Eng. **34**(1), 135–154 (2018)
8. del Pino, R., Katsumata, S.: A new framework for more efficient round-optimal lattice-based (partially) blind signature via trapdoor sampling. In: Dodis, Y., Shrimpton, T. (eds.) CRYPTO 2022. LNCS, vol. 13508, pp. 306–336. Springer, Cham (2022). https://doi.org/10.1007/978-3-031-15979-4_11
9. Fuchsbauer, G., Hanser, C., Kamath, C., Slamanig, D.: Practical round-optimal blind signatures in the standard model from weaker assumptions. In: Zikas, V., De Prisco, R. (eds.) SCN 2016. LNCS, vol. 9841, pp. 391–408. Springer, Cham (2016). https://doi.org/10.1007/978-3-319-44618-9_21
10. Fuchsbauer, G., Hanser, C., Slamanig, D.: Practical round-optimal blind signatures in the standard model. In: Gennaro, R., Robshaw, M. (eds.) CRYPTO 2015. LNCS, vol. 9216, pp. 233–253. Springer, Heidelberg (2015). https://doi.org/10.1007/978-3-662-48000-7_12
11. Ghadafi, E.: Efficient round-optimal blind signatures in the standard model. In: Kiayias, A. (ed.) FC 2017. LNCS, vol. 10322, pp. 455–473. Springer, Cham (2017). https://doi.org/10.1007/978-3-319-70972-7_26
12. Hanzlik, L., Kluczniak, K.: A short paper on blind signatures from knowledge assumptions. In: Grossklags, J., Preneel, B. (eds.) FC 2016. LNCS, vol. 9603, pp. 535–543. Springer, Heidelberg (2017). https://doi.org/10.1007/978-3-662-54970-4_31
13. Hanzlik, L., Kluczniak, K.: Two-move and setup-free blind signatures with perfect blindness. In: Baek, J., Zhang, R. (eds.) Proceedings of the 4th ACM International Workshop on ASIA Public-Key Cryptography, APKC@AsiaCCS 2017, Abu Dhabi, United Arab Emirates, 2 April 2017, pp. 1–11. ACM (2017)
14. Hanzlik, L., Loss, J., Wagner, B.: Rai-Choo! evolving blind signatures to the next level. In: Hazay, C., Stam, M. (eds.) EUROCRYPT 2023. LNCS, vol. 14008, pp. 753–783. Springer, Cham (2023). https://doi.org/10.1007/978-3-031-30589-4_26

15. Katsumata, S., Nishimaki, R., Yamada, S., Yamakawa, T.: Round-optimal blind signatures in the plain model from classical and quantum standard assumptions. In: Canteaut, A., Standaert, F.-X. (eds.) EUROCRYPT 2021. LNCS, vol. 12696, pp. 404–434. Springer, Cham (2021). https://doi.org/10.1007/978-3-030-77870-5_15
16. Lyubashevsky, V., Nguyen, N.K., Plancon, M.: Efficient lattice-based blind signatures via Gaussian one-time signatures. In: Hanaoka, G., Shikata, J., Watanabe, Y. (eds.) PKC 2022. LNCs, vol. 13178, pp. 498–527. Springer, Cham (2022). https://doi.org/10.1007/978-3-030-97131-1_17
17. Merkle, R.C.: A digital signature based on a conventional encryption function. In: Pomerance, C. (ed.) CRYPTO 1987. LNCS, vol. 293, pp. 369–378. Springer, Heidelberg (1988). https://doi.org/10.1007/3-540-48184-2_32
18. Song, C., Yin, X., Liu, Y.: A practical electronic voting protocol based upon oblivious signature scheme. In: 2008 International Conference on Computational Intelligence and Security, CIS 2008, Suzhou, China, 13–17 December 2008, Volume 1 - Conference Papers, pp. 381–384. IEEE Computer Society (2008)
19. Tso, R., Okamoto, T., Okamoto, E.: 1-out-of-n oblivious signatures. In: Chen, L., Mu, Y., Susilo, W. (eds.) ISPEC 2008. LNCS, vol. 4991, pp. 45–55. Springer, Heidelberg (2008). https://doi.org/10.1007/978-3-540-79104-1_4
20. You, J.S., Liu, Z.Y., Tso, R., Tseng, Y.F., Mambo, M.: Quantum-resistant 1-out-of-n oblivious signatures from lattices. In: Cheng, C.M., Akiyama, M. (eds.) IWSEC 2022. LNCS, vol. 13504, pp. 166–186. Springer, Cham (2022). https://doi.org/10.1007/978-3-031-15255-9_9
21. Zhou, Y., Liu, S., Han, S.: Generic construction of 1-out-of-n oblivious signatures. IEICE Trans. Inf. Syst. **105–D**(11), 1836–1844 (2022)

Compact Identity-Based Signature and Puncturable Signature from SQISign

Surbhi Shaw[✉] and Ratna Dutta

Department of Mathematics, Indian Institute of Technology Kharagpur,
Kharagpur 721302, India
surbhi_shaw@iitkgp.ac.in, ratna@maths.iitkgp.ac.in

Abstract. Puncturable signature (PS) offers a fine-grained revocation of signing ability by updating its signing key for a given message m such that the resulting punctured signing key can produce signatures for all messages except for m. In light of the applications of PS in proof-of-stake blockchain protocols, disappearing signatures and asynchronous transaction data signing services, this paper addresses the need for designing practical and efficient PS schemes. Existing proposals pertaining to PS suffer from various limitations, including computational inefficiency, false-positive errors, vulnerability to quantum attacks and large key and signature sizes. To overcome these challenges, we aim to design a PS from isogenies. We first propose an *Identity-Based Signature* (IBS) by employing the Short Quaternion and Isogeny Signature (SQISign). We provide a rigorous security analysis of our IBS and prove it is secure against *unforgeability under chosen identity and chosen message attacks*. More interestingly, our IBS achieves the most compact key and signature size compared to existing isogeny-based IBS schemes. Leveraging our proposed IBS, we introduce the *first* Short Quaternion and Isogeny Puncturable Signature (SQIPS) which allows for selective revocation of signatures and is supported by a comprehensive security analysis against *existential forgery under chosen message attacks with adaptive puncturing*. Our PS scheme SQIPS provides resistance from quantum attacks, enjoys small signature size and is free from false-positive errors.

Keywords: Puncturable signature · Isogenies · Identity-based signature · Post-quantum cryptography

1 Introduction

With the proliferation of digital technology and the widespread adoption of online transactions, ensuring the privacy and security of sensitive data has emerged as a paramount concern. Cryptographic techniques lay the foundation for secure transactions by protecting the integrity and confidentiality of digital communications. Digital signatures are of particular importance among these cryptographic techniques as they enable parties to verify the authenticity and integrity of communications over the Internet. Puncturable signature (PS)

© The Author(s), under exclusive license to Springer Nature Singapore Pte Ltd. 2024
H. Seo and S. Kim (Eds.): ICISC 2023, LNCS 14561, pp. 282–305, 2024.
https://doi.org/10.1007/978-981-97-1235-9_15

is a variant of digital signature proposed by Bellare, Stepanovs and Waters [1] at EUROCRYPT 2016. It offers a fine-grained revocation of signing ability by updating the secret key with selective messages. In contrast to a conventional digital signature, PS includes an additional algorithm known as Puncture which enables the signer to create punctured secret key with messages chosen by itself. Precisely, with the punctured secret key that has been punctured at a specific message m, the signer can sign on any message except for the punctured message m. The security definition of a PS requires that the adversary cannot forge signatures on punctured messages even though the punctured secret key is compromised.

Applications. Puncturable signatures have been identified as a versatile cryptographic primitive with numerous applications. These include improving the resilience of proof-of-stake blockchain protocols, designing disappearing signatures and securing asynchronous transaction data signing services. We delve deeper into these applications and their significance below:

- Proof of Stake (PoS) and Proof of Work (PoW) are two consensus mechanisms used in blockchain networks to validate transactions. While PoW requires substantial computational power, PoS relies on participants' cryptocurrency stake, resulting in a more energy-efficient approach. However, the majority of existing PoS protocols are prone to long-range attacks [7,9]. In this attack, the attacker can tweak the historical records of the blockchain which could lead to double-spending of cryptocurrency or the deletion of prior transactions. PS provide a viable solution to construct practical PoS blockchain resilient to long-range attacks by enabling the selective revocation of past signatures. By puncturing prior used signatures associated with a specific stakeholder, the potential for an attacker to leverage accumulated stakes from the past and manipulate the blockchain's history is reduced. This prevents the forging of past signatures and deter long-range attacks.
- Puncturable signatures are essential building blocks for designing disappearing signature [10] in the bounded storage model. A disappearing signature refers to a signature scheme where the signature becomes inaccessible or "disappears" once the streaming of the signature stops. In the context of bounded storage model, a disappearing signature ensures that the signature can only be verified online and cannot be retained by any malicious party.
- Asynchronous transaction data signing services involve the signing and verification of transaction data in a non-interactive manner without necessitating all parties involved to be online simultaneously [15]. In this context, messages may be delayed and participants may not be available simultaneously due to factors like connectivity issues or delivery failures. PS have applications in ensuring the integrity and authenticity of transaction data in asynchronous signing services. By using PS, the transaction session identity can serve as a prefix that is subsequently punctured after the honest user signs the transaction data. This ensures that no other signature can exist for messages with the same prefix, thereby upholding the integrity of the transaction data.

Related Works. Several studies have been carried out pertaining to PS, exploring their potential applications and security properties. The notion of PS was first proposed by Bellare et al. [1] in 2016. However, their proposed scheme was based on indistinguishability obfuscation which resulted in excessive computational overhead, rendering the scheme impractical. In a subsequent work, Halevi et al. [11] proposed a PS by combining a statistically binding commitment scheme with non-interactive zero-knowledge proofs. Their approach differed from the conventional PS schemes as it involved updating the public key instead of the secret key during each puncture operation which posed significant challenges in practical deployment. In 2020, Li et al. [13] presented a PS using a bloom filter that surpasses prior schemes in terms of signature size and algorithm efficiency. Additionally, the authors explored the application of PS in proof-of-stake blockchain protocols, specifically addressing the issue of long-range attacks caused by secret key leakage [7,9]. However, their proposed scheme faced a notable challenge in the form of non-negligible false-positive errors, stemming from the probabilistic nature of the bloom filter data structure. Moreover, their proposed scheme was based on the Strong Diffie-Hellman (SDH) assumption in bilinear map setting and is thus susceptible to quantum attacks due to Shor's algorithm [18]. In light of the devastating consequences that quantum computers have had on the security of classical cryptosystems, Jiang et al. [12] proposed a generic construction of PS from identity-based signatures (IBS). Moreover, they presented different instantiations of their generic construction from lattice-based, pairing-based and multivariate-based assumptions. More precisely, their lattice-based instantiation leverages the efficient IBS proposed by Tian and Huang [19] and is based on the Short Integer Solution (SIS) assumption. Their pairing-based instantiation uses the identity-based version of Paterson's signature [20] which is based on the Computational Diffie-Hellman (CDH) assumption. The instantiation over multivariate assumption relies on ID-based Rainbow signature [4].

Contributions. The existing proposals for PS are undesirable for practical applications. Some PS schemes have large key and signature sizes as they rely on heavy cryptographic structures, making them computationally expensive and inefficient. The PS based on bloom filter suffers from non-negligible false-positive errors, providing economical benefits to the attackers in blockchain. Some PS schemes are prone to quantum attacks raising significant security concerns. To address these limitations, it is imperative to develop improved and more practical approaches to PS. In this work, we identify a gap in the existing literature, noting the absence of a construction for PS from isogenies. The emergence of isogeny-based cryptography as a promising candidate for post-quantum cryptosystems, characterized by its compact key sizes compared to other alternatives, has motivated us to focus on the design of an isogeny-based PS scheme. The compactness of isogeny-based cryptography makes it particularly appealing for practical applications, where efficiency and scalability are crucial factors. To show an instantiation of the generic construction of PS proposed by Jiang et al. [12], we seek an IBS scheme from isogenies. One of the main technical challenges encountered during our research is the absence of a suitable IBS based on isogenies to instantiate the generic construction. Though there exist two constructions of IBS from isogenies in the literature, none appears to be a suitable candidate to design PS. Peng et al. [16] proposed the first construction of IBS from isogenies. Unfortunately, their IBS scheme was proven to be flawed by Shaw and Dutta [17] who provided a viable fix and designed an IBS scheme from ID-based identification scheme. However, we find that the IBS scheme of [17] has a large key and signature size, rendering it unsuitable for blockchain applications. Furthermore, both the prior IBS schemes are based on *Commutative Supersingular Isogeny Diffie-Hellman* (CSIDH) based group action [2] which suffers from a subexponential attack [5] leading to poor concrete efficiency. The somewhat unsatisfactory state-of-art motivates us to first design an IBS from isogenies with compact key and signature size.

The most recent and sophisticated *Short Quaternion and Isogeny Signature* (SQISign) by De Feo et al. [6] is the starting point in designing our IBS. The signature scheme SQISign is derived from a one-round, high soundness, interactive identification protocol. The combined size of the signature and public key of SQISign are an order of magnitude smaller than all other post-quantum signature schemes. We then employ our proposed IBS to design our PS from isogenies.

Thus, our main contributions in this paper are two-fold, as summarized below:

- *Firstly,* we design an IBS scheme from SQISign which we refer to as *Short Quaternion and Isogeny Identity-based Signature* (SQIIBS). We provide a rigorous security reduction showing it is secure against unforgeability under chosen identity and chosen message attacks (UF-IBS-CMA). We compare our scheme with the existing IBS schemes from isogenies and show that our scheme outperforms existing schemes in terms of key size and signature size which thereby reduces the storage and communication cost.
- Secondly, we employ our identity-based signature scheme SQIIBS to construct our PS from isogenies which we refer to it as Short Quaternion and Isogeny Puncturable Signature (SQIPS). We prove our scheme to be secure against *existential unforgeability under chosen message attacks with adaptive puncturing* (UF-CMA-AP). We also compare the features of our scheme with the existing PS schemes. Our scheme works for a pre-determined time of key punctures since the range of prefix space is fixed in advance. The size of the punctured secret key decreases linearly as the times of key puncture increase. Our scheme involves an efficient puncture operation that only contain a conversion from a bit string to a decimal integer and the deletion of a part in the current secret key. More positively, our scheme provides quantum security, enjoys small signature size and is free from false-positive errors.

2   Preliminaries

Let $\lambda \in \mathbb{N}$ denotes the security parameter. By $i \in [T]$, we mean i belongs to the set $\{1, 2, \ldots, T\}$. The symbol $\#S$ denotes the cardinality of S. By $\mathsf{bin}(x)$, we mean the binary representation of x. A function $\epsilon(\cdot)$ is negligible if for every positive integer c, there exists an integer k such that for all $\lambda > k$, $|\epsilon(\lambda)| < 1/\lambda^c$.

2.1   Quaternion Algebras, Orders and Ideals

Quaternion Algebras. For $a, b \in \mathbb{Q}^* = \mathbb{Q} \setminus \{0\}$, the quaternion algebra over $\mathbb{Q}$, denoted by $H(a,b) = \mathbb{Q} + i\mathbb{Q} + j\mathbb{Q} + k\mathbb{Q}$, is defined as a four-dimensional non-commutative vector space with basis $\{1, i, j, k\}$ such that $i^2 = a$, $j^2 = b$ and $k = ij = -ji$. Every quaternion algebra $H(a,b)$ is associated by a standard convolution $g : H(a,b) \to H(a,b)$ given by $g : \alpha = a_1 + a_2 i + a_3 j + a_4 k \to a_1 - a_2 i - a_3 j - a_4 k = \bar{\alpha}$. The *reduced norm* $\mathsf{nr} : H(a,b) \to \mathbb{Q}$ of a standard convolution g is the map $\mathsf{nr} : \alpha \to \alpha g(\alpha)$. In this work, we are interested in the quaternion algebra $\mathcal{B}_{p,\infty} = H(-1, -p)$ for some prime p.

Ideals and Orders. A *fractional ideal* $I = \alpha_1 \mathbb{Z} + \alpha_2 \mathbb{Z} + \alpha_3 \mathbb{Z} + \alpha_4 \mathbb{Z}$ is a $\mathbb{Z}$-lattice of rank four with $\{\alpha_1, \alpha_2, \alpha_3, \alpha_4\}$ a basis of $\mathcal{B}_{p,\infty}$. The *norm* of I, denoted by $\mathsf{nr}(I)$, is defined as the largest rational number such that $\mathsf{nr}(\alpha) \in \mathsf{nr}(I)\mathbb{Z}$ for any $\alpha \in I$. The *conjugate ideal* $\bar{I}$ of I is given by $\bar{I} = \{\bar{\alpha} \,|\, \alpha \in I\}$. An *order* is a subring of $\mathcal{B}_{p,\infty}$ that is also a fractional ideal. A *maximal order* $\mathcal{O}$ is an order that is not properly contained in any other order. The *left order* of a fractional ideal I, denoted by $\mathcal{O}_L(I)$, is defined as $\mathcal{O}_L(I) = \{\alpha \in \mathcal{B}_{p,\infty} \,|\, \alpha I \subseteq I\}$. Similarly, *right order* of a fractional ideal I, denoted by $\mathcal{O}_R(I)$, is defined as $\mathcal{O}_R(I) = \{\alpha \in \mathcal{B}_{p,\infty} \,|\, I\alpha \subseteq I\}$. Here I is said to be a left $\mathcal{O}_L(I)$-ideal or a right $\mathcal{O}_R(I)$-ideal or an $(\mathcal{O}_L(I), \mathcal{O}_R(I))$-ideal. An *Eichler order* is the intersection of two maximal orders inside $\mathcal{B}_{p,\infty}$. A fractional ideal I is called *integral* if $I \subseteq \mathcal{O}_L(I)$ or $I \subseteq \mathcal{O}_R(I)$. Two left $\mathcal{O}$-ideals I and J are *equivalent* if there exists $\beta \in \mathcal{B}_{p,\infty} \setminus \{0\}$ such that $I = J\beta$ and is denoted by $I \sim J$. A *special extremal order* is an order $\mathcal{O}$ in $\mathcal{B}_{p,\infty}$ which contains a suborder of the form $R + jR$ where $R = \mathbb{Z}[\omega] \subset \mathbb{Q}[i]$ is a quadratic order and ω has smallest norm in $\mathcal{O}$.

2.2   Elliptic Curves, Isogenies and Deuring's Correspondence

Isogenies. Let E_1 and E_2 be two elliptic curves over a finite field F. An *isogeny* from E_1 to E_2 is a non-constant morphism $\varphi : E_1 \to E_2$ over F satisfying $\varphi(\Theta_{E_1}) = \Theta_{E_2}$ where Θ_{E_i} is the point at infinity of the curve E_i for $i = 1, 2$. The *degree* of the isogeny φ, denoted by $\deg(\varphi)$ is its degree as a rational map. A non-zero isogeny $\varphi : E_1 \to E_2$ is called *separable* if and only if $\deg(\varphi) = \#\mathsf{ker}(\varphi)$ where $\mathsf{ker}(\varphi) = \varphi^{-1}(\Theta_{E_2})$ is the kernel of φ. An isogeny φ is said to be *cyclic* (non-backtracking) if its kernel is a cyclic group. For any isogeny $\varphi : E_1 \to E_2$, there exists a unique *dual isogeny* $\hat{\varphi} : E_2 \to E_1$ satisfying $\varphi \circ \hat{\varphi} = [\deg(\varphi)]$, the multiplication-by-$\deg(\varphi)$ map on E_2. An isogeny from an elliptic curve E to itself is called an *endomorphism*. The set of all endomorphisms of E forms a ring under pointwise addition and composition, called the *endomorphism ring* of E and is denoted by $\mathsf{End}(E)$. For a supersingular elliptic curve E, the endomorphism ring $\mathsf{End}(E)$ is isomorphic to an order in a quaternion algebra. The *j-invariant* of an elliptic curve $E : y^2 = x^3 + Ax + B$ over F is given by $j(E) = 1728\frac{4A^3}{4A^3 + 27B^2}$.

Theorem 2.21 [2]. *Given a finite subgroup G of an elliptic curve E_1, there exists a unique (up to F-isomorphism) elliptic curve E_2 and a separable isogeny $\varphi : E_1 \to E_2$ such that $\mathsf{ker}(\varphi) = G$ and $E_2 := E_1/G$ with $\deg(\varphi) = \#\mathsf{ker}(\varphi)$.*

Throughout this work, we focus on supersingular curves over $F = \mathbb{F}_{p^2}$. We fix the curve $E_0 : y^2 = x^3 + x$ over $\mathbb{F}_{p^2}$ which has special extremal endomorphism ring $\mathsf{End}(E_0) = \mathcal{O}_0 = \langle 1, i, \frac{i+j}{2}, \frac{1+k}{2} \rangle$ where $i^2 = -1$, $j^2 = -p$ and $k = ij$.

Deuring's Correspondence: *Deuring's correspondence* [8] establishes a one-to-one correspondence between the set of isomorphism classes of supersingular curves over $\mathbb{F}_{p^2}$ and the set of ideal classes of a given maximal order. Under this correspondence, we look into the connection between ideals in maximal orders of quaternions and separable isogenies between supersingular curves over $\mathbb{F}_{p^2}$.

Theorem 2.22. *Let $\varphi : E_0 \to E_1$ be a separable isogeny and $\mathcal{O}_0 = \mathsf{End}(E_0)$ and $\mathcal{O}_1 = \mathsf{End}(E_1)$ are the maximal orders corresponding to the endomorphism rings of E_0 and E_1. Then we define the corresponding left $\mathcal{O}_0$-ideal $I_\varphi = \{\alpha \in \mathcal{O}_0 \,|\, \alpha(P) = \Theta_{E_0} \text{ for all } P \in \mathsf{ker}(\varphi)\}$. Conversely, given a left $\mathcal{O}_0$-ideal I, we can define the kernel $E_0[I] = \cap_{\alpha \in I} E_0[\alpha] = \{P \in E_0 \,|\, \alpha(P) = \Theta_{E_0} \text{ for all } \alpha \in I\}$ and compute the separable isogeny $\varphi_I : E_0 \to E_0/E_0[I]$ that corresponds to I.*

Lemma 2.23 [6]. *Let $\mathcal{O}$ be a maximal order, I be a left $\mathcal{O}$-ideal and $\beta \in I \setminus \{0\}$. Then $\chi_I(\beta) = I \frac{\bar{\beta}}{nr(I)}$ is a left $\mathcal{O}$-ideal equivalent to I and has norm $\frac{nr(\beta)}{nr(I)}$.*

Pushforward and Pullback Isogeny. Consider three elliptic curves E_0, E_1, E_2 over $\mathbb{F}_{p^2}$ and two separable isogenies $\varphi_1 : E_0 \to E_1$ and $\varphi_2 : E_0 \to E_2$ of coprime degrees N_1 and N_2 respectively. The *pushforward of φ_1 by φ_2* is denoted by $[\varphi_2]_*\varphi_1$ and is defined as the separable isogeny $[\varphi_2]_*\varphi_1$ from E_2 to some new curve E_3 such that $\mathsf{ker}([\varphi_2]_*\varphi_1) = \varphi_2(\mathsf{ker}(\varphi_1))$ and $\deg([\varphi_2]_*\varphi_1) = N_1$. Similarly, the *pushforward of φ_2 by φ_1* is denoted by $[\varphi_1]_*\varphi_2$ and is defined as the separable isogeny $[\varphi_1]_*\varphi_2 : E_1 \to E_3$ such that $\mathsf{ker}([\varphi_1]_*\varphi_2) = \varphi_1(\mathsf{ker}(\varphi_2))$ and $\deg([\varphi_1]_*\varphi_2) = N_2$. *Pullback isogeny* is the dual notion of pushforward isogeny. Consider two separable isogeniers $\varphi_1 : E_0 \to E_1$ and $\rho_2 : E_1 \to E_3$ of coprime degrees. The pullback of ρ_2 by φ_1 is denoted by $[\varphi_1]^*\rho_2$ and is defined as the separable isogeny $[\varphi_1]^*\rho_2$ from E_0 to a new curve E_4 satisfying $[\varphi_1]^*\rho_2 = [\hat{\varphi}_1]_*\rho_2$.

The pushforward and pullback terms can be extended to ideals as well. Consider a $(\mathcal{O}_0, \mathcal{O}_1)$-ideal J and a $(\mathcal{O}_0, \mathcal{O}_2)$-ideal K where $\mathcal{O}_0 = \mathsf{End}(E_0)$, $\mathcal{O}_1 = \mathsf{End}(E_1)$ and $\mathcal{O}_2 = \mathsf{End}(E_2)$. The *pushforward of J by K*, denoted by $[K]_*J$ is the ideal $I_{[\varphi_K]_*\varphi_J}$ corresponding to the pushforward isogeny $[\varphi_K]_*\varphi_J$. Consider a $(\mathcal{O}_1, \mathcal{O}_3)$-ideal L where $\mathcal{O}_1 = \mathsf{End}(E_1)$, $\mathcal{O}_3 = \mathsf{End}(E_3)$, then the *pullback of L by J*, denoted by $[J]^*L$ is defined as $[J]^*L = [\bar{J}]_*L$.

Lemma 2.24 [6]. *Let I is an ideal with left order $\mathcal{O}_0$ and right order $\mathcal{O}$ and J_1, J_2 be $\mathcal{O}_0$-ideals with $J_1 \sim J_2$ and $\gcd(nr(J_1), nr(J_2), nr(I)) = 1$. Suppose that $J_1 = \chi_{J_2}(\beta)$ and $\beta \in J_2 \cap \mathcal{O}_0 \cap \mathcal{O}$. Then $[I]_*J_1 \sim [I]_*J_2$ and $[I]_*J_1 = \chi_{[I]_*J_2}(\beta)$.*

2.3 SigningKLPT Algorithm

We briefly review below the sub-algorithms invoked by the algorithm SigningKLPT. The details of which can be found in the work of De Feo et al. [6].

Cornacchia$(M) \to (x, y)$: This algorithm on input $M \in \mathbb{Z}$ either outputs $\perp$ if M cannot be represented as $f(x, y)$ or returns a solution (x, y) to $f(x, y) = M$.

EquivalentPrimeIdeal$(I) \to L \sim I$: This algorithm takes as input a left $\mathcal{O}_0$-ideal I represented by Minkowski reduced basis [14] $(\delta_1, \delta_2, \delta_3, \delta_4)$. It chooses an integer m, generates a random element $\delta = \Sigma_i x_i \delta_i$ with $x_i \in [-m, m]$ and checks if $\frac{\mathrm{nr}(\delta)}{\mathrm{nr}(I)}$ is a prime number. If not, it continues to generate random δ until it finds a $\delta \in I$ for which $\frac{\mathrm{nr}(\delta)}{\mathrm{nr}(I)}$ is a prime number. The algorithm outputs the ideal $L = \chi_I(\delta) = I\frac{\bar{\delta}}{\mathrm{nr}(I)}$ equivalent to I and of prime norm.

EquivalentRandomEichlerIdeal$(I, N) \to L \sim I$: This algorithm takes as input a left $\mathcal{O}_0$-ideal I and an integer N and finds a random equivalent left $\mathcal{O}_0$-ideal L of norm coprime to N.

FullRepresentInteger$_{\mathcal{O}_0}(M) \to \gamma$: This algorithm takes input an integer $M \in \mathbb{Z}$ with $M > p$ and outputs an element $\gamma \in \mathcal{O}_0$ with $\mathrm{nr}(\gamma) = M$ as follows.

  i. Sets $m' = \lfloor \sqrt{\frac{4M}{p}} \rfloor$ and samples a random integer $z' \in [-m', m']$.

  ii. Sets $m'' = \lfloor \sqrt{\frac{4M}{p} - (z')^2} \rfloor$ and samples a random integer $t' \in [-m'', m'']$.

  iii. Sets $M' = 4M - p\big((z')^2 + (t')^2\big)$ and runs Cornacchia(M') until Cornacchia returns a solution (x', y') to $f(x', y') = M'$.

  iv. If $x' \neq t' \pmod 2$ or $z' \neq y' \pmod 2$ then go back to Step (i).

  v. The algorithm outputs $\gamma = x + yi + z\frac{i+j}{2} + t\frac{1+k}{2} \in \mathcal{O}_0$ of norm M where $x = \frac{x'-t}{2}, y = \frac{y'-z}{2}, z = z'$ and $t = t'$.

IdealModConstraint$(I, \gamma) \to (C_0 : D_0)$: On input a left $\mathcal{O}_0$-ideal I of norm N and an element $\gamma \in \mathcal{O}_0$ of norm Nn, this algorithm outputs a projective point $(C_0 : D_0) \in \mathbb{P}^1(\mathbb{Z}/N\mathbb{Z})$ satisfying $\gamma\mu_0 \in I$ with $\mu_0 = (C_0 + \omega D_0)j \in Rj$.

EichlerModConstraint$(I, \gamma, \delta) \to (C_0 : D_0)$: This algorithm takes input a left $\mathcal{O}_0$-ideal I of norm N, elements $\gamma, \delta \in \mathcal{O}_0$ of norms coprime to N and outputs a projective point $(C_0 : D_0) \in \mathbb{P}^1(\mathbb{Z}/N\mathbb{Z})$ satisfying $\gamma\mu_0\delta \in I$ where $\mu_0 = (C_0 + \omega D_0)j \in Rj$.

FullStrongApproximation$_{\mathcal{S}}(N, C, D) \to \mu$: Taking as input a prime N, integers C, D and a subset $\mathcal{S} \subset \mathbb{N}$, this algorithm outputs $\mu \in \mathcal{O}_0$ of norm in $\mathcal{S}$ satisfying $2\mu = \lambda\mu_0 + N\mu_1$ where $\mu_0 = (C_0 + \omega D_0)j \in Rj$, $\lambda \in \mathbb{Z}$ and $\mu_1 \in \mathcal{O}_0$. When $\mathcal{S} = \{d \in \mathbb{N} : d|D\}$ for some $D \in \mathbb{N}$, we simply write FullStrongApproximation$_D$.

CRT$_{M,N}(x, y) \to z$: This is the algorithm for Chinese Remainder Theorem which takes as input $x \in \mathbb{Z}_M$, $y \in \mathbb{Z}_N$ and returns $z \in \mathbb{Z}_{MN}$ satisfying $z \equiv x \pmod M$ and $z \equiv y \pmod N$ where M and N are coprime to each other.

We now describe the algorithm SigningKLPT$_{\ell^e}(I_\tau, I)$ [6] which takes as input a prime l, a fixed $e \in \mathbb{N}$, a left $\mathcal{O}_0$ and a right $\mathcal{O}$-ideal I_τ of norm N_τ and a left $\mathcal{O}$-ideal I and outputs an ideal $J \sim I$ of norm ℓ^e. The steps involved in the algorithm SigningKLPT are illustrated in Fig. 1 and explicitly described below.

  1. Runs the algorithm EquivalentRandomEichlerIdeal(I, N_τ) to generate a random ideal $K \sim I$ with $gcd(\mathrm{nr}(K), N_\tau) = 1$. We denote the right order of the ideal K (or I) by $\mathcal{O}_2$.

2. Performs the pullback of the $(\mathcal{O}, \mathcal{O}_2)$- ideal K by the $(\mathcal{O}_0, \mathcal{O})$-ideal I_τ to obtain a $(\mathcal{O}_0, \mathcal{O}')$-ideal $K' = [I_\tau]^* K$ where $\mathcal{O}' = \mathrm{End}(E')$ for some curve E'.

3. Computes an ideal $L = K'\frac{\bar{\delta}'}{\mathrm{nr}(K')} = \chi_{K'}(\delta') \leftarrow \mathsf{EquivalentPrimeIdeal}(K')$ equivalent to K' but of prime norm N for some $\delta' \in K'$. (See Lemma 2.23)

4. Chooses $e_0 \in \mathbb{N}$ and runs the algorithm $\mathsf{FullRepresentInteger}_{\mathcal{O}_0}(N\ell^{e_0})$ to obtain an element $\gamma \in \mathcal{O}_0$ such that $\mathrm{nr}(\gamma) = N\ell^{e_0}$. Sets $e_1 = e - e_0 \in \mathbb{N}$.

5. Finds the projective point $(C_0 : D_0) \in \mathbb{P}^1(\mathbb{Z}/N\mathbb{Z}) \leftarrow \mathsf{IdealModConstraint}(L, \gamma)$ satisfying $\gamma\mu_0 \in L$ where $\mu_0 = (C_0 + \omega D_0)j \in Rj$.

6. Chooses $\delta \in \mathcal{O}_0$ with $\gcd(\mathrm{nr}(\delta), N_\tau) = 1$ and runs the algorithm $\mathsf{EichlerModConstraint}(\mathbb{Z} + I_\tau, \gamma, \delta)$ on input the ideal $\mathbb{Z} + I_\tau$ of norm N_τ and elements $\gamma, \delta \in \mathcal{O}_0$ of norms coprime to N_τ to find the projective point $(C_1 : D_1) \in \mathbb{P}^1(\mathbb{Z}/N_\tau\mathbb{Z})$ satisfying $\gamma\mu_1\delta \in \mathbb{Z} + I_\tau$ where $\mu_1 = (C_1 + \omega D_1)j \in Rj$.

7. Computes $C \leftarrow \mathrm{CRT}_{N,N_\tau}(C_0, C_1)$ where C is the solution modulo NN_τ to the system of congruences $C \equiv C_0 \pmod{N}$ and $C \equiv C_1 \pmod{N_\tau}$ and $D \leftarrow \mathrm{CRT}_{N,N_\tau}(D_0, D_1)$ where D is the solution modulo NN_τ to the system of congruences $D \equiv D_0 \pmod{N}$ and $D \equiv D_1 \pmod{N_\tau}$. If $\ell^e p(C^2 + D^2)$ is not a quadratic residue, go back to Step 4 and repeat the process.

8. Executes the algorithm $\mathsf{FullStrongApproximation}_{\ell^\star}(NN_\tau, C, D)$ to generate $\mu \in \mathcal{O}_0$ of norm ℓ^{e_1} where $\ell^\star = \{\ell^\alpha : \alpha \in \mathbb{N}\}$.

9. Sets $\beta = \gamma\mu$, obtains the $(\mathcal{O}_0, \mathcal{O}')$-ideal $\chi_L(\beta) = L\frac{\bar{\beta}}{\mathrm{nr}(L)}$ (See Lemma 2.23) and computes the $(\mathcal{O}, \mathcal{O}_2)$- ideal $J = [I_\tau]_*\chi_L(\beta)$ by using pushforward of the ideal $\chi_L(\beta)$ by the $(\mathcal{O}_0, \mathcal{O})$-ideal I_τ. (See Lemma 2.24)

10. The algorithm then returns the ideal $J \sim I$.

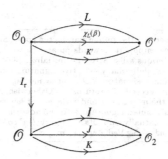

Fig. 1. Pictorial description of $\mathsf{SigningKLPT}$ algorithm

Correctness. Step 5 and Step 8 ensure $\beta \in L$ whereas Step 6 ensures $\beta \in \mathbb{Z} + I_\tau$. Also we have, $\mathrm{nr}(\beta) = \mathrm{nr}(\gamma)\mathrm{nr}(\mu) = N\ell^{e_0}\ell^{e_1} = N\ell^e$ which implies $\mathrm{nr}(J) = \mathrm{nr}([I_\tau]_*\chi_L(\beta)) = \frac{\mathrm{nr}(\beta)}{\mathrm{nr}(L)} = \frac{N\ell^e}{N} = \ell^e$. Also, Lemma 2.24 applied to $\chi_L(\beta) =$

$L\frac{\bar{\beta}}{\mathrm{nr}(L)} = \chi_{K'}(\delta')\frac{\bar{\beta}}{\mathrm{nr}(L)} = K'\frac{\bar{\delta}'}{\mathrm{nr}(K')}\frac{\bar{\beta}}{\mathrm{nr}(L)} = \chi_{K'}(\frac{\overline{\beta\delta'}}{\mathrm{nr}(L)})$ implies that $[I_\tau]_*\chi_L(\beta) \sim [I_\tau]_* K'$. This proves $J \sim K$ and we also have $K \sim I$, which implies $J \sim I$.

2.4 Signature Scheme

Definition 2.41. A *signature scheme* associated with a message space $\mathcal{M}$ is a tuple of probabilistic polynomial-time (PPT) algorithms Sig = (Setup, KeyGen, Sign, Verify) with the following syntax:

Sig.Setup(1^λ) $\to$ pp : A trusted party taking input 1^λ outputs the public parameter pp and makes it publicly available.

Sig.KeyGen(pp) $\to$ (sk, pk) : On input pp, the user runs this algorithm to generate a signing and verification key pair (sk, pk).

Sig.Sign(pp, sk, m) $\to \sigma$: Taking input pp, sk and a message $m \in \mathcal{M}$, the signer executes this algorithm to generate a signature σ on the message m.

Sig.Verify(pp, pk, m, σ) $\to$ Valid/Invalid : On input pp, pk, $m \in \mathcal{M}$ and a signature σ, the verifier checks the validity of the signature σ on m.

Correctness. For all pp $\leftarrow$ Sig.Setup(1^λ), all (sk, pk) $\leftarrow$ Sig.KeyGen(pp) and all signature $\sigma \leftarrow$ Sig.Sign(pp, sk, m), it holds that

$$\text{Sig.Verify}(\text{pp}, \text{pk}, m, \sigma) = \text{Valid}$$

Definition 2.42. A signature scheme Sig is secure against *existential unforgeability under chosen-message attacks* (UF-CMA) if for all PPT adversary $\mathcal{A}$, there exists a negligible function ϵ such that

$$\text{Adv}^{\text{UF-CMA}}_{\text{Sig}, \mathcal{A}}(\lambda) = \Pr[\mathcal{A} \text{ wins in } \text{Exp}^{\text{UF-CMA}}_{\text{Sig}, \mathcal{A}}(\lambda)] < \epsilon$$

where the experiment $\text{Exp}^{\text{UF-CMA}}_{\text{Sig}, \mathcal{A}}(\lambda)$ is depicted in Fig. 2.

Setup: The challenger $\mathcal{C}$ generates the public parameter pp $\leftarrow$ Sig.Setup(1^λ) and secret-public key pair (sk, pk) $\leftarrow$ Sig.KeyGen(pp). It forwards pp and pk to the adversary $\mathcal{A}$ while keeps sk secret to itself. It also maintains a list SList and initializes SList to $\emptyset$.

Query Phase: $\mathcal{A}$ issues polynomially many adaptive signature queries to the following oracle:
  – $\mathcal{O}_\text{S}(\text{sk}, \cdot)$: On receiving a signature query on a message m, the challenger $\mathcal{C}$ checks if $m \notin \mathcal{M}$. If the check succeeds, it returns $\bot$. Otherwise, it computes a signature $\sigma \leftarrow$ Sig.Sign(pp, sk, m) on the message m under the secret key sk and updates SList $\leftarrow$ SList $\cup$ $\{m\}$. It returns the computed signature σ to the adversary $\mathcal{A}$.

Forgery: The adversary $\mathcal{A}$ eventually submits a forgery (m^*, σ^*). The adversary $\mathcal{A}$ wins the game if $m^* \notin$ SList and Valid $\leftarrow$ Sig.Verify(pp, pk, m^*, σ^*).

Fig. 2. $\text{Exp}^{\text{UF-CMA}}_{\text{Sig}, \mathcal{A}}(\lambda)$: Existential unforgeability under chosen-message attack

2.5 SQISign: An Isogeny-Based Signature Scheme

The signature scheme SQISign [6] comprises of four PPT algorithms (Setup, KeyGen, Sign, Verify) having the following interface:

SQISign.Setup(1^λ) $\to$ pp_sgn: A trusted authority runs this algorithm on input a security parameter 1^λ and performs the following steps:

i. Chooses a prime p and fixes the supersingular curve $E_0 : y^2 = x^3 + x$ over $\mathbb{F}_{p^2}$ with special extremal endomorphism ring $\mathsf{End}(E_0) = \mathcal{O}_0 = \langle 1, i, \frac{i+j}{2}, \frac{1+k}{2} \rangle$.

ii. Picks a smooth number $D = 2^e$ where $2^e > p^3$.

iii. Picks an odd smooth number $D_c = \ell^e$ where ℓ is a prime and $e \in \mathbb{N}$ and computes $\mu(D_c) = (\ell + 1) \cdot \ell^{e-1}$.

iv. Samples a cryptographic hash function $\mathcal{H}_1 : \mathbb{F}_{p^2} \times \{0,1\}^* \to [\mu(D_c)]$.

v. Samples an arbitrary function $\Phi_{D_c}(E, s)$ that maps a curve E and an integer $s \in [\mu(D_c)]$ to a non-backtracking isogeny of degree D_c from E [3].

vi. Sets the public parameter $\mathsf{pp_{sgn}} = (p, E_0, D_c, D, \mathcal{H}_1, \Phi_{D_c})$.

$\mathsf{SQISign.KeyGen(pp_{sgn})} \to (\mathsf{sk}, \mathsf{pk})$: On input $\mathsf{pp_{sgn}}$, the key generation algorithm run by a user generates a signing-verification key pair $(\mathsf{sk}, \mathsf{pk})$ as follows:

i. Picks a random isogeny $\tau : E_0 \to E_A$ of degree N_τ.

ii. Sets the signing key $\mathsf{sk} = \tau$ and verification key $\mathsf{pk} = E_A$.

$\mathsf{SQISign.Sign(pp_{sgn}, sk}, m) \to \sigma$: Taking input $\mathsf{pp_{sgn}}$, signing key $\mathsf{sk} = \tau$ and a message $m \in \{0,1\}^*$, the signer generates a signature σ on m as follows:

i. Picks a random commitment isogeny $\psi : E_0 \to E_1$.

ii. Computes $s = \mathcal{H}_1(j(E_1), m)$ and sets the challenge isogeny $\Phi_{D_c}(E_1, s) = \varphi$ where $\varphi : E_1 \to E_2$ is a non-backtracking isogeny of degree D_c.

iii. Computes $\bar{I}_\tau$, I_τ, I_ψ and I_φ corresponding to $\hat{\tau}$, τ, ψ and φ respectively.

iv. The signer having the knowledge of $\mathcal{O} = \mathsf{End}(E_A)$ through $\mathsf{sk} = \tau$ and $\mathcal{O}_2 = \mathsf{End}(E_2)$ through $\varphi \circ \psi : E_0 \to E_2$, executes the algorithm $\mathsf{SigningKLPT_{2^e}}(I_\tau, I)$ described in Sect. 2.3 on input the $(\mathcal{O}_0, \mathcal{O})$-ideal I_τ and the left $\mathcal{O}$-ideal $I = I_\varphi I_\psi \bar{I}_\tau$ to obtain a $(\mathcal{O}, \mathcal{O}_2)$-ideal $J \sim I$ of norm $D = 2^e$.

v. Constructs a cyclic isogeny $\eta : E_A \to E_2$ of degree D corresponding to the ideal J such that $\hat{\varphi} \circ \eta$ is cyclic. The signature is the pair $\sigma = (E_1, \eta)$.

$\mathsf{SQISign.Verify(pp_{sgn}, pk}, m, \sigma) \to \mathsf{Valid/Invalid}$: The verifier verifies the validity of the signature $\sigma = (E_1, \eta)$ on the message m as follows:

i. Computes $s = \mathcal{H}_1(j(E_1), m)$ and then recovers the isogeny $\Phi_{D_c}(E_1, s) = \varphi$.

ii. Checks if η is an isogeny of degree D from E_A to E_2 and that $\hat{\varphi} \circ \eta : E_A \to E_1$ is cyclic.

iii. If all the checks succeed returns Valid, otherwise returns $\mathsf{Invalid}$.

Correctness. It follows from the correctness of $\mathsf{SigningKLPT}$ algorithm.

3   Security Aspect of SQISign

To prove the security of the signature scheme $\mathsf{SQISign}$, the authors resort to a computational assumption that formalises the idea that the isogeny η corresponding to the ideal J returned by the algorithm $\mathsf{SigningKLPT}$ is indistinguishable from a random isogeny of the same degree. Before defining the problem formally, we analyze the structure of η.

Lemma 3.01 [6]. *Consider the ideal L and element $\beta \in L$ computed as in steps 3, 9 respectively of the algorithm* SigningKLPT *described in Sect. 2.3. The isogeny η corresponding to the output J of* SigningKLPT *algorithm is equal to $\eta = [\tau]_* \iota$ where ι is an isogeny of degree ℓ^e satisfying $\beta = \hat{\iota} \circ \varphi_L$.*

We recall the following notations before defining the (computationally) indistinguishable problem underlying the security of SQISign.

$\mathcal{U}_{L,N_\tau}$: For a given ideal L of norm N, $\mathcal{U}_{L,N_\tau}$ denotes the set of all isogenies ι computed in Lemma 3.01 from elements $\beta = \gamma\mu \in L$ where γ is any possible output of the algorithm FullRepresentInteger$_{\mathcal{O}_0}$ and μ is computed by algorithm FullStrongApproximation in Step 8 of SigningKLPT.

$\mathcal{P}_{N_\tau}$: We define $\mathcal{P}_{N_\tau} = \bigcup_{\mathcal{C} \in \text{Cl}(\mathcal{O})} \mathcal{U}_{\mathcal{C},N_\tau}$ where we write $\mathcal{U}_{\mathcal{C},N_\tau}$ for $\mathcal{U}_{L,N_\tau}$ where $L \leftarrow$ EquivalentPrimeIdeal$(\mathcal{C})$ for an equivalence class $\mathcal{C}$ in the ideal class group $\text{Cl}(\mathcal{O}_0)$ of $\mathcal{O}_0$.

$\text{Iso}_{D,j(E)}$: Denotes the set of cyclic isogenies of degree D whose domain is a curve inside the isomorphism class of E.

$[\tau]_*\mathcal{P}$: Denotes the subset $\{[\tau]_*\varphi \mid \varphi \in \mathcal{P}\}$ of $\text{Iso}_{D,j(E_0)}$ where $\mathcal{P}$ is a subset of $\text{Iso}_{D,j(E)}$ and $\tau : E \to E_0$ is an isogeny with $\gcd(\deg(\tau), D) = 1$.

$\mathcal{K}$: a probability distribution on the set of cyclic isogenies whose domain is E_0, representing the distribution of SQISign private keys.

Definition 3.02 [6]. *Let p be a prime and D be a smooth integer. Let $\tau : E_0 \to E_A$ be a random isogeny drawn from $\mathcal{K}$ and let N_τ be its degree. Let* Oracle$_\tau$ *be an oracle sampling random elements in $[\tau]_*\mathcal{P}_{N_\tau}$. Let η be an isogeny of degree D whose domain curve is E. Given $p, D, \mathcal{K}, E_A, \eta$ and a polynomial number of queries to* Oracle$_\tau$, *the Real or Random Isogeny problem is to determine where*

1. *whether η is uniformly random in $\text{Iso}_{D,j(E_A)}$*
2. *or η is uniformly random in $[\tau]_*\mathcal{P}_{N_\tau}$.*

Informally speaking, the problem states that the ideals output by the algorithm SigningKLPT are indistinguishable from uniformly random ideals of the same norm. The hardness assumption underlying the security of SQISign is the Real or Random Isogeny problem defined in Definition 3.02.

Theorem 3.03 [6]. *The scheme* SQISign *is* UF-CMA *secure under the hardness of Real or Random Isogeny Problem defined in Definition 3.02.*

3.1   Identity-Based Signature

Definition 3.11. An *identity-based signature* is a tuple IBS = (Setup, Extract, Sign, Verify) of four PPT algorithms with the following syntax:

IBS.Setup$(1^\lambda) \to (\text{pp}_{\text{ibs}}, \text{msk})$: The key generation centre (KGC) on input 1^λ generates a public parameter pp_{ibs} and a master secret key msk.

IBS.Extract(pp_{ibs}, msk, id) $\to$ usk_{id}: The KGC runs this key extract algorithm on input the public parameter pp_{ibs}, the master secret key msk and user identity id. It generates the user secret key usk_{id} for the given identity id.

IBS.Sign(pp_{ibs}, usk_{id}, m) $\to$ σ: Taking input the public parameter pp_{ibs}, user secret key usk_{id} and a message m, the signer executes this randomized algorithm and outputs a signature σ on the message m.

IBS.Verify(pp_{ibs}, id, m, σ) $\to$ Valid/Invalid: The verifier runs this deterministic algorithm on input the public parameter pp_{ibs}, an identity id, a message m and a signature σ to verify the validity of the signature σ.

Correctness. For all $(pp_{ibs}, msk) \leftarrow$ IBS.Setup(1^λ), all $usk_{id} \leftarrow$ IBS.Extract(pp_{ibs}, msk, id), all m and all id, it holds that

$$\text{IBS.Verify}(pp_{ibs}, id, m, \text{IBS.Sign}(pp_{ibs}, usk_{id}, m)) \to \text{Valid}.$$

Definition 3.12. An IBS scheme is said to be secure against *unforgeability under chosen identity and chosen message attacks* (UF-IBS-CMA) if for all PPT adversary $\mathcal{A}$, there exists a negligible function ϵ such that

$$\text{Adv}_{IBS,\mathcal{A}}^{UF\text{-}IBS\text{-}CMA}(\lambda) = \Pr[\mathcal{A} \text{ wins in } \text{Exp}_{IBS,\mathcal{A}}^{UF\text{-}IBS\text{-}CMA}(\lambda)] < \epsilon$$

where the experiment $\text{Exp}_{IBS,\mathcal{A}}^{UF\text{-}IBS\text{-}CMA}(\lambda)$ that formalizes the unforgeability game is described in Fig. 3.

Setup: The challenger $\mathcal{C}$ takes input the security parameter 1^λ and generate $(pp_{ibs}, msk) \leftarrow$ IBS.Setup(1^λ). It gives the public parameter pp_{ibs} to $\mathcal{A}$ while keeps the master secret key msk secret to itself. Also it maintains three lists Klist, Clist and Mlist and initializes each to $\emptyset$.

Query Phase: $\mathcal{C}$ responds to polynomially many adaptive queries made by $\mathcal{A}$ as follows:
  – *Oracle* $\mathcal{O}_{Extract}(\cdot)$: On receiving a query on a user identity id from $\mathcal{A}$, $\mathcal{C}$ checks whether (id, usk_{id}) $\in$ Klist. If so, it returns usk_{id} and appends id to Clist. Otherwise, it generates $usk_{id} \leftarrow$ IBS.Extract(pp_{ibs}, msk, id), returns usk_{id} and appends (id, usk_{id}) to Klist and id to Clist.
  – *Oracle* $\mathcal{O}_{Sign}(\cdot)$: On receiving a query on a message m and a user identity id from $\mathcal{A}$, $\mathcal{C}$ computes usk_{id} as in the extraction query, except for appending identity id to Clist. It then computes a signature $\sigma \leftarrow$ IBS.Sign(pp_{ibs}, usk_{id}, m) and appends (m, id, σ) to Mlist.

Forgery: The adversary $\mathcal{A}$ eventually outputs a message m^*, user identity id^* and a forge signature σ^*. The adversary $\mathcal{A}$ wins the game if IBS.Verify(pp_{ibs}, id^*, m^*, σ^*) $\to$ Valid with the restriction that $id^* \notin$ Clist and $(m^*, id^*, \cdot) \notin$ Mlist.

Fig. 3. $\text{Exp}_{IBS,\mathcal{A}}^{UF\text{-}IBS\text{-}CMA}(\lambda)$: Unforgeability under chosen identity and chosen message attacks

3.2   Puncturable Signature Scheme

Definition 3.21. A *puncturable signature* is a tuple PS = (PS.Setup, PS.Puncture, PS.Sign, PS.Verify) of PPT algorithms associated with a message space $\mathcal{M}$ and prefix space $\mathcal{P}$ that satisfy the following requirements. Note that, if $x \in \mathcal{P}$, then there exists some $m \in M$ with prefix x and every message m has a unique prefix.

PS.Setup(1^λ) $\to$ (pp_{ps}, sk_0): On input 1^λ, the signer executes this algorithm to generate the public parameter pk_{ps} and initial secret key sk_0.

PS.Puncture(sk, x') → sk′: The signer takes as input its secret key sk and a prefix $x' \in \mathcal{P}$ and runs this randomized algorithm to output an updated secret key sk′. We say the prefix x' has been punctured and refer the updated secret key sk′ as a punctured secret key.

PS.Sign($\mathsf{pp_{ps}}$, sk, m) → Σ/ ⊥: Taking input $\mathsf{pp_{ps}}$, secret key sk and a message $m \in \mathcal{M}$, the signer runs this randomized algorithm to generate a signature Σ if the prefix $x' \in \mathcal{P}$ has not been punctured. Otherwise, it returns ⊥.

PS.Verify($\mathsf{pp_{ps}}$, m, Σ) → Valid/Invalid: This is a deterministic algorithm that takes as input the public parameter $\mathsf{pp_{ps}}$, a message m and a signature Σ. It outputs Valid if Σ is a valid signature on m and Invalid otherwise.

Correctness. The scheme PS is correct if it satisfies the following conditions:

i. For any message $m \in \mathcal{M}$, any prefix $x' \in \mathcal{P}$ and any $(\mathsf{pp_{ps}}, \mathsf{sk_0}) \leftarrow$ PS.Setup(1^λ), it holds that PS.Verify($\mathsf{pp_{ps}}$, m, PS.Sign($\mathsf{pp_{ps}}$, $\mathsf{sk_0}$, m)) → Valid where $\mathsf{sk_0}$ is the initial non-punctured secret key.

ii. For any message $m \in \mathcal{M}$ with prefix $x' \in \mathcal{P}$ which has been punctured with secret key sk, it holds that PS.Verify($\mathsf{pp_{ps}}$, m, PS.Sign($\mathsf{pp_{ps}}$, sk′, m)) → Invalid where sk′ ← PS.Puncture(sk, x') is the punctured secret key corresponding to the prefix x'.

iii. For any message $m \in \mathcal{M}$ with prefix $x \in \mathcal{P}$ which has not been punctured, we have PS.Verify($\mathsf{pp_{ps}}$, m, PS.Sign($\mathsf{pp_{ps}}$, sk′, m)) → Valid where sk′ ← PS.Puncture(sk, x') is the punctured secret key corresponding to the prefix $x' \neq x$ of a message m' with $m' \neq m$.

Definition 3.22. A puncturable signature scheme PS is secure against *existential unforgeability under chosen-message attacks with adaptive puncturing* (UF-CMA-AP) if for all PPT adversary $\mathcal{A}$, there exists a negligible function ϵ such that

$$\mathsf{Adv}^{\mathsf{UF\text{-}CMA\text{-}AP}}_{\mathsf{PS}, \mathcal{A}}(\lambda) = \Pr[\mathcal{A} \text{ wins in } \mathsf{Exp}^{\mathsf{UF\text{-}CMA\text{-}AP}}_{\mathsf{PS}, \mathcal{A}}(\lambda)] < \epsilon$$

where the experiment $\mathsf{Exp}^{\mathsf{UF\text{-}CMA\text{-}AP}}_{\mathsf{PS}, \mathcal{A}}(\lambda)$ is described in Fig. 4.

Setup: The challenger $\mathcal{C}$ takes input the security parameter 1^λ and generates $(\mathsf{pp_{ps}}, \mathsf{sk_0}) \leftarrow$ PS.Setup(1^λ). It forwards $\mathsf{pp_{ps}}$ to $\mathcal{A}$ while keeps sk secret to itself. It also maintains the set $\mathcal{Q}_{\mathsf{sig}}$ for signed messages and the set $\mathcal{Q}_{\mathsf{pun}}$ for punctured prefixes and initializes each to $\emptyset$.
Query Phase: The adversary $\mathcal{A}$ issues polynomially many adaptive queries to the oracles $\mathcal{O}_{\mathsf{Puncture}}(\mathsf{sk}, \cdot)$ and $\mathcal{O}_{\mathsf{Sign}}(\mathsf{pp_{ps}}, \mathsf{sk}, \cdot)$ as follows:
  – $\mathcal{O}_{\mathsf{Puncture}}(\mathsf{sk}, \cdot)$: Upon receiving a query on prefix x', the challenger $\mathcal{C}$ generates a punctured secret key sk′ ← Puncture(sk, x') and updates $\mathcal{Q}_{\mathsf{pun}} \leftarrow \mathcal{Q}_{\mathsf{pun}} \cup \{x'\}$.
  – $\mathcal{O}_{\mathsf{Sgn}}(\mathsf{sk}, \cdot)$: On receiving a signature query on a message m with prefix $x' \in \mathcal{P}$, the challenger $\mathcal{C}$ checks if $x' \in \mathcal{Q}_{\mathsf{pun}}$. If the check succeeds, it returns ⊥. Otherwise, it computes the signature $\Sigma \leftarrow$ PS.Sign($\mathsf{pp_{ps}}$, sk, m) on the message m and updates $\mathcal{Q}_{\mathsf{sig}} \leftarrow \mathcal{Q}_{\mathsf{sig}} \cup \{m\}$. It returns the computed signature Σ to the adversary $\mathcal{A}$.
Challenge: The adversary $\mathcal{A}$ sends a target prefix x^* to the challenger $\mathcal{C}$ and issues additional puncture and signature queries as described in the Query phase.
Corruption Query: $\mathcal{C}$ returns the current secret key sk* if $x^* \in \mathcal{Q}_{\mathsf{pun}}$ and ⊥ otherwise.
Forgery: The adversary $\mathcal{A}$ eventually submits a forgery (m^*, Σ^*, x^*) where x^* is the prefix of m^*. $\mathcal{A}$ wins the game if $m^* \notin \mathcal{Q}_{\mathsf{sig}}$, $x^* \in \mathcal{Q}_{\mathsf{pun}}$ and Valid ← PS.Verify($\mathsf{pp_{ps}}$, m^*, Σ^*).

Fig. 4. $\mathsf{Exp}^{\mathsf{UF\text{-}CMA\text{-}AP}}_{\mathsf{PS}, \mathcal{A}}(\lambda)$: Existential unforgeability under chosen-message attacks with adaptive puncturing

4   Our Identity-Based Signature from SQISign

In this section, we propose our identity-based signature from SQISign. We refer to our scheme as *Short Quaternion and Isogeny Identity-based Signatures* (SQIIBS).

SQIIBS.Setup(1^λ) $\to$ (pp_{ibs}, msk): A KGC on input the security parameter 1^λ generates the public parameter pp_{ibs} and a master secret key msk as follows:

i. Same as the algorithm SQISign.Setup described in Sect. 2.5. Additionally, it picks a random isogeny $\tau_1 : E_0 \to E_A^{(1)}$.

ii. Publishes the public parameter $pp_{ibs} = (p, E_0, D_c, D, \mathcal{H}_1, \Phi_{D_c}, E_A^{(1)})$ and keeps the master secret key msk $= \tau_1$ secret to itself.

SQIIBS.Extract(pp_{ibs}, msk, id) $\to$ usk_{id}: On input the public parameter $pp_{ibs} = (p, E_0, D_c, D, \mathcal{H}_1, \Phi_{D_c}, E_A^{(1)})$, master secret key msk $= \tau_1$ and an identity id, the KGC executes this algorithm to generate the user secret key usk_{id} as follows:

i. Picks a random isogeny $\tau_2 : E_0 \to E_A^{(2)}$.

ii. Selects a random commitment isogeny $\psi_1 : E_0 \to E_1^{(1)}$.

iii. Computes $s_1 = \mathcal{H}_1(j(E_1^{(1)}), \text{bin}(j(E_A^{(2)})))\|\text{id})$ and sets $\Phi_{D_c}(E_1^{(1)}, s_1) = \varphi_1$ where $\varphi_1 : E_1^{(1)} \to E_2^{(1)}$ is a non-backtracking isogeny of degree D_c.

iv. Computes the ideals $\bar{I}_{\tau_1}$, I_{τ_1}, I_{ψ_1} and I_{φ_1} corresponding to the isogenies $\hat{\tau}_1$, τ_1, ψ_1 and φ_1 respectively.

v. The KGC having the knowledge of $\mathcal{O}^{(1)} = \text{End}(E_A^{(1)})$ through τ_1 and $\mathcal{O}_2^{(1)} = \text{End}(E_2^{(1)})$ through $\varphi_1 \circ \psi_1 : E_0 \to E_2^{(1)}$, executes the SigningKLPT$_{2^e}(I_{\tau_1}, I_1)$ algorithm (Sect. 2.3) on input the $(\mathcal{O}_0, \mathcal{O}^{(1)})$-ideal I_{τ_1} and a left $\mathcal{O}^{(1)}$-ideal $I_1 = I_{\varphi_1} I_{\psi_1} \bar{I}_{\tau_1}$ to obtain a $(\mathcal{O}^{(1)}, \mathcal{O}_2^{(1)})$-ideal $J_1 \sim I_1$ of norm $D = 2^e$.

vi. Constructs the isogeny $\eta_1 : E_A^{(1)} \to E_2^{(1)}$ of degree D corresponding to the ideal J_1 such that $\hat{\varphi}_1 \circ \eta_1 : E_A^{(1)} \to E_1^{(1)}$ is cyclic and sets $\text{cert}_{id} = (E_1^{(1)}, \eta_1)$.

vii. Issues the user secret key $usk_{id} = (\tau_2, \text{cert}_{id} = (E_1^{(1)}, \eta_1))$.

SQIIBS.Sign(pp_{ibs}, usk_{id}, m) $\to \sigma$: On input $pp_{ibs} = (p, E_0, D_c, D, \mathcal{H}_1, \Phi_{D_c}, E_A^{(1)})$, user secret key $usk_{id} = (\tau_2, \text{cert}_{id})$ and a message $m \in \{0, 1\}^*$, the signer generates a signature σ on m as follows:

i. Picks a random commitment isogeny $\psi_2 : E_0 \to E_1^{(2)}$.

ii. Computes $s_2 = \mathcal{H}_1(j(E_1^{(2)}), m)$ and sets the challenge isogeny $\Phi_{D_c}(E_1^{(2)}, s_2) = \varphi_2$ where $\varphi_2 : E_1^{(2)} \to E_2^{(2)}$ is a non-backtracking isogeny of degree D_c.

iii. Computes the ideal $\bar{I}_{\tau_2}$, I_{τ_2}, I_{ψ_2} and I_{φ_2} corresponding to the isogenies $\hat{\tau}_2$, τ_2, ψ_2 and φ_2 respectively.

iv. The signer having the knowledge of $\mathcal{O}^{(2)} = \text{End}(E_A^{(2)})$ through τ_2 and $\mathcal{O}_2^{(2)} = \text{End}(E_2^{(2)})$ through $\varphi_2 \circ \psi_2$, executes the algorithm SigningKLPT$_{2^e}(I_{\tau_2}, I_2)$ described in Sect. 2.3 on input the $(\mathcal{O}_0, \mathcal{O}^{(2)})$-ideal I_{τ_2} and a left $\mathcal{O}^{(2)}$-ideal $I_2 = I_{\varphi_2} I_{\psi_2} \bar{I}_{\tau_2}$ to obtain a $(\mathcal{O}^{(2)}, \mathcal{O}_2^{(2)})$-ideal $J_2 \sim I_2$ of norm D.

v. Constructs the isogeny $\eta_2 : E_A^{(2)} \to E_2^{(2)}$ of degree D corresponding to the ideal J_2 such that $\hat{\varphi}_2 \circ \eta_2 : E_A^{(2)} \to E_1^2$ is cyclic and sets $\bar{\sigma} = (E_1^{(2)}, \eta_2)$.

vi. Extracts $\mathsf{cert}_{\mathsf{id}}$ from $\mathsf{usk}_{\mathsf{id}}$ and sets the signature $\sigma = (\bar{\sigma}, E_A^{(2)}, \mathsf{cert}_{\mathsf{id}})$.

$\mathsf{SQIIBS.Verify}(\mathsf{pp}_{\mathsf{ibs}}, \mathsf{id}, m, \sigma) \to \mathsf{Valid/Invalid}$: The verifier employing $\mathsf{pp}_{\mathsf{ibs}} = (p, E_0, D_c, D, \mathcal{H}_1, \Phi_{D_c}, E_A^{(1)})$ verifies the validity of signature $\sigma = (\bar{\sigma}, E_A^{(2)}, \mathsf{cert}_{\mathsf{id}})$ on $m \in \{0, 1\}^*$ as follows:

i. Parses $\sigma = (\bar{\sigma} = (E_1^{(2)}, \eta_2), E_A^{(2)}, \mathsf{cert}_{\mathsf{id}} = (E_1^{(1)}, \eta_1))$.

ii. Computes $s_1 = \mathcal{H}_1(j(E_1^{(1)}), \mathsf{bin}(j(E_A^{(2)}))) \| \mathsf{id}$ and $s_2 = \mathcal{H}_1(j(E_1^{(2)}), m)$.

iii. Recovers the isogenies $\Phi_{D_c}(E_1^{(1)}, s_1) = \varphi_1$ and $\Phi_{D_c}(E_1^{(2)}, s_2) = \varphi_2$.

iv. Checks if η_1 is an isogeny of degree D from $E_A^{(1)}$ to $E_2^{(1)}$ and that $\hat{\varphi}_1 \circ \eta_1 : E_A^{(1)} \to E_1^{(1)}$ is cyclic.

v. Checks if η_2 is an isogeny of degree D from $E_A^{(2)}$ to $E_2^{(2)}$ and that $\hat{\varphi}_2 \circ \eta_2 : E_A^{(2)} \to E_1^{(2)}$ is cyclic.

vi. If all the checks succeed returns Valid, otherwise returns $\mathsf{Invalid}$.

Correctness. The correctness of our proposed scheme SQIIBS follows immediately from the correctness of $\mathsf{SQISign}$ signature described in Sect. 2.5.

4.1 Efficiency

A theoretical comparison of our scheme SQIIBS with the existing works on IBS from isogenies is provided in Table 1 and Table 2. We compare our scheme with the CSIDH-based IBS scheme by Peng et al. [16] as well as the recently proposed IBS scheme by Shaw et al. [17]. Table 2 depicts that the secret key size and signature size of the existing IBS scheme grows with the value of S_1. The exponential size of $S_1 = 2^{n_1-1}$ leads to large key and signatures, making them impractical for real-life applications. The user secret key in our scheme comprises of an elliptic curve over the field $\mathbb{F}_{p^2}$ and two isogenies of degree 2^e. The elliptic curve is represented by its j-invariant and thus it is of size $2 \log p$. As discussed in [6], an isogeny of degree 2^e can be compressed to e bits where $e = \frac{15}{4} \log p$. Thus the user secret key is of size $2 \log p + 2(\frac{15}{4}) \log p = 2 \log p + \frac{15}{2} \log p$. The signature in our scheme comprises of three elliptic curves over $\mathbb{F}_{p^2}$ and two isogenies of degree 2^e. Thus, the signature in our scheme is of size $3(2 \log p) + 2(\frac{15}{4}) \log p = 6 \log p + \frac{15}{2} \log p$. Our scheme enjoys improved efficiency in terms of key and signature sizes which thereby reduces the storage and communication cost.

4.2 Security Analysis

Theorem 4.21. *Our proposed scheme* SQIIBS *is* UF-IBS-CMA *secure as the underlying signature scheme* $\mathsf{SQISign}$ *is* UF-CMA *secure.*

Table 1. Comparison of our SQIIBS with existing IBS schemes

Scheme	Security Analysis	Rejection Sampling	Security
Peng et al.'s IBS [16]	✗	✓	CSIDH
Shaw et al.'s IBS [17]	✓	✗	CSI-FiSh
Our Work	✓	✗	SQISign

CSIDH = Commutative Supersingular Isogeny Diffie-Hellman, CSI-FiSh = Commutative Supersingular Isogeny based Fiat-Shamir signature, SQISign = Short Quaternion and Isogeny Signature.

Table 2. Comparison of secret and signature size of our SQIIBS with existing IBS schemes from isogenies

Scheme	$|\mathsf{usk}_{id}|$	$|\sigma|$
Peng et al.'s IBS [16]	$nT_1S_1\log(2I_1+1)+T_1S_1\log p$	$T_1T_2[n\log(2I_2+1)+\log S_1]+T_1S_1\log p$
Shaw et al.'s IBS [17]	$T_1S_1[\log S_0+\log N]$	$T_1T_2[\log N+\log S_1]+T_1S_1\log p$
Our Work	$2\log p+\frac{15}{2}\log p$	$6\log p+\frac{15}{2}\log p$

Here $n \in \mathbb{N}$, p is a prime, $I_0, I_1 = \delta_0 I_0, I_2 = \delta_1 I_1, T_1, T_2, S_0 = 2^{\eta_0}-1$ and $S_1 = 2^{\eta_1}-1$ are integers with $T_1 < S_0$ and $T_2 < S_1$. N is the size of ideal class group for CSIDH-512 parameter set.

Proof. Let us assume that there exists an adversary $\mathcal{A}$ that wins the UF-IBS-CMA game with non-negligible probability. At the end of the game, $\mathcal{A}$ outputs a valid forgery (m^*, id^*, σ^*) where $\sigma^* = (\bar{\sigma}^*, (E_A^{(2)})^*, \mathsf{cert}_{id^*})$. We employ the adversary $\mathcal{A}$ as a subroutine to design an adversary $\mathcal{B}$ that breaks the UF-CMA security of the signature scheme SQISign. To complete the security reduction, $\mathcal{B}$ simulating the IBS security game with $\mathcal{A}$ must embed the public key given to $\mathcal{B}$ by its UF-CMA challenger $\mathcal{C}$ into some part of the "target" which $\mathcal{A}$ takes as a target of forgery. There are two attack points in our construction. The adversary $\mathcal{A}$ may either take the public parameter pp_{ibs} provided by $\mathcal{B}$ or it reuses the components cert_{id^*} and $(E_A^{(2)})^*$ of the answer of the signing oracle on id^* and message $m \neq m^*$ for its forgery. We denote the later event as "REUSE". Then the advantage of $\mathcal{A}$ is given by $\Pr[\mathsf{Success}] = \Pr[\mathsf{Success}|\neg\mathsf{REUSE}] + \Pr[\mathsf{Success}|\mathsf{REUSE}]$ where $\mathsf{Success}$ is the event that $\mathcal{A}$ wins in $\mathsf{Exp}_{\mathsf{IBS},\mathcal{A}}^{\mathsf{UF\text{-}IBS\text{-}CMA}}(\lambda)$. For each of the two cases $\neg\mathsf{REUSE}$ and REUSE, we give reductions as follows:

Case 1 $\Pr[\mathsf{Success}|\neg\mathsf{REUSE}]$: We describe below how the UF-CMA adversary $\mathcal{B}$ plays the role of the challenger and simulates the experiment $\mathsf{Exp}_{\mathsf{IBS},\mathcal{A}}^{\mathsf{UF\text{-}IBS\text{-}CMA}}(\lambda)$.

Setup: The UF-CMA challenger $\mathcal{C}$ generates the public parameter $\mathsf{pp}_{\mathsf{sgn}} = (p, E_0, D_c, D, \mathcal{H}_1, \Phi_{D_c})$ by executing the algorithm SQISign.Setup(1^λ) and computes a secret-public key pair $(\mathsf{sk}, \mathsf{pk}) \leftarrow$ SQISign.KeyGen$(\mathsf{pp}_{\mathsf{sgn}})$ where $\mathsf{sk} = \tau_1$ and $\mathsf{pk} = E_A^{(1)}$ and forwards $\mathsf{pp}_{\mathsf{sgn}}$ and pk to the adversary $\mathcal{B}$. It keeps sk secret to itself. The challenger $\mathcal{C}$ also maintains a list SList and initializes SList to $\emptyset$. Upon receiving $\mathsf{pp}_{\mathsf{sgn}} = (p, E_0, D_c, D, \mathcal{H}_1, \Phi_{D_c})$ and $\mathsf{pk} = E_A^{(1)}$

from $\mathcal{C}$, $\mathcal{B}$ sets $\mathsf{pp}_{\mathsf{ibs}} = (p, E_0, D_c, D, \mathcal{H}_1, \Phi_{D_c}, E_A^{(1)})$ and sends it to $\mathcal{A}$. It also initializes the lists Klist, Clist, Mlist to $\emptyset$.

Query Phase: The adversary $\mathcal{B}$ responds to polynomially many adaptive queries made by $\mathcal{A}$ to the oracles $\mathcal{O}_{\mathsf{Extract}}$ and $\mathcal{O}_{\mathsf{Sign}}$ as follows:

- *Oracle $\mathcal{O}_{\mathsf{Extract}}(\cdot)$*: On receiving a query on a user identity id from $\mathcal{A}$, $\mathcal{B}$ checks whether $(\mathsf{id}, \mathsf{usk}_{\mathsf{id}}) \in$ Klist. If there exists such a pair in Klist, it returns $\mathsf{usk}_{\mathsf{id}}$ to $\mathcal{A}$ and appends id to CList. If $(\mathsf{id}, \mathsf{usk}_{\mathsf{id}}) \notin$ Klist, $\mathcal{B}$ picks a random isogeny $\tau_2 : E_0 \to E_A^{(2)}$ and queries its signing oracle $\mathcal{O}_{\mathsf{Sign}}(\mathsf{sk} = \tau_1, \cdot)$ simulated by $\mathcal{C}$ on the message $\mathsf{bin}(j(E_A^{(2)}))\|\mathsf{id}$. Upon receiving the signature $\mathsf{cert}_{\mathsf{id}} = (E_1^{(1)}, \eta_1)$ from $\mathcal{C}$, the adversary $\mathcal{B}$ sets $\mathsf{usk}_{\mathsf{id}} = (\tau_2, \mathsf{cert}_{\mathsf{id}})$ and returns it to $\mathcal{A}$. The adversary $\mathcal{B}$ also appends $(\mathsf{id}, \mathsf{usk}_{\mathsf{id}})$ to Klist and id to Clist. The challenger $\mathcal{C}$ appends $\mathsf{bin}(j(E_A^{(2)}))\|\mathsf{id}$ in Slist.

- *Oracle $\mathcal{O}_{\mathsf{Sign}}(\cdot)$*: On receiving a query on a message $m \in \{0,1\}^*$ and a user identity id from $\mathcal{A}$, $\mathcal{B}$ retrieves the pair $(\mathsf{id}, \mathsf{usk}_{\mathsf{id}})$ from Klist where $\mathsf{usk}_{\mathsf{id}} = (\tau_2, \mathsf{cert}_{\mathsf{id}})$ is the user secret key corresponding to id. If $(\mathsf{id}, \mathsf{usk}_{\mathsf{id}}) \notin$ Klist, $\mathcal{B}$ picks a random isogeny $\tau_2 : E_0 \to E_A^{(2)}$ and queries its signing oracle $\mathcal{O}_{\mathsf{S}}(\mathsf{sk} = \tau_1, \cdot)$ on the message $\mathsf{bin}(j(E_A^{(2)}))\|\mathsf{id}$. Upon receiving the signature $\mathsf{cert}_{\mathsf{id}} = (E_1^{(1)}, \eta_1)$ under $\mathsf{sk} = \tau_1$ from $\mathcal{C}$, $\mathcal{B}$ sets $\mathsf{usk}_{\mathsf{id}} = (\tau_2, \mathsf{cert}_{\mathsf{id}})$. It then executes $\bar{\sigma} = (E_1^{(2)}, \eta_2) \leftarrow \mathsf{SQISign.Sign}(\mathsf{pp}_{\mathsf{sgn}}, \tau_2, m)$, sets the signature $\sigma = (\bar{\sigma}, E_A^{(2)}, \mathsf{cert}_{\mathsf{id}})$ and sends it to $\mathcal{A}$. It also appends (m, id, σ) to Mlist.

Forgery: The adversary $\mathcal{A}$ eventually outputs a message m^*, user identity id^* and a forge signature σ^* where $\sigma^* = (\bar{\sigma}^*, (E_A^{(2)})^*, \mathsf{cert}_{\mathsf{id}^*})$. If $\mathcal{A}$ wins the UF-IBS-CMA game with non-negligible probability then $(m^*, \mathsf{id}^*, \sigma^*)$ must be a valid forgery. Thus, $\mathsf{IBS.Verify}(\mathsf{pp}_{\mathsf{ibs}}, \mathsf{id}^*, m^*, \sigma^*) \to$ Valid where $\mathsf{id}^* \notin$ Clist and $(m^*, \mathsf{id}^*, \cdot) \notin$ Mlist. The adversary $\mathcal{B}$ submits $\mathsf{bin}(j((E_A^{(2)})^*))\|\mathsf{id}^*, \mathsf{cert}_{\mathsf{id}^*}$ as a forgery to its own challenger $\mathcal{C}$.

The event ¬REUSE means $(\mathsf{id}^*, \mathsf{usk}_{\mathsf{id}^*}) \notin$ Klist where $\mathsf{usk}_{\mathsf{id}^*} = (\tau_2^*, \mathsf{cert}_{\mathsf{id}^*})$. This implies that $(\mathsf{bin}(j((E_A^{(2)})^*))\|\mathsf{id}^* \notin$ Slist . Hence, the adversary $\mathcal{B}$ has output the valid forgery $(\mathsf{bin}(j((E_A^{(2)})^*))\|\mathsf{id}^*, \mathsf{cert}_{\mathsf{id}}^*)$ such that $\mathsf{SQISign.Veriy}(\mathsf{pp}_{\mathsf{sgn}}, E_A^{(1)}, \mathsf{bin}(j((E_A^{(2)})^*))\|\mathsf{id}^*, \mathsf{cert}_{\mathsf{id}}^*) \to$ Valid. From the security of SQISign, it follows that $\Pr[\mathsf{Success}|\neg\mathsf{REUSE}]$ is negligible.

Case 2 $\Pr[\mathsf{Success}|\mathsf{REUSE}]$: In this case the adversary $\mathcal{A}$ reuses the components $\mathsf{cert}_{\mathsf{id}^*}$ and $(E_A^{(2)})^*$ of the answer of the signing oracle query on identity id^* and message $m \neq m^*$ for its forgery.

Setup: The UF-CMA challenger $\mathcal{C}$ generates the public parameter $\mathsf{pp}_{\mathsf{sgn}} = (p, E_0, D_c, D, \mathcal{H}_1, \Phi_{D_c})$ by executing the algorithm $\mathsf{SQISign.Setup}(1^\lambda)$ as in **Case 1** and computes a secret-public key pair $(\mathsf{sk}, \mathsf{pk}) \leftarrow \mathsf{SQISign.KeyGen}(\mathsf{pp}_{\mathsf{sgn}})$ where $\mathsf{sk} = \tau_2$ and $\mathsf{pk} = E_A^{(2)}$ and forwards

pp_{sgn} and pk to the adversary $\mathcal{B}$. It keeps sk secret to itself. The challenger $\mathcal{C}$ maintains a list SList and initializes SList to $\emptyset$. Upon receiving $pp_{sgn} = (p, E_0, D_c, D, \mathcal{H}_1, \Phi_{D_c})$ and $pk = E_A^{(2)}$ from the challenger $\mathcal{C}$, the adversary $\mathcal{B}$ picks a random isogeny $\tau_1 : E_0 \to E_A^{(1)}$, sets $pp_{ibs} = (p, E_0, D_c, D, \mathcal{H}_1, \Phi_{D_c}, E_A^{(1)})$, $msk = \tau_1$ and sends pp_{ibs} to $\mathcal{A}$. It initializes the lists Klist, Clist, Mlist to $\emptyset$ and chooses $r \leftarrow \{1, 2, \ldots, q(\lambda)\}$ where $q(\lambda)$ is the maximum number of queries by $\mathcal{A}$.

Query Phase: The adversary $\mathcal{B}$ responds to polynomially many adaptive queries to the oracles $\mathcal{O}_{Extract}$ and $\mathcal{O}_{Sign}$ made by $\mathcal{A}$. Let id' be the identity for which the rth signing query of $\mathcal{A}$ was made.

- *Oracle* $\mathcal{O}_{Extract}(\cdot)$: If $\mathcal{A}$ ever makes an extract query for the identity id', the experiment is aborted. On receiving a query on a user identity $id \neq id'$ from $\mathcal{A}$, $\mathcal{B}$ checks whether $(id, usk_{id}) \in$ Klist. If there exists such a pair in Klist, it returns usk_{id} and appends id to CList. If $(id, usk_{id}) \notin$ Klist, it picks a random isogeny $\bar{\tau}_2 : E_0 \to \overline{E}_A^{(2)}$ and uses $msk = \tau_1$ to compute $\overline{cert}_{id} = (\overline{E}_1^{(1)}, \bar{\eta}_1) \leftarrow$ SQISign.Sign$(pp_{sgn}, \tau_1, bin(j(\overline{E}_A^{(2)}))||id)$. It then sets $usk_{id} = (\bar{\tau}_2, \overline{cert}_{id})$ and returns it to $\mathcal{A}$. It appends (id, usk_{id}) to Klist and id to Clist.

- *Oracle* $\mathcal{O}_{Sign}(\cdot)$: The adversary $\mathcal{B}$ receives signing queries on pairs (m, id) from the adversary $\mathcal{A}$. For the rth signing query on (id', m) by $\mathcal{A}$, $\mathcal{B}$ first checks whether $(m, id', \sigma) \in$ Mlist. If there exists such a tuple, the adversary $\mathcal{B}$ aborts the experiment. Otherwise, $\mathcal{B}$ computes $cert_{id'} = ((E_1^{(1)})', \eta_1') \leftarrow$ SQISign.Sign$(pp_{sgn}, \tau_1, bin(j(E_A^{(2)}))||id')$ using $msk = \tau_1$ and queries its signing oracle $\mathcal{O}_S(sk = \tau_2, \cdot)$ on m. Upon receiving the signature $\bar{\sigma} = (E_1^{(2)}, \eta_2)$ on m from $\mathcal{C}$ under secret key $sk = \tau_2$, $\mathcal{B}$ sets $\sigma' = (\bar{\sigma}, E_A^{(2)}, cert_{id'})$ and sends it to $\mathcal{A}$. The adversary $\mathcal{B}$ updates the Mlist with (m, id', σ') and the challenger $\mathcal{C}$ updates Slist with m. For the ith query where $i \in \{r+1, \ldots, q(\lambda)\}$, on identity id' and a message m' by $\mathcal{A}$, the adversary $\mathcal{B}$ checks whether $(m', id', \sigma') \in$ Mlist. If such a tuple exists, $\mathcal{B}$ answers the query from the Mlist, otherwise it proceeds as in the rth signing query.

  Upon receiving a query on a message m and identity $id \neq id'$, $\mathcal{B}$ retrieves the pair (id, usk_{id}) from Klist where $usk_{id} = (\bar{\tau}_2, \overline{cert}_{id})$ is the user secret key corresponding to id. If $(id, usk_{id}) \notin$ Klist, it picks a random isogeny $\bar{\tau}_2 : E_0 \to \overline{E}_A^{(2)}$ and uses its master secret key $msk = \tau_1$ to compute $\overline{cert}_{id} = (\overline{E}_1^{(1)}, \bar{\eta}_1) \leftarrow$ SQISign.Sign$(pp_{sgn}, \tau_1, bin(j(\overline{E}_A^{(2)}))||id)$ and sets $usk_{id} = (\bar{\tau}_2, \overline{cert}_{id})$. It then computes the signature $\bar{\sigma} = (\overline{E}_1^{(2)}, \bar{\eta}_2) \leftarrow$ SQISign.Sign$(pp_{ibs}, \bar{\tau}_2, m)$ on m and sets $\sigma = (\bar{\sigma}, \overline{E}_A^{(2)}, \overline{cert}_{id})$ and sends it to $\mathcal{A}$. It appends (m, id, σ) to Mlist.

Forgery: If $\mathcal{A}$ eventually outputs a message m^*, user identity id^* and a forge signature σ^* where $\sigma^* = (\bar{\sigma}^*, (E_A^{(2)})^*, cert_{id^*})$ and the experiment was never aborted, $\mathcal{B}$ submits (m^*, σ^*) as a forgery to its own challenger $\mathcal{C}$. If $\mathcal{A}$ wins the

UF-IBS-CMA game with non-negligible probability then $(m^*, \mathrm{id}^*, \sigma^*)$ must be a valid forgery. Thus, we have IBS.Verify$(\mathsf{pp}_{\mathrm{ibs}}, \mathrm{id}^*, m^*, \sigma^*) = \mathsf{Valid}$, $\mathrm{id}^* \notin \mathsf{Clist}$ and $(m^*, \mathrm{id}^*, \cdot) \notin \mathsf{Mlist}$. Note that the condition $(m^*, \mathrm{id}^*, \cdot) \notin \mathsf{Mlist}$ means that the adversary $\mathcal{B}$ never queried its signing oracle $\mathcal{O}_S(\tau_2, \cdot)$ on m^*.

With probability at least $1/q(\lambda)$, the experiment is not aborted and $\mathrm{id}' = \mathrm{id}^*$. The success probability of $\mathcal{B}$ in forging a signature for SQISign is thus at least $\Pr[\mathsf{Success}|\mathsf{REUSE}]/q(\lambda)$. From the security of SQISign, it follows that this quantity must be negligible. Since q is polynomial in λ, we must have $\Pr[\mathsf{Success}|\mathsf{REUSE}]$ is negligible as well.

5   Puncturable Signature: Concrete Construction

We now describe our Short Quaternion and Isogeny Puncturable Signature (SQIPS) leveraging our scheme SQIIBS described in Sect. 4. Let $\mathcal{M} = \{0,1\}^*$ denotes the message space and $\mathcal{P} = \{0,1\}^l \subseteq \mathcal{M}$ be the prefix space of our PS.

SQIPS.Setup$(1^\lambda) \to (\mathsf{pp}_{\mathrm{ps}}, \mathsf{sk}_0)$: On input 1^λ, the signer executes this algorithm to generate the public parameter $\mathsf{pk}_{\mathrm{ps}}$ and initial secret key sk as follows:

i. Invokes the algorithm SQIIBS.Setup(1^λ) to compute the key pair $(\mathsf{pp}_{\mathrm{ibs}}, \mathsf{msk})$ as follows:
   - Chooses a prime p and fixes the supersingular curve $E_0 : y^2 = x^3 + x$ over $\mathbb{F}_{p^2}$ with special extremal endomorphism ring $\mathcal{O}_0 = \langle 1, i, \frac{i+j}{2}, \frac{1+k}{2} \rangle$.
   - Picks a smooth number $D = 2^e$ where $2^e > p^3$.
   - Picks an odd smooth number $D_c = \ell^e$ where ℓ is a prime and computes $\mu(D_c) = (\ell+1) \cdot \ell^{e-1}$.
   - Samples a cryptographic hash function $\mathcal{H}_1 : \mathbb{F}_{p^2} \times \{0,1\}^* \to [1, \mu(D_c)]$.
   - Samples an arbitrary function $\Phi_{D_c}(E, s)$ that maps a pair (E, s) of an elliptic curve E and an integer $s \in [1, \mu(D_c)]$ to a non-backtracking isogeny of degree D_c from E [3].
   - Picks a random isogeny $\tau_1 : E_0 \to E_A^{(1)}$.
   - Sets $\mathsf{pp}_{\mathrm{ibs}} = (p, E_0, D_c, D, \mathcal{H}_1, \Phi_{D_c}, E_A^{(1)})$ and $\mathsf{msk} = \tau_1$.
ii. For each prefix $x' \in \{0,1\}^l$, executes the algorithm SQIIBS.Extract$(\mathsf{pp}_{\mathrm{ibs}}, \mathsf{msk} = \tau_1, x')$ to compute the key $\mathsf{usk}_{x'}$ and stores it in an array T of size 2^l.
   - Picks a random isogeny $\tau_2 : E_0 \to E_A^{(2)}$.
   - Selects a random commitment isogeny $\psi_1 : E_0 \to E_1^{(1)}$.
   - Computes $s_1 = \mathcal{H}_1(j(E_1^{(1)}), \mathrm{bin}(j(E_A^{(2)}))\|x')$ and sets the challenge isogeny $\Phi_{D_c}(E_1^{(1)}, s_1) = \varphi_1$ where $\varphi_1 : E_1^{(1)} \to E_2^{(1)}$ is a non-backtracking isogeny of degree D_c.
   - Computes the ideals $\bar{I}_{\tau_1}, I_{\tau_1}, I_{\psi_1}$ and I_{φ_1} corresponding to the isogenies $\hat{\tau}_1, \tau_1, \psi_1$ and φ_1 respectively.

- The signer having the knowledge of $\mathcal{O}^{(1)} = \mathsf{End}(E_A^{(1)})$ through τ_1 and $\mathcal{O}_2^{(1)} = \mathsf{End}(E_2^{(1)})$ through $\varphi_1 \circ \psi_1$, runs the $\mathsf{SigningKLPT}_{2^e}(I_{\tau_1}, I_1)$ algorithm (Sect. 2.3) on input the $(\mathcal{O}_0, \mathcal{O}^{(1)})$-ideal I_{τ_1} and a left $\mathcal{O}^{(1)}$-ideal $I_1 = I_{\varphi_1} I_{\psi_1} \bar{I}_{\tau_1}$ to obtain a $(\mathcal{O}^{(1)}, \mathcal{O}_2^{(1)})$-ideal $J_1 \sim I_1$ of norm $D = 2^e$.
- Constructs the isogeny $\eta_1 : E_A^{(1)} \to E_2^{(1)}$ of degree D corresponding to the ideal J_1 such that $\hat{\varphi}_1 \circ \eta_1$ is cyclic and $\mathsf{cert}_{x'} = (E_1^{(1)}, \eta_1)$.
- Issues the user secret key $\mathsf{usk}_{x'} = (\tau_2, \mathsf{cert}_{x'} = (E_1^{(1)}, \eta_1))$.

iii. Sets $T[\mathsf{ind}_{x'}] = \mathsf{usk}_{x'}$ where $\mathsf{ind}_{x'} = (x')_{10} \in \{0, 1, \ldots, 2^l - 1\}$ is the decimal representation of the binary string x'.

iv. Sets the public parameter $\mathsf{pp}_{\mathsf{ps}} = \mathsf{pp}_{\mathsf{ibs}}$ and secret key $\mathsf{sk} = T$.

$\mathsf{SQIPS.Puncture}(\mathsf{sk}, x') \to \mathsf{sk}'$: The signer on input the secret key $\mathsf{sk} = T$ and a prefix $x' \in \{0,1\}^l$, computes $\mathsf{ind}_{x'} = (x')_{10}$ and sets $T[\mathsf{ind}] = 0$. It returns the updated punctured secret key $\mathsf{sk}' = T$ where the value corresponding to the index ind of the array T is made 0.

$\mathsf{SQIPS.Sign}(\mathsf{pp}_{\mathsf{ps}}, \mathsf{sk}, m) \to \Sigma/ \perp$: Taking input $\mathsf{pp}_{\mathsf{ps}} = (p, E_0, D_c, D, \mathcal{H}_1, \Phi_{D_c}, E_A^{(1)})$, secret key $\mathsf{sk} = T$ and a message $m \in \{0,1\}^*$, the signer either generates a signature Σ if the prefix x' of m has not been punctured or it returns $\perp$.

i. Returns $\perp$ if $T[\mathsf{ind}_{x'}] = 0$.

ii. If $T[\mathsf{ind}_{x'}] \neq 0$, it retrieves the value $\mathsf{usk}_{x'} = (\tau_2, \mathsf{cert}_{x'} = (E_1^{(1)}, \eta_1)) = T[\mathsf{ind}_{x'}]$ from the array and executes the algorithm $\mathsf{SQIIBS.Sign}(\mathsf{pp}_{\mathsf{ibs}}, \mathsf{usk}_{x'}, m)$ as follows to generate a signature on m.

   - Picks a random commitment isogeny $\psi_2 : E_0 \to E_1^{(2)}$.
   - Computes $s_2 = \mathcal{H}_1(j(E_1^{(2)}), m)$ and $\Phi_{D_c}(E_1^{(2)}, s_2) = \varphi_2$ where $\varphi_2 : E_1^{(2)} \to E_2^{(2)}$ is a non-backtracking challenge isogeny of degree D_c.
   - Computes the ideal $\bar{I}_{\tau_2}, I_{\tau_2}, I_{\psi_2}$ and I_{φ_2} corresponding to the isogenies $\hat{\tau}_2, \tau_2, \psi_2$ and φ_2 respectively.
   - The signer having the knowledge of $\mathcal{O}^{(2)} = \mathsf{End}(E_A^{(2)})$ through τ_2 and $\mathcal{O}_2^{(2)} = \mathsf{End}(E_2^{(2)})$ through $\varphi_2 \circ \psi_2$, runs the $\mathsf{SigningKLPT}_{2^e}(I_{\tau_2}, I_2)$ algorithm (Sect. 2.3) on input the $(\mathcal{O}_0, \mathcal{O}^{(2)})$-ideal I_{τ_2} and a left $\mathcal{O}^{(2)}$-ideal $I_2 = I_{\varphi_2} I_{\psi_2} \bar{I}_{\tau_2}$ to obtain a $(\mathcal{O}^{(2)}, \mathcal{O}_2^{(2)})$-ideal $J_2 \sim I_2$ of norm $D = 2^e$.
   - Constructs the isogeny $\eta_2 : E_A^{(2)} \to E_2^{(2)}$ of degree D corresponding to the ideal J_2 such that $\hat{\varphi}_2 \circ \eta_2 : E_A^{(2)} \to E_1^{(2)}$ is cyclic. It sets $\bar{\sigma} = (E_1^{(2)}, \eta_2)$.
   - Extract $\mathsf{cert}_{x'}$ from $\mathsf{usk}_{x'}$ and sets the signature $\sigma = (\bar{\sigma}, E_A^{(2)}, \mathsf{cert}_{x'})$.

iii. Returns the puncturable signature $\Sigma = \sigma$.

$\mathsf{SQIPS.Verify}(\mathsf{pp}_{\mathsf{ps}}, m, \Sigma) \to \mathsf{Valid}/\mathsf{Invalid}$: This algorithm takes as input $\mathsf{pp}_{\mathsf{ps}} = (p, E_0, D_c, D, \mathcal{H}_1, \Phi_{D_c}, E_A^{(1)})$, a message $m \in \{0,1\}^*$ and a signature $\Sigma = \sigma = (\bar{\sigma}, E_A^{(2)}, \mathsf{cert}_{x'})$ where $x' \in \{0,1\}^l$ is the prefix of the message $m \in \{0,1\}^*$. It outputs Valid if Σ is a valid signature on m and $\mathsf{Invalid}$ otherwise.

i. Executes the algorithm SQIIBS.Verify as follows to check the validity of the signature $\Sigma = \sigma = (\bar{\sigma}, E_A^{(2)}, \text{cert}_{x'})$ on m.

- Parses $\sigma = (\bar{\sigma} = (E_1^{(2)}, \eta_2), E_A^{(2)}, \text{cert}_{x'} = (E_1^{(1)}, \eta_1))$.
- Computes $s_1 = \mathcal{H}_1(j(E_1^{(1)}), \text{bin}(j(E_A^{(2)})) \| x')$ and $s_2 = \mathcal{H}_1(j(E_1^{(2)}), m)$.
- Recovers the isogenies $\Phi_{D_c}(E_1^{(1)}, s_1) = \varphi_1$ and $\Phi_{D_c}(E_1^{(2)}, s_2) = \varphi_2$.
- Checks if η_1 is an isogeny of degree D from $E_A^{(1)}$ to $E_2^{(1)}$ and that $\varphi_1 \circ \eta_1 : E_A^{(1)} \to E_1^{(1)}$ is cyclic.
- Checks if η_2 is an isogeny of degree D from $E_A^{(2)}$ to $E_2^{(2)}$ and that $\varphi_2 \circ \eta_2 : E_A^{(2)} \to E_1^{(2)}$ is cyclic.
- If all the checks succeed returns Valid, otherwise returns Invalid.

Correctness. The correctness of our puncturable signature scheme SQIPS from isogenies follows from the correctness of our identity-based signature SQIIBS.

5.1 Comparison of Our Scheme SQIPS with the Existing Puncturable Signatures

In Table 3, we compare our scheme with the existing schemes on PS. The PS scheme by Li et al. [13] is based on the τ-Strong Diffie-Hellman assumption (τ-SDH) in bilinear map setting and is proven secure in the random oracle model (ROM). Their scheme employs the probabilistic bloom filter data structure and suffers from non-negligible false-positive errors. Jiang et al. [12] designed a pairing-based PS which is free from false positive errors and is secure under the hardness of the Computational Diffie-Hellman (CDH) assumption in the standard model (SDM). However, none of these schemes are resistant to quantum attacks. The PS schemes from lattices and MPKC proposed by Jiang et al. [12] enjoy post-quantum security and are based on the hardness of Short Integer Solution (SIS) and Multivariate Quadratic polynomial (MQ) assumptions respectively. Our isogeny-based PS is post-quantum secure as it is based on SQISign cryptosystem and is also free from false-positive errors.

Table 3. Comparison of the existing puncturable signature schemes

Instantiation	Assumption	Security Model	Post-quantum	False-positive errors
Li et al. [13]	τ-SDH	ROM	✗	✓
Pairing Inst. [12]	CDH	SDM	✗	✗
Lattice Inst. [12]	SIS	ROM	✓	✗
Multivariate Inst. [12]	MQ		✓	✗
Our Isogeny Inst	SQISign	ROM	✓	✗

5.2 Security Analysis

Theorem 5.21. *Our proposed puncturable signature* SQIPS *is* UF-CMA-AP *secure as the underlying identity-based signature* SQIIBS *is* UF-IBS-CMA *secure.*

Proof. Let us assume that there exists a PPT adversary $\mathcal{A}$ that wins the experiment $\mathsf{Exp}_{\mathsf{SQIPS},\mathcal{A}}^{\mathsf{UF\text{-}CMA\text{-}AP}}(\lambda)$ depicted in Fig. 4 with a non-negligible advantage. We design an adversary $\mathcal{B}$ who simulates the PS security experiment $\mathsf{Exp}_{\mathsf{SQIPS},\mathcal{A}}^{\mathsf{UF\text{-}CMA\text{-}AP}}(\lambda)$, exploits $\mathcal{A}$ as a subroutine and wins the IBS security experiment $\mathsf{Exp}_{\mathsf{SQIIBS},\mathcal{B}}^{\mathsf{UF\text{-}IBS\text{-}CMA}}(\lambda)$ with the same advantage. Let $\mathcal{C}$ denotes the challenger for the security experiment $\mathsf{Exp}_{\mathsf{SQIIBS},\mathcal{B}}^{\mathsf{UF\text{-}IBS\text{-}CMA}}(\lambda)$.

Setup: The challenger $\mathcal{C}$ on input the security parameter 1^λ, computes $(\mathsf{pp}_{\mathsf{ibs}}, \mathsf{msk}) \leftarrow \mathsf{SQIIBS.Setup}(1^\lambda)$ and sends $\mathsf{pp}_{\mathsf{ibs}}$ to $\mathcal{B}$. Additionally, $\mathcal{C}$ executes the algorithm $\mathsf{SQIIBS.Extract}(\mathsf{pp}_{\mathsf{ibs}}, \mathsf{msk}, x')$ to compute the key $\mathsf{usk}_{x'}$ for each prefix $x' \in \{0,1\}^l$ and forms the array $T[\mathsf{ind}_{x'}] = \mathsf{usk}_{x'}$. Also it initiates three lists Klist, Clist and Mlist to $\emptyset$. Upon receiving the public parameter $\mathsf{pp}_{\mathsf{ibs}}$ from its own challenger $\mathcal{C}$, the adversary $\mathcal{B}$ sets $\mathsf{pp}_{\mathsf{ps}} = \mathsf{pp}_{\mathsf{ibs}}$ and forwards it to $\mathcal{A}$. It also initializes the sets $\mathcal{Q}_{\mathsf{sig}}$ for signed messages and $\mathcal{Q}_{\mathsf{pun}}$ for punctured prefixes to ϕ.

Query Phase: The adversary $\mathcal{A}$ issues polynomially many adaptive queries to the following oracles $\mathcal{O}_{\mathsf{Puncture}}(\mathsf{sk}, \cdot)$ and $\mathcal{O}_{\mathsf{Sgn}}(\mathsf{sk}, \cdot)$.

- $\mathcal{O}_{\mathsf{Puncture}}(\mathsf{sk} = T, \cdot)$: Upon receiving a query on prefix x', the challenger $\mathcal{C}$ updates $\mathcal{Q}_{\mathsf{pun}} \leftarrow \mathcal{Q}_{\mathsf{pun}} \cup \{x'\}$.
- $\mathcal{O}_{\mathsf{Sgn}}(\mathsf{sk} = T, \cdot)$: On receiving a signature query on a message $m \in \{0,1\}^*$, the adversary $\mathcal{B}$ checks if $x' \in \mathcal{Q}_{\mathsf{pun}}$ where x' is the prefix of m. If the check succeeds, it returns $\perp$. Otherwise, it issues a signature query on (m, x') for a with message m and identity x' to $\mathcal{C}$. The challenger $\mathcal{C}$ extracts $T[\mathsf{ind}_{x'}] = \mathsf{usk}_{x'}$ from $\mathsf{sk} = T$, computes the signature $\Sigma \leftarrow \mathsf{SQIIBS.Sign}(\mathsf{pp}_{\mathsf{ibs}}, \mathsf{usk}_{x'}, m)$ and sends it to $\mathcal{B}$ who forwards it to $\mathcal{A}$. The adversary $\mathcal{B}$ updates $\mathcal{Q}_{\mathsf{sig}} \leftarrow \mathcal{Q}_{\mathsf{sig}} \cup \{m\}$.

Challenge: The adversary $\mathcal{A}$ sends a target prefix $x^* \in \{0,1\}^l$ to the adversary $\mathcal{B}$ which $\mathcal{B}$ forwards to $\mathcal{C}$ as the target identity. The adversary $\mathcal{A}$ can issue additional puncture and signature queries as described in the Query phase.

Corruption Query: Upon receiving a corruption query on $x^* \in \{0,1\}^l$, the adversary $\mathcal{B}$ returns $\perp$ if $x^* \notin \mathcal{Q}_{\mathsf{pun}}$. Otherwise, $\mathcal{B}$ queries its extract oracle $\mathcal{O}_{\mathsf{Extract}}(\cdot)$ for each prefix $x' \in \{0,1\}^l \setminus \{x^*\}$ and updates the array T with the response $\mathsf{usk}_{x'} \leftarrow \mathsf{SQIIBS.Extract}(\mathsf{pp}_{\mathsf{ibs}}, \mathsf{msk}, x')$ from $\mathcal{C}$ by setting $T[\mathsf{ind}_{x'}] = \mathsf{usk}_{x'}$. For each $x' \in \mathcal{Q}_{\mathsf{pun}}$, the adversary $\mathcal{B}$ deletes the related key by setting $T[\mathsf{ind}_{x'}] = 0$ and returns the current secret key $\mathsf{sk} = T$ to $\mathcal{A}$.

Forgery: $\mathcal{A}$ eventually submits a forgery (m^*, Σ^*, x^*) where x^* is the prefix of m^*. $\mathcal{B}$ uses the forgery of $\mathcal{A}$ to frame its own forgery (m^*, x^*, Σ^*).

If the adversary $\mathcal{A}$ wins the game then we have $m^* \notin \mathcal{Q}_{\mathsf{sig}}$, $x^* \in \mathcal{Q}_{\mathsf{pun}}$ and $\mathsf{Valid} \leftarrow \mathsf{SQIPS.Verify}(\mathsf{pp}_{\mathsf{ps}}, m^*, \Sigma^*)$. The condition $m^* \notin \mathcal{Q}_{\mathsf{sig}}$ means that $(m^*, x^*, \cdot) \notin \mathsf{Mlist}$. Also note that the adversary $\mathcal{B}$ has not made any extraction query on x^*, thus $x^* \notin \mathsf{Clist}$. Moreover, $\mathsf{Valid} \leftarrow \mathsf{SQIPS.Verify}(\mathsf{pp}_{\mathsf{ps}}, m^*, \Sigma^*)$ implies that $\mathsf{Valid} \leftarrow \mathsf{SQIIBS.Verify}(\mathsf{pp}_{\mathsf{ibs}}, m^*, \Sigma^*)$.

References

1. Bellare, M., Stepanovs, I., Waters, B.: New negative results on differing-inputs obfuscation. In: Fischlin, M., Coron, J.-S. (eds.) EUROCRYPT 2016, Part II. LNCS, vol. 9666, pp. 792–821. Springer, Heidelberg (2016). https://doi.org/10.1007/978-3-662-49896-5_28
2. Castryck, W., Lange, T., Martindale, C., Panny, L., Renes, J.: CSIDH: an efficient post-quantum commutative group action. In: Peyrin, T., Galbraith, S. (eds.) ASIACRYPT 2018, Part III. LNCS, vol. 11274, pp. 395–427. Springer, Cham (2018). https://doi.org/10.1007/978-3-030-03332-3_15
3. Charles, D.X., Lauter, K.E., Goren, E.Z.: Cryptographic hash functions from expander graphs. J. Cryptol. **22**(1), 93–113 (2009)
4. Chen, J., Ling, J., Ning, J., Ding, J.: Identity-based signature schemes for multivariate public key cryptosystems. Comput. J. **62**(8), 1132–1147 (2019)
5. Childs, A., Jao, D., Soukharev, V.: Constructing elliptic curve isogenies in quantum subexponential time. J. Math. Cryptol. **8**(1), 1–29 (2014)
6. De Feo, L., Kohel, D., Leroux, A., Petit, C., Wesolowski, B.: SQISign: compact post-quantum signatures from quaternions and isogenies. In: Moriai, S., Wang, H. (eds.) ASIACRYPT 2020. LNCS, vol. 12491, pp. 64–93. Springer, Cham (2020). https://doi.org/10.1007/978-3-030-64837-4_3
7. Deirmentzoglou, E., Papakyriakopoulos, G., Patsakis, C.: A survey on long-range attacks for proof of stake protocols. IEEE Access **7**, 28712–28725 (2019)
8. Deuring, M.: Die typen der multiplikatorenringe elliptischer funktionenkörper. In: Abhandlungen aus dem mathematischen Seminar der Universität Hamburg, vol. 14, pp. 197–272. Springer, Heidelberg (1941)
9. Gaži, P., Kiayias, A., Russell, A.: Stake-bleeding attacks on proof-of-stake blockchains. In: 2018 Crypto Valley Conference on Blockchain Technology (CVCBT), pp. 85–92. IEEE (2018)
10. Guan, J., Zhandry, M.: Disappearing cryptography in the bounded storage model. In: Nissim, K., Waters, B. (eds.) TCC 2021, Part II. LNCS, vol. 13043, pp. 365–396. Springer, Cham (2021). https://doi.org/10.1007/978-3-030-90453-1_13
11. Halevi, S., Ishai, Y., Jain, A., Komargodski, I., Sahai, A., Yogev, E.: Non-interactive multiparty computation without correlated randomness. In: Takagi, T., Peyrin, T. (eds.) ASIACRYPT 2017, Part III. LNCS, vol. 10626, pp. 181–211. Springer, Cham (2017). https://doi.org/10.1007/978-3-319-70700-6_7
12. Jiang, M., Duong, D.H., Susilo, W.: Puncturable signature: a generic construction and instantiations. In: Atluri, V., Di Pietro, R., Jensen, C.D., Meng, W. (eds.) ESORICS 2022, Part II. LNCS, vol. 13555, pp. 507–527. Springer, Cham (2022). https://doi.org/10.1007/978-3-031-17146-8_25
13. Li, X., Xu, J., Fan, X., Wang, Y., Zhang, Z.: Puncturable signatures and applications in proof-of-stake blockchain protocols. IEEE Trans. Inf. Forensics Secur. **15**, 3872–3885 (2020)
14. Minkowski, H.: Uber die positiven quadratischen Formen und iiber Kettenbruchanliche Algorithmen. Ges. Abh. I, pp. 243–260
15. Pass, R., Seeman, L., Shelat, A.: Analysis of the blockchain protocol in asynchronous networks. In: Coron, J.-S., Nielsen, J.B. (eds.) EUROCRYPT 2017, Part II. LNCS, vol. 10211, pp. 643–673. Springer, Cham (2017). https://doi.org/10.1007/978-3-319-56614-6_22
16. Peng, C., Chen, J., Zhou, L., Choo, K.K.R., He, D.: CsiIBS: a post-quantum identity-based signature scheme based on isogenies. J. Inf. Secur. Appl. **54**, 102504 (2020)

17. Shaw, S., Dutta, R.: Identification scheme and forward-secure signature in identity-based setting from isogenies. In: Huang, Q., Yu, Y. (eds.) ProvSec 2021. LNCS, vol. 13059, pp. 309–326. Springer, Cham (2021). https://doi.org/10.1007/978-3-030-90402-9_17

18. Shor, P.W.: Polynomial-time algorithms for prime factorization and discrete logarithms on a quantum computer. SIAM Rev. **41**(2), 303–332 (1999)

19. Tian, M., Huang, L.: Identity-based signatures from lattices: simpler, faster, shorter. Fund. Inform. **145**(2), 171–187 (2016)

20. Yi, P., Li, J., Liu, C., Han, J., Wang, H., Zhang, Y., Chen, Y.: An efficient identity-based signature scheme with provable security. Inf. Sci. **576**, 790–799 (2021)

High Weight Code-Based Signature Scheme from QC-LDPC Codes

Chik How Tan and Theo Fanuela Prabowo[✉]

Temasek Laboratories, National University of Singapore, Singapore, Singapore
{tsltch,tsltfp}@nus.edu.sg

Abstract. We propose a new Hamming metric code-based signature scheme (called HWQCS) based on quasi-cyclic low density parity-check (QC-LDPC) codes. We propose the use of high error on QC-LDPC codes for constructing this signature and analyse its complexity. We show that HWQCS signature scheme achieves EUF-CMA security in the classical random oracle model, assuming the hardness of the syndrome decoding problem and the codeword finding problem for QC-LDPC codes. Furthermore, we also give a detailed security analysis of the HWQCS signature scheme. Based on the complexities of solving the underlying problems, the public key size and signature size of the HWQCS signature scheme are 1568 bytes and 4759 bytes respectively at 128-bit security level.

Keywords: code-based cryptography · signature · QC-LDPC codes

1 Introduction

Code-based cryptography is based on the problem of decoding random linear codes, which is referred to as the syndrome decoding problem and is known to be NP-hard [11]. The most common code-based cryptosystems are the McEliece cryptosystem [29] and the Niederreiter cryptosystem [32], which are equivalent in terms of their security. Solving the NP-hard syndrome decoding problem is believed to be hard even for quantum computers. Over the years, a number of code-based cryptographic schemes have been proposed. These include some promising key encapsulation mechanisms called BIKE [4], Classic McEliece [12] and HQC [1], which become fourth-round candidates in the NIST call for post-quantum cryptography standardization.

Unlike encryption and key encapsulation mechanisms, the construction of code-based digital signature schemes seems to be more challenging. This is indicated by the absence of code-based signature scheme in the second round onwards of the NIST PQC standardization. The most common techniques to construct signatures are based on two generic frameworks, which are, hash-and-sign constructions and Fiat-Shamir framework [22] constructions. The hash-and-sign construction requires some trapdoor functions, such as CFS [17] and Wave [19]. On the other hand, Fiat-Shamir framework construction does not necessarily use trapdoor functions in general, such as Stern [40], CVA [15], MPT [30], CVE

H. Seo and S. Kim (Eds.): ICISC 2023, LNCS 14561, pp. 306–323, 2024.
https://doi.org/10.1007/978-981-97-1235-9_16

[8], cRVDC [9], etc. However, most of them are inefficient or have large key or signature sizes. Furthermore, some of the proposed code-based signatures were even found to be insecure. For example, the KKS [23], RZW [36], CVE [8], MPT [30], Durandal [3] and SHMWW [38], are shown to be insecure in [6,18,24,33,34] and [5,41] respectively.

Recently, there is a new technique to construct signature schemes, which is called MPC (multiparty computation) in the head paradigm. This approach combines secret key sharing scheme and identification scheme in the multi-party computations setting, for example, CCJ signature [14], FJR signature [21], etc. The purpose of this construction is to reduce the signature size. But most of the signature size is still around eight thousand bytes. Therefore, it is still a challenge to construct signature schemes with practical signature size and public key size.

In this paper, we proposed a new signature scheme (called HWQCS) based on quasi-cyclic low density parity-check (QC-LDPC) codes. The proposed signature scheme is based on the Fiat-Shamir transformation and introduces high weight error on QC-LDPC codes. HWQCS signature scheme resists Prabowo-Tan's attack [34] on MPT-like signature scheme [30]. This is achieved by signing a message depending on a new ephemeral secret key for each signature rather than relying only on a fixed secret key. So, each signature can be viewed as a one-time signature. Furthermore, this signature is also secure against Bit-Flipping algorithm attack and statistical attack.

The organization of this paper is as follows. In Sect. 2, we provide a brief review of the properties of linear codes, quasi-cyclic codes and also define the syndrome decoding problem, etc. In Sect. 3, we propose a new high weight signature scheme (called HWQCS) which is based on 2-quasi-cyclic codes. We also provide security proof of the proposed HWQCS signature scheme under the random oracle model. In Sect. 4, we give a detailed analysis of various possible attacks on the proposed signature scheme HWQCS. In Sect. 5, we examine the public/secret key size and signature size for various security levels. Finally, the paper is concluded in Sect. 6.

2   Preliminaries

In this paper, let n, k be integers, denote by $\mathbb{F}_2$ the finite field of two elements, let $\mathbf{a} = (a_1, \ldots, a_n) \in \mathbb{F}_2^n$ be a vector in $\mathbb{F}_2^n$.

2.1   Linear Codes

Definition 1. *Let* $\mathbf{a} = (a_1, \ldots, a_n) \in \mathbb{F}_2^n$. *The* support *of* $\mathbf{a}$ *is the set consisting of all indices* $i \in \{1, \ldots, n\}$ *such that* $a_i \neq 0$. *The* Hamming weight *of* $\mathbf{a}$, *denoted by* wt($\mathbf{a}$) *is the cardinality of its support. The* Hamming distance *between* $\mathbf{a}$ *and* $\mathbf{b}$, *denoted by* d($\mathbf{a}, \mathbf{b}$) *is defined as* wt($\mathbf{a} - \mathbf{b}$), *i.e., the number of coordinates* $\mathbf{a}$ *and* $\mathbf{b}$ *differs on.*

Definition 2. *Let* k *and* n *be two positive integers with* $k \leq n$. *An* $[n, k]$-*linear code* $\mathcal{C}$ *of length* n *and dimension* k *is a linear subspace of dimension* k *of the vector space* $\mathbb{F}_2^n$. *The rate of the code* $\mathcal{C}$ *is* $R = \frac{k}{n}$.

Definition 3. *Let C be an $[n, k]$-linear code of length n and dimension k. We call its* minimum distance δ *the minimum Hamming weight of a non-zero codeword in C, i.e.,*

$$\delta = \min\{\mathrm{wt}(\mathbf{a}) \mid \mathbf{a} \in C, \mathbf{a} \neq \mathbf{0}\}$$
$$= \min\{\mathrm{wt}(\mathbf{a} - \mathbf{b}) \mid \mathbf{a}, \mathbf{b} \in C, \mathbf{a} \neq \mathbf{b}\}.$$

We sometimes refer to C as an $[n, k, \delta]$-code if δ is known.

Definition 4. *A matrix $G \in \mathbb{F}_2^{k \times n}$ is said to be a generator matrix of an $[n, k]$-linear code C if its rows form a basis of C. Then, $C = \{\mathbf{u}G \mid \mathbf{u} \in \mathbb{F}_2^k\}$. The parity-check matrix of C is $H \in \mathbb{F}_2^{(n-k) \times n}$ such that $GH^T = 0$ or $\mathbf{c}H^T = 0$ for all $\mathbf{c} \in C$. Furthermore, G and H are said to be in systematic form if they are written as*

$$G = [I_k \quad A] \quad \text{resp.} \quad H = [I_{n-k} \quad B],$$

for some $A \in \mathbb{F}_2^{k \times (n-k)}$ and $B \in \mathbb{F}_2^{(n-k) \times k}$.

Problem 1 (Syndrome Decoding Problem (SDP)). *Given a matrix $H \in \mathbb{F}_2^{(n-k) \times n}$, a vector $\mathbf{s} \in \mathbb{F}_2^{n-k}$ and an integer $w > 0$ as input. The Syndrome Decoding problem is to determine a vector $\mathbf{e} \in \mathbb{F}_2^n$ such that $\mathrm{wt}(\mathbf{e}) \leq w$ and $\mathbf{s} = \mathbf{e}H^T$.*

Problem 2 (Codeword Finding Problem (CFP)). *Given a matrix $H \in \mathbb{F}_2^{(n-k) \times n}$, and an integer $w > 0$ as input. The Codeword Finding problem is to determine a vector $\mathbf{e} \in \mathbb{F}_2^n$ such that $\mathrm{wt}(\mathbf{e}) = w$ and $\mathbf{e}H^T = 0$.*

The SDP problem and CFP problem are well known and was proved to be NP-complete by Berlekamp, McEliece and van Tilborg in [11].

The first generic decoding method to solve SDP is called the Information Set Decoding (ISD) method, introduced by Prange [35] (denoted as Pra62) in 1962. It is the best known algorithm for decoding a general linear code. Since then, several improvements of the ISD method have been proposed for codes over the binary field, such as LB88 [25], Leon88 [26], Stern88 [39], Dum91 [20], and more recently by BLP11 [13], MMT11 [27], BJMM12 [7], MO15 [28]. The computational complexity of solving the syndrome decoding problem is quantified by the work factor $\mathcal{WF}_{\mathcal{A}}(n, k, w)$, which is defined as the average cost in binary operations of algorithm $\mathcal{A}$ to solve it. The work factor of Pra62 is given as follows.

$$\mathcal{WF}_{\mathsf{Pra62}}(n, k, w) = \frac{\min\{\binom{n}{w}, 2^{n-k}\}}{\binom{n-k}{w}}.$$

When $w = o(n)$, then $\mathcal{WF}_{\mathsf{Pra62}}(n, k, w) = \frac{\binom{n}{w}}{\binom{n-k}{w}}$ and $\frac{1}{w} \log_2 \frac{\binom{n}{w}}{\binom{n-k}{w}} \approx c$, where $c := -\log_2(1 - \frac{k}{n})$. Therefore, we have $\mathcal{WF}_{\mathsf{Pra62}}(n, k, w) \approx 2^{cw(1+o(1))}$.

Among the variants of solving algorithms for the syndrome decoding problem, the following result from [42] shows that their work factors are asymptotically the same.

Proposition 1 [42]. *Let k and w be two functions of n such that $\lim_{n\to\infty} \frac{k}{n} = R$, $0 < R < 1$, and $\lim_{n\to\infty} \frac{w}{n} = 0$. For any algorithm $\mathcal{A}$ among the variants of Pra62, Stern88, Dum91, MMT11, BJMM12 and MO15, their work factors are asymptotically the same as*

$$\mathcal{WF}_{\mathcal{A}}(n, k, w) = 2^{cw(1+o(1))}, \quad \text{where } c = -\log_2(1 - R)$$

when n tends to infinity.

2.2 Quasi-cyclic Linear Codes

Let $\mathbb{F}_2$ be the finite field of two elements and let $\mathcal{R} := \mathbb{F}_2[x]/(x^k - 1)$ be the quotient ring of polynomials over $\mathbb{F}_2$ of degree less than k. Given $a = a_0 + a_1 x + \dots + a_{k-1} x^{k-1} \in \mathcal{R}$, we denote $\mathbf{a} := (a_0, a_1, \dots, a_{k-1}) \in \mathbb{F}_2^k$. Let $\mathcal{R}^* = \{a \in \mathcal{R} \mid a \text{ is invertible in } \mathcal{R}\}$. Let $\mathcal{V}$ be a vector space of dimension k over $\mathbb{F}_2$. Denote $\mathcal{V}_{k,w} := \{a \in \mathcal{R} = \mathbb{F}_2[x]/(x^k - 1) \mid \text{wt}(\mathbf{a}) = w\}$. We sometimes abuse the notation by interchanging $\mathbf{a}$ with $a \in \mathcal{R}$.

Definition 5 (Circulant Matrix). *Let $\mathbf{v} = (v_0, \cdots, v_{k-1}) \in \mathcal{V}$, a circulant matrix defined by $\mathbf{v}$ is*

$$V := \begin{bmatrix} v_0 & v_1 & \dots & v_{k-1} \\ v_{k-1} & v_0 & \dots & v_{k-2} \\ \vdots & \vdots & \ddots & \vdots \\ v_1 & v_2 & \dots & v_0 \end{bmatrix} \in \mathbb{F}_2^{k \times k}.$$

For $\mathbf{u}, \mathbf{v} \in \mathcal{R}$, the product $\mathbf{w} = \mathbf{uv}$ can be computed as $\mathbf{w} = \mathbf{u}V = \mathbf{v}U$, and $w_l = \sum_{i+j=l \bmod k} u_i v_j$ for $l = 0, \cdots, k-1$, where $\mathbf{w} = (w_0, \cdots, w_{k-1})$. To find the weight of $\mathbf{uv}$, we first compute the probability that $w_i = 1$, say p', then $\text{wt}(\mathbf{w}) = p' * k$. Now, we compute the probability that $w_i = 1$ as follows.

Lemma 1 [34]. *Let $\mathbf{u} \in \mathcal{V}_{k,\omega_u}$, $\mathbf{v} \in \mathcal{V}_{k,\omega_v}$ and $\mathbf{w} = \mathbf{uv} = (w_0, \cdots, w_{k-1})$. Denote the probability that $w_i = 1$, for $i \in \{0, \cdots, k-1\}$, as $P(k, \omega_u, \omega_v)$. Then*

$$P(k, \omega_u, \omega_v) = \frac{1}{\binom{k}{\omega_v}} \sum_{\substack{1 \le l \le \min(\omega_u, \omega_v) \\ l \text{ odd}}} \binom{\omega_u}{l} \binom{k - \omega_u}{\omega_v - l}.$$

Definition 6 (Quasi-Cyclic Codes). *A linear block code $\mathcal{C}$ of length lk over $\mathbb{F}_2$ is called a quasi-cyclic code of index l if for any $\mathbf{c} = (\mathbf{c}_0, \cdots, \mathbf{c}_{l-1}) \in \mathcal{C}$, the vector obtained after applying a simultaneous circular shift to every block $\mathbf{c}_0, \cdots, \mathbf{c}_{l-1}$ is also a codeword.*

Definition 7 (Systematic 2-Quasi-Cyclic Codes, 2-QC Codes). *A systematic 2-quasi-cyclic $[2k, k]$-code has generator matrix of the form $[H \ I_k] \in \mathbb{F}_2^{k \times 2k}$ and parity check matrix $[I_k \ H^T] \in \mathbb{F}_2^{k \times 2k}$.*

Due to the quasi-cyclic structure of a code, any blockwise circular shift of a codeword is also a codeword. So, any circular shift of a syndrome will correspond to a blockwise circular shift of the error pattern. It has been shown in [37] that the work factor of the ISD algorithm for solving the syndrome decoding problem and the codeword finding problem for 2-quasi-cyclic codes for $n = 2k$ are

$$\mathcal{WF}_{A,2QCSD}(n, k, w) := \frac{\mathcal{WF}_A(n, k, w)}{\sqrt{n-k}} = 2^{c[1/2 + w(1+o(1))] - (\log_2 n)/2}$$

and

$$\mathcal{WF}_{A,2QCCF}(n, k, w) := \frac{\mathcal{WF}_A(n, k, w)}{n-k} = 2^{c[1 + w(1+o(1))] - \log_2 n}$$

respectively. Since the methods and the work factors for solving the syndrome decoding problem and the codeword finding problem for 2-quasi-cyclic codes require exponential time, therefore, we assume that the syndrome decoding problem and the codeword finding problem on quasi-cyclic codes are hard problems. We define the decisional codeword finding problem for 2-quasi-cyclic codes as follows.

Problem 3 (Decisional Codeword Finding Problem for 2-Quasi-Cyclic Codes (2QC-DCFP)). *Given a matrix* $[I_k \ h] \in \mathbb{F}_2^{k \times 2k}$, *and an even integer* $w > 0$ *as input, decide if there exists* $h_0, h_1 \in \mathcal{R}$ *such that* $\text{wt}(h_0) = \text{wt}(h_1) = w/2$ *and*
$$(h_0, h_1) \begin{bmatrix} I_k \\ h \end{bmatrix} = 0.$$

In the special case of 2-quasi-cyclic codes with parity check matrix $H = [h_0 \ h_1] \in \mathbb{F}_2^{k \times 2k}$, where (h_0, h_1) and e are of low weight approximate to $\sqrt{2k}$, we have what is called the quasi-cyclic low density parity check (QC-LDPC) codes. These codes are commonly used in the construction of key encapsulation mechanisms and signatures, such as BIKE [4] and HQC [1]. The Bit-Flipping algorithm [43] is used to decode an error e in BIKE.

On the other hand, for our signature (proposed in Sect. 3), we have $n = 2k$, $H = [I_k \ c]$ and $e = (e_1, e_2)$ is of high weight such that $\text{wt}(e) \gg \sqrt{n}$, $\frac{\text{wt}(e)}{n} < \frac{1}{2}$, $\frac{\text{wt}(e_1)}{k} + \frac{\text{wt}(ce_2)}{k} > \frac{1}{2}$ and $\text{wt}(c) < \sqrt{k}$. Experimental results show that the Bit-Flipping algorithm [43] is unable to obtain e correctly in this case (many bits are decoded incorrectly). Up to our knowledge, there is no efficient decoding algorithm for high weight error. Therefore, we define the following problem and assume that it is a hard problem.

Problem 4 (Syndrome Decoding Problem for High Weight on QC-LDPC Codes (HWQC-LDPC-SDP)) . *Let* ω *be integer,* $n = 2k$, $H = [I_k \ c]$ *and* $e = (e_1, e_2)$ *is of high weight such that* $\omega = \text{wt}(e) \gg \sqrt{n}$, $\frac{\text{wt}(e)}{n} < \frac{1}{2}$, $\frac{\text{wt}(e_1)}{k} + \frac{\text{wt}(ce_2)}{k} > \frac{1}{2}$ *and* $\text{wt}(c) < \sqrt{k}$. *Given* $H \in \mathbb{F}_2^{k \times 2k}$, $s \in \mathbb{F}_2^k$ *and* ω *as input. The syndrome decoding problem for high weight on QC-LDPC code is to determine* e *such that* $\text{wt}(e) = \omega$ *and* $s = eH^T$.

3   HWQCS Signature Scheme

In this section, we present the Hamming-metric code-based digital signature scheme from QC-LDPC codes with high weight errors, which we call the HWQCS signature scheme. The HWQCS signature scheme is based on the hardness of the syndrome decoding problem and the codeword finding problem on quasi-cyclic codes. Furthermore, the HWQCS signature scheme is different from the MPT signature scheme [30] and is resistant to Prabowo-Tan's attack [34] as each signature can be thought of as a one-time signature with a new ephemeral secret key, while the MPT signature is based on a fixed secret key.

A signature scheme consists of three algorithms: KeyGen, Sign and Verify.

- KeyGen: Given a security parameter λ, the key generation algorithm returns a key pair (pk, sk) where pk and sk are the public key and the secret key respectively.
- Sign: The algorithm, on input a message m and the secret key sk, returns a signature σ.
- Verify: Given a message m, a public key pk and a signature σ as input, the algorithm returns either 0 or 1 depending on whether the signature σ is valid or not.

Before we describe a HWQCS signature scheme, we first define the required parameters. Let $k, \omega_f, \omega_u, \omega_e, \omega_c, \omega_s, \omega_t$ be integers as public parameters. The HWQCS signature scheme is described as follows.

Algorithm 1: Key Generation of HWQCS Signature Scheme

Input   : k, ω_f, security parameter λ
Output: $pk = (\mathbf{h})$
1 Choose random $\mathbf{f}_1, \mathbf{f}_2 \in \mathcal{V}_{k,\omega_f}$ and both are invertible
2 Compute $\mathbf{h} := \mathbf{f}_1^{-1}\mathbf{f}_2$ in $\mathcal{R}^*$
3 The public key is $pk = (\mathbf{h})$ and the secret key is $sk = (\mathbf{f}_1, \mathbf{f}_2)$

Algorithm 2: Signing of HWQCS Signature Scheme

Input : $k, \omega_f, \omega_u, \omega_e, \omega_c, \omega_s, \omega_t$, message m, $pk = (\mathbf{h})$ and $sk = (\mathbf{f}_1, \mathbf{f}_2)$
Output: signature σ

1 Choose random $\mathbf{e}_1, \mathbf{e}_2 \in \mathcal{V}_{k,\omega_e}$ and $\mathbf{u}_1, \mathbf{u}_2 \in \mathcal{V}_{k,\omega_u}$

2 Compute $\mathbf{b} := (\mathbf{e}_1, \mathbf{e}_2) \begin{bmatrix} \mathbf{h} \\ \mathbf{h}^{-1} \end{bmatrix}$ in $\mathcal{R}$

3 Compute $\mathbf{c} := \mathcal{H}(m\|\mathbf{b}\|(\mathbf{u}_1\mathbf{f}_2 + \mathbf{u}_2\mathbf{f}_1)\|pk) \in \mathcal{V}_{k,\omega_c}$

4 Compute $\mathbf{s}_i := \mathbf{u}_i\mathbf{f}_i + \mathbf{c}\mathbf{e}_i$ in $\mathcal{R}$ for $i = 1, 2$

5 **if** $\mathrm{wt}(\mathbf{s}_1) > \omega_s$ or $\mathrm{wt}(\mathbf{s}_2) > \omega_s$ or $\mathrm{wt}(\mathbf{u}_1\mathbf{f}_2 + \mathbf{u}_2\mathbf{f}_1) > \omega_t$ **then**

6 | repeat from Step 1

7 **else**

8 | the signature is $\sigma = (\mathbf{c}, \mathbf{b}, \mathbf{s}_1, \mathbf{s}_2)$

9 **end if**

Algorithm 3: Verification of HWQCS Signature Scheme

Input : message m, pk, signature $\sigma = (\mathbf{c}, \mathbf{b}, \mathbf{s}_1, \mathbf{s}_2)$
Output: validity of the signature

1 **if** $\mathrm{wt}(\mathbf{s}_1) > \omega_s$ *or* $\mathrm{wt}(\mathbf{s}_2) > \omega_s$ **then**

2 | the signature is invalid

3 **else**

4 | Compute $\mathbf{t} := (\mathbf{s}_1, \mathbf{s}_2) \begin{bmatrix} \mathbf{h} \\ \mathbf{h}^{-1} \end{bmatrix} - \mathbf{c}\mathbf{b}$ in $\mathcal{R}$

5 | Compute $\mathbf{c}' := \mathcal{H}(m\|\mathbf{b}\|\mathbf{t}\|pk) \in \mathcal{V}_{k,\omega_c}$

6 | **if** $\mathbf{c}' = \mathbf{c}$ and $\mathrm{wt}(\mathbf{t}) \leq \omega_t$ and $\mathbf{t} \neq 0$ *in* $\mathcal{R}$ **then**

7 | | the signature is valid

8 | **else**

9 | | the signature is invalid

10 | **end if**

11 **end if**

Correctness:

$$\mathbf{t} = (\mathbf{s}_1, \mathbf{s}_2) \begin{bmatrix} \mathbf{h} \\ \mathbf{h}^{-1} \end{bmatrix} - \mathbf{c}\mathbf{b}$$
$$= (\mathbf{u}_1\mathbf{f}_2 + \mathbf{c}\mathbf{e}_1\mathbf{h}) + (\mathbf{u}_2\mathbf{f}_1 + \mathbf{c}\mathbf{e}_2\mathbf{h}^{-1}) - \mathbf{c}(\mathbf{e}_1\mathbf{h} + \mathbf{e}_2\mathbf{h}^{-1})$$
$$= \mathbf{u}_1\mathbf{f}_2 + \mathbf{u}_2\mathbf{f}_1$$

We define the notion of existential unforgeability under adaptive chosen message attack as follows.

Definition 8 (EUF-CMA Security). *A signature scheme is existential unforgeable under adaptive chosen message attack (EUF-CMA) if given a public key* pk *to any polynomial-time adversary* $\mathcal{A}$ *who can access the signing oracle* Sign(sk, ·) *and query a number of signatures, then the adversary* $\mathcal{A}$ *can produce a valid signature* σ *for a message* m *which has not been previously queried to the* *signing oracle only with negligible success probability (the success probability is denoted as* Pr[Forge]*).*

The advantage Adv of an adversary $\mathcal{A}$ in successfully solving a problem is defined as follows.

Definition 9. *The advantage of an adversary $\mathcal{A}$ in solving a problem* B *denoted as* Adv(B) *is defined as the probability that $\mathcal{A}$ successfully solves problem* B.

We define the following assumptions which are used to prove the security of the proposed signature scheme.

Assumption 1 (Syndrome Decoding for 2-Quasi-Cyclic Code (2QC-SDP) Assumption). *The syndrome decoding for 2-quasi-cyclic code assumption is the assumption that the advantage of an adversary $\mathcal{A}$ in solving* 2QC-SDP *is negligible, i.e.* Adv(2QC-SDP) $< \epsilon_{\text{2QC-SDP}}$.

Assumption 2 (Codeword Finding for 2-Quasi-Cyclic Codes (2QC-CFP) Assumption). *The codeword finding for quasi-cyclic codes assumption is the assumption that the advantage of an adversary $\mathcal{A}$ in solving* 2QC-CFP *is negligible, i.e.* Adv(2QC-CFP) $< \epsilon_{\text{2QC-CFP}}$.

Assumption 3 (Decisional Codeword Finding for 2-Quasi-Cyclic Codes (2QC-DCFP) Assumption). *The decisional codeword finding for 2-quasi-cyclic codes assumption is the assumption that the advantage of an adversary $\mathcal{A}$ in solving* 2QC-DCFP *is negligible, i.e.* Adv(2QC-DCFP) $< \epsilon_{\text{2QC-DCFP}}$.

Assumption 4 (Syndrome Decoding for High Weight on QC-LDPC Codes (HWQC-LDPC-SDP) Assumption). *The syndrome decoding for high weight of QC-LDPC codes assumption is the assumption that the advantage of an adversary $\mathcal{A}$ in solving* HWQC-LDPC-SDP *is negligible, i.e.* Adv(HWQC-LDPC-SDP) $< \epsilon_{\text{HWQC-LDPC-SDP}}$.

Theorem 1. *Under the* 2QC-SDP, 2QC-DCFP, 2QC-CFP, HWQC-LDPC-SDP *assumptions, the* HWQCS *signature scheme with parameters* $(k, \omega_f, \omega_u, \omega_e, \omega_c, \omega_s, \omega_t)$ *is secure under the* EUF-CMA *model in the classical random oracle model.*

Proof. We consider a chosen-message EUF adversary $\mathcal{A}$ against the HWQCS signature scheme. To prove the security, adversary $\mathcal{A}$ interacts with the real signature scheme and makes a sequence of experiments. The adversary $\mathcal{A}$ is first given a public key **h**. $\mathcal{A}$ made q_s signing queries and $q_{\mathcal{H}}$ hash ($\mathcal{H}$) queries. Finally, $\mathcal{A}$ outputs a message/signature pair such that the message has not been queried previously to the signing oracle. Let $\text{Pr}_i[\text{Forge}]$ be the probability of an event in experiment i that $\mathcal{A}$ obtains a valid signature of a message that has not been queried previously to the signing oracle. Let $\text{Pr}_0[\text{Forge}]$ be the success probability of an adversary $\mathcal{A}$ at the beginning (Experiment 0). Our goal is to give an upper-bound of $\text{Pr}_0[\text{Forge}]$.

Experiment 1. During the course of the experiment, if there is a collision in $\mathcal{H}$, then we abort the experiment. The number of queries to the hash oracle or the signing oracle throughout the experiment is at most $q_s + q_{\mathcal{H}}$. Thus,

$$| \Pr_0[\text{Forge}] - \Pr_1[\text{Forge}] | \leq 1 - \left(\frac{\binom{k}{\omega_c} - 1}{\binom{k}{\omega_c}} \right)^{\binom{q_s + q_{\mathcal{H}}}{2}} \approx \frac{(q_s + q_{\mathcal{H}})^2}{\binom{k}{\omega_c}}.$$

Experiment 2. During the course of the experiment, $\mathcal{A}$ received a number of signatures $\sigma_j = (\mathbf{c}, \mathbf{b}, \mathbf{s}_1, \mathbf{s}_2)_j$ for $j = 1, \cdots, q_s$. If $\mathcal{A}$ could solve for $(\mathbf{e}_1, \mathbf{e}_2)_j$ from $\mathbf{b}_j = (\mathbf{e}_1, \mathbf{e}_2)_j \begin{bmatrix} \mathbf{h} \\ \mathbf{h}^{-1} \end{bmatrix}$ for some j, then $\mathcal{A}$ could forge a new signature. But, the probability that $\mathcal{A}$ could solve it is bounded by $\epsilon_{\text{2QC-SDP}}$. Thus,

$$| \Pr_1[\text{Forge}] - \Pr_2[\text{Forge}] | \leq \epsilon_{\text{2QC-SDP}}.$$

Experiment 3. During the course of the experiment, $\mathcal{A}$ received a number of signatures $\sigma_j = (\mathbf{c}, \mathbf{b}, \mathbf{s}_1, \mathbf{s}_2)_j$ for $j = 1, \cdots, q_s$. If $\mathcal{A}$ could solve for $(\mathbf{u}_i \mathbf{f}_i, \mathbf{e}_i)$ from $(\mathbf{s}_i)_j = (\mathbf{u}_i \mathbf{f}_i, \mathbf{e}_i)_j \begin{bmatrix} \mathbf{I}_k \\ \mathbf{c}_j \end{bmatrix}$ for $i = 1, 2$ for some j, then $\mathcal{A}$ could forge a new signature. But, the probability that $\mathcal{A}$ could solve it is bounded by $\epsilon_{\text{HWQC-LDPC-SDP}}$. Thus,

$$| \Pr_2[\text{Forge}] - \Pr_3[\text{Forge}] | \leq 2\epsilon_{\text{HWQC-LDPC-SDP}}.$$

Experiment 4. In this experiment, a public key $\mathbf{h}$ is replaced by a random $\mathbf{h}' \in \mathcal{R}^*$. To distinguish Experiment 4 from Experiment 3, the adversary must in fact distinguish a well-formed public key $\mathbf{h} = \mathbf{f}_1^{-1} \mathbf{f}_2$ from a random invertible element of $\mathcal{R}$. Thus, we have

$$| \Pr_3[\text{Forge}] - \Pr_4[\text{Forge}] | \leq \epsilon_{\text{2QC-DCFP}}.$$

Furthermore, in this experiment, an adversary $\mathcal{A}$ has no signature information on $\mathbf{h}'$ and needs to solve a codeword finding problem for 2-quasi-cyclic codes in order to forge a signature. Thus,

$$| \Pr_4[\text{Forge}] | \leq \epsilon_{\text{2QC-CFP}}.$$

Combining the above experiments, the success probability of the adversary $\mathcal{A}$ is

$$| \Pr_0[\text{Forge}] | \leq \sum_{i=0}^{3} | \Pr_i[\text{Forge}] - \Pr_{i+1}[\text{Forge}] | + | \Pr_4[\text{Forge}] |$$

$$\leq \epsilon_{\text{2QC-CFP}} + \epsilon_{\text{2QC-DCFP}} + 2\epsilon_{\text{HWQC-LDPC-SDP}} + \epsilon_{\text{2QC-SDP}} + \frac{(q_s + q_{\mathcal{H}})^2}{\binom{k}{\omega_c}}.$$

4   Security Analysis

Let λ be the security level. For the security analysis, we consider two common types of attacks, namely, key recovery attacks and signature forgeries.

4.1   Key Recovery Attack

Finding the secret key $(\mathbf{f}_1, \mathbf{f}_2)$ from the public key $\mathbf{h} = \mathbf{f}_1^{-1}\mathbf{f}_2$ is equivalent to finding the codeword $(\mathbf{f}_1, \mathbf{f}_2)$ with parity check matrix $[\mathbf{h} \quad \mathbf{I}_k]$ such that $(\mathbf{f}_1, \mathbf{f}_2) \begin{bmatrix} \mathbf{h} \\ \mathbf{I}_k \end{bmatrix} = \mathbf{0}$. The work factor of solving the codeword finding problem for quasi-cyclic parity-check codes is

$$\mathcal{WF}_{A,2\text{QCCF}}(2k, k, 2\omega_f) = 2^{c[1+2\omega_f(1+o(1))]-\log_2 2k}, \qquad \text{where } c = 1.$$

Therefore, we can prevent key recovery attack by choosing the parameters such that $1 + 2\omega_f(1 + o(1)) - \log_2 2k \geq \lambda$, where λ is the security level.

Another method to find the secret key $(\mathbf{f}_1, \mathbf{f}_2)$ is by performing exhaustive search for $\mathbf{f}_1$ and checking whether $\mathbf{f}_1\mathbf{h}$ is of small Hamming weight w_f. The complexity of performing this exhaustive search is $\binom{k}{\omega_f}$. So, we must choose the parameters such that $\log_2 \binom{k}{\omega_f} \geq \lambda$, where λ is the security level.

Based on the above, we choose the parameters such that

$$\min \left\{ \log_2 \binom{k}{\omega_f}, \ 1 + 2\omega_f(1 + o(1)) - \log_2 2k \right\} \geq \lambda.$$

This ensures that the scheme is resistant against key recovery attacks.

4.2   Signature Forgery

4.2.1 Collision

For a signature scheme based on the Schnorr scheme, it is important to address the issue of collisions between different messages. In order to prevent collisions, one way is to use a collision-free hash function. Another way is to use a secure hash function such that the collision is minimal, that is, satisfying $\log_2 \binom{k}{\omega_c} \geq 2\lambda$, where λ is the security level.

4.2.2 Forgery From Known Signature

We consider the following methods to forge a signature.

4.2.2.1 Forgery via Syndrome Decoding Algorithm

From a given signature, we have $\mathbf{b} = \mathbf{e}_1\mathbf{h} + \mathbf{e}_2\mathbf{h}^{-1}$, $\mathbf{s}_i = \mathbf{u}_i\mathbf{f}_i + \mathbf{c}\mathbf{e}_i$, where $i = 1, 2$. Equivalently, $\mathbf{b} = (\mathbf{e}_1, \mathbf{e}_2) \begin{bmatrix} \mathbf{h} \\ \mathbf{h}^{-1} \end{bmatrix}$, $\mathbf{s}_i = (\mathbf{u}_i\mathbf{f}_i, \mathbf{e}_i) \begin{bmatrix} \mathbf{I}_k \\ \mathbf{c} \end{bmatrix}$ for $i = 1, 2$.

(1) One may use syndrome decoding algorithms to recover $(\mathbf{e}_1, \mathbf{e}_2)$ from $\mathbf{b} = (\mathbf{e}_1, \mathbf{e}_2) \begin{bmatrix} \mathbf{h} \\ \mathbf{h}^{-1} \end{bmatrix}$. The work factor is

$$\mathcal{WF}_{\mathcal{A},2\text{QCSD}}(2k, k, 2w_e) = 2^{c[1/2 + 2w_e(1+o(1))] - (\log_2 2k)/2}, \quad \text{where } c = 1.$$

In order to prevent this attack, we choose k, w_e such that

$$1/2 + 2w_e(1 + o(1)) - (\log_2 2k)/2 \geq \lambda,$$

where λ is the security level.

(2) One may also use syndrome decoding algorithms to recover $(\mathbf{e}_1, \mathbf{e}_2, \mathbf{u}_1\mathbf{f}_1, \mathbf{u}_2\mathbf{f}_2)$ from

$$\begin{bmatrix} \mathbf{b} \\ \mathbf{s}_1 \\ \mathbf{s}_2 \end{bmatrix} = \begin{bmatrix} \mathbf{h} & \mathbf{h}^{-1} & \mathbf{0}_k & \mathbf{0}_k \\ \mathbf{c} & \mathbf{0}_k & \mathbf{I}_k & \mathbf{0}_k \\ \mathbf{0}_k & \mathbf{c} & \mathbf{0}_k & \mathbf{I}_k \end{bmatrix} \begin{bmatrix} \mathbf{e}_1 \\ \mathbf{e}_2 \\ \mathbf{u}_1\mathbf{f}_1 \\ \mathbf{u}_2\mathbf{f}_2 \end{bmatrix}$$

Note that the weight of $(\mathbf{e}_1, \mathbf{e}_2, \mathbf{u}_1\mathbf{f}_1, \mathbf{u}_2\mathbf{f}_2)$ is $\omega = 2(w_e + \text{wt}(\mathbf{u}_1\mathbf{f}_1))$. So, the work factor is

$$\mathcal{WF}_{\mathcal{A},4\text{QCSD}}(4k, k, \omega) = \frac{\min\{\binom{4k}{\omega}, 2^{4k-k}\}}{\binom{4k-k}{\omega}\sqrt{4k-k}} = \frac{\min\{\binom{4k}{\omega}, 2^{3k}\}}{\binom{3k}{\omega}\sqrt{3k}}.$$

(3) Another method to find the ephemeral secret $(\mathbf{e}_1, \mathbf{e}_2)$ is by performing exhaustive search on $\mathbf{e}_1$ and checking whether $\mathbf{e}_2 = \mathbf{b}\mathbf{h} + \mathbf{e}_1\mathbf{h}^2$ is of small Hamming weight w_e. The complexity of performing this method is $\binom{k}{w_e}$. In order to prevent this attack, we choose k, w_e such that $\log_2 \binom{k}{w_e} \geq \lambda$, where λ is the security level.

Suppose an adversary can recover $(\mathbf{e}_1, \mathbf{e}_2)$ using any of the above methods. Then, the adversary obtains $\mathbf{u}_i\mathbf{f}_i = \mathbf{s}_i - \mathbf{c}\mathbf{e}_i$ for $i = 1, 2$. Afterwards, he can forge a new signature by generating new $\mathbf{b}' = \mathbf{e}_1'\mathbf{h} + \mathbf{e}_2'\mathbf{h}^{-1}$ and setting $\mathbf{s}_i' = \mathbf{u}_i\mathbf{f}_i + \mathbf{c}'\mathbf{e}_i'$, for $i = 1, 2$.

Based on the above analysis, in order to resist forgery attacks with security level λ, we choose the parameters k, ω, ω_e satisfying the following conditions:

$$\min\left\{\log_2\binom{k}{\omega_e}, \; 1/2 + 2\omega_e(1 + o(1)) - (\log_2 2k)/2, \log_2 \frac{\min\{\binom{4k}{\omega}, 2^{3k}\}}{\binom{3k}{\omega}\sqrt{3k}}\right\} \geq \lambda.$$

4.2.2.2 Forgery via Bit-Flipping Algorithm

Given a signature, we have $\mathbf{s}_i = \mathbf{u}_i\mathbf{f}_i + \mathbf{c}\mathbf{e}_i$, where $i = 1, 2$. One may try to apply the bit-flipping algorithm on $\mathbf{s}_i = (\mathbf{u}_i\mathbf{f}_i, \mathbf{e}_i)\begin{bmatrix}\mathbf{I}_k \\ \mathbf{c}\end{bmatrix}$ for $i = 1, 2$ to recover $\mathbf{e}_i$.

In this case, $n = 2k$, $H = \begin{bmatrix}\mathbf{I}_k \\ \mathbf{c}\end{bmatrix}$ and the threshold $\tau = \lfloor\rho\cdot\omega_c\rfloor$, where ρ is the probability that $(\mathbf{e}_i)_j = (\mathbf{s}_i)_j = 1$ for $j \in \{0, \cdots, k-1\}$ and will be given in the following proposition.

Proposition 2. *If $\mathbf{c}_0 = 1$ and $(\mathbf{s}_i)_j = 1$, then $\rho = Prob[(\mathbf{e}_i)_j = (\mathbf{s}_i)_j = 1]$ is equal to*

$$(1 - P(k, \omega_u, \omega_f)) * (1 - P(k, \omega_c - 1, \omega_e - 1)) + P(k, \omega_u, \omega_f) * P(k, \omega_c - 1, \omega_e - 1).$$

Proof. If $\mathbf{c}_0 = 1$, then

$$(\mathbf{s}_i)_j = (\mathbf{u}_i\mathbf{f}_i + \mathbf{c}\mathbf{e}_i)_j = (\mathbf{e}_i)_j + \sum_{l=0}^{k-1}(\mathbf{u}_i)_l(\mathbf{f}_i)_{j-l \bmod k} + \sum_{\substack{0\leq l\leq k-1 \\ l\neq j}} \mathbf{c}_l(\mathbf{e}_i)_{j-l \bmod k}.$$

Note that the probability that $(\mathbf{u}_i\mathbf{f}_i)_j = 1$ and $\sum_{l\neq j}(\mathbf{c}_i)_l(\mathbf{e}_i)_{j-l \bmod k} = 1$ are $P(k, \omega_u, \omega_f)$ and $P(k, \omega_c - 1, \omega_e - 1)$ respectively. Hence, the probability that $(\mathbf{e}_i)_j = (\mathbf{s}_i)_j = 1$ is

$$(1 - P(k, \omega_u, \omega_f)) * (1 - P(k, \omega_c - 1, \omega_e - 1)) + P(k, \omega_u, \omega_f) * P(k, \omega_c - 1, \omega_e - 1).$$

As in Problem 4, we choose the parameters such that $wt(\mathbf{u}_i\mathbf{f}_i) + \omega_e \gg \sqrt{2k}$, $\frac{wt(\mathbf{u}_i\mathbf{f}_i)+wt(\mathbf{c}\mathbf{e}_i)}{k} > \frac{1}{2}$ and $\omega_c \ll \sqrt{k}$. With this choice of parameters, the bit-flipping algorithm will not be able to decode correctly to obtain $\mathbf{e}_i$ for $i = 1, 2$. Hence, one cannot obtain $\mathbf{u}_i\mathbf{f}_i$ and forge a new signature.

4.2.3 Forgery Without Knowing Any Signature

Note that an adversary can generate $\mathbf{b} = \mathbf{e}_1\mathbf{h} + \mathbf{e}_2\mathbf{h}^{-1}$. To forge a signature, the adversary has to produce $\mathbf{s}_i$ of low weight. As the adversary needs to produce $\mathbf{u}_i\mathbf{f}_i$ of low Hamming weight and $\mathbf{u}_1\mathbf{f}_1\mathbf{h}$ such that $\mathbf{u}_2\mathbf{f}_2\mathbf{h}^{-1}$ are also of low Hamming weight, therefore $wt(\mathbf{u}_i\mathbf{f}_i)$ must be set to low. In order to ensure this, we need to define the normal distribution and present the following lemma and corollary.

Let $\mathcal{N}(0, \sigma^2)$ be the normal distribution with mean 0 and standard deviation σ. Its density function is $\rho_\sigma(x) = (\frac{1}{\sqrt{2\pi\sigma^2}})e^{-\frac{x^2}{2\sigma^2}}$ for $x \in \mathbb{R}$.

Lemma 2 [16]. *For $k > 2$, $Z \sim \mathcal{N}(0, \sigma^2)$, then*

$$\Pr[|z| > k\sigma \mid z \leftarrow Z] \leq \frac{1}{2}(e^{-k^2} + e^{-\frac{k^2}{2}}).$$

Corollary 1. (1) *For $\kappa > 2$, $Y \sim \mathcal{N}(\mu, \sigma^2)$, then $\Pr[|y - \mu| > \kappa\sigma \mid y \leftarrow Y] \leq \frac{1}{2}(e^{-\kappa^2} + e^{-\frac{\kappa^2}{2}})$.*
(2) *Let n be a large positive integer and $0 < p < 1$. If Y is a binomial distribution with parameters n and p (denoted $\mathrm{Bin}(n, p)$), then Y approximates to $\mathcal{N}(\mu, \sigma^2)$, where $\mu = np$ and $\sigma = \sqrt{np(1-p)}$.*
(3) *In (2), if $0 < l < p < 1$ and $\kappa = \frac{(p-l)\sqrt{n}}{\sqrt{p(1-p)}}$, then*

$$\Pr[|y - np| > (p - l)n \mid y \leftarrow Y] \leq \frac{1}{2}(e^{-\kappa^2} + e^{-\frac{\kappa^2}{2}}) < e^{-\kappa^2/2}.$$

Setting $n = k$, $p = \frac{1}{2}$ and $l < \frac{1}{2}$ in Corollary 1 (3), we have $\Pr[|y - \frac{k}{2}| > (\frac{1}{2} - l)k \mid y \leftarrow \mathrm{Bin}(k, p)] < e^{-\kappa^2/2}$. To ensure that the probability is negligible, we should choose κ such that $\kappa = (1 - 2l)\sqrt{k}$ and $\frac{1}{2}(e^{-\kappa^2} + e^{-\kappa^2/2}) < e^{-\kappa^2/2} < 2^{-\lambda}$, that is,

$$\frac{\kappa^2}{2}\log_2 e > \lambda \implies \kappa > \sqrt{\frac{2\lambda}{\log_2 e}}.$$

Letting $\kappa_0 = \sqrt{\frac{2\lambda}{\log_2 e}}$, we have

λ	128	192	256
κ_0	13.320	16.314	18.838

This means that if an adversary randomly picks an element $\mathbf{a}$ in place of $\mathbf{u}_i \mathbf{f}_i$ for $i = 1, 2$, then the probability that $|\mathrm{wt}(\mathbf{a}) - \frac{k}{2}| \leq \kappa\sqrt{k/4}$ is more than $1 - 2^{-\lambda}$. Hence, by selecting appropriate l, k such that $(1 - 2l)\sqrt{k} \geq \kappa_0$, we can ensure that the adversary cannot find $\mathbf{a}$ of weight less than lk. Therefore, it is not possible to forge a signature with probability more than $2^{-\lambda}$.

5   Parameters Selections

Based on the above security analysis, the parameters $(k, \omega_f, \omega_u, \omega_e, \omega_c, \omega_s)$ of the signature scheme must be chosen properly in order to achieve λ-bit computational security. The following conditions are to be fulfilled:

$$\min\left\{\log_2\binom{k}{\omega_f}, \; 1 + 2\omega_f(1 + o(1)) - \log_2 2k\right\} \geq \lambda,$$

$$\log_2\binom{k}{\omega_c} \geq 2\lambda,$$

$$\min\left\{ \log_2 \binom{k}{\omega_e}, \frac{1}{2} + 2\omega_e(1 + o(1)) - \frac{\log_2 2k}{2}, \log_2 \frac{\min\{\binom{4k}{\omega}, 2^{3k}\}}{\binom{3k}{\omega}\sqrt{3k}} \right\} \geq \lambda,$$

$$(1 - 2l)\sqrt{k} > \sqrt{\frac{2\lambda}{\log_2 e}},$$

$$\text{wt}(\mathbf{u}_i\mathbf{f}_i) + \omega_e \gg \sqrt{2k},$$

$$\frac{\text{wt}(\mathbf{u}_i\mathbf{f}_i) + \text{wt}(\mathbf{ce}_i)}{k} > \frac{1}{2}.$$

We now set the parameters ω_s and ω_t. Let $p_s := \Pr[(\mathbf{s}_i)_j = 1] = P(k, \omega_u, \omega_f)(1 - P(k, \omega_c, \omega_e)) + (1 - P(k, \omega_u, \omega_f))P(k, \omega_c, \omega_e)$ and $p_t := \Pr[(\mathbf{u}_1\mathbf{f}_1 + \mathbf{u}_2\mathbf{f}_2)_j = 1] = 2P(k, \omega_u, \omega_f)(1 - P(k, \omega_u, \omega_f))$. Suppose $\omega_s := \left\lceil k \cdot p_s + \kappa\sqrt{kp_s(1 - p_s)} \right\rceil$ and $\omega_t := \left\lceil k \cdot p_t + \kappa\sqrt{kp_t(1 - p_t)} \right\rceil$ for some $\kappa > 0$ to be determined later. Note that $\text{wt}(\mathbf{s}_i)$ can be estimated to follow $\text{Bin}(k, p_s) \sim \mathcal{N}(kp_s, kp_s(1 - p_s))$. Thus, $\Pr[\text{wt}(\mathbf{s}_i) > \omega_s] \leq \Pr\left[|\text{wt}(\mathbf{s}_i) - kp_s| > \kappa\sqrt{kp_s(1 - p_s)}\right] \leq \frac{1}{2}(e^{-\kappa^2} + e^{-\kappa^2/2})$ by Corollary 1 (1). Similarly, we have $\Pr[\text{wt}(\mathbf{t}) > \omega_t] \leq \frac{1}{2}(e^{-\kappa^2} + e^{-\kappa^2/2})$. We require that a user can generate at most 2^{72} signatures. As $\frac{1}{2}(e^{-10^2} + e^{-10^2/2}) \approx 2^{-73.1}$, we may take $\kappa = 10$, i.e. we set

$$\omega_s := \left\lceil k \cdot p_s + 10\sqrt{kp_s(1 - p_s)} \right\rceil, \qquad \omega_t := \left\lceil k \cdot p_t + 10\sqrt{kp_t(1 - p_t)} \right\rceil.$$

This ensures that $\Pr[\text{wt}(\mathbf{s}_i) > \omega_s] < 2^{-73.1}$ and $\Pr[\text{wt}(\mathbf{t}) > \omega_t] < 2^{-73.1}$.

The parameters for various security levels are given in the following Table 1.

Table 1. The parameters of the HWQCS signature

Name	λ	k	ω_f	ω_u	ω_e	ω_c	ω_s	ω_t	$\frac{\text{wt}(s)}{k}$	$\frac{\text{wt}(uf)}{k}$	$\frac{\text{wt}(t)}{k}$
Para-1	128	12539	145	33	141	31	5390	5484	0.3863	0.2694	0.3937
Para-2	192	18917	185	41	177	39	8123	8267	0.3938	0.2779	0.4013
Para-3	256	25417	201	51	191	51	10894	10999	0.3978	0.2786	0.4019

To compute the size of HWQCS signature scheme, the public key size is $\lceil k/8 \rceil$ bytes, the secret key size is $2 * \lceil \lceil \log_2 k \rceil * \omega_f/8 \rceil$ bytes and the signature size is $3 * \lceil k/8 \rceil + \lceil \lceil \log_2 k \rceil * \omega_c/8 \rceil$ bytes. We list their sizes for various security levels in Table 2.

As listed in Table 2, the public key size, secret key size and signature size of the proposed signature scheme HWQCS-I are 1568 bytes, 508 bytes and 4759 bytes respectively for 128-bit classical security level.

We provide comparison of the key sizes and signature size for various code-based signature schemes in Table 3.

Table 2. Size of Signature Schemes (at certain classical security levels)

Scheme	Security	Size (in Bytes)		
		PK	SK	Sg
HWQCS-I	128	1,568	508	4,759
HWQCS-II	192	2,365	694	7,169
HWQCS-III	256	3,178	754	9,630

Table 3. Comparison of Various Code-based Signature Schemes (at certain classical security levels)

Scheme	PK size	SK size	Sg size	C.Sec
HWQCS-I	1.568 KB	508 B	4.759 KB	128
Durandal-I19 [3]	15.25 KB	2.565 KB	4.060 KB	128
WAVE23 [31]	3.60 MB	2.27 MB	737 B	128
CCJ23 [14]	90 B	231 B	12.52 KB	128
SDitH23 [2]	120 B	404 B	8.26 KB	128
BG23 [10]	1 KB	2 KB	13.5 KB	128
cRVDC19 [9]	0.152 KB	0.151 KB	22.480 KB	125
CVE18 [8]	7.638 KB	0.210 KB	436.600 KB	80

In Table 3, it can be observed that the signature size of the proposed signature scheme HWQCS-I is smaller than the other signature schemes except for the WAVE23 signature scheme [31] and the Durandal-I19 signature scheme [3]. However, it should be noted that the public key sizes for both the WAVE23 and Durandal-I19 signature schemes exceed ten thousand bytes. These are larger than that of the signature scheme HWQCS-I. Moreover, recently there is an attack on Durandal-I19 [6] which requires it to increase its parameter sizes.

Although the public key size of the CCJ23 signature scheme [14] and the SDitH23 signature scheme [2] are relatively small, but their signature sizes are more than eight thousand bytes. Overall, the proposed signature scheme HWQCS-I has shorter combined key and signature sizes than other signature schemes.

6   Conclusion

In this paper, we constructed a new Hamming metric code-based signature scheme (called HWQCS signature scheme). The security of HWQCS signature is based on the hardness of the syndrome decoding problem and the codeword finding problem on 2-quasi-cyclic codes, as well as on high error for quasi-cyclic low parity-check codes respectively. We provided security proof of the HWQCS signature scheme under the random oracle model and gave detailed analysis on the security of the HWQCS signature scheme against Bit-Flipping attack and statistical attack. Furthermore, we also provided concrete parameter choices for the HWQCS signature scheme and compared its key sizes and signature size to other existing signature schemes. The signature scheme HWQCS-I outperforms other code-based signature schemes with a public key size of 1568 bytes, secret key size of 508 bytes and signature size of 4759 bytes at 128-bit security level.

References

1. Aguilar-Melchor, C., et al.: Hamming Quasi-Cyclic (HQC). Submission to the NIST post quantum standardization process (2017). https://www.pqc-hqc.org/doc/hqc-specification_2021-06-06.pdf
2. Aguilar-Melchor, C., et al.: The Syndrome Decoding in the Head (SD-in-the-Head) Signature Scheme. Submission to the NIST call for additional post-quantum signatures (2023). https://csrc.nist.gov/csrc/media/Projects/pqc-dig-sig/documents/round-1/spec-files/SDitH-spec-web.pdf
3. Aragon, N., Blazy, O., Gaborit, P., Hauteville, A., Zémor, G.: Durandal: a rank metric based signature scheme. In: Ishai, Y., Rijmen, V. (eds.) EUROCRYPT 2019, Part III. LNCS, vol. 11478, pp. 728–758. Springer, Cham (2019). https://doi.org/10.1007/978-3-030-17659-4_25
4. Aragon, N., et al.: BIKE: Bit Flipping Key Encapsulation. Submission to the NIST post quantum standardization process (2017). https://bikesuite.org/files/v5.0/BIKE_Spec.2022.10.10.1.pdf
5. Aragon, N., Baldi, M., Deneuville, J.C., Khathuria, K., Persichetti, E., Santini, P.: Cryptanalysis of a code-based full-time signature. Des. Codes Crypt. **89**(9), 2097–2112 (2021). https://doi.org/10.1007/s10623-021-00902-7
6. Aragon, N., Dyseryn, V., Gaborit, P.: Analysis of the security of the PSSI problem and cryptanalysis of the Durandal signature scheme. In: Handschuh, H., Lysyanskaya, A. (eds.) CRYPTO 2023. LNCS, vol. 14083, pp. 127–149. Springer, Cham (2023). https://doi.org/10.1007/978-3-031-38548-3_5
7. Becker, A., Joux, A., May, A., Meurer, A.: Decoding random binary linear codes in $2^{n/20}$: how $1 + 1 = 0$ improves information set decoding. In: Pointcheval, D., Johansson, T. (eds.) EUROCRYPT 2012. LNCS, vol. 7237, pp. 520–536. Springer, Heidelberg (2012). https://doi.org/10.1007/978-3-642-29011-4_31
8. Bellini, E., Caullery, F., Hasikos, A., Manzano, M., Mateu, V.: Code-based signature schemes from identification protocols in the rank metric. In: Camenisch, J., Papadimitratos, P. (eds.) CANS 2018. LNCS, vol. 11124, pp. 277–298. Springer, Cham (2018). https://doi.org/10.1007/978-3-030-00434-7_14
9. Bellini, E., Caullery, F., Gaborit, P., Manzano, M., Mateu, V.: Improved Veron identification and signature schemes in the rank metric. In: IEEE International Symposium on Information Theory, pp. 1872–1876 (2019). https://doi.org/10.1109/ISIT.2019.8849585
10. Bidoux, L., Gaborit, P.: Compact post-quantum signatures from proofs of knowledge leveraging structure for the PKP, SD and RSD problems. In: El Hajji, S., Mesnager, S., Souidi, E.M. (eds.) C2SI 2023. LNCS, vol. 13874, pp. 10–42. Springer, Cham (2023). https://doi.org/10.1007/978-3-031-33017-9_2
11. Berlekamp, E., McEliece, R., van Tilborg, H.: On the inherent intractability of certain coding problems (coresp.). IEEE Trans. Inf. Theory **24**(3), 384–386 (1978). https://doi.org/10.1109/TIT.1978.1055873

12. Bernstein, D.J., et al.: Classic McEliece: conservative code-based cryptography. Submission to the NIST post quantum standardization process (2017). https://classic.mceliece.org/mceliece-rationale-20221023.pdf

13. Bernstein, D.J., Lange, T., Peters, C.: Smaller decoding exponents: ball-collision decoding. In: Rogaway, P. (ed.) CRYPTO 2011. LNCS, vol. 6841, pp. 743–760. Springer, Heidelberg (2011). https://doi.org/10.1007/978-3-642-22792-9_42

14. Carozza, E., Couteau, G., Joux, A.: Short signatures from regular syndrome decoding in the head. In: Hazay, C., Stam, M. (eds.) EUROCRYPT 2023. LNCS, vol. 14008, pp. 532–563. Springer, Cham (2023). https://doi.org/10.1007/978-3-031-30589-4_19

15. Cayrel, P.L., Véron, P., El Yousfi Alaoui, S.M.: A zero-knowledge identification scheme based on the q-ary syndrome decoding problem. In: Biryukov, A., Gong, G., Stinson, D.R. (eds.) SAC 2010. LNCS, vol. 6544, pp. 171–186. Springer, Berlin (2011). https://doi.org/10.1007/978-3-642-19574-7_12

16. Chiani, M., Dardari, D., Simon, M.K.: New exponential bounds and approximations for the computation of error probability in fading channels. IEEE Trans. Wireless Commun. $\mathbf{2}$(4), 840–845 (2003)

17. Courtois, N.T., Finiasz, M., Sendrier, N.: How to achieve a McEliece-based digital signature scheme. In: Boyd, C. (ed.) ASIACRYPT 2001. LNCS, vol. 2248, pp. 157–174. Springer, Heidelberg (2001). https://doi.org/10.1007/3-540-45682-1_10

18. D'Alconzo, G., Meneghetti, A., Piasenti, P.: Security issues of CFS-like digital signature algorithms. arXiv preprint arXiv:2112.00429 (2021). https://arxiv.org/abs/2112.00429

19. Debris-Alazard, T., Sendrier, N., Tillich, J.P.: Wave: a new family of trapdoor one-way preimage sampleable functions based on codes. In: Galbraith, S.D., Moriai, S. (eds.) ASIACRYPT 2019. LNCS, vol. 11921, pp. 21–51. Springer, Cham (2019). https://doi.org/10.1007/978-3-030-34578-5_2

20. Dumer, I.: On minimum distance decoding of linear codes. In: Proceedings of the 5th Joint Soviet-Swedish International Workshop Information Theory, pp. 50–52 (1991)

21. Feneuil, T., Joux, A., Rivain, M.: Syndrome decoding in the head: shorter signatures from zero-knowledge proofs. In: Dodis, Y., Shrimpton, T. (eds.) CRYPTO 2022. LNCS, vol. 13508, pp. 541–572. Springer, Cham (2022). https://doi.org/10.1007/978-3-031-15979-4_19

22. Fiat, A., Shamir, A.: How to prove yourself: practical solutions to identification and signature problems. In: Odlyzko, A.M. (ed.) CRYPTO 1986. LNCS, vol. 263, pp. 186–194. Springer, Heidelberg (1987). https://doi.org/10.1007/3-540-47721-7_12

23. Kabatianskii, G., Krouk, E., Smeets, B.: A digital signature scheme based on random error-correcting codes. In: Darnell, M. (ed.) Cryptography and Coding 1997. LNCS, vol. 1355, pp. 161–167. Springer, Heidelberg (1997). https://doi.org/10.1007/BFb0024461

24. Lau, T.S.C., Tan, C.H., Prabowo, T.F.: Key recovery attacks on some rank metric code-based signatures. In: Albrecht, M. (ed.) IMACC 2019. LNCS, vol. 11929, pp. 215–235. Springer, Cham (2019). https://doi.org/10.1007/978-3-030-35199-1_11

25. Lee, P.J., Brickell, E.F.: An observation on the security of McEliece's public-key cryptosystem. In: Barstow, D., et al. (eds.) EUROCRYPT 1988. LNCS, vol. 330, pp. 275–280. Springer, Heidelberg (1988). https://doi.org/10.1007/3-540-45961-8_25

26. Leon, J.: A probabilistic algorithm for computing minimum weight of large error-correcting codes. IEEE Trans. Inf. Theory $\mathbf{34}$(5), 1354–1359 (1988)

27. May, A., Meurer, A., Thomae, E.: Decoding random linear codes in $\tilde{O}(2^{0.054n})$. In: Lee, D.H., Wang, X. (eds.) ASIACRYPT 2011. LNCS, vol. 7073, pp. 107–124. Springer, Heidelberg (2011). https://doi.org/10.1007/978-3-642-25385-0_6

28. May, A., Ozerov, I.: On computing nearest neighbors with applications to decoding of binary linear codes. In: Oswald, E., Fischlin, M. (eds.) EUROCRYPT 2015. LNCS, vol. 9056, pp. 203–228. Springer, Heidelberg (2015). https://doi.org/10.1007/978-3-662-46800-5_9

29. McEliece, R.J.: A public-key cryptosystem based on algebraic coding theory. DSN PR 42-44, California Institute of Technology (1978)

30. Meneghetti, A., Picozzi, C., Tognolini, G.: A post-quantum digital signature scheme from QC-LDPC codes. IACR Cryptology ePrint Archive 2022/1477 (2022). https://eprint.iacr.org/2022/1477

31. Sendrier, N.: Wave parameter selection. IACR Cryptology ePrint Archive 2023/588 (2023). https://eprint.iacr.org/2023/588

32. Niederreiter, H.: Knapsack-type cryptosystems and algebraic coding theory. Probl. Control Inf. Theory **15**, 159–166 (1986)

33. Otmani, A., Tillich, J.P.: An efficient attack on all concrete KKS proposals. In: Yang, B.-Y. (ed.) PQCrypto 2011. LNCS, vol. 7071, pp. 98–116. Springer, Heidelberg (2011). https://doi.org/10.1007/978-3-642-25405-5_7

34. Prabowo, T.F., Tan, C.H.: Attack on a code-based signature scheme from QC-LDPC codes. In: El Hajji, S., Mesnager, S., Souidi, E.M. (eds.) C2SI 2023. LNCS, vol. 13874, pp. 136–149. Springer, Cham (2023). https://doi.org/10.1007/978-3-031-33017-9_9

35. Prange, E.: The use of information sets in decoding cyclic codes. IRE Trans. Inf. Theory **8**(5), 5–9 (1962)

36. Ren, F., Zheng, D., Wang, W.: An efficient code based digital signature algorithm. Int. J. Netw. Secur. **19**(6), 1072–1079 (2017). https://doi.org/10.6633/IJNS.201711.19(6).24

37. Sendrier, N.: Decoding one out of many. In: Yang, B.-Y. (ed.) PQCrypto 2011. LNCS, vol. 7071, pp. 51–67. Springer, Heidelberg (2011). https://doi.org/10.1007/978-3-642-25405-5_4

38. Song, Y., Huang, X., Mu, Y., Wu, W., Wang, H.: A code-based signature scheme from the Lyubashevsky framework. Theor. Comput. Sci. **835**, 15–30 (2020). https://doi.org/10.1016/j.tcs.2020.05.011

39. Stern, J.: A method for finding codewords of small weight. In: Cohen, G., Wolfmann, J. (eds.) Coding Theory 1988. LNCS, vol. 388, pp. 106–113. Springer, Heidelberg (1989). https://doi.org/10.1007/BFb0019850

40. Stern, J.: A new identification scheme based on syndrome decoding. In: Stinson, D.R. (ed.) CRYPTO 1993. LNCS, vol. 773, pp. 13–21. Springer, Heidelberg (1994). https://doi.org/10.1007/3-540-48329-2_2

41. Tan, C.H., Prabowo, T.F.: A new key recovery attack on a code-based signature from the Lyubashevsky framework. Inf. Process. Lett. **183**(106422), 1–7 (2024). https://doi.org/10.1016/j.ipl.2023.106422

42. Torres, R.C., Sendrier, N.: Analysis of information set decoding for a sub-linear error weight. In: Takagi, T. (ed.) PQCrypto 2016. LNCS, vol. 9606, pp. 144–161. Springer, Cham (2016). https://doi.org/10.1007/978-3-319-29360-8_10

43. Vasseur, V.: Post-quantum cryptography: a study of the decoding of QC-MDPC codes. Ph.D. thesis, Université de Paris (2021)

Author Index

H. Seo and S. Kim (Eds.): ICISC 2023, LNCS 14561, pp. 325–326, 2024.
https://doi.org/10.1007/978-981-97-1235-9

Printed in the United States
by Baker & Taylor Publisher Services

Printed in the United States
by Baker & Taylor Publisher Services